A HISTORY OF
EDUCATIONAL THOUGHT

Second Edition

Frederick Mayer

CHARLES E. MERRILL BOOKS, INC., COLUMBUS, OHIO

to
Michael Birnkrant
one of the truly great men
of our time

Library of Congress Catalog Card Number 66-14407

2 3 4 5 6 7 8 9 10 11 12 13–72 71 70 69 68 67

Printed in the United States of America

Preface

Today, the theory and history of education are of universal interest. We have come to realize that educational practice must be illuminated by critical examination. We have learned that without a consideration of goals and purposes, education is bound to suffer from a grave limitation of vision.

In this book I have explored the religious as well as the philosophical foundations of educational thought. For many centuries, religious and educational instruction were one; in modern times, men like Pestalozzi and Froebel have been encouraged in their educational reforms by their religious idealism. Basically, education and religion appeal to the same drives. Both are concerned with man as he ought to be; both are hindered by materialism; both demand a reconstruction of the heart as well as of the mind. Both depend upon the inspiration of exceptional leaders. Both are concerned not merely with the present, but with the distant future. Both demand a genuine ethical viewpoint which goes beyond expediency. For we cannot understand the history of educational thought without understanding its religious foundations.

My approach to the philosophical foundations of educational thought has been cosmopolitan. To be cosmopolitan in education means to cultivate an open mind, welcoming new truths and new insights wherever found. I have tried to reveal the impact on education of philosophical ideas not only of Christians, but also of Mohammedans, and of the ancient Chinese, Greeks, and Indians. Only as we learn do we progress; only as we overcome prejudice do we become enlightened. The Orient can teach us the virtue of contemplation which we need desperately in our activistic culture.

The last three centuries have brought spectacular scientific advancement. Science as the method of controlling nature dates back to the Renaissance, but it promises no magic vistas, and, in unenlightened hands, it may become a tool of total destruction. On the other hand, the scientific method, applied to our institutional system, may create a real change in the habits of mankind. It may develop genuine open-mindedness; it may bring about a spirit of mutuality; it may intensify the hypothetical temper which has been the foundation of our scientific advancement. However, science alone is not enough; we need genuine morality and genuine spirituality. Only when we use science for the betterment of man, when education, philosophy, and religion unite, will a new age dawn for humanity.

The theme of this book is the development of creativity as a basic concept in educational thought. Man's quest for education represents at the same time his search for creativity. To be creative implies a capacity for self-definition, the ability to discipline one's powers, the vision of new goals, and the application of this vision to daily existence. Creative education represents an affirmation of man; it symbolizes an unwavering faith in his intellectual and moral capacities, so that the gulf between the realm of ideals and actuality can be narrowed. Creative education is the process by which man utilizes the greatness which he finds within himself.

When an educator discusses the history and theories of education, he reveals much about his own value structure and his own world view. What matters in education is not merely factual competence but valuational boldness. A theorist performs only a minor function when he comments upon the ideas of the past and when he strives for academic respectability. His main function is to anticipate the horizons of the future. As Heidegger asserted, the philosopher is the guardian of being because he, above all, lives for the future and thus helps to define human destiny.

I wish to acknowledge all those who have helped to make this book possible. I am endebted to the numerous publishers who have generously consented to the republication of selections for which they hold copyrights. My profound thanks go to the following for reading all or part of the book and offering many helpful criticisms and suggestions: Professors William H. Kilpatrick, Teachers College, Columbia University; Lester B. Sands, University of California, Santa Barbara, Everett J. Kircher and Bernard Hehl, The Ohio State University, and Emery Stoops, University of Southern California.

Frederick Mayer

Preface to the Second Edition

I have been deeply gratified by the reception of the *History of Educational Thought*. It is my belief that a historical study should not be the prelude to an attitude of neutrality and that the student needs more than a factual basis for education. In an age of profound turmoil, he needs a creative perspective so that he can contribute to the affirmative forces of civilization and so that he can view his vocation with dedication and enthusiasm.

I regard the study of education as the crucial foundation of the curriculum. Education includes more than a historical, philosophical, psychological and sociological background; it goes beyond methodology. Education aims at the creation of the enlightened individual and the enlightened society.

In the revision of the book I have expanded the sections on the relationship between education and society and the impact of art and science on education. Furthermore there is a new chapter on the relationship between American philosophy and education. Specific questions have been added to test the knowledge of the student and to evoke new areas of interest.

I hope that the pioneers of the past like Comenius, Pestalozzi, and Froebel will inspire the student to continue the struggle for democracy in education. We have the choice of being guided by authoritarianism, which means education by the few, which leads to the closed society, which implies indoctrination and rigid standards or to seek the vistas of creative democracy leading to the open society and to the expansion of educational opportunities for all.

Jefferson one time was asked whether the education of the élite or the education of the common people should be stressed. His answer was that "it is safer to have a whole people respectably enlightened than a few in a high state of science, and the many in ignorance. This last is the most dangerous state in which a nation can be."

I want to thank my friends at Charles E. Merrill, especially Julia Estadt and R. Frank Bitner, for their great interest in the book and for their splendid work as publishers in expanding the ideals of American education.

F.M.

Contents

Part 4

Ideals of American Education
Chapter

Part 5

Conclusion
Chapter

A HISTORY OF
EDUCATIONAL THOUGHT

Part 1

Introduction

Chapter 1

An Approach to Education

DILEMMAS

Ours is an age of disenchantment. The optimism which characterized part of the nineteenth century has been undermined by wars and depressions and the rise of dictatorships. World War I was fought by some Americans in the belief that the world could be made safe for democracy, yet today democracy in Europe is more embattled than it was in 1914. World War II was fought to establish fundamental freedoms for men everywhere, and yet today there is a wholesale escape from freedom on the part of many nations in Europe and in Asia.

We all know that our scientific progress has been astounding. Indeed, more progress has been made in the physical and natural sciences since 1900 than in the last 5000 years. Yet this advancement has not been accompanied by ethical progress and by a growing sensitivity towards the needs of others. Technology in our time is like a Leviathan; we have almost become slaves to machines. We have more comforts than ever, but we are profoundly uncomfortable as we face the future. We have more ways and better means to amuse ourselves, yet many of us feel a sense of profound emptiness.

The dilemma of modern man is perhaps best represented by Albert Camus in *The Stranger*. The main character of the book is a young man who feels no fundamental emotions. He does not love anyone. When his mother dies, he does not mourn; he does not even miss her. He is interested in a girl because he needs a purge for his biological needs. To him she is an object, not someone to be cherished. Then, in a moment of passion he kills an Arab. He is convicted of murder and sentenced to die. At last, when he realizes that his time is limited, he awakens to the value of human existence. But the awakening has come too late.

In *The Fall,* Camus again describes the feeling of futility which so many of us experience. The central character of this book is a Parisian lawyer who is apparently very successful and quite humanitarian. One night, on his way home from a routine day at his office, he sees a girl at the railing of a bridge. She is a picture of desolation. After he passes her, he hears a cry for help. He knows that she is drowning. For a moment he debates with himself whether he should help her, but he decides to walk on. This act of cowardice torments him; he gives up his practice and starts to confess his sins. His great hope is that he might have another chance to save the girl, but he knows that even if given such a second chance his cowardice again would conquer him. Again, the water would be too cold, and he would be too late.

Camus concludes that modern man lives by pretension, that he covers his selfishness with the mantle of convention. Man's tragedy is his lack of involvement and concern. He preaches love, but in reality he is a slave to his own egocentric desires.

AGE OF VIOLENCE

An outstanding feature of the past hundred years has been the rise of the *mass-man.* Whether in Nazi Germany, in Soviet Russia, or even in parts of our own civilization, he is the man who subconsciously hates civilization, who prefers a psychological jungle to civilized laws. The mass-man can read and write and has enjoyed the rudiments of civilization, but he is full of prejudices and lives an unexamined life.

Educational reformers in the eighteenth century, like Voltaire, Basedow, and Montesquieu, hoped that through the proper use of reason man could build Utopia. However, we know today the immensity of the obstacles that lie along the road to a world governed by reason. We have seen the shadows of prejudice and bigotry lengthen under the auspices of the very educational systems to which we look for enlightenment. Forests of irrationality still pose a continual threat to future progress, and, indeed, even to progress already achieved.

We are living in a twilight atmosphere, suspended between a new age and obsolete superstitions. It is doubtful whether the sensitive individual is better off in our time than in the age of Socrates or whether creativity flourishes more today than in Greek civilization. We see many parallels between our own dilemmas and those of ancient nations. Like them, we are threatened by violence and war.

War, more than any other force, threatens the progress of civilization. It creates tribal loyalties, it subordinates the individual to the state, and it impedes the progress of free inquiry. The effect of war upon a sensitive individual is described by Erich Maria Remarque in *All Quiet on the Western Front*. The hero of the book, is a young German of eighteen. His early humanistic education developed within him a deep reverence for learning: mathematics, history, and Latin appeared to possess intrinsic values. He was inflamed by idealism. Then, he volunteered for the Western front. Amidst trench warfare and the constant danger of destruction, the academic life he had so cherished appeared wholly visionary and useless. Life had been reduced to a biological process in which only survival mattered.

SIGNIFICANCE OF EDUCATION

Education is the best defense against war and destruction. Yet education can be either a positive or a negative force in history. Educational thinkers like Comenius appealed to the idealism of mankind, and they attempted to apply reason to man's institutional life. In an age which believed in rigid class divisions in education, Comenius believed that all should be educated. But thinkers like Machiavelli used education to promote the seeds of war and to uphold the power of unscrupulous rulers. To Machiavelli, man was a creature dominated by self-interest; reason was only a tool in the struggle for power.

Still, we must not underestimate the affirmative power of the great teacher in history. Think of Buddha, who became the teacher of the Orient; or of Confucius, who taught a way of life which lasted for many centuries; or of Socrates, who became the gadfly of Athens: here we have examples of men who inspired by their idealism. Long after they died their ideas lived. Thus Henry Adams could justly remark that the teacher affects eternity.

Most of the great teachers of the past have been men of hope. Buddha spoke of equality even amidst the ravages of the caste system. Socrates felt that man has a divine spark in his soul. Jesus preached that all human beings can be taught, for they are all the children of God. Erasmus thought that scholarship would create a brave new world of peace. Comenius envisioned a universal system of knowledge and a universal college based on genuine Christian ideals. Pestalozzi had such pity for the children of the poor that he educated them in the most idealistic manner. Froebel created the kindergarten, because he had boundless love for children.

In some respects, we seem closer to the realization of these ideals in our time than in previous periods: national frontiers today are obsolete; nations are closer together because they are all threatened by extinction;

technology is aiding us through educational television; travel is made much easier for us than ever before, and the time may come when we shall go to high school and college in six or seven different countries. But our basic problems are still the same: we are threatened by bigotry and intolerance; almost one half of the world is illiterate, and there is still a vast gap between the haves and have-nots; our population is increasing at such a rapid rate that we shall have difficulty producing an adequate food supply. In an age when understanding and mutuality are more imperative than ever before the seeds of suspicion remain frighteningly strong.

ALTERNATIVES

There are three main methods by which we may seek to solve the world's problems. The first is revolution. This means violent upheaval. The example of the French revolution and the experiments of Lenin and Stalin lead us to fear that such violence may create but another tyranny. The revolutionary all too often has a Machiavellian perspective and justifies any method to accomplish his goal. In the end, he may establish an oppressive government that is almost as regressive as the previous regime. The great educators of the past, like Socrates, Erasmus, and Tolstoy, have pointed out that change must come from *within* and that it must be based upon ethical principles.

The second means by which we may seek a solution to the world's problems is war. Heraclitus in Greece remarked that war is the father of all things and that it creates the seeds for progress. Hegel remarked that war decides the destiny of the world. Nietzsche once said that war is the essence of civilization. But today we know that a major conflict would spell the end of civilization. After millions of human beings have been killed in the twentieth century, our dilemmas are just as pronounced as in the nineteenth century. An atomic war would be an unparalleled nightmare for humanity.

Our third alternative is education. It works slowly, in an evolutionary manner. It creates no sudden Utopias. It offers no magic remedies. It gives no categorical promises. It demands effort and discipline. It awakens man to his own creative possibilities—to what William James called the "wider self." Education, rightly considered, is man's most formidable tool for survival.

QUESTIONS FOR DISCUSSION AND INVESTIGATION

1. Explain how the optimism of the nineteenth century gradually faded into the disenchantment as characterized by the twentieth century.

2. How is modern man's dilemma represented in Camus' *The Stranger?*

3. In what way is man's lack of involvement described in Camus' *The Stranger* and *The Fall?* How might this theme tie in with the events of your own community?

4. Define the term "mass-man" and indicate the symptoms of its recent growth in our era.

5. What are some of the obstacles that lie along the path to reason?

6. Explain the phrase "living in a twilight atmosphere."

7. Why does war threaten the progress of civilization more than any other force?

8. Enumerate a few historical teachers, some who promoted the negative side and others who stood for the positive side of education.

9. Name the three alternatives by which we may seek to solve the world's problems and compare their ends and means.

10. In what way is education man's most formidable tool for survival?

Chapter 2

The Aims of Education

THE MEANING OF EDUCATION

Education has been defined in various ways. Plato thought that "a good education consists in giving to the body and to the soul all the beauty and all the perfection of which they are capable." Herbert Spencer believed that "education has for its object the formation of character." Horace Mann felt that "education alone can conduct us to that enjoyment which is, at once, best in quality and infinite in quantity." Thomas Henry Huxley thought that "education is the instruction of the intellect in the laws of nature, under which I include not merely things and their forces, but men and their ways, and the fashioning of the affections and of the will into an earnest and loving desire to move in harmony with these laws."

One of the most famous contemporary views of education is that of John Dewey. He regards education as a reconstruction of experience which gives meaning to our existence and which aids us in the direction of subsequent experience. But Dewey himself realized the inadequacy of his definition because *experience* is a very broad term of many meanings, almost as broad as the term *life*. Experience may be directed, as the experiments of Hitler and Mussolini indicate, through indoctrination and propaganda as well as through rational training. Education, I believe, demands a *qualitative* concept of experience. *Thus, we should regard education as a process leading to the enlightenment of mankind.*

This definition implies not merely intellectual growth as a criterion for education, but also emotional maturity and ethical awareness. Thus,

7

education is incomplete without the formation of critical habits. The definition further implies the need for a continuous re-examination of educational methods and objectives.

One may object that this definition neglects the importance of vocational training. How can vocational efficiency add to the enlightenment of mankind? The answer is that human progress depends upon techniques as much as upon intellectual stimulation. Without vocational skills and technological efficiency, education tends to be an exercise in contemplation and abstraction. The purpose of education is not merely to contribute to the continuity of culture, but also to change peacefully and rationally the *material* foundations of civilization.[1]

EDUCATION VS. INDOCTRINATION. Let us consider the difference between education and indoctrination. Indoctrination depends upon the closed mind and preconceived viewpoints, whereas education is open-minded and accepts no absolutes. Indoctrination appeals mainly to our emotional biases, while education appeals primarily to our rational capacities. Indoctrination gives us only partial knowledge, while education seeks complete knowledge. Indoctrination is intensely subjective, whereas education tends to be an objective process.

Dogmatism is the keynote of indoctrination, while tolerance is the watchword of education. The conclusions of indoctrination lead to rigidity and compulsion; the conclusions of education are subject to scientific verification and thus are *tentative*.

Education, as Dewey often pointed out, is not the preparation for life, but represents the continuous changes and processes of life. To identify education with book knowledge is a rather narrow view, for education often arises in the matrix of practical activity. Education implies not merely discipline of thinking, but also a passion for creativity.

THE AGENCIES OF EDUCATION

Most of us recognize the importance of the family in the diffusion of education. Our primary attitudes are shaped in the home and much of our later success depends upon the cultural atmosphere and stimulation of the home.

The community, likewise, aids in the diffusion of knowledge. Certain communities, like Boston, have a tradition of education, while others, especially small agricultural communities, may not regard education as essential. The resources of the large city, particularly its libraries, universities, and museums, aid in intellectual and esthetic growth. Many small communities lack this type of stimulation, and thus tend to be more narrow intellectually than some of the larger cities.

---

[1] Cf. John Dewey, *Democracy and Education,* and *Experience and Education.*

National differences, to a large extent, condition the development of education. Thus, Russia emphasizes totalitarianism in education, while the United States cherishes democratic ideals. South American countries frequently have at least indirect ecclesiastical control over education, while the United States system of education is based upon the principle of *separation of state and church.*

Religious factors, however, cannot be excluded from education. In our own time we are well aware of the rapid growth of parochial education, to a great extent sponsored by the Roman Catholic Church. Denominational colleges have made a significant contribution to higher education in the United States. We must remember that religious organizations were responsible for the founding of the early colleges. Thus, the Congregationalists established Harvard, the Anglicans gave impetus to the founding of King's College (Columbia), and the Presbyterians were active in the establishment of Princeton.

The economic system of a country plays a great role in determining the prevalent educational structure. Capitalism encourages private support of education, as evidenced by the activities of such great foundations as the Rockefeller, Ford, and Carnegie foundations. On the other hand, under a fascist economic system the state controls all activities of education; private support is extremely limited.

Certainly our occupations and vocations influence our outlook upon education. In Greece, for instance, education was mainly a preparation for leisure; thus philosophy to the Athenians was the noblest subject. However, in recent times the gospel of labor has conditioned our educational views; thus, today, education is more vocational and less literary and philosophical. The newspaper, as we all know, has significantly influenced our education systems, perhaps less through the editorial page than through the comic section, which has become a universal medium of entertainment. Newspapers in the nation range from the staid and objective *New York Times* to the tabloids which specialize in sex, crime, and sensationalism.

The radio, like the press, is not only an agency of entertainment, but also transmits matters of informational and educational value. Through the facilities of radio networks we are exposed to lectures, plays, and musical presentations. Millions enjoy such broadcasts as the performances of the Metropolitan Opera and the New York Philharmonic. Panels and discussion groups provide an opportunity for various political parties to voice their views. News commentators illuminate the trends of current events.

The library, another agency of culture and educational diffusion, preserves the books and manuscripts of the past and stores the valuable documents of the present. The free public library is one of the bastions of the democratic way of life; here rich and poor, young and old, meet on the basis of equality—all engaged in the search for knowledge and truth.

It would be impossible to omit the contribution of the motion picture and television to the stimulation of American education and culture. Many great motion pictures give a dramatic view of man's life and present important moral implications. The motion picture is fundamental in shaping the mores of American youth; millions of American girls will imitate their favorite actress, while boys will often speak and act like Marlon Brando. Television promises to be an even greater force than the cinema in shaping popular education. It is possible that a television set may become part of the regular classroom equipment, and that television will greatly aid the teaching process.

We all know the educational effects of travel. Through our travels we come into direct contact with the people of foreign nations as well as people of various sections of our own country. Thus, through travel we often overcome prejudice and bias, and develop a cosmopolitan and broadminded philosophy of life. Whereas formal education tends to be abstract and theoretical, travelling provides a sense of *immediacy and directness.*

We often learn more through play than in our regular classroom. We realize today that education fails if it does not prepare us for a creative use of leisure time.

The mores which exist in our city or nation may influence our outlook upon education. In the study of Middletown by the Lynds it was established that poetry and the arts were thought to be more suitable to women than to men. This may explain the fact that poetry has not become too popular in this nation, for there exists a general feeling that men should not be interested in the arts. Man's function is to earn a living, not to think about impractical subjects. Confucius thought that no one is truly educated who does not appreciate poetry; however, our utilitarian civilization tends to view the poet as being impractical and much less important than the businessman.

We cannot omit the influence of war upon education. Usually, war intensifies the mood of chauvinism and encourages the development of applied science, while it inhibits the advancement of the humanities. War thus contributes to the cultural lag, and adds to the discrepancy between the moral and scientific development of man.

Technology, like war, exerts another important influence upon education. Technology creates new inventions which improve the teaching process and which aid in the art of communication. Often technology becomes an idol of the educator who believes in mechanical solutions, instead of stressing the importance of inspired and inspiring teaching.

We may conclude that education involves not merely the formal school environment, but also the informal agencies of communication.

We learn through multiple sources; education thus is pluralistic rather than monistic. All this implies that the school cannot exist in an atmosphere of isolation, and that it must contribute to social change and social advancement.

THE HISTORICAL AIMS OF EDUCATION

The goals of education have differed in various historical periods. In primitive society, education enforced the status quo and became the bastion of tradition. While primitive education was conservative, modern education tends to be progressive and looks to the future rather than to the past.

Hebrew civilization stressed the religious purpose of education. Through education a correct knowledge of God was to be achieved. Education taught not only the fundamentals of ethics, but was also concerned with history, dietary laws, and the meaning of the ritual. The rabbi was not only a spiritual leader, but also a teacher who would comment upon the meaning of religious laws and the nature and destiny of man.

In Athens, the purpose of education was both rational enlightenment and preparation for citizenship. No infallible book was acknowledged; religion was subordinated to philosophy. Sparta, on the other hand, regarded militarism as the goal of education and specialized in the art of warfare rather than in the arts of peace.

In Rome, education was more practical than in Athens. Romans stressed the obligations of citizenship rather than the pursuit of speculative philosophy. The Roman ideal in education was to produce an individual who would sacrifice for his fatherland, who would be temperate and moderate in his habits, and who would never be discouraged by reverses.

In the Middle Ages the spiritual qualities of education were foremost. It was thought that this life was only a preparation for the beyond. Thus, education aided in asceticism, in curbing our natural appetites and passions, and in preparing us for celestial bliss. The sciences in the Middle Ages were subordinated to theology, which was regarded as the queen of the sciences and as the most significant part of knowledge.

During the Renaissance a different ideal of education emerged. Now the natural capacities of man were glorified; education emphasized individualism rather than spiritual collectivism. The educated man of the Renaissance, as Castiglione indicates, could speak several languages, was versed in the art of love, and looked down upon the rustic manners of the medieval knights.[2]

---

[2] Cf. William T. Waugh, *History of Europe*, ch. 21; Henry O. Taylor, *Thought and Expression in the 16th Century*, vol. 1, ch. 1.

In modern times there is a heavy emphasis on the scientific goals of education. Did not Bacon point out that knowledge means power over nature? Did not science revolutionize the physical world? Did not science give us the basis of the industrial revolution? Modern education, as Thorndike tells us, is based upon psychology and biology, rather than theology.

TENTATIVE GOALS

Several attempts have been made to describe the aims of education. Thus, in 1918, the Commission of the Reorganization of Secondary Education pointed to seven basic goals of education.

Good health
Command of fundamental processes
Worthy home membership
Vocational efficiency
Civic efficiency
Worthy use of leisure
Ethical character

In 1933, a committee of the National Education Association formulated social-economic goals to be realized through education. Among the members of the commission were Leon C. Marshall, Robert C. Moore, Edward A. Ross, John Dewey, and Fred J. Kelly. According to the commission, the goals to be achieved were the following:

Hereditary strength
Physical security
Participation in a growing civilization
   a. Development of skills and techniques
   b. Development of values, standards and meaningful philosophies
A dynamic, flexible personality
   a. Personal initiative
   b. Discriminating viewpoints and choice
   c. Flexibility of thought and conduct
   d. Individual differences
   e. Need for co-operation
Suitable occupation
Economic security
Mental security
Equality of opportunity
Freedom
Fair play

The Educational Policies Commission in 1938 issued an important report on *The Purposes of Education in American Democracy*. The report centers upon four major areas.

1. *Self-realization:* an inquiring mind; command of fundamental processes, such as speech, reading, writing, arithmetic; sight and hearing; health knowledge and habits; interest in public health; recreation; intellectual and esthetic interests; formation of character.

2. *Human relationships:* respect for humanity; friendship; co-operation; courtesy; appreciation of the home; conservation of the home; homemaking; democracy in the home.

3. *Economic efficiency:* the importance of good workmanship; occupational efficiency; occupational adjustment; occupational appreciation; personal economics; consumer judgment; efficiency in buying; consumer protection.

4. *Civic responsibility:* the need for social justice; social activity; social understanding; critical judgment; tolerance; social application of science; world citizenship; understanding of the principles of conservation as related to the national resources; devotion to democracy.

THE BROAD GOALS OF EDUCATION

The main aims of education can be summarized under fifteen headings. Naturally these objectives are tentative.

1. *Reflective thinking* is a primary need. Few of us are aware of the resources of our mind, and thus we spend most of the time in day dreams, rationalizing our pre-conceived beliefs. Reflective thinking involves an attitude of objectivity whereby we formulate tentative theories and try to verify them in a laboratory manner. Reflective thinking is a purposeful activity; it changes, as Dewey points out, an indeterminate into a determinate situation.

2. *Appreciation of culture* should be emphasized. Education is incomplete without the enjoyment of the arts and humanities. A knowledge of the great works of art of the past may illuminate our appreciation of the present. The alarming trend in education, as Whitman indicates, is the reign of vulgarity. Often a monistic viewpoint exists which equates industrial arts with Sophocles, Edgar Guest with Robinson Jeffers, Dale Carnegie with Socrates, and Michelangelo with an illustrator of the *Saturday Evening Post*. Appreciation implies more than a recognition of the great works of art; it means a transvaluation of our attitudes whereby art becomes a way of life and conditions our basic values and goals.

3. *Development of creativity* should be stimulated. Too often education is concerned merely with the imitation of the past; too often education stresses discipline for the sake of discipline; too often the individuality of the student is overlooked; too often the educational process is so boring and anemic that it kills our creative drives. Creativity demands not only insight, but concentration and dedication. Thus, Thomas

Wolfe would revise his novels many times; when he was engaged in creative work all other interests and concerns would be secondary. The teacher can aid creativity by stimulating students, by uncovering hidden talents, and by respecting the originality and individuality of his students. The goal of the teacher should be to lead the student from passivity to activity, and from imitation to creativity.

4. *Understanding and application of science* are significant, because science, perhaps more than any other field, has contributed to the advancement of civilization. At the same time, the new scientific weapons have created immense dangers for the survival of man. Science thus offers no magic solutions and no magic Utopias for modern man.

A clear distinction should be made between the *scientific method* and *technology*. The scientific method is open-minded, tentative, tolerant and abhors absolute conclusion. It can be used in the natural as well as in the social sciences. Technology, on the other hand, represents the application of science. From a moral viewpoint, it may have either constructive or destructive effects. For example, an airplane may be used for transportation or for purposes of mass destruction.

The task of education is to give us a balanced view of science, to see both its possibilities and limitations.

5. *Contact with great ideas* is another aim of education. We learn by critical thinking as well as by doing. Many philosophers have been concerned mainly with abstractions; they have looked upon ideas as things-in-themselves. Ideas, it must be remembered, are functional and they initiate social change, as in the case of Darwin and Freud.

Contact with great ideas leads us away from the immediate and gives us perspective regarding our own time and our own culture. However, the emphasis in our educational thinking should not primarily be upon description of events and ideas, but rather upon the ways and means through which life can be changed and improved.

6. *Moral and spiritual values* cannot be excluded from the educative process. Yet, moral and spiritual values are often regarded in a rather narrow manner. Teachers are frequently subjected to a multitude of tabus, especially in small towns. They are evaluated by their conformity, rather than by their sense of originality.

A commentator stated recently that he wanted to preserve the spiritual values of our civilization. When I asked him how this would be accomplished, he replied that he wanted to banish writers like Steinbeck and Hemingway from the high school anthologies, for writers such as these present a "perverted view of life."

Genuine spirituality implies quite a different perspective than that represented by the commentator. Genuine spirituality implies a questioning spirit and an identification with the highest symbols of cultures. Like Jesus and Buddha, the truly spiritual teacher will regard all men as equal and he will disregard the barriers of race, religion and nationality.

7. *Fundamental skills* are basic in education. Yet these skills do not just imply a mastery of reading, writing, and arithmetic, but they include an emphasis upon the art of communication and the development of esthetic sensitivity. To be able to read, write legibly and understand the bases of mathematics—all these capacities are not to be equated with genuine education. A more significant measure of genuine education would be the ability to critically analyze literature, distinguish between propaganda and truth, and arrive at rational decisions.

8. *Vocational efficiency* has become a primary concern of modern education. We are interested not only in the enjoyment of life, but also in how we can best make a living. Unfortunately, we often choose the wrong profession; as a result we feel frustrated and may develop a severe neurosis.

Once we realize that we are in the wrong career field we may react as violently as Gauguin, who sacrificed respectability and economic success to devote himself to art, both in the garrets of Paris and in the wilderness of various South Sea Islands.

Vocational efficiency should not be equated with economic success; otherwise we are dominated by the idol of materialism. Often, important professions, like teaching, are certainly not the most remunerative careers. We should develop a respect for all, as much for the mechanic as for the banker, as much for the poet as for the scientist.

9. *Effective education* implies a better adjustment to family life. Through education we can improve our appreciation of the home and we can become more considerate of others. We become aware of the destructive ways of conflict and of the importance of mutual sharing and understanding. Confucius already pointed out that the educated man should set an example, not merely in his thinking, but also in his conduct.

Education can change both the spiritual and physical aspects of the home. It can create a more esthetic atmosphere, and it can improve our homemaking capacities. It can also change our basic attitudes; we may cease to regard our own needs and desires as primary and instead learn to cooperate with others.

10. *Effective citizenship* is best achieved through education. Citizenship implies more than the fulfillment of elementary political duties—it implies the need for tolerance and social justice and the development of a genuine social conscience. Effective citizenship demands not only a verbal allegiance to democracy, it requires also the daily application of democratic principles in the home, in the classroom, in business, and in political affairs.

11. Without *physical and mental health* all the other objectives are superficial and visionary. While good health, to some extent, depends upon our heredity, modern science has made immense strides. Through correct habits, emphasizing the interdependence of the mind and body, we can achieve not only a long life, but also a healthy and happy life.

Mental health requires a balanced perspective and the avoidance of extremes. If we are sadistic or masochistic, if we hate others, if we are imperialistic in our behavior, if we act on an infantile plane, then, certainly, psychological conflicts are bound to occur.

Education can become the tool of maturity. It should be, as Spinoza said, a reflection upon life rather than upon death; it should indicate our possibilities—both physical and mental—rather than our limitations.

12. Genuine education ought to change our *personality*. Whitehead once stated that being interesting is more important than being factually correct. If education has made us boring and uninteresting then it has missed its goal. Real knowledge should make us more dynamic and fascinating, we should radiate our zest and yearning for truth.

13. Education ought to give us *permanent interests*. Activities that are confined merely to the classroom are superficial. If we only read the books that are assigned we are inferior students; we should read on our own and become imbued with the *adventure* of knowledge.

Our leisure time interests ought to reflect our yearning for education. Certainly, sports, movies, an active social life are to be recommended; still, all these activities are not ends in themselves and are inferior to cultural activities, which raise our level of understanding and sensitivity.

14. *The achievement of peace* is one of the fundamental objectives of education. Any system of education which contributes to mistrust among nations and which glorifies chauvinism and military force is to be condemned. Thus, we read in *All Quiet on the Western Front* about the education system of Germany before 1914. Technically, it was proficient. The German youths had an excellent classical background and a comprehensive knowledge of science, but their minds were poisoned by myths about the superiority and infallibility of the German fatherland.

15. Education aims at a *perpetual renaissance* of man. It indicates that man is the measure of the universe, that knowledge is an infinite process, and that creativity must radiate and not be confined to the few. As educators it is our task to create not only original minds in art, literature, music, philosophy, religion, and science, but also to develop an interested audience which can appreciate creativeness.

Education thus looks to the future; it indicates that man has not finished his task, rather that he has only begun. Education is not the prelude to despair and cynicism, but the eternal overture to hope and expectancy.

QUESTIONS FOR DISCUSSION AND INVESTIGATION

1. What significance lies in the belief of education as a qualitative concept rather than as a quantitative concept?

2. What is the difference between education and indoctrination?

3. Enumerate the agencies of education in a given community.

4. How do war and technology influence education?

5. Compare and contrast the educational aims of the Middle Ages and of the Renaissance; of Athens and of Rome; of Hebrew civilization and of modern times.

6. What are the seven basic goals of education, as described in 1918 by the Commission of the Reorganization of Secondary Education?

7. Enumerate the "Purposes of Education in American Democracy" as presented by the Educational Policies Commission in 1938.

8. Give the fifteen headings under which are listed the broad goals of education.

9. Distinguish between scientific method and technology.

10. Discuss this statement: "Education is not the prelude to despair and cynicism, but the eternal overture to hope and expectancy."

Chapter 3

Education for Progress

In every period education has reflected the values of society. Thus in Sparta it developed warriors who had little interest in literature and the arts; in Athens a more universal view of culture was stressed; while in Rome patriotic values were emphasized in the school system. In the Middle Ages the teacher was the servant of ecclesiasticism, and he was expected to follow the dictates of orthodoxy. If he expressed too many independent ideas he would be persecuted and would live a precarious existence. In later periods he was to be dominated by national authorities and hence his task was to glorify the idols of the tribe. Therefore, a teacher in Germany was expected to stress the supremacy of the German way of life and in France the teacher was to uphold the glories of French culture. In times of peace the teacher occasionally could point to the deficiencies in the national way of life, but no real dissent was allowed in wartime. Such dissent was equated with treason.

The result has been that authoritarian education and philosophy have deepened the culture lag of modern times. They have contributed to the cult of chauvinism and militarism. They have created millions of youngsters who worship before the altar of national power and expediency. The predictions of Hobbes and Machiavelli have been fulfilled, for both thinkers realized that in the end the modern totalitarian state would tolerate no opposition and would become a Leviathan which would dominate all activities and yearnings of its citizens.

CHANGE AND CULTURE

What impresses us is the constancy of change. When Heraclitus expressed the statement that the "universe is in a constant state of flux," he developed the theory of relativity. The concept of change is especially important in our own time. When we think about the last 150 years in America, is it not true that progression has been present everywhere? Think of the change in technology, from the horse to space travel.

There is a story of an old lady who had observed her 95th birthday, and someone suggested she go on an airplane trip. She was a determined lady. She said, "No, God doesn't want me to fly; he just wants me to watch television." In our time, we take many inventions such as television for granted. We do not want to intimate that they have had an entirely beneficial result; television as yet is in its infancy and it is to be hoped it will not experience premature senility.

Flux is the dominant trait of modern life. Think of the cities around us, the new housing developments; and certainly it is true that transition prevails. This change creates great emotional and philosophic problems, one of which is adjustment; for we find almost everywhere a lack of security. Our grandfathers and grandmothers knew about the structure of the future, but in an age of the hydrogen bomb we do not know very much about the next century—not even about tomorrow.

Emerson anticipated our dilemma when he wrote:

"Yes, we have a pretty artillery of tools now in our social arrangement: we ride four times as fast as our fathers did; travel, grind, weave, forge, plant, till and excavate better. We have new shoes, gloves, glasses and gimlets; we have the calculus; we have the newspaper, which does its best to make every square acre of land and sea give an account of itself at your breakfast table; we have money, and paper money; we have language—the finest tool of all, and nearest to the mind. Much will have more. Man flatters himself that his command over Nature must increase. Things begin to obey him. We are to have the balloon yet, and the next war will be fought in the air. We may yet find a rose water that will wash the Negro white. He sees the skull of the English race changing from its Saxon type under the exigencies of American life.

"Tantalus, who in old times was seen vainly trying to quench his thirst with a flowing stream which ebbed whenever he approached it, has been seen again lately. He is in Paris, in New York, in Boston. He is now in great spirits; thinks he shall reach it yet; thinks he shall bottle the wave. It is however getting a little doubtful. Things have an ugly look still. No matter how many centuries of culture have preceded, the new man always finds himself standing on the brink of chaos, always in a crisis. Can anybody remember when the times were not hard, and money not scarce? Can anybody remember when sensible men, and the right sort of men, and the right sort of women were plentiful? Tantalus begins to think steam a delusion, and galvanism no better than it should be.

"Many facts concur to show that we must look deeper for our salvation than to steam, photographs, balloons or astronomy. These tools have some questionable properties. They are reagents. Machinery is aggressive. The weaver becomes a web, the machinist a tool."[1]

---

1 *Works and Days*

As we look at modern man we find that he has more conveniences than ever before and yet he is dissatisfied. He can travel more than his ancestors, but his views tend to be parochial. He is exposed to more agencies of communication, such as radio and television, but he has little to communicate. He achieves more prosperity and has more worldly goods, but he is suffering from spiritual poverty. He joins a multitude of organizations and yet he tends to be lonely. His conscience is more enlightened and yet he tolerates incredible callousness. He talks more about peace and yet is unwilling to compromise on crucial issues which may promote war. He believes that he is tolerant, still he harbors a multitude of prejudices. To Eugene O'Neill, one of the great modern writers, the *Hairy Ape* is the symbol of modern man, for like the main character in O'Neill's play, modern man is guided by subterranean impulses which he cannot control and which threaten his happiness and integrity.

Undoubtedly, today we have more cultural institutions than ever before, yet we produce relatively few awakened individuals. This does not imply that in the 18th century or before more cultured individuals were created, rather that we are not meeting the main challenge of our time which demands reason, moderation, and a sense of self-limitation.

It is questionable whether man can survive with a conventional educational system. Conventional education, especially in the totalitarian nations, is guided by narrowness and self-interest. It is dominated by political leaders who are swayed by the expediency of the moment. It teaches proficiency rather than self-examination. It produces graduates who are interested in success rather than wisdom. It creates specialists who are uninterested in the wider issues of humanity and who will serve any authority as long as they are paid and find a degree of security .

In *Brave New World Revisited* Huxley pictures the modern world as a totalitarian paradise. Indoctrination has replaced impartial investigation, propaganda controls the market-place. It appears that Dr. Goebbels has become the main guide of modern man. Decisions are made by the few for the many. In the meantime modern man moves from crisis to crisis, just a step away from ultimate catastrophe.

THE CRISIS IN CULTURE

In the United States the same ambivalent tendencies which plague society infest our cultural institutions. *Middletown, Middletown in Transition,* and *The Lonely Crowd* are studies not merely of the lags of our social structure but of the deficiencies of our cultural institutions. We may have the same status seeking in education as in business. We may find the same impersonality in higher education as in many of the major cities.

Culture is hindered by an emphasis on bigness. We are intoxicated by numbers. Trustees rate a professor by the number of books which he publishes rather than by his ability to inspire students and be a sage. Professors have often a mechanical view of our students and judge them by grades and achievement tests rather than by inward growth and genuine creativity.

In this way society produces the indifferent student and the anemic teacher. The indifferent student goes through the motions of learning, but he is not really challenged and involved. He remains forever an outsider. Education is a process which he endures so that he can become successful in life and improve his earning power.

The indifferent teacher may be proficient in his subject matter but he feels no existential excitement. He is judgmental in his approach to his students. He is concerned with conformity. In every way he is looking forward to retirement. He follows the rules of the game, but he sees little relevance in the educational process.

This atmosphere of indifference in our time can be noted in the escapism which prevails in most motion pictures and television plays. We are producing more and more spectators who are passive about life. Democracy demands intense participation, yet political elections, especially on the local level, evoke a relatively anemic response. Newspapers feature social columns and sports events; they exaggerate scandal and corruption. The crucial international issues of our time attract only a minority of readers.

The task of education is to transform the market place and to make democracy a reality. This can be done only when the school leads society and when it attempts to make education the major concern of modern man.

To accomplish this goal, a creative perspective is needed. This implies total education and a universalization of our ideals. Just as Epicurus taught the young and the old, the wise and the foolish, slaves and freemen, so today we must not be worried so much about rigid standards of achievement but rather about standards of humanity. We must learn that education is tested by the way we perceive and by the way we live. The fact that there are so many malignant fanatics in our time indicates that reason has only been a footnote in man's existence. With prejudice making so many converts, an enlightened view of man is imperative. Thus the teacher must be more than a scholar and a practitioner of the intellect; he must be like a therapist who fights against neurotic anxiety and superstition.

Our schools are successful if they produce truly happy individuals. To do this their environment must be more relaxed and humane; the individual, whether he has an I.Q. of 80 or 180, should be respected. Originality of expression is to be emphasized on all levels. The dominant objective must not be how many students can be eliminated, rather how many can find abiding enjoyment through education and the humanities.

Some might say that this is a utopian ideal. Are not most condemned to a mediocre life? Is not great culture the result of the élite? Are not the masses mainly interested in sensate desires? The answer is that education has usually been a fragmentary enterprise and has been guided by a philosophy of negation and authoritarianism. Some educators feel that if the students dislike a subject they become more disciplined; in reality they usually become objectors to learning.

One of the most promising aspects of learning in our time is adult education. To be sure, some of the adult programs are trivial and some of the subjects taught encourage a specialized view of life. But adult education on the highest level is a pattern for all learning. For adult education is concerned with universality, emphasizes real discussion, and tries to overcome the class barriers which plague our society. Adult education, based on an appreciation of diversity, becomes the foundation of democracy. The awakened adult understands that knowledge is not a luxury but the substance of life. He realizes, as Epicurus did, that the mind is the source of real joy and happiness and that when he neglects the mind he opens the door to oblivion. He realizes that it is not enough to memorize and to accumulate facts. What is important is to apply wisdom to daily living.

To appreciate culture, to universalize ideals, to live without superstition in an atmosphere of peace, to banish anxiety, to grasp the preciousness of the present, to be cheerful regardless of the varying fortunes of fate, to treasure humanity, to enjoy the adventure of living—these are the imperatives of creative education for our age.

Thoreau expressed these thoughts poetically when he wrote:

"If the day and the night are such that you greet them with joy, and life emits a fragrance like flowers and sweet-scented herbs, is more elastic, more starry, more immortal,—that is your success. All nature is your congratulation, and you have cause momentarily to bless yourself. . . . The true harvest of my daily life is somewhat as intangible and indiscernible as the tints of morning or evening. It is a little star-dust caught, a segment of the rainbow which I have clutched."[1]

---

1 *Walden*

QUESTIONS FOR DISCUSSION AND INVESTIGATION

1. How has education reflected in every historical period the values of society?

2. Explain how authoritarian education and philosophy have deepened the cultural lag of modern times.

3. Give examples of how flux is the dominant trait of modern life.

4. What signs of Emerson's time inspired him to anticipate our own dilemmas?

5. What was Tantalus' spirit of philosophy and education and how is it manifested today?

6. Cite examples of the growing paradoxes in modern life.

7. Why is it considered to be doubtful whether man can survive with a conventional education system?

8. Cite reasons as to why "bigness" hinders culture.

9. What is the great task of education?

10. Why is adult education one of the most promising aspects of learning, particularly in our time?

Chapter 4

The Vocation of the Teacher

In a period of crisis and transition the position of the teacher is more significant than at any other time. Today, the American teacher represents the hope of our society. We look to education to solve the perplexing problems of our time. The threat of war, the ravages of delinquency, the crises of marriage, the rise in mental illness—all these problems can be solved only through a concentrated investment in education.

What is the function of the teacher? What are his responsibilities? How should he conceive of his task? What should be his basic philosophy of life? What can he learn from educational history and theory?

ENTHUSIASM. Teaching is not merely an intellectual process. Man, as Aristotle maintained, may be a rational animal, but at the same time feelings are fundamental in our behavior. We must be conscious of fundamental motives, such as the drives for security, response, recognition, new experience, and cooperation. Too many students in our schools merely endure education. They conform to the ritual, they study the assignments, and they may get acceptable grades. But they are not enthusiastic about school. As a result, culture to them becomes a luxury instead of being an imperative.

Some teachers, likewise, are not sufficiently enthusiastic about their vocation. They are governed by routine. They feel frustrated because of economic pressure. With only a limited vision of the opportunities of teaching these teachers are not able to become unforgettable events in the lives of their students.

To teach profoundly is to experience the attractions of love. Plato one time remarked that love rises from a physical to a spiritual realm, that it moves from a specific to a universal area. In the highest stage of love, the individual forgets about his selfhood and his own desires and wishes. This type of love is often experienced by the dedicated teacher who lives for a higher cause, a teacher who sees the schoolroom as a representation of the drama of life. He sees education as man's eternal quest to transcend his limitations and to live by ideals instead of being seduced by the idols of immediacy. He looks upon education as man's most precious good, for it represents the possibilities of the future.

The student knows almost instinctively how the teacher feels about him. If the teacher is indifferent and lethargic, the student will reciprocate with an attitude of boredom. On the other hand, when the teacher really loves his work, then students will be inspired and they will realize the significance of education for their own development.

IDEALS

To love teaching does not imply vague sentimentality. The wise teacher knows how to encourage and how to criticize, how to praise and how to uncover areas of weakness. He never allows smugness and self-righteousness. He sees to it that the brilliant student develops a sense of social responsibility and, at the same time, that the slow learner does not lose interest in the process of knowledge. The wise teacher is aware of the importance of good habits without which success cannot be achieved. Not all parts of knowledge can be dramatized; education demands effort and application. Hard work, concentration, rigorous efforts, respect for scholarship—these attitudes make learning important. To be "too easy" with students is a temptation which the wise teacher must overcome. Students are grateful to their teacher when he demands real effort and real dedication.

CREATIVITY. *Teaching is one of the most creative professions of mankind.* When we think of creativity we usually consider the realm of art and science, and we recall literary giants, like Aeschylus and Goethe, painters like Da Vinci and Van Gogh, and scientists like Newton and Einstein. But the most important area of creativity lies in the field of human relations. The teacher has the privilege to see growth in action. Often he watches a student develop from an attitude of passivity to one of enthusiastic participation. A shy girl thus may never take part in class discussions; suddenly she may be awakened and may become an alert individual, imbued with the importance of ideas. In kindergarten a child may be utterly selfish and may never share his toys. Then, because of the influence of a dedicated teacher, such a child may become an altruistic human being.

The importance of the teacher is celebrated in *Rugby Chapel*, which Matthew Arnold dedicated to his father:

> *"And through thee I believe*
> *In the noble and great who are gone;*
> *Pure souls honour'd and blest*
> *By former ages, who else—*
> *Such, so soulless, so poor,*
> *Is the race of men whom I see—*
> *Seem'd but a dream of the heart,*
> *Seem'd but a cry of desire.*
> *Yes! I believe that there lived*
> *Others like thee in the past,*
> *Not like the men of the crowd*
> *Who all round me to-day*
> *Bluster or cringe, and make life*
> *Hideous, and arid, and vile;*
> *But souls temper'd with fire,*
> *Fervent, heroic, and good,*
> *Helpers and friends of mankind . . ."*

Arnold continues with his praise:

> *"Then, in such hour of need*
> *Of your fainting, dispirited race,*
> *Ye, like angels appear,*
> *Radiant with ardor divine.*
> *Beacons of hope, ye appear!*
> *Langour is not in your heart,*
> *Weakness is not in your word,*
> *Weariness is not on your brow.*
> *Ye alight in our van; at your voice,*
> *Panic, despair, flee away.*
> *Ye move through the ranks, recall*
> *The stragglers, refresh the outworn,*
> *Praise, reinspire the brave.*
> *Order, courage, return.*
> *Eyes rekindling, and prayers,*
> *Follow your steps as ye go.*
> *Ye fill up the gaps in our files,*
> *Strengthen the wavering line,*
> *Stablish, continue our march,*
> *On, to the bound of the waste,*
> *On, to the City of God."*

TO TEACH PROFOUNDLY IS TO INSPIRE. Teaching is the most dramatic form of inspiration. Emerson once remarked that there are two types of teachers. One type speaks from the outside; he is concerned with facts and measurements. The other type speaks from the depth of his soul; he is the prophet of inwardness. He is guided by an inner vision which he exemplifies in his actions and which he communicates to his students. As teachers we can inspire only when we realize our responsibilities and our opportunities. If we look upon our task as a form of drudgery then we become technicians who only preserve knowledge instead of expanding it.

To be inspired in teaching means to anticipate the future. It is to live for a larger cause which has unlimited possibilities. It is to find a true happiness and a lasting joy. It is to be a guardian of progress and a servant of humanity.

As we survey the story of education, we shall find it to be a story of achievement and failure, enlightenment and superstition, progress and traditionalism, creativity and stagnation. The story shows that educational progress is not inevitable, but that it must be safeguarded by every generation. The past then becomes a prelude to redefinition and reexamination so that a more creative future can be achieved.

QUESTIONS FOR DISCUSSION AND INVESTIGATION

1. Why is the teacher's position most significant during times of crisis and transition?

2. Explain how culture for too many students tends to become a luxury instead of an imperative.

3. Describe the teacher who is not enthusiastic about his vocation.

4. Explain the statement, "To teach profoundly is to experience the attractions of love"?

5. Explain the importance of interaction between teacher and student.

6. What are the qualities of a wise teacher?

7. Why is teaching one of the most creative professions of mankind?

8. Describe the spirit of Matthew Arnold's poem *Rugby Chapel*.

9. What is Emerson's distinction between the two types of teachers?

10. How can a more creative future be achieved in terms of more effective education?

Part 2

Ancient
and
Medieval Education

Chapter 5

Foundations of Indian Religion and Education

THE SPIRIT OF INDIAN PHILOSOPHY

Indian philosophy is primarily dominated by metaphysical interests. Most Indian thinkers are not satisfied with the consideration of superficial and transitory events; rather, they seek for an unchanging and eternal essence. Unlike Chinese philosophy with its ethical interests, Indian philosophy deals above all with the problems of reality. Man, in Indian thought, is subordinated to the universe; life itself becomes a pilgrimage, almost an interlude in the cosmic process.

It has often been remarked that this interest in metaphysics destroys a truly ethical perspective on the part of the Indian thinker, and that it serves as a rationalization for existing social evils. However, this charge is only partially correct. It is true that much of Indian philosophy, especially Hinduism, provided religious justification for the caste system. Other Indian philosophers, above all Buddha, vigorously attacked the prevailing social system, including the institution of the caste. The more we study Indian philosophy in its educational implications, the more we shall appreciate its bold ethical teachings and its sublime concept of the nature and destiny of man.

WORLD OF BEING. Noteworthy in Indian thinking is its *vast time perspective*. The destiny of the individual is evaluated not according to momentary considerations, not even according to historical factors; rather again and again it is pointed out, especially in the *Upanishads,* that reality is beyond space and time. *Thus the world of becoming is subordinated to the world of being.* It is difficult for the Westerner to appreciate this perspective since he is so intensely conscious of historical events and, in most cases, he has such a well developed time consciousness. The Indian thinker, on the other hand, tries to grasp reality as a whole. Imbued with the theory of reincarnation, he sees life on earth only as a fragmentary and partial process, as one step in a cosmic drama which has as its goal the extinction of all separateness and individuality.[1]

IMPERSONAL FORCE. This brings us to another salient factor of Indian philosophy—its impersonal basis. Whereas the Western mind usually regards personality as the highest category, and personal fulfillment as the ideal existence, the Indian thinkers, from Buddha to Shankara, look upon selfhood as a lower category of being; they believe that the self is in a constant state of flux. According to most Indian thinkers, real education cannot be obtained if we abide by the demands of the individual ego because real education demands the obliteration and absorption of the self in a larger unity.

In most cases, the Indian thinker does not worship God as a personal being; in fact, atheistic trends are strong in many systems, including Buddhism and the Sankhya philosophy. This does not indicate a secular bent; instead it appears that the Indian thinker is intoxicated with a detached intellectual love of God. He feels, like Spinoza, that the universe does not reveal personal features, but an impersonal force which transcends all limitations of space, time, and physical existence.

LIFE OF SPIRIT. For real education, the Indian thinkers recommend, above all, emancipation from material goals and desires. Progress is not to be evaluated according to wealth, fame, or physical power. Social improvement is secondary, for the Indian thinker believes in the cultivation of the spirit and emphasizes cosmic values through which man realizes his essential self.

In fact, there is a definite contrast in Indian philosophy between the life of the senses and the life of the spirit. The life of the senses gratifies only our physical desires, brings about at best an animal happiness, and is, essentially, a superficial existence. The life of the spirit, which demands constant discipline and unending application, leads to true contentment, gives a knowledge of eternal life, and, in penetrating all appearances and all superficiality, reveals the illusion of multiplicity and the basic oneness of the universe.

TOLERANCE. Compared with Western philosophy, the Indian system of education permits more variety and tolerance when it treats philosophical conclusions.[2] Again and again, Indian thinkers point out that truth appears on various levels and that it is impossible for one man to have

---

[1] For an excellent introduction to Indian philosophy see Hiriyanna, *Outlines of Indian Philosophy*; Carus, *The Gospel of Buddha*; Radhakrishnan, *Indian Philosophy*, 2 vols.

[2] Many prominent schools of thought, especially the Buddhists and the Sankhya, presented vigorous arguments against the existence of God.

a monopoly on wisdom and scientific knowledge. A generous allowance is made for man's innate limitations; consequently, the categories of reason are frequently subordinated to the demands of intuition and insight. Thus, Indian thinkers do not accept the conclusion of science as absolutely valid, for, in the highest stages of knowledge, science is replaced by mysticism, and reason yields to an intuitive appreciation of reality.[3]

While religious controversies have cost millions of lives in the West, religious debates, at least in earlier times, were carried on in a far more broad-minded spirit in India. Hinduism, especially, was able to absorb a variety of other religious theories. The various gods of India intermingled and thus became extremely cosmopolitan.

PESSIMISM. Indian philosophy has often been charged with being overly pessimistic. Schopenhauer derived much of his doloristic wisdom from the thinkers of the *Upanishads* and from Buddhism. The Indians certainly did not accept the optimistic belief that this is the best of all possible worlds. Indian pessimism, however, is not synonymous with a spirit of negativism and placidity. Rather, it is symbolic of a *profound dissatisfaction with the existing world.* The spirit of pessimism demands transcendence—the conquest of the lower self, of fame, of riches, and of the yearning for social approval. It reminds man of his eternal origin and his eternal destiny. In short, Indian thought presents us with a truly universal perspective. It demands that we turn away from the finite, from all that is transitory and perishable, and that instead we concentrate upon eternal ideas and eternal verities.

THE VEDAS

Indian philosophy is expressed on a rudimentary level by the *Vedas* which were mainly religious hymns; literally translated, "veda" stands for knowledge. The main Vedas which have come down to us are: 1. the *Rig-Veda,* which contained mainly lyrical hymns of testimony and praise; 2. the *Sama-Veda,* which contained instructions regarding melodies; 3. the *Yajur-Veda,* which dealt with the proper procedure in sacrifice; and 4. the *Atharva-Veda,* which contained some detailed instructions regarding the best ways of attaining magical results in religion.

POLYTHEISM. A basic theme of the *Vedas* is the spirit of polytheism.[4] Practically all the forces of nature were worshipped, not only animate but inanimate objects. Especially significant among the Veda gods was *Agni,* the god of fire, who anything but restrained, revealed almost Dionysian emotions. The flame which he wielded brought him close to mankind and represented the force of eternity.

---

3 Cf. Cyril Edwin Joad, *Counter-Attack from the East, The Philosophy of Radhakrishnan*.

4 For a discussion of the spirit of the Vedas consult Arthur B. Keith, *The Religion and Philosophy of the Veda and Upanishads,* 2 vols.

Varuna was the sky god who, at first, had mainly physical functions; later he was regarded in a moral light. Varuna punished those who transgressed moral laws and rewarded those who were righteous in their behavior.

Another important God was *Indra,* the deity of thunder and storm, who usually was pictured as a great hero, capable of accomplishing magical feats of strength. Disdaining temperance, Indra had an enormous love for wine; it was popular belief that his aid could best be gained by the drinking of the soma-juice, through which man absorbed the divine presence.

It was frequently stated in the *Vedas* that the favor of the gods could best be achieved through material gifts; hence, we have a separation of morality and theology.[5] The priests were in charge of the divine formulas. In order to be saved, man had to pay the priests sufficiently and subject himself to their education. Only in this manner would the divine secrets be revealed to him.

PANTHEISM. Still, at least in one hymn of the *Vedas* a rather amazing philosophic spirit begins to emerge. It is called the *Song of Creation.*

> *"THEN was not non-existent nor existent: there*
> *was no realm of air, no sky beyond it.*
> *What covered it, and where? and what gave shelter?*
> *Was water there, unfathomed depth of water?*
>
> *Death was not then, nor was there aught immortal:*
> *no sign was there, the day's and night's divider*
> *That one thing, breathless, breathed by its own*
> *nature: apart from it was nothing whatsoever.*
>
> *Darkness there was: at first concealed in darkness,*
> *this All was indiscriminated chaos.*
> *All that existed then was void and formless: by*
> *the great power of warmth was born that unit.*
>
> *Thereafter rose desire in the beginning, Desire,*
> *the primal seed and germ of spirit.*
> *Sages who searched with their heart's thought*
> *discovered the existent's kinship in the non-existent.*
>
> *He, the first origin of this creation, whether*
> *he formed it all or did not form it,*
> *Whose eye controls this world in highest heaven*
> *he verily knows it, or perhaps he knows not."* [6]

---

[5] This point is especially evident in the *Atharva-Veda.*

[6] *The Song of Creation,* Book X, 129.

This hymn reveals a touch of pantheism. There is no absolute separation between the creative power and nature—both are intermingled. It is important to note that the gods, according to this hymn, did not exist in the beginning. Perhaps they themselves did not know the secret of life. Thus, in addition to pantheism, we have a significant note of skepticism, which challenged both the power of God and the knowledge of man.

Another significant note of this hymn is its emphasis upon desire as the basic foundation of the universe. Advancement comes through desire and is nourished by its volcanic force; without desire there can be no self-consciousness. Desire is the connecting link between the finite and the infinite. In the beginning there was only a fathomless abyss; now there are definite forms guided by desire. Psychologically, desire stands for more than intellectual knowledge—it stands for unending activity and for boundless craving. But as we shall see later in Buddhism, desire is regarded as the principle of evil, for it brings about multiplicity and separateness.

MORALITY. The moral ideals of the *Vedas* are based on theological foundations. Righteousness, thus, is determined by the will of the gods—those who sin are punished by the deities. Generally, we find a rather external sense of morality; as yet the sense of inwardness, of the subjective sense of right or wrong, has not developed. Compared with the *Upanishads* there is less asceticism in the *Vedas*. Life is to be enjoyed to the utmost and mortification of the body is disregarded. Religious ritual is to increase the power of man over nature.

UPANISHADS

The philosophical and educational spirit of India appears in its full glory and splendor in the *Upanishads*. The date of the *Upanishads* has not been established with certainty. It is believed that one hundred and eight of these discourses were written between 800 and 400 B.C. It is a mistake to think of them as systematic opinions on reality; frequently, they are full of inconsistencies and sometimes reveal a rather naive concept of the external world. But, in many places, they embody some of the most profound observations ever made in philosophy.

Generally, the tone of the *Upanishads* is impersonal. In vain do we look for a Socrates or a Plato. The dominant thinker is Yajnavalkya, a sage and educator, who leaves earthly pleasures behind, including two wives, in order to become a philosopher.

KNOWLEDGE. To appreciate the educational philosophy of the *Upanishads,* we must understand the nature of the questions which are raised by these discourses. The first question deals with man's knowledge. How can man know reality—how can he understand the essence of the universe? The authors of the *Upanishads* gave an extremely modern answer; in some ways they anticipated Bergson. Man knows reality, not through the intellect, but through intuition. The intellect sees everything as being related, but reality is beyond relations. In short, we have almost a God-intoxicated spirit.

To understand God, it is useless to cultivate detailed and analytical learning. Words are incapable of expressing the splendor of the universe and the majesty of reality. The best attitude resembles the openness of the child which disdains idle disputes and is receptive to all the impressions of life.

Thus, the *Upanishads* favor a state of mysticism. The soul loses its sense of separateness, for the spiritual vision obliterates all phenomenal distinctions. The real self is not attained through book knowledge nor through scientific investigation, but can only be achieved through spontaneous illumination.

This implies that man has within himself a *divine spirit*. The task of education then is to liberate this unique capacity. In the religious life, "the unknown becomes known." This does not mean that the intellect is to be entirely disregarded, but it is to be supplemented and intensified by the resources of mystic insight.

The nature of this insight cannot be described verbally, only through the use of symbolic terms. Later we shall find again how the mystics of the West used allegory to describe the highest stages of knowledge. If we are asked to define the nature of reality, *silence* is the best answer. Thus, when a sage was asked by a king to explain Brahman, he did not answer at all. When asked a second time, the sage reminded the king that the real self "is peaceful, quiet."

NATURE OF SELF. Another important question in the *Upanishads* is concerned with the nature of the self. Again and again, the thinkers of the *Upanishads* emphasize that the empirical self is not real. The ego, which we feel and which directs our emotions, is only a bundle of sensations. When we dream, we experience a world which appears to be absolutely real, but when we wake up, it appears to us as a vague memory.

The *Upanishads* develop the doctrine of the universal soul, *Brahman,* to which the individual soul, *Atman,* will be reunited after Maya (the illusion of time and space) is conquered. Thus, the real self is universal and cannot be touched by the ravages of time. *Atman* and *Brahman,* subjective and objective reality, are the same. Brahman is imperishable, unchangeable, and eternal.[7] It can only be defined in impersonal terms, for Brahman is not a personal god.

Those who find Brahman are beyond life and death. Man's essential nature neither is created nor does it die. Spiritual education reminds us

---

[7] Cf. Deussen, *The System of the Vedanta*, p. 94.

of the unity of life: "If the killer thinks that he kills, if the killed thinks that he is killed, they do not understand; for this one does not kill, nor is that one killed. The self, smaller than small, greater than great, is hidden in the heart of that creature. A man who is free from desires and free from grief, sees the majesty of the Self by the grace of the Creator. Though sitting still, he walks far; though lying down, he goes everywhere. Who, save myself, is able to know that God who rejoices and rejoices not? The wise man who knows the Self as bodiless within the bodies, as unchanging among changing things, as great and omnipresent, does never grieve." [8]

EVIL. How can we account for evil? How can we explain the imperfection of the universe? How can we understand the nature of sin? According to the authors of the *Upanishads,* evil is essentially bound up with individuality.[9]

Man acts in a wicked way when he places his own interest first and when he disregards the welfare of the universe. Since God is reflected everywhere, evil, as such, does not have metaphysical reality. Still, from an ethical standpoint we cannot deny evil, and man must struggle hard to achieve goodness.

To make the matter clear, we can say that evil is everything that isolates man from God and from the essential sources of His being. Whereas the good man identifies himself with God, to the evil man the universe is contained in his own fragmentary experiences. When he fails, the universe is cruel and wicked, for he sees himself as the only actor on the stage. The good man, however, realizes the inevitable chain which guides all human destiny; he is a part of a vast unit, identifies himself with others, and guides his will by the dictates of God.

How can morality be achieved? Not through pleasure, according to the *Upanishads,* nor through the exercise of our physical capacities. The life of the senses is secondary to the life of the spirit. Perfection cannot be achieved without constant ordeals. In fact, the path to truth and and knowledge and education is like the edge of a razor. Throughout our existence we must struggle against our lower impulses, against greed, physical lust, willfulness, pride, and arrogance. Such a life requires unending education. Still, the final goal justifies our abandonment of lower desires.

CAUSE AND EFFECT. Another fundamental concept in the *Upanishads* is *Karma,* the law of cause and effect. Whatever we do, whatever we accomplish, whatever we decide has a definite bearing upon our personalities. The moral law is as fixed and absolute as the natural law. If we perform evil deeds, our character will be evil; if we perform good deeds, our inner self will become good.

[8] *Katha Upanishad* (tr. by F. Max Müller).

[9] In Indian philosophy there is no concept of original sin; man is held responsible for his own shortcomings.

Opposed to the religious philosophy of the *Vedas,* which has a rather external view of morality and which stresses sacrifices, the *Upanishads* emphasize an inward concept of morality. No one can escape the law of Karma; not only men are guided by it, but even animals.

The question arises now whether Atman, the essential and individual self, is also bound by the laws of Karma. The *Upanishads'* answer is negative. Again and again it is pointed out that man's soul is *free;* we are determined as long as we act according to .selfish purposes. Only by acting in a disinterested, almost Spinozistic way, do we achieve freedom. When we identify ourselves with God, we achieve true liberation. Separated from God, we are subject to the laws of nature and to the laws of Karma. When God enters our life, when we become truly emancipated, we transcend the laws of cause and effect. Thus, we become part of an eternal kingdom in which true freedom reigns.

It may be asked now whether Karma is controlled by the gods. Can it be compared with God's providence? Again, the *Upanishads'* answer is negative. The law of Karma, like the Greek concept of fate, dominates even the gods. Karma is an unconscious principle which makes divine interference in the universe impossible. This eliminates a belief in miracles, for they would change the natural order of the universe. The gods, according to the *Upanishads,* do not act in an arbitrary manner. They do not intervene like Jehovah, rather they, too, are guided by the laws of cause and effect.

REINCARNATION. The theory of immortality is another basic doctrine found in the *Upanishads.* Reincarnation dominates all those who are not truly emancipated. The kind of rebirth is determined by the nature of our previous life. For example, those who have sinned and who have transgressed upon the laws of morality will live a lower kind of existence; they may even become dogs. On the other hand, those who have lived a sublime life may become priests or warriors.

The ultimate educational goal of the *Upanishads* is release from the cycle of reincarnation. This is called *Moksha,* which implies obliteration of all individuality and complete oneness in Brahman. This is not a personal heaven, nor does it constitute the fulfillment of material desires; rather *Moksha* implies the obliteration of all separateness and multiplicity. The self, which has temporarily lost its identity with reality, now regains its original nature. This process can be compared with the rivers that disappear into the ocean. To the uninitiated layman, *Moksha* appears as annihilation, but to the truly educated man it is the realization of all desires and all wishes. For now we are no longer part of the cycle of birth and death: we have achieved eternal peace and tranquility.

THE BHAGAVAD-GITA

The poetic expression of the *Upanishads* is found in the *Bhagavad-Gita,* which may be compared to the Christian *New Testament.* The tone of the Gita is anything but provincial; instead it has sympathy for all kinds of worship and almost all types of belief.

The concept of love found in the Gita teaches us that man cannot find himself except through total self-surrender. The will of God, thus, is the real criterion for all human acts and all human desires.

Ethics, in the Gita, are subordinated to metaphysics. Above all, we must realize the majesty of God who appears in everything. The Supreme Being which transcends space and time is without beginning and without end.

Real education should teach us to beware of sense objects: "He whose mind is not agitated in calamities and who has no longing for pleasure, free from attachment, fear, and anger, he indeed is said to be a saint of steady wisdom. He who is free from all attachment and neither rejoices on receiving good or is vexed on receiving evil, his wisdom is well-established." [10]

There are two ways through which salvation can be achieved. One is the path of meditation; the other is the path of action. Generally, the spirit of the Gita leans closer to the path of action than the spirit of the *Upanishads*. We must perform certain acts, for action is superior to inaction; in fact, without action our bodily functions would cease.

Interesting and moving are the doubts of Arjuna who is tortured by the idea that in war he would slay his own relatives. Again and again he asks, "What value is there in warfare?" He is a pacifist, for he feels that violence does not create real morality.

Krishna, who is the god in the story, explains to Arjuna that the real self is not subject to death, for man's inner essence cannot be destroyed. As in the *Upanishads,* there is a clear lesson that man's destiny transcends life and death and that the most important task is the realization of the true self.

With great fervor Krishna denounces all those who fall in the path of evil; he tells about the path of wisdom, which is the fulfillment of education.

"Endowed with pure understanding; subduing self by firmness; relinquishing sound and other sense-objects; abandoning longing and aversion; restoring to a secluded spot; eating little; controlling body, speech, and mind; ever steadfastly engaged in meditation and concentration; endowed with dispassion; forsaking egoism, power, pride, lust, anger and possession; freed from the notion of "mine," and tranquil: one is thus fit to become one with Brahman. Becoming one with Brahman, serene-minded, he neither grieves nor desires; alike to all beings, he attains supreme devotion to Me. He who, with supreme devotion to Me, will declare this deeply profound secret to My devotees, doubtless he shall come unto Me." [11]

[10] *Bhagavad-Gita,* Chapter II.

[11] *Ibid,* Chapter XVIII.

EDUCATIONAL IDEALS

The Hindu educational ideal was severe. A student had to obey and follow his teacher in every way. Students were frequently subjected to corporal punishment, and were called on to practice ascetism. In the *Laws* of Baudhayana a student is commanded to avoid light speech, dancing, and playing musical instruments; he is to assist the teacher, even when "the latter is making his toilet."

Various types of schools developed. There were private schools established by gurus who taught their disciples. There were Parishads, which were assemblies of learned Brahmins. Tols became noted: they were one-room, one-teacher educational centers, surrounded by huts in which students lived. Forest colleges, which stressed the virtue of contemplation, attracted many famous scholars. Temple schools, which stressed religious instruction, arose after 500 A.D. Secular knowledge was cultivated by the court schools. Mathas and Vidyapathas were monastic centers which concentrated upon the knowledge of the *Vedas* and the *Upanishads*. Mathas were orthodox centers of Brahmin learning, while the Vidyapathas were more liberal in their religious leanings.

Among the important Brahmin universities that were established in that era, the most famous ones were located at Benares, Nadia, and Taksasila. There the natural and physical sciences were studied as well as logic, literature, philosophy, and religion. Teachers were held in great respect, and they were supposed to be ascetic, learned and gentle in their behavior. Scholarship, for them, was a way of life.

THE IDEALS OF BUDDHA

In Buddha (563-483 B.C.) we find one of the outstanding and most provocative saints in history. He was not only a man of unusual religious insight but also a philosopher and educator of great depth and penetration.[12]

Numerous legends surround his birth. Thus, we hear of many miracles, such as the healing of diseased and blind, and we hear of kings who came from all parts of the world to celebrate his birth. He was brought up amidst luxury, and, as a member of the nobility, received an excellent education. Seldom has a man been so privileged; almost anything his heart desired was given to him. He was happily married, adored his child, and never lacked any material comfort.

Still, he was tormented by the evil which he saw around him. Evil appeared to him in three forms: old age, sickness, and death. Even with

---

12 Cf. Thomas, *The Life of Buddha;* Windisch, *Mara und Buddha;* Rhys Davids, *Buddhist India;* Oldenberg, *Buddha, Sein Leben, Seine Lehre;* Kern, *Manual of Indian Buddhism.*

all the wealth and glory in the world, he would not be able to conquer death and he would not be able to find his essential self.

This crisis in his life produced a climactic decision. He resolved to leave his wife and his new-born child, and he became a hermit. For six years he mortified his body, ate very little, neglected his appearance; in fact, he even slept among corpses. To get accustomed to this type of life, he wore hair cloth. Living in this manner he hoped to find salvation. Still, the enlightenment for which he was searching did not come.

Finally, disgusted with austerities, he realized that the middle road was the best solution. Neither asceticism nor self-indulgence would bring about true peace of mind. The key to his teachings lay in the four-fold truth..

1. *Life is sorrow and full of pain.* The great events of life, birth, sickness, old age, and death, are all equally painful.

2. *Sorrow is caused by desire.* Desire is exhibited in the pleasure which we find in this existence; it is manifested in the yearning for passion, in craving for existence, even in craving for non-existence.

3. *The pain which we observe is not ultimate and may be removed.* Instead of desire we must seek non-attachment. To Buddha, life is a virtual hell, but there is an escape from this hell which can be found through moral means, not through metaphysical exercises.

4. *The escape from sorrow is represented by the eight-fold path.*

1. *Right views* imply that we must understand the nature of the self and the nature of the universe. Those who believe that the self is eternal are utterly deluded, for the self is in a constant state of flux.

2. Besides right views we need *right aspirations.* Thus, we must abandon the life of pleasure and cultivate the resources of our inner spirit. We are not to bear malice towards any creature, animate or inanimate.[13]

3. *Right words* demand that we abandon all lies. We are not to speak harshly of others, nor are we to engage in trivial gossip.

4. *Right conduct* emphasizes, above all, the rule of pacifism; under no circumstances are we ever to take someone else's life. Furthermore, we are not to appropriate the goods of others. As for sensual indulgence and physical passion, such activities are expressly forbidden by Buddha.

5. *Right livelihood* deals with the occupations which we can enter.[14] The choice of professions is to be guided by moral dictates. For example, we are to avoid the slave trade, and we are not to engage in the sale of harmful drugs.

---

13 Cf. Neumann, *Reden Buddhas,* i, 215.

14 Cf. Winternitz, *Der ältere Buddhismus,* p. 81. Buddha makes greater demands upon the monks than upon the laity.

6. *Right effort* demands that we cultivate the correct type of motives. We must guard against spiritual indifference and lethargy and earnestly search for truth. Like Kant, Buddha emphasized the importance of good will, for if our thoughts are pure, happiness results, and we achieve true peace of mind.

7. *Right mindfulness* demands self-discipline. The great man is not one who conquers others but one who conquers his own self. The body, according to Buddha, is not autonomous, rather it is to be guided by the mind.

8. The last link of the eight-fold path is *right concentration.* Now we are emancipated from all transitory pleasures and from the life of the senses; the mind is in a state of ecstasy and concentrates upon Nirvana.

Buddha constantly reminds us that we are to shun evil.

"A MAN should hasten towards the good, and should keep his thought away from evil; if a man does what is good slothfully, his mind delights in evil. If a man commits a sin, let him not do it again; let him not delight in sin: the accumulation of evil is painful. If a man does what is good, let him do it again; let him delight in it: the accumulation of good is delightful." [15]

Who is the wise man? Not a man who has been born in a noble family or who is blessed by riches:

"The man who wears dirty raiments, who is emaciated and covered with veins, who meditates alone in the forest, him I call indeed a Brahmana. Him I call indeed a Brahmana who, after cutting all fetters, never trembles, is free from bonds and unshackled. Him I call indeed a Brahmana who, even here, knows the end of his own suffering, has put down his burden, and is unshackled. Him I call indeed a Brahmana whose knowledge is deep, who possesses wisdom, who knows the right way and wrong and has attained the highest end." [16]

Basic in Buddhism are five moral rules:
1. We are not to kill any living being.
2. We are not to covet or appropriate someone else's property.
3. We are not to engage in falsehood.
4. We are not to indulge in intoxicating drinks.
5. We are not to engage in unchastity.

Extremely significant is Buddha's concept of religious authority. While he did not deny the popular gods and while he sympathized with the worship of the masses, he believed that salvation only comes through reliance upon our own powers. "Be ye a refuge unto yourself"—is the

---

[15] *The Dhammapada,* (tr. by F. Max Müller) Chapter IX.

[16] *Ibid.,* Ch. XXVI.

keynote of Buddhist thinking. Prayers are entirely in vain, for happiness or unhappiness are not caused by divine forces. As for a future life, Buddha denied the existence of a heaven, hell, or purgatory.

Buddha rejected both the cosmological and teleological proofs for the existence of God. There is no first cause. Just as a seed develops into a full grown plant, just as man develops naturally, so the universe exists as an autonomous unit. The world is not caused by an outside force. In fact, according to Buddha, we do not need ultimate explanations—it is enough if we can describe the relations of phenomena. Even if we accept a first cause, our mind demands that the first cause itself be originated, which creates an insoluble paradox.

As for the teleological proof for the existence of God, Buddha felt that the universe is too imperfect to allow for a creator; nature itself does not reveal the providence of God—every event is determined by laws. When we speak of evil we are only using human biases; for nature is beyond good and evil and is in every way the expression of the law of cause and effect.

Will the saint survive after death? Buddha denies personal immortality; man is not characterized by a conscious personal ego; the self, just as nature, is in a perpetual state of change. Still, Buddha accepts the concept of reincarnation; hence, *there is not continuity of personality but continuity of action.* Man's character, thus, transcends the limitations of space and time.

The ultimate goal of Buddha was to find *Nirvana.* It is difficult to describe this ultimate state since it transcends verbal predications. In the Buddhist teachings it is used in the following ways:

1. As a release from rebirth.
2. The overcoming of all individuality and all consciousness.
3. The extinction of selfhood.
4. The merging of the individual with the principles of reality.
5. A state of heaven which man experiences after death.[17]

We may now ask what differences existed between the teachings of Buddha and the beliefs of the authors of the *Upanishads.* We find that Buddha did not accept revelation; to him there were no sacred scriptures; there existed no infallible word that man had to accept. Also, Buddha was more positivistic than the teachers of the *Upanishads;* to him the problems of metaphysics were secondary; what mattered, above all, was man's moral life. As to the problems of infinity and free will, they could not be solved by man's finite intellect. Unlike the authors of the *Upanishads,* Buddha rejected asceticism. The way to education is not reserved to the priests or to one group of people, but can be found by all.

---

17 Cf. Stcherbatsky, *The Conception of Buddhist Nirvana.*

Likewise, in his attitude regarding the caste system, Buddha revealed his unusual independence. The real struggle in life is between those who accept the dictates of morality and those who are guided by selfish desires. While he was not primarily a social reformer he made it clear that ultimate religion was a matter of individual responsibility, not of social organization and ecclesiastical ritual.

With eloquence Buddha stressed the positive aspects of the moral life.[18] The enlightened man is not bound by fear or by attachment to transitory goals; he is guided by a deep sense of compassion which includes all parts of creation.

HINAYANA, MAHAYANA, AND ZEN-BUDDHISM

HINAYANA BUDDHISM. The philosophy of *Hinayana Buddhism* is a rather austere form of Buddhism. To the Hinayana Buddhists, Buddha is primarily a teacher, not a god. They maintain that enlightenment may be achieved without the aid of any deity; Buddha thus is to be worshipped mainly because he gave us the supreme example of the religious life. Prominent in Hinayana Buddhism is the ideal of asceticism. The educated man will live a celibate life apart from society; if he engages in social intercourse he cannot realize true tranquillity.

What is the goal of man? What is the aim of his existence? According to Hinayana Buddhism, the goal of man is the extinction of consciousness—a state identified with Nirvana. This can be achieved through a concentrated meditation on the four-fold truth. We note again that this emancipation can be accomplished through one's *own power,* not through external aid.

Important in Hinayana Buddhism is the emphasis on the change which governs the universe; there are no permanent entities or permanent substances. Whatever we perceive is in a state of flux. Frequently, Hinayana Buddhism made a concession to the popular beliefs and thus developed polytheistic ideals. The gods, however, are not eternal or immortal and they are subordinated to Buddha himself. In Hinayana Buddhism, the gods mediate between Buddha and the worshipper. This is quite different from the Christian concept of God who is all-powerful.

MAHAYANA BUDDHISM. The philosophy of *Mahayana Buddhism,* unlike Hinayana Buddhism, is extremely colorful. Mahayana Buddhism elevates Buddha into a saviour and speaks of saints who could have attained Nirvana but instead have chosen to aid human beings. These saints have such compassion that they will rescue even the worst sinner

---

18 For a critical survey of Buddhist ethical teachings consult Hopkins, *Ethics of India;* Pratt, *The Pilgrimage of Buddhism,* Tachibana, *The Ethics of Buddhism,* Poussin, *La Morale Bouddhique.*

and make salvation possible for all. As in Catholicism, the saints mediate between man and God and their spiritual achievements compensate for the limitations of the common man.

Theistic features dominate Mahayana Buddhism. There is a heaven and a hell; paradise is regarded as a form of personal existence. Survival after death is not a delusion, but a definite fact.

Education in Mahayana Buddhism represents an attempt to achieve sainthood. The wise man combines knowledge and moral fervor. He fights a perpetual war against the forces of ignorance.

In Mahayana Buddhism, we find much metaphysical speculation. Usually, speculation is in the direction of idealism—*to be is to be perceived*. A distinction is made between absolute truth which can be known only by the enlightened saints whereas the common man can know only relative truth.

ZEN-BUDDHISM. The teachings of *Zen-Buddhism* stress, above all, the independence of the individual. Devoted to nature, Zen-Buddhists protest against the artificiality of city life; no wonder that most Buddhist temples can be found on isolated mountains. Detachment is the keynote to Zen-Buddhism. We are not to be moved by selfish desires or by the love of possessions. The Zen ideal is one of spiritual poverty. This is a state of the mind rather than of physical possession.[19]

In many ways, Zen-Buddhism reminds us of the conclusions of Socrates. It holds that the individual contains within himself the seeds of truth. Education thus implies the clearing away of all biases and prejudices; this process necessitates a return to nature. We learn more from the contemplation of majestic mountains than from the lectures of learned scholars. Real knowledge is based on intuition and unites an understanding of nature with a comprehension of the self.

To be more concrete, in Zen education a disciple may ask a master a question and receive what appears to be a nonsensical answer. According to Zen principles, plain answers are to be avoided. Rather, the disciple may be asked to study under various teachers; thus his vision will expand and his intellectual horizon will be broadened. Travel will bring him into contact with eminent masters and he will learn about new ways of living. At the same time, he will appreciate the simplicity of nature. One day, as he contemplates nature, his question may be answered and he may achieve an insight into the nature of life. All this will happen spontaneously, for the Zen teacher believes that the student has to achieve his own conclusions and find his own path to truth.

In the end, the disciple returns to his first master, convinced that education has a symbolic meaning and that truth transcends verbal state-

---

[19] Cf. Watts, *The Spirit of The Zen*, pp. 57-60. Zen Buddhism became especially popular in China.

ments. He is grateful to the master; he has found his own way to wisdom and he has not been indoctrinated with preconceived viewpoints.

The Zen concept of education reminds us of progressive education. Both viewpoints stress the importance of the learner, both believe that our nature is creative, and that interest is to guide our intellectual development. However, Zen-Buddhism emphasizes the importance of intuition, while progressive leaders of education, like Kilpatrick, believe in the supremacy of the scientific method.

BUDDHIST EDUCATIONAL IDEALS

Buddhist students are not selected on the basis of caste; rather, the ideal of equality is cherished. The Buddhist child starts his studies at the age of six and completes them at about the age of twenty. Then he begins advanced studies consisting of literature, philosophy, metaphysics, science and other courses. If he wants to enter a university, he has to pass rigorous tests.

Among the famous Buddhist universities we find Nalanda, which developed around 425 A.D. It is said to have attracted over 10,000 students and had a teaching staff of 1500. Students did not have to pay for tuition and lodging. There were several gates through which applicants had to pass and there they were subjected to a difficult test by a Dean of Admissions. More than seventy per cent failed the examination.

Nalanda attracted not only students but scholars who came to dispute ideas or wanted a center for quiet study. Both the sciences and philosophy were cultivated; law received only a secondary emphasis.

Buddhism developed monasteries in which education flourished. Monasteries were open both to those who wanted to lead an ascetic life as well as to students who wanted to pursue knowledge.

The aim of Buddhist education was to produce a compassionate individual who emancipated himself from egocentricity. The scholar had to be an example in virtue and in loving-kindness. His main interest was to be in morality rather than in metaphysics.

OTHER SYSTEMS

JAINISM. Closely related to Buddhism is *Jainism* which was founded by Vardhamāna. Based upon a realistic system of knowledge, Jainism emphasizes the relativity of truth. Ordinary human beings can only know the relations of events, while absolute truth can be found only through the redeemer. The ideal of Jainism is to live the life of the Arhats who are not subject to rebirth and who live far away from the struggle and strife of man.[20]

---

[20] For a discussion of the ethical values of Jainism see Jaini, *Outlines of Jainism;* Stevenson, *The Heart of Jainism.*

The theology of the Jains denies the existence of God, for we cannot explain why God should be uncaused. They combined atheism with a belief in an eternal universe and, like Buddha, they appealed to natural laws rather than to theological intervention. At the same time, they believed in saints to whom people could pray. Yet even these saints were not immortal nor were they the absolute lords of the universe. In every way they were like human beings, only they lived a more blissful existence.

Fundamental in the education of Jainism is Ahimsa—the responsibility not to harm or kill any living beings.[21] Thus the Jains take the following vows:

To preserve all life
Not to engage in falsehood
Never to steal
To remain chaste
Not to subject themselves to sensuous experiences

It can readily be seen that there is a strong note of asceticism in Jainism, since its fundamental object is emancipation from all pleasures.
MATERIALISM. More secular than Jainism is the school of *materialism* championed by the *Charvakas*.[22] They stressed that matter is the fundamental principle of the universe, denied the reality of the soul, and reduced mental states to their physiological origin. With vigor they denied that any sacred book exists; the idea of the supreme self likewise rests upon an illusion. The only knowledge which is trustworthy can be found through the senses, which are the criteria for all our inferences regarding the external world.

In ethics, the Charvakas stressed the relativity of all behavior. They attacked the religious leaders because the latter frequently favored asceticism and thus hindered man's natural development. Happiness, the materialists thought, cannot be found through spiritual exercises; rather it should be sought through the senses.

Education, they asserted, should be motivated by skepticism. We are to learn to rely upon ourselves and to avoid the illusory security of conventional religion.

Their religious philosophy was based on frank atheism. *There is no God, no providence and no rebirth.* If we want to understand the universe, we should not resort to supernatural explanations; rather, we should be guided by scientific hypotheses. The Charvakas made it clear that religion is based on fear and that it hinders, rather than advances, human knowledge.

VAIŚESIKA. Related to the materialistic system is the *Vaiśesika* system. Its author, Kanāda, believed that all phenomena are composed of

---

21 Cf. Winternitz, *History of Indian Literature,* II·
22 Cf. *Sarvadarśanasaṅgraha,* translated by Cowell and Gough.

atoms which he regarded as eternal and indestructible. He denied the existence of a personal god, for he thought that the atoms are guided by deterministic laws.[23] His followers, however, tried to explain the changes in the universe by appealing to God's providence, since He arranged the universe according to teleological patterns.

NYĀYA. The *Nyāya* system, unlike Kanāda, was more concerned with logic than with the structure of the universe. It tried to reduce all logical arguments to fundamental propositions of which, according to that school, there are five. Knowledge, however, is not an end in itself and has as its goal emancipation from the world of the senses. In fact, knowledge has a practical educative function. Gautama, the founder of this system, apparently did not believe in God and he thought that man could attain salvation without the aid of supernatural intervention.

PŪRVA MĪMĀMSĀ. More conventional than the Nyāya system was the school *of Pūrva Mīmāmsā*. Severely orthodox, it reacted against all forms of impiety.[24] If man wants to find himself he should not trust the resources of rationalistic education; rather, he should accept the sacred scriptures, especially the *Vedas* and the *Upanishads*. He should subordinate himself to the dictates of authority; only in this way could he find certainty. The author of the system, Jaimini, protested against all forms of rationalism. He made it clear that human reason only leads to pride and arrogance, whereas genuine education produces an attitude of humility and leads to the recognition of man's finite standing in the universe.

SĀMKHYA. More philosophical than this system was the *Sāmkhya* philosophy, believed to have been founded by Kapila. Like Buddha, Kapila did not accept the existence of God. There is no creation, according to Kapila, for the universe is eternal. Those who argue for the existence of God are bound by a paradox; if we accept God's perfection why should he create a universe; on the other hand, if God is finite and imperfect, we cannot believe in a supreme force. Furthermore, the imperfection of the universe, the presence of evil, and the problems of sin—all indicate that the universe could not have been created by a beneficent deity.

In his ethical theory Kapila was a pessimist like Buddha. All the so-called goods of life are illusions; wealth is impermanent, fame transitory, and joy unreliable. How, then, can we be emancipated? Kapila replies that we must recognize the basic freedom of the soul. *The individual perishes but the spirit remains the same* and is not determined by birth and

---

[23] The goal in this system is *Moksha,* which implies a cessation of rebirth and the liberation from all sorrow and desire.

[24] It stressed that salvation comes through action, *Karma,* while the other orthodox systems emphasized the role of knowledge.

death. Man, thus, should become an objective spectator who, through genuine education, sees through the vanity of existence.

Metaphysically, the Sāṃkhya philosophy is based on a dualistic foundation. There are two basic forces—Prakrti, the material substance, and Purusa, the spirit. Kapila speaks of evolution determined by naturalistic laws; the spiritual principle, however, is not affected by the material world. Eternal and omnipresent, it stirs to action the material world. The state of evolution is cyclical and leads from creation to decay, and back to a new universe.

SHANKARA. Perhaps the most profound system in Indian philosophy is that of Shankara.[25] It is impossible for reason to prove the existence of God; we can only postulate a personal god as a requisite for morality. A supreme force symbolizes our need for security and satisfies our demand for piety. The personal god, however, is not the ultimate reality. Thus, the philosopher realizes that the supreme being is impersonal. Raised above all personal attributes, it stands beyond moral qualities; eternal and unlimited, it is the real source of the universe.

On the other hand, the phenomenal world is part of the veil of maya, for ultimately we realize that space and time do not have metaphysical reality. Our mind is limited by the categories of space and time; thus, we necessarily think according to the demands of multiplicity when the universe in reality is *one*. The universal reality, Brahman, can be reached not through science or logic but through philosophy; its aim is to liberate man from multiplicity. When the self is absorbed in Nirvana, we realize that individuality is an illusion.

How can wisdom be achieved? Shankara makes it clear that we must abandon worldly goods, act in disinterested manner, and see the identity of Atman and Brahman. Spiritual education, rather than good deeds, brings about the release of the individual from the chain of rebirth.

Shankara, like many other Indian philosophers, believed in the usefulness of the Yogi system. The philosophy of this system was elaborated by Patanjali. The Yogi system, which has as its aim complete enlightenment and separation from sense phenomena,[26] consists of the following eight steps:

All *selfishness must be transcended*. This means that man is to give up the love for material goods and instead cultivate the resources of the spirit. Furthermore, he must respect all living beings and not kill anyone.

---

[25] He is usually ranked above Rāmānuja, another brilliant thinker who was more pluralistic in his philosophy and who represents more the theistic emphasis in Indian thinking. Cf. Radhakrishnan, *Indian Philosophy*, II, 690 ff.; Das Gupta, *A History of Indian Philosophy*, III, 286 ff.

[26] Cf. Das Gupta, *Yoga as Philosophy and Religion*.

Yoga demands certain *sanitary rules,* especially bodily purification. The mind likewise is to be trained; hence, piety and study are recommended.

Correct posture is extremely important. In this way all bodily movement can be abolished. Perfect stillness is to be achieved.

Control of the breath is recommended. This is called Pranayama. In this way we learn that we must empty our mind.

The next stage is that of *abstraction.* We have achieved a mastery of the body; we are no longer attached to sense objects.

Now, we reach the level of *concentration,* called Dharana. In this stage the mind concentrates upon one concept; all specific thoughts are excluded. In this way we feel that there is no material substance, but that the world is our idea. Such idealism banishes all sensuous thoughts and all craving for material objects.

The next stage is that of *meditation.* To bring about this condition, the Yogi recommends the repetition of the sacred word *om.* Through this word we realize the importance of introspection.

The final phase is trance *contemplation.* The mind now becomes part of totality. This state cannot be described intellectually; only the Yogi can understand it.

To the Indian thinkers, Yoga is, above all, an *educational* discipline. It teaches us control of our body and our mind. It combines psychological and spiritual principles; Yoga is to man's spirit what wisdom is to man's mind. Note how the Yogi moves from the concrete to the abstract, from practical matters to contemplation, which is the goal of genuine education.

There are certain obstructions which must be overcome before complete release is obtained. They are: *ignorance*—lack of knowledge of the eternal; *egoism*—when the seer regards himself as part of the instrument of seeing; *attachment*—concentration on pleasure; *aversion*—concentration on pain; *clinging to life*—emphasis on self-preservation.

By meditation and ascetic education man may realize his divine destiny and thus become like Brahman. Dissociated from all material longings, man attains a knowledge of the oneness of the universe and is emancipated from his physical limitations.

CONTRIBUTIONS OF INDIAN PHILOSOPHY AND EDUCATION

1. Indian philosophy is based on *speculative insight.* There is no essential opposition between faith and reason, between education and religion, between revelation and scientific knowledge. The highest state of knowledge is intuition through which man achieves a realization of the oneness of the universe.

2. The *moral education* of the Indian thinkers is on the highest plane. Morality, especially in Buddhism, is not based on supernatural foundation, rather it excludes the concept of divine anger and divine providence. There is a heavy emphasis on inwardness; hence, the subjective motive is dominant, both in the *Upanishads* and in Buddhism.

3. Especially impressive is the concept of *compassion* which we find in Buddhism. Compassion brings about a sense of identification; the educated man does not isolate himself from the universe but seeks to conquer evil wherever he finds it. His sense of sympathy is so strong that it extends to all beings, even to animals.

4. Indian thought contributes a strain of *pacifism,* especially in Buddhism and Jainism. Absolute respect for living beings is stressed. It is pointed out that the best way to resist evil is through non-violence, a gospel which Gandhi used so successfully in modern times.

5. Important also in Indian philosophy is the *law of Karma,* the law of cause and effect. The universe thus is not ruled by the providence of a supreme being, rather by the moral law which punishes all sins and which rewards good deeds. Our character creates its own heaven and its own hell.

6. Indian philosophy teaches the *unreality of the material world.* Ultimate reality transcends the life of the senses—our mind itself is finite and limited. Where we see multiplicity, as Shankara shows, oneness exists. The best way of life, educationally, is the life of the Yogi whose mind becomes independent of all material desires.

7. Indian thought contributes an *impersonal world view.* According to the Indian mind, only the untutored think of a creator and of a personal god; the truly educated man, however, sees God beyond space and time and beyond all personal categories. In this way, there is a close relationship between Indian thinkers and Western mystics, like Eckhart and Tauler, who likewise believed that God in his essence is impersonal.

8. *There is a strong note of pantheism* in Indian thinking. Thus, in the *Upanishads* we find that *Atman* and *Brahman* are one; the subjective self and the objective reality are identified.

9. The goal of Indian thinking is not a personal heaven, rather *absorption in the world stream.* We may call it *Moksha* or *Nirvana,* but in any case it means the loss of all individuality and all separateness. The Indian sage seeks for release from rebirth, for he regards life as a doubtful blessing.

10. Indian philosophy is basically *pessimistic.* This is brought out most clearly by Buddha who regarded all earthly life as a form of sorrow. But the Indian thinkers agree that this sorrow may be overcome and that evil is not ultimate. In a way, sorrow, according to the Indian mind, has a positive function, for it indicates that man is a wanderer and pilgrim,

and that if he wants to find real enlightenment he must conquer all selfishness, all partiality, and all passion for material goods.

It is impossible to separate Indian religion, philosophy and education. The Indian teacher is a holy man as well as a man of wisdom. He teaches, by indirection, that attachment to the senses is to be overcome and that worldly strivings are to be subordinated to spiritual ideals.

William James recommended that American educators could benefit from the contemplative spirit of the Indian teacher. We are so immersed in action and utilitarianism that we lose sight of ultimate goals and we are often overcome by the idols of immediacy. Indian education teaches us that we find ourselves as we subordinate ourselves to a greater cause; without serenity, calmness, and detachment, education may become a futile process.

In *The Meeting of East and West*, F. S. C. Northrop makes a distinction between Eastern culture, which stresses immediate experience and emphasizes an ineffable "esthetic continuum," and Western culture, which is interested in particular objects and in the inference and abstraction created by logical thinking. He concludes that the East, especially India, should study Western science, and that the West should study Eastern religion.

Still, we must beware of generalizations. Strains of materialism were as evident in India as in the West. The moral idealism which Northrop saw as a manifestation of a universal continuum in Eastern culture was not always evident in practice. Thus Vivekananda maintained that "no society puts its foot on the neck of the wretched so mercilessly as does India."

In India, the creative process in education was hindered by the caste system, by extreme poverty, and by the absence of a systematic interest in technology. On the other hand, India pioneered a creative approach towards spirituality. India demonstrated the need for meditation and quiet reflection, if man is to find an abiding meaning in life and in education.

QUESTIONS FOR DISCUSSION AND INVESTIGATION

1. List and discuss the qualities of Indian philosophy which manifest a distinctly metaphysical approach to life.

2. Describe the religious ideals of the *Vedas*.

3. Give the basic philosophical tenets as set down in the *Upanishads*.

4. What important educational concepts may be discovered in the *Bhagavad-Gita*?

5. Explain the Hindu educational ideal.

6. Discuss Buddha's basic approach to life as shown in the four truths, and relate this approach to his concepts on education.

7. Trace the line of metaphysical and educational development through Hinayana, Mahayana, and Zen-Buddhism.

8. What essentially are the ideals of Buddhist students?

9. List and briefly define the other systems of Indian religion.

10. Name the main contributions of Indian philosophy and education.

Chapter 6

Chinese Ideals

THE EDUCATIONAL AIM

Through the ages, unity of the family provided the foundation for Chinese education. The Chinese were taught to respect age and superior achievement. As Confucius pointed out, states could prosper only when filial piety prevailed and when a system of etiquette governed social life. Chinese education emphasized the past, rather than the present.

While the Indian ideal of scholarship taught the virtues of non-attachment and the overcoming of desire, the Chinese scholars believed in the enjoyment of life in this world. This did not imply enjoyment to an extreme but rather, the sense of moderation and balance.

What is the difference between the educated and the uneducated individual? According to the Chinese view, the educated man has respect for knowledge, while the ignorant man follows irrational passions. Knowledge, however, is not to be worshipped for its own sake; it is important as the prelude to correct ethical action.

China did not develop a national system of education. Private schools were created which prepared students to pass state examinations. The main types of educational centers were elementary schools and academies which gave advanced instruction. Elementary classes were usually conducted in the teacher's house.

The educational training of the Chinese was divided into three periods. The first period stressed the art of writing and literature. In the second period, the nine sacred books were studied; in the third period,

59

the student advanced in his skills and concentrated upon philosophical and moral ideals.

The discipline in Chinese schools, as in Indian schools, was firm, and corporal punishment was frequently used. Teachers stressed repetition and students were instructed and encouraged to imitate the teacher. Since the past was the model, originality and inventiveness were discouraged.

THE SPIRIT OF CHINESE PHILOSOPHY AND RELIGION

Chinese philosophy is characterized by its tolerant and eclectic spirit. Chinese scholars respect a variety of opinions, for they feel that truth cannot be monopolized by one nation or one religious group. Consequently, there is little dogmatism in Chinese thought. Philosophical and religious controversies are not fought with the sword; there is no persecution of heretics.

The tolerance of the Chinese is based to a great extent on their educational training. Confucianism, thus, teaches that the superior man is eager to learn and that he is moderate in his behavior. The gentleman in China has a sense of propriety and does not try to impose his opinion on others. He sees the grayness of most issues and consequently avoids extreme partisanship.

Religious worship in China is founded on individual rather than on congregational factors; the church is not an absolute institution. Basically, a strain of individualism dominates Chinese social relationships and this individualism extends to man's relationship with God. The family is a cornerstone of Chinese religion, and the purpose of the family is to insure the continuity of the ancestral relationship rather than the welfare of the individual. Respect for ancestors can influence man's life on earth. Furthermore, ancestor worship adds stability to man's social life. The family is often responsible for the conduct of its members, and when family relations rest upon a sound basis then, Confucius teaches, the state can prosper.

Whereas Indian philosophy rests upon a metaphysical basis, the Chinese are primarily concerned with moral problems.[1] Ethics replaces theology; in vain do we look for an Aquinas or a Shankara in China. The Chinese educator feels that it is useless to discuss the attributes of God and that it is impossible to rely upon revelation. He identifies morality and faith; thus, the educated man would be religious and the religious man would be truly educated.

---

[1] For a survey of Chinese moral ideals see Rawlinson, *Chinese Ethical Ideals;* Fung Yu-lan, *A Comparative Study of Life Ideals.*

To the Chinese, religion is not a separate subject but includes *all aspects of life*. The belief in God is strong, although God is frequently regarded as an impersonal force, as "Heaven" or "Providence." Belief in God implies faith in the validity of moral laws. Thus, the Chinese feel that those who follow the dictates of heaven will be rewarded and prosper, while those who violate the laws of morality will be inevitable failures.

CONFUCIUS

Chinese philosophy has been championed most effectively by Confucius (551-478 B.C.), whose life was dedicated to the search for a perfect government.[2] His father, a member of a distinguished family that was related to Emperor Huang-ti, passed away while Confucius was still in his infancy. Confucius helped to support his mother by working after school; still, he took his education seriously and became especially proficient in archery and music. When his mother died, he showed his feelings for her by mourning for twenty-seven months. Thus, in his personal life, he did not always practice his teachings. He married at the age of seventeen; apparently, it was an unhappy marriage, and so he was divorced four years later.

At the early age of twenty he became an overseer of the fields of the kingdom of Lu and the authorities became aware of his talents. He started his career as a teacher two years later, teaching, above all, three subjects: history, etiquette, and poetry. He did not charge a stipulated fee, but demanded from every student whatever he could pay without hardship.

When Confucius visited Laotse, the old philosopher apparently tried to discourage him from reforming the existing governmental system. The Duke of Tsi considered the possibility of employing Confucius until one of his advisers told him that Confucius was too pedantic and too intent upon ceremony.

Later, Confucius had more luck in the state of Lu. He was made chief magistrate of an important town, then he became superintendent of public works; finally, he became Minister of Crime. He was so efficient that criminal activities were curtailed and honesty governed the state of Lu. Strangers came from all over China in search of the perfect government which at last had been established.

However, two neighboring princes conspired against the Duke of Lu, and, to tempt him, they sent him a number of sing-song girls as well as a collection of splendid horses. Now the Duke of Lu showed little

[2] Cf. F. Gabelentz, *Confucius und seine Lehre;* Soothill, *The Three Religions of China;* F. Legge, *The Life and Teachings of Confucius;* Vol. I of the *Chinese Classics,* 3 Vols.

interest in the government affairs of that town; Confucius gave him an ultimatum: Either the sing-song girls would leave, or Confucius would resign. The ruler did not hesitate and Confucius left his governmental position.

From 496-483 B.C., Confucius travelled from one principality to another, always in search of a perfect government. He was offered a tempting position by the Duke of Wu, but he did not approve of the moral standards of the latter, and so he refused the position. He returned to the state of Lu when he was sixty-eight years old and lived there in semiretirement until he died in 478 B.C.

Among his contributions to mankind are the five classics, including the *Book of Songs*, the *Book of History*, the *Book of Changes*, the *Book of Spring and Autumn*, and the *Book of Rites*. With the exception of the *Book of Spring and Autumn*, these works were mostly written by his disciples.

Traditionally, we think of Confucius as a formalist who followed the ways of the past. However, this viewpoint is not justified, for above all Confucius believed in sincerity. Manners and morals were to be united; reform was to come through the efforts of the superior man. Opposed to all types of dogmatism and narrow-mindedness, he believed in the constant cultivation of the *self*. Thus, there is a strong *personal* element in the system of Confucius.

He describes his own educational development in the following passages:

> "The Master said, 'At fifteen, I had my mind bent on learning.
> 'At thirty, I stood firm.
> 'At forty, I had no doubts.
> 'At fifty, I knew the decrees of Heaven.
> 'At sixty, my ear was an obedient organ for the reception of truth.
> 'At seventy, I could follow what my heart desired, without transgressing what was right.' " [3]

> "If a man keeps cherishing his old knowledge, so as continually to be acquiring new, he may be a teacher of others." [4]

What is knowledge?

> "When you know a thing, to hold that you know it; and when you do not know a thing, to allow that you do not know it: —this is knowledge." [5]

> "The leaving virtue without proper cultivation: the not thoroughly discussing what is learned; not being able to move toward righteousness of which a knowledge is gained; and not being able to change what is not good: —these are the things which occasion my solicitude." [6]

---

3 *Analects,* Book II iv, I
4 *Ibid.,* Book II xi.
5 *Ibid.,* Book II, xvii.
6 *Ibid.,* Book VII, iii.

Education, Confucius taught, demands an inquiring mind:

> "I do not open up the truth to one who is not eager to get knowledge, nor help out anyone who is not anxious to explain himself. When I have presented one corner of a subject to anyone, and he cannot from it learn the other three, I do not repeat my lesson." [7]

An important concept in Confucianism is *filial piety,* which requires an attitude of obedience on the part of the son. However, the father is not to exercise his rule dictatorially. Filial piety demands self-restraint on the part of the individual; thus, he has to subordinate himself to the welfare of the family.

In his religious philosophy, Confucius, like Buddha, had no patience with metaphysical disputes. He felt that no absolute answers could be obtained on the question of the existence of God. He counseled his followers to adhere to the traditional ritual and to act as if the ancestors were present. When someone asked him how the spirits were to be served, he replied that this was a useless question, for "we are to serve men first." We are to concentrate upon the facts of this life, not upon supernatural beings.

Still, this does not mean that Confucius was a nihilist. On the contrary, he saw a fundamental unity in the universe; hence he felt that the laws of morality and the laws of nature were one. Thus, the thief could not escape from the consequences of his evil actions, just as no one could deny the law of gravity.

What, then, is wisdom according to Confucianism? The answer is quite definite. Wisdom consists in realizing our limitations and in the acceptance of man's fundamental ignorance. Being a humanist, Confucius maintained that we must *first* serve man rather than supernatural beings. We should respect the laws of Heaven, although our mind can never understand them completely.

Education, according to Confucius, is founded upon morality. We must try to conquer ourselves, investigate our thoughts, and be perfectly sincere in our quest for truth. When the individual achieves peace, then he can order his family life. If the family life is harmonious, then the states can experience prosperity. If the states are at peace, then the empire can achieve tranquillity.

The moral method of Confucius is opposed to the ethics of the commissar. Reform does not come about through social legislation or through revolution; rather it depends upon the efforts of the individual. We must improve ourselves first—only then can we try to reform society.

In educational, as well as in spiritual matters, the Golden Mean is all important. This implies a careful regard for the laws of propriety. The gentleman avoids all excesses and all extreme passions.

---

[7] *Ibid.,* Book VII, viii.

The educational system of Confucius is based upon his doctrine of the superior man. The ideal man does not live in an ivory tower, but he tries to reform society. He is respectful, righteous, and always sincere in his thoughts. Confucius contrasts the superior man and the common man:

> "What the gentleman seeks is in himself. What the mean man seeks is in others. The gentleman is dignified, but does not wrangle. He is sociable but not a partisan.
> "The gentleman does not promote a man simply on account of his words, nor does he put aside good words because of the man." [8]
> "The master said, 'The object of the superior man is truth. Food is not his object. There is plowing: —even in that there is sometimes want. So with learning: —emolument may be found in it. The superior man is anxious lest he should not get truth; he is not anxious lest poverty should come upon him.' " [9]

Notice that Confucius did not believe in asceticism. Salvation is not to be gained through mortification of the flesh or through renunciation of material goods. Thus the scholar replaces the Yogi, and etiquette replaces the striving for metaphysical knowledge.

The superior man, who represents the best of education, tries to perfect both his mind and his character.

> "The superior man has nine things which are subjects with him of thoughtful consideration. In regard to the use of his eyes, he is anxious to see clearly. In regard to the use of his ears, he is anxious to hear distinctly. In regard to his countenance, he is anxious that it should be benign. In regard to his demeanor, he is anxious that it should be respectful. In regard to his speech, he is anxious that it should be sincere. In regard to his doing of business, he is anxious that it should be reverently careful. In regard to what he doubts about, he is anxious to question others. When he is angry, he thinks of the difficulties (his anger may involve him in). When he sees gain to be got, he thinks of righteousness." [10]

The superior man is in awe before three things. First, he has a sense of awe when he deals with the ordinances of Heaven. Secondly, the superior man is awed when confronted by great men. Thirdly, the superior man stands in awe when he encounters words of wisdom.

Confucius felt great disdain in regard to the controversies of philosophy. Having no use for obscure passages and foggy thinking, he demanded a rectification of names; thus a father who neglected his duties should not be called a father; a prince who abdicated his power should not be called a prince. In short, verbal meaning should correspond to

[8] *Ibid.*, Book XV xx, xxi, xxii.
[9] *Ibid.*, Book XV, xxxi.
[10] *Ibid.*, Book XVI, x.

actual function. As for theological controversies, Confucius thought that they were too unimportant and their subject matter too obscure. He was concerned mainly with social relationships and not with man's understanding of the beyond.

His moral ideals were reflected in his concept of government. He maintained that rulers should be exemplary in their conduct and that the princes should employ only the most efficient and scrupulous ministers. He looked forward to an educational utopia in which there would be eternal peace and in which no poverty existed. In this state no man would be oppressed and the rights of all would be safeguarded. The community would rank above the demands of the individual and all would realize their essential identity and would act for the welfare of the group. This utopia is based on secular foundations; unlike the utopia of the Hebrew prophets, it is dominated by humanistic rather than supernatural foundations.

MOTSE

The spiritual emphasis is stronger in Motse than Confucius. Motse believed in universal love and he felt that this love could reform the existing institutions.[11] While Confucius felt that the universe is guided by impersonal laws, Motse accepted the existence of a *personal* god. As a theist, he felt that God intervened in the life of individuals. In fact, he believed not only in God but in the existence of ghosts and spirits as well. To those who objected to his concept of religion, he replied that religion has practical consequences, for it improves man's behavior and gives stability to the state.

Motse asserted that the teacher should avoid harsh forms of discipline and that he should be an example of love and kindness. Education is to appeal to man's heart rather than to his sense of etiquette.

TAOISM

While Motse believed in organized society, Laotse took refuge in nature. Scholars are divided in the controversy over the authorship of the *Tao-Te-Ching,* although traditionally Laotse has been regarded as its author.

What we know about Laotse's life is mostly derived from Sze-ma-Tsien who tells us that Laotse was born about 604 B.C. in the province of Honan. He became librarian at the court of Chou. He was visited in 517 B.C. by Confucius who wanted to learn about his philosophy. Later, Laotse wandered through the empire, always in search of seclusion.

---

11 Cf. Mei Yi-Pao, *The Ethical and Political Works of Motse.*

Sze-ma-Tsien describes the meeting of Laotse and Confucius in detail. We do not know whether the report is true; apparently Laotse advised Confucius to give up all desire to reform the empire, for the political leader should be like the merchant and not make an exhibit of his designs. He told Confucius to abandon all pride and ambition and to think of his ancestors whose deeds were forgotten and whose bones had become dust.

Laotse composed the *Tao-Te-Ching* at the request of Yin Hse, a gate-keeper, who had detained Laotse before he undertook his wanderings. The gate-keeper wanted to know about the principles of morality and how man is to conduct himself if he is to live a meaningful life.

One of Laotse's basic principles is the concept of *Tao*. Tao is not a personal force, nor is it transcendent; rather it is pantheistic and revealed everywhere: in man, animals, plants, in the infinite and infinitesimal. It is the supreme moral law which is the standard for all our actions and all of our aspirations.

Words cannot define Tao.

"The Tao that can be trodden is not the enduring and unchanging Tao. The name that can be named is not the enduring and unchanging name. (Conceived of as) having no name, it is the Originator of heaven and earth; (conceived of as) having a name, it is the Mother of all things . . . Always without desire we must be found, if its deep mystery we would sound; but·if desire always within us be, its outer fringe is all that we shall see . . . Under these two aspects, it is really the same; but as development takes place, it receives the different names. Together we call them the Mystery. Where the Mystery is the deepest is the gate of all that is subtle and wonderful." [12]

Tao is everywhere: it includes all parts of life.

"The Tao is (like) the emptiness of a vessel; and in our employment of it we must be on our guard against all fulness. How deep and unfathomable it is, as if it were the Honoured Ancestor of all things!

"We should blunt our sharp points, and unravel the complications of things; we should attemper our brightness, and bring ourselves into agreement with the obscurity of others. How pure and still the Tao is, as if it would ever so continue!" [13]

The concept of education which we find in Laotse is quite different from that of Confucius. The insight of the intellectual is to be rejected, for his knowledge is essentially superficial and fragmentary. The best way of life is a way of ignorance, not of scientific knowledge. The more we educate people, according to Laotse, the more we tend to corrupt them.[14]

---

12 *The Sacred Books of China,* trans. James Legge, vol. XXXIX of *The Sacred Books of the East,* ed. F. Max Müller, p. 47, part I, Ch. I.

13 *Ibid.*

14 A more extreme interpretation of Laotse can be found in Hu Shih, *The Development of the Logical Method in Ancient China.* Hu Shih calls Laotse a nihilist.

The ideal life, thus, is that of the peasant who lives away from the luxury of urban existence. Government is to be reduced to a minimum and is to be guided by spontaneous goodness. The watchword of Taoism is *laissez-faire,* non-interference with the laws of nature.

Under no circumstances are philosophers to rule a nation, for they would only corrupt the people.

"The ancients who showed their skill in practising the Tao did so, not to enlighten the people, but rather to make them simple and ignorant.

"The difficulty in governing the people arises from their having much knowledge. He who (tries to) govern a state by his wisdom is a scourge to it; while he who does not (try to) is a blessing.

"He who knows these two things finds in them also his model and rule. Ability to know this model and rule constitutes what we call the mysterious excellence (of a governor). Deep and far-reaching is such mysterious excellence, showing indeed its possessor as opposite to others, but leading them to a great conformity to him." [15]

In many ways Laotse comes close to the Christian concept of ethics and education. Thus he recommended that we are not to respond to evil by evil, but that we should overcome evil through kindness. He felt that, ultimately, the poor and persecuted would prevail, for physical power is impermanent and the weak would gain a lasting victory through submission.

CHUANG-TZE

Like Laotse, Chuang-tze believed in the life of nature. According to tradition, he refused public office twice, since he felt that organized governments only corrupted the character of man. The wise man, according to Chuang-tze, lives a life of tranquillity; unburdened by property, he is able to cultivate his inner spirit.

Like Laotse, Chuang-tze maintained that Tao, the principle of reality, cannot be defined and is beyond all distinctions. In his theory of knowledge he maintained that man can never know reality completely. Since man is limited, he must be content with an understanding of his ignorance.

In his theory of reality Chuang-tze was an agnostic. We cannot know whether a supreme being exists, for our intellect presents us with phenomenal facts; we can understand only relations; we have *no* knowledge of the unconditioned. Furthermore, he denied free will; the universe, he stated, is guided by deterministic laws which man cannot change.

Famous is the story of Chuang-tze dreaming that he was a butterfly. As he was dreaming he was not aware that he was a man. Then he woke up and he was conscious again of being human. The question that arises

---

[15] *Sacred Books*, Book II, LXV.

now is whether or not our existence is real. Chuang-tze hints at the fact
that our present existence may be part of the veil of Maya, a step in the
endless transformation of life. It appears that existence merges into non-
existence and non-existence is replaced by new types of existences.

With our finite minds we think of contradictions and opposites, but
when we look at the universe from the standpoint of Tao, which represents real education, these contradictions are lost and instead we see oneness. From the standpoint of nature there is no good or evil; the infinite
and infinitesimal are one. Thus, we can find the secret of the universe in
nature as well as in the mind of man.

OTHER SYSTEMS

MENCIUS. While Chuang-tze preached the way of nature, Mencius was
more concerned with politics. Mencius believed, like Rousseau, that man
is good and that he is corrupted by evil institutions. Like Confucius,
Mencius was mainly a positivist who had no patience with metaphysical
arguments. As a pacifist, Mencius condemned all forms of warfare; with
vehemence he preached the doctrine of popular sovereignty. With his
democratic tendencies he felt that the people should oppose oppressive
rulers.

In his educational theory, Mencius showed pragmatic leanings.
Knowledge has to be applied through practice and education has to be exemplified by the ruler.

Our moral conduct reveals the will of heaven:

> Wan Chang said, "(It is said that) Yao gave the empire to Shun; was it
> so?" Mencius replied, "No; the emperor cannot give the empire to another."
> "Yes; but Shun possessed the empire. Who gave it to him?" "Heaven
> gave it to him," was the reply.
> "Heaven gave it to him; did (Heaven) confer the appointment on him
> with specific injunctions?"
> (Mencius) said, "No; Heaven does not speak. It simply showed its will
> by his (personal) conduct, and by (his conduct of) affairs." [16]

HSÜN-TZE. Hsün-tze, unlike Mencius, believed that man is evil. Laws
are framed to correct man's deficiencies; education is absolutely necessary if man is to conquer himself. The natural state of man, according
to this thinker, is one of *warfare*. Our love of gain and of conquest is not
a part of society but is derived from our original nature. If we followed
our native impulses, we would go back to savagery and destroy civilization.

---

[16] *Sacred Books*, Book V, part 1, Ch. 5.

The task of education, according to Hsün-tze, is to restrain the evil impulses of man. Education is a form of social control and adds to the cohesive power of society. He almost anticipated John Dewey in his concept of nature, for he felt that man's best chances for advancement lay in increasing his control over the external world. Nature is not to be admired, but to be controlled. It is up to us to transform nature so that it will obey human desires and human wants. Nature, in short, is not to be the standard for our activities; we are not to stand in awe before it; rather we are to use it for our own welfare and advancement.

YANG-CHU. The atheistic trend in Chinese thought is expressed in Yang-Chu. He was certain that God does not exist and that all the tales about a future life are fallacious. This is our only existence; what happens after death no-one can know.

Yang-Chu's educational philosophy was based on hedonistic principles; we are to be guided by our desires and pleasures. Those who believe that the virtuous prosper most do not have a sense of actuality, for it appears frequently that the wicked rule supreme. Unlike Epicurus, Yang-Chu did not think very highly of the pleasures of the mind; rather he put his trust in bodily sensations. While Confucius and Motse spoke against the life of physical enjoyment, Yang-Chu had a high regard for the demands of the flesh. We are not to be disturbed by thoughts of propriety nor by the demands of etiquette; rather we are to gratify our physical cravings.

Since Yang-Chu realized that life is full of suffering, he stated that the only thing that makes our existence worthwhile is the expectation of pleasure. When pleasure comes our way we should try to explore it completely; education, thus, is a systematic approach to the enjoyment of life.

CHU-HSI. Such a hedonistic philosophy did not satisfy the demands of Chinese life, and Confucius remained the outstanding influence in Chinese culture. In the Middle Ages, Confucius found two outstanding interpreters—Chu-Hsi and Wang Yang-Ming. Chu-Hsi, who lived in the twelfth century, developed a system of metaphysical dualism. The universe is guided by two forces, *Yang* and *Yin*. All things are the product of law and motion, form and substance. The universe is not without God, who remains impersonal and is identified with T'ien. Nature is not guided by irrational providence, but by rational laws.

Turning to the moral law, Chu-Hsi believed that it is derived from natural phenomena. The educated man understands the laws of nature.[17] When he realizes the harmony of man and the universe, he experiences a state of complete tranquillity.

---

[17] Cf. Joseph Percy Bruce, *The Philosophy of Human Nature by Chu Hsi*.

WANG YANG-MING. More idealistic than Chu-Hsi was Wang Yang-Ming who believed, above all, in *self-knowledge* in education. Reality is not to be found in external things, but in the self, for the mind is a mirror and a summary of the universe.[18] If man wants to achieve a complete education he should not study the physical sciences; rather he should cultivate his inner resources.

Wang Yang-Ming did not speak of a personal god; he identified God with moral laws, which have a definite relationship to man's life. Occasionally, he spoke of the anger of God and he tells us that God rewards those who are good. Thus, there is a personal touch in Wang Yang-Ming's philosophy.

CONTRIBUTIONS OF CHINESE PHILOSOPHY

In Chinese philosophy, as has been shown, ethics triumphed over metaphysics. Thus, the goal of philosophy was not the attainment of God, but the achievement of a moral perspective. Unlike Indian thinkers, the Chinese preferred the middle road; this spirit was especially evident in Confucianism.

In China the priest was subordinated to the educator. The latter was not only a man who knew the classics and was eager to learn, but he was also accomplished in virtue and tried to achieve sublime character traits. Impatient with metaphysical subtleties, he concentrated upon human relationships and served God by serving man.

Also of importance in Chinese philosophy is the concept of the *Tao,* which can almost be compared with Spinoza's "Substance." We can find it, according to Chuang-tze, in the greatest as well as in the smallest, in the infinite as well as in the infinitesimal. In the *Tao* all multiplicity vanishes and all separateness is transcended.

A naturalistic element emerged in Chinese philosophy, especially in Chuang-tze, who emphasized that life and death are part of the same process and who had no patience with supernatural explanations. The naturalistic trend became even stronger in Yang-Chu who denied the existence of God and personal immortality.

Almost all Chinese thinkers were unanimous in pointing to the limitations of man's mind. This means that no certainty can be achieved in intellectual matters. Thus, opposing views were tolerated and there was no sense of heresy.

Generally, God was regarded as an impersonal force. It must be remembered, however, that Motse believed in a personal god who intervened in the life of man. It is noteworthy that the laws of heaven and scientific laws were identical. Hence, man's moral concepts were not artificial but had metaphysical reality.

---

18 Cf. Henke, *The Philosophy of Wang Yang-Ming.*

The approach to philosophy was usually not on an intellectual basis in Chinese thought. Thus, Laotse emphasized the inadequacy of the intellect and the importance of intuition. In the ultimate stage of knowledge, analysis is utterly inadequate; instead we must depend upon spontaneous insight.

To the Chinese philosophers education has definite social consequences. Hence, it is not enough to believe in certain doctrines and to adhere to formal rituals, but education must change our conduct and transform our inner being. What strikes the modern observer is the pragmatic content of Chinese educational ideals. Pragmatism is a philosophy which stresses application and concreteness and which believes that ideas are tested by consequences. Likewise, the Chinese stressed the importance of practical education and applying scholarly ideals to daily existence.

The same thought was expressed by Kilpatrick in *Philosophy of Education*. Kilpatrick maintained that we learn only what we use and what becomes part of us. The wise teacher creates concomitant interests which transcend the subject matter; he is concerned about the long range results of education. The same emphasis was given by Chinese scholars who wanted to make education a living process.

The important difference, however, between pragmatism and Chinese thought lies in the high regard of the present on the part of pragmatists as against the traditionalism of the Chinese. This conservatism was both a source of stability and a source of weakness in Chinese culture. It created strong family ties and at the same time produced a culture lag which became noticeable in modern times.

The educated class in China was bound by tradition. Filial piety was its ideal. An elaborate ritual governed its conduct. A thinker, like Motse, might point to social reforms, but he was neglected. Later Confucianists would show some tolerance for Taoism and Buddhism, but to them family loyalty was most important; innovations were regarded as being dangerous. The examinations for government office required a detailed knowledge of the classics. Originality in thought and education was not tolerated.

In China, then, creative ideas were stymied for centuries by too much conservatism. But China demonstrated the importance of the role of the scholar, who, in that civilization, was regarded with veritable awe. No great educational system can ever be developed which underrates the importance of the teacher. In stressing the role of the teacher, China made a permanent contribution to civilization.

QUESTIONS FOR DISCUSSION AND INVESTIGATION

1. What has been the educational aim of the Chinese?

2. Discuss the tolerant and eclectic spirit in Chinese philosophy.

3. Relate Confucius' ethical codes of philosophy to his views on education.

4. Define Confucius' concept of the superior man in education.

5. Compare and contrast the philosophy of Confucius and Motse; of Confucius and Laotse.

6. Discuss the concept of Tao and relate its approach to the way one might practice education.

7. Explain the philosophical views of Chuang-Tze.

8. Discuss some of the other systems of Chinese philosophy and education.

9. Discuss the contributions of Chinese philosophy to education.

10. In what way does Kilpatrick share some of the Chinese concepts of life and education?

Chapter 7

Foundations of Near Eastern Ideals

EGYPTIAN RELIGIOUS PHILOSOPHY

In ancient Egypt, religion governed all aspects of life. The Egyptians worshipped animals as well as men. Egyptian priests had a powerful position and frequently dominated the political, economic and educational affairs of that nation.[1]

Above all, the Egyptians stressed the concept of immortality. They thought that man's body could be preserved after death. Their view of immortality, however, was not spiritual, for survival after death was regarded as a concrete existence which would perpetuate the pleasures of this earth. No wonder that Egyptian funeral chambers contained so many earthly goods. Education itself, to the Egyptians, was a preparation for the after-life.

The after-life was conceived in two ways: either man would live in a glorious place called the "Happy Field of Food" where luxury prevailed and where he could live in material abundance; or he would be thrust into dark rivers where crocodiles would devour him. To obtain immortality it was necessary to buy the magic charms which the priest guarded and also it was indispensable to buy the *Book of the Dead*. In this work a certain moral spirit appears, as seen in the following quotation:

[1] Cf. Albert A. Trever, *History of Ancient Civilization*, I, 50; James H. Breasted, *The Development of Religion and Thought in Ancient Egypt*.

"I am not a doer of wrong to men.
I am not one who slayeth his kindred.
I am not one who telleth lies instead of truth.
I am not conscious of treason.
I am not a doer of mischief.
I do not exact as the first fruits of each day more work than should be done
*   for me.*
My name cometh not to the Bark of the god who is at the Helm.
I am not a transgressor against the god.
I am not a tale-bearer.
I am not a detractor.
I am not a doer of that which the gods abhor.
I hurt no servant with his master.
I cause no famine.
I cause not weeping.
I am not a murderer.
I give not orders for murder.
I cause not suffering to men.
I reduce not the offerings in the temples.
I lessen not the cakes of the gods.
I rob not the dead of their funereal food.
I am not an adulterer."

The religion of the Egyptians was polytheistic. Among the main gods we find the sun god, called Rah or Reh, the source of life, who had created men to be happy and blissful, but in their evil ways they had sinned against the providence of Rah, and now they lived in the spirit of darkness. There was Osiris, the god of the Nile, and Isis who was pictured as his loyal sister and wife. Her worship was especially colorful since it was thought that through her intervention death could be conquered. In addition, there were countless minor deities.

ATON. The best example of monotheism in Egypt can be found in the work of Amenhotep IV, who was disgusted with the prevalent idolatry and the immorality of the priests, and announced there was only one God who ruled supreme: Aton. Amenhotep IV changed his name to Ikhnaton, and he composed a hymn to the new god which indicated that Aton is truly universal.

"Thy dawning is beautiful in the horizon of the sky,
O living Aton, Beginning of life!
When thou risest in the eastern horizon,
Thou fillest every land with thy beauty.
Thou are beautiful, great, glittering, high above every land,
Thy rays, they encompass the lands, even all that thou hast made.
Thou art Re, and thou carriest them all away captive;
Thou bindest them by thy love.
Though thou art far away, thy rays are upon earth;
Though thou art on high, thy footprints are the day."

What is noteworthy in this concept of God is not only its high concept of spirituality, but also the universal power ascribed to Aton. Aton is not merely the god of the Egyptians; he also governs other nations and protects men as well as animals. As a majestic spirit, he is the creator of life and his perfection is the standard of all human evaluation. Aton demands wisdom more than formal knowledge.

Ikhnaton thought that he might convert the Egyptians to this new religion, and he tried to banish the old deities. Superstition was to cease; the priests were to live a moral life. Education was to teach genuine morality. But his attempted reform failed and the old religion remained triumphant.

EDUCATION IN EGYPT. Egyptian education in early times was handled by the family. The father instructed his children in the ways of piety and morality, and they were taught obedience to the pharaoh.

In the Middle Kingdom three types of schools developed. There were the temple schools, supervised by priests who taught children the elements of writing. Then we find court schools, established by the official rulers to train the successors to the throne. The court schools placed heavy emphasis on etiquette. The third type of school was established by the various government departments and stressed political and social knowledge.

Liberal education was neglected by the Egyptians since their system of education was primarily vocational. The stress on vocational education was as strong in ancient Egypt as in modern America.

Egyptian educational methods stressed harsh punishments. The lazy student was severely punished. An early clay tablet, written by a student to a teacher, declared: "Thou didst beat me and knowledge entered my head."

In every way, Egyptian education and religion were united. The basic aim of both education and religion was to develop morality in this life and piety towards the gods.

PERSIAN IDEALS

ZOROASTER. The moral fervor appears more strongly in Persian than in Egyptian religion. The most prominent prophet of this faith was Zoroaster, about whose life we have few reliable facts.[2] His birth, c. 660 B.C., like that of Buddha, is surrounded by legend. Like Buddha, he was tempted by the devil and, as a man with a proclivity for meditation, he loved solitude. He endured persecution until the high priest of Iran accepted his religion. Zoroaster's doctrines are contained in the *Zend-Avesta*.[3]

---

[2] On Zoroastrianism see Buch, *Zoroastrian Ethics*; Dhalla, *History of Zoroastrianism*.

[3] The *Zend-Avesta* can be divided into five sections: (1) the Yasna—chapters of liturgy and revelation. (2) the Vispered—other parts of liturgy. (3) the Vendidad—chapters dealing with moral ideals and theology. (4) the Yashts—hymns of praise and prophecy. (5) Khordah-Avesta—collection of prayers.

In Zoroastrian religion we find a definite spirit of dualism. The god of light, Ahura-Mazda, fights against Satan, Ahriman. This is not only an individual struggle but a conflict in which the entire universe takes part. Mazda is assisted by good spirits, while Ahriman enjoys the support of a host of demons.

This dualism had important consequences. Later it entered Jewish religion, and it became prominent in Christianity. Thus, we have the seeds of the Augustinian concept of history, the struggle between good and evil, between the city of God and the city of the devil.

Zoroaster considered religion as identical with education. The most important virtue was piety, to honor God. Also, man was to be kind to his neighbor, and he was to spread righteousness. The most dangerous sin, according to the code of Zoroaster, was *heresy*. Here we have a spirit of dogmatism which is absent in most Chinese religions.

In Zoroastrianism, we have a clear concept of the after-life. There is a day of judgment which is almost as terrifying as the judgment day of the *Book of Revelation*. The good would live in a blissful heaven called the *Abode of Song*, where men would enjoy the companionship of beautiful women; whereas the wicked would live in an eternal hell where incredible tortures await them.

The monotheistic spirit of Zoroastrianism is revealed in a hymn to Mazda.

> "This I ask Thee, O Ahura! Tell me aright: Who by generation was the first father of the Righteous Order within the world? Who gave the recurring sun and stars their undeviating way? Who established that whereby the moon waxes, and whereby she wanes, save Thee? These things, O Great Creator! would I know, and others likewise still.
>
> "This I ask Thee, O Ahura! Tell me aright, who from beneath hath sustained the earth and the clouds above that they do not fall? Who made the waters and the plants? Who to the wind has yoked on the storm-clouds, the swift and fleetest two? Who, O Great Creator! is the inspirer of the good thoughts within our souls?
>
> "This I ask thee, O Ahura! tell me aright; who, as a skilful artisan, hath made the lights and the darkness? Who, as thus skilful, hath made sleep and the zest of waking hours? Who spread the Auroras, the noontides and midnight, monitors to discerning man, duty's true guides? How may my soul with joyfulness increase in goodness? Let it thus be." [4]

In this hymn, we find that Mazda is not merely the ruler of the universe but also a spiritual force. To serve him, we must not only pay attention to his ritual, but we must purify our thoughts and search our hearts. In short, Mazda becomes the moral force which governs all parts of life and all aspects of the universe.

---

[4] *Ibid., Yasna,* XLIV, 3-8.

PERSIAN EDUCATION. Persian education was based upon theological ideals. The Persian aim was to develop moral character and righteousness. For the man, bravery was especially important, while women were to be examples in gentleness.

The first part of Persian education began in the home and was supervised by women. Boys were taught the importance of self-control; girls were instructed in the elements of domestic science. At the age of five the boy was taught the elements of religion; he was told that he had to wage a constant fight against the forces of evil (Ahriman).

At the age of fifteen, another phase of education started during which military training was stressed. This lasted for five or six years after which the boy became a citizen.

Those boys who wanted to become priests studied philosophy, science, and the sacred scriptures. A specialized curriculum was also developed for advisors to the great king; there men were instructed in the elements of finance and statesmanship.

Persian education was mainly vocational. It neglected the liberal arts and it over-emphasized physical fitness. The Persians were prepared for war, but they could not live creatively in times of peace.

THE HEBREW IDEALS

Even more formative than the Persians in the development of Western ideals was the influence of Hebrew religion, which, to a large extent, supplied the formulation of the moral and religious code of modern man.

What are the basic differences between Hebrew and Oriental religion? First, we note the emphasis upon *personality* in the Hebrew faith. While the Orient, especially Hinduism, usually regards personality as a subordinate category, in Hebrew thought the individual is all important and salvation lies in the fulfillment of personality, not in the negation of the self.

Second, the emphasis upon the *fatherhood of God* is significant in Hebrew religion. Oriental faiths regard God as a cosmic principle, and some, like Buddhism, deny the existence of a Supreme Being. In Hebrew religion, on the other hand, there is a vivid and intensely emotional relationship between man and God, and the supreme being becomes a dramatic participant in human history.

Third, *indeterminism* plays a larger role in Hebrew religion than in Oriental faiths. The Hebrew ideal of freedom means that man is not a victim of fate, but that he can shape his own destiny. His character is not fixed by a series of transmigrations, but it is the result of his own actions and ideals.

Fourth, there is a fiercely *nationalistic tone* in Hebrew religion. The Hebrew concept of a chosen people had an enormous influence on the religious and political development of the West. This concept usually gives only lip service to universal ideals, and in action it practices a fierce type of nationalism. On the other hand, we find a rather cosmopolitan spirit in Taoism, Confucianism, Hinduism, and Buddhism.

Fifth, the concept of *sin* stamps Hebrew religion. While in Oriental religion the failings of man are mostly regarded as the products of ignorance, in Hebrew religion, sin is viewed as a conscious defiance of the will of God—an action which merits harsh punishment. This sense of sin is intensely emotional in Hebrew religion and it results in the abasement of the individual before his creator.

It appears, according to some scholars, that the Hebrews derived their God from the Midianite-Kenites, a nomadic tribe which came into contact with the Hebrews. It is probable that Jehovah was a God of fertility who inhabited fiery volcanoes.

EARLY HISTORY. The early beginning of Hebrew history is shrouded in legend. Abraham, Isaac, and Jacob were tribal leaders who lived a migratory existence. They were at the head of a group of people which had a high concept of sexual morality, but which was subject to many superstitions. The *Old Testament* thus tells us that all kinds of objects and spirits were worshipped, and that magic found many adherents. Totemism and fetishism flourished among the Hebrew tribes. We find frequent references in the early part of the *Old Testament* to sacred stones and pillars and it was thought that certain wells were inhabited by divine spirits. The Hebrews also worshipped animals, including the bull and the sheep. Even snakes were regarded as sacred; in fact, the snake became the symbol of virility.

The social organization of the tribes was *patriarchal*. The father was the absolute head of the family; his word was law and could not be challenged. Gradually, as civilization grew more advanced among the Hebrews, the status of women improved; later, puritanical prophets, like Amos, inveighed against the dissipations of the female sex.

MOSES. The outstanding single influence of early times was Moses, who became the leader in the exodus from Egypt. The exodus was full of miracles which were ascribed to the power of Jehovah. At this time, the high priest was Jathro, whose daughter was married to Moses; but later Moses and Aaron were in charge of the ritual. Moses had to remind the people constantly to abide by the laws of God and to be grateful for their blessings. Yet they considered the worship of the old idols as an extremely satisfying experience; only slowly did they develop a new concept of God.

JEHOVAH. While Jehovah was the god of the patriarchs, his name was first revealed to Moses. Jehovah could not be seen in person; anyone who saw him face to face could not live. He was revealed through lightning, storms and earthquakes. Man could only know his manifestations, not his essence.

Jehovah, it was thought in early Hebrew history, was not the only God; there were other deities; however, he was the mightiest. Moses often stressed his physical attributes; later, the prophets dwelled more upon his spiritual traits.

Moses made it clear that there was a vast difference between man and Jehovah. Jehovah had super-human powers. He could wield the thunderstorm and he could easily kill those who offended him.

It was a common belief that Jehovah's presence dwelled among the Hebrews. The symbol of his presence was the sacred arc which was taken along by the tribes through their nomadic journeys.

The early view of the Hebrews regarding the moral attributes of Jehovah is rather limited. He often changes his mind, and, to some extent, regrets the creation of man. He appears to approve deceit on the part of Jacob in his relationship with Laban, and he kills the first-born children of the Egyptians—an action which can scarcely be approved on moral grounds.

As the protector of the Hebrews, Jehovah promotes their welfare and punishes their enemies. Occasionally he becomes extremely stern, especially when dealing with enemies of the Hebrews. He certainly is not a pacifist, for he believes that war is justified. Moses regarded Jehovah as a God of War who took delight in the slaughter of his enemies. When his anger becomes strong, Jehovah threatens to exterminate the Hebrews. For example, when the Hebrews worship the Golden Calf, Jehovah wants to destroy them. Only with difficulty does Moses persuade Jehovah to moderate his wrath.

The early view of Jehovah stressed his power to punish. When the Hebrews violate his commandments, he will punish not only the guilty, but his wrath will extend to their children and grandchildren. He is so determined that his commandments be followed, that he utters awe-inspiring curses in cases of transgression. For example, he threatens the Hebrews that, should they disobey him, they shall be cursed in all their activities and they shall be ruined by deadly diseases.

THE COVENANT. Jehovah's relationship with the Hebrew people was intensely personal and was symbolized by the covenant, which promised them prosperity and power in return for their worship. To the average Hebrew, the covenant meant that he was a member of a chosen race, that he had a special destiny, and that he could look down on other nations and other races.

Yet, there was also a more profound implication of the covenant. It was a contract between the Hebrews and God. It demanded absolute loyalty. If the Hebrews lived up to the covenant, then they would be prosperous, and they would experience an era of peace and goodwill; however, if they violated the covenant they would be exposed to turmoil, chaos, and destruction.

The covenant was not merely a social, but also an individual contract. It meant that every member of the Hebrew faith had a personal obligation to God. While this personal element was not so strong in early Hebrew life, it became the central message of the prophets who dwelled upon the subjective relationship between man and God.

Moreover, the concept of the covenant created a definite religious philosophy of history. While Greek historians, like Thucydides, gave a thoroughly naturalistic account of history and traced the decline and rise of institutions to economic and political factors, the Hebrew historian looked upon all temporal events as being guided by God. He looked back to a distant past when man was in paradise, free from sin and corruption. Then he described man's life on earth, full of toil and sorrow, and Man's salvation, made possible through the revelation of God; both became the beginning and the end of history.

As the Hebrews came into contact with other nations, especially the Babylonians, Persians, and Greeks, their concept of life expanded. The prophets, especially Isaiah, pointed to a God of love who is the ruler of all nations. They maintained that God desired, above all, an inward attitude of spirituality and was not concerned about sacrifice. As Isaiah states:

"Fasting and feasting I cannot endure.
My whole being hates your new moons and your festal seasons;
They are a burden upon me; I am tired of them.
So, when you spread out your hands, I will hide my eyes from you;
Even though you make many prayers, I will not listen . . .
Wash yourselves clean! Put away the evil of your doings from before my eyes;
Cease to do evil, and learn to do good!
Seek justice, and restrain the oppressor!"

And Micah, a contemporary of Isaiah, declares:

"With what shall I come before the LORD,
And bow myself before God most high?
Shall I come before him with burnt-offerings,
With calves a year old?
Will the LORD be pleased with thousands of rams,
With myriads of streams of oil?
Shall I give my first born for my transgression,
The fruit of my body for the sin of my soul?
You have been told, O man, what is good,
And what the LORD requires of you:
Only to do justice, and to love mercy,
And to walk humbly with your God?"

The prophets differed in their concepts of God. To Amos, He was a stern protector of moral ideals; to Isaiah, He was an imperious ruler of all nations. To Jeremiah, He was an all powerful father who knew the motives of His children. To Ezekiel, He was an impartial judge, and to Deutero-Isaiah, He was a savior. But all prophets agreed that, ideally, the Hebrews would lead other nations in the path of righteousness.

EDUCATIONAL VIEWS

Hebrew education in early times was handled mainly by the father. After the exile in Egypt, the synagogue became the central place of instruction. The main emphasis was upon memorization: The child had to know the letter of the law. Originality was discouraged.

Children were regarded as being naturally inclined to have wayward impulses and, therefore, had to be rigorously disciplined. Still, great teachers, like Hillel, were extremely humane in their disciplinary methods.

Educational life was divided into four periods. The first period, up to the age of six, was mainly conducted in the home. The child learned basic moral attitudes, was introduced into the basic ritual, and was told stories about the glories of Hebrew culture.

The second period was under the supervision of the scribe in the synagogue. Now religious instruction was intensified, and the child was taught the basic fundamentals of reading, writing and arithmetic.

The third period, from ages ten to sixteen, concentrated upon the mastery of the law. The student was in close contact with the rabbi, the spiritual leader of the community.

The fourth period was concerned with higher education. At the age of sixteen, the more intelligent boys associated themselves with teachers like Gamaliel and Hillel, and they learned the intricacies of the law. Education in this phase involved an intellectual interchange of ideas between teacher and student.

Hebrew education was guided by the ideal of wisdom. Thus, we read in the book of Proverbs:

"My son, if you receive my words,
And store my commands within you,
Inclining your ear to wisdom,
And applying your mind to reason;
If you seek her as silver,
And search for her as for hidden treasures—
Then will you understand reverence for the Lord,
And will discover the knowledge of God . . .

"For when wisdom finds a welcome within you,
And knowledge becomes a pleasure to you,

> *Discretion will watch over you,*
> *Reason will guard you—*
> *Saving you from the way of evil men."*

Wisdom is man's supreme good:

> *"How happy is the man who finds wisdom,*
> *The man who gains understanding!*
> *For her income is better than income of silver,*
> *And her revenue than gold.*
> *She is more precious than corals,*
> *And none of your heart's desires can compare with her.*
> *Long life is in her right hand,*
> *In her left are riches and honor."*

Creativity in the Hebrew civilization was hindered by heavy reliance on orthodox religious standards. On the other hand, the intimate contact between teacher and student brought about an intense interest in education. The example of the Hebrews indicates that more important than worldly power is *interest in ideas,* that more significant than material achievement is a *unifying ideal of life.*

QUESTIONS FOR DISCUSSION AND INVESTIGATION

1. Why was religion emphasized in ancient Egypt?

2. What was the most predominant example of monotheism in Egypt and why did it not survive?

3. Give the types of schools which developed under Egyptian education.

4. Discuss the spirit of dualism and its consequences in Zoroastrian religion.

5. How does Persian education compare with the Egyptian approach to teaching?

6. Explain the basic differences between Hebrew and Oriental religion.

7. Trace the historical development of Hebrew religion.

8. What implications did the covenant bear for the basic concepts of religion and education?

9. Trace the development of the Hebrew's educational ideas.

10. What were the chief advantages and disadvantages of Hebrew religion and education?

Chapter 8

Greek Educational Thought

BACKGROUND

The educational ideals of Athens were influenced by its social structure. The city had a population of about 100,000 freemen, 60,000 to 70,000 slaves, and 45,000 foreigners. The latter did not enjoy the privileges of full citizenship but took part in the educational and commercial activities of the city state. Athens, at first, was ruled by a landed aristocracy, but, after the Peloponnesian war, democratic tendencies prevailed. Throughout Athenian history a conflict existed between the aristocracy and the lower classes. Thus anarchy and tyranny were constant dangers. No wonder that in his *Politics* Aristotle preferred the government of the middle class as the ideal form of political administration.

Athenian boys were educated in the home until they reached the age of six, at which time they entered a formal school. Here they were instructed in physical exercises, to perfect their bodies, as well as in music, a term which included all the arts. The ideal of Greek education was not professionalism in the arts but enjoyment and participation. Athenian education was literary rather than religious. Its goals were the cultivation of the sciences and of the humanities. Among the subjects stressed were reading, writing, arithmetic, poetry, the sciences, and moral and metaphysical philosophy.

The life of an Athenian schoolboy is described by Plato in *The Protagoras:*

"Education and admonition commence in the first years of childhood, and last to the very end of life. Mother and nurse and father and tutor are quarreling about the improvement of the child as soon as ever he is able to understand them; he cannot say or do anything without their setting forth to him that this is just and that is unjust; this is honourable, that is dishonourable; this is holy, that is unholy; do this and abstain from that. And if he obeys, well and good; if not, he is straightened by threats and blows, like a piece of warped wood. At a later stage they send him to teachers, and enjoin them to see to his manners even more than to his reading and music; and the teachers do as they are desired. And when the boy has learned his letters and is beginning to understand what is written, as before he understood only what was spoken, they put into his hands the works of great poets, which he reads at school; in these are contained many admonitions, and many tales, and praises, and encomia of ancient famous men, which he is required to learn by heart, in order that he may imitate or emulate them and desire to become like them. Then, again, the teachers of the lyre take similar care that their young disciple is temperate and gets into no mischief; and when they have taught him the use of the lyre, they introduce him to the poems of other excellent poets, who are the lyric poets; and these they set to music, and make their harmonies and rhythms quite familiar to the children's souls, in order that they may learn to be more gentle, and harmonious, and rhythmical, and so more fitted for speech and action; for the life of man in every part has need of harmony and rhythm. Then they send them to the master of gymnastic, in order that their bodies may better minister to the virtuous mind, and that they may not be compelled through bodily weakness to play the coward in war or on any other occasion. This is what is done by those who have the means, and those who have the means are the rich; their children begin education soonest and leave off latest." [1]

As Athens expanded, a divison took place in the levels of education. Oratory became a most important subject of inquiry. Isocrates, one of the great teachers of Athens, regarded oratory as the most important study of man. He maintained that education should be practical; its highest aim should be the creation of the public speaker with a broad, liberal education. To Isocrates, the communicative elements of education were most significant, and in this view he represents the spirit of fourth century Athens.

In secondary education grammar was cultivated. At the same time, arithmetic and geometry had an important place in the curriculum. A specialized teacher called the *grammaticus* was employed in Athens.

While early Athenian education stressed physical education as an end in itself, professionalism in sports became more and more significant

---

[1] *Protagoras.*

in later education. Xenophon, famous Greek historian, believed in heavy emphasis on military training because he felt that a state should control all activities of its citizens. Thus, he shows great admiration for the Spartans, who tolerated no political opposition and exercised strong state control. Physical prowess, as he points out in his *Cyropaedia,* is far superior to literary skill.

In 335 B.C., Athens passed a law which made military training compulsory for all boys upon reaching the age of eighteen. For a period of two years they were to serve the state. In 300 B.C., the training period was reduced to one year; later, compulsory military service was abolished altogether.

Higher education in Athens grew out of the schools established by the various philosophers. Four schools are especially noteworthy: The Academy, where Plato taught, stressed mathematics and literary studies. The Lyceum, where Aristotle instructed a large group of disciples, stressed the biological sciences. The Epicurean school was founded by Epicurus, a philosopher who stressed ethics and insisted that the highest pleasure was that of the mind. The Stoic school, started by Zeno, stressed the importance of resignation and self-control and attracted a wide audience, especially in the Hellenistic era. In these schools teaching methods were rather informal, a close comradeship existed between instructor and student.

The weakness of Athenian educational practice was revealed in the treatment of women who received only the rudiments of education. They were usually confined to the home and, if they had enough wealth, spent most of their time gossiping and supervising the slaves.

Another weakness of Athenian education was the lack of application of educational ideals. This was largely due to the Athenian's regard of labor as an inferior activity. Thus we find that the Greeks have developed many of the theories which have furthered the progress of Science, but they seem to have neglected the realm of application.

GREEK EDUCATIONAL IDEALS

Greek education was guided by a rationalistic emphasis. Since there was no infallible authority, since there was no organized priesthood, free inquiry could flourish. This freedom developed a spirit of tolerance unequaled by other civilizations.

However, there were limitations to this tolerant attitude. Anaxagoras, one of the pre-socratic thinkers, was persecuted because of his scientific views. Socrates had to take the hemlock, because some Athenians felt that he was corrupting the youth of his time, and that he was subversive to established religion and government.

The Greek ideal of education upheld a combination of physical and intellectual excellence. Both the mind and the body had to be trained; both intellect and physical prowess had to be cultivated.

The educated man, according to the Greeks, would stress the pleasures of this world, but would never go to extremes. He would cultivate reason because this was man's most important quality. Asceticism, denial of the flesh, were attitudes to be avoided. Thus, as Aristotle maintained, the wise man would seek enough material satisfaction, friendship, and the good things of life so that his existence would be enriched.

The Greek mind was at home in the world and conceived of moral laws as being part of physical laws. Nature and morality were identified as one. The good man acted according to the laws of nature, while the evil man violated the laws of the universe. Even the gods were dominated by the concept of fate. They had a definite function in life, but when they overstepped their function other gods usually effected their punishment. The idea of *limitation* was extended to man; in fact, to the Greeks the finite was good, while the infinite was regarded as the principle of evil. The sin of Prometheus was his attempt to overstep his limits; consequently, he was punished by the gods.

Greek thought, unlike Christianity, was based on a naturalistic spirit. Life was to be enjoyed to the fullest. What happened after this life was, at best, uncertain. The Greeks believed that the life beyond would be in a vague, shadowy place called Hades—an austere and somber existence that did not hold any promises.

Greek ideals resulted in an integrative concept of education. The best life was one which led to a full adjustment of man to his environment. The Greeks did not think that social duties were to be avoided; the educated man, thus, would be a good citizen and certainly would not avoid public responsibility. He would not be overly modest; in fact, the Greeks did not have that sense of humility which we find in Christian tradition. For example, the truly educated man, according to Aristotle, is conscious of his perfection and regards modesty as a sign of weakness.

RATIONALISM AND THE SOPHISTS

The Sophists lived in a period when Athenian life shifted from an agrarian to a commercial basis. Economic change produced philosophical questioning. Thus, the Sophists believed in the relativity of truth and challenged any absolute standards of morality.

In a famous statement, Protagoras maintained that we can never have certain knowledge regarding the existence of the gods. There are two things that hinder us—"the obscurity of the subject matter and the shortness of man's life." As a skeptic, Protagoras neither affirmed nor denied existence of religious truths. As a humanist, Protagoras believed that man is the measure for all things. In other words, man is to study only those subjects that lead to human advancement. On the other hand, when certain knowledge is not possible, man should avoid all dogmatic conclusions.

In regard to orthodox religion we can find similar skepticism in the beliefs of Thrasymachus, who felt that there are no categorical moral laws and that the concepts of ethics are merely products of human legislation. What is good is pleasant, whereas what is evil leads to pain. The gods themselves have no regard for human beings. If they cared for man, according to Thrasymachus, they would have instilled in man absolute principles of morality, and they would have made him righteous. However, when we look at society, we see that unrighteousness prevails and that there is no indication of divine intervention.

The Sophists enriched the Athenian curriculum by stressing the art of public speaking. They became the first lawyers of modern civilization. To the Sophists, the humanities were the core of education. But as skeptics, they opposed absolutism. Thus, Gorgias taught:

1. *Nothing (Absolute) exists.*
2. *Even if it existed, it could not be known.*
3. *Even if it could be known, it could not be communicated.*

Since the Sophists were paid teachers, many of their contemporaries accused them of selling truth to the highest bidder. But all in all, we cannot deny that the Sophists injected into education a certain element of excitement.

SOCRATES

Socrates (470?-399 B.C.), unlike the Sophists, believed that truth is absolute. According to Socrates, the task of the teacher is to ask questions and to probe the ideas of mankind. Most individuals are governed by prejudice, not by truth, and they live in a world of unreality. The beginning of education then is the recognition of limitation; we do not know and, thus, we are more wise than those who live by pretension.

"Know thyself" was the keynote to the educational teachings of Socrates. The unexamined life is not worth living, and reason is man's guide to emancipation. Virtue and knowledge are one in the philosophy of Socrates. Virtue leads to right habits, while knowledge gives us a correct picture of man, the universe, and God.

The teacher, according to Socrates, is the leader of civilization. He must pursue truth even when his contemporaries oppose him. Integrity, above all, is demanded from the schoolmaster.

Socrates was primarily a moralist in education. He was generally uninterested in science. Unlike the early Greek thinkers, he considered nature as less important than the problem of man.

In his teachings, he used the dialectical method. This method brings out truth through a process of intellectual definition and finally achieves an absolute definition. The dialectic method was used by medieval educators who believed in logic rather than in the experimental method.

Why did Socrates become the supreme model for later educators? Why was his influence so pronounced? Why was he admired so greatly by Plato and Aristotle? It appears that Socrates was not merely a theorist. but he lived according to his educational ideals. He believed that the rich and the poor, the wise and the ignorant, the young and the old—all need real education. To Socrates, education was a spontaneous process; it required neither formal school nor organized student body. Plato tells us that Socrates taught most effectively when he attended banquets and when he would discuss abstract concepts as virtue, truth, and immortality.

Socrates became important as an educational critic. He made it clear that many of Athens' leaders were ignorant and guided by irrational idols. He opposed the government of the people, for they were inclined to be swayed by emotions. He found that the professional philosophers were too arrogant about their beliefs and that they would readily accept the expediency of the moment. Socrates was more concerned about the problem of man than the nature of the universe; if man does not find himself of what value is cosmological knowledge?

His interest in teaching and education caused him to neglect practical matters. All his life he was a poor man—a fact which greatly distressed his wife. But he considered intellectual growth more important than external riches. Knowledge, to Socrates, was a good in itself. It banished anxiety. It created true serenity. It brought about emotional balance. Thus, he was unafraid to die: death would be either an eternal sleep, undisturbed by dreams, or a journey to a better world.

What strikes the modern observer is the dignity of Socrates. No reverse could change his basic attitude. When he was tried by the Athenians he did not appeal to emotion and prejudice, but he remained objective and without fear. To Socrates, morality was not an abstract ideal, but a pattern to be realized in daily living.

The function of the teacher, according to Socrates, is to awaken the average man. The majority, he felt, is guided by irrational thoughts and lethargy, and lives in a cave of half-truths and illusions. Once the student is stirred, and once he becomes aware, he sees a new meaning in life. He probes and he questions. He is guided by curiosity and takes pleasure in intellectual inquiry. Yet education, Socrates maintained, has ultimately a social function. What matters is not our own brilliance, but how we radiate our ideas and how we change society so that morality and intelligence are combined.

To Socrates, the teacher is anything but a specialist. Education, philosophy, ethics, and religion all are basically one and aim at the creation of a rational individual. The most important task of the teacher, he maintained, is to be the conscience of his time. This means that he must cherish the ideals of knowledge even when he faces social disapproval and persecution.

To the conservatives, Socrates appeared as an innovator. Ironically, Aristophanes pictured him as one of the Sophists who perverts truth. Thus, in the *Clouds*, Socrates is portrayed as an atheistic teacher who, in a conversation with Strepsiades, claims that Zeus does not exist.

STREPSIADES: . . . Whence comes then the thunderbolt, pray?

SOCRATES: When a wind that is dry, being lifted on high, is suddenly pent into these,
It swells up their skin, like a bladder, within, by Necessity's changeless decrees:
Till, compressed very tight, it bursts them outright, and away with an impulse so strong,
That at last by the force and swing of its course, it takes fire as it whizzes along.

STREPS: That's exactly the thing that I suffered one spring, at the great feast of Zeus, I admit:
I'd a paunch in the pot, but I wholly forgot about making the safety-valve slit.
So it spluttered and swelled, while the saucepan I held, till at last with a vengeance it flew:
Took me quite by surprise, dung-bespattered my eyes, and scalded my face black and blue! . . . .

SOCR: Now then you agree in rejecting with me the Gods you believed in when young.
And *my* creed you'll embrace: *"I believe in wide Space, in the eloquent Tongue."*

STREPS: If I happened to meet another God in the street, I'd show the cold shoulder, I vow.
No libation I'll pour: not one victim more on their altars I'll sacrifice now.[2]

The picture of Socrates which we find in Plato is quite different. It appears that, unlike Democritus, Socrates was uninterested in scientific philosophy. Thus, he could not agree with Anaxagoras and was disappointed when he found out that Anaxagoras did not make use of the principle of Nous.

. . . "It seemed to me that his case was very like that of one who should say that Socrates, in all he does, acts with intelligence, and then, when he tried to give the reasons of any particular action of mine, should begin by saying that the reason why I am sitting here now is that my body is composed of bones and sinews; and while my bones are hard and have joints which

---

2 Aristophanes, *Clouds*, 218

separate them, my sinews, which, together with the flesh and the skin which
contains them, enfold the bones, can be contracted and relaxed; and so when
my bones swing in their sockets, my limbs, relaxing and contracting the
sinews, make me able to bend myself at this moment, and that is the reason
of my sitting here in a bent posture. . . ." 3

Socrates was certain that the universe was a moral order and that it
had a definite purpose. He could not agree with a mechanistic interpretation of life, for intellect and morality meant the same: The intelligent
man would be moral; the moral man would exhibit true knowledge.

The religious strains of Socrates are intensified when we read Xenophon. Thus Xenophon tells us that Socrates had a definite prescription
for prayer.

"His formula of prayer was simple: 'Give me that which is best for me,'
for, said he, 'the gods know best what good things are—to pray for gold or
silver or despotic power were no better than to make some particular throw
at dice or stake in battle or any such thing the subject of prayer, of which
the future consequences are manifestly uncertain.'

"If with scant means he offered but small sacrifices he believed that he
was in no wise inferior to others who make frequent and large sacrifices from
an ampler store. It were ill surely for the very gods themselves, could they
take delight in large sacrifices rather than in small, else often times must the
offerings of bad men be found acceptable rather than of good; nor from the
point of view of men themselves would life be worth living if the offerings
of a villain rather than of a righteous man found favor in the sight of
Heaven. His belief was that the joy of the gods is greater in proportion to
the holiness of the giver." 4

The courageous tone of Socrates is evident in his famous defense.
The Athenians among other charges had accused him of impiety but he
showed that he believed in the gods, indeed, he thought that he was
guided by a divine voice. He felt that there are duties which transcend
life.

"The truth is, Athenians, that, wherever a man's post may be, whether
he has chosen it himself as the best place for him or been sent there by a superior, there it is his duty to remain at all risks, without thinking of death or
anything else except dishonour. When the officers whom you elected to be
my superiors at Potidaea, at Amphipolis, and at Delium stationed me at my
post, I stayed there, like anyone else, at the risk of death; and it would be
strange if fear of death or of anything whatever should make me a deserter
now, when heaven, as I believe, has laid upon me the duty to spend my life
in seeking wisdom and in examining myself and others. Such conduct would
be strange indeed; and I should really deserve to be put on my trial for not

---

3 Plato, *Phaedo.*

4 Xenophon, *Recollections of Socrates,* i. 3.

believing in gods; for I should be disobeying the oracle, fearing death, and thinking myself wise when I was not; for it is to think you know what you do not know. No one knows whether death may not be the greatest good a man can have; yet men fear it as if they were certain it was the worst of evils. What is this but folly—that shameful folly of thinking we know what we do not know? Here again I am, perhaps, superior to the ordinary man; if I were to make any claim to be wiser than others, it would be because I do not think I have any sufficient knowledge of the other world, when in fact I have none. What I do not know is that it is bad and dishonourable to do wrong and to disobey a superior, be he man or god. Accordingly, when I am confronted by evils which I know to be evils, I will never take fright and run away from a thing which, for anything I know, may be a good." [5]

To Socrates, education demanded adherence to ideals—his function was to teach wisdom to the Athenians. Socrates made it clear that he would rather obey heaven than the citizens of Athens.

"Athenians, I hold you in much affection and esteem; but I will obey heaven rather than you, and, so long as breath and strength are in me, I will never cease from seeking wisdom or from exhorting you and pointing out the truth to any of you whom I may chance to meet, in my accustomed words: 'My good friend, you are a citizen of Athens, a great city famous for wisdom and strength; are you not ashamed to spend so much trouble upon reaping up riches and honour and reputation, while you care nothing for wisdom and truth and the perfection of your soul?' And if he protests that he does care for these things, I shall not immediately release him and go my way; I shall question and cross-examine and test him, and if I think he does not possess the virtue he affects, I shall reproach him for holding the most precious things cheap, and worthless things dear . . .

"For I have no other business but to go about persuading you all, both young and old, to care less for your bodies and your wealth than for the perfection of your souls, and to make that your first concern, and telling you that goodness does not come from wealth, but wealth and every other good thing, public or private, comes to mankind from goodness.[6]

There are basic similarities between Socrates and Jesus. Both suffered a tragic death, both believed in humility, both accepted an inner voice, and both had an intense sense of vocation. But Socrates, as a teacher, used mainly the method of reason, while Jesus appealed to faith.

PLATO

Plato (427-347 B.C.), the great student of Socrates, gave a new interpretation of the Socratic theory of knowledge. To Plato what was real was not the individual, the transitory and the flux of the external world

---

[5] Plato, *Apology.*
[6] *Ibid.*

—rather the general Forms or Ideas, which are eternal, unchanging, and completely perfect. These Forms are also ideal standards of evaluation and they indicate the meaning of absolute perfection.[7]

The Forms are climaxed by the concept of the Idea of the Good. The Idea of the Good should not be conceived as a personal force; it can only be compared with the sun which gives light to all parts of creation. Plato made it clear that the Idea of the Good is higher than existence and truth; in fact, it even surpasses the concept of God.

The Platonic view of knowledge turns away from mere opinion. When we use our senses we obtain only a fallible account of the universe; reliable knowledge depends on understanding, which provides for a scientific interpretation of reality. The highest type of knowledge is philosophy which sees reality as a whole. Philosophy is concerned not with empirical facts but with a synthesis of reality. While the sciences analyze, philosophy tries to obtain a complete view of reality.

It must be pointed out that Plato was vigorously opposed to popular religion. He blamed Homer for picturing the gods in an unfavorable light. Other poets, like Hesiod, likewise show that frequently the wicked are rewarded while the virtuous suffer.

Plato feels that the popular religious teachings would lead to a disintegration of morality and would ultimately produce atheism. How do we know that God exists? Can we believe in God? Plato maintains that the universal acceptance of the existence of God indicates its definite empirical foundation. Another Platonic argument appeals to the existence of motion: bodies do not move themselves, they need a teleological principle which comes from the outside. Just as the soul is man's ruling principle, so God rules the universe. Furthermore, Plato points to the remarkable order displayed in the universe which cannot be accidental but implies the providence of a supreme force.

The philosophy of Plato rests upon his belief in the immortality of the soul. How do we know that the soul is immortal? How can we be certain that it will not perish through death? Plato argues that the soul is not dependent upon the body, rather it is the dominant force in the body. The soul is unalterable and cannot be destroyed through successive reincarnations. The central idea of the soul is that of life, which excludes the idea of death. From a logical standpoint, Plato appeals to the identity of opposites. The existence of life demands the existence of death, whereas the existence of death demands the existence of life. Also, death can only touch those substances which are composite; it cannot touch a simple substance—the soul. The soul, imprisoned in the

---

7 The synthesis of the Forms corresponds to the concept of God. Cf. P. E. More, *Religion of Plato*, pp. 119 ff. J. Adam, *Republic of Plato* II, pp. 50-51; John Burnet, *Greek Philosophy*, Part I, 232.

body, longs for eternal union; it naturally transcends the limitations of human existence.

Furthermore, Plato points out that while bodies are moved from the outside, the soul is completely autonomous and contains its own principle of motion. Not dependent on external forces, it can neither be created nor destroyed, and thus it transcends the categories of space and time.

Plato definitely accepts the theory of reincarnation. The type of life after death is determined by our existence on earth. Our character produces a continuity throughout our pilgrimage in the universe. Hence, the evil man may become an animal while the good man may become a philosopher in another existence. The fate of the soul on earth is essentially somber and melancholy; therefore, the aim of the soul is to regain its original purity. The world process ends with the absorption of the soul in the world stream, a condition which approximates the Buddhist Nirvana, and which can scarcely be expressed in philosophical terms.

Plato, in his later philosophy, especially in the *Laws,* almost advocates a theocratic government. Heresy is to be strictly punished; religion is to be the center of the state. The rulers of the state are to be especially trained in theology. This parallels medieval beliefs which usually upheld the supremacy of religion. The status of the priesthood in the Middle Ages reminds us of the role of the philosopher kings in Plato's *Republic.*

Plato's educational philosophy rests upon his political ideals. In the *Republic* he describes three classes: the philosopher kings who rule, the guardians who defend the state, and the common people who do the menial work. Plato feels that education, ethics, politics, and economics form an indissoluble unit, for how could a Utopia be established without a correspondence between theory and practice?

Many modern theorists of education show certain weaknesses in their isolation of education as a specialized study, and in their preoccupation with details of philosophy or curriculum construction. They overlook the fact that we are determined by social values and that society cannot be changed merely by intellectual ideas. In this way, Plato was far more realistic than many modern thinkers, for the author of the *Republic* stressed the interrelatedness of all aspects of life.

Plato believes in an integrative approach to life. Thus, knowledge rises from opinion, which is fallible, to reason, which generalizes and establishes laws, to intuition, which sees the universe in its totality. Is not our sense perception a prelude to the nature of Ideas, which are eternal? Is not the specific the prelude to generalization? Is not human existence a yearning for spirituality?

To Plato, the state represents the highest interests of the individual. Hence, the state would establish educational standards and could use any means, even lies, to indoctrinate the citizens. This indicates certain Machiavellian undertones in Plato's philosophies.

In all his beliefs, Plato was inspired by the educational standards of Sparta. In this city state simplicity was the keynote; individualism was outlawed; men and women received the same basic training. From birth, boys were taught how to endure hardship and how to become brave in battle. The arts, especially music, were used to inspire patriotism; music, however, was limited to strict Doric rhythms. This was indeed a paradise for those who believed in austerity as a way of life.

Plato feels that Athenian education contributed to anarchy. He especially opposes the conventional stress upon Homeric literature. In Homer, according to Plato, the just are frequently not rewarded, bravery is not always recognized, and the gods are portrayed in a very skeptical light. As a result, both the young people and adults develop a false conception of man, society, and religion.

Traditionalism, thus, is a prominent feature of Plato's philosophy and is especially emphasized in *The Laws:*

"The argument says that to change from anything except the bad is the most dangerous of all things; this is true in the case of the seasons and of the winds, in the management of our bodies and the habits of our minds—true of all things except, as I said before, of the bad. He who looks at the constitution of individuals accustomed to eat any sort of meat, or drink any drink, or do any work which they could get, may see that they are at first disordered but afterwards, as time goes on, their bodies grow adapted to them, and they learn to know and like variety, and have good health and enjoyment of life; and if ever afterwards they are confined again to a superior diet, at first they are troubled with disorders, and with difficulty become habituated to their new food. A similar principle we may imagine to hold good about the minds of men and the nature of their souls. For when they have been brought up in certain laws, which by some Divine Providence have remained unchanged during long ages, so that no one has any memory or tradition of their ever having been otherwise than they are, then every one is afraid and ashamed to change that which is established." [8]

This conservatism even extends to music, as the following selection indicates:

"There are many ancient music compositions and dances which are excellent, and from these the government may freely select what is proper and suitable; and they shall choose judges of not less than fifty years of age, who shall make the selection, and any of the old poems which they deem sufficient they shall include; any that is deficient or altogether unsuitable, they

[8] Plato, *Laws.*

shall either utterly throw aside, or examine and amend, taking into their counsel poets and musicians, and making use of their poetical genius; but explaining to them the wishes of the legislator in order that they may regulate dancing, music, and all choral strains, according to his mind; and not allowing them to indulge, except in some minor matter, their individual pleasures and fancies. Now, the irregular strain of music is always made ten thousand times better by attaining to law and order, and rejecting the honied Muse—not however that we mean wholly to exclude pleasure, which is the characteristic of all music. And if a man be brought up from childhood to the age of discretion and maturity in the use of the orderly and severe music, when he hears the opposite he detests it, and calls it illiberal; but if trained in the sweet and vulgar music, he deems the opposite cold and displeasing." [9]

While women played only a minor part in Athenian education, Plato recommended that, essentially, they should receive the same training as men. This was indeed a revolutionary suggestion, and it scandalized many of his contemporaries. He also recommended a communistic system of property sharing for the philosopher kings who were to have no individual possessions. He favored eugenics and recommended that infants who were unfit should not be allowed to live. His view of the family was extremely unorthodox. He considered the family an inferior institution, and he believed that marriage should be regulated by the state. Only slaves were to be permitted to lead an unrestricted family life. He also thought that nursing and the bringing up of children were important enough not to be left to the discretion of private individuals.

Plato described exact levels of education. He emphasized the importance of infancy—education up to the age of three, during which time the child can already develop good habits and be taught by example; it is important to stress the ideal of bravery at this early age. From ages three to six, the child undergoes informal education; now, disciplinary measures should be used freely if the child misbehaves. At this stage the child is introduced to fairy-tales, but care should be taken that only ennobling stories are told to him. From ages six to thirteen, boys are separated from girls; from now on boys associate only with their own group. The curriculum is to expand and, besides morals, should include music, letters, mathematics, and religion. At the age of thirteen, boys receive more specialized instruction in mathematics, poetry and instrumental music. Plato warns against the use of the enfeebling Lydian rhythms as music should strengthen the boy's character.

From ages sixteen to twenty, boys should concentrate upon military training and strenuous physical exercise. Plato felt that, compared with the Spartans, the Athenians were inadequately prepared for war.

[9] Ibid.

After the age of twenty, only the superior students would continue their educational program. They would study the relationship between the various sciences in order to better understand the unitary aspects of life. At the age of thirty, the future philosopher kings would study philosophy and dialectics, and, at the age of thirty-five, they would be equipped to lead the state. Then, at fifty, they would retire to a life of contemplation.

There is a strain of mysticism in Plato's educational philosophy, however, it is not of an emotional, ecstatic variety. This sense of mysticism does not imply that the senses are to be neglected, rather, that life is a spiral leading from the present to eternity, from the immediate to more distant perspectives.

Plato felt that peace, prosperity, and happiness could only be achieved by rule of the "wisest." But intelligence alone is not the sole factor necessary for good government; even more important factors are morality and dedication to the welfare of others.

Many of Plato's concerns and beliefs are meaningful and applicable in our times. He believed that education was essentially the vision of man's greatness and that there could be no progress in a mediocre environment. He wanted the state to expose children to the beautiful; thus, their life would be ennobled.

To Plato, schooling has two parts: the training of the body, and the training of the soul; both are equally important. The formal organization of education would be supervised by a superintendent who would hold office for five years; he is to have two assistants: a director of music for the supervision of the arts, and a director of gymnastics to supervise the physical development of the future citizens.

One strong point of Plato's scheme of education lies in his recognition of the importance of individual differences. There cannot be the same training for all. In the United States, on the other hand, we have given to all students essentially the same scholastic diet; we have neglected the superior student. We have not realized the importance of great teachers and we certainly have not recognized their worth. Only by understanding the importance of inspiration, living greatness, and an ennobling atmosphere can we build a truly significant system of education.

However, Plato's weakness lies in his totalitarian tendencies. He had contempt for the masses; his vision of art was limited; his educational Utopia, like Sparta, would make only insignificant contributions to the progress of mankind. The negative inclinations of Plato have been eloquently described by Popper in *The Open Society and its Enemies*. Still, we must recognize the genius of Plato, who, in the *Republic*, developed a blueprint for modern times. He was largely ignored by the educational leaders of the Middle Ages, but, when he was rediscovered by the humanists, his influence led to the expansion of the Renaissance curriculum.

ARISTOTLE

Whereas Plato stressed the reality of universals, Aristotle (384-322 B.C.) was concerned above all with specific things.[10] His main interest lay in the science of biology, and his philosophy was stimulated by his research in natural science. But to appreciate the philosophy of Aristotle, we must understand certain fundamental terms.

Aristotle believes that all substances, with the exception of God, are made up of Form and Matter. Form is identified with actuality, while Matter is identified with potentiality. God is pure Form or Pure Actuality.

Aristotle tells us that there are four types of causes: 1. material cause, 2. efficient cause, 3. formal cause, and 4. final cause. This doctrine can be clarified by a concrete example. Imagine an artist who is trying to erect a statue. The content of the statue is the material cause; the artist is the efficient cause; the form of the statue is the formal cause, while the goal of the artist represents the final cause. Now, according to Aristotle, the most important cause is the *final cause*.

This doctrine has important consequences. It implies a rejection of a mechanistic philosophy. The universe cannot be interpreted according to absolute laws, rather it exhibits definite levels. The highest levels determine the function of the lower levels, and all levels are dominated by the climax of creation: *God*. The doctrine also implies that the actual is prior to the potential. The purpose of the artist determines the nature of the product which he creates; the plan of the universe determines the content of the universe. According to Aristotle, God is completely *immutable*. He is not a personal deity in the Christian sense, nor does he possess a sense of morality. His main activity is a meditation upon his own perfection.

We must not omit Aristotle's adherence to the geocentric hypothesis. Aristotle firmly believed that the earth was the center of the universe; he was certain that there could not be more than one heaven and that outside the heaven there could be no place or void. His teleological interpretation of science had a significant impact upon many medieval thinkers who likewise were mostly concerned with the religious purpose of science, rather than with the practical application of scientific knowledge.

---

[10] Cf. Zeller, *Aristoteles und die alten Peripatetiker;* Mure, *Aristotle;* Ross, *Aristotle;* Taylor, *Aristotle;* Stocks, *Aristotelianism.*

From an educational standpoint, it is important to understand Aristotle's doctrine of immortality. Aristotle did not believe in personal survival after death. He considered the intellect to be composed of a potential or *passive reason* and an *active reason*. The passive reason is determined by physical forces and, when the body disappears, the passive reason likewise suffers extinction.

The active reason is truly immortal. Consequently, when we apprehend the truth we become timeless spectators of our existence. Whatever is personal, on the other hand, does not survive after death. Our sensations, our memories, and our consciousness are all destroyed when we pass away. The active reason, according to Aristotle, is not dependent on any outside force. It transcends time and space. In using the active reason, man becomes like God and absorbs part of God's majesty.

The Aristotelian ideal of education is based upon a definite view of man. Aristotle maintains that man's most important attribute is his rational capacity, hence, he believed in the cultivation of the intellect. The emotional life is only the prelude to our rational development. Man is endowed with three souls: a vegetative soul, an animal soul, and a rational soul. The rational soul, most important of the three, has two parts: one is practical, the other is theoretical. The rational soul is the faculty which allows man to make judgments and evaluations.

Aristotle considers leisure the most important element in education. Only in times of leisure can man contemplate and speculate and become conscious of his higher powers. Labor is a secondary activity; in this respect, Aristotle represents the Athenian view of life.

According to Aristotle, the state is the fulfillment of our social drives. Hence, the state is to be in charge of education, and it should prohibit all vulgar activities.

> "That education should be regulated by law and should be an affair of state is not to be denied, but what should be the character of this public education, and how young persons should be educated, are questions which remain to be considered. For mankind are by no means agreed about the things to be taught, whether we look to virtue or the best life.
>
> "Neither is it clear whether education is more concerned with intellectual or with moral virtue. The existing practice is perplexing; no one knows on what principle we should proceed—should the useful in life, or should virtue, or should the higher knowledge be the aim of our training; all three opinions have been entertained. Again, about the means there is no agreement; for different persons, starting with different ideas about the nature of virtue, naturally disagree about the practice of it.
>
> "There can be no doubt that children should be taught those useful things which are really necessary, but not all things; for occupations are divided into liberal and illiberal; and to young children should be imparted only such kinds of knowledge as will be useful to them without vulgarizing them. And any occupation, art, or science, which makes the body or soul

or mind of the freeman less fit for the practice or exercise of virtue, is vulgar; wherefore we call those arts vulgar which tend to deform the body, and likewise all paid employments, for they absorb and degrade the mind." [11]

Youth is to be protected from all debasing influences:

"A freeman who is fond of saying or doing what is forbidden, if he be too young as yet to have the privilege of a place at the public tables, should be disgraced and beaten, and an elder person degraded as his slavish conduct deserves. And since we do not allow improper language, clearly we should also banish pictures or tales which are indecent. Let the rulers take care that there be no image or picture representing unseemly actions, except in the temples of those Gods at whose festivals the law permits even ribaldry, and whom the law also permits to be worshiped by persons of mature age on behalf of themselves, their children, and their wives. But the legislator should not allow youth to be hearers of satirical iambic verses or spectators of comedy until they are of an age to sit at the public tables and to drink strong wine; by that time education will have armed them against the evil influences of such representations." [12]

To Aristotle, the best government is government of the middle class. The most moral way of life is life according to the golden mean, a life of moderation. Unlike Plato, Aristotle is less opposed to a more sophisticated type of music because he realized it could play an important role in the curriculum.

"The question what is or is not suitable for different ages may be easily answered; nor is there any difficulty in meeting the objection of those who say that the study of music is vulgar. We reply (1) in the first place, that they who are to be judges must also be performers, and that they should begin to practice early, although, when they are older, they may be spared the execution; they must have learned to appreciate what is good and to delight in it, thanks to the knowledge which they acquired in their youth. As to (2) the vulgarizing effect which music is supposed to exercise, this is a question (of degree), which we shall have no difficulty in determining, when we have considered to what extent freemen who are being trained to political virtue should pursue the art, what melodies and what rhythms they should be allowed to use, and what instruments should be employed in teaching them to play, for even the instrument makes a difference. The answer to the objection turns upon these distinctions; for it is quite possible that certain methods of teaching and learning music do really have a degrading effect . . .

"The right measure will be attained if students of music stop short of the arts which are practiced in professional contests, and do not seek to acquire those fantastic marvels of execution which are now the fashion in such contests, and from these have passed into education. Let the young pursue

---

11 Aristotle, *Politics*.
12 *Ibid*.

their studies until they are able to feel delight in noble melodies and
rhythms, and not merely in that common part of music in which every slave
or child and even some animals find pleasure." [13]

How do we learn? Aristotle, interested in a systematic presentation
of knowledge, shows that our mind rises from the specific to the universal, from the particular to the general. Experience is to be our guide
and induction is to guide our reasoning. He emphasizes that, without a
correct method, education and philosophy cannot progress.

In education, according to Aristotle, three principles are to be kept
in mind. The first is *nature* which is the foundation of our biological
activities and which gives us our emotional drives. The second is *habit,*
which implies a control of our irrational activities. Children tend to act
instinctively, as do animals; only by instilling good habits in their lives
can they progress in a creative manner.

In this respect, Aristotle had a far more realistic perspective than
some contemporary twentieth century educators. Interest alone is not an
adequate motive in the education of children. For real knowledge and
real creativity, discipline is also essential. We learn from the Aristotelian concept of education how character is built through right associations and how reason can be established through self-control.

But the important part of education, according to Aristotle, is the
third principle: *the cultivation of the intellect.* Reason can understand
the totality of life; it can give order to chaos. When we use our reason
we virtually achieve a divine status and we rise above the trivialities of
the present.

Education, Aristotle maintains, can be divided into several phases.
At first, from birth to age seven, the child should be brought up in a
healthy manner. Special attention should be paid to his physical development; he should be taught how to endure hardship. Association
with slaves should be avoided.

A break takes place when the child reaches the age of five. As Aristotle states in the *Politics:*

"The next period lasts to the age of five; during this no demand should
be made upon the child for study or labor, lest its growth be impeded; and
there should be sufficient motion to prevent the limbs from being inactive.
This can be secured, among other ways, by amusement, but the amusement
should not be vulgar or tiring or riotous. The Directors of Education, as
they are termed, should be careful what tales or stories the children hear,
for the sports of children are designed to prepare the way for the business
of later life, and should be for the most part imitations of the occupations
which they will hereafter pursue in earnest. Those are wrong who (like

---

[13] *Ibid.*.

Plato) in the *Laws* attempt to check the loud crying and screaming of children, for these contribute towards their growth, and, in a manner, exercise
their bodies. Straining the voice has an effect similar to that produced by the
retention of the breath in violent exertions. Besides other duties, the Directors of Education should have an eye to their bringing up, and should take
care that they are left as little as possible with slaves. For until they are
seven years old they must live at home; and therefore, even at this early age,
all that is mean and low should be banished from their sight and hearing." [14]

From the age of seven to puberty, the child is exposed to an extensive curriculum which includes the study of the fundamentals of music
and gymnastics as well as reading, writing, and arithmetic. During the
next phase, from puberty to age seventeen, the boy would study rhetoric,
grammar, literature, and geography, as well as instrumental music and
mathematics. Now the stress would be upon exact knowledge. The climax of education comes after the boy reaches age twenty-one. Only the
really superior students may continue with their studies. Now the young
man would develop truly encyclopedic interests as he would study the
biological and physical sciences, psychology and ethics, and rhetoric as
well as philosophy. The knowledge of these subjects would give him a
complete concept of man and the universe. The school founded by
Aristotle, the *Lyceum,* stressed the knowledge of science and had a more
empirical foundation than Plato's Academy.

The aim of education, in Aristotle's view, is to guide youngsters so
that they "love which they ought to love and hate which they ought to
hate." Education is concerned not merely with a fragmentary concept of
man, but with the development of all his capacities—physical, moral,
and intellectual. The wise man, according to Aristotle, would combine
theory and practice, intuition and scientific knowledge. Thus, Aristotle's
view of man and knowledge is similar to the Renaissance conception,
which stressed the development of all our capacities.

The Aristotelian view of education may be compared to that of
Confucius. Both believed in the golden mean; both were concerned
with right habits; both had confidence in the powers of reason. However, they differed greatly in one respect: Aristotle was less concerned
with tradition and with the past, but more interested in religion and in
metaphysics, than the great Chinese thinker.

It has often been stated that a fundamental gulf exists between the
world view and the educational ideals of Plato and those of Aristotle.
Plato maintained that art has a secondary reality; it is to be strictly
regulated. Aristotle believes that art is an incentive to creative living;
in watching dramas or listening to music our emotions would be stirred;
a catharsis would take place, and we would expand our vision and see

---

[14] *Ibid.*

life on a cosmic plane. Aristotle also opposes professionalism in art, since art is to be the sport of the gentleman.

While Plato is essentially concerned with the realm of forms, Aristotle stresses specific experience. According to Aristotle, life is development, from lower forms to higher forms, from inorganic existence to man. Of utmost significance is man's *purpose,* for it defines his function in the universe.

Aristotle considers the ideal of justice as a basic concept of education and politics. The aim of the legislator is to produce good men, which implies that education is tested by *actual* results, not by theories.

The basic weakness of Aristotle's educational ideal is its anti-democratic tendencies. He had a low opinion of women, he defended slavery, and he had contempt for the culture of other nations. Furthermore, he neglected the importance of vocational training, a necessary supplement to any liberal education.

The greatness of Aristotle lay in his emphasis upon reason. By the use of reason man surpasses his animal nature; through rational insight emotional impulses can be controlled. Reason, used pragmatically, can remold the conditions of existence. Even Freud, who glorified man's animal impulses, stated in a letter that "there is no control of our passions except through intelligence."

In his educational ideals, Aristotle symbolized the Athenian view of life, which stressed moderation and a balanced concept of man and his intellectual powers. In Athens, there was no infallible theology. There was not one standard of morals and religion. The Athenians believed in free inquiry, and thus they laid the seeds for our own intellectual development.

Man's most formidable asset is curiosity, which is a truly explosive force. It makes us eternally restless, so that we seek and yearn and never stand still. To cultivate curiosity in education is to cultivate a power which goes beyond life and death and which gives meaning to the uncertainty of human existence.

Santayana one time remarked that the life of reason was most perfectly embodied by the Greeks, even though it was limited by political insecurity and by the struggle between totalitarianism and democracy. But the Greeks, especially thinkers like Aristotle, were more creative than perhaps any other civilization; to them education became a way of life; unending curiosity became man's most important trait in his quest for the good life.

THE DECLINE OF PHILOSOPHY

The death of Aristotle (322 B.C.) concurs with the end of that period in Greek history known as the *Hellenic* period. During the period that followed, commonly known as the *Hellenistic* period, the general concerns of thinkers changed radically. Philosophers emphasized ethical ideals rather than detached and objective views of reality. An important aspect of the philosophies of that period was the obvious conflict between faith and reason, between skepticism and religion.

At this time, the important contributions of Hellenistic Civilization included such items as city planning, the building of aqueducts, and the creation of cosmopolitan cities like Alexandria. As knowledge became more specialized, scholars arose who commented upon more particular aspects of culture. In mathematics, Euclid and Appolonius deserve special notice; in technology, Hero of Alexandria was outstanding; in geography, Strabo, Posidonius, and Eratosthenes were significant contributors, while Ptolemy, Hipparchus, and Aristarchus of Samos achieved eminence in astronomy. Archimedes, a universal genius, made brilliant contributions both to physics and mathematics.

Eric Fischer, in *The Passing of the European Age,* notes the similarities between Hellenistic civilization and the United States. Both civilizations, he maintains, were governed by the ideal of practicality; both stressed economic enterprise; both were inventive in the field of technology; both depended on other cultures for the source of their speculative theories.

Individuals in Hellenistic times travelled as much as we do today. A student might study at several centers of higher learning, including Alexandria and Athens. But philosophy, as Oswald Spengler noted in *The Decline of the West,* became more specialized and became often a systematic escape from reality. The mystery cults which arose are comparable, according to Toynbee, to the impact of Oriental religion upon the modern mind.

Hellenistic civilization, despite its splendor and luxury, was less creative than Hellenic civilization. It lacked refinement, it was too concerned with bigness. Alexandria had less freedom than Athens under Pericles. A social caste system prevented a vigorous exchange of intellectual viewpoints. Education became a prelude to specialization instead of being regarded as a good in itself. Hellenistic scholars, like some American scholars, were so imbued with the glories of the past that they neglected the creative possibilities of the present.

QUESTIONS FOR DISCUSSION AND INVESTIGATION

1. Trace the influence of the social structure on the educational ideals of Athens.

2. Explain the Sophists' views on life and education.

3. Compare Socrates' major premises in life with those of the Sophists and discuss his profound influence on the education of that time.

4. According to Socrates, what is the function of the teacher?

5. Explain Plato's views on religion, politics, and morality.

6. Compare and contrast Plato's ideas on education with those of the United States.

7. Define Aristotle's four types of causes and discuss the consequences of this doctrine.

8. How does Aristotle relate philosophical reasoning to his principles on education?

9. Compare and contrast the world views of Plato and Aristotle on education.

10. Why did philosophy eventually decline in Athens?

Chapter 9

The Age of Quintilian

Roman education was at first dominated by the family. In the Roman family the father was supreme and his word was like an edict of the state. The ideal of Roman education was to cultivate manliness and self-control. Individualism was not tolerated in the early Roman republic. As Rome expanded, the Greek influence became more significant. After 272 B.C. many Greek scholars came to Rome, among them, Livius Andronicus, who translated many Greek writings into Latin and who popularized Greek literature, and Plautus, who specialized in the translation of Greek comedy themes. Later, Cato, the Censor, attempted to arrest the Greek influence, but he was unsuccessful.

There are important parallels in the development of Roman and American education. Both systems started in an atmosphere of puritanism. Both emphasized utilitarian endeavors. Both were rather uninterested in speculation; instead they emphasized practical subjects. Both were faced by complex social problems, such as juvenile waywardness. Both made the most significant contributions in the field of technology.

In Rome three types of schools developed. On the elementary level the *litterator* taught the elements of reading and writing. On the secondary level the *grammaticus* instructed students in the fundamentals of the liberal arts. In more advanced education, schools of *Rhetoric* developed which often were liberally endowed by Roman emperors.

Roman professional education was extensive: In legal education the natural rights of all human beings and equality before the law became important legal concepts. At Constantinople, Theodosius established a professorship of law. Justinian continued this tradition, and his code of laws influenced medieval scholars, especially at the University of Bologna. In medical education, Galen stressed the empirical method, and his ideas influenced the scholars of the Middle Ages and of the Renaissance. Medieval instruction in medicine was on a high level at Rome; the Roman physicians were highly skilled in pharmacology and surgery.

Compared with Greek education, Roman schools were too practical, and under too much state control, especially after the first century A.D. The most important subject in the Roman curriculum was rhetoric, often taught in an uninspiring manner. Generally, teachers were paid a low salary. Juvenal, the great Roman satirist, complains that teachers in Rome received only a jockey's wage.

To quote Juvenal directly:

"Do you teach? Bowels of iron is what a teacher needs when each pupil stands up in turn and recites the self-same things in the self-same way. The same daily fare again and again—it is death to the wretched master. 'What would I not give,' cries he, 'that the boy's father might listen to him as often as I do.' And you live in a hole no blacksmith would put up with . . ." [1]

CICERO

Opposed to the original spirit of early Greek thinking, Romans practiced eclecticism—the tendency to combine various viewpoints. This is represented especially by Cicero (106-43 B.C.). He was well-trained in Greek thought, and he was an orator of note, but he had no original ideas on life and education. He was concerned, like many thinkers of his time, with rhetoric—the science of public speaking. The good orator, according to Cicero, should be well-grounded in a humanistic education. The good orator should also be able to stir his audience.

STOICISM

Stoics, like Seneca, Marcus Aurelius, and Epictetus influenced ancient education. They taught that evil has no metaphysical reality. In their arguments for the non-existence of evil they showed that evil is educational and that the world is improved by apparent tragedies. Furthermore, they explained that evil and good are interdependent. The virtuous, according to the Stoics, will never be overcome by evil but will triumph in spite of misfortune. Ethically, the Stoics believed in self-sufficiency and extolled the virtue of *apathy*. The mind is to control all emotions. The educated man, then, will not yield to hope or regret and will cultivate the independence of his own soul.

---

1 *Satires.*

The Stoics extend their philosophy to social matters. They preached the brotherhood of man and accepted the concept of natural law which was extended to all human beings. They believed in following the dictates of duty, an aspect of man's divinity.

The piety of the Stoics is revealed in the following hymn by Aratus, which was dedicated to Zeus:

"With Zeus let our song begin! Him never may we men leave
Unpraised! Full of Zeus are all the streets,
All the gathering-places of men; full is the sea,
Full the harbours. In all respects we have need of Zeus, all of us,
For we are also His offspring, and He, being gracious to men,
Signifieth that is favourable, and waketh up the peoples to work,
Reminding them of livelihood. He telleth it, when the clod is best
For oxen and for mattocks; He telleth it, when the seasons are favourable.
Both for the planting of trees and for the strewing of seed of every kind.
For He Himself established the signs of these things in the heavens,
When He ordered the stars; and He took thought to provide for the year,
Stars, which most chiefly should signify things made,
As touching the seasons, unto men, in order that all things might grow
soundly.
Wherefore Him always first and Him last they propitiate." [2]

The Stoics had great respect for the popular gods which they explained in a symbolic fashion. Also, they worshipped the stars, and they peopled the universe with spirits who mediate between man and the deities. However, the Stoics did not have a definite doctrine of immortality. According to Zeno, the founder of Stoicism, the souls of the virtuous do not perish after death, while Chrysippus felt that only the Stoic philosophers would be immortal.

The lyrical spirit of Stoicism is perhaps best revealed in Epictetus, once a slave of one of Nero's followers. Although he was tortured by ill health, Epictetus was certain that man should praise God. Indeed, man and God are comrades.

"If these statements of the philosophers are true, that God and men are akin, there is but one course open to men, to do as Socrates did: never to reply to one who asks his country 'I am an Athenian,' or 'I am a Corinthian,' but 'I am a citizen of the universe'. . . . When a man has learnt to understand the government of the universe, and has realized that there is nothing so great or sovereign or all-inclusive as this frame of things wherein men and God are united, and that from it come the seeds from which are sprung, not only my own father or grandfather, but all things that are begotten and that grow upon earth, and rational creatures in particular—for these alone are by nature fitted to share in the society of God, being connected with Him by the bond of reason—why should he not call himself a citizen of the universe and a son of God?[3]

[2] Aratus, *Phaenomena.*

[3] Epictetus, *Discourses*, I. ix. 1-7.

Stoicism influenced Christian thinking by developing a God-centered philosophy of life. Furthermore, the Stoics anticipated the internationalism of the church. The Stoic doctrine which states that all are part of the natural law is comparable to the Christian doctrine that all are children of God. Furthermore, the Stoics believed in resignation to the will of God—a view well-adapted to the spread of Christianity.

In education, the Stoics preached the importance of dignity. Intellectual ideals are secondary to right moral action. The educated man, in his self-control and poise, is to be an example to the irrational masses.

EPICUREANISM

While Stoicism had great respect for popular religion, the Epicureans gave a scientific account of the universe and regarded the popular faith as an obstacle to the educational progress of man.[4] A rational perspective, according to the Epicureans, demands the elimination of the fear of God and dread of death.

Why should we be afraid of death? Why should death have such horror for us? The Epicureans thought that death involves only a transformation and is an entirely natural process. Death is not to be feared, for whatever lives must die; whatever is created must again become part of the elements.

Metaphysically, the doctrines of the Epicureans were based on the atomism of Democritus. However, the Epicureans taught that the atoms are not determined but contain within themselves the principle of *free will*. The greatest pleasure is the pleasure of the mind; extreme passions are to be avoided; friendship is more important than love. The ultimate state to be attained is *ataraxia,* which may be translated as serenity. The educated man will not cultivate social approval, rather he will live apart from society and treasure his own tranquillity.

According to the Epicureans, gods exist but they, as man, are also composed of atoms. These gods do not intervene in human affairs, they are not infinite, nor did they create the universe. The task of man is to imitate the blissful existence of the gods and, like them, cultivate an attitude of perfect tranquillity.

The Epicureans appealed to science instead of theology. Thus, Lucretius, in his great poem *De Rerum Natura,* presents us with an outline of evolution.

---

4 The founder of this movement was Epicurus (342-270 B.C.), one of the most brilliant Greek philosophers. Cf. Hicks, *Stoic and Epicurean;* Pater, *Marius the Epicurean.*
5 Lucretius, *De Rerum Natura.*

According to Lucretius, Epicurus was an educational prophet:

> *"When Man's life upon earth in base dismay,*   6
> *Crushed by the burden of RELIGION, lay,*
> *Whose face, from all the regions of the sky,*
> *Hung, glaring hate upon mortality,*
> *First one Greek man against her dared to raise*
> *His eyes, against her strive through all his days;*
> *Him noise of Gods, nor lightnings, nor the roar*
> *Of raging heaven subdued, but pricked the more*
> *His spirit's valiance, till he longed the Gate*
> *To burst of this low prison of man's fate.*
> *And thus the living ardour of his mind*
> *Conquered, and clove its way; he passed behind*
> *The world's last flaming well, and through the whole*
> *Of space uncharted ranged his mind and soul."* [5]

PLUTARCH

Plutarch (45-125 A.D.) contributed to educational theory by his *Moralia,* or the *Education of Children.* He felt that the wise teacher should cultivate memory, correct habits, and intensify instruction. Without discipline a student could not progress. Schoolmasters should be examples in their way of life.

"When our boys are old enough to be put into the hands of pedagogues, great care must be taken that we do not hand them over to slaves, or foreigners, or flighty persons. For what happens nowadays in many cases is highly ridiculous: good slaves are made farmers, or sailors, or merchants, or stewards, or money-lenders; but if they find a winebibbing, greedy, and utterly useless slave, to him parents commit the charge of their sons, whereas the good tutor ought to be such a one as was Phoenix, the tutor of Achilles. The point, also, which I am now going to speak about is of the utmost importance. The schoolmasters we ought to select for our boys should be of blameless life, of pure character, and of great experience. For a good training is the source and root of gentlemanly behavior. And just as farmers prop up their trees, so good schoolmasters prop up the young by good advice and suggestions, that they may become upright. How one must despise, therefore, some fathers, who, whether from ignorance or inexperience, before putting the intended teachers to the test, commit their sons to the charge of untried and untested men." [6]

Young men, according to Plutarch, ought to be disciplined.

"I have often censured the introducers of bad habits, who have set over boys pedagogues and preceptors, but have given to youths full liberty, when they ought, on the contrary, to have watched and guarded them more than

[6] *Moralia.*

boys. For who does not know that the offenses of boys are petty and easily cured, and proceed from the carelessness of tutors or want of obedience to preceptors; but the faults of young men are often grave and serious, as gluttony, and robbing their fathers, and dice, and revelings, and drinking-bouts, and licentiousness. Such outbreaks ought to be carefully checked and curbed. For that prime of life is prodigal in pleasure, and frisky, and needs a bridle, so that those parents who do not strongly check that period, are foolishly, if unawares, giving their youths license for vice." [7]

QUINTILIAN

The Roman ideal of character and education is best represented by Quintilian. His emphasis on self-control, his dislike of speculation, his practical bent—all stamp him as a Roman citizen. He was born in Spain at Calagurris in 35 A.D.; he studied at Rome, where later he became a famous teacher of rhetoric and was rewarded for his efforts by emperor Vespasian.

To Quintilian, the only worth-while life is that of action. Contemplation was for the scholar who wanted to escape from reality. The philosopher failed when he tried to reform society according to his own dictates and ideals. Quintilian cited the example of history and showed that, usually, philosophers had not won fame in public assemblies.

Note the profound difference between Quintilian and Plato. Plato considered education as the study of immaterial truth; society was to be governed by a philosopher king. To Quintilian the philosopher at best was inferior to the experienced statesman and his role in life was a secondary one.

Quintilian divides philosophy into three fields, all three of which are important for the orator. First, the study of dialectics—the laws of reasoning; second, ethics—the laws of justice; and third, physics. However, Quintilian did not think of physics as a science; rather it was a study of the ways of providence. Quintilian thought that the universe had a moral purpose and that it is our duty to find the divinity which is within our soul. Physics would inspire the orator who thus would cherish a religious interpretation of life.

To become an orator, according to Quintilian, an individual should seek virtue above all other considerations. He should defend the interests of his client and he should never espouse falsehood. He should study the emotions of the audience and at the same time cultivate the techniques of public speaking. Mere specialized knowledge of speech was not adequate, for Quintilian believed that the orator should have a wide educational background.

In the twentieth century, Winston Churchill is certainly one of the outstanding orators. The reasons for his success in public speaking are

---

[7] *Ibid.*

complex. He expresses himself in dramatic terms; he has the ability to coin new terms; his eloquence is almost epic and reminds us of Shakespeare and Milton. Quintilian was undoubtedly right when he told us that public speaking is one of the foundations of education.

Quintilian tells us that in a child's development the early training is especially important.

"Let a father, then, as soon as his son is born, conceive, first of all, the best possible hopes of him; for he will thus grow the more solicitous about his improvement from the very beginning; since it is a complaint without foundation that 'to a very few people is granted the faculty of comprehending what is imparted to them, and that most, through dullness of understanding, lose their labor and their time.' For, on the contrary, you will find the greater number of men both ready in conceiving and quick in learning; since such quickness is natural to man; and as birds are born to fly, horses to run, and wild beasts to show fierceness, so to us peculiarly belong activity and sagacity of understanding; whence the origin of the mind is thought to be from heaven.

"But dull and unteachable persons are no more produced in the course of nature than are persons marked by monstrosity and deformities; such are certainly but few. It will be a proof of this assertion, that, among boys, good promise is shown in the far greater number; and, if it passes off in the progress of time, it is manifest that it was not natural ability, but care, that was wanting." [8]

The morals of children are easily corrupted. Our mistake, Quintilian maintains, is that we indulge them too much. We provide too many luxuries for them, and, as a result, they lack genuine appreciation. Like Socrates, Quintilian believed that simplicity is to be stressed on all levels of education.

Quintilian, progressive for his time, objected to corporal punishment, which, he believed, only created fear and an attitude of submission. The wise teacher would use a method of positive rewards and thus appeal to the idealism of students. Corporal punishment of students meant failure on the part of teachers. Education was to be conducted in such a way that the student would develop a sense of honor and a sense of integrity.

Quintilian held that all parts of knowledge were interrelated: a boy should not only know the elements of reading, writing and arithmetic; he should also be familiar with poetry and science.

"In regard to the boy who has attained facility in reading and writing, the next object is instruction from the grammarians. Nor is it of importance whether I speak of the Greek or Latin grammarian, though I am inclined to think that the Greek should take the precedence.

---

[8] *Institutes of Oratory*, Book I.

"Both have the same method. This profession, then, distinguished as it is, most compendiously, into two parts, the art of *speaking correctly* and the *illustration of the poets,* carries more beneath the surface than it shows on its front.

"For not only is the *art of writing* combined with that of speaking, but *correct reading* also precedes illustration, and with all these is joined the exercise of *judgment,* which the old grammarians, indeed, used with such severity, that they not only allowed themselves to distinguish certain verses with a particular mark of censure, and to remove, as spurious, certain books which had been inscribed with false titles, from their sets, but even brought some authors within their canon, and excluded others altogether from classification. Nor is it sufficient to have read the poets only; every class of writers must be studied, not simply for matter, but for words, which often receive their authority from writers. Nor can grammar be complete without a knowledge of music, since the grammarian has to speak of meter and rhythm; nor if he is ignorant of astronomy, can he understand the poets." [9]

Quintilian's educational plan of instruction consists of three levels. The first level of instruction is composed of the three R's and Latin and Greek grammar; Quintilian placed special emphasis on the study of Greek at an early stage of a child's development.

"I prefer that a boy should begin with the Greek language, because he will acquire Latin, which is in general use, even though we tried to prevent him, and because, at the same time, he ought first to be instructed in Greek learning, from which ours is derived. Yet I should not wish this rule to be so superstitiously observed that he should for a long time speak or learn only Greek, as is the custom with most people; for hence arise many faults of pronunciation, which is viciously adapted to foreign sounds, and also of language, in which when Greek idioms have become inherent by constant usage, they keep their place most pertinaciously even when we speak a different tongue. The study of Latin ought therefore to follow at no long interval, and soon after to keep pace with the Greek; and thus it will happen, that, when we have begun to attend to both tongues with equal care, neither will impede the other." [10]

The second level of instruction includes oratory, literature, geometry, astronomy, music, and philosophy. The third level, for exceptional students only, is the school of Rhetoric which corresponds to a modern university. Here the curriculum includes logic, history, literary criticism, dialectic and, above all, public-speaking. These schools would aim to turn out a man who has the eloquence of the lawyer, and who uses theoretical knowledge for the advancement of his professional life.

The inadequacy of Quintilian's educational plan lies in his disregard of speculation. Education thus becomes a pedestrian matter. Quin-

---

9 *Ibid.*
10 *Ibid.*

tilian reminds us of many American educators who are so concerned with activities and practical matters that they lose sight of the real purposes and ideals of the educative process. Quintilian, seduced by immediacy, was a victim of limited vision.

His example should be a warning to us. Education should stress the art of communication, but, even more, it must emphasize intellectual and moral qualities. Education is basically a vision, not a methodology; it is a vision of man's awareness and potentialities; man can only find himself when he cultivates the inward spark. To be too practical in education, or in philosophy, is to be misled by the idols of the tribe; it is to lose direction and a sense of purpose.

PHILO

The religious influence upon educational philosophy is best illustrated by the philosophies of Philo. Philo, a resident of Alexandria, is noted for his attempts to combine Judaism with Greek philosophy. Philo believed that reason was to be subordinated to revelation, and that teachers were less important than prophets who spoke directly for God.[11]

God, according to Philo, is completely *transcendent*. We cannot know His essence; still, God's providence dominates the universe. He uses intermediaries, the logoi, to mediate between man and Himself. Furthermore, Philo believed in numerous spirits, both good and evil, who represent the basic dualism of the universe.

It is a mistake, according to Philo, to believe that the universe is eternal. God's relationship to the world is like that of a father; in this respect Philo anticipates Christian thinking.

Philo, like St. Augustine, regarded life on this earth as a pilgrimage in which the holy man withdraws from this world and turns his attention upon eternal essences. We can find ourselves only through the love of God, and our existence is made worthwhile by the possibility of the vision of His splendor. Education has a spiritual function, and it shows how reason should be subordinated to faith.

NEO-PLATONISM

Plotinus, the founder of Neo-Platonism, studied at Alexandria under Saccas, one of the most famous teachers of ancient civilization. Plotinus took part in Emperor Gordian's campaign against the Persians; in 244 A.D. he opened up a school of Philosophy in Rome. His students were extremely enthusiastic about his instruction which appealed to their sense of idealism. Some of them were so impressed by his lectures that they called him "the most divine Plotinus."

---

11 For a more extensive treatment of Philo see Frederick Mayer, *History of Ancient and Medieval Philosophy*.

Real education, according to Plotinus, demands good citizenship and ethical conduct. Yet, more important than social virtues is man's mystical sense and his quest for the *One,* the principle of reality. Since man is a pilgrim on earth and estranged from the principle of unity, real knowledge implies "a flight of the alone to the Alone."

The fundamental concepts of Plotinus are: the transcendence of God, the immortality of the soul, the reality of mysticism, the non-existence of evil, and the monistic structure of the universe.[12]

Plotinus also stresses his belief in three basic realities in the universe—the *One,* which is beyond existence and which cannot be described in verbal terms, the *Nous,* and the *World-Soul.*

The soul, according to Plotinus, is independent of the body, incorporeal, everlasting, and not dependent on its physical environment. Thus, the soul exists before we come into this world and after we leave it. Like Plato, Plotinus believes in reincarnation. Those who have abandoned themselves to physical pleasures will become animals, while those who have been truly educated are suitably rewarded. The ultimate destiny of the soul is to overcome multiplicity and to become part of the majesty of the *One.*

The final state of the soul cannot be expressed in verbal terms. We can only use mystical language:

> "Many times it has happened: Lifted out of the body into myself; becoming external to all other things and self-encentered; beholding a marvellous beauty; then, more than ever, assured of community with the loftiest order; enacting the noblest life, acquiring identity with the divine; stationing within It by having attained that activity; poised above whatsoever within the Intellectual is less than the Supreme: yet there comes the moment of descent from intellection to reasoning, and after that sojourn in the divine, I ask myself how it happens that I can now be descending, and how did the soul ever enter into my body, the soul which, even with the body, is the high thing it has shown itself to be." [13]

Neo-Platonism, like most of the philosophies of later classical times, teaches the supremacy of the spirit, and it points out that man's life on this earth is essentially an interlude. It subordinates reason to intuition, the body to the soul, and man to the ineffable majesty of God.

Mortification of the flesh was not as significant in the system of Plotinus as in the philosophy of later Neo-Platonists, like Iamblichus. However, even Plotinus was ashamed of his body, and he believed strongly in the discipline of his soul. The dualism between body and soul was intensified later in Christian thought, which, in the Middle Ages, glorified the virtues of celibacy.

---

12 Cf. Inge, *The Philosophy of Plotinus,* 2 vols.
13 Plotinus, *Enneads.*

To the Neo-Platonists, evil did not have a cosmic status: its existence added to the perfection of the universe. The same concept appears in Christian orthodoxy which expressed belief in the providence of God; the universe will ultimately be dominated by the forces of goodness.

From an educational standpoint, Neo-Platonism is important because it stressed subordination of rational knowledge to spiritual understanding. The task of the teacher thus is to overcome the temptations of this life. The demands of the body are gradually neglected while the worth of man's spirit is emphasized more and more. Like the medieval educators, the Neo-Platonists pointed out the significance of self-discipline; truth could not be found without curbing the sensual side of man.

In Neo-Platonism we reach the twilight of ancient philosophy and education. It symbolizes a note of escapism, a trend away from concerns with this life, and a concentration upon spiritual matters. It marks a lack of creativity in Roman thinking.

The decline of philosophy was part of the decline of freedom. "As to liberty," asserted Plutarch, "we have that which the government leaves us." Tacitus remarked that "genius died by the same blow that ended public liberty."

After the second century A.D., Rome ceased to be creative in intellectual matters. Encyclopedists and copyists dominated its culture. Eloquence was stressed for its own sake. The vital issues of the day were not discussed. H. G. Wells remarked once that "the incuriousness of the Roman rulers was more massive even than their art."

THE DECLINE OF ROME. The decline of Rome was due mainly to economic factors, as Rostovtzeff points out. Rome was a parasitical city which encouraged large estates for the few and economic slavery for the many. Tiberius Gracchus remarked that "the wild animals that range over Italy have a hole, but the men who fight and die for Italy . . . have not a clod of earth to call their own." Some emperors, like Antoninus Pius, debased the currency; others, like Diocletian and Constantine, tried to fight inflation with artificial economic controls. In the third and fourth centuries, as Rostovtzeff describes, Rome developed an economic and social caste system which made a healthy economy impossible.

While Rome was creative in its system of government and laws, it lacked imagination in its education and in its philosophical speculations. Roman education was far more limited than that of Athens. Ultimately, Rome paid the price for being too practical. It was seduced by foreign ideologies, first by Greek philosophies, then by mystery cults. Later Roman education failed to meet the social challenge and did not imbue the young Roman with the ideal of social service; instead Rome permitted a decline of morale which led to a feeling of complete futility on the part of the most sensitive Roman citizens. The decline of Rome can be ascribed to its system of education almost as much as to any other cause.

QUESTIONS FOR DISCUSSION AND INVESTIGATION

1. Compare the development of Roman education with American education; with Greek education.

2. What did the Stoics offer to ancient education?

3. Where did the Stoics stand in relation to social philosophy?

4. What influence did the Stoics have on Christianity?

5. Compare and contrast Epicureanism and Stoicism.

6. What did Plutarch emphasize in education?

7. What Roman characteristics in philosophy and education are attributed to Quintilian?

8. Describe the religious views of Philo as put forth in his writings.

9. Discuss the beliefs of the Neo-Platonists.

10. What were the philosophical weaknesses in education which contributed to Rome's decline?

Chapter 10

The Ideals of Jesus

THE SIGNIFICANCE OF JESUS

The impact of Jesus upon educational history in the West is enormous. He influenced groups as diverse as the Quakers and the Jesuits; his impact was strong upon the deists, who believed in reason, as well as upon the pietists, who favored emotion as the keynote of religion. Orthodox believers like Loyola, felt his power, and liberals, like Schweitzer, regarded Jesus as the inspiration for their philosophical and humanitarian labors.

Jesus was bound to be misunderstood. He lived in a period of profound social upheaval. The Jews were oppressed by the Romans, and they looked for a leader to free them from the foreign yoke. Hebrew religion at the time of Jesus was intensely legalistic: to know the law was to be saved. Many of the most pious individuals were Pharisees—spiritual exhibitionists who proclaimed their virtue, their righteousness, and their superiority. In reality, they lacked the most important virtue: inwardness.

We must not forget the gulf between the ideals of the inhabitants of a city like Jerusalem and the concepts of life cherished by the people of a rural community like Nazareth. The city inhabitants, more sophisticated than their country neighbors, often imitated Roman manners and Roman behavior. The rural inhabitants, on the other hand, were simple in their faith.

The keynote of the character of Jesus is his sincerity. He appeals to the heart. He shows that what matters are not our material possessions, it is our spirit that counts. He is an idealist because he believes

125

that man is the child of God and that within himself man holds a kingdom of unlimited possibilities.

Jesus believed that all people are teachable: the rich and the poor, the scholars and the ignorant. Yet, real education and real religion—and to Jesus the two activities were identical—requires the openness of a child. How often does the scholar lose his enthusiasm and his capacity for awareness; how often does he debate endlessly about minor points.

Jesus was bound to be misunderstood. He wanted a faith based upon unqualified love, a love which respected no barriers of race, religion and nationality, a love which included all in the common bonds of fellowship. The test of this love was action: how would it change the ideals and patterns of the individual? Yet many of his followers were particularistic in their allegiance. They stressed that they alone, the elect, could find salvation and that anyone who disagreed with them was bound for hell-fire.

EDUCATIONAL IMPACT

Why was Jesus so successful as an educator? He used a simple method; he told innumerable parables; he appealed to the moral idealism of his audience. The universe was his textbook, and every day afforded a new lesson. His schoolroom was the open field and the market place.

Like Socrates, Jesus believed in the identity of virtue and knowledge. The moral man would know the essence of the universe and the man who understood nature would love God. Was not life itself a miracle? Were not human beings expressions of divine creativity?

Pascal, during the Renaissance coined the phrase, "The heart has reasons that reason does not know." Jesus was guided by intuition, not by analytical knowledge. He felt the needs of his disciples and they experienced his dedication and sincerity.

Education can be advanced in two ways. The first way is through science and analytical knowledge, whereby real progress can be made. But we all know that analysis and intellectual knowledge may be empty and lead to conceit. We realize, as we become philosophically aware, that intellect and knowledge may not create happiness, for the more we ponder the more we may experience a Faustian sense of dissatisfaction. Our analysis may lead to constant neuroses and to a feeling of complete disenchantment.

The second way in which education may be advanced, is through the wisdom of the heart. This is the road of Buddha and Jesus. Such wisdom goes to the center of things; it establishes harmony and a sense of contentment. It creates balance and perspective. It leads away from the knowledge of facts to understanding and compassion. Education thus becomes a way of living rather than an empty theory.

Modern psychology teaches us the importance of warmth and love. If we read books like Fromm's *The Art of Loving,* Frankl's *Doctor and the Soul,* Menninger's *Love Against Hate*—we find a common emphasis upon the importance of warmth, understanding and kindness. The child who is unloved, the student who is not encouraged, the teacher who finds no emotional meaning in his work—all are bound for serious emotional maladjustment. To learn how to love, as Jesus teaches, is to become truly educated.

The educational ideals of Jesus rest upon his moral insights. The essential factor in our relationship with our neighbors is our motive: our heart must be pure. Hatred can never be conquered by hatred, but only through love. Suspicion would create more suspicion, envy would only lead to more unhappiness. We must love our neighbor the way God loves us. Even when we err, even when we are wayward, even when we stray from the path of righteousness, God will treat us with mercy.

Man, according to Jesus, needs few goods to be happy and to find meaning in life. Attachment to material goods is only a hindrance. It is difficult for the rich man to find the path to salvation. Honor and fame only create illusory goals. We should not worry about tomorrow, for today is important; today is the time for decision and creative action.

All this is extremely important in education. We preach spirituality and respect for the individual, yet most of the time we are so concerned about buildings, equipment, and other material considerations, that we neglect the teacher and the student. We provide for the comforts of the body, but we neglect the welfare of the soul. We look upon laboratories and stadiums as signs of progress, when they may only hide an empty spirit. We do not know the core of education; thus, many of our institutions of higher learning are centers of organized confusion.

The educational lesson of Jesus is that we must cultivate the individual. This demands more than lip service. We must be conscious of the individual not only as an intellectual being, but as an emotional being desiring something more than knowledge.

Real education is existential: it demands a living encounter between teacher and student, just as Jesus pictured the encounter between man and God.

Contemporaries of Jesus believed God to be a force of fear who punished human beings for their transgressions. They thought that He was localistic and that He had his favorites among nations. Jesus taught that God is everywhere and that He can be worshipped everywhere. He demands not sacrifice and slavish obedience, but an upright heart. We honor God by loving our neighbor; God is not confined to one nation or to one civilization; He controls the universe.

Some thinkers might say that the knowledge of God is unessential in our concept of education. But if we translate the ideals of Jesus in a broader way and in a more profound manner, knowledge and understanding of God becomes one of the central problems of education. The question is: Does education give us the perspective of universality? Are we worshipping false idols, like mere utilitarian pursuits, or are we conscious of the centrality of human personality? Is our philosophy of education based upon materialism or the love of God? This does not imply endorsement of one concept of religion or theology, for man must always be open to new experiences and must be a constant explorer. However, this does imply that education must be concerned with the present as well as with the future. Education must be concerned with man's total personality and his total adjustment.

Jesus was educated at home and in the synagogue. He was in intimate contact with his teachers. To Jesus, the teacher was the representative of God, for he brought forth what is best in man. Jesus converted others by using informal conversation. In simple statements, as, for instance, "Man does not live by bread alone," Jesus could express in few words what philosophers would state in volumes. Thus, Jesus, rather than formalizing the educational process as we know it today, made it part of our entire life, of all our concerns and all our ideals.

The great teachers of mankind, like Buddha, Confucius, and Jesus were all *personalistic* in their approach: they taught by example. They appealed to the many, not just to the elite. They believed in democracy, for they had faith that all could learn and that wisdom was universal. They spoke with firmness and not merely as debaters. They were inspired by an inner vision which they communicated to their audience.

Most teachers have little vision; they are mainly technicians. They are guided by routine and dominated by intellectual slumber. Thoreau once said that he had met few individuals who were awake; this remark he applied to teachers. But how can we teach when we ourselves are lethargic and indifferent? Jesus teaches us that we cannot communicate what we do not feel and that we cannot reach others when we ourselves live an isolated life. Our words are empty, our formulas are meaningless, if they are not exemplified by action.

Jesus reminds us of the importance of sympathy in education. He never talked down to his audience; He always respected their ability; He saw life through their perspective. Sympathy is the prelude to wisdom, and understanding is the basis of progress.

One may object that modern man can only advance through technical training since knowledge is becoming more complicated all the time. Thus, it will be impossible to be guided by the simple educational philosophy of Jesus. The answer is: We still are confused about the nature and destiny of man. We still want inner security; we still need warmth and love; we still yearn for permanent satisfactions; we still have not conquered the conflicts within and the conflicts without which threaten the very existence of our society. A teacher, like Jesus, must have a vision of his importance and see beyond technical details. His task is not merely to impart knowledge, but to develop patterns for behavior. He must stir his students, and this can only be achieved when he really understands them and becomes part of their life.

INFLUENCE

The stamp of Jesus upon educational history in the West can never be erased. To the medieval educators, like St. Augustine, He was the great disciplinarian who taught how to avoid evil and how to find the path to God. To mystics, like Eckhart, He taught the importance of self-sacrifice and abandonment to utter poverty; that the acknowledgment of ignorance is the beginning of wisdom.

To Renaissance scholars, like Erasmus, Jesus was a more religious version of Socrates who demonstrated how the scholar must avoid folly and hypocrisy. To the leaders of the Reformation, Jesus became the symbol of a living faith who demanded education of the poor and the rich. To Comenius, Jesus was the symbol of mysticism; He showed that universal understanding was possible. To the Jesuits, Jesus indicated the importance of discipline so that damnation can be avoided. To Quakers, like George Fox and William Penn, Jesus was the symbol of love; all men are educable.

Pietists, like Philipp J. Spener and August Herman Francke, were encouraged in their educational reforms, especially in their regard for the common people, by the example of Jesus. Pestalozzi was inspired by His example as he cared for the children of the poor and for orphans. Froebel looked upon Jesus as the ideal educator who had demonstrated the unity of man and God, and who had shown that life has unlimited possibilities.

The example of Jesus indicates the importance of creativity exemplified in action. Beyond methodology, beyond formal knowledge, is the living vision of greatness. We move forward in educational history when we stress essentials, when we feel the inspiration of great ideas and great ideals, and when we overcome all forms of lethargy and indifference.

QUESTIONS FOR DISCUSSION AND INVESTIGATION

1. Name a few of the many varying groups on which Jesus exerted his profound influence.

2. Explain the keynote of Jesus' character.

3. What are Jesus' religious and educational goals?

4. Why was Jesus a great success as an educator?

5. What are the two ways in which education may be advanced?

6. According to Jesus, what are man's greatest chances for finding happiness?

7. Compare Jesus' concept of God to that of his contemporaries.

8. How does Jesus prove that knowledge and understanding of God become the central problems of education?

9. Explain the characteristics that make Buddha, Confucius, and Jesus the great teachers of all time.

10. What is the significance of Jesus for our time?

Chapter 11

Educational Foundations
of Orthodoxy

THE EARLY CHURCH

The religious doctrines of Jesus and His apostles were relatively simple and uncomplicated; but, with the expansion of Christianity and with growing ideological competition from the Greek thinkers, it became necessary to define its doctrinal content.

The attack came from within as well as from without. The problem of heresy has tormented Christian institutions almost from the beginning of their establishment.

GNOSTICS. Important among the heretics were the *Gnostics* who owed much to Neo-Platonism and Oriental patterns of thinking. The Gnostics objected to the theology of the Old Testament, which they regarded as an expression of an inferior religious spirit. A dualism prevailed in their philosophy of religion, which taught that the struggle between good and evil has cosmic significance. They identified the principle of evil with our bondage to our material environment, which could only be overthrown through Jesus, who reconciled God and man. Education, to the Gnostics, was the method whereby evil could be overcome.

Like the Neo-Platonists, the Gnostics believed in emanation; man must abandon the realm of flesh and instead dedicate himself to the world of the spirit. While they believed in ethical commandments, they also stressed magic and secret initiation rites.

The dualism of the Gnostics was again found in the *Manicheans*, who likewise regarded the world as an arena which saw a vivid conflict

133

between good and evil. This movement exerted a strong influence upon the greatest of the earliest theologians, St. Augustine.

OTHER HERESIES. Innumerable heresies were caused by the doctrine of the Trinity. There were the Sabellians who emphasized the unity of the divine person and held that Father, Son, and Holy Spirit were mainly three manifestations of the same underlying substance. The Montanists, who wanted to go back to the ideals of Christ, were in favor of an ascetic way of life and thought that they were guided by the special intervention of the Holy Ghost. To the Arians, Christ was similar, not identical to God. Christ represented the Divine Logos. The more we would share in the work of the Logos, the more we could attain an understanding of truth. In their educational theories the Arians stressed reason more than their contemporaries did.

CLEMENT. Among the early theologians and church fathers, Clement, like Justin Martyr, had a high regard for philosophy. Unlike Tertullian, he thought that faith should be rational and he did not maintain that we should believe in that which is absurd. In his educational theory, he stressed the importance of the inner motive, and that outward acts are less significant than the attitude of our heart. He did not favor celibacy over family life, and he lacked the austerity which we find in so many of the early Western philosophers of Christianity.

In his concept of deity, Clement upheld the absolute transcendence of God, who is beyond all human predication. We can only say that God is not like man in any way. As for man's soul, Clement believed that it comes into the world in an immaculate condition and evil is due to our own free choice. It is important to notice that Clement rejected original sin, a doctrine which was upheld with vigorous emphasis by St. Augustine.

ORIGEN. Origen, another early Church father, shared Clement's abiding love for education. Most of the writings of the Bible he interpreted in an allegorical spirit. This did not mean that he was ashamed of the Christian religious works; on the contrary, he treasured them immensely; however, he did think that truth frequently is revealed in a symbolic manner and that Christians could learn from the teachers of antiquity.

As for God, we cannot know Him in His essence; we can know only His manifestations. God is reached not through scientific knowledge nor through an analysis of nature, but through a humble acceptance of Jesus Christ.

Later theologians sharply attacked Origen for his view that the soul is pre-existent and that the universe is not created but is eternal. He also felt that hellfire is not everlasting and, ultimately, only goodness prevails. In short, Origen adhered to a symbolic interpretation of religion, stressing God's transcendence together with the eternity of the universe and the pre-existence of the soul.

DIONYSIUS. The independent trend of speculation was more noticeable in Eastern Christianity than in the West, especially in Dionysius, the Areopagite who gave a Neo-Platonic interpretation of Christianity. He denied the doctrine of creation and spoke instead of emanation. To him, the source of reality was beyond all predication, and life was a cyclical process which led from the oneness of God to multiplicity and back again to divine unity.

In Dionysius we have a strain of pantheism; there is no absolute distinction betwen the universe and God. Naturally, this negates the concept that God is far away and that man is a product of original sin. The pantheistic tendency was strong also in Maximus, the Confessor, who openly attacked a theistic interpretation of reality. On the other hand, John of Damascus upheld a more orthodox type of philosophy and believed in the use of images, which he thought aided religious worship and brought about a sense of identification with the divine forces.

ICONOCLASM. John of Damascus came into conflict with the policy of the Byzantine state which, under Leo III, prohibited the use of image worship. Leo III ordered the churches purged of all images and the pictures of the saints destroyed. Those attempting to carry out his edict were lynched by the fanatical masses; finally, troops crushed the riots. Serious disturbances also broke out in Italy and Greece. The Western Church protested violently against the edict of Leo III. In 843, the images were restored in the Eastern Church. However, the split between Eastern and Western Christianity did not heal and has persisted to the present.

EASTERN VS. WESTERN CHURCH. What were the main sources of friction between the Eastern and Western Church? First ranks the problem of authority. The patriarch at Constantinople believed that he was a universal ruler since he governed over 28 provinces. Usually, his policies were linked with those of the Byzantine Empire. On the other hand, the Pope refused to acknowledge the sovereignty of the patriarch, and attempts were made again and again to destroy the independence of the Byzantine church.

In second place ranks the controversy over the Balkans. The Byzantine church was largely responsible for the conversion of the Slavs; this was done largely through the work of Cyril and Methodius. Through educational and missionary endeavors, the Byzantine church ultimately governed a vast territory stretching from the Baltic Sea to Constantinople; out of it developed the Russian church, which, under Soviet domination, has been one of the insistent foes of Roman Catholicism.

In the third place, doctrinal disputes led to a definite schism between East and West. The Byzantine church would not allow its priests to shave their beards, use unleavened bread in the mass, or eat eggs during Lent. All these matters may appear trivial to a modern observer, but in the Middle Ages the details of the religious ritual were regarded with great concern.

The philosophers of the Byzantine church, like John of Damascus and Michael Psellus, served to transmit Greek knowledge to the West. They preserved learning in an age of chaos and insecurity. Generally, they were more interested in metaphysical speculation, more pantheistic in their concept of God, and less willing to accept the doctrine of pre-destination than the Christian thinkers of the West.

THE RISE OF WESTERN CHRISTIAN PHILOSOPHY

While the Eastern Church fathers believed in speculation, the Western Church fathers stressed the rule of law and absolute authority. Thus Irenaeus (140-202 A.D.) maintained that man can only be reconciled to God through the work of Christ. Man had fallen through original sin and deserved damnation, but Christ made possible a restoration of man's original nature. The Christian faith can only be achieved through the Church which guarantees its continuity and strengthens its authority.

The Latin Church father Tertullian firmly maintained that Catholicism is the only religion for mankind. All other faiths, he declared, are false and pervert essential truth. In every way, Tertullian was opposed to Greek education, for Greek philosophy emphasized the power of reason which is subversive to religious ideals. What man needs most is faith, even faith in that which appears to be absurd. The relationship between man and God should be like the relationship between a subject and his emperor. Any rebellion, then, on the part of man, will be strictly punished by God. Tertullian emphasized that man's soul was created by God; however, in declaring man's soul to be material, he became a heretic according to the orthodox Catholic doctrine, a doctrine which stressed the incorporeal and spiritual nature of the soul.

The power of the Church was advanced in the early centuries by Cyprian, Bishop of Carthage, who fought strenuously against all heretics. He asserted that the bishops are directly appointed by God. Ambrose, Bishop of Milan, likewise expanded the realm of the Catholic Church. Throughout his life, he fought for the interests of the Church and dared to defy emperors in his promotion of the welfare of the faith. It was partly his influence that converted St. Augustine to Catholicism. Ambrose systematized the educational structure of the Western Church.

ST. JEROME. Another of the Western Church fathers, St. Jerome, was exposed to the temptations of Roman life until he became a hermit. He advised his followers to live the life of celibacy. His concern with the problems of Christian education caused him to urge asceticism as the best way of life for the teacher. In writing on the education of girls, St. Jerome insisted that they be trained in domestic arts, and that they be protected from all secular pleasures.

EARLY CHRISTIAN EDUCATION

The early Christians considered preaching and teaching to be of equal importance. They made exact provisions for the training of educational leaders through an apprenticeship system. In their catechumen schools they taught the fundamentals of doctrine. All persons who wanted to become members of the faith had to join these schools. There the students were taught from the Bible, from the sayings of the Apostles, and also from *The Epistle of Barnabas.*

Scholastic centers developed which attracted many students, and which became famous throughout the ancient world. One such center was at Alexandria, where Clement and Origen were teaching. Both these men were hospitable to the ideas of free thought and tried to reconcile them with Christian viewpoints. Another center was established at Caesarea, where Eusebius wrote his *Ecclesiastical History.* A third school, located at Antioch, gained fame for its historical studies of the Bible. A fourth center was established at Edessa; this Macedonian city later became the seat of the Nestorians, a group which promoted a liberal version of Christianity. A fifth school, located at Nisibis, stressed the values of monasticism in promoting learning. Here, scholars translated the Greek thinkers into Syrian and thus became agents of culture diffusion.

ST. AUGUSTINE AND THE SEARCH FOR RELIGIOUS EDUCATION

St. Augustine ranks among the most profound and influential of all the Christian philosophers.[1] However, his acceptance of Christianity did not come at once: a Christian mother and pagan father were among many factors which caused his long hesitation before joining Catholicism.

His religious pilgrimage reflected a wide variety of intellectual currents. As a student, he believed in the pleasures of the world with an essentially hedonistic outlook. Then, through reading one of the treatises of Cicero, he became interested in philosophy. Later, he joined the Manicheans, for he could not accept the Old Testament view of morality. Conscious of the great dualism between good and evil, he thought that the Manichean faith had the best explanation for the existence of evil. After his disillusionment with the Manicheans, he became a skeptic. He doubted man's ability to find an absolute standard of truth, although he

---

[1] Cf. McCabe, *St. Augustine and His Age.* Figgis, *The Political Aspects of St. Augustine's City of God.*

still accepted the existence of God. From Skepticism, he turned to Neo-Platonism with its view of God's transcendence and its concept of emanation. This movement proved to be his bridge to Christianity. After his conversion, he became a fanatical enemy of all heresies and all attempts to subvert Catholic dogma.

The educational record of the experiences of St. Augustine can be found in the *Confessions,* one of the masterpieces of religious autobiography. St. Augustine described with eloquence the harsh educational system which prevailed in his childhood:

"If I proved idle in learning, I was soundly beaten. For this procedure seemed wise to our ancestors: and many, passing the same way in days past, had built a sorrowful road by which we too must go, with multiplication of grief and toil upon the sons of Adam.

"As a boy I fell into the way of calling upon You, my Help and my Refuge; and in those prayers I broke the strings of my tongue—praying to You, small as I was but with no small energy, that I might not be beaten at school. And when You did not hear me (*not as giving me over to folly*), my elders and even my parents, who certainly wished me no harm, treated my stripes as a huge joke, which they were very far from being to me. Surely, Lord, there is no one so steeled in mind or cleaving to You so close—or even so insensitive, for that might have the same effect—as to make light of the racks and hooks and other torture instruments (from which in all lands men pray so fervently to be saved) while truly loving those who are in such bitter fear of them. Yet my parents seemed to be amused at the torments inflicted upon me as a boy by my masters, though I was no less afraid of my punishments or zealous in my prayers to You for deliverance. But in spite of my terrors I still did wrong, by writing or reading or studying less than my set tasks. It was not, Lord, that I lacked mind or memory, for You had given me as much of these as my age required; but the one thing I revelled in was play; and for this I was punished by men who after all were doing exactly the same things themselves. But the idling of men is called business; the idling of boys, though exactly like, is punished by those same men." [2]

He shows how he was motivated by vanity:

"Yet in acting against the commands of my parents and schoolmasters, I did wrong, O Lord my God, Creator and Ruler of all things, but of sin not Creator but Ruler only: for I might later have made good use of those lessons that they wanted me to learn, whatever may have been their motive in wanting it. I disobeyed, not because I had chosen better, but through sheer love of play: I loved the vanity of victory, and I loved too to have my ears tickled with the fictions of the theatre which set them to itching ever more burningly: and in my eyes a similar curiosity burned increasingly for the games and shows of my elders. Yet those who put on such shows are held in high esteem. And most people would be delighted to have their sons grow up to give similar shows in their turn—and meanwhile fully concur in the

2 From *The Confessions of Saint Augustine,* translated by F. J. Sheed, Copyright 1943, Sheed and Ward, Inc., New York.

beatings those same sons get if these shows hinder study: for study is the way to prosperity necessary for giving them! Look down in mercy, Lord, upon such things; and set us free who now beseech Thee: and not only us, but those also who have never besought Thee—that they may turn to Thee and be made free." [3]

He tells how he hated Greek, but enjoyed Latin. He favored strict discipline in learning:

"The drudgery of learning a foreign language sprinkled bitterness over all the sweetness of the Greek tales. I did not know a word of the language: and I was driven with threats and savage punishments to learn. There had been a time of infancy when I knew no Latin either. Yet I learnt it without threat or punishment merely by keeping my eyes and ears open, amidst the flatterings of nurses and the jesting and pleased laughter of elders leading me on. I learned it without the painful pressure of compulsion, by the sole pressure of my own desire to express what was in my mind, which would have been impossible unless I had learnt words: and I learnt them not through people teaching me but simply through people speaking: to whom I was striving to utter my own feelings. All this goes to prove that free curiosity is of more value in learning than harsh discipline. But by Your ordinance, O God, discipline must control the free play of curiosity—for Your ordinance ranges from the master's cane to the torments suffered by the martyrs, and works that mingling of bitter with sweet which brings us back to You from the poison of pleasure that first drew us away from You." [4]

Classical learning, Augustine stated, may corrupt morals:

"In this matter of classical studies how woeful are you, O torrent of established custom. Who can resist you or when will you run dry? How long will you continue to roll the sons of Eve into that vast and terrible sea in which even those who mount the cross scarcely escape drowning? In you I read of Jove, both as the God of thunder and as an adulterer. How could he be both? But so the story goes: and so sham thunder is made to legitimize and play pander to real adultery: yet these robed and gowned masters are furious when Cicero, a man trained in their own school, protests: 'Homer invented these stories, ascribing things human to the Gods: would that he had brought down things divine to us.' It would have been even truer to say that Homer invented them, attributing divinity to the vilest of men, with the result that crimes are held not to be crimes, and those who do commit them are regarded as acting not like abandoned men but like Gods from Olympus.

"And still, O torrent from hell, the sons of men pay fees to be hurled into you in order that they may learn such things. And there is great interest when this sort of teaching is carried on publicly in the forum under the very eye of laws allotting salaries to the masters over and above the fees paid by the pupils." [5]

---

3 *Ibid.*, I, x.

4 *Ibid.*, I, xiv.

5 *Ibid.*, I, xvi.

He tells about his wrong-doings and how they symbolize man's proclivity for evil:

"These were the ways of the world upon whose threshold I stood as a boy, and such was the arena for which I was training—more concerned to avoid committing a grammatical error than to be void of envy in case I did commit one and another did not. This I say and confess to Thee, O My God: and in this I was praised by those whom my one idea of success was to please. I did not see the whirl of vileness into which I had been cast away from Thy eyes: for what was more unclean than I, seeing that I did not win the approval even of my own kind: I told endless lies to my tutors, my masters and my parents: all for the love of games, the craving for stage shows, and a restlessness to do what I saw done in these shows.

"I stole from my parents' cellar and table, sometimes because I was gluttonous myself, sometimes to have something to give other boys in exchange for implements of play which they were prepared to sell although they loved them as much as I.

"Is this boyhood innocence? It is not, Lord. I cry Thy mercy, O my God. Yet as we leave behind tutors and masters and nuts and balls and birds and come to deal with prefects and kings and the getting of gold and estates and slaves, these are the qualities which pass on with us, one stage of life taking the place of another as the greater punishments of the law take the place of the schoolmaster's cane." [6]

BASIC IDEAS

EXISTENCE OF GOD. St. Augustine built his philosophy upon the intellectually provable existence of God. For the order of the universe indicates a creator; our conscience leads us to believe in a divine moral force. Creation itself indicates contingency and demands a necessary cause. Furthermore, St. Augustine maintained, our knowledge is relative and finite; we cannot be certain of anything unless we have an absolute standard of truth: God. The skeptics only have to open their eyes and see the order of nature, to listen to the voice of mankind which universally and eloquently proclaims that God exists.

How can we find God? Is knowledge sufficient? Is the road of philosophy the only road? St. Augustine answers that knowledge itself is not adequate. Above all, we must *love* God. The search for the supreme principle is profoundly emotional and transcends intellectual desires and interests. In the highest stage of knowledge, we have a mystical experience; we feel the presence of a divine light which reveals the splendor and majesty of God.

The man who experiences this illumination realizes that scientific analysis is secondary. He can only feel the presence of God; he cannot

---

6 *Ibid.,* I, xix

describe it in intellectual terms. He sees life from a new viewpoint, not from the standpoint of fragmentary and partial truth but from the perspective of an all-embracing principle of reality.

IMMORTALITY OF THE SOUL. Together with the existence of God, the spirituality of the soul was vigorously affirmed by St. Augustine. He denied that the soul is material and that it existed in another form before man was born. The soul itself is a copy of the Divine Trinity. Its three manifestations, memory, understanding, and will, mirror the three aspects of the Trinity. Through self-examination and contemplation, we can substantiate the truths which authority has transmitted to us.

St. Augustine believed that the immortality of the soul could be established by reason. He claimed that the soul is the principle of life and is superior to the body; hence, when the body dies, the soul continues. Identifying soul and reason, he maintained that reason transcends the limitations of matter. Since reason is eternal, the soul likewise must be eternal. The soul, furthermore, is part of eternal truths, which are not bound by spatial and temporal limitations. Just as certain laws of the universe always prevail, so the soul will be everlasting.

The philosophy of St. Augustine depends on the authority of the Church. We are frail and insecure as long as we are outside of it; within, we find comfort, grace and salvation. The Church, as a distributor of the sacraments, has a unique function in life, for the sacraments mediate between man and God. It does not matter whether the priests lead a blameless life or one of immorality, for the sacraments are valid regardless of the moral standards of the administrators.

With all his power, St. Augustine led the fight against individualism. The edicts of the Church are not to be disobeyed, its fundamental doctrines are not to be questioned, and its basic tenets are not to be challenged. As the link between Christ and man, the Church stands throughout the centuries as a visible expression of God's purpose in the universe.

The question now arises whether or not the Church has national limits. Should its work be confined only to Europe? St. Augustine answers in the negative: he was certain that the function of the Church was universal, and he looked forward to the day when there would be only one Church, one sacramental system, and one system of philosophy.

The political ideals of St. Augustine are best represented by the *City of God*. This work was written under the impact of the Vandal invasion of Rome, an act which caused immense suffering to the Romans and which shook their faith in the Christian religion. To St. Augustine, the sacking of Rome was only an incident in a vast world of drama. For life on earth is essentially a prelude to life in the beyond. This is merely a journey, infinite from the standpoint of the present but infinitesimal from the viewpoint of God. The power of kings and emperors, which most men admire and worship, is shattered by the providence of God who has no respect for earthly fortunes.

In St. Augustine's view of history, there is a perpetual opposition between the *city of God* and the *city of the devil*. Outwardly, the city of God appears to be defeated, for the world is frequently dominated by the wicked, but in reality the city of God will triumph and the sinners will be punished through God's justice.

God, according to St. Augustine, is not a transcendent force, rather He takes part in shaping history. He sees to it that the arrogance of earthly rulers is punished. This, according to St. Augustine, explains the disintegration of the Roman Empire, for it had defied the laws of morality and now was reaping the results of its crimes. History ends with the members of the city of the devil being punished, while those who belong to the city of God enjoy infinite bliss.

In this dualistic concept of history there can be no neutrality. Every man had to make up his mind and join either the forces of righteousness or the legions of doom. This was not a solitary struggle; the good were aided by angels, the saints, and by the power of the Church; the evil forces were supported by the devil and were under the influence of the most corrupt and treacherous men of all ages.

In Augustine's moral ideals the puritanical strain is only too evident. Thus he inveighed against the temptations of the flesh, identifying original sin with Adam's temptation by Eve. What is to be preferred— the life of the hermit or the life of family relations? St. Augustine had no doubts in regard to this problem: Any relationship with women undermines men's love of God; it is impossible to love the flesh and the spirit at the same time. Hence, asceticism is the only road for those who really want to dedicate themselves to the service of God.

Few thinkers have been more aware of the ever-present reality of sin than St. Augustine. Sin represents a rebellion against the majesty of God; it comes, thus, in a thousand different forms, subjectively and objectively. As slaves of desire, we frequently crave that which is incompatible with our salvation.

St. Augustine was deeply pessimistic regarding human merit. In fact, since the fall of Adam all of us have deserved damnation. He made it clear that God, from the beginning, had elected most men for damnation, while only the minority was destined for heaven. This doctrine of predestination at once caused much controversy, for it made God's will arbitrary and detracted from the freedom of the will. The Pelagians took the opposite viewpoint and insisted that man's free will can attain salvation. However, the Church maintained a middle road between the Pelagians and St. Augustine and tried to give hope to the individual that through faith in the sacraments, Christ, and good works, salvation could be achieved.

EDUCATIONAL PRINCIPLES

Augustine, influenced by Plato, believed that truth can be grasped only by the few. Truth is not relative but absolute, and it is taught through the Church. The task of education is to avoid independent judgment and to subordinate private ideas to ecclesiastical organization.

Real truth can be found through mystical knowledge when our mind has been purified by prayer and contemplation. Most individuals are guided by their senses, and thus they become victims of illusion and falsehood.

The Christian scholar should be acquainted with literature, rhetoric, logic, arithmetic, ethics, and natural philosophy; these subjects are not to be studied as ends in themselves and care should be taken that they do not corrupt the scholar's faith. They are, however, only preludes to the study of Church doctrines.

Even the study of mathematics may be helpful. Augustine felt that the Bible was full of number symbolism, and that mathematics was a tool of clear thinking. Science, in general, could be a method of combating superstition.

He warns the Christian again and again not to be seduced by classical learning. Classical studies are full of error and falsehood and overemphasize man's rational powers.

Learning cannot be promoted without discipline. The teacher has to control the child and, if necessary, has to use the cane and the strap. Thus the pupil learns to control his evil impulses and becomes conscious of the importance of obedience. Augustine, constantly aware of original sin, believed that children were naturally evil; therefore, their nature had to be changed by the schoolmaster.

AUGUSTINE'S INFLUENCE

The influence of Augustine can scarcely be overestimated. His ideas inspired many great medieval thinkers, especially Anselm. While Aquinas rejected the Platonism of the bishop of Hippo, he shared with the latter a basic faith in the authority of the Church and a strong hatred of all forms of heresy. Duns Scotus, theologist of the fourteenth century, followed St. Augustine in his belief about the separation of faith and reason, as well as in his insistence that man is nothing, while God is all-powerful.

The impact of St. Augustine on Calvin produced a system of thought which stressed the sovereignty of God, the depravity of man, and the idea that man is predestined to either heaven or hell. Like St. Augustine, Calvin emphasized the importance of puritanism. Was not the flesh an obstacle in man's search for salvation? Did not earthly pleasures alienate man from God?

In the United States, Jonathan Edwards absorbed the spirit of Augustinianism. With eloquence Edwards pictured the tortures of damnation. Like the bishop of Hippo, Edwards believed that hell-fire was an actual reality and that most individuals would land in hell rather than in heaven.

In a more sophisticated vein, Reinhold Niebuhr, in *The Nature and Destiny of Man,* represents an Augustinian version of history. Niebuhr pictures man as a rebel against God, and he is certain that, without faith, man is doomed and civilization will perish.

Many religious existentialists have claimed Augustine as one of their foremost saints. Augustine indicated that man's personal awareness of God is most significant and that life demands a religion of the heart rather than of the intellect. We are still wrestling with the same problem that agitated the bishop of Hippo: How can man find security in a world governed by flux and rebellion?

Augustine as an educator influenced both Catholic and Protestant ideas. By pointing out the need for discipline and puritanism he made education a rigorous process. By subordinating free inquiry to orthodoxy he made education a form of indoctrination. This view is still cherished by many religious teachers in the twentieth century.

St. Augustine as well as the scholars that followed in his footsteps were not interested in new ideas. They wanted to preserve the orthodoxy of the past. Living in a period of turmoil, they were conservators rather than creators. Still, the West owes them a debt, for they laid the foundations of both Protestant and Catholic education.

QUESTIONS FOR DISCUSSION AND INVESTIGATION

1. Name and define the main heresies which arose from the early Christian institutions.

2. Explain the main sources of friction between the Eastern and Western Church.

3. Describe the figures who were responsible for the rise of Western Christian philosophy.

4. What ideas and schools were established in early Christian education?

5. Define Saint Augustine's responses to the early education in his life.

6. Trace Saint Augustine's line of reasoning in proving the existence of God.

7. Discuss his concept of the immortal soul in relation to the authority of the Church.

8. What is Saint Augustine's dualistic philosophy of history?

9. Name some of the later figures whom Augustine deeply influenced.

10. Compare and contrast the views of Saint Augustine and Socrates.

Chapter 12

Education and Medieval Thought

EARLY EDUCATORS

During the early Middle Ages, education was in a chaotic state. The invasions, the feudal system, and the low economic status of most people made learning very difficult.

However, there are some scholars that stand out. One of these, Isidore of Seville (560-636 A.D.), attempted to classify knowledge in an encyclopedia called the *Etymologies*. Another contributor to the rebirth of learning was Alcuin, a scholar whom Charlemagne had placed in charge of his palace school.

Alcuin's teaching methods have been preserved in a sample syllabus which he prepared for the instruction of Pepin, the son of Charlemagne.

"1. General questions and answers.

P. What is writing?   A. The custodian of history.

P. What is speech?   A. The interpreter of the soul.

P. What produces speech?   A. The tongue.

P. What is the tongue?   A. The whip of the air.

P. What is air?   A. The guardian of life.

P. What is life?   A. The joy of the good, the sorrow of the evil, the expectation of death.

P. What is death?   A. An inevitable event, an uncertain journey, a subject of weeping to the living, the fulfilment of wills, the thief of men.

P. What is man?	A. The slave of death, a transient traveller, a host in his dwelling.
P. What is man like?	A. Like a fruit-tree.
P. How is man placed?	A. Like a lantern exposed to the wind.
P. Where is he placed?	A. Between six walls.
P. Which are they?	A. Above, below; before, behind; right, left.
P. To how many changes is he liable?	A. To six.
P. Which are they?	A. Hunger and satiety; rest and work; waking and sleeping.
P. What is sleep?	A. The image of death.
P. What is the liberty of man?	A. Innocence.
P. What is the head?	A. The top of the body.
P. What is the body?	A. The domicile of the soul." [1]

Notice that the questions are very general and that the answers tend to be vague. In contrast to the Greek scholars, Alcuin believed in a symbolic interpretation of man and the universe, and he slighted the contributions of empirical science. Thus, he gave no exact account of the sun when he discussed its structure, but merely defined it "as the splendor of the universe." Like most scholars of his age, his interests were dominated by religious concerns.

MAURUS. Alcuin's favorite student was Rabanus Maurus, a young scholar who built a library at Fulda and who contributed to the preservation of learning. Maurus considered the seven liberal arts as basic in man's education. In an essay he described the importance of the various subjects.

First he turned to grammar which

"takes its name from the written character, as the derivation of the word indicates. The definition of grammar is this: Grammar is the science which teaches us to explain the poets and historians; it is the art which qualifies us to write and speak correctly. Grammar is the source and foundation of the liberal arts. It should be taught in every Christian school, since the art of writing and speaking correctly is attained through it. How could one understand the sense of the spoken word or the meaning of letters and syllables, if one had not learned this before from grammar? How could one know about metrical feet, accent, and verses, if grammar had not given one knowledge of them? How should one learn to know the articulation of discourse, the advantages of figurative language, the laws of word formation, and the correct forms of words, if one had not familiarized himself with the art of grammar?" [2]

---

[1] Alcuin, *Disputation of Pepin.*

[2] Rhabanus Maurus, *Education of the Clergy*, translated in F. V. Painter, *Great Pedagogical Essays* (New York: The American Book Company, 1905). Reprinted by permission.

Next he discusses Rhetoric.

"According to the statements of teachers, rhetoric is the art of using secular discourse effectively in the circumstances of daily life. From this definition rhetoric seems indeed to have reference merely to secular wisdom. Yet it is not foreign to ecclesiastical instruction. Whatever the preacher and herald of the divine law, in his instruction, brings forth in an eloquent and becoming manner; whatever in his written exposition he knows how to clothe in adequate and impressive language, he owes to his acquaintance with this art. Whoever at the proper time makes himself familiar with this art, and faithfully follows its rules in speaking and writing, needs not count it as something blameworthy. On the contrary, whoever thoroughly learns it so that he acquires the ability to proclaim God's word, performs a true work. Through rhetoric anything is proved true or false. Who would have the courage to maintain that the defenders of truth should stand weaponless in the presence of falsehood, so that those, who dare to represent false, should know how by their discourse to win the favor and sympathy of the hearers, and that, on the other hand, the friends of truth should not be able to do this; that those should know how to present falsehood briefly, clearly, and with the semblance of truth, and that the latter, on the contrary, should clothe the truth in such an exposition, that listening would become a burden, apprehension of the truth a weariness, and faith in the truth an impossibility?" [3]

Then he turns to Dialectic which

"is the science of the understanding, which fits us for investigations and definitions, for explanations, and for distinguishing the true from the false. It is the science of sciences. It teaches how to teach others; it teaches learning itself; in it the reason marks and manifests itself according to its nature, efforts, and activities; it alone is capable of knowing; it not only will, but can lead others to knowledge; its conclusions lead us to an apprehension of our being and of our origin; through it we apprehend the origin and activity of the good, of Creator and creature; it teaches us to discover the truth and to unmask falsehood; it teaches us to draw conclusions; it shows us what is valid in argument and what is not; it teaches us to recognize what is contrary to the nature of things." [4]

The next subject which Maurus discusses is arithmetic, the science of numbers.

"Those with whom Plato stands in especial honor will not make bold to esteem numbers lightly, as if they were of no consequence for the knowledge of God. He teaches that God made the world out of numbers. And among us the prophet says of God, 'He forms the world by number.' And in the Gospel the Savior says, 'The very hairs of your head are all numbered.'

3 *Ibid.*
4 *Ibid.*

. . . Ignorance of numbers leaves many things unintelligible that are expressed in the Holy Scripture in a derivative sense or with a mystical meaning." 5

Then he gives an exposition of geometry which

"found realization at the building of the tabernacle and the temple; the same measuring rod, circles, spheres, hemispheres, quadrangles, and other figures were employed. The knowledge of all this brings to him, who is occupied with it, no small gain for his spiritual culture." 6

Maurus had high praise for music.

"Music is the science of time intervals as they are perceived in tones. This science is as eminent as it is useful. He who is a stranger to it is not able to fulfil the duties of an ecclesiastical officer in a suitable manner. A proper delivery in reading and a lovely rendering of the Psalms in the church are regulated by a knowledge of this science." 7

The religious tone of Maurus is evident in his discussion of astronomy:

"There remains yet astronomy which, as some one has said, is a weighty means of demonstration to the pious, and to the curious a grievous torment. If we seek to investigate it with a pure heart and an ample mind, then it fills us, as the ancients said, with great love for it. For what will it not signify, that we soar in spirit to the sky, that with penetration of mind we analyze that sublime structure, that we, in part at least, fathom with the keenness of our logical faculties what mighty space has enveloped in mystery! The world itself, according to the assumption of some, is said to have the shape of a sphere, in order that in its circumference it may be able to contain the different forms of things. Thus Seneca, in agreement with the philosophers of ancient times, composed a work under the title, 'The Shape of the Earth.'
"Astronomy, of which we now speak, teaches the laws of the stellar world. The stars can take their place or carry out their motion only in the manner established by the Creator, unless by the will of the Creator a miraculous change takes place." 8

In the tenth century, Gerbert, who later became Pope Sylvester, encouraged classical learning. Unlike St. Augustine, he felt that there was no essential conflict between the Church and antique knowledge.

Medieval education was dominated by the conflict between those who believed that only universals are real and those who stressed the reality of specific facts. Anselm, bishop of Canterbury, believed in the

5 *Ibid.*
6 *Ibid.*
7 *Ibid.*
8 *Ibid.*

reality of universals, while Roscellinus stressed nominalism. Educationally, this preoccupation turned the scholars away from empirical study
and thus they occupied their minds with abstract logical principles.

Education in the Middle Ages was also governed by the theology of
the Church, which stressed orthodoxy and excommunicated heretics. At
the same time, political security was limited. Incessant wars between
feudal lords made learning extremely difficult.

EDUCATION FOR KNIGHTHOOD

Knighthood was one of the most significant institutions of the Middle Ages. In the twelfth century, John of Salisbury declared emphatically
that knighthood was divinely instituted; Caxton later maintained that
knighthood was the earliest device of God to ensure the recovery of
mankind from the consequences of the Fall. Ideally, knighthood became
a way of life with formal traditions, a definite education, and a world
view of its own. The Bible itself was regarded as a source of knightly virtue. Stories, like those of Abraham, of Jonas and the Whale, of Daniel
and the Lion, were popular because they appealed to the romantic imagination of the aristocracy. Just as the monks made a recluse out of
Joseph, so did the knights fashion Joshua into a chevalier. Mary with her
unblemished virtues and her merciful ways was appealed to for protection. One might pray also to the saints, particularly to St. Michael, the
personal antagonist of Satan, to St. James, St. George, and St. Martin,
who had been selected as heavenly paragons of aristocratic virtues. Chiv-
alric education consequently was imbued with a religious tincture. From
baptism to death in battle, the knight came in contact with religious
ideals, not for the purpose of acquiring scholastic education, but to ensure religion's protection against evil powers.

Early education of medieval knights began in the home. His mother,
or the local priest, taught the young boy simple prayers as well as obedience to his elders. When the boy was seven years old, he usually was sent
to the castle of a secular lord or to the palace of a prominent churchman.
This second stage in education, though it varied from country to country
and depended upon individual choice, seemed to have been quite common. As a page the boy shared duties with other members of the household. His task consisted of attending the lord and his lady; from the latter
he was able to learn the rudiments of etiquette and receive instruction in
knightly behavior. Sometimes he even procured some elementary lessons
in the Seven Liberal Arts, but this part of his education was generally
overlooked. Most of the time there were wandering singers from whom
the page might learn how to sing and play the harp. A more prominent
part of his training consisted of outdoor activities such as boxing, wrestling, and horseback riding.

Before his elevation to knighthood, the youth had to spend several years as a squire. Now he spent less time with the Lady for the master of the house demanded his services. The many menial tasks that he had to perform included waiting on tables and helping to dress his Lord. His duty was to be near him at the battlefield as well as in the tournament. Furthermore, he was ordered to take good care of the war horse and the other equipment, besides taking strenuous exercises in the various sports in order to increase his physical dexterity. In the evening hours, after having devoted most of the day to his master, he could practice the arts of music and poetry.

Finally, when the squire reached knighthood, he would concentrate upon physical exercise, and he would generally neglect his esthetic interests. An excellent example of medieval knighthood was Godfrey of Bouillon. Until he went on the first crusade he led the usual knightly existence which consisted largely of engaging in border warfares with his neighbors. In these feudal wars we can scarcely find a justification for the lavish praise bestowed upon Godfrey by the chroniclers and poets. In Palestine, Godfrey, who had been one of the first nobles to take up the cross, distinguished himself by blind fanaticism. He was so powerful, that, to the delight of all the Crusaders, he once, with his sword, split a Saracen into two parts; Godfrey seemed to be most satisfied when he killed his enemies by the hundred.

But the superhuman prowess and strength is just one part of Godfrey's character, although it counted for his popularity with the common people and made some of his more critical contemporaries forget his other faults. The same Godfrey could walk barefoot to the Church of the Resurrection after he had slaughtered hundreds of Saracens. William of Tyre writes, that as Godfrey went to the church, he wept tears of joy and sang hymns of penitence. When, later, he became the first ruler of the kingdom of Jerusalem, he refused to wear a crown because it reminded him of Christ who had been forced to wear a crown of thorns. Although Godfrey's rule lasted only for a few months, his exploits were celebrated in all the countries of Western Christendom; centuries later, Caxton ranked Godfrey as the third greatest knight of the world, next to Charlemagne and Arthur.

This mixture of piety and fanaticism which thus distinguished Godfrey of Bouillon was common to many medieval knights. In general, they impeded the progress of education because they valued skill in warfare above proficiency in learning.

EDUCATIONAL INSTITUTIONS

Among the various educational institutions developed in the Middle Ages, the most important were the Cathedral schools, usually established at episcopal centers. Important Cathedral schools developed at Paris, Tours, Chartres, Orléans, Rheims, Canterbury, and Toledo. Collegiate schools were usually administered by large churches and attracted mainly candidates for the priesthood. In monastic schools, two types of students were eligible: those who wanted to enter monastic life were called *oblati;* those who merely wanted professional instruction were called *externi.* The oblati were not obliged to pay tuition fees, but the parents of the externi had to pay for their instruction by making special donations to the Church.

Among the more specialized schools of the Middle Ages are the Song Schools, which appealed to poor boys, and which gave educational instruction to those who aided the musical services of the Church. Chantry schools were endowed by members of the local aristocracy who would establish a chapel in memory of a departed ancestor, and who would employ a priest who also might act as an educator. Another type of religious school was the parish school. We know, for instance, that in 1257 the priests in Breslau established a parish school which specialized in the teaching of Latin grammar.

Not all schools in the Middle Ages were under church control. The merchant and craft guilds created special schools for their members; noblemen founded schools for the education of their sons. In Italy, especially, lay grammar schools flourished, and in Ireland similar institutions specialized in law and history. At the end of the Middle Ages, burgher vernacular schools became more prominent. These schools were dominated by a practical philosophy of education, and they stressed arithmetic and the liberal arts. They appealed especially to sons of the middle class.

Education of women played a minor part in the Middle Ages. Nuns were taught the rudiments of reading and writing. Some of them became great scholars, but most of them received little beyond thorough manual training. Castle schools for daughters of the aristocracy provided training in etiquette and physical education. In Italy, the education of women was on a higher plane than in most European nations. At Salerno, for instance, women were even admitted to the medical school.

One of the most memorable women in the Middle Ages was Héloïse, the French abbess who has been immortalized in literature. Her letters reveal her as a most profound scholar and an expert in Greek and philosophy.

MASTER AND STUDENT

The relationship between master and student is illustrated by a colloquy written by Abbott Elfric in 1005. It shows the frequent use of physical punishment and the rudimentary state of learning in the Middle Ages.

"Boys.   Master, we children ask you to teach us to speak correctly for
                we are unlearned and speak corruptly.
MASTER.   What do you want to say?
BOYS.   What do we care what we say so long as we speak correctly
                and say what is useful, not old-womanish or improper.
MASTER.   Will you be flogged while learning?
BOYS.   We would rather be flogged while learning than remain ig-
                norant; but we know that you will be kind to us and not flog
                us unless you are obliged.
MASTER.   I ask you what you are saying to me. What work have you?
FIRST BOY.   I am a professed monk and I sing seven times a day with the
                brethren and I am busy with reading and singing; and mean-
                while I want to learn to speak Latin.
MASTER.   You boy, what did you do today?
BOY.   I did many things. At night when I heard the bell, I got out
                of bed and went to church and sang the nocturne with the
                brethren. Then we sang the martyrology and lauds; after that,
                prime and the seven psalms with litanies and first mass; next
                tierce, and did the mass of the day; after that we sang sext,
                and ate and drank and slept; and then we got up again and
                sang nones, and now here we are before you ready to listen to
                what you tell us.
MASTER.   When will you sing vespers or compline?
BOY.   When it's time.
MASTER.   Were you flogged today?
BOY.   I was not, because I was very careful.
MASTER.   And how about the others?
BOY.   Why do you ask me that? I daren't tell you our secrets. Each
                one knows whether he was flogged or not.
MASTER.   Where do you sleep?
BOY.   In the dormitory with the brethren.
MASTER.   Who calls you to nocturnes?
BOY.   Sometimes I hear the bell, and get up; sometimes my master
                wakes me with a ground-ash.
MASTER.   All you good children and clever scholars, your teacher ex-
                horts you to keep the commandments of God, and behave
                properly everywhere. Walk quietly when you hear the church
                bells and go into church, and bow to the holy altars, and
                stand quietly and sing in unison, and ask pardon for your
                sins, and go out again without playing, to the cloister or to
                school." [9]

The dialogue indicates that education was a servant of the Church.
Its purpose was to inspire students so that they would lead a moral life
and obey the commandments of the religious leaders. Self-expression was
not allowed; play activities were regarded as being frivolous. The ideal

---

[9] A. F. Leach, *Educational Charters* (New York: G. P. Putnam's Sons, 1911), pp. 37 ff.

student was one who dedicated himself to a life of self-denial and sacrifice.

ABELARD

Among the scholars who changed medieval education, Peter Abelard (1079-1142) has an important place. Undoubtedly, he ranks among the great teachers of mankind. Audacious in his viewpoints, he challenged the dominant ideas of his time. His books were burned; several times he was forbidden to teach. Bernard of Clairvaux, who represented the orthodoxy of the Church, regarded Abelard as a dangerous influence and wanted to silence him completely.

His work *Sic et Non* (Yes and No) was a fundamental event in medieval education. The keynote to the work was doubt. In his introduction Abelard explained the purpose of the work.

"In truth, constant or frequent questioning is the first key to wisdom; and it is, indeed, to the acquiring of this (habit of) questioning with absorbing eagerness that the famous philosopher, Aristotle, the most clear-sighted of all, urges the studious when he says: 'It is perhaps difficult to speak confidently in matters of this sort unless they have often been investigated. Indeed, to doubt in special cases will not be without advantage.' For through doubting we come to inquiry, and through inquiry we perceive the truth. As the Truth Himself says: 'Seek and ye shall find, knock and it shall be opened unto you.' And He also, instructing us by His own example, about the twelfth year of His life wished to be found sitting in the midst of the doctors, asking them questions, exhibiting to us by His asking of questions the appearance of a pupil, rather than, by preaching, that of a teacher, although there is in him nevertheless, the full and perfect wisdom of God." [10]

Abelard raised 158 questions regarding basic beliefs. They are less controversial in our time, but in the Middle Ages they were constantly debated. The following questions are representative of Abelard's skeptical spirit:

"Should human faith be based on reason, or no?
Is God one, or no?
Is God a substance, or no?
Does the first Psalm refer to Christ, or no?
Is sin pleasing to God, or no?
Is God the author of evil, or no?
Is God all-powerful, or no?
Can God be resisted, or no?
Has God free will, or no?
Was the first man persuaded to sin by the devil, or no?" [11]

---

10 *Sic et Non.*
11 *Ibid.*

In his views, Abelard revealed a remarkable tolerance regarding other faiths. He had great admiration for Greek philosophers, especially for Plato and Socrates, and he maintained that his own age could profit from the rationality of Greek education. To Abelard, Christianity was not so much an institutionalized way of life as an educational attitude based on *love and compassion*.

In his ethical doctrines, Abelard emphasized the *subjective* nature of morality. The goodness of an act is determined by the motive, not by its consequences. When we act in the spirit of ill-will, no profitable results can occur. The criterion of morality is man's conscience, the infallible voice of God, superior to political and ecclesiastical authorities.

While Abelard rebelled against the Church, his philosophy led to a reformulation of orthodox theology in the thirteenth century.

As a teacher, he attracted thousands of students and he contributed to the development of the University of Paris. Throughout history, Abelard has been regarded as the representative of independent inquiry.

SCHOLASTICISM AND UNIVERSITIES

To appreciate the educational achievements of scholasticism in the thirteenth century, it is necessary to understand the intellectual currents which produced it. We find now that medieval civilization was reaching a climax. Early opinions were systematized; consequently, we have more coherence in the philosophies of the thirteenth century than in the previous period.

Outside influences contributed to the formation of this synthesis. The rediscovery of some of the most important books of Aristotle changed the outlook of many theologians. It produced an incessant conflict between those who believed in the Platonic interpretation of the universe, and those who, like Aquinas, tried to combine Aristotle with Christian tradition.

The twelfth and thirteenth centuries saw the rise of universities. Medieval universities were organized like guilds, and they were concerned with scholarship rather than with buildings. Students had to study hard and had few conveniences. There were three main universities: the University of Salerno specialized in medicine; another, at Bologna, concentrated upon the study of law; a third university, located at Paris, emphasized theology.

The universities at Oxford, Naples, and Rome had only a secondary standing in the Middle Ages as compared with the University of Paris.

Medieval teaching methods were based upon the formal lecture which would be memorized by students. Occasionally, students debated philosophical points among each other; sometimes students and masters would hold public disputations. Examinations were strict; when a candidate was examined for the Doctor's degree, the examinations frequently lasted a week or more.

Students were in control at the University of Bologna, while the teachers dominated life at the University of Paris. However—and this was true of all the schools—student life was not always on a scholastic level. Many students attended the university just for social reasons and enjoyed the life of the senses.

THE QUEST FOR CERTAINTY

The salient problem of thirteenth century education centered around the intellectual revolution associated with the recovery of the physical and metaphysical doctrines of Aristotle. A new avenue of knowledge was opened up which had to be connected with the far flung foundations of Christian dogma that were based upon a Platonic philosophy as expounded by St. Augustine. Aristotle became the eminently authoritative scholar for the scholastics in the natural world, i.e., in matters where reason reigned instead of revelation.

The fundamental doctrinal content of scholasticism may be briefly stated in the following points. In the first place, the system was imbued with a theistic philosophy and emphasized the majesty of God. The universe was conceived as the creation of God whose providence was constantly evident. The scholastics fought any attempts to bridge the gap between Creator and created beings.

Second, scholasticism made a *distinction between revelation and reason.* Revelation can attain knowledge of reality, while reason is valid in its own sphere when concerned with its proper object.

Scholastic ethics were strongly anti-deterministic and gave full sway to man's free will, leaning towards a *personalistic* morality.[12]

Completely antithetic to scholasticism were other schools of thought whose metaphysical doctrines were monistic, pantheistic, and deterministic. They found their best expression in *Averrhoism,* which propounded a universal determinism, limited God's freedom by necessity, and held forth the co-eternal existence of the intelligences.

Some of the Averrhoist doctrines were obviously anti-Christian and could not be implanted in Christianity without destroying the supernatural functions of the faith. For example, the Averrhoists believed that each human being has his own body and his own sensible soul, but that

---

[12] General surveys of scholasticism can be obtained in J. Rickaby, *Scholasticism;* W. Turner, *History of Philosophy,* 237-420; and M. Grabmann, *Die Philosophie des Mittelalters.*

there is only one active intellect which exists separately from all individual members of the race. This "race-mind" enters into a temporary union with the sensible soul and is alone immortal, while the soul, the center of physical individuality, perishes with the body.

If the Averrhoist system, an Arabic interpretation of peripateticism, had prevailed in Christian theology, the whole structure of rewards and punishments would have collapsed. It would have undermined the faith of the ordinary believer. Against such doctrines, the theologians fought shoulder to shoulder, recognizing the common danger.

The thirteenth century is one in which the results of the study of previous generations were classified and synthesized. This holds true for philosophy as well as for other sciences. Vincent of Beauvais wrote an enormous encyclopedia, the *Speculum Quadruplex,* which treated many subjects in voluminous books. Jacopo de Voragine gathered together, in the *Golden Legend,* the stories of the lives of the saints. In legal science, Accursius wrote the *Glossa Ordinaria,* a compilation of the opinions and commentaries of his predecessors. Medieval civilization had reached the zenith of its development, and scholars wanted to blend and interfuse the works of the past.

In the camp of the scholastics, the classification of education was carried out most accurately and scientifically. After starting with the analytical sciences, scholastics proceeded to consider philosophy, and then theology, the queen of sciences "whose light lends brilliance to all fields of knowledge."

By the middle of the thirteenth century, the list of the particular sciences taught at Paris included astronomy, botany, physiology, zoology, physics, and chemistry. It would be absurd to suppose that these sciences resembled their modern form and were free from superstition. But the fact that they were on the curriculum indicates that scholars started from sense experience. The study of these sciences supplied them with valuable illustrations for enlivening their abstract deductions. What scholars lacked was primarily an attitude of detachment, as they often exhibited evidences of bias in their scientific discussions.

But of utmost importance for the student were the Seven Liberal Arts. These were divided into the trivium, which comprised dialectic, grammar, and rhetoric, and the quadrivium, comprising arithmetic, geometry, astronomy, and music.

Since the quadrivium required more technical knowledge than the trivium, only a few schools, such as the school at Chartres under the direction of John of Salisbury, were successful in their instruction. In addition to the traditional Seven Arts, civil and canon law had become autonomous studies in the twelfth century; medicine was still regarded as a semi-science, just as it had been in the early Middle Ages.

However, the scholastics were not content with these subject areas and consequently turned to philosophy, the subject that presented a *synthetic* view of the whole scientific field. The scholastics believed that philosophy was concerned with all existence, potential and actual, thereby bridging the gap between the particular sciences. Not only did philosophy unite the discordant branches of knowledge in one comprehensive system, but it also presented a point of view from which to judge them all.

Following the example set by Aristotle, the scholastics divided philosophy into a theoretical and a practical part. The theoretical part comprised physics, mathematics, and metaphysics; the practical part dealt with logic, ethics, and esthetics. The theoretical function of philosophy was the study of the universe through the use of abstract principles. There was no emphasis on the practical relationship of these principles; there was no thought of subordinating them to a utilitarian end. On the other hand, the practical function of philosophy was not the study of the universal order for its own sake, but rather a study of how to bring philosophy into relationship with our concrete needs.

Still, the classification of knowledge was not complete: the crowning story was lacking. All knowledge formed an introduction to the study of *theology*, which rested upon an elaborate foundation. To neglect this noblest science, according to the medieval point of view, was like building a cathedral without a roof.

Theology was considered *superior* to all other sciences. Thus, the teachers of theology at Paris, for instance, needed special qualifications, stricter than those for any other course of study. Such a field was not to be approached lightly and could not be understood by an uneducated or lethargic mind.

THE IDEALS OF AQUINAS

It became the task of St. Thomas Aquinas (1225-1274) to give a complete formulation of Catholic doctrine and education. His philosophy produced a synthesis of medieval knowledge; it united the realms of reason and faith, science and theology, nature and the beyond.

INFLUENCE. It may be asked now why his work has had such a lasting influence, why Aquinas has made such a great impact upon modern times? In the first place, Aquinas appealed not only to tradition but freely used the resources of his own reasoning power. His mind was truly encyclopedic; the orderliness and the logical consistency of his observations have scarcely been surpassed in philosophy.

In the second place, Aquinas pictured an orderly universe. There was a function for all levels and all creatures. The task of man was to utilize his reason and to glorify God. The life of the lower levels is made meaningful by the existence of God whose actions govern all parts of the universe.

In the third place, the philosophy of Aquinas was anti-mechanistic. The universe is not governed by blind chance nor by necessity; rather, the universe reveals the majesty of God; nothing occurs without His intervention.

In the fourth place, Aquinas accepted the leadership of the Church. He had an insistent sense of insecurity and felt that, without the Church, no salvation could be attained. Modern man may be more independent and more individualistic, but in times of crisis he usually escapes to the haven of institutionalism.

Furthermore, Aquinas built his philosophy upon a definite scientific foundation. His outlook was not that of the twentieth century scientist for he did not believe in an experimental approach to science. To him, as to Aristotle, the main purpose of science was *explanation rather than the control of nature*. Thus, Aquinas built his philosophy upon sense experience. The road to truth lay from the particular to the universal, from the specific to the general. Thus, we do not start with innate ideas, but with the facts of sense experience.

IMMORTALITY. To Aquinas, man's soul was truly immortal. In the main, he repeated the arguments of the previous theologians regarding the immortality of the soul; however, he added an interesting argument which depends on man's desire. He claimed that we all wish that existence should not be limited to life on earth, and we naturally desire immortality. God, being good, will not disappoint our desire and will make possible our resurrection which means that after death the soul again will have a bodily form.

Since man has a soul, he is a rational creature. Is the body superior to the soul? Aquinas answered in the negative, for he believed that the soul is the ruling capacity of the body. Like St. Augustine, he stressed the fact that the soul does not emanate but is created by God. Aquinas taught that all substances are composed of matter and form. Certain Franciscan philosophers have stated that man can have several forms; however, Aquinas asserted that man has only one form. Angels are superior to men for they have pure Form, whereas man is a union of Matter and Form. We should remember that Matter represents potentiality, while Form represents actuality.

EXISTENCE OF GOD. A basic principle in the philosophy of Aquinas is his argument for the existence of God. Actually, he uses five arguments to demonstrate his reasoning. The first depends on the nature of motion. It appears that the things which we see in motion are not self moved. *To explain motion we need a first mover: God.*

The second argument depends on the nature of causation. Nothing in this universe causes itself; we need a connection between causes and effects. Since we cannot accept an infinite regress of causation, *our mind arrives at a first cause: God.*

The third argument is based on the nature of possibility and necessity. The possible, he maintains, is not autonomous, but depends on something which is necessary. We must postulate a being *which has its own necessity; this being is God.*

The fourth argument is founded on the nature of gradation. We find a hierarchy of goods; relative standards demand an absolute standard. The highest is the cause of lower beings; *the highest principle is God.*

The fifth argument appeals to divine purposes; the universe reveals not a mechanistic order but a teleological arrangement. This cannot be due to accident. *The universe reveals divine purpose and must be traced back to God.*

According to Aquinas, God is the source of all perfection, all goodness, all existence, and all truth. God created the world to mirror His own perfection. The evil which we see is only apparent; through evil, goodness triumphs; through evil, the universe attains a more varied appearance.

It is interesting to notice the relation between faith and reason in Aquinas. Reason can tell us that God exists but it cannot prove the resurrection of the body and the atonement of Christ. Reason, also, is unable to destroy the essential foundation of Christianity which stands above it. Aquinas divided sciences into three parts—physical, metaphysical and mathematical; the most important of these sciences is *metaphysical knowledge.*

EDUCATIONAL IMPLICATIONS. Aquinas felt that the task of knowledge is the study of first principles. Those who have been influenced by Aquinas have generally been concerned more with universal principles than with specific facts.

The religious views of Aquinas had significant implications for moral education. The most important virtue is charity which implies not merely giving freely to the poor but also love for one's neighbor. The highest form of love, however, is devotion to God.

Like St. Augustine, Aquinas thundered against the heretics. The Church must try to convert them; if they persist in their errors they are to be excommunicated and, if necessary, their life is to be taken.

Generally, Aquinas supported the patriarchal system of the Middle Ages. The father is to be the head of the household; wives should obey their husbands. The foundation of the state, according to Aquinas, is the family. Hence, when the family is disrupted, social chaos is inevitable. Also, the teacher in the schools is to exercise the same type of authority over his students as the father over his household.

SOCIAL CONSIDERATIONS. Important for future ages was his opposition to divorce and birth control. The Catholic Church has, to this
date, generally adhered to his viewpoint on these subjects. For Aquinas,
the family was an indissoluble unit. He felt that divorce violated the commandments of God and of Christ and that socially it would lead to the
breakdown of civilization. Likewise, birth control would be injurious to
the individual and to the state; it would also be in opposition to moral
laws. The best state of man, according to Aquinas, is that of asceticism;
family life is a secondary existence. Above all, the temptations of the
flesh must be avoided. Man alone, not the devil, is the cause of all sin.
But on the whole, Aquinas was less puritanical than the Puritan reformers of New England.

In his social philosophy, Aquinas emphasized the moral nature of
statehood. It is the task of the ruler to preserve the integrity of the citizens. Aquinas opposed the principles of power politics. The best political
unit, he believed, is the small state in which the ruler is pious, avoids
warfare, and is an example to his subjects.

These views differ radically from the philosophies of Machiavelli
and Hobbes. The latter believed that power is a goal in itself, that the
end justifies the means, and that social relations cannot be governed by
moral precepts. Aquinas, however, felt that morality should dominate all
relationships and that man can never negate the foundations of ethics.

RELIGIOUS VIEWS. In every way, Aquinas was a loyal son of the
Church. He acknowledged the absolute power of the Pope and the necessity of the sacraments. If man wanted to obtain salvation, all the sacraments, including baptism, confirmation, the eucharist, penance, extreme
unction, ordination, and marriage, were essential. The sacraments are
parts of divine grace—they bind together nature and God, man and the
supernatural. Reason cannot explain their essential elements; only faith
can understand them.

While the Eastern theologians, like Origen and Clement, frequently
regarded Christ as a metaphysical force, Aquinas considered Jesus a living
reality. Jesus made possible our salvation; when we follow Jesus, we are
delivered from the devil; our original sin is overcome. To Aquinas, Jesus
was the supreme teacher.

EDUCATIONAL PHILOSOPHY. Aquinas produced a treatise entitled
De Veritate (On Truth), in which he asserted that education depended
on potential qualities. One type of potentiality is actualized from the
outside and demands the instruction of the teacher; another type of potentiality develops intrinsically. To illustrate this principle let us imagine
a student who, after reading a book, suddenly develops a new theory of
psychology. This theory has arisen out of his own consciousness and
represents an internal process. But, if that same student would have been

inspired by a teacher to learn about the laws of psychology, we would call this essentially an external process.

Aquinas believed that all of us are endowed with the light of reason, which indicates the majesty of God. When this light shines brightly, education prospers.

What then is the role of the teacher? How should he instruct? Aquinas answers that the teacher should be conscious of the majesty of God and thus develop the innate capacities of students. To teach, then, is to mediate between God and man. Right education is based on the ideals of the Church and is a symbol of divine truth; wrong teaching is alienation from God and represents vicious intellectual pride.

EVALUATION

The weakness of medieval education was its lack of interest in the experimental sciences. Truth was regarded as an absolute standard. Heresy was not to be tolerated. Knowledge was to be a rigorous process; it was not to be enjoyed: Thus, as Rashdall points out, the sense of beauty was not cultivated adequately in the Middle Ages.

The curriculum of the medieval schools was limited when compared with the Athenian schools in the time of Socrates and Plato. Philosophy in the Middle Ages was subordinated to theology. The liberal arts were studied in a formal manner. The horizon of the medieval student was narrow compared with that of the Athenian student. But above all, lack of freedom caused a certain timidity in intellectual matters.

We read about the excesses of medieval students. These were caused primarily by a lack of provision for their recreational activities. When they rioted they expressed opposition, not only to the university authorities but to the medieval way of life. The stress upon asceticism as an ideal of life prevented a balanced attitude towards human existence.

Still, medieval education, as represented by Aquinas, laid the groundwork for modern civilization. Robert Hutchins one time pointed to the medieval university of Paris as the ideal university. Medieval scholars were creative because they treasured the realm of the spirit, because they were willing to sacrifice to obtain an education. Thus, they could look beyond the limitations of their own time.

QUESTIONS FOR DISCUSSION AND INVESTIGATION

1. Give the names of the early educators and explain their roles in the forming of medieval education and thought.

2. Describe the life of knighthood which contributed one of the most significant institutions in the Middle Ages.

3. Describe the educational institutions developed in the Middle Ages.

4. What is the relation between master and student according to Abbott Elfric?

5. What significant role does Abelard play in instigating a newly creative, more revolutionary system of education?

6. Why did scholasticism arise as part of the medieval structure?

7. What is the fundamental doctrinal content of scholasticism in its quest for certainty?

8. Why has Thomas Aquinas had such a long-lasting influence on western civilization?

9. Delineate Aquinas' principles for proving the existence of God.

10. What was Aquinas' educational philosophy?

Chapter 13

Educational Philosophy of Mohammedanism

THE FAITH OF MOHAMMED

To appreciate the work of Mohammed, we must understand his environment. He was born in 570 A.D. in Arabia, a country which at that time was still largely in an uncivilized condition. The social organization was patriarchal; the man was the absolute head of the family. National ideals, as yet, were absent; the fundamental social unit was the tribe. Superstition was dominant, expressed in a fervent belief in magic. Peace was constantly disturbed by blood feuds and internal warfare between the tribes.

The two most important communities in ancient Arabia were Medina, known especially for its date growing industry, and Mecca, regarded as a holy city. Mecca contained a sacred stone which, it was thought, had been delivered to Abraham by the angel Gabriel. The temple in Mecca was the center of local polytheism; hundreds of gods and idols were represented in this famous shrine of worship. This was the social and religious environment of Mohammed,[1] a man who by the time of his death in 632 A.D. had stirred the national consciousness of Arabia.

In his youth, Mohammed was extremely poor, and he was never able to obtain an adequate education. His fortune improved after he entered the service of a wealthy widow. When he was twenty-nine he married her, although she was eleven years his elder. Now that he had wealth and in-

---

[1] Cf. Margoliouth, *Mohammed and the Rise of Islam;* Hitti, *The Origins of the Islamic State;* Arnold, *The Caliphate.*

fluence, he did not change his habits, but remained as unassuming as before.

Later in his life, Mohammed experienced several intense visions; one day, while meditating in a cave near Mecca, he felt that he had received the call to be God's messenger. The heavenly voice told him that he was God's prophet, and it was his task to spread the message of Allah. Mohammed was convinced that this revelation was divine. However, the people of Mecca did not want to listen to his message. Thus, in 622 A.D., he had to leave Mecca and journey to Medina. This flight, the *Hegira*, marks an epoch in the history of Mohammedanism.

At Medina he was extremely successful in spreading his religious message, and, soon, popular support began to strengthen his movement. A mosque was built and a code of laws was adopted which contained his essential beliefs. Every form of education was to be based on religious principles. Thus, the leaders of Medina were to be the messengers of God.

In 630 A.D. Mohammed was able to conquer Mecca. He destroyed the idols; however, he preserved the sacred temple with its Black Stone. His movement spread like wildfire; when he died, it was certain that it would become an international religion.

BELIEFS OF MOHAMMED

THE KORAN. The concepts of Mohammed can be found in the *Koran*, regarded as infallible by the orthodox Moslems, who believe that God Himself has revealed His teachings in these scriptures. Arranged in one hundred and fourteen chapters, the *Koran* is one of the most eloquent examples of educational and religious literature. It has a lofty concept of God and is almost lyrical in expressing man's appreciation for God's blessings. However, there are also notes of pessimism in the *Koran* which indicate that life on earth is not an unmixed blessing.

ALLAH. What are the central tenets of the faith? The most important principle is the belief in Allah. Mohammedanism is a monotheistic religion and vigorously rejects the doctrine of the Trinity.

Allah has seven attributes.

1. Allah is identified with *life*. His own existence is truly eternal, and he transcends space and time. The world depends upon his providence; if he wishes he can destroy the universe. His majesty would not suffer if all faithful would desert him, so great is his glory.

2. Allah is *knowledge* which exists throughout eternity. Nothing transpires in the universe that is not known by him. With one glance he knows the past, present, and future. We honor Allah by cultivating education.

3. Allah is identified with *power*. Thus he can accomplish all types of miracles. This explains why he can raise the dead, and why he can change the laws of nature. If he wants to destroy the earth he can accomplish this without effort.

4. Allah is identified with *will*. Whatever occurs in the universe, whatever transpires is dominated by his will, which has existed throughout all time. It is uncreated; all our actions, good or evil, pious or irreligious, are guided by his direction.

5. *Hearing* is part of Allah's attributes. All the sounds in the universe can be heard by Allah who, however, has no mechanical facilities for hearing; he does not need an ear, for his spiritual power is independent of bodily needs.

6. *Seeing*—although Allah has no eyes, he perceives all events. Whereas ordinary mortals are exposed to darkness, there is only light for Allah.

7. Allah is identified with *speech*. Not that he speaks in a human manner, rather he communicates through Gabriel, who is the intermediary between Allah and mankind.

There is no exact agreement as to whether these attributes are physically real or merely allegories. The rationalists thought that Allah's attributes are dependent upon man's intellectual interpretation and they are merely symbolic representations of reality.

Another important doctrine of the Mohammedans is the belief in angels who mediate between God and man. These angels are beyond material needs and do not need any physical food for their existence.

It is the function of the good angels to protect men. On the one hand, the angels of the right record the benevolent deeds of man; on the other hand, the angels of the left record his wicked deeds. After man dies, two angels come to his grave and ask him about his beliefs. To be saved, he must give the right answers about the nature of God and the name of the prophet.

Mohammedanism also has a devil, who is assisted by evil spirits. The devil is called Shaitin. Once upon a time he was in Paradise, but he was expelled when he refused to acknowledge the power of Allah.

Mohammedanism believes in the inspiration of the prophets. Naturally, Mohammed is the main prophet; all together there are twenty-eight prophets including twenty-two from the Old Testament. Jesus is included among the prophets, but he does not rank as high as Mohammed.

Can man completely understand the decrees of God? Can he comprehend God's ultimate ends? Mohammed answers that God's mind transcends human limitations, and that his wisdom cannot be fully understood by mankind.

While the orthodox Mohammedan believes in absolute fatalism, some sects believe in a limited form of free will and maintain that evil and injustice are not caused by God, but rather by man. Man is to blame if he is unsuccessful in life.

This belief in predestination has far-reaching philosophical and educational implications. It supports the prevalent social and economic system, for, if God has ordered all relations and all events, why should man rebel? It causes a vast time consciousness. The 'now' was only part of an enormous chain—the past, present, and future were all linked together. Why worry about momentary suffering? Why complain about transitory evils? Why worry about educational progress when all events are predetermined? Why use the resources of reason when faith is all important?

At the same time we must not neglect the ethical injunctions of Mohammedanism. Thus, Mohammedanism provides for a strong family system, for moderate habits, and for charity toward the underprivileged members of society. Again and again, Mohammed warned against idolatry, emphasizing the fact that no other gods could exist except Allah. He did not believe in blood revenge; acts of injustice were to be met by love and affection. He banned intoxicating drinks and tried to eliminate the practice of infanticide, which, in former times, had prevailed so freely among the Arabian tribes.

According to Mohammed, all believers were equal before Allah. Thus, no organized priesthood could develop. Not the church, but the *Koran* was the center of Mohammedanism.

Sins are classified into two main divisions. Among the major sins we find heresy, murder, adultery, magic, and gambling. These sins require genuine repentance. The worst sin is disbelief in God, for it leads to damnation and is, therefore, unpardonable.

On the other hand, the minor sins are mostly individual failings. Among them we find dissipation and acts of lust. We can make up for them by performing good works. Regarding sexual morality, there is far less puritanism in Mohammedanism than in orthodox Christianity. Probably the system of polygamy and the subordination of women allowed for more erotic freedom than Western religions were willing to recognize.

Other duties which Mohammedans must perform, include repeating the creed five times every day, and bowing in the direction of Mecca. Liberal almsgiving is stressed, for charity is part and parcel of Mohammedanism. Also, fasts are prescribed, especially during the days of the month of Ramadan. Every faithful Mohammedan is to journey to Mecca at least once in his life-time, if that is at all possible.

RELIGIOUS EDUCATION

ALFARABI. In Mohammedan philosophy, we find a constant struggle between those who believed in faith and accepted the inspired message of the *Koran,* and those who were guided by reason and were more inclined in the direction of philosophy. One of the most important of the Moslem philosophers was Alfarabi, who gave a Neo-Platonic interpretation to Mohammedanism. In many ways his reasoning parallels that of the Scholastics. Like them, he maintains that we cannot know God completely, for God is infinitely perfect.

In his educational philosophy, Alfarabi stressed the importance of reason. God is the spirit of truth and we honor him best by cultivating our philosophical powers. The teacher is the representative of Allah on earth.

AVICENNA. Another philosopher, who also made great contributions in medicine, was Avicenna. Like Alfarabi, he believed in the omnipotence of God, and he thought that man has value and dignity only insofar as he identifies himself with the Supreme Being. Avicenna believed in personal immortality; the soul is not corrupted by matter. Mystical strains emerge in his philosophy; thus reason is supplemented by intuition. In the highest stage of knowledge, we feel a divine illumination which no words or phrases can fully describe. According to Avicenna, the main purpose of education is to cultivate mysticism.

AL-GAZZALI. The mystical strains in Mohammedanism were heightened by Al-Gazzali. In his youth he had a great love for critical knowledge, and he studied every type of philosophy and religion. For a while he became a skeptic, and he believed in the relativity of all standards. He divided the searchers for truth into four classes: 1. scholastics, 2. believers in esoteric doctrines, 3. professional philosophers, 4. Sufis. He made it clear that the Scholastics did not have enough faith to defend religious ideals; thus they could not give certainty to man. As for those who believed in esoteric doctrines, their knowledge was shallow and often full of fraud. Al-Gazzali was bitter especially against professional educators and philosophers. The doctrine they taught was irrelevant, for, essentially, they tended to be subversive. Consequently, he wrote a book entitled *The Destruction of the Philosophers.*

The only approach to wisdom that offered him satisfaction was that of the Sufis, the mystics; theirs was truly the path to salvation. They replaced reason by faith and scientific knowledge by intuition. To achieve a realization of God, man did not need theology, rather he must achieve a recognition of the divine reality which governs the universe.

Al-Gazzali felt that real education demands asceticism. We are to abandon all lusts of the flesh, and we are to give up the striving for honor and worldly applause. Through fasting and mortification of the flesh, we turn away from sense objects and see the overwhelming majesty of God.

AVERRHOES. Quite different from Al-Gazzali was Averrhoes, who put his reliance upon philosophy. As the outstanding Moslem commentator on Aristotle, he followed the Greek sage in not accepting personal immortality; only the active intellect is immortal. What remains after death is that part of reason which we share with other beings.

Averrhoes felt that philosophy could deepen religious truth, and that it could give an allegorical interpretation of religious ideals. To defend himself against heresy, he accepted the standpoint of the double truth. This means that something may be true in philosophy and education and yet may be false in theology.

The orthodox suspected him because of his rationalism and, more so, because of his belief in emanation and his rejection of the concept of creation out of nothing. He maintained that the universe was eternal and could not be destroyed by Allah.

His doctrines caused an immense stir, not only in Mohammedan circles, but also in the West where they led to endless heresies. They contributed to the reinterpretation of Aristotle, which, through Pomponazzi in the Renaissance, led to a more naturalistic viewpoint regarding the Greek philosopher.

Averrhoes believed in the cause of enlightenment. The real teacher, he maintained, is emancipated from superstition and he understands the symbolic nature of truth. He will look upon knowledge as an eternal process, not as a final attainment.

THE SIGNIFICANCE OF MOHAMMEDANISM

Mohammedanism is one of the most monotheistic religions of the world. Whereas orthodox Christianity upholds the concept of the Trinity, Mohammedanism recognizes only one God. The Mohammedans believe that salvation lies in obedience to the will of Allah, while damnation occurs when we defy his will.

In most cases, Mohammedanism has led to a theocratic form of government with religion and the state being identified. This gives great power to the ruling classes and gives rise to traditionalism in social customs. However, liberal Mohammedan theologians point out that the *Koran* allows for a separation of state and church.

Mohammedanism, like Christianity, believes in supernaturalism. The destiny of the individual on earth, thus, is insignificant as compared with his fate after death. Heaven and hell are not spiritual, but material states. Even in heaven a patriarchal organization exists. Yet supernaturalism did not convert all Mohammedan thinkers. Thus, a frank note of Epicureanism existed in the *Rubaiyat* of Omar Khayyam who believed that the present is all important, and sinners and saints share the same fate.

In Mohammedanism, as in Christianity, an intense struggle rages between the traditionalists and the progressives. The traditionalists uphold the absolute infallibility of the *Koran* and object to modern education and to industrial progress. The liberals, on the other hand, want to change Mohammedanism so that it can be accommodated to the modern age and to modern educational methods.

However, the Moslem concept of fate stands in the way of individual betterment. Thus, the individual is powerless in regard to God's decrees. Allah sends to men whatever they deserve; his decisions are not to be questioned. Still, in Mohammedanism there is a basic democratic element. There is no privileged priesthood; there are no sacraments; there is no infallible interpreter of the truth except Mohammed. All men are equal before the sight of God, whose majesty encompasses heaven and earth.

EDUCATIONAL CONTRIBUTIONS

During the Middle Ages, Moslem culture and learning was far superior to Western civilization. The Moslems translated the Greek classics into Arabic, they cultivated high standards of learning, and they were tolerant when it came to new ideas. This spirit, unfortunately, did not continue in modern times.

Among the sciences, medicine reached a relatively high state of development; the outstanding scientific work of the time was Avicenna's *Canon of Medicine.* Roger Bacon owed a major debt to Moslem scientists who were pioneers in mathematics, physics, and chemistry.

Generally, the empirical spirit governed Arabic scholarship. Scholarship should be verified and controlled by experiments. Historical studies were cultivated, and Arabic educators expanded our knowledge of geography.

Universities arose which stressed both scientific and religious knowledge. At Bagdad, in 830 A.D., a House of Wisdom was established—a combination of advanced center of learning and museum. In the Middle Ages, Arabic universities were far more liberal and progressive than in modern times.

The art of literature found expression in such works as *Arabian Nights* and the *Rubaiyat.* We must not forget that Omar Khayyam was not only a poet, but also a scientist of note. While Al-Gazzali favored faith, Omar Khayyam strikes a note of skepticism.

> *"Why, all the Saints and Sages who discuss'd*   6
> *Of the Two Worlds so wisely—they are thrust*
> *Like foolish Prophets forth; their Words to Scorn*
> *Are scatter'd, and their Mouths are stopt with Dust.*

Myself when young did eagerly frequent
Doctor and Saint, and heard great argument
About it and about: but evermore
Came out by the same door where in I went.

With them the seed of Wisdom did I sow,
And with mine own hand wrought to make it grow;
And this was all the Harvest that I reap'd—
"I came like Water, and like Wind I go."

Into this Universe, and Why not knowing
Nor Whence, like Water willy-nilly flowing;
And out of it, as Wind along the Waste,
I know not Whither, willy-nilly blowing." [2]

The Arabs contributed to the Renaissance by their translations of Greek thinkers and by their encouragement of scholarship. By the fifteenth century they became more intolerant; in fact, when they captured Constantinople in 1453, many of the famous Greek scholars fled to find refuge in the Italian city states.

In general, Moslem education is an example of the relationship of freedom and creativity in education. When Moslem rulers, like Haroun al Rashid, encouraged freedom of expression, the arts and sciences prospered. When freedom was curbed, and when orthodoxy prevailed Moslem learning declined. As long as freedom of inquiry is limited, no real advancement in knowledge is possible.

---

[2] *Rubaiyat*

QUESTIONS FOR DISCUSSION AND INVESTIGATION

1. What part does the environment play in influencing the birth of Mohammed's works?

2. What significance does the *Koran* bear for the Moslem?

3. List and describe the seven attributes of Allah.

4. Compare and contrast the Islamic concept of angel and devil to that of orthodox Christianity.

5. What profound and far-reaching implications does the belief in predestination have on the Moslem way of life?

6. What was Alfarabi's interpretation of Mohammedanism?

7. Contrast the approach of Al-Gazzali and Averrhoes in Mohammedanism.

8. Explain the statement that "Mohammedanism is one of the most monotheistic religions of the world."

9. How does the Moslem concept of fate stand in the way of individual betterment?

10. Why did the superior Moslem culture of the Middle Ages not continue in the modern era?

Part 3

Foundations
of
Modern Education

Chapter 14

Renaissance Ideals of Education

The Renaissance represents a new period in man's culture. Its break with the Middle Ages was gradual, yet it created a new world view. Whereas the Middle Ages had advocated mortification of the body, Renaissance scholars strongly asserted that life is to be enjoyed to the utmost.

The middle class became more important during the Renaissance; nationalism and glorification of wealth became permanent aspects of European civilization. The invention of printing created a broader foundation for universal education. Women, who had played a rather inferior role in the Middle Ages, now took a prominent place in culture and, like Margaret of Navarre, contributed to the advancement of learning.

While the Middle Ages had maintained a moralistic conception of man, art became the main vehicle of interpretation during the Renaissance. The artist, like da Vinci, became the leader of society. Man's body, earlier regarded as the source of sin, was glorified by the artist and became the object of detailed anatomic study.

The status of man changed. Human perfection was glorified; dignity was emphasized; man, as Pico della Mirandola showed, became the center of the universe.

Furthermore, we find a new conception of the gentleman. The medieval gentleman was usually illiterate, interested only in sports and warfare. The Renaissance gentleman treasured education and was an expert in the art of love. It was the ideal of the period to develop the complete man and to cultivate both the arts and the sciences.

The attitude of the Renaissance period brought about a revolution in the thinking of man. The provincial population of the Middle Ages, having pictured the earth as the center of the universe, was now confronted with a heliocentric perspective. The work of Copernicus, Galileo, Brahe, and Kepler aided in the emergence and final victory of this world view.

At first, the new scientific ideas were ridiculed, their proponents were persecuted; well known are the sufferings of Galileo at the hands of the Inquisition. Finally, in the age of Newton, the heliocentric viewpoint was taken for granted by the educated world. Not only had the universe changed, but so had man lost status as lord of creation. More and more scholars were conscious of man's infinitesimal position in the vast astronomical world.

Yet the thinkers had various reactions to the new world concept: To Bruno, it meant a ready acceptance of pantheism; to Gassendi, Epicureanism was the only alternative; to Bayle, skepticism seemed to be the best answer. Pascal, who laid the foundations for the calculus, considered faith as the only valid solution. But his belief in revelation was different from the medieval acceptance of the dogmas of the Church. For the scholars of the Middle Ages it was natural to adhere to absolute standards; for Pascal it was an escape caused by despair.

The new universe was dominated by laws, not by miracles. It was far more sober than the picturesque world of Aquinas and Dante. Faith in miracles continued, only now miracles were based upon the foundations of science. Were not the alchemists seeking for the philosopher's stone and for perpetual health and prosperity? Did they not combine in their work magic with chemistry?

Theology had been displaced as queen of the sciences. The humanist laughed at the old fashioned utterances of the theologians. The students at the universities were enraptured by the study of languages and the sway of the physical sciences, instead of by the issues of theology.

Aristotle was dethroned. In the Middle Ages, he had been an authority not only in religion, but also in science; he had been regarded as the master of those who knew. His scholastic and spiritual reign, although not completely ended, was at least challenged. The revolt was violent on the part of Ramus and, when his logic challenged the Aristotelian foundations of knowledge, the theology of the Church was likewise imperilled.

The new method in science respected the facts of nature; it ceased to be an allegory and instead became an experiment. Particulars were emphasized instead of generalities; patience became a prime virtue for the scientists. In the *Discourse on Method,* Descartes tells how he constantly checked and reviewed his conclusions. Here we find the beginning of the hypothetical method of modern science.

All these advances created an unbounded spirit of confidence in man's ability. Thus, the Renaissance, to a great extent, was an age of optimism. It was the feeling of the times that no discovery and no scientific advance lay beyond human achievement.

It is strange that modern civilization started with such a naive faith in man's possibilities. For today a spirit of skepticism has arisen in regard to man's ability to control nature. But it is easy to explain this Renaissance spirit of self-confidence: it was in this period that man, at the early stages of his emancipation, was overwhelmed by the novelty of his inventions.

ITALIAN SCHOLARS

One of the scholars who influenced the development of the Renaissance was Petrarch. He was a supporter of the classics and, in his poetry, an exponent of secular ideals. He maintained that, in many ways, classical scholarship was superior to that of his own time. He was opposed to an educational system which glorified asceticism. Instead, he urged the cultivation of the arts and sciences.

Vittorino da Feltre was a famed classical scholar and noted mathematician at Mantua; his school included training in the sciences as well as in the humanities and religion. In each field he expounded the humanistic concept of life.

Petrus Paulus Vergerius distinguished himself in the field of literature which he regarded as the basic study of the educational curriculum. Guarino of Verona founded a school at Ferrara, which was a preparatory academy for teaching religion and which emphasized high literary standards.

Castiglione, in *The Courtier,* outlined the etiquette of the new educational system, maintaining that learning and good manners should be joined and that the aristocrat should be a model to others in his cultural interests.

EDUCATIONAL REFORMERS

Among educational reformers, Rabelais deserves an honored place. Born in 1494 in Touraine, he soon joined a monastery; later he became too independent for the order and, instead, devoted himself to medicine.

The keynote to education, as Rabelais maintains in *Gargantua* is "do what thou wilt." He wanted to establish an ideal school which was to be a "coeducational monastery." There were to be no clocks and no compulsion. Only fair and personable ladies were to be admitted, and only intelligent and personable men students were to be allowed in this educational center.

Rabelais made it clear that he wanted no ascetics and no rules of poverty, chastity and obedience. He thought that the students at Thélème would exercise their freedom wisely and would learn foreign languages as well as various sciences.

According to Rabelais, coercion in education was the great evil. Away with corporal punishment! Away with scholastic rules! Away with the worship of the past! We need an educational system based on the glories of the present.

Just as utilitarian in his emphasis, although more religious than Rabelais, was Juan Louis Vives (1492-1540), a Spanish thinker who remained faithful to Catholicism. Among the books by Vives we find *On Instruction of a Christian Woman, Concerning the Teaching of the Arts, On a Plan for Study of Youth,* and *Concerning the Mind.* He exerted a profound influence on Comenius by his advocacy of the vernacular in learning, and by his concern for the education of women. Vives made it clear that the progress of education depends on methodology. Learning should start with the simple and the concrete, and then move to more abstract matters.

Peter Ramus (1515-1572) was a noted scholar who felt that the influence of Aristotle had to be limited. He favored a logic based on induction and considered literature as the basis of instruction. He was a professor at Paris, where he ended tragically: as a Protestant he was killed during the massacre of Saint Bartholomew. To Ramus, as to Vives, methodology was the starting point of knowledge. Knowledge must be concrete and instrumental in the daily life of man.

In England, Thomas Elyot (1490-1546) popularized the new ideals of education. In the *Governour* he outlined the rules for the instructions for a future aristocrat. He should be taught moral virtue as well as the humanities and the sciences. At the same time, his poise should be developed so that he may act like a gentleman on all occasions. He should be an expert in sports, especially hunting, for the scholarly life as such was not a goal of the landed gentry.

The Renaissance ideal of education was eloquently represented by Sir Phillip Sidney, who combined poetic proclivities with manliness and unexcelled bravery. In his many-sided genius, Sidney represented the aspiration to excellence, a spirit much admired during the Renaissance.

ERASMUS AND HUMANISM

The victory of the scientific spirit was made possible by the northern Humanists of the Renaissance. Most of them, like Reuchlin and Erasmus, were pious Christians and still accepted faith in God as the primary condition in life. They had great respect for authorities, especially for Greek and Roman scholars. Colet worshipped Socrates like a saint; Reuchlin enjoyed nothing better than the study of the Hebrew language. The latter had a persistent enemy in Pfefferkorn, a Jewish convert to Christianity, who wanted to destroy all Jewish literature. Pfefferkorn was defeated in the end, and the study of Hebrew prospered at the European universities.

The Humanists did much to popularize scholarship. Now the universities became social and political storm centers as well as agencies of active religious reform. Unfortunately, the humanists were too concerned with exactness and scholarship. They venerated Greek and Latin authorities almost to the same degree as the theologians venerated the works of the Church Fathers.

At the same time, scholarship became more cosmopolitan. Desiderius Erasmus (1466?-1536) was a traveller in many lands; he often admitted that he was a citizen of Europe, not of any one nation. During his lifetime he taught at Cambridge and lived at Paris, Venice, and Basel. Everywhere scholars followed him, and his letters and books reached a wide audience.

Erasmus believed that man is the center of the universe. He had strong faith in God, but, hating superstition, he fought a constant warfare with the theologians. He felt that hypocrisy governs most of mankind and that the educator has to beware of conceit.

Especially important, from an educational standpoint, are his *On the Education of a Christian Prince, On Christian Matrimony, Colloquies,* and *Upon the Method of Right Instruction.* Unlike Machiavelli, Erasmus believed that the prince should be a moral example for his subjects and that he should cultivate the arts of peace, rather than those of war. Erasmus, like many other humanists, believed that women should be educated for real knowledge would strengthen family ties. His *Colloquies* were a popular introduction to Latin literature, and they were among the most important textbooks of his time. In *Upon the Method of Right Instruction,* Erasmus urged the systematic training of teachers. How could civilization progress without adequate schoolmasters?

How could students advance? First, their innate capacities had to be stimulated; in this, nature was to be the guide. Second, guidance had to be consistent; this could be best determined by the teacher's love for the student. Third, the student had to practice what he learned. Wisdom, according to Erasmus, is applied knowledge.

The aim of education in the system proposed by Erasmus is independent judgment. This combines honesty and real knowledge. We must not rely on the ancients; rather we must learn to stand on our own feet and deal intelligently with the problems of our own time.

Erasmus made an important contribution to the study of motivation. If a teacher used force and coercion, he would motivate his students in a negative manner. He would become a positive influence if he set a scholarly example. It is easy to use the rod as a tool of discipline; yet it is far more important to use moral inspiration, so that the student may want to learn.

His *Praise of Folly* sets forth one of the most eloquent pleas for a new educational system. Since folly dominates all aspects of society, self-examination is needed. The rich, especially, are governed by folly:

> "There is another very pleasant sort of madness whereby persons assume to themselves whatever of accomplishment they discern in others. Thus the happy rich churl in Seneca, who had so short a memory, that he could not tell the least story without a servant standing by to prompt him, and was at the same time so weak that he could scarce go upright, yet he thought he might adventure to accept a challenge to a duel, because he kept at home some lusty, sturdy fellows whose strength he relied upon instead of his own." [1]

So are professors:

> "It is almost needless to insist upon the several professors of arts and sciences, who are all so egregiously conceited, that they would sooner give up their title to an estate in lands than part with the reversion of their wits; among these, more especially stage-players, musicians, orators, and poets, each of which, the more of duncery they have, and the more of pride, the greater is their ambition: and how notoriously soever dull they be, they meet with their admirers; nay, the more silly they are the higher they are extolled; Folly (as we have before intimated) never failing of respect and esteem. If therefore every one, the more ignorant he is, the greater satisfaction he is to himself, and the more commended by others, to what purpose is it to sweat and toil in the pursuit of true learning, which shall cost so many gripes and pangs of the brain to acquire, and when obtained, shall only make the laborious student more uneasy to himself and less acceptable to others?" [2]

Nations are subject to Folly:

> "As nature in her dispensation of conceitedness has dealt with private persons, so has she given a particular snatch of self-love to each country and nation. Upon this account it is that the English challenge the prerogative of having the most handsome women, of being the most accomplished in the science of music, and of keeping the best tables. The Scotch brag of their gentility, and pretend the genius of their native soil inclines them to be good disputants. The French think themselves remarkable for complaisance and good breeding; the Sorbonists of Paris pretend before any others to have made the greatest proficiency in polemic divinity. The Italians value themselves for learning and eloquence; and like the Grecians of old, account all the world barbarians compared to themselves; to which piece of vanity the inhabitants of Rome are more especially addicted, pretending themselves to

---

[1] *In Praise of Folly*
[2] *Ibid.*

be owners of all those heroic virtues, which their city so many ages since was deservedly famous for." 3

Flattery and self-love govern man:

"But not to mention any more, I suppose you are already convinced how great an improvement and addition to the happiness of human life is occasioned by self-love; the next step to which is flattery; . . . so the same currying and humoring of others is termed flattery.

"Flattery, it is true, is now looked upon as a scandalous name, but it is by such only as mind words more than things. They are prejudiced against it upon this account, because they suppose it jostles out all truth and sincerity, whereas indeed its property is quite contrary, as appears from the examples of several brute creatures. What is more fawning than a spaniel? And yet what animal is more faithful to its master? What is more fond and loving than a tame squirrel? And yet what is more sportive and inoffensive? This little frisking creature is kept up in a cage to play withal, while lions, tigers, leopards, and such other savage emblems of rapine and cruelty are shown only for their great rarity, and otherwise yield no pleasure to their respective keepers.

"There is indeed a pernicious and destructive sort of flattery wherewith rookers and sharks work their several ends upon such as they can make a prey of, by decoying them into traps and snares beyond recovery." 4

Erasmus stated that learning should be concerned less with flattery and ornamentation, but more with the Socratic spirit. Humility, to Erasmus, is the most important trait of the scholar.

To some extent, his educational scheme was one-sided. He neglected the physical sciences and he had little regard for physical education. He was so intoxicated by the classics that he considered them as the whole substance of education.

The task of the teacher, Erasmus maintained, is to develop a Christian philosophy of education which can be understood by all:

"Other philosophies, by the very difficulty of their precepts, are removed out of the range of most minds. (But) no age, no sex, no condition of life is excluded from (comprehending the Christian philosophy of life). The sun itself is not more common and open to all than is the teaching of Christ. For I utterly dissent from those who are unwilling that the sacred Scriptures should be read by the unlearned and translated into their vulgar tongues. . . . I long that the husbandman should sing portions of them to himself as he follows the plough, that the weaver should hum them to the tune of his shuttle, that the traveller should beguile with their story the tedium of the journey." 5

3 *Ibid.*
4 *Ibid.*
5 *Ibid.*

MACHIAVELLI AND EDUCATION FOR NATIONALISM

In addition to the cosmopolitan ideal, best represented by Erasmus, we find that the Renaissance also holds the seeds of modern nationalism. As the Church weakened, the state took over. Indeed, the religious revolts were motivated, to a great extent, by nationalistic considerations. The state developed its own mythology and its own moral system. As yet, the struggle between the states was not on a world-wide basis; thus, Niccolo Machiavelli (1469-1527) takes the city-state as the fundamental unit for his discussion.

In the Renaissance, also, thinkers were more frank than the medieval scholastics in regard to the economic drives of man. Machiavelli indicates the importance of property in politics; revolutions have been brought about because of inadequate economic policies on the part of the ruler.

There was, furthermore, a frank recognition of a dual concept of morality. What was valid for the common people could not be applied to princes; what was praiseworthy in private conduct could not be applied to the state. The divine right of kings placed the king beyond the dictates of ordinary morality; in fact, what was good and right and just was determined by the ruler, not by the customs of society.

The educational ideals of power politics are best represented by Machiavelli's two main works, the *Discourses on Livy,* and *The Prince.* What strikes the reader at once is Machiavelli's secular tone. To him life was not a metaphysical process, but was determined by biology and economics. He minimized the altruistic drives of man and stressed the fact that self-interest guides the human race. According to Machiavelli, we are all egotists: we think of our own advancement before we give a thought to others.

While religious leaders pointed to love and compassion, Machiavelli regarded these traits as enfeebling. Men who are dominated by idealistic motives are usually conquered by the strong, who are without scruples. We find this same viewpoint later in Spengler, who felt that pacifism merely represented a stage of cultural disintegration and, thus, foreshadowed the death of a particular civilization.

Machiavelli was a caustic critic of the papacy. He stated that the nearer people live to Rome, the more they are inclined to be atheistic.

"We Italians then owe to the Church of Rome and to her priests our having become irreligious and bad; but we owe her a still greater debt, and one that will be the cause of our ruin, namely, that the Church has kept and still keeps our country divided. Certainly a country can never be united and happy, except when it obeys wholly one government. The Church, then, not having been powerful enough to be able to master all Italy, not having permitted any other power to do so, has been the cause why Italy has never been able to unite under one head, but has always remained under a number of princes and lords, which occasioned her so many dissensions and so much weakness that she became a prey not only to the powerful barbarians, but of whoever chose to assail her. This we other Italians owe to the Church of Rome, and to none other." [6]

Machiavelli was certain that the masses could be easily controlled. He noted that people change frequently and that their memories are short-lived. The best type of education would appeal to the lowest drives of man and would simplify all issues.

His moral, or immoral, advice to the princes was extremely penetrating. He said, for example, that a prince should not be concerned if he is called a miser.

"This niggardliness is one of those vices which enable him to reign. If it is said that Caesar attained the empire through liberality, and that a great many others have reached the highest positions through being liberal or being thought so, I would reply that you are either a prince already or else on the way to become one. In the first case, this liberality is harmful; in the second, it is certainly necessary to be considered master over Rome, but if after attaining it he had lived and had not moderated his expenses, he would have destroyed that empire. And should any one reply that there have been many princes, who have done great things with their armies, who have been thought extremely liberal, I would answer by saying that the prince may either spend his own wealth and that of his subjects or the wealth of others." [7]

It may be asked whether it is better for the prince to be feared or loved. Machiavelli replied that if a choice must be made, fear is to be preferred. A prince must not be

"thought changeable, frivolous, effeminate, timid, and irresolute; which a prince must guard against as a rock of danger, and so contrive that his actions show grandeur, spirit, gravity, and fortitude; and as to the government of his subjects, let his sentence be irrevocable, and let him adhere to his decisions so that no one may think of deceiving or cozening him." [8]

A prince should promote the arts and education and at the same time entertain the people.

"A prince must also show himself a lover of merit, give preferment to the able, and honour those who excel in every art. Moreover he must encourage his citizens to follow their callings quietly, whether in commerce, or agriculture, or any other trade that men follow, so that this one shall not refrain from improving his possessions through fear that they may be taken

---

[6] *The Discourses on Livy*, Ch. XII.

[7] *The Prince*, Ch. XVI.

[8] *Ibid.*, Ch. XIX.

from him, and that one from starting a trade for fear of taxes; but he should offer rewards to whoever does these things, and to whoever seeks in any way to improve his city or state. Besides this, he ought, at convenient seasons of the year, to keep the people occupied with festivals and shows; and as every city is divided either into guilds or into classes, he ought to pay attention to all these groups, mingle with them from time to time, and give them an example of his humanity and munificence, always upholding, however, the majesty of his dignity, which must never be allowed to fail in anything whatever." [9]

The prince, however, should not tolerate opposition. He should see to it that his opponents are eliminated. This can be done either through bribery or through forceful means. Advisers are to be encouraged to be truthful; however, they are to be reminded that, in the last analysis, the prince decides.

In every way, the prince is to be guided by expediency. Machiavelli made it clear that there are no absolute standards of morality; what should determine the conduct of the prince is the desire to maintain and expand his power. *The end justifies the means; the issue is not virtue or vice, but success or failure.*

If all else fails, Machiavelli stated, the ruler can always create a state of emergency. Thus, the opposition is silenced, at least for the moment, and the emotion of patriotism takes over. War is entirely natural and legitimate in statecraft. Armies in many cases are indispensable for national policy; they may be used both internally and externally. Machiavelli believed in the citizen army, which, he thought, would be far more reliable than the mercenaries who fought only for adequate pay and who frequently went over to the other side.

Strangely enough, there is a touch of idealism in Machiavelli. He admired the simplicity and stoicism of the ancient Romans, and he thought that a degree of public spiritedness is possible. The morality of power was to transform the character of the citizens. He appealed to the Medici at the end of the *Prince* to drive the barbarians out of Italy: "This opportunity must not, therefore, be allowed to pass, so that Italy may at length find her liberator." [10]

To Machiavelli, as to modern fascist educators, the goal of instruction was the creation of blind patriotism. The people are to be taught obedience to such a degree that they will be willing to die for the state. The prince is to determine both the content and the structure of the educational system.

---

9 *Ibid.*, Ch. XXI.
10 *Ibid.*, Ch. XXVI.

MONTAIGNE

Michel de Montaigne (1533-1592) deserves a distinguished place among the Renaissance educators. His essays have become famous, and his *Of the Education of Children* is a classic in educational literature.

According to Montaigne, life is the schoolmaster. He emphasized the value of individualism and considered faith of far less importance than reason. He wanted the whole man to be educated.

Montaigne was an indefatigable traveller. Wherever he went, he wisely noted how customs and ideals differed in various nations.

Books to Montaigne were not the primary means of education. We learn most from people, especially when our powers of observation are sharp. Often the scholar takes his field too seriously and becomes a narrow specialist. Thus, the grammarian knows only grammar, and the logician is only interested in Aristotle. Sometimes, scholarship is so enervating and tiresome that it creates anemic individuals. Knowledge will not protect us from evil, for man feels before he thinks; he is guided by passion rather than intellect.

The development of the educated man, according to Montaigne, depends on his physical excellence. Without good health the mind cannot develop. The educated man should cultivate the arts and the sciences. He must avoid puritanism like a deadly sin. This does not imply a life dedicated to sensate pleasures, but rather a sense of moderation. His morals are to be trained and developed the same way that his esthetic sensitivity is sharpened.

In regard to religion, Montaigne was loyal to its teachings, but had no fervent faith. Did not Epicurus live a good life without supernaturalism? Were not the Greek thinkers more enlightened than many scholastic philosophers? To Montaigne, man is to be guided by good sense and by a sense of proportion; religion only too often had impeded educational progress.

Learning, Montaigne maintained, must be an *active* process. Memorization should be avoided. We should travel intellectually as well as physically. Every season, every social event, every encounter with a new person can be an educative experience. Being alert and conscious of our environment we may read with more profound interest. The great author demands not imitation but critical analysis.

Montaigne exhibited a remarkably modern spirit. Avoiding the dualism of the medieval educators, he claimed that the body and the mind have the same needs. Education is not an abstract external process, but one which involves a change in our basic attitudes. The value of education, to Montaigne, is that it facilitates the full enjoyment of life.

The young man, Montaigne stated, should be taught in the following way:

"Let his conscience and virtue be eminently manifest in his speaking, and have only reason for their guide. Make him understand, that to acknowledge the error he shall discover in his own argument, though only found out by himself, is an effect of judgment and sincerity, which are the principal things he is to seek after; that obstinacy and contention are common qualities, most appearing in mean souls; that to revise and correct himself, to forsake an unjust argument in the height and heat of dispute, are rare, great, and philosophical qualities. Let him be advised; being in company, to have his eye and ear in every corner, for I find that the places of greatest honor are commonly seized upon by men that have least in them, and that the greatest fortunes are seldom accompanied with the ablest parts. . . . Let him be taught to be curious in the election and choice of his reasons, to abominate impertinence, and consequently, to affect brevity; but, above all, let him be lessoned to acquiescence and submit to truth so soon as ever he shall discover it, whether in his opponent's argument, or upon better consideration of his own; for he shall never be preferred to the chair for a mere clatter of words and syllogisms, and is no further engaged to any argument whatever, than as he shall in his own judgment approve it: nor yet is arguing a trade, where the liberty of recantation and getting off upon better thoughts, are to be sold for ready money." [11]

The world is our mirror, according to Montaigne:

"This great world which some do yet multiply as several species under one genus, is the mirror wherein we are to behold ourselves, to be able to know ourselves as we ought to do in the true bias. In short, I would have this to be the book my young gentleman should study with the most attention. So many humors, so many sects, so many judgments, opinions, laws and customs, teach us to judge aright of our own, and inform our understanding to discover its imperfection and natural infirmity, which is no trivial speculation. So many mutations of states and kingdoms, and so many turns and revolutions of public fortune, will make us wise enough to make no great wonder of our own. So many great names, so many famous victories and conquests drowned and swallowed in oblivion, render our hopes ridiculous of eternizing our names by the taking of half-a-score of light horse, or a henroost, which only derives its memory from its ruin." [12]

Knowledge and theory must be combined:

"Epicurus, in the beginning of his letter to Meniceus, says, 'That neither the youngest should refuse to philosophize, nor the oldest grow weary of it.' Who does otherwise seems tacitly to imply, that neither the time of living

[11] *Of the Education of Children.*
[12] *Ibid.*

happily is not yet come, or that it is already past. And yet, for all that, I would not have this pupil of ours imprisoned and made a slave to his book; nor would I have him given up to the morosity and melancholic humor of a sour-ill-natured pedant; I would not have his spirit cowed and subdued, by applying him to the rack, and tormenting him, as some do, fourteen or fifteen hours a day, and so make a pack-horse of him. Neither should I think it good, when, by reason of a solitary and melancholic complexion, he is discovered to be overmuch addicted to his book, to nourish that humor in him; for that renders him unfit for civil conversation, and diverts him from better employments. And how many have I seen in my time totally brutified by an immoderate thirst after knowledge? Carneades was so besotted with it, that he would not find time as so much as to comb his head or to pare his nails. Neither would I have his generous manners spoiled and corrupted by the incivility and barbarism of those of another. The French wisdom was anciently turned into proverb: 'early, but of no continuance.' And, in truth, we yet see, that nothing can be more ingenious and pleasing than the children of France; but they ordinarily deceive the hope and expectation that have been conceived of them; and grown up to be men, have nothing extraordinary or worth taking notice of: I have heard men of good understanding say, these colleges of ours to which we send our young people (and of which we have but too many) make them such animals as they are." [13]

Montaigne believed in humane discipline:

"As to the rest, this method of education ought to be carried on with a severe sweetness, quite contrary to the practice of our pedants, who, instead of tempting and alluring children to letters by apt and gentle ways, do in truth present nothing before them but rods and ferrules, horror and cruelty. Away with this violence! away with this compulsion! than which, I certainly believe nothing more dulls and degenerates a well-descended nature. If you would have him apprehend shame and chastisement, do not harden him to them: inure him to heat and cold, to wind and sun, and to dangers that he ought to despise; wean him from all effeminacy and delicacy in clothes and lodging, eating and drinking, accustom him to everything, that he may not be a Sire Paris, a carpet-knight, but a sinewy, hardy, and vigorous young man. I have ever from a child to the age wherein I now am, been of this opinion, and am still constant to it. But among other things, the strict government of most of our colleges has evermore displeased me; peradventure, they might have erred less perniciously on the indulgent side. 'Tis a real house of correction of imprisoned youth.' They are made debauched, by being punished before they are so." [14]

Montaigne almost sounds like a twentieth century educator. In his advanced system he anticipated the ideals of modern pragmatism.

---

[13] *Ibid.*
[14] *Ibid.*

EVALUATION OF HUMANIST EDUCATION

The advantage of the new system of education lay in its enthusiasm for the classics. The classical ideal represented a way of life based on moderation and the enjoyment of this world. Exact ideals of scholarship were glorified and the scholar was regarded as the leader of civilization.

But the new system also brought about the degeneration of the study of literature, a stress on empty memorization, and an emphasis on a limitation of the past.

However, in the history of humanity reformers have often become traditional, and their fervor has frequently been diminished through apparent success. Actually pedantic, many Renaissance scholars were as regressive as the scholastics whom they criticized so vigorously. On the other hand, this criticism cannot be made of educators like Montaigne and Ramus who believed in a universal scheme of instruction.

Still, the Renaissance is closer to the twentieth century than almost any age. It posed severe dilemmas which still torture modern man: What is the relationship of knowledge to morality? What is more important: general education or specific knowledge? Which is to be the center of education: science or literature? What is the relationship between intellectual and esthetic excellence? All these questions are of perennial importance in the history of education.

In order to live up to the Renaissance ideal of *virtu*, man found it necessary to develop all his interests: physical, mental, esthetic, and spiritual. Thus, there was a need for real creativity. In addition, the emphasis on self-expression and of confidence in man helped to make humanism one of the most significant movements in the history of education.

QUESTIONS FOR DISCUSSION AND INVESTIGATION

1. Give examples of the change of world view between the Middle Ages and the Renaissance.

2. Why might the Renaissance be called an age of optimism?

3. List the Italian scholars who influenced the development of the Renaissance.

4. What views did Rabelais have regarding education?

5. In what way did the Humanist scholar Erasmus help develop the scientific spirit, rationalism, and cosmopolitanism?

6. Explain how Machiavelli represents the more atheistic, nationalistic concepts. as compared to the medieval ideas.

7. What is *The Prince's* stand on education?

8. Discuss Montaigne's belief that life is the schoolmaster.

9. Explain Montaigne's assumption that knowledge and theory must be combined.

10. List the advantages and disadvantages of Humanist education.

Chapter 15

Education and the Reformation

BASIC CAUSES

It is a mistake to think that the Reformation came about suddenly. It was preceded by centuries of agitation on the part of heretical groups, such as the Waldensians and the Albigensians; the causes that produced it were economic and social as well as religious.

The Reformation coincided with the rise of a new age. Instead of feudalism there was the growth of a capitalistic economy; instead of complete domination by the aristocracy, the middle class became more and more powerful. Furthermore, the discovery of printing helped to make religious knowledge available to all. At that time, the Church was suffering from various abuses. Among them we find the immorality of the clergy, the great schisms with several contenders for the papacy, the papacy itself falling short of its high calling, and the growing materialism among the Church officials.

Intellectually, the Reformation was conditioned by new philosophies of life. The mystics, like Joachim of Fiore and Eckhart, believed in a personal approach to God, which involved the abandonment of all material desires and temporal powers of the Church. The nominalists, like Ockham, challenged the concept of universal truths. They held that only particulars are real; this meant an emphasis upon the individual worshipper, not on the Church organization. The humanists stressed the importance of man rather than of the supernatural, and, like Erasmus, were often satirical regarding scholastic doctrines. The conciliar movement tried to strengthen the democratic forces of the Church and held that church councils, rather than the pope, were supreme. Rebels, like Huss and Wycliffe, urged that the Church should go back to the simplicity of Christ, and they favored an encouragement of the nationalistic forces within Catholicism.[1]

LUTHER

Martin Luther (1483-1546), more than any other reformer, produced the new outlook in religion and education.[2] He was well educated and had a brilliant mind. Besides intelligence, he had intense moral earnestness. Since he could not stomach the sale of indulgences, he posted, in 1517, his famous ninety-five theses. Catholic doctrine held that the merit of the saints can make up for some of the sins of mankind; thus, our stay in purgatory might be shortened by indulgences. Luther, however, maintained:

"God remits guilt to no one whom He does not, at the same time, humble in all things and bring into subjection of His vicar, the priest.

The power which the pope has, in a general way, over purgatory, is just like the power which any bishop or curate has, in a special way, within his own diocese or parish.

The pope does well when he grants remission to souls (in purgatory), not by the power of the keys (which he does not possess), but by way of intercession.

They preach man (rather than God) who say that so soon as the penny jingles in the money-box, the soul flies out (of purgatory).

It is certain that when the penny jingles into the money-box, gain and avarice can be increased, but the result of the intercession of the Church is in the power of God alone.

Who knows whether all the souls in purgatory wish to be bought out of it? . . .

They will be condemned eternally, together with their teachers, who believe themselves sure of their salvation because they have letters of pardon.

Men must be on their guard against those who say that the pope's pardons are that inestimable gift of God by which man is reconciled to Him;

For these 'graces of pardon' concern only the penalties of sacramental satisfaction, and these are appointed by man.

They preach no Christian doctrine who teach that contrition is not necessary in those who intend to buy souls out of purgatory or to buy confessionalia.

Every truly repentant Christian has a right to full remission of penalty and guilt, even without letters of pardon.

Every true Christian, whether living or dead, has part in all the blessings of Christ and the Church, and this is granted him by God, even without letters of pardon."

---

[1] Cf. Flick, *The Decline of the Medieval Church,* I, 293 ff; Barnes, *The History of Western Civilization,* I, 710 ff.
[2] Cf. Thomas M. Lindsay, *History of the Reformation,* 2 vols; Preserved Smith, *The Age of the Reformation.*

The 95 theses contained subtle attacks against the papacy:

"This unbridled preaching of pardons makes it no easy matter, even for learned men, to rescue the reverence due to the pope from slander, or even from the shrewd questionings of the laity.

To wit:—'Why does not the pope empty purgatory, for the sake of holy love and of the dire need of the souls that are there, if he redeems an infinite number of souls for the sake of miserable money with which to build a Church? The former reasons would be most just; the latter is most trivial.'

Again:—'Why does not the pope, whose wealth is to-day greater than the riches of the richest, build just this one church of St. Peter with his own money, rather than with the money of poor believers?'

Again:—'What greater blessing could come to the Church than if the pope were to do a hundred times a day what he now does once, and bestow on every believer these remissions and participations?'

To repress these arguments and scruples of the laity by force alone, and not to resolve them by giving reasons, is to expose the Church and the pope to the ridicule of their enemies, and to make Christians unhappy."

As time went on Luther became more and more radical. In a treatise entitled *To the Christian Nobility of the German Nation,* he attacked the concept that the pope is superior to church councils, that spiritual power ranks above temporal power, and that no one could interpret the Bible but the pope. Luther maintained emphatically that there is no real difference between spiritual and secular power, for all Christians belonged to the *spiritual estate.* The bishops have neither special privileges nor special status; according to Luther, potentially, every man is his own priest.

Also, Luther was emphatic regarding the ability of every Christian to interpret the Bible. He could find no scriptural evidence for the claim that only the pope could interpret the holy scriptures. To appreciate the Bible we need faith and understanding, and this can be achieved by the layman as well as by the priest, by the lowly as well as by the aristocrat.

Church councils, Luther stated, do not need to be called by the pope. Thus, he showed that the Council of Nicaea was called together by the emperor. The church council ranks above the pope, and when the pope violates the laws of morality, the council has the right to depose him.

It is interesting to note Luther's attitude regarding the sacramental system. He accepted only two sacraments: the Lord's Supper and baptism. He rejected ordination, extreme unction, confirmation, and the Catholic concept of penance; also, he reinterpreted the meaning of the Lord's Supper. He objected to the Catholic doctrine of transubstantiation. Thus, the words of the priest cannot change the bread and wine into the body and blood of Christ; rather this sacrament is to be interpreted spiritually: it is to strengthen our spiritual faith in Jesus Christ. Baptism symbolizes our faith in God. By itself it has no magic validity, for only when the power of spiritual regeneration is present does it strengthen man.

The cardinal concept of Luther was his emphasis on *justification by faith,* rather than, and more important than, good works. We are not saved without complete dependence on God. Man, the fallen creature, needs God's forgiveness and mercy for salvation. The faith of Luther was emotional rather than intellectual; often he was tormented by thoughts of the devil and experienced intense temptations. Thus a certain dualism in his character persisted. However, he had complete trust in Jesus Christ, who was a visible symbol of God's concern for mankind. The atonement of Jesus had meaning for all, for it indicated that man's sins could be forgiven and that man could be reborn.

What was the standard of truth? It was not the decisions of the church councils nor the pronouncements of the church fathers; rather Luther believed in the Bible's authority. The Bible was to be the inspiration for the Christian life, the guide to God, and the aid to man's moral enlightenment. The Church, to him, was not an authoritarian hierarchy; *its head was not the pope, but Jesus Christ.* All believers are equal in the sight of God. Thus the preachers become guides rather than absolute leaders in the religious scheme of Luther.

Like St. Augustine, Luther was conscious of man's lusts and failings. Faith itself is due to God's mercy, not to man's merits. God in his own inscrutable way determines those who will receive his divine grace.

When Luther died in 1546, his denomination already had invaded most of Northern and Central Germany. It had spread to the Baltic provinces and had become well established in the Scandinavian countries.

From a social standpoint Lutheranism, at first, did not result in a liberal attitude. During the Peasants' War, Luther supported the aristocracy, and he wrote pamphlets against what he called the "thieving peasants." Furthermore, Lutheranism was willing to subordinate itself to the state, an act which did not always have constructive results in religion.

EDUCATIONAL IMPLICATIONS

Luther made an important contribution to education by translating the Bible into German. Thus, it was made available to a broader audience and became the real textbook of the German nation.

Whereas schools in the Middle Ages were controlled by the Church, Luther maintained that schools should be governed by the state. He even urged the princes of his time to force parents to send their children to school. Not only would this promote morality, but it would also add to the stability of the state.

Luther regarded the existing educational institutions as extremely inadequate. In the first place, they over-emphasized scholasticism which, to Luther, was a decadent method of philosophy. In the second place, they overrated rhetoric; this gave man an exaggerated pride of his accomplishments. In the third place, they endangered the moral development of young people. Especially, the universities, according to Luther, were "dens of iniquity."

Education, to Luther, rested upon the instruction a child received at home. The first commandment was to honor our parents. The debt we owed to them had to be clearly recognized. A wayward child had to be disciplined; otherwise, Satanic impulses would find expression and complete delinquency would result. This did not imply that the rod should be used constantly by the teacher; on the contrary, Luther urged a more humane form of discipline. All in all, inspiration was the best method of education.

In discussing the curriculum of the various schools Luther maintained that elementary schools should stress religion as well as Latin, history and music. Luther especially favored music in the curriculum, because it could inspire moral sentiments in children. The catechism, which he translated into the vernacular, was to be taught to children. Even girls were to receive some form of education, with particular emphasis on the instruction in religion.

Luther also urged a thorough reform of universities. The study of the Holy Bible was to become the core of the university curriculum. Opposed to scientific investigation, he followed the geocentric emphasis of Ptolemy. Among the subjects of study which he recommended were Latin, Greek, Hebrew, rhetoric, logic and poetry. The main aim of university education was spiritual: It was to prepare candidates for the clergy.

The educational chasm between Luther and Erasmus was deep. Erasmus was a strong believer in the classics and in independent thinking; Luther favored the role of faith and to him the Bible was the textbook for man. Unlike Erasmus, Luther had little sympathy for the learning of the ancients who, he thought, had a rather inferior system of morality.

In a letter to the Mayors and Aldermen of Germany he reminded them of the importance of education:

"It is indeed a sin and shame that we must be aroused and incited to the duty of educating our children and of considering their highest interests, whereas nature itself should move us thereto, and the example of the heathen affords us varied instruction. There is no irrational animal that does not care for and instruct its young in what they should know, except the ostrich, of which God says, She leaveth her eggs in the earth, and warmeth them in the dust; and is hardened against her young ones, as though they were not hers. And what would it avail if we possessed and performed all else, and became perfect saints, if we neglect that for which we chiefly live, namely, to care for the young? In my judgment there is no other outward offense that in the sight of God so heavily burdens the world, and deserves such heavy chastisement, as the neglect to educate children.

"Parents neglect this duty from various causes. In the first place, there are some who are so lacking in piety and uprightness that they would not do it if they could, but, like the ostrich, harden themselves against their own offspring, and do nothing for them. In the second place, the great majority of parents are unqualified for it, and do not understand how children should be brought up and taught. In the third place, even if parents were qualified and willing to do it themselves, yet on account of the other employments and household duties, they have no time for it, so that necessity requires us to have teachers for public schools, unless each parent employ a private instructor.

"Therefore it will be the duty of the mayors and councils to exercise the greatest care over the young. For since the happiness, honor, and life of the city are committed to their hands, they would be held recreant before God and the world, if they did not day and night, with all their power, seek its welfare and improvement." [3]

Languages are to be studied to frustrate the designs of the devil.

"But you say again, if we shall and must have schools, what is the use to teach Latin, Greek, Hebrew, and other liberal arts? Is it not enough to teach the Scriptures, which are necessary to salvation, in the mother tongue? To which I answer: I know, alas! that we Germans must always remain irrational brutes, as we are deservedly called by surrounding nations. But I wonder why we do not also say: of what use to us are silk, wine, spices, and other foreign articles, since we ourselves have an abundance of wine, corn, wool, flax, wood, and stone in the German states, not only for our necessities, but also for embellishment and ornament? The languages and other liberal arts, which are not only harmless, but even a greater ornament, benefit, and honor than these things, both for understanding the Holy Scriptures and carrying on the civil government, we are disposed to despise; and the foreign articles which are neither necessary nor useful, and which besides greatly impoverish us, we are unwilling to dispense with. Are we not rightly called German dunces and brutes?

"Indeed, if the languages were of no practical benefit, we ought still to feel an interest in them as a wonderful gift of God, with which he has now blessed Germany almost beyond all other lands. We do not find many instances in which Satan has fostered them through the universities and cloisters; on the contrary, these institutions have fiercely inveighed and continue to inveigh against them. For the devil scented the danger that would

---

[3] Martin Luther, *Letter to the Mayors and Aldermen of All the Cities of Germany in Behalf of Christian Schools*, translated in F. V. Painter, *Great Pedagogical Essays* (New York: American Book Company, 1905). Reprinted by permission.

threaten his kingdom, if the languages should be generally studied. But since he could not wholly prevent their cultivation, he aims at least to confine them within such narrow limits that they will of themselves decline and fall into disuse." [4]

The study of the gospel and of languages must be joined together:

"Therefore, my beloved countrymen, let us open our eyes, thank God for his precious treasure, and take pains to preserve it and to frustrate the design of Satan. For we can not deny that, although the Gospel has come and daily comes through the Holy Spirit, it has come by means of the languages, and through them must increase and be preserved. For when God wished through the apostles to spread the Gospel abroad in all the world, he gave the languages for that purpose; and by means of the Roman empire he made Latin and Greek the language of many lands, that his Gospel might speedily bear fruit far and wide. He has done the same now. For a time no one understood why God had revived the study of the languages; but now we see that it was for the sale of the Gospel, which he wished to bring to light and thereby expose and destroy the reign of Antichrist. For the same reason he gave Greece a prey to the Turks, in order that Greek scholars, driven from home and scattered abroad, might bear the Greek tongue to other countries, and thereby excite an interest in the study of languages.

"And let this be kept in mind, that we shall not preserve the Gospel without the languages. The languages are the scabbard in which the word of God is sheathed. They are the casket in which this jewel is enshrined; the cask in which this wine is kept; the chamber in which this food is stored. And, to borrow a figure from the Gospel itself, they are the baskets in which this bread and fish and fragments are preserved. If through neglect we lose the languages (which may God forbid), we shall not only lose the Gospel, but it will finally come to pass that we shall lose also the ability to speak and write either Latin or German." [5]

Finally, Luther urged the establishment of educational libraries:

"This must be taken into consideration by all who earnestly desire to see such schools established and the languages preserved in the German states; that no cost nor pains should be spared to procure good libraries in suitable buildings, especially in the large cities that are able to afford it. For if a knowledge of the Gospel and of every kind of learning is to be preserved, it must be embodied in books, as the prophets and apostles did, as I have already shown. This should be done, not only that our spiritual and civil leaders may have something to read and study, but also that good books may not be lost, and that the arts and languages may be preserved, with which God has graciously favored us.

"All the kingdoms that have been distinguished in the world have bestowed care upon this matter, and particularly the Israelites, among whom Moses was the first to begin the work, who commanded them to preserve the

---

[4] *Ibid.*
[5] *Ibid.*

book of the law in the ark of God, and put it under the care of the Levites, that any one might procure copies from them. He even commanded the king to make a copy of this book in the hands of the Levites. Among other duties God directed the Levitical priesthood to preserve and attend to the books. Afterwards Joshua increased and improved this library, as did Samuel subsequently, and David, Solomon, Isaiah, and many kings and prophets. Hence have come to us the Holy Scriptures of the Old Testament, which would not otherwise have been collected and preserved, if God had not required such diligence in regard to it." [6]

BUGENHAGEN

Johann Bugenhagen (1485-1558) was a professor at Wittenberg who made important contributions to Protestant education. He favored Latin schools as well as reading and writing schools in the vernacular. Like Luther, Bugenhagen favored religious instruction as the nucleus of education.

He urged that special schools be established for girls, who should be taught domestic science as well as the rudiments of the liberal arts.

He gave impetus to the establishment of libraries, which, he thought, would aid the cause of popular culture.

In the organization of schools he urged that they be put under the control of town councils. Fees should be charged so that buildings could be erected and teachers paid. He made it clear that only teachers of the highest moral character are to be employed.

JOHANN STURM

More humanistic than Bugenhagen was Sturm (1507-1589) who established a famous gymnasium at Strassburg. Sturm regarded Cicero as the model educator and, thus, he especially emphasized Latin and Greek literature at the gymnasium. Scholarship to him was a way of life and was best obtained through a knowledge of the classics. The organization of Sturm's gymnasium was systematic; each grade had a formal curriculum. It soon became the model for many schools in Europe and many aristocrats sent their children to Sturm's gymnasium.

CALVINISM

The outstanding theologian of the Protestant faith was John Calvin (1509-1564). He studied theology at the Sorbonne and law at Orleans. He had the opportunity to put his religious ideals into practice when he became the virtual moral dictator of Geneva. During his reign the city

---
[6] *Ibid.*

was transformed completely; it became almost as puritanical as Florence under Savonarola.[7]

The doctrines of Calvin are stated succinctly in the *Institutes of the Christian Religion*. This work systematized Protestant doctrine and presented it almost in a legal fashion.

At the outset, Calvin explains that man's main task is to glorify God. "Our wisdom, in so far as it ought to be deemed true and solid wisdom, consists almost entirely of two parts: the knowledge of God and of ourselves." [8]

Calvin made it clear that God does not have physical qualities. His essence is entirely spiritual.

"The doctrine of Scripture concerning the immensity and the spirituality of the essence of God, should have the effect not only of dissipating the wild dreams of the vulgar, but also of refuting the subtleties of a profane philosophy. One of the ancients thought he spoke shrewdly when he said that everything we see and everything we do not see is God (Seneca Praef. lib. i. Quaest. Nat.). In this way he fancied that the Divinity was transfused into every separate portion of the world. But although God, in order to keep us within the bounds of soberness, treats sparingly of his essence, still, by the two attributes which I have mentioned, he at once suppresses all gross imaginations, and checks the audacity of the human mind. His immensity surely ought to deter us from measuring him by our sense, while his spiritual nature forbids us to indulge in carnal or earthly speculation concerning him." [9]

Calvin, like St. Augustine, stresses the absolute sovereignty of God. God's will determines what is good and what is evil. This is quite different from the intellectualism which we find in Aquinas, who emphasized God's goodness rather than God's will. Calvin accepted the doctrine of the Trinity, and with vigor prosecuted Servetus, a Unitarian. God's providence includes all creatures and all regions of the universe; he is all-powerful, all-knowing, and present everywhere.

Likewise Calvin believed in the immortality of the soul. He tried to prove immortality by appealing to the force of conscience, its innate knowledge of God, its eternal capacities, its wondrous activities in sleep; above all he tried to prove it by an appeal to scripture.

Most impressive is Calvin's insistence upon man's depravity. Again and again he speaks of original sin. This depravity is part of our nature and conditions our tendency towards wickedness. Only the sacrifice of Christ gives us hope that we may be saved. However, salvation is not due to our own merit, but solely to the mercy of God. For, in reality, all of us deserve the torture of hellfire.

[7] Cf. Doumerque, *Calvin;* Harkness, *John Calvin: The Man and his Ethics.*
[8] Calvin, *Institutes of the Christian Religion*, p. 47.
[9] *Ibid.*, pp. 146-147.

Like St. Augustine, Calvin had a vivid consciousness of the devil. He believed in the existence of the devil, and that he is the author of all wickedness.

"One thing which ought to animate us to perpetual contest with the devil is, that he is everywhere called both our adversary and the adversary of God. For, if the glory of God is dear to us, as it ought to be, we ought to struggle with all our might against him who aims at the extinction of that glory. If we are animated with proper zeal to maintain the Kingdom of Christ, we must wage irreconcilable war with him who conspires its ruin. Again, if we have any anxiety about our own salvation, we ought to make no peace nor truce with him who is continually laying schemes for its destruction. But such is the character given to Satan in the third chapter of Genesis, where he is seen seducing man from his allegiance to God, that he may both deprive God of his due honour, and plunge man headlong in destruction." [10]

The church, according to Calvin, is not made up of bishops and popes, but of the elect, who appear to be in the minority. Divine law takes precedence over secular law; political officials are to be guided by the elect who shall rule in the name of God.

HISTORICAL MARKS OF CALVINISM. From a historical standpoint, Calvin's insistence upon *predestination* is most significant. This means that God predestines some men for heaven and others for hellfire. Those who are to be saved do not experience this fate because of their own actions, rather because of the inscrutable decrees of God. Like St. Augustine, Calvin believed that God's actions transcend human understanding. We can only resign ourselves to the will of God, for disobedience is a great sin.

The Bible is substantiated by the sacrifices of the saints; however it cannot be understood except through faith.

"Again, with what confidence does it become us to subscribe to a doctrine attested and confirmed by the blood of so many saints? They, when once they had embraced it, hesitated not boldly and intrepidly, and even with great alacrity, to meet death in its defence. Being transmitted to us with such an earnest spirit, who of us shall not receive it with firm and unshaken conviction? It is therefore no small proof of the authority of Scripture, that it was sealed with the blood of so many witnesses, especially when it is considered that in bearing testimony to the faith, they met death not with fanatical enthusiasm, (as erring spirits are sometimes wont to do,) but with a firm and constant, yet sober godly zeal." [11]

Calvin gave powerful impetus to the forces of puritanism. He stressed a way of life based on self-control, self-denial, and the shunning

10 *Ibid.*, pp. 204-215.
11 *Ibid.*, p. 109.

of all physical pleasures. Sexual lusts, gambling, frivolity, and all forms of luxury were to be avoided; instead sobriety, industry and frugality are to be upheld. Calvin asserted that ethical ideals are to be practiced by all. Thus, as virtual dictator of Geneva, he ordered the civil authorities to enforce a puritanical way of life. Before he came to Geneva, the citizens enjoyed a rather hedonistic way of life; under Calvin's rule, women had to give up their make-up, taverns were closed, dancing and music were censored, and drama was forbidden. Attendance at church was compulsory, and an interruption of the sermon brought punishment.

ECONOMIC ASPECTS OF CALVINISM. From an economic standpoint, the growth of Calvinism encouraged the rise of capitalism.[12] Calvin himself believed that morality should govern business relations, but some of the Calvinistic preachers glorified success, and they identified wealth and virtue. Accordingly, they taught that the rich man received his material rewards because of superior ability and moral earnestness, while the poor man was punished for his sloth.

This contrasts with the medieval ideals of poverty and rejection of all material goods. The Calvinistic businessman, however, wanted to be successful, constantly tried to increase his worldly possessions and, in this way, tried to find favor in the eyes of God. Yet he was not to enjoy his money-making activities, for enjoyment led to pride and disobedience. The Calvinists had almost an Augustinian sense of sin. They were conscious of the innumerable failings of man; again and again they showed that man could not raise himself without divine aid, and that, if he relied upon his own capacities, damnation was certain.

The doctrines of Calvin had an important influence upon the American character. The Puritans of New England reflected the teachings of the author of the *Institutes of the Christian Religion*.

EDUCATIONAL IDEALS

The educational ideals of Calvin were spread through the establishment of a gymnasium and an academy at Geneva. The gymnasium was like Sturm's school at Strassburg, except that less emphasis was placed upon the classics. The academy corresponded to a university, and it taught such subjects as physics, mathematics, logic, rhetoric, Greek, Hebrew, and ethics. Needless to say, the scientific teachings were highly traditional and were based upon deductive rather than inductive principles.

The academy had as its rector Corderius, who had been one of Calvin's teachers. Academy discipline was severe. School opened and closed with prayer. On Wednesday the student body heard a sermon, Saturday

12 Cf. Tawney, *Religion and the Rise of Capitalism.*

afternoon the catechism was studied and Sunday was given over to religious worship. Students who were inattentive or wayward were punished.

The academy was the model for early American universities, especially Harvard. It developed some of the outstanding Protestant leaders of early modern times. Its curriculum was hard, but it lacked imagination.

Calvin favored education for all in religion; the gymnasium and the academy, however, were open only to boys of superior ability. Calvin opposed higher education for women, their place was in the home and knowledge would only corrupt them.

Like Luther, Calvin believed that education was a tool against the devil who often used pagan knowledge to tempt man; it was also a form of moral discipline through which we could control our lower instincts.

The teacher, according to Calvin, has the same functions as the preacher. His task is to curb the waywardness of man and to develop patterns of absolute obedience to God. Calvin favored the use of physical punishment, for this was mild as compared with the eternal torments of hellfire. Since man is naturally evil, he had to be controlled; education had to root out the evil impulses of children.

EDWARDS AND CALVINISM

In the United States, Jonathan Edwards, one of the outstanding educators and theologians, was a strong exponent of Calvinism. Edwards believed in the reality of hell and the ineffable majesty of God.

However, in Edwards there are also softer strains which indicate the influence of Platonism. In the ultimate experience of God, intuition prevails, and we perceive God's mercy. Edwards was tender when he dealt with the saints, but extremely harsh when he criticized the actions of the sinners.

Theologically, the fame of Edwards rests, above all, on his treatise on free will. In it he showed that God's predestination moves all, and that real freedom lies not in capricious choices but in following the will of God, the beginning and end of creation.

The teachings of Calvinism spread to the Netherlands and to France, where the Huguenots endured persecution in accepting this denomination. In Scotland, John Knox defied Mary Stuart, and his influence later led to the conversion of Scotland to Calvinism. In England, the Calvinistic influence was revealed through the Puritans, Separatists, and the Presbyterians.

LIBERAL SECTS OF THE REFORMATION

The Reformation also produced radical movements, which were persecuted both by the Protestants and by the forces of the Counter-Reformation. Calvinism especially opposed the Arminians, a religious group that believed in man's free will and rejected the concept of predestination. In the United States, their theology had an important influence on the development of liberalism in education.

The Socinians believed that man is good, and not the product of original sin. They regarded Christ primarily as a teacher; they denied the doctrine of the Trinity and the concept of predestination.

More vocal and emotional than these two sects were the Anabaptists, who rejected infant baptism in favor of adult baptism. They stressed the importance of conversion, which they regarded literally as a "new" birth. Frequently they were pacifists, on many occasions, refused to take up arms. They denounced oaths; and their leaders preached a gospel of equality. Most of them had little formal education, and they were so inspired by faith in God that they were willing to endure the most cruel type of persecution.

QUAKERS. Indirectly, the Protestant Reformation also stimulated the rise of the Society of Friends. As represented by its outstanding leaders, such as John Woolman and George Fox, this group believed in the goodness of man, in complete compassion for all, and in help for the poor and underprivileged. As pacifists, the Quakers did not support any kind of warfare, rather they urged universal peace. The religion of the Quakers was unorganized; instead of ritual, they stressed silent prayer and meditation.

The religious ideal of the Quakers had wide-spread social reverberations. It tended to result in humanitarianism and social legislation, and in constant attempts to outlaw slavery and oppression in industry. These attempts have continued throughout our century. Thus, today, we find the Quakers in the vanguard of progressive causes. Wherever persecution and injustice prevail, we can find the helping hand of the Quakers, who believe that man contains within himself the seeds of God's spirit.

Their colleges, like Haverford, emphasize a liberal spirit and are open to all races. The Quaker educational ideal stresses equality and simplicity. A humane form of discipline is used by Quaker teachers who believe in the rule of love.

THE RESULTS OF THE REFORMATION

It is difficult to evaluate the long-range results of the Reformation. To some extent, they were negative; thus we find a constant multiplication of sects, a return to Biblical literalism, and a puritanism of morals, which increased the instability of Western man. Indirectly, the Reformation encouraged the forces of nationalism; for instance, the Peace of Westphalia resulted in a concept whereby the princes would decide the religion of their subjects.

It has often been remarked that Puritanism stimulated an acquisitive economy; property rights were placed above human rights, and moral obligations to the individual were often forgotten. Catholic thinkers, like Maritain, speak of the Reformation as an unfortunate incident. They feel that it impoverished the spiritual life of man and destroyed the esthetic splendor of the Middle Ages. They charge that Protestantism contributed to the chaos and split-personality of the modern mind; hence, they urge a return to the medieval unity.

However, it must not be forgotten that the Protestant Reformation had many *constructive results*. It encouraged the dignity of the individual, who could face God directly without intercession of the priesthood. It contributed to reform within the Catholic Church, which solidified its dogmas and strengthened its administrative process.

Moreover, the common man became able to take a more active part in religion. He could understand the prayers that were said, and his education was furthered by instruction by the Church authorities. Jesus, who had been a rather distant symbol of religion, became more vital and, once again, he occupied the center of Christian worship.

The liberal sects of the Reformation have often been overlooked; however, they contributed much to the emancipation of modern man. They showed that religious experience is open to all. By their rejection of original sin, they appealed to the creative drives of man, and, like the Quakers, they translated their ideals into action. Thus, they resurrected the simple spirit of Christ, and, like him, had love for their neighbor and even for their enemies.

In education, the Reformation encouraged the use of the vernacular. The basis of popular education was expanded and thus the Reformation aided the forces of democracy.

THE SPIRIT OF PROTESTANT PHILOSOPHY AND ITS RELATIONSHIP WITH CATHOLIC PHILOSOPHY

There are significant similarities as well as differences between Protestant and Catholic philosophy. Both systems emphasize that man's destiny is not fulfilled on earth, but only in the beyond. However, in Protestantism there is only a heaven and a hell, while Catholicism introduces the purgatory as an intermediate stage during which man can prepare himself for heaven.

Both systems emphasize the inadequacies of man, however Protestantism goes back to St. Augustine rather than to Aquinas; Calvinism especially emphasizes man's original sin. Both systems believe in a spiritual interpretation of the universe; this means that the world is governed by final causes. Such a view excludes a purely scientific description of nature and man. To understand man we must turn to God, and remain conscious of the final purposes of man's existence.

Both systems reject metaphysical dualism; while the devil exists, he is not on the same level as God. Evil, thus, has no reality in the cosmic scheme. Protestantism is largely based upon the Bible, it holds that the Bible can be interpreted without the intercession of the Church. Religious leadership, according to Protestantism, depends upon the call of God, not upon ecclesiastical office. This awareness of God is frequently emotional, as can be seen by the pietism which is found in the Baptists and Methodists. Furthermore, the Protestants believe that the miraculous intervention pictured in the Old and New Testaments did not continue throughout the Middle Ages. Thus, they refused to acknowledge the saints of the Church. In fact, Protestant worship was much more austere and simple than the Catholic ritual.

This austerity can be partly explained by Puritanism, a concept especially furthered by the Calvinists. Puritanism increased awareness of the temptations of sex, and created an antagonism toward all forms of luxury. The puritanical philosophy encouraged constant self-examination on the part of the individual who frequently suffered from an agonized conscience. Socially, it frequently led to an encouragement of the capitalistic virtues. In Catholicism, on the other hand, the weaknesses of the flesh were regarded with a more tolerant eye. What counted most was not man's sexual morality, but man's moral education. Thus, heresy was a more grave crime than adultery, for heresy touched man's mind, while adultery mainly affected his body.

Basically, the emphasis of Protestantism was nominalistic. The relationship between God and the individual was all-important. The individual, partly as a result of Protestantism, felt a new sense of freedom and independence. Thus, the Protestant Reformation contributed to the separation of state and church as well as to freedom of conscience. On the other hand, Catholicism depended upon a realistic epistemology; according to this viewpoint, the universal element has more reality than the individual. Salvation, thus, is achieved through the ecclesiastical institution, not through the efforts of the individual.

JESUIT EDUCATION

The ideals of Catholicism are best represented in Jesuit education. The founder of the order was St. Ignatius Loyola (1491-1556) who believed in rigorous discipline. In a work called *De Ratio Studiorum,* Loyola systematically presented the Jesuit educational ideals.

The aim of the Jesuits was to develop an educational system which was both thorough and profound. Its teachers were extremely well trained: they had to study sixteen to nineteen years before they could become instructors. Their work was constantly supervised by superiors to prevent the development of heresy.

Generally, the Jesuits were interested in secondary and higher education. The classics formed the substance of the curriculum, while the sciences played a secondary role. Repetition and memorization, as well as thorough review, were favorite teaching methods. Students were encouraged to compete with each other and intellectual excellence was recognized.

Christian doctrine was taught not just one day, but every day. It had "to be learnt by heart in all the classes." The teacher had to examine his conscience every day, and he had to be a model in his moral and spiritual virtues.

The Jesuit schools were among the best in the seventeenth century, and they have made a distinguished contribution to American education. Jesuit teachers were often the most dedicated classicists and the most inspiring philosophers. Their weakness lay in their acceptance and profession of only one viewpoint. Students who, like Voltaire, attended Jesuit schools often rebelled against their discipline. However, we should not underestimate the educational contributions of the Jesuits, for they realized that without self-discipline, creativity cannot advance. The lessons of the past must be learned if the present is to be understood and mastered.

QUESTIONS FOR DISCUSSION AND INVESTIGATION

1. Give the basic causes for the rise of the Reformation.

2. What was Luther's contribution to education and in what ways did he differ with Erasmus?

3. Compare the contributions of Bugenhagen, Sturm, and Calvin in the Protestant Movement.

4. Describe Calvin's theological stand in the Protestant faith.

5. How does one account for the spread of Calvin's educational ideals?

6. What was Jonathan Edward's version of Calvinism?

7. Explain how the Protestant Reformation stimulated the rise of the Quakers.

8. Name the negative and constructive effects of the Reformation.

9. Compare and contrast the philosophies of Protestantism and Catholicism.

10. What was the aim of Jesuits regarding education?

Chapter 16

Significance of the New Science

From an intellectual viewpoint, modern civilization probably has been conditioned most strongly by the development of science. In the Middle Ages, man's primary concern was the beyond; there was little interest in nature for its own sake. Outstanding scientists, like Roger Bacon, were frequently regarded with suspicion. Bacon thought that the new science could be combined with the old theology—in fact, that it would strengthen the dogmas of the church.[1] However, the leaders of Catholicism did not share his opinion; it followed Aristotle and Aquinas rather than endorsing an experimental approach to knowledge.

As scholasticism waned, we find a new group of scholars, impatient with tradition and determined to apply their knowledge concretely. While the Scholastics were mainly monks, the new scholars came from the middle class; they were interested in concrete matters rather than abstract theological speculations.

The emergence of strong national states created enough stability and order in order that scientific progress could be safeguarded. Wealthy princes, such as Charles II of England and the Medici of Florence, frequently patronized the new sciences.

The universe of the Renaissance expanded immeasurably. Gone was the localism of the Middle Ages; geographical discoveries produced a mass of new information; interest in alien ideas grew constantly. New concepts developed and were applied not only to the social sciences, but also to the physical world.

---

[1] The three great works of Roger Bacon are *Opus Majus, Opus Minus,* and *Opus Tertium.*

At the same time, the progress of science was facilitated through the invention of better scientific instruments. The barometer, the telescope, the microscope, and the micrometer—all contributed to the foundation of modern experimental science.

Whereas theology had been the most significant subject in the Middle Ages, mathematics now occupied the minds of men. Mathematics did not tolerate vagueness and mystical emotion; rather it upheld exact observation and a severe discipline of the human mind.

Scientists formed societies which interchanged ideas and advanced new theories. These societies often transcended national boundaries. Thus, modern science started in an atmosphere of genuine internationalism.

Progress in science left no room for the old logic. Sir Francis Bacon, for example, held Aristotelian logic to be only pseudo-knowledge based on generalizations—worth nothing in man's conquest of nature. The new knowledge was based on the observation of facts which lead to tentative conclusions. In other words, it was *inductive* rather than *deductive,* and it was motivated by doubt rather than faith.

Scientific progress also left behind the old cosmology. The heliocentric theory advanced by Copernicus meant that the earth rotated around the sun rather than the sun around the earth. The geocentric viewpoint of the Middle Ages was therefore replaced by a new perspective, which made man almost an infinitesimal creature living in infinite space and time.

Progress such as this depended to a large extent on co-operative research. While history books reveal the eminent achievements of Copernicus, Brahe, Kepler, and Newton,[2] we must not forget that their work was made possible by hundreds of unknown research workers. Standardization of knowledge and interchange of information was made possible through the invention of printing. Thus, a scientist in one country was not isolated from his colleagues, and, when successful experiments were made, they would be known almost at once in other nations.

The popular imagination caught and accepted the unbounded sweep of science. Nothing seemed impossible, nothing seemed beyond the reach of science.

BRUNO

Giordano Bruno (1548-1600) was the most characteristic exponent of the new scientific perspective.[3] Soon after he became eighteen years old,

---

2 Also we should remember the achievements of Harvey in medicine, Fracastoro in physics, and Napier in mathematics.

3 See McIntyre, *Giordano Bruno;* Frith, *Life of Bruno.*

his independent mind, as well as doubts regarding the doctrine of the Trinity, caused him to give up his life as a Dominican monk. He was suspected by Protestants and Catholics alike. His constant travels led him to England, where he had little regard for the standard of education at Oxford; later travels took him to France, Germany, and Switzerland. In 1593, he accepted a fateful offer to come to Venice, and there he died in 1600, burned at the stake for heresy.

To Bruno, the new astronomy was the guide to all philosophy and education. He scorned the miracles of the Old Testament, and compared them to the myths of Greek mythology. While his colleagues venerated Aristotle, he felt that Aristotle was a roadblock to knowledge. Bruno certainly did not believe in a physical paradise or a physical hell, and in most ways showed an amazing disregard for orthodoxy.

The keynote to his thinking was his belief in infinity. There is not one world, but an infinite number of worlds which are all unbounded: space itself is infinite.

This concept of infinity also stamps the modern mind. It is the foundation of Goethe's *Faust,* who tried to transcend the limits of his environment. Notice how this contrasts with the Greek belief in man's limitation.

Bruno was a strong proponent of pantheism: the universe and God are one. To please the theologians, probably, he distinguished between the term, *natura naturans,* when God is regarded as a cause of creation, and, *natura naturata,* when we see nature as an effect of God.

His pantheistic gospel constituted a severe danger both to Protestantism and Catholicism; if God and man are identified, what room is there for traditional religion? What happens to the sacraments? Does man need faith to be saved? No wonder that the proponents of the orthodox doctrine persecuted him so severely.

How can we conceive of God? Bruno answers that God is not a personal being, and that His attributes are transcendent. When we try to describe God according to human ideals, we detract from His dignity. Reality is beyond logic; we can only use negative terms in defining the attributes of God.

During the Middle Ages, matter was considered as a principle of negation. Disregarding this, Bruno had a dynamic concept of matter. Destruction is impossible; death involves only a transformation of material properties. This means that man is not to be ashamed of his corporeal nature, for matter and spirit go together—both are necessary.

Bruno applied his metaphysical concepts to moral education. Ignorance was the worst sin, for it led to an alienation from God and prevented the progress of society. Even when the search for knowledge is hindered by orthodoxy, man must persevere in his quest. Truth itself has metaphysical reality, for in finding the real principles of knowledge, man shares God's eternal wisdom.

Could these views be spread to all? Would they be understood by the masses? Bruno, like Averrhoes, believed that contemplative philosophy and the search for reason were only designed for the elite; the masses, on the other hand, had to depend on theology. This exclusiveness is similar to the spirit found in the Renaissance mind, which frequently felt disdain for the ideas of the common people.

Bruno himself did not regard his viewpoint as being subversive to true religion. Like Spinoza, he was awed by the majesty and infinite aspects of God; man was infinitesimal, while God was infinite. Bruno regarded the life of reason as far more significant than theological disputes. Theological controversies only lead to sterile debates and do not contribute to the advancement of man's knowledge. Reason itself has not merely a contemplative function, rather it must be applied so that man can fully explore the resources of nature.

Man's destiny, according to Bruno, is two-fold. His body is dominated by the laws of the physical world and, at death, will be transmuted into different elements. However, man's soul becomes part of God's essence; it returns to the original unity, and thus symbolizes the oneness of the universe. While the soul represents the divinity of God, the material world stands for multiplicity. Insofar, then, as man lives the life of the spirit and dedicates himself to eternal truths, he achieves a measure of immortality.

Bruno's ideas can be applied to formal education. Man should think for himself; the schoolmaster should be a model of independent thinking. The present, rather than the past, is to be the center of the curriculum.

The primary aim of education, according to Bruno, is to banish prejudice. There are no infallible masters. Neither Aristotle nor the Church fathers are to be obeyed. *Education thus implies a constant reconstruction of knowledge.*

BACON

Sir Francis Bacon lacked the imaginative power of Bruno; Bacon's approach to knowledge and education was detailed and analytical with a keen sense of reality.

In many ways, Bacon was the prototype of the Renaissance man. He believed in the pursuit of power and frequently sacrificed moral principles to achieve his goals. Thus, he was even willing to betray one of his best friends, the Earl of Essex. Bacon certainly lacked lofty idealism; he was too keen a judge of human nature to be deceived by man's ideals; inevitably, he saw the failings and shortcomings of society.

If educational progress is to prevail, Bacon stated, man had to change his attitude regarding nature, and not rely upon the past. Even the Greeks were not to be trusted, for they had shown too much interest in the principles of metaphysics. To an even lesser degree can we depend upon the scholars of the Middle Ages, for they thought that science has a subordinate function in the service of theology. The medieval theologians, according to Bacon, were dominated by dogmatism; their own desires and ideals determined their conclusions. Worst of all, the medieval theologians were constantly searching for final purposes which have no place in the sciences. Man's knowledge is limited; hence, he cannot understand the ultimate end of nature or of God.

Knowledge, Bacon stated, is not an esthetic capacity; it is to be used concretely and experimentally. Therefore, we should not make any generalizations regarding nature but rather investigate nature dispassionately and understand the laws which it obeys.

Bacon urged a separation of philosophy and theology. While theology deals with faith and rests upon the laws of God, philosophy is based upon the empirical world. The task of theology is to preserve the faith of the masses, and to contradict the claims of the atheists. Theology inevitably goes back to first principles, which, however, cannot be substantiated by rational means.

Man has two souls—one material, and one spiritual. We can understand our material soul; however, reason cannot define the spiritual soul. Metaphysically, Bacon had great sympathy for the materialism of Democritus; however, he did not extend this naturalistic concept to the existence of God.

To Bacon, as to most English thinkers, religion was more a matter of social convention than of the heart. He had no use for fervent piety; God is to be worshipped in a thoroughly rational manner. He felt that profound knowledge would lead to religion by demonstrating the order and providence of the universe. However, superficial knowledge would lead to atheism.

Bacon asserted that there cannot be absolute agreement in spiritual philosophy. Inevitably, various sects will declare that they have found the key to truth. The rational man will respect the beliefs of his neighbors, and, in the main, will be guided by the prevailing concepts of faith.

IDOLS. The kingdom of the sciences, according to Bacon, is like the kingdom of God. It can only be entered through a thorough transformation of knowledge. This concept led to his attack on so-called idols, which, he believed, prevented the full progress of society.

The first idols are those of the *tribe,* which are derived from man's social environment. Frequently, we project our own prejudices upon the universe. Knowledge, Bacon made clear, does not arise objectively, but is conditioned by the society in which we live. Hence education, religious and economic institutions, govern our thinking. For example, when we live in a Protestant country we believe that Protestantism is the only type of religion, whereas, if we were Moslems, we would feel that Islam has achieved the highest truth.

The idol of the *cave* deals with man's specific prejudices; our private experiences condition our outlook upon the universe. Some of us live in the past, for we feel that the present is an age of insecurity. Others look forward to the future, which they believe will result in a real Utopia. We have a fondness for certain personal prejudices, which can often be explained by childhood experiences.

The idol of the *market place* stands for the confusion of words. Often disputes of scholars are concerned with terminology rather than subject matter. Here Bacon lashes at theology, which was full of vague and unexamined statements. When these terms are used in science, they obscure, rather than clarify, knowledge. Thus, Bacon hinted at a reconstruction of education. If knowledge is to advance in any field, it must be based upon intellectual clarity and upon a correspondence between meaning and object.

The fourth idol is the idol of the *theatre,* which stands for the constant domination of the past. In education we are guided by tradition; we repeat the same formulas, the same ideas, and the same teachings that our ancestors did.

INVALID PHILOSOPHIES. In the main, there are three types of philosophy which are to be avoided. The first is that of Aristotle, with his misuse of logic, who fashioned the world out of 'categories.'

> "Just as dangerous is the empirical school, which is based upon a few experiments. The empirical school of philosophy gives birth to dogmas more deformed and monstrous than the Sophistical or Rational school. For it has its foundations not in the light of common notions (which though it be a faint and superficial light, is yet in a manner universal, and has reference to many things) but in the narrowness and darkness of a few experiments." [4]

Even worse is the corruption of philosophy by theology:

> "The corruption of philosophy by superstition and an admixture of theology is far more widely spread, and does the greatest harm, whether to entire systems or to their parts. For the human understanding is obnoxious to the influence of the imagination no less than to the influence of common notions. For the contentious and sophistical kind of philosophy ensnares the understanding; but this kind, being fanciful and timid and half poetical, misleads it more by flattery." [5]

[4] *Novum Organum*, LXIV.
[5] *Ibid.*, LXV.

Note that Bacon tried to make a clear distinction between faith and reason. Whenever theology intervenes in natural philosophy, regression is bound to occur. His own method of induction was founded on a careful enumeration and selection of specific facts, finally arriving at a law which governs the behavior of phenomena.

This method indicated that the philosophy of the Middle Ages was based on an invalid foundation. Did not the scholastics start with universal assumptions? Did they not misuse terms such as active reason and substantial forms? Did they not regard science as a subordinate subject?

SECULAR FOUNDATION. Bacon's scientific revolution was that he used a method based upon observation instead of *a priori* principles. In short, he gave a secular foundation to knowledge. This secular spirit is exhibited in his essay on *Studies:*

"Studies serve for delight, for ornament, and for ability. Their chief use for delight is in privateness and retiring; for ornament, is in discourse; and for ability, is in the judgment and disposition of business. For expert men can execute, and perhaps judge of particulars, one by one; but the general counsels, and the plots and marshaling of affairs, come best from those that are learned. To spend too much time in studies is sloth; to use them too much for ornament is affectation; to make judgment wholly by their rules is the humor of a scholar. They perfect nature, and are perfected by experience." [6]

Studies have a pragmatic value. They make for the full enjoyment of life.

"Crafty men condemn studies, simple men admire them, and wise men use them, for they teach not their own use; but that is a wisdom without them and above them, won by observation. Read not to contradict and confute, nor to believe and take for granted, nor to find talk and discourse, but to weigh and consider. Some books are to be read only in parts; others to be read, but not curiously; and some few to be read wholly, and with diligence and attention. Some books also may be read by deputy and extracts made of them by others; but that would be only in the less important arguments, and the meaner sort of books; else distilled books are like common distilled waters, flashy things. Reading maketh a full man, conference a ready man, and writing an exact man. And therefore, if a man write little, he had need have a present wit; and if he read little, he had need have much cunning, to seem to know that he doth not. Histories make men wise, poets witty, the mathematics subtle, natural philosophy deep, moral grave, logic and rhetoric able to contend." [7]

Bacon predicted a new type of educational system which anticipates the modern university. He suggested in the *New Atlantis* that a scientific

[6] "Of Studies."
[7] *Ibid.*

institute be founded which would cultivate inventions and promote new ideas. Its approach would be experimental; the emphasis of study would be on the present, rather than the past.

In his academic ideas, Bacon, like Peter Ramus, suggested that complex problems be taken up only after simple issues had been solved. He urged a thorough study of nature and much preferred the study of modern languages to delving into the classics.

Bacon had great respect for the work of Richard Mulcaster. As head of Saint Paul's School, Mulcaster tried to expand the bases of popular education and urged higher standards for teacher preparation. Both men considered education as man's supreme achievement.

DESCARTES

In René Descartes (1596-1650) we find a clear attempt to apply mathematical principles to education.[8] To Descartes mathematics possessed a clarity and inevitability, which made it the most important subject of inquiry. At the same time, he still labored under the influence of Scholasticism. He was brought up in a Jesuit school and regarded himself as a faithful Catholic. He felt that mathematical knowledge was not an end in itself, but that it served to demonstrate the existence of God and the orderly nature of the universe.

He envisioned a new foundation for Catholicism, which was to be based upon mathematical demonstration, not upon theological subtleties. But Descartes was unable to replace Aquinas, and his philosophy was regarded with suspicion by the Church.

His independent tone is revealed in his *Discourse on Method:*

"I revered our Theology, and aspired as much as any one to reach heaven: but being given assuredly to understand that the way is not less open to the most ignorant than to the most learned, and that the revealed truths which lead to heaven are above our comprehension, I did not presume to subject them to the impotency of my Reason; and I thought that in order competently to undertake their examination, there was need of some special help from heaven, and of being more than man.

"Of Philosophy I will say nothing, except that when I saw that it had been cultivated for many ages by the most distinguished men, and that there is not a single matter within its sphere which is not still in dispute, and nothing, therefore, which is above doubt, I did not presume to anticipate that my success would be greater in it than that of others; and further, when I considered the number of conflicting opinions touching a single matter that may be upheld by learned men, while there can be but one true, I reckoned as well-nigh all that was only probable." [9]

8 C. F. Fischer, *Descartes and His School;* Haldane, *Descartes, His Life and Times.*
9 *Discourse on Method.*

As to the other Sciences,

> "inasmuch as these borrow their principles from Philosophy, I judged
> that no solid superstructures could be reared on foundations so infirm; and
> neither the honour nor the gain held out by them was sufficient to determine
> me to their cultivation: for I was not, thank Heaven, in a condition which
> compelled me to make merchandise of Science for the bettering of my for-
> tune; and though I might not profess to scorn glory as a Cynic, I yet made
> very slight account of that honour which I hoped to acquire only through
> fictitious titles. And, in fine, of false Sciences I thought I knew the worth
> sufficiently to escape being deceived by the professions of an alchemist, the
> predictions of an astrologer, the impostures of a magician, or by the artifices
> and boasting of any of those who profess to know things of which they are
> ignorant." [10]

DOUBTS. Descartes initially doubted everything, including his own existence. When we doubt our own existence, we cannot doubt the doubting, and we become aware of the thinking process. Thus, we understand
the famous statement of Descartes, "I think, therefore, I am." This viewpoint has far-reaching consequences, not only for philosophy, but also for
religion. In the first place, it indicates a subjective bias. We start philosophy not by an investigation of nature, but by a search for the essence of
the self. This subjective tendency became especially strong in idealism;
however, it also dominates existentialism, which often denies the existence of God.

Secondly, this statement indicates that man is defined by his reason.
Voluntaristic philosophers would emphasize the opposite "I feel, therefore, I am." They detract from the rationality of the world, and affirm the
value of intuition, rather than the value of reason.

The starting point of Descartes is *man,* not God. Here again he
anticipates the main trend of modern thinking, which is based on man's
needs, rather than on the providence of God.

How do we know that God exists? Descartes resurrected the philosophical argument of Anselm. We have an idea of perfection, and this
idea would not be perfect unless it existed. Furthermore, we are finite,
and, thus, we cannot be the author of an infinite idea. Even our doubts
ultimately point to the existence of an absolute truth.

Descartes asserted that the universe is made up of three substances:
one is absolute: God; the other two, mind and matter, are relative, for
they are created by God. While God is the efficient cause of matter, he is
the *teleological* cause of mind. Mind and matter have no properties in
common; thus, we find a *dualistic* spirit in Descartes.

EDUCATIONAL VIEWS. The method of Descartes had profound consequences for education, for he maintained that valid knowledge cannot

---

[10] *Ibid.*

be achieved without the purging of all prejudices. What we want to believe should not influence our thinking; we are to be guided by reason alone, not by our hopes and desires. Descartes' scientific bent was exemplified by the rules which he made for his own conduct. He believed in the avoidance of all extremes, was not afraid to be guided by probability when absolute conclusions could not be achieved, and he adhered to those moral views approved by society. At the same time, he cultivated a sense of independence from external circumstances. Thus, conquest of the self came before the conquest of the universe; in all, he showed a Stoic spirit.

Descartes enumerates four rules for the achievement of real education.

"The *first* was never to accept anything for true which I did not clearly know to be such; that is to say, carefully to avoid precipitancy and prejudice, more in my judgment than what was presented to my mind so clearly and distinctly as to exclude all ground of doubt.

"The *second,* to divide each of the difficulties under examination into as many parts as possible, and as might be necessary for its adequate solution.

"The *third,* to conduct my thoughts in such order that, by commencing with objects the simplest and easiest to know, I might ascend by little and little, and, as it were, step by step, to the knowledge of the more complex; assigning in thought a certain order even to those objects which in their own nature do not stand in a relation of antecedence and sequence.

"And the *last,* in every case to make enumerations so complete, and reviews so general, that I might be assured that nothing was omitted." [11]

Thus, it can be seen that the system of Descartes mediated between the beliefs of the Middle Ages and the scientific viewpoint of modern times. He still believed in the value of scholastic deductions; he had faith in a personal God and in the immortality of the soul, but, through his use of mathematics and his mechanical interpretation of the universe, he prepared the way for the thorough-going scientific rationalism of Spinoza.

SPINOZA

The system of Baruch Spinoza (1632-1677) ranks among the most profound in philosophy.[12] It was Spinoza's ideal to develop a philosophy based upon mathematical deduction; reason was to encompass all aspects of the universe. He believed in the dignity of man, and, throughout his life, he emphasized *freedom of thought.*

There was immense tragedy in his life. He was excommunicated from the Jewish faith for his unorthodox religious opinions. He was

---

[11] *Discourse on Method,* Part II.

[12] Regarding Spinoza's philosophy see Caird, *Spinoza;* Martineau, *A Study of Spinoza;* Pollock, *Spinoza, His Life and Philosophy.*

charged with believing that God may have a body, that angels may be merely fictions of the imagination, and that the doctrine of immortality was not a necessary part of the Old Testament. He interpreted the Bible in a critical manner, pointing out its contradictions. He tried to disprove the reality of miracles, for he thought they negated the concept of a rational universe.

To Spinoza, religion was a very simple matter. Its basic foundation was the love of man and the love of God. He had no use for abstruse theological discussions.

Like Bacon and Hobbes, Spinoza insisted that religion should be subordinated to the state. This measure would be justified, he thought, since it would decrease religious persecution. He respected the faith of others, and he expected his opponents to have tolerance for his own viewpoint. He was certain that no group had an exclusive knowledge of truth nor an exclusive possession of God. Above all, he pointed out that beliefs are private. Thus, an individual cannot be coerced to accept certain theological doctrines. Dogmatism inevitably leads to a regression in science and education.

While Descartes was a dualist, Spinoza was a *monist*. There is only one substance, God. Substance is completely autonomous, eternal, and beyond space and time.

The relationship between God and the universe does not resemble the relationship between Jehovah and the Hebrews. Strictly speaking, there is no creation. The relationship between God and nature is entirely mathematical. We can look at nature from two viewpoints. On the one hand, when we look at nature from the perspective of God, we call it *natura naturans;* when we look at it from the perspective of man, we call it *natura naturata.* Spinoza emphasized again and again that we cannot apply any human traits to God who is beyond all human limitations. We cannot even say that God is self-conscious, for this would imply a limitation.

Like Bruno, Spinoza believed in the concept of infinity. The standard of evaluation, therefore, is the infinite, not the finite. Finite modes are contingent, while God is eternal.

There are an infinite number of attributes; however, we can know only two, thought and extension. The attributes are intermediary stages between modes and God. Modes are only aspects of the divine substance.

Spinoza vigorously denied the doctrine of free will. Everything in the universe is *determined;* the idea of free will rests upon man's ignorance, upon the belief that he can be independent of God.

In his ethical education Spinoza starts with self-preservation. Our aim, thus, is to increase our well being. The man who is guided by passions and lusts will inevitably be in bondage. Freedom is achieved through intellectual understanding and genuine education, and, above all, through the love of God.

STAGES OF KNOWLEDGE. To achieve real education, there are three stages. The first is based on opinion; in this stage no certainty can be achieved. Most people, it appears, are guided by their neighbors, and they willingly share their mutual ignorance. More important than opinion is understanding, the second stage of knowledge. Now we understand the orderly nature of the universe, and we are able to relate causes and effects. The highest stage of knowledge, however, is that of intuition; through it we look at the universe as a whole, and we transcend everything that is fragmentary and partial.

LIFE OF REASON. While the Protestant theologians emphasized the limitations of the human mind, Spinoza believed that man can have an adequate knowledge of God. By using his reason man becomes divine and he sees all things under the aspect of eternity.

The life of reason, according to Spinoza, is the life of the educated man. Reason indicates the foolishness of any subjection to envy, anger, revenge, and hatred; all these passions are irrational and tend to enslave man. Reason also indicates that we should never base our religious beliefs upon fear. The superstitious person is the most unhappy, for he is constantly afraid of the anger of God.

Reason leads to detachment. The man of true wisdom and education will not pay too much attention to the present, nor will he be disturbed by momentary reverses. So enlightened is he that he faces death unafraid and without trembling.

INTELLECTUAL LOVE. The spiritual system of Spinoza is climaxed by his concept of the intellectual love of God. This love is not based on any expectation of rewards. God, according to Spinoza, is beyond morality; He does not reward the virtuous and punish the wicked. The love of God, then, is a good in itself, for through it we transcend the finite and become part of the infinite.

When we love God we are not envious of anyone. We do not detract from the knowledge of other thinkers, for God is in all things, and His wisdom is manifested in all nations.

Spinoza, at the end of his *Ethics*, indicates how difficult the road is and how rare real education is.

> "Whence it appears, how potent is the wise man, and how much he surpasses the ignorant man, who is driven only by his lusts. For the ignorant man is not only distracted in various ways by external causes without ever gaining the true acquiescence of his spirit, but moreover lives, as it were unwitting of himself, and of God, and of things, and as soon as he ceases to suffer, ceases also to be.

> "Whereas the wise man, in so far as he is regarded as such, is scarcely at all disturbed in spirit, but, being conscious of himself, and of God, and of things, by a certain eternal necessity, never ceases to be, but always possesses true acquiescence of his spirit.

"If the way which I have pointed out as leading to this result seems exceedingly hard, it may nevertheless be discovered. Needs must it be hard, since it is so seldom found. How would it be possible, if salvation were ready to our hand, and could without great labour be found, that it should be by almost all men neglected? But all things excellent are as difficult as they are rare." [13]

It is strange to observe the reaction of later times to Spinoza. In his own century he was regarded as a subversive in religion; later, Hume attacked him most sharply. Goethe, however, found great meaning in Spinoza's philosophy. Novalis called him the God-intoxicated man; and, in our own time, Einstein regarded himself as a true follower of Spinoza. Spinoza has also exerted an immense influence upon such diverse twentieth century thinkers as Santayana and Morris Cohen.

Why does Spinoza have such great appeal to modern times? Why has his influence become so strong? In the first place, he relied upon reason, not upon revelation. He felt that man contains within himself the seeds of divinity. Secondly, he pictured a deterministic universe. Modern science, likewise, gives us a view of nature which is thoroughly law-abiding with no room for caprice and special intervention. Thirdly, he tried to get away from all anthropomorphism; God is beyond love and hatred. The man who truly loves God does not expect to be loved in return. Finally, Spinoza pictured the great advantages of the life of reason. Since modern man has lost his supernatural foundations, he seeks a substitute. In the Spinozistic life of detachment, compassion, and objectivity, man finds a perennial meaning and a foundation for tranquillity.

Spinoza made only indirect contributions to education. He showed the importance of freedom of inquiry; no system is infallible. Education, according to Spinoza, is the ability to achieve perspective and to become detached regarding one's own status in the universe.

During his lifetime he was offered a professorship at the University of Heidelberg on the condition that he would conform to the standards and beliefs of that institution. He refused because he valued intellectual independence and freedom. The aloneness of Spinoza is a symbol of the solitude which many great educators have experienced in history.

The relationship between ethics and science which Spinoza discussed is still a tortuous problem in our time. Does the scientist have a responsibility towards society? Should he be concerned about the social use of his inventions? Should he take part in political affairs? These questions are just as important today as they were in the seventeenth century. Certainly, as Spinoza realized, there can be no creative system of education in which the realm of facts and that of values are separated and in which scientists cultivate an attitude of social irresponsibility.

---

[13] *Ethics,* Part V.

QUESTIONS FOR DISCUSSION AND INVESTIGATION

1. What was the background of the Renaissance which stimulated the rise of the new science?

2. Explain Giordano Bruno's beliefs, which contributed to the new scientific perspective.

3. Describe Bruno's metaphysical concepts.

4. What were Sir Francis Bacon's ideas on the advancement of education?

5. Name and define the three types of philosophy which, according to Bacon, should be avoided.

6. Explain Bacon's revolutionary approach to knowledge.

7. How did Descartes' mathematical principles apply to education and Catholicism?

8. What profound implications does Descartes' premise of doubting have for philosophy, religion, and education?

9. What were Spinoza's basic religious and philosophic tenets?

10. Explain the importance of Spinoza's intellectual love of God.

Chapter 17

Comenius

INFLUENCES

Among the educational reformers through the ages John Comenius deserves a high place. His life history (1592-1670) was marred by persecution and he lived amidst the agonizing impact of the Thirty Years War. He was born in Nivnitz as a member of the Moravian Brethren. His early education was extremely inadequate. He entered a seminary at twenty at Herborn, Nassau to study for the ministry. A tireless traveller, he visited England and Sweden. Several years he spent in Poland where he was rector of a gymnasium. The later years of his life were spent in Amsterdam where he was active in the work of his denomination.

Among his works we find *The Great Didactic, The School of Infancy, The Gates of Tongues Unlocked, The Palace of Authors, The World of Sensible Things Pictured,* and *The Vestibule.* In all of them we find a close connection between his religious views and his educational ideals.

Among the influences which conditioned his life was his deep mystical faith. As a member of a minority group which was inspired by the ideals of Huss he felt a deep personal relationship with God. His mysticism demanded absolute dedication to religious goals. He was certain that, basically, education should have a Christian orientation, otherwise it would be a journey in vanity.

He had Utopian tendencies which were representative of the view of his times. Sir Thomas More, in *Utopia,* had pictured an ideal society in which education was cherished and in which there was no division of

property. Campanella, in *The City of the Sun,* had urged a more humane and progressive system of instruction. Johann Valentin Andrea, in
The Christian City, had spoken of an ideal commonwealth in which love
was cherished and in which education was for all. Sir Francis Bacon, in
The New Atlantis, had spoken of a scientific commonwealth.

Bacon's influence was especially strong on Comenius. Like Bacon,
Comenius believed that knowledge was power, and he stressed useful
subjects. Like Bacon, Comenius believed in progress through science
rather than through the humanities. An avid reader, Comenius enjoyed
especially the books of Plato, Cicero, Plutarch, and Quintilian. He
praised the advanced ideas of the Catholic humanist, Vives, and found
much stimulation in them. He was not a classicist; this, perhaps, was
fortunate for the advancement of education, for he was conscious of the
limitations of language training and literary studies. His guide was the
empiricism of Bacon rather than the humanism of Erasmus.

RATICH. Most directly he was influenced by Ratich (1571-1635) who
believed in the use of the vernacular and disliked compulsion in education. Ratich, who favored a system of experimental learning, was opposed to the empty memorization which prevailed in his time. Ratich
stressed the importance of student interest, and that without correct
methodology no real progress could be achieved in education.

BASIC BELIEFS

Essentially, Comenius was an optimist. While most theologians of
his time stressed man's evil and waywardness, Comenius emphasized
man's greatness. To be sure, life was a battleground between good and
evil, but he was certain that the good would prevail. Perhaps he was too
optimistic about the capacities of people to learn, for he suggested a system of pansophic education which implied that everyone should learn
everything. He looked forward to universal learning, symbolized by an
encyclopedia of knowledge to which major scholars would contribute. He
even wanted to found a college which would be a world scientific center
and a beacon of enlightenment. He not only had an abstract faith in
education, but throughout his life he wanted to actualize his ideals and
further the progress of civilization through practical action.

With his faith in the innate equality of all, Comenius tolerated no
class distinctions in education. Christianity was not an abstract ideal or a
system of theology; it demanded action based upon the faith that all human beings can participate in education. As a liberal, he did not recognize the aristocracy; class privileges had no place in a sound educational
scheme. He dreamt of a Christian Republic in which all were united
through knowledge and faith.

Some critics have seen a Platonic strain in the teachings of Comenius, for like Plato, Comenius believed in an ideal state. Unlike Plato, however, Comenius believed in equality; humanity could only progress when genuine democracy prevailed. Morality and wisdom were not the monopoly of any group, rather they belonged to all.

GOALS. The goal and aim of education, according to Comenius, is to make human beings Christ-like. This means training for life, not merely for a profession. This also implies a correspondence of action and ideal; virtue is the heart of the educative process. Comenius can be called a God-intoxicated thinker, for to him God was the beginning and the end of education.

With fervor, Comenius opposed the learning of his time. It caused snobbishness, it was impractical, and it alienated man from God. Education is mankind's hope; if rightly interpreted, it could establish a heaven on earth.

How can this goal be accomplished? How can these high ideals be put into practice? Comenius answers that education should shift from the home to the school. Students should be educated in groups. In this way, the teacher would become more influential. Exact organization and schedule was to guide school life. Teachers were to be chosen who loved scholarship and who had real regard for children.

Most schoolmasters of his time were strict disciplinarians. This attitude was deplorable, according to Comenius, who compared the child to a growing plant whose progress had to be carefully and lovingly guided.

He proposed four types of educational institutions. The first was the *School of the Mother's Knee,* which represented the training a child received at home. It was important that parents were constructive examples for their children and that religious and moral ideals were emphasized in the home. The second institution that he proposed was the *Vernacular School,* which would stress the study of the mother tongue, rather than of the classics. At the same time, the arts and science should not be neglected. The third type of school, *the Latin School,* was for the better students; it would stress Greek, Latin, and Hebrew as well as the fundamentals of science, literature and the arts. The fourth school, *University and Travel,* would create the leaders of society; this school would be for the best students who were to be encouraged to make original investigations and to explore the ideals and morals of various nations.

While Comenius believed, like his contemporaries, that the mind consists of faculties, he emphasized that knowledge is not innate, but is derived from our sense experience. This means that the student can be guided by experience and that his mind is a tablet upon which the teacher exerts a powerful influence. Mere information was not enough; what was important in the educative process was to stir the imagination of youngsters; here he anticipated the conclusions of Whitehead in *The Aims of Education*.

Comenius was influenced by Vives in his stress upon memory. He felt that practice would strengthen the child's memory and that if we established correct intellectual habits in childhood they would be of inestimable benefit in adult life. As a believer in visual impressions, he thought that object lessons would strengthen the child's intellectual life.

Like modern pragmatic educators, he stressed the importance of action. *Learn by doing* was the key to his system. We learn to write by writing, and we learn to reason by reasoning. But action alone was not enough; the critical and speculative capacities of students had to be cultivated. This was the function of reason which provided the basis for judgment.

More than any thinker of his time, Comenius stressed the interrelatedness of rational and emotional factors. The scholar who only treasured intellect would have only a minor impact upon life. On the other hand, the practical man would fail because he overlooked the importance of reason. To Comenius, learning was an unending process which demanded interest and curiosity on the part of the student.

PRINCIPLES. His educational method is summarized in nine principles which follow the order of nature.
The first principle is:

> "*Nature observes a suitable time.*—For example: a bird that wishes to multiply its species, does not set about it in winter, when everything is stiff with cold, nor in summer when everything is parched and withered by the heat; nor in autumn, when the vital force of all creatures declines with the sun's declining rays, and a new winter with hostile mien is approaching; but in spring, when the sun brings back life and strength to all. Again, the process consists of several steps. While it is yet cold the bird conceives the eggs and warms them inside its body, where they are protected from the cold; when the air grows warmer it lays them in its nest, but does not hatch them out until the warm season comes, that the tender chicks may grow accustomed to light and warmth by degrees." [1]

The schools did not follow this principle:

> "In direct opposition to this principle, a twofold error is committed in schools.
> 1. The right time for mental exercises is not chosen.
> 2. The exercises are not properly divided, so that all advance may be made through the several stages needful, without any omission. As long as the

---

[1] *The Great Didactic.*

boy is still a child he cannot be taught, because the roots of his understanding are still too deep below the surface. As soon as he becomes old, it is too
late to teach him, because the intellect and the memory are then failing . . .

"We conclude, therefore, that

1. The education of men should be commenced in the springtime of life,
that is to say, in boyhood (for boyhood is the equivalent of spring, youth
of summer, manhood of autumn, and old age of winter).

2. The morning hours are the most suitable for study (for here again the
morning is the equivalent of spring, midday of summer, the evening of
autumn, and the night of winter).

3. All the subjects that are to be learned should be arranged so as to suit the
age of the students, that nothing which is beyond their comprehension be
given them to learn." [2]

The second principle is:

"*Nature prepares the material, before she begins to give it form.*—For
example: the bird that wishes to produce a creature similar to itself first
conceives the embryo from a drop of its blood; it then prepares the nest in
which it is to lay the eggs."[3]

He emphasized that to change prevalent attitudes:

"1. Books and materials necessary for teaching be held in readiness.

2. That the understanding be first instructed in things, and then taught to
express them in language.

3. That no language be learned from a grammar, but from suitable authors.

4. That the knowledge of things precede the knowledge of their combina-
tions.

5. And that examples come before rules." [4]

The third principle is:

"*Nature chooses a fit subject to act upon, or first submits one to a
suitable treatment in order to make it fit.*—For example: a bird does not
place any object in the nest in which it sits, but an object of such a kind
that a chicken can be hatched from it; that is to say, an egg. If a small stone
or anything else falls into the nest, it throws it out as useless. But when the
process of hatching takes place, it warms the material contained in the egg,
and looks after it until the chicken makes its way out." [5]

The schools violate this principle

"not because they include the weak of intellect (for in our opinion all
the young should be admitted into the schools) but far more because:

---

2 *Ibid.*
3 *Ibid.*
4 *Ibid.*
5 *Ibid.*

1. These tender plants are not transplanted into the garden, that is to say, are not entirely entrusted to the schools, so that none, who are to be trained as men, shall be allowed to leave the workshop before their training is complete.

2. The attempt is generally made to engraft that noblest graft of knowledge, virtue and piety, too early, before the stock itself has taken root; that is to say, before the desire to learn has been excited in those who have no natural bent in that direction.

3. The side-shoots or root-suckers are not removed before the grafting takes place; that is to say, the minds are not freed from all idle tendencies by being habituated to discipline and order."

Rectification.—It is therefore desirable:

"1. That all who enter schools persevere in their studies.

2. That, before any special study is introduced, the mind of the student be prepared and made receptive of it.

3. That all obstacles be removed out of the way of schools.

'For it is of no use to give precepts,' says Seneca, 'unless the obstacles that stand in the way be removed.' " 6

The fourth principle is:

"*Nature is not confused in its operations, but in its forward progress advances distinctly from one point to another.*" 7 [This means that] "We should put off the study of Greek until Latin is mastered, since it is impossible to concentrate the mind on any one thing, when it has to busy itself with several things at once.

"That great man, Joseph Scaliger, was well aware of this. It is related of him that (perhaps on the advice of his father) he never occupied himself with more than one branch of knowledge at once, and concentrated all his energies on that one. It was owing to this that he was able to master not only fourteen languages, but also all the arts and sciences that lie within the province of man. He devoted himself to these one after the other with such success that in each subject his learning excelled that of men who had given their lives to it. And those who have tried to follow in his footsteps and imitate his method, have done so with considerable success.

"Schools, therefore, should be organized in such a manner that the scholar shall be occupied with only one object of study at any given time." 8

The fifth principle is:

"*In all the operations of nature development is from within.*—For example: in the case of the bird it is not the claws, or the feathers, or the skin that is first formed, but the inner parts; the outer parts are formed later, at the proper season.

6 *Ibid.*
7 *Ibid.*
8 *Ibid.*

"In the same way the gardener does not insert his graft into the outer bark nor into the outside layer of wood, but making an incision right into the pith, places the graft as far in as it will go." [9]

[This means that the scholar] "should first understand things and then remember them and that the teacher should be conscious of all methods of knowledge." [10]

The sixth principle is:

"*Nature, in its formative processes, begins with the universal and ends with the particular.*—For example: a bird is to be produced from an egg. It is not the head, an eye, a feather, or a claw that is first formed, but the following process takes place. The whole egg is warmed, the warmth produces movement, and this movement brings into existence a system of veins, which mark in outline the shape of the whole bird (defining the parts that are to become the head, the wings, the feet, etc.). It is not until this outline is complete that the individual parts are brought to perfection.

"An artist proceeds in the same way. He does not begin by drawing an ear, an eye, a nose, or a mouth, but first makes a charcoal sketch of the face or of the whole body. If he be satisfied that this sketch resembles the original, he paints its with light strokes of the brush, still omitting all detail. Then, finally, he puts in the light and shade, and, using a variety of colors, finishes the several parts in detail." [11] [This means:] "(i.) Each language, science or art must be first taught in its most simple elements that the student may obtain a general idea of it. (ii.) His knowledge may next be developed further by placing rules and examples before him. (iii.) Then he may be allowed to learn the subject systematically with the exceptions and irregularities; and (iv.), last of all, may be given a commentary, though only where it is absolutely necessary. For he who has thoroughly mastered a subject from the beginning will have little need of a commentary, but will soon be in the position to write one himself." [12]

The seventh principle is:

"*Nature makes no leaps, but proceeds step by step.*—It follows therefore: (i.) That all studies should be carefully graded throughout the various classes, in such a way that those that come first may prepare the way for and throw light on those that come after.

(ii.) That the time should be carefully divided, so that each year, each month, each day, and each hour may have its appointed task.

(iii.) That the division of the time and of the subjects of study should be rigidly adhered to, that nothing may be omitted or perverted." [13]

---

9 *Ibid.*

10 *Ibid.*

11 *Ibid.*

12 *Ibid.*

13 *Ibid.*

The eighth principle states:

"If nature commences anything it does not leave off until the operation is completed.—It follows therefore:

1. That he who is sent to school must be kept there until he becomes well informed, virtuous, and pious.
2. That the school must be situated in a quiet spot, far from noise and distractions.
3. That whatever has to be done, in accordance with the theme of study, must be done without any shirking.
4. That no boys, under any pretext whatever, should be allowed to stay away or to play truant." [14]

The ninth principle states:

"Nature carefully avoids obstacles and things likely to cause hurt.—For example, when a bird is hatching eggs it does not allow a cold wind, much less rain or hail to reach them. It also drives away snakes, birds of prey, etc.

"In the same way the builder, so far as is possible, keeps dry his wood, bricks, and lime, and does not allow what he has built to be destroyed or to fall down.

"So, too, the painter protects a newly-painted picture from wind, from violent heat, and from dust, and allows no hand but his own to touch it.

"The gardener also protects a young plant by a railing or by hurdles, that hares or goats may not gnaw it or root it up.

"It is therefore folly to introduce a student to controversial points when he is just beginning a subject; that is to say, to allow a mind that is mastering something new to assume an attitude of doubt. What is this but to tear up a plant that is just beginning to strike root? (Rightly does Hugo say: 'He who starts by investigating doubtful points will never enter into the temple of wisdom.') But this is exactly what takes place if the young are not protected from incorrect, intricate, and badly written books as well as from evil companions." [15]

[Schools should be careful:]
"(i.) That the scholars receive no books but those suitable for their classes.

(ii.) That these books be of such a kind that they can rightly be termed sources of wisdom, virtue, and piety.

(iii.) That neither in the school nor in its vicinity the scholars be allowed to mix with bad companions.

"If all these recommendations are observed, it is scarcely possible that schools should fail to attain their object." [16]

---

14 *Ibid.*
15 *Ibid.*
16 *Ibid.*

SOCIAL FUNCTION. To Comenius education has a social function. Love is in direct proportion to knowledge. As he states in *The Great Didactic:* "The seeds of knowledge, of virtue, and of piety are naturally implanted in us." [17] He defined man as a teachable animal. According to Comenius, education was not the acceptance of the past but the anticipation of the future. As a Utopian thinker he urged reform in government and in economics. As long as nations made war upon each other there could be little progress. He looked forward to universal books, a universal college, universal language, and universal schools.

We have today the United Nations as a platform for peace. But we are still far removed from the dream of Comenius who urged real world unity. He realized that education is always threatened by provincialism and bigotry, and that violence and ignorance anywhere threaten the advancement of humanity.

We can be molded by violence or by peace. Violence usually creates more conflicts as Comenius experienced in his own lifetime. For real education, peace is not a luxury, but a dire necessity. Only in an atmosphere of peace can knowledge triumph; only in times of peace can reason be truly cultivated. The objection may be made that war aids technology, but, usually, only weapons of destruction are furthered; the final result may be the extinction of humanity.

Comenius urged men of good-will to unite; teachers, ministers, statesmen, and merchants were to create a society based upon love and charity. The human race was to be invigorated; a truly creative concept of life was to be established. Comenius urged that more money should be spent for schools, that the best investment of society lay in great teachers, and that aids for instruction, especially text-books, should be liberally provided. Religion is to govern the school system; it is to follow Jesus, not the dictates of orthodoxy.

This was the dream of Comenius; it was ambitious and profound. He was a mystic with a vivid sense of actuality and a teacher who wanted to reform society. He realized that creative education is man's highest good.

---

[17] *Ibid.*

QUESTIONS FOR DISCUSSION AND INVESTIGATION

1. Enumerate a few life circumstances which conditioned Comenius' beliefs in education.

2. What preceding educational reformers most directly influenced Comenius and how?

3. What were Comenius' basic beliefs in religion and education?

4. What are the goals of education according to Comenius?

5. List and describe the four types of educational institutions which he proposed.

6. What important ideas did he have regarding the interrelatedness of rational and emotional factors?

7. Name and describe his nine principles on education.

8. Explain the statement that "Nature . . . begins with the universal and ends with the particular."

9. How does Comenius relate nature and education in his ninth principle?

10. Explain Comenius' belief in education as a social function.

Chapter 18

The Age of Locke

THE ENGLISH BACKGROUND

One of the most important religious organizations in Europe is the Anglican church, established by law and by the desires of Henry VIII. Since it represents a compromise it is well suited to the English temperament. The English intellectual, throughout modern times, has not inclined towards deep pious feeling. True, occasionally a man like Blake may echo the mysticism of Tauler, but Blake is an exception in the English cultural scene, where sanity and balance are more appreciated than emotional excesses.

The Church of England faced opposition by those who believed in the extremes of the Reformation. The Puritans, who represented the middle class, favored the establishment of a Calvinistic theology in England. Intensely moralistic, they protested against the dissipations of the aristocracy. The Puritans saw the evils of the world in elaborate dress, in immoral stage plays, in lewd humor, and in sexual irregularity. At the same time, the Puritans championed a democratic form of government, by which they meant government of the middle class. The aristocracy, on the other hand, as represented by men like Hobbes, stressed the divine rights of kings and the complete limitation of freedom in political and religious affairs. The policy of Charles I followed this viewpoint, and he established inquisitorial courts whose function was to eliminate heresy.

After the Glorious Revolution a religious compromise prevailed which was represented by the Articles of Toleration. John Locke's philosophy stood for the victory of a more enlightened and broad-minded attitude. There is no doubt, however, that Locke was motivated by a strong religious faith. He did not doubt the existence of God, the spiritual nature of man, and his need for immortality. Moreover, he believed in revelation. Still, the main emphasis of his thought was upon sanity and tolerance in religion.

John Locke (1632-1704) was a political liberal. Governments, according to him, are not instituted to perpetuate the rights of the ruling class; rather they are designed for the happiness and welfare of man. The contract theory of John Locke held that when the ruler became a tyrant, the people had a right to rebel. Not for a moment did John Locke favor a government of the masses, for he thought that the end of civil rule was the protection of private property.

In the eighteenth century, such a philosophy seemed to be rather radical, although in the twentieth century, it would be considered conservative. To the founders of American Independence, John Locke's *Two Treatises on Civil Government* were almost as authoritative as the Bible, for Locke provided them with a philosophical justification for the rebellion against absolutism.

LOCKE'S ENVIRONMENT

Locke is therefore one of the most important thinkers of mankind. This is not due so much to his speculative depth as to his sanity. He expressed a middle of the road spirit both in philosophy and in education.

To appreciate his educational ideals, we must examine his general philosophical concepts. Locke did not believe in the doctrine of innate ideas; the mind is a blank tablet. Nor did he accept the doctrine that man is naturally depraved; he felt that all of us have capacities for betterment and improvement. Instead of a metaphysical account of man, he looked upon life through psychological eyes. Pointing to the limitations of reason, he showed how we must be guided by experience.

Among his books are such works as *Essay Concerning Human Understanding, Two Treatises on Government,* and *Letters Concerning Toleration.* In the field of education, his most important work was *Some Thoughts Concerning Education.*

EARLY INFLUENCES. Locke was influenced especially by Montaigne who felt that the study of books was secondary to the study of mankind. Other influences include Samuel Hartlib, who had written a utopia popularizing the ideas of Comenius, William Petty, who had called for a reorganization of education in order to give recognition to the mechanical arts, and Daniel Defoe, who wanted to establish a literary academy similar to the French Academy.

Locke also felt the impact of earlier thinkers like Milton who urged the study of useful subjects and who believed in freedom of inquiry. He studied the ideas of Mulcaster who favored stress upon the vernacular and who believed that all teaching be adapted to the needs of students. Locke also studied with approval Roger Ascham's book *The School-master* which urged a humane system of discipline and improvements in the study of languages.

BELIEFS

Above all, Locke opposed the system of scholastic philosophy which still prevailed in his period. Scholasticism created generalizations without a factual basis and prevented progress in the sciences. To regard Aristotle as the master of knowledge, to revere without criticism, was an act of folly, according to Locke.

At the same time, he opposed the prevalent stress upon the humanistic curriculum. The classical languages, he maintained, had only an ornamental value; they were of little use to the gentleman of leisure and to the merchant. Likewise, he had little use for rhetoric for it created too many disputations and developed a false conceit on the part of students.

He anticipated the modern science of semantics. Again and again he reminds us that words are emotionally charged and that they should be carefully defined, if education is to advance. It is better, Locke maintained, to have a few definite ideas than to express many ideas in vague terms. An excellent stylist, he had contempt for the involved language he found so often in the philosophical and educational literature of his time.

AIMS OF EDUCATION

What is the aim of education? Locke replies that human beings should cultivate a sound mind in a sound body. Without physical health our mental accomplishments would be secondary, without a wise mind physical strength would create no lasting satisfactions. As Locke states eloquently:

"He whose mind directs not wisely will never take the right way; and he whose body is crazy and feeble will never be able to advance in it. I confess there are some men's constitutions of body and mind so vigorous, and well framed by nature that they need not much assistance from others; but by the strength of their natural genius, they are, from their cradles, carried towards what is excellent; and, by the privilege of their happy constitutions, are able to do wonders. But examples of this kind are but few; and I think I may say that of all the men we meet with, nine parts of ten are good or evil, useful or not, by their education. It is that which makes the great difference in mankind.

"I imagine the minds of children as easily turned this or that way as water itself; and though this be the principal part, and our main care should be about the inside, yet the clay cottage is not to be neglected. How necessary health is to our business and happiness, and how requisite a strong constitution, able to endure hardships and fatigue, is to one that will make any figure in the world, is too obvious to need any proof. What concerns the body and health reduces itself to these few and easily observable rules. Plenty of open air, exercise, and sleep; plain diet, no wine or strong drink, and very little or no physic; not too warm and strait clothing." [1]

Self-control is a vital element in education, according to Locke.

"The great mistake I have observed in people's breeding their children has been that this has not been taken care enough of in its due season; that the mind has not been made obedient to discipline, and pliant to reason, when at first it was most tender, most easy to be bowed. Parents being wisely ordained by nature to love their children, are very apt, if reason watch not that natural affection very warily—are apt, I say, to let it run into fondness. They love their little ones, and it is their duty: but they often with them cherish their faults too. They must not be crossed, forsooth; they must be permitted to have their wills in all things: and they being in their infancies not capable of great vices, their parents think they may safely enough indulge their little irregularities, and make themselves sport with that pretty perverseness, which they think well enough becomes that innocent age. But to a fond parent, that would not have his child corrected for a perverse trick, but excused it, saying it was a small matter, Solon very well replied: 'Aye, but custom is a great one.'" [2]

Locke favored reasoning rather than corporal punishment for children.

"This they are capable of understanding; and there is no virtue they should be excited to, nor fault they should be kept from, which I do not think they may be convinced of; but it must be by such reasons as their age and understanding are capable of, and those proposed always in very few and plain words.

"Beating is the worst, and therefore the last means to be used in the correction of children; and that only in cases of extremity, after all gentler ways have been tried, and proved unsuccessful: which, if well observed, there will be very seldom any need of blows. For, it not being to be imagined that a child will often, if ever, dispute his father's present command in any particular instance; and the father not interposing his absolute authority,

---

1 *Some Thoughts Concerning Education.*
2 *Ibid.*

in peremptory rules, concerning either childish or indifferent actions, wherein his son is to have his liberty; or concerning his learning or improvement, wherein there is no compulsion to be used: there remains only the prohibition of some vicious actions, wherein a child is capable of obstinacy, and consequently can deserve beating; and so there will be but very few occasions of that discipline to be used by any one who considers well, and orders his child's education as it should be." 3

A good teacher in Locke's system is concerned with the book of the world.

"The great work of a governor is to fashion the carriage and form the mind; to settle in his pupil good habits, and the principles of virtue and wisdom; to give him, by little and little, a view of mankind; and work him into a love and imitation of what is excellent and praiseworthy; and, in the prosecution of it, to give him vigor, activity, and industry. The studies which he sets him upon are but, as it were, the exercises of his faculties, and employment of his time, to keep him from sauntering and idleness, to teach him application, and accustom him to take pains, and to give him some little taste of what his own industry must perfect. For who expects that under a tutor a young gentleman should be an accomplished critic, orator, or logician; go to the bottom of metaphysics, natural philosophy, or mathematics; or be a master in history or chronology? though something of each of these is to be taught him: but it is only to open the door that he may look in, and, as it were, begin an acquaintance, but not to dwell there; and a governor would be much blamed that should keep his pupil too long, and lead him too far in most of them. But of good breeding, knowledge of the world, virtue, industry, and a love of reputation, he can not have too much; and if he have these, he will not long want what he needs or desires of the other." 4

A teacher should love his student.

"The great skill of a teacher is to get and keep the attention of his scholar: whilst he has that, he is sure to advance as fast as the learner's abilities will carry him; and without that, all his bustle and pother will be to little or no purpose (as much as may be) the usefulness of what he teaches him; and let him see, by what he has learned, that he can do something which he could not do before; something which gives him some power and real advantage above others, who are ignorant of it. To this he should add sweetness in all his instructions; and by a certain tenderness in his whole carriage, make the child sensible that he loves him, and designs nothing but his good; the only way to beget love in the child, which will make him hearken to his lessons, and relish what he teaches him." 5

---

3 *Ibid.*
4 *Ibid.*
5 *Ibid.*

UPPER CLASSES. According to Locke, education for the upper classes has four major goals: First, virtue, which implies a knowledge of right and wrong, thus following the dictates of conscience. Moral ideals, Locke maintained, depend on our religious training. We should study the Bible, be inspired by its lofty dictates, and follow the decrees of God.

The second concept which Locke cherished was that of wisdom. Unlike Spinoza, Locke did not believe that man could get a complete view of the universe. Wisdom was a practical rather than a theoretical activity; it meant the ability to conduct our affairs in a skillful manner and to be in control of our environment. Locke felt that most philosophers had been anti-social in their attitude, and he recommended public service as an excellent outlet for the gentleman.

The third quality which he cherished was good breeding, which is part and parcel of the English character. Good breeding implies a sense of dignity. The gentleman would be neither too proud nor too humble. His manners would be spontaneous and he would exhibit self-control under all situations.

The fourth quality which Locke favored was learning, but to him it was far less important than the others. Learning could only produce outward knowledge; what mattered was action and prudent behavior.

Locke made a clear distinction between the education of the scholar and that of a gentleman. The gentleman was to concentrate on practical matters, while the scholar would cultivate the classical languages.

LOWER CLASSES. When he discussed the education of the lower classes, he showed a limited vision. He favored a scheme whereby children of the poor are to be taken away from their parents, to be educated in working schools from ages three to fourteen. The advantage of such a plan would be its economy. Children would be disciplined, and they would not be delinquent. They should be taught simple handicrafts, and they should be encouraged in thrift and hard work. For their moral edification they would be instructed in the precepts of the Bible. At the same time, the mothers of the children would have enough time to earn a living. For the poor, Locke favored no academic learning, rather he recommended apprenticeship training which would start early in the morning and end late at night.

CURRICULUM. There has been a debate among scholars whether Locke was a mental disciplinarian. It is evident that Locke wanted education to be interesting; he disliked memorization because it presents the mind with specific facts rather than with general knowledge.

In regard to the subjects of the curriculum, Locke was especially impressed by the study of the English language. This was far more important to him than a knowledge of the classics. To speak one's mother tongue well was the first obligation of the gentleman.

He favored the study of both the physical and biological sciences. Anatomy had a special place in his educational scheme, for when we become conscious of our bodily structure we become more aware of our physical functions.

Mathematics he recommended because of its clarity and logical order. The lesson of mathematics is that we must overcome our prejudices and reason objectively. Locke believed that the progress of science would depend on the advancement of mathematics.

Geography Locke favored, because it broadens the outlook of the gentleman who thus would become more cosmopolitan in his outlook upon life. Furthermore, it stimulates our desire for adventure. For history Locke had a special fondness. It stirs our imagination and shows how the present is determined by the past. Locke was especially interested in the moralists of ancient times, like Seneca and Marcus Aurelius, who could be models for later periods.

In his discussion of the arts, Locke favored the applied rather than the fine arts. He had little use for poetry. A gentleman might enjoy painting, but Locke thought that cabinet-making and gardening might be more practical on a country estate.

GENTLEMEN. How can we distinguish between the gentleman and the ordinary man? Locke would reply that the gentleman is interested in all aspects of life; he has a broad education. He has excellent manners. The ordinary man, on the other hand, is usually a specialist in one field of endeavor and generally lacks poise.

To become a gentleman, one must, above all, control one's passions. According to Locke, man naturally is a being who likes pleasure and hates pain. Yet his reason would tell him that some pleasures should be avoided so that life could have a maximum meaning. Nothing is as important as the curbing of our desires, so that we may live like free men rather than like serfs.

This ideal of education, according to Locke, should be started in early youth. Teachers should use the method of social approval and reward those acts which are praiseworthy and punish those which are undesirable. A child does not like to be disgraced, and will therefore seek encouragement and approval from his elders. However, as Locke states, the teacher should not rely merely upon precept, but, if necessary, he should enforce obedience. Respect for authority, is the foundation of education and of civilization.

EVALUATION

The weaknesses of Locke's philosophy are apparent. He was mainly concerned with the upper classes; he had little faith in the capacities of the common man. He represented the class spirit of seventeenth century England.

Still, his work contributed to the educational emancipation of England. He destroyed the hold of humanism and scholasticism. He was influential in the spread of the sciences and in the practical application of educational ideals.

Locke asked fundamental questions regarding creativity in education. Should education produce scholars or educated individuals who were at home in the world? What is more important: virtue or learning? Should the classics or the sciences be the foundation of the curriculum? Should formal logic be stressed or should the study of mathematics be cultivated? Should the teacher emphasize obedience or freedom on the part of the student? Is general education more important than the development of specific skills?

These questions are as important in our own time as they were in Locke's period.

QUESTIONS FOR DISCUSSION AND INVESTIGATION

1. Explain the circumstances which gave rise to a compromising position on the part of the Anglican Church.

2. Why was John Locke considered to be a political liberal?

3. What philosophical concepts of Locke differed from the philosophers preceding his time?

4. Name the early influences on Locke's thinking.

5. Why did Locke reject the system of scholastic philosophy and the stress on the humanistic curriculum?

6. In what way did he anticipate the science of semantics?

7. Discuss Locke's views regarding the curriculum.

8. What were to be the four major goals for the education of the upper classes?

9. According to Locke, what is the distinction between the gentleman and the ordinary man?

10. List the negative and positive contributions of Locke's philosophy of education.

Chapter 19

Rousseau and the Education of Nature

WHATEVER IS, IS RIGHT

The assumptions of the eighteenth century mark a definite break with the medieval traditions. Humanism, still maintained, to some extent, a religious philosophy of life. However, the outlook of the eighteenth century liberals was based upon a strictly mathematical interpretation of the universe. The cornerstones of this faith were reason, progress, and peace. Reason was exemplified by the infallible nature of the natural law, progress, by man's march toward enlightenment; peace was a Utopian condition which would eventually guarantee the full development of European culture.

The liberals of the eighteenth century were too optimistic. For one thing they misunderstood the basic emotional features of life. Reason is an activity which can appeal only to a minority. Nature does not reveal eternal laws; rather it is part of the structure of indeterminacy. There is no correspondence between knowledge and virtue. The outlook of modern psychology, especially of Freudianism, underlines the power of the subconscious currents of life, which indicates that many of our cherished truths are merely rationalizations.

The God of the eighteenth century tended to be extremely staid, almost like a complacent English country gentleman who is not too concerned with the affairs of the universe. It seems, however, that the majority of people like to have a colorful and human God, who is concerned with mankind.

The religion of the Deists was immortalized by Alexander Pope in his *Essay on Man:*

> *"All are but parts of one stupendous whole,*
> *Whose body Nature is, and God the soul;*
> *That, changed through all, and yet in all the same;*
> *Great in the earth as in the ethereal frame.*
>
> .   .   .   .
>
> *As full, as perfect, in vile man that mourns,*
> *As the rapt seraph that adores and burns:*
> *To him no high, no low, no great, no small;*
> *He fills, he bounds, connects and equals all.*
>
> .   .   .   .
>
> *And spite of pride, in erring reason's spite*
> *One truth is clear, Whatever is, is right."* [1]

ROUSSEAU'S BACKGROUND

In his outlook, Pope differed greatly from Jean Jacques Rousseau (1712-1778), whose influence upon modern culture cannot be minimized. With Rousseau, modern politics, religion, and education reach their full expression.

The story of Rousseau's life is truly fantastic. Extremely unstable, he alienated many of his friends. He was subject to a split personality. On the one hand, he was extremely enlightened, and he had a keen intellect; on the other hand, he was suspicious of rational ideas and he suffered from a persecution complex. He began his career as a Calvinist, later turned towards Catholicism, and afterwards returned to Calvinism. He ended his life as a man who believed in the religion of nature, which, intolerant of denominationalism, was denounced by orthodox Protestants and Catholics alike. His philosophical reputation was not established until his middle years, when he won first prize in an essay contest held by the Academy at Dijon. In his essay Rousseau maintained that civilization had corrupted man. This caused the cynic Voltaire to reply that never before had anyone glorified savagery so much, that he was almost tempted to walk on his fours. Rousseau never had the opportunity to enjoy his literary triumphs, for he had to flee France because of his radical political ideas. He found temporary asylum in Prussia, later in Switzerland; but his enemies were well organized, and his books were burned in France as a danger to public morality.

Rousseau, in his *Confessions,* believed that he was motivated by the noblest impulses. But when we read his autobiography and become conscious of one love affair after another and of the fact that his own children were brought up in an orphanage, we cannot admire his character.

---

1 *Essay on Man.*

He married a most ignorant woman, Thérèse Le Vaseur, who could neither read nor write, and who had the standards of a woman of the streets in Paris. He married her because of his own sense of inadequacy. Naturally, his waywardness continued. Ironically enough, he celebrated the joys of married love in *La Nouvelle Heloise,* and he declared that marriage should represent an indissoluble union. Love, he maintained, is never to be taken lightly. It is to govern all of man's relations in politics, education, and social relations. But Rousseau could hate more fervently than he could love. Thus, in the most bitter terms he attacked his literary enemies, among them Voltaire.

Rousseau and Voltaire are fascinating studies, mainly because of their contrasting views of life and education. While Voltaire believed in the advantages of civilization, Rousseau stressed the benefits of primitive life. Whereas Voltaire believed in progress, Rousseau maintained that progress was an illusion and that man had been retarded with the advances of scientific knowledge. Voltaire stressed the importance of the arts and the humanities, while Rousseau felt that knowledge corrupted man and that the arts contributed to the spirit of sophistication. Education, to Voltaire, meant the cultivation of the mind, an understanding of the past so that its errors could be avoided. To Rousseau, education depended on the wisdom of the heart so that the child would not be corrupted by the false standards of society.

No wonder that Voltaire wrote to a friend that Rousseau "resembles a philosopher as a monkey resembles a man." Yet when Rousseau was attacked by the French and Swiss authorities, Voltaire defended Rousseau with the claim that freedom was an absolute good and that humanity could only advance when a diversity of ideas and a multitude of opinions were being encouraged. When the persecution of Rousseau became even more intense, Voltaire invited him to stay at his country place.

CIVILIZATION AND POLITICS

The dilemmas of civilization were described by Rousseau most eloquently in his *Discourse on the Origin of Inequality Among Men,* in which he changed the dominant ideas of French and European philosophy. Most thinkers believed that the arts and sciences had aided humanity and had been responsible for overcoming primitive superstitions. In championing the opposite viewpoint, Rousseau insisted that civilization represented a constant state of war and that it only produced a parasitical aristocracy which had enslaved the common people.

While Hobbes had maintained that the state of nature was one of war, a view echoed by Voltaire, Rousseau glorified the noble savage. In the state of nature, he maintained, man lived in peace and was unfettered by convention. He was not tortured by avarice and greed. His body was strong, for it was not infeebled by modern conveniences. The noble savage had sharp senses and thus he learned from nature. He was never bored. He needed no artificial amusements. He cultivated his intuition rather than his reason, for life was completely uncomplicated. He was in a state of serenity and at peace with nature and with himself. The noble savage, according to Rousseau, was naturally good; selfishness arose with the advancement of civilization which evaluated everything according to material standards.

Ever since Rousseau's essay, the issue of civilization has been a fundamental problem in the philosophy of history and in education. Some theorists, like Pestalozzi, believed in the natural goodness of man, and they wanted a school system which would embody a minimum of restraint. Thoreau, in the United States, believed in the return to nature, for society represented a state of organized confusion and quiet desperation. The test of a man, according to Thoreau, lay in the things he could do without. Only by simplifying his way of life could man find permanent meaning and happiness. Tolstoy in Russia studied the ideas of Rousseau and he came to the conclusion that civilization had encouraged false standards of morality and education and had developed an oppressive social system. Thus Tolstoy, like Rousseau, celebrated the joys of a simple peasant existence in which man lived close to nature and avoided the corruptions and artificialities of city life. Education, according to Tolstoy, should be based on sincerity and perfect frankness with children; there should be no artificial barriers between students and teachers, for they were to follow the dictates of their hearts rather than the shallow standards of society.

Rousseau compared the states of civilized man and his savage ancestor:

"The savage and the civilized man differ so much in the bottom of their hearts and in their inclinations, that what constitutes the supreme happiness of one would reduce the other to despair. The former breathes only peace and liberty; he desires only to live and be free from labor. Even the *ataraxia* of the Stoic falls far short of his profound indifference to every other object. Civilized man, on the other hand, is always moving, sweating, toiling and racking his brains to find still more laborious occupations; he goes on in drudgery to his last moment and even seeks death to put himself in a position to live, or renounces life to acquire immortality. He pays his court to men in power, whom he hates, and to the wealthy, whom he despises; he stops at nothing to have the honor of serving them; he is not ashamed to value himself on his own meanness and their protection; and, proud of his slavery, he speaks with disdain of those who have not the honor of sharing it. What a sight would the perplexing and envied labors of a European minister of State present to the eyes of a Caribbean! But, for him to see into the motives of all this solicitude, the words power and reputation would have to bear some meaning in his mind; he would have to know that there are men who set a value on the opinion of the rest of the world—who can be made happy and satisfied with themselves rather on the testimony of other people than on their own. In reality, the source of all these differences is, that the savage lives within himself, while the social man lives constantly outside himself, and only knows how to live in the opinion of others, so that he seems to receive the consciousness of his existence merely from the judgment of others concerning him." [2]

The conclusion is inevitable. Civilization increases the misery of the common man and develops a parasitical ruling class.

"It follows from this survey, that, as there is hardly any inequality in the state of nature, all the inequality which now prevails owes its strength and growth to the development of our faculties and the advance of the human mind, and becomes at last permanent and legitimate by the establishment of property and laws. Secondly, it follows that moral inequality, authorized by positive right alone, clashes with natural right, whenever it is not proportionate to physical inequality; a distinction which sufficiently determines what we ought to think of that species of inequality which prevails in all civilized countries, since it is plainly contrary to the law of nature, however, defined, that children should command old men, fools wise men, and that the privileged few should gorge themselves with superfluities while the starving multitude are in want of the bare necessities of life." [3]

Rousseau had a direct impact upon the French revolution, and Robespierre held him in great esteem. For Rousseau believed that revolutions were inevitable and that the common man had the right to rebel. To him property rights were unimportant. He attacked both monarchies and democracies. He charged that monarchies were usually led by incapable rulers, while democracies were dominated too much by men of wealth. He made an important distinction between the forms of government which may vary and the state which remains the same. He maintained that the state represents the general will, which is symbolic of its sovereignty and coercive power. The general will ensures continuity and cohesion. The ideas of the citizens, on the other hand, are subject to change. The doctrine of the general will gave a totalitarian slant to Rousseau's philosophy and influenced German theorists like Hegel and Treitschke who stressed the supremacy of the state. This doctrine found a ready reception in Nazi Germany which regarded the state as an absolute power superior to the interests of the individual citizens.

Rousseau encouraged the rise of nationalism. He felt that cosmopolitanism was a decadent philosophy and that it represented a false philosophy of life: Thus, he encouraged the Poles to rebel against foreign

---

[2] *Discourse on the Origin of Inequality Among Men.*
[3] *Ibid.*

rulers. It must be understood that in the eighteenth century nationalism had constructive effects. It led to educational reforms; it even increased democratic tendencies in France and Germany. In our time, however, excessive nationalism has the most destructive possibilities and it constantly creates seeds for war and universal destruction.

Albert Schweitzer maintains that, ever since the enlightenment, humanity has travelled along a false path which made its journey extremely perilous. In the enlightenment most thinkers regarded themselves as good Europeans. Voltaire believed in humanity more than in his own nation. Goethe advocated the study of comparative literature so that all forms of provincialism and national conceit could be overcome. Goethe admired Napoleon even though he had made war upon Germany. During the enlightenment, thinkers like Voltaire were actually the guardians of civilization. But Rousseau, who sensed the deficiencies of civilization and whose criticism of the weaknesses of society was admirable, went to another extreme and thus opened the door to nationalistic emotions which threaten the progress of modern man.

IDEALS

Rousseau's influence upon education in modern times is so great that, some believe, he almost accomplished a Copernican revolution in that field. We can divide the history of education into two periods: before Rousseau and after Rousseau. This is not due to the soundness of his theories, but rather to their spectacular tendencies. More than anyone before his time Rousseau championed the ideals of romanticism which he applied to education.

To appreciate Rousseau's educational ideals we should become acquainted not only with *Émile*, his masterwork, but also with his *Confessions*, *The New Heloise*, *The Social Contract*, and his essay on the *Origin of Inequality Among Men*.

As the prophet of simplicity, Rousseau believed in rural living. How calm and peaceful village life could be! How far away it was from the confusion of the big city! How virtuous were its citizens! Rousseau felt that the center of education is family life; this meant a firm husband and an acquiescent, gentle wife. The only remedy for the artificiality of city life was a return to the calmness of country living.

In all these thoughts Rousseau sounds very much like Laotse, the great Chinese thinker. Both believed in intuition; both stressed the wisdom of the heart; both trusted ignorance rather than knowledge; both reacted against city life; and both were suspicious of formal definitions. The great difference, however, is that Rousseau also glorified the emotion of nationalism and that he believed in state coercion of the citizens, while Laotse believed that the state, in any form, and patriotism were abominable inventions.

EDUCATIONAL BACKGROUND

Education in the time of Rousseau was still extremely formal. The schoolmaster was an absolute authority; memorization was encouraged and learning was notably stereotyped. Since the classics were the center of the curriculum, the sciences were slighted. Children were regarded as being naturally wayward who had to be disciplined and strictly controlled.

To be sure, there were progressive tendencies. The Jansenists urged a system of education based upon moral regeneration. Fénélon, who was enthusiastic about the possibilities of education for women, was opposed to all forms of austerity and wanted to make education as pleasant as possible. Abbé de La Salle, who had founded The Institute of the Brothers of the Christian Schools at Rouen in 1684, held such advanced ideas that the interests of the pupils rather than those of the teacher became the center of the curriculum.

In Germany, Basedow (1723-1790) had similar ideas. He believed that the poor and rich should enjoy the same education and he urged that children be taught according to their interests and outlook. He wanted better trained teachers with a humanitarian concept of life and this explains his founding of the Philanthropium at Passau.

In short, the ideas of Rousseau were part of the *Zeitgeist*, the spirit of the times. He stated these ideas in a stark form to make them dramatic. He made it clear that the beginning and end of education is not the adult, but the child; the child has his own interests and lives in his own world, and the values of children are completely different from those of adults. Society had erred in regarding its educational standards as absolutes. They were only postulates; more important than society was the individual, whose integrity should be cherished.

Rousseau, like many progressive thinkers who followed him, believed that we must start with the present in education. School is not a preparation for living; it is an exercise in living. The child, above all, must be shielded from the vices of society so that his virtues can develop.

Education can be regarded as an external process or as internal development. Like Pestalozzi, Rousseau believed that it is inward growth. We cannot impose standards; we cannot impart information mechanically; we can only develop the natural tendencies of children and excite their curiosity.

Rousseau pointed to four stages in the development of the child, who repeats the growth of the race. Till the child reaches the age of five the main emphasis should be upon *physical* activities whereby we try to harden the body of the child. Artificial conventions are to be avoided and the child is to experience life directly. In this stage the child is similar to an animal. Above all, Rousseau recommended the avoidance of rational activities, for knowledge only too often inhibits man.

The second phase, from ages five to twelve, corresponds to the *savage* state of humanity. Now the child is aware of his separate identity. Book-knowledge is to be curbed; Rousseau felt that it created pedants unfit for life. He warns teachers *not* to reason with the youngster who is to learn from experience. The keynote is "do nothing." At the same time, the child, with a natural curiosity, will start to explore the world and his surroundings, and will pick up the first elements of language, writing and reading.

The third phase of development, from ages twelve to fifteen, corresponds to the *rational* stage of humanity. Now the youngster is able to evaluate and form critical judgments. *Robinson Crusoe* should be the text for this period. The sciences, especially astronomy, agriculture, and the manual arts, are to be stressed; the child will learn by doing. Hence, the teacher should encourage manual activities. The test of the subjects studied lies in their utility; if they only had an ornamental value, Rousseau would eliminate them.

The *social* stage is from ages fifteen to twenty. Now religious concerns are dominant for adolescents, who are to be taught a system of natural religion, whereby they may find God through nature, not through orthodox theology. At the same time, they would develop a natural interest in the opposite sex. Their studies should make use of real situations, for we learn best by acting in a natural way; we become philosophers by being reflective and we develop religious ideals by acting in a charitable manner. Rousseau sounds like Kilpatrick, the famous American educator, when he says that we learn what we live in our daily existence.

Living to Rousseau implies action. As he states in *Émile:*

> "In the natural order of things, all men being equal, the vocation common to all is the state of manhood; and whoever is well trained for that, cannot fulfil badly any vocation which depends upon it. Whether my pupil be destined for the army, the church, or the bar, matters little to me. Before he can think of adopting the vocation of his parents, nature calls upon him to be a man. How to live is the business I wish to teach him. On leaving my hands he will not, I admit, be a magistrate, a soldier, or a priest; first of all he will be a man. All that a man ought to be he can be, at need, as well as any one else can. Fortune will in vain alter his position, for he will always occupy his own.
>
> "Our real study is that of the state of man. He among us who best knows how to bear the good and evil fortunes of this life is, in my opinion, the best

educated; whence it follows that true education consists less in precept than in practice. We begin to instruct ourselves when we begin to live; our education commences with the commencement of our life; our first teacher is our nurse. For this reason the word "education" had among the ancients another meaning which we no longer attach to it; it signified nutriment.

"To live is not merely to breathe, it is to act. It is to make use of our organs, of our senses, of our faculties, of all the powers which bear witness to us of our own existence." [4]

"O men, be humane! it is your highest duty; be humane to all conditions of men, to every age, to everything not alien to mankind. What higher wisdom is there for you than humanity? Love childhood; encourage its sports, its pleasures, its lovable instincts. Who among us has not at times looked back with regret to the age when a smile was continually on our lips, when the soul was always at peace? Why should we rob these little innocent creatures of the enjoyment of a time so brief, so transient, of a boon so precious, which they cannot misuse? Why will you fill with bitterness and sorrow these fleeting years which can no more return to them than to you? Do you know, you fathers, the moment when death awaits your children? Do not store up for yourselves remorse, by taking from them the brief moments nature has given them. As soon as they can appreciate the delights of existence, let them enjoy it. At whatever hour God may call them, let them not die without having tasted life at all." [5]

We must in all our endeavors reverse the current practices, according to Rousseau. Moral instruction must be negative.

"We are now within the domain of morals, and the door is open to vice. Side by side with conventionalities and duties spring up deceit and falsehood. As soon as there are things we ought not to do, we desire to hide what we ought not to have done. As soon as one interest leads us to promise, a stronger one may urge us to break the promise. Our chief concern is how to break it and still go unscathed. It is natural to find expedients; we dissemble and we utter falsehood. Unable to prevent this evil, we must nevertheless punish it. Thus the miseries of our life arise from our mistakes . . ."

"The only moral lesson suited to childhood and the most important at any age, is never to injure any one. Even the principle of doing good, if not subordinated to this, is dangerous, false, and contradictory. For who does not do good? Everybody does, even a wicked man who makes one happy at the expense of making a hundred miserable; and thence arise all our calamities. The most exalted virtues are negative." [6]

Rousseau stated that we must respect children. Words without a knowledge of things are a waste of time.

---

[4] *Émile.*

[5] *Ibid.*

[6] *Ibid.*

"Respect children, and be in no haste to judge their actions, good or evil. Let the exceptional cases show themselves such for some time before you adopt special methods of dealing with them. Let nature be long at work before you attempt to supplant her, lest you thwart her work. You say you know how precious time is, and do not wish to lose it. Do you not know that to employ it badly is to waste it still more, and that a child badly taught is farther from being wise than one not taught at all? You are troubled at seeing him spend his early years in doing nothing. What! is it nothing to be happy? Is it nothing to skip, to play, to run about all day long? Never in all his life will he be so busy as now.

"Pedagogues, who make such an imposing display of what they teach, are paid to talk in another strain than mine, but their conduct shows that they think as I do. For after all, what do they teach their pupils? Words, words, words. Among all their boasted subjects, none are selected because they are useful; such would be the sciences of things, in which these professors are unskillful." [7]

Clarity is the goal of education:

"Bear in mind always that the life and soul of my system is, not to teach the child many things, but to allow only correct and clear ideas to enter his mind. I do not care if he knows nothing, so long as he is not mistaken. To guard him from errors he might learn, I furnish his mind with truths only. Reason and judgment enter slowly; prejudices crowd in; and he must be preserved from these last. Yet if you consider science in itself, you launch upon an unfathomable and boundless sea, full of unavoidable dangers. When I see a man carried away by his love for knowledge, hastening from one alluring science to another, without knowing where to stop, I think I see a child gathering shells upon the seashore. At first he loads himself with them; then, tempted by others, he throws these away, and gathers more. At last, weighed down by so many, and no longer knowing which to choose, he ends by throwing all away, and returning empty-handed." [8]

Émile, instructed by Rousseau's concepts leads almost a utopian life.

"In a word, Émile has every virtue which affects himself. To have the social virtues as well, he only needs to know the relations which make them necessary; and this knowledge his mind is ready to receive. He considers himself independently of others, and is satisfied when others do not think of him at all. He exacts nothing from others, and never thinks of owing anything to them. He is alone in human society, and depends solely upon himself. He has the best right of all to be independent, for he is all that any one can be at his age. He has no errors but such as a human being must have; no vices but those from which no one can warrant himself exempt. He has a sound constitution, active limbs, a fair and unprejudiced mind, a heart free and

7 *Ibid.*
8 *Ibid.*

without passions. Self-love, the first and most natural of all, has scarcely manifested itself at all. Without disturbing any one's peace of mind he has led
a happy, contented life, as free as nature will allow." [9]

Real democracy is to be practiced by the teacher. Education is to be
measured by action, especially by our capacity to love and to engage in
useful endeavors.

"In a word, teach your pupil to love all men, even those who despise
them; let him not belong to any class, but be at home in all. Speak before
him of the human race with tenderness, even with pity, but never with contempt. Man, do not dishonor man!

"When the critical age approaches, bring before young people scenes
that will restrain and not excite them; give a chance to their nascent imagination by objects which, far from inflaming their senses, will repress the activity of them. Remove them from great cities where the dress and immodesty
of women will hasten and anticipate the lessons of nature, where everything
presents to their eyes pleasures which they ought to be acquainted with only
when they know how to choose them. Take them back to their first dwelling-
place, where rural simplicity lets the passions of their age develop less rapidly;
or if their taste for the arts still attaches them to the city, prevent in them,
by this taste itself, a dangerous idleness. Carefully choose their associations,
their occupations, and their pleasures; show them only touching but modest
pictures, which will move without demoralizing them, and which will nourish
their sensibilities without stirring their senses." [10]

EVALUATION

What strikes the reader are the modern tendencies of Rousseau. He
was the father of modern child psychology; he laid the foundations for a
new curriculum; he emphasized the importance of play activities; he saw
that the child must unfold from within; he knew that languages had to
be taught in a new way; and he believed that curiosity and utility are
the foundations of the curriculum.

Still, the weaknesses of his system are apparent; he restricted the
activities of teachers who are to be only minor parts of education. We
know today that firm guidance is one of the primary tasks of education
and that, if it is not exercised by teachers, it will be carried on by the
agencies of communication and the cultural mores, which will lead to
mediocre standards for the individual and society.

Furthermore, Rousseau overlooked the importance of reason. To be
sure, reason may be perverted; intellectual discipline may be overdone

---

[9] *Ibid.*
[10] *Ibid.*

and the child may be taught useless facts; still, reason is man's most glorious possession; without it he is like an animal. "I think, therefore, I am" remarked Descartes, and while reality may not be intellectual it is explored best through the resources of reason. This does not imply a separation of reason and emotion; this would be a major mistake. What is needed in a sound system of education is to make emotions rational and to intensify reason through the development of our creative drives. Of all the capacities of man reason has the most explosive potentialities; undoubtedly, Rousseau underestimated its possibilities.

There is a direct line between Rousseau, Kant and Pestalozzi; his impact on contemporary education, especially in the United States, is immense. He is the prophet of freedom and of laissez-faire, but we must realize that the freedom to be creative in education also demands a sense of responsibility and a sense of social dedication.

QUESTIONS FOR DISCUSSION AND INVESTIGATION

1. What are the assumptions of the eighteenth century which mark a definite break with the medieval traditions?

2. Discuss the view of God during the eighteenth century.

3. Give a brief account of Rousseau's life.

4. Contrast the views of Rousseau and Voltaire.

5. What are Rousseau's beliefs regarding the noble savage and civilization?

6. Explain Rousseau's impact on the French Revolution.

7. What aspects of his beliefs constituted a revolutionary approach in the field of education?

8. Describe the educational background in Rousseau's time.

9. Point out the utopian tendencies which one might discover in reading *Émile*.

10. Describe the positive and negative contributions of Rousseau in the educational field.

Chapter 20

The Philosophy of Idealism

BASIC ASSUMPTIONS

The philosophy of idealism accepted a law-abiding universe, which depended on the perception of the human mind. It was a universe which was friendly to human wishes, which promoted the good, and which ultimately destroyed the evil. The God of idealism lacked the awe-inspiring sovereignty of Calvin's deity.

According to idealistic philosophers, evil is not ultimate, nor does it have metaphysical reality; it is usually identified with man's lower drives, with hedonism, whereby man abandons himself to sensuous cravings. From an intellectual standpoint, they often traced evil to materialistic philosophy. Generally, an optimistic tone prevails in idealism. This faith, so strongly expressed by Leibniz, emerges again in Hegel, who thought that in his time governmental and social institutions had reached real perfection.

Most idealists of early modern times were tender-minded. They felt that man possessed free will, that he could make intelligent choices, and that he had infinite capacity for self-improvement. Whereas in the twentieth century we often see life as a chaotic and disorderly process, the idealists saw life as rational, and they obeyed the laws of the intellect. No wonder that Schopenhauer's philosophy caused so much opposition, for Schopenhauer announced that the will, the principle of reality, does not obey the dictates of reason, but is a blind and irrational force.

265

Generally, the idealists stressed the dignity of the individual. However, in absolute idealism the collective group was emphasized, and this tendency had a marked influence upon the development of Marxism.

In regard to science, the idealists had a rather condescending attitude. They were certain that science was not the key to ultimate truth, and that it only pictured cause-and-effect relationships.

There are two types of idealism in modern philosophy. One is subjective and it is represented by Berkeley, who maintained *that to be is to be perceived*. The other type of idealism is represented by Hegel in his *Phenomenology of Mind*. Hegel, a philosopher at the University of Berlin, asserted that the *rational is real and the real is rational*. To Hegel, life and history represent the unfolding of the absolute. His twentieth century followers, like Croce and Gentile, stress the importance of history which to them has both a transcendental and an empirical reality.

In their ethical theory, the idealists tend to emphasize that *moral laws are absolute*. This viewpoint is best represented in Kant's *Critique of Practical Reason*. Kant held that every person is to be regarded as an end in himself, that moral laws could be universalized, and that our sense of duty is innate. Kant was interested in the motives of behavior, and he believed that, without good will, genuine moral action was not possible.

In their religious philosophy, the idealists tend to be conservative. Most idealist philosophers were Protestants, and thus they stressed the importance of faith. They were more interested in the practical application of religion than in abstruse problems of theology. A more liberal version of idealism can be found in Adler's "Ethical Culture" movement.

Probably the best representation of the esthetic concepts of idealism can be found in Schopenhauer's *World As Will and Idea*. Schopenhauer held that in ordinary existence, we are tortured by passions and irrational feelings, but in esthetic apprehension, we rise beyond the immediate, and we become disinterested and objective. *"Art,"* he maintained, *"is concerned with universal forms"* and like Plato, he spoke of ideas which go beyond temporal existence. The highest form of art, according to Schopenhauer, is music. "Its values form a direct contact with reality. That music acts directly upon the will . . . may be explained from the fact that, unlike all the other arts, it does not express the Ideas or grades of the objectification of the will, but directly the *will* itself." [1]

In their social views, idealists are usually conservatives. Hegel, in his defense of absolutism, is an excellent representative of this tendency. Hegel maintained that the best system of government was an absolute monarchy, that the community was superior to the individual, and that

---

[1] *The World as Will and Idea*, iii, p. 232.

freedom was less important than discipline. Hegel has been very much admired by totalitarian nations who have stressed the sovereignty and supremacy of the state. However, to be fair to idealism, it should be pointed out that some idealists, like Froebel, had very liberal ideas in philosophy and education, and that they contributed greatly to the progressive movements of our time.

LEIBNIZ

The idealistic spirit is well represented by the philosophy of Gottfried von Leibniz (1646-1716), who was unusually talented both in philosophy and mathematics, and who, already as a boy, showed great genius.[2] Among his works we find *Monadology, Discourses on Metaphysics, New System of Nature, Principles of Nature and Grace, New Essays,* and *The Theodicy.*

In his theory of knowledge he made a sharp distinction between universal truths which have eternal validity and which are prior to experience, and the truths of experience which are contingent. The truths of reason depend upon the principle of contradiction, while empirical truths rely upon the principle of sufficient reason.

Leibniz believed in the principle of *pluralism* in metaphysics; thus instead of one substance, as in Spinoza, there are an infinite number of substances. Behind the substances he found not inert matter, but force; spirituality is at the very heart of the universe. The basic force-centers, Leibniz called *Monads.*

According to Leibniz, these Monads do not interact with each other. They exist in complete isolation, yet each mirrors the universe. How are the Monads unified? How do they represent the world so completely? Leibniz's answer is the principle of *pre-established harmony.*

The philosophy of Leibniz was bolstered by his confidence that God exists. Essentially, he used four arguments to prove the existence of the Supreme Being. The first proof is ontological. Leibniz believed that the concept of the greatest being necessitates existence, and that God as the subject of perfection must exist.

The second proof was based on the cosmological argument. In the universe contingency prevails, but contingency depends upon necessity. We need a necessary cause and that cause is God. The third proof is derived from the nature of eternal truth. The laws of mathematics, according to Leibniz, are beyond contingency. For example, the statement 'four times five is twenty' is true regardless of any empirical exemplification of this law. Now, eternal truth must be contained in an eternal

---

[2] Cf. Russell, *The Philosophy of Leibniz;* Dewey, *Leibniz's New Essays.*

mind: God. The fourth proof is derived from the teleological argument. That the Monads mirror the universe so perfectly cannot be accidental: It requires the pre-established harmony of the Monad of Monads: God.

Leibniz points out that there is only one God, and He is the source both of possibility and of necessity.

Famous is the optimism of Leibniz, who stated that this is the best of all possible worlds. If it were a perfect world, man could have no free will. Our world is suited to our desires and appetites. Naturally, the pessimists of the nineteenth century sharply attacked this statement; Schopenhauer even commented that this is the worst of all possible worlds. Already during Leibniz's lifetime, his optimism had been satirized by Voltaire in *Candide*.

The optimism of Leibniz is not accidental. As we have seen, it is part and parcel of the idealistic spirit, for the idealist feels that he must justify God's ways with man, and, if possible, try to give a rational explanation for the existence of the evils in the universe.

EDUCATION. Leibniz was interested in the promotion of science, and he thought that mathematics was a model for education. He wanted definite ideas in education, not vague Aristotelianism. He felt that reason was the best tool of reform and that, eventually, it would create a new culture.

Leibniz divided education into four parts. The first part he compared with the domestication of animals, for the young child has to be disciplined. Until the pupil is six, Latin, the vernacular, and basic history should be the substance of his education; then, from age six to twelve, the pupil should attend public school and learn history, mathematics, the sciences, music, and also physical education. From age twelve to eighteen, the youngster should attend a university, provided he has scholastic ability. Now, the classical languages, French, Italian, Hebrew, as well as dramatics are important. The fourth period would start at age eighteen, or in some cases at age twenty, and it should center upon travel to other nations.

In regard to teaching, Leibniz stressed the importance of habit as well as the significance of interest. He even advocated the use of visual material. "To learn by playing" was one of his favorite phrases which he used in his *Methodus nova discendoe docendoeque jurisprudentioe,* one of the important treatises on education in early modern times.

KANT

Immanuel Kant (1724-1804) expressed his idealism in a more critical manner than did Leibniz. Kant's background reflected an early pietistic upbringing. His parents were devout Christians, and they educated their child in the fundamentals of religion. While his intellect might have questioned his early faith, his emotions were never emancipated from it.

Among the main intellectual influences which had left their mark on Kant were Rousseau, Newton, the Leibnizian-Wolffian philosophy, and David Hume. He was especially indebted to Rousseau, because the latter championed the dignity of man, preached a philosophy based on feeling, and, like Kant, developed educational ideals based on faith.

Newton influenced Kant as a model scientific thinker. What Newton had done for the physical sciences, Kant wanted to accomplish for philosophy.

The Leibnizian-Wolffian philosophy supplied the technical setting for Kant. Like Leibniz and Wolff, he was interested not in the content of experience, but in the invariable forms of experience.

Hume awoke him from his dogmatic slumber. When Hume challenged the principle of causality, Kant had to re-examine the rationalistic foundations of knowledge, and his critical method was an attempt to mediate between empiricism and rationalism.[3]

Among the important books of Kant are *Prolegomena to Any Future Metaphysics, Critique of Pure Reason, Critique of Practical Reason* and *Critique of Judgment.* From the standpoint of education, we should especially note his *Pedagogy.*[4]

Kant approached philosophy from an epistemological standpoint; hence, he was primarily concerned with the problem of knowledge. He made it clear that the objects do not exist by themselves, but are determined by our *cognition.* His philosophy is called transcendental; this means that it deals not with the content of phenomena, but with the *a priori* knowledge which we have of them. Before we proceed, let us make a clear distinction between *a priori* and *a posteriori* knowledge. *A priori* knowledge occurs prior to experience, whereas *a posteriori* knowledge depends upon experience.

In addition, Kant made a distinction between analytical and synthetic judgments. In analytical judgments the predicate is implied by the subject; for example, the triangle contains three angles. Analytical judgments do not add anything new to our knowledge. However, in synthetic judgments the predicate is not contained in the subject, and, thus, they add new factors to our knowledge.

Kant showed that science and metaphysics depend upon the validity of *synthetic a priori* judgments. This is illustrated, for example, by the

---

[3] Cf. Caird, *The Philosophy of Kant;* Ward, *A Study of Kant;* Wenley, *Kant and his Philosophical Revolution;* Saenger, *Kants Lehre vom Glauben;* Schweitzer, *Die Religionsphilosophie Kants.*

[4] Among Kant's minor works we find *Dreams of a Spirit Seer* and *De mundi sensibilis atque intelligibilis forma et principiis.*

law of gravity. Incidentally, Kant maintained that synthetic a priori judgments have a different validity in the physical and natural sciences than in metaphysics; in the latter they should be used with caution and as mere postulates.

We can sketch only briefly the stages of Kant's system of knowledge as a prelude to his educational theory. In the *Transcendental Esthetic* he shows that space and time are *a priori* forms of intuition; we would call them forms of perception. This means that our perception of the external world comes in an orderly spatial and temporal manner. However, he made it clear that space and time cannot be applied to God, and are only valid within the realm of phenomena.

The understanding, Kant explains in the *Transcendental Analytic,* depends upon four kinds of categories: quantity, quality, relation, and modality. *Quantity* is subdivided into unity, plurality, and totality. *Quality* contains reality, negation, and limitation. *Relation* is subdivided into substance, cause, and reciprocity; *modality* contains the categories of possibility, existence, and necessity. These categories are not based on experience but are *a priori*. Still, these categories cannot be applied to God; thus, we cannot speak of God as a substance, and we cannot treat the concept of God according to the categories of causality.

The concept of the self is made possible by postulating the transcendental unity of apperception. This means that we are conscious of our own existence, and that the self is not merely a bundle of sensations.

Yet, reason tries to transcend the understanding, and it attempts to achieve a view of totality. Thus, three Ideas result, dealing with 1. the universe as a whole, 2. the soul, and 3. God.

When we reason about the universe as a totality, contradictions or antinomies result. There are four antinomies: the first deals with the possibility of creation. The thesis holds that the world must be created in time, and be contained in finite space. The antithesis states that the world is infinite and eternal. The second antinomy deals with the indivisibility of the universe. The thesis maintains that the world is divisible into parts which are ultimately irreducible, while the antithesis states that the world can be divided indefinitely. The third antinomy treats the problem of freedom. The thesis maintains freedom, while the antithesis upholds necessity. The fourth antinomy deals with the problem of the creator. The thesis holds that there is a necessary force which has created the universe, and which is the cause of the universe. The antithesis maintains that no necessary being exists.

Kant pointed out that our reason is unable to deal adequately with these paradoxes. Regarding the possibility of freedom, he tried to make an important compromise. He maintained that while necessity may apply to the world of phenomena, freedom rules in the unconditioned realm, the world of the thing-in-itself.

When Kant turns to the problem of the soul, he likewise shows his skeptical temper; paradoxes result, which are called *paralogisms*. I cannot know myself as a metaphysical subject; I can know my inner being only through the categories. In short, even the concept of identity depends upon an analytic proposition.

His skepticism regarding the existence of the soul has significant consequences. Remember that the scholastic theologians accepted the existence of the soul as a definite principle of knowledge, and they thought they could describe its attributes. However, Kant points out that our reason can say nothing definite about the existence of the soul, and that when we philosophize about it, our knowledge ends in contradictions.

When he turns to the arguments for the existence of God, he unleashes a veritable philosophical barrage. Thus, he attacks the ontological proof for the existence of God. We cannot bridge the gap between thought and existence. I can think of a millionaire, yet this does not create a necessity for the existence of a millionaire, Furthermore, since the existence of God is a synthetic judgment, it may be denied without logical contradiction. Also, we must experience existence; conception of an idea is not enough.

It may be asked now, whether the conclusion of Kant's theoretical system is atheistic? The answer is an emphatic no. We may not be able to demonstrate philosophically that our soul is immortal and that God exists, but our theoretical judgment is only one aspect of our being— more important is our practical judgment. Kant, showing the limits of philosophical insight, thus paves the way for a more definite faith. The Ideas of reason have a regulative significance. We must act in such a way as if God existed, as if we had freedom, and as if our life were not terminated by death. Morality creates its own structure and its own needs.

The moral laws are discussed in detail in the *Critique of Practical Reason*. Kant is concerned not with the content of moral laws, but with their forms. Foremost is the categorical imperative which states that we should act in a way that our actions can become maxims of universal behavior. We might object to this law by saying that a man who steals would violate the categorical imperative. Yet Kant feels that not even the thief would want to have his behavior universalized.

Kant made it clear that every man is to be treated as an end in himself, and that man has an innate dignity. Thus, he is not to be a tool for unscrupulous legislators, nor is he to be used as cannon fodder for the princes, nor is the integrity of the student to be violated. Kant would never agree to the doctrine that the end justifies the means. Above all, he emphasized good will both in philosophy and education. Unlike the pragmatists, he believed in the motive rather than in the consequences of moral action.

It may be asked now whether such morality can be established by legislation and whether the state should coerce its citizens to act morally. Kant did not believe in force. Morality must be produced through *education* and must be founded upon an intense sense of duty.

The greatness of man, according to Kant, lies in his moral power which gives meaning to human destiny. Man's moral nature imbued Kant with hope for the future, and he thought that, eventually, the laws of morality would prevail, not only in religion, but also in politics and in international relations.

Important are his three postulates of morality. First is the postulate of freedom. When I engage in a moral action, when I follow the sense of duty, I act as if I were free. If my behavior were completely determined, I could not become conscious of the dignity of the moral law. Freedom itself cannot be proven by knowledge, but depends on *faith*. Freedom, to Kant, does not mean caprice; it stands for subordination to the sense of duty. The second postulate is the immortality of the soul; the third is the existence of God.

What is the significance of these postulates? What is their meaning for philosophy? They indicate that belief in God, human freedom, and the immortality of the soul make possible an adequate moral life. Thus, if this existence were the only one, virtue would not be rewarded and vice would not be punished. The concept of the future life, however, establishes an adequate scale of values. This type of thinking encouraged the development of an empirical theology based on the experience of God's grace rather than on intellectual definition.

Kant defines religion as the recognition of all duties as divine commands. It must be pointed out that his philosophy stressed duty rather than a knowledge of divinity; religion, according to Kant, depends on morality. Religious systems, be they Christian or pagan, must be judged by their contribution to man's moral ideals. What happens then to prayer? Can man appeal to God? Kant answers that prayer cannot change the order of nature, and cannot lead to God's intervention in human existence. It can only strengthen man's moral capacities. He denied the possibility of miracles, for the realm of phenomena is governed by the principle of causality. Miracles, thus, would be against the laws of nature.

Kant did not believe in original sin in the Augustinian sense. Original sin does not lie in the fall of Adam, rather in man's deceitfulness.

Since man did not fall from grace, he did not need a divine savior. Kant consequently stressed Christ's *human* qualities.

How are we saved? How can we enjoy eternal bliss? According to Kant, not by theological dogmas, nor by the acceptance of sacraments, but by moral and educational training and by following our sense of duty. Generally Kant gave a subjective explanation of ecclesiastical doctrines. He did not believe in the existence of the devil, nor did he accept the existence of a physical hell—good and evil refer to our heart which is the source of all true morality.

It is no wonder that his religious views were regarded with suspicion. The education minister of Frederick William II censored Kant and threatened him with extreme measures. Kant promised not to publish his views; however, after Frederick William II died, Kant broke his silence.

To Kant, God was not an arbitrary force. He was not a Jehovah sitting on a throne and punishing mankind for their sins, rather God was a moral force within man. The dictates of God were known through our conscience, which served as the arbiter when conflicting choices had to be made.

Since theological doctrines have only symbolic value, no one could be coerced to accept them. Thus Kant believed in freedom of conscience. A man's beliefs were not to be determined by the state; they were his private matter. Morality itself could not be produced through social reform; it could only be created through man's insight and through his acceptance of a universal sense of duty.

EDUCATIONAL VIEWS. To Kant education was of utmost importance. Through education we become truly human and we develop the patterns of civilization. We should educate with a view toward the future, for man is evolving, and he has within himself seeds of perfection. In educating the child, we should insure the safeguard of his independence. At the same time, the child is to be trained in a truly moral manner. Moralization implies to "acquire that type of mind which chooses good aims only."

To accomplish this goal, Kant disapproved of state education, and he also opposed control on the part of princes. Philosophers and educators should combine and develop the ideals of a new school system based upon moral law and the dignity of the individual. In his educational thought, Kant stressed especially the importance of discipline.

"Discipline or training transforms animal nature into human nature. An animal is by instinct all that it ever can be; some other reason has already provided everything for it. But man needs a reason of his own. Having no instincts, he has to work out a plan of conduct himself. Since, however, he is not able to do this at once, but comes into the world undeveloped, others must do it for him.

"Through its own efforts the human race is by degrees to develop all the natural endowments of man. One generation educates the next. The beginning of this process may be looked for either in a rude and unformed, or in a perfect and cultivated condition. If we assume the latter, man must afterwards have degenerated and lapsed into barbarism.

"Discipline prevents man from being turned aside by his animal impulses from humanity, his appointed end. It must restrain him, for example, from venturing wildly and thoughtlessly into danger. Discipline thus is merely negative, namely, the process by which man is deprived of his brutality. Instruction, on the contrary, is the positive part of education." [5]

Children need control, according to Kant:

"Discipline subjects man to the laws of mankind, and lets him feel their constraint. But this must take place early. Thus children are at first sent to school, not so much to learn anything, as to become accustomed to sitting still and obeying promptly what they are told, to the end that later in life they may not actually and instantly follow all their impulses." [6]

Kant opposed Rousseau and regarded civilization as a prerequisite for education.

"We see this among savage nations which, though they may live in subjection to Europeans a long time, yet never adopt European customs. With them, however, this is not a noble love of freedom, as Rousseau and others imagine, but a kind of savagery, in which the animal, so to speak, has not yet developed its humanity. Man should therefore accustom himself early to submit to the dictates of reason. If a man in his youth is allowed to follow his own will without opposition, he will retain a certain lawlessness through life. And it is no advantage to such a man to be spared in his youth through a superabundant motherly tenderness, for later on he will meet with all the more opposition on every side and everywhere encounter rebuffs, when he enters into the business of the world.

"It is a common mistake in the education of the great that, because they are destined to rule, they should never meet with opposition in their youth. Owing to his love of freedom, man needs to have his native roughness smoothed down; but with animals instinct renders this unnecessary." [7]

Culture is primary to Kant:

"Culture includes discipline and instruction. These, so far as we know, no animal needs; for none of them learn anything from their elders, except the birds, which are taught by them to sing. It is a touching sight to watch

---

5 *Pedagogy.*

6 *Ibid.*

7 *Ibid.*

the mother bird singing with all her might to her young ones, which like children at school, try to produce the same tones out of their tiny throats.

"Man can become man only by education. He is nothing but what education makes him. It is to be noted that man is educated only by men who themselves have been educated." [8]

Education, to Kant, implies constant improvement.

"There are many undeveloped powers in man; and it is our task to unfold these natural gifts in due proportion, to develop humanity from its germinal state, and to lead man to a realization of his destiny. Animals unconsciously fulfill their destiny themselves. Man must strive to attain it, but this he can not do, unless he has a conception as to the object of his existence. The fulfillment of his destiny is absolutely impossible to the individual. In times past men had no conception of the perfection to which human nature might attain. We ourselves have not yet become perfectly clear on the subject. This much, however, is certain: no individual man, whatever may be the culture of his pupils, can insure the fulfillment of their destiny. To succeed in this high end, not the work of individuals, but that of the whole human race, is necessary." [9]

[Education is a supreme art,] "the practice of which can become perfect only through many generations. Each generation, provided with the knowledge of the preceding one, can more and more bring about an education, which will develop man's natural gifts in due proportion and relation to their end, and thus advance the whole human race towards its destiny. Providence has willed that man shall develop the good that lies hidden in his nature, and has spoken, as it were, thus to him: 'Go forth into the world, I have equipped thee with all potencies of good. It is for thee to develop them, and thus thy happiness and unhappiness depend upon thyself alone.' " [10]

Man, Kant taught, must develop his moral sense:

"Providence has not placed a fully formed goodness in him, but merely capabilities without moral distinction. Man's duty is to improve himself; to cultivate his mind, and when he is evil, to develop moral character. Upon reflection we shall find this very difficult. Hence education is the greatest and most difficult problem to which man can devote himself." [11]

Kant favored an enlightened system of education:

"Man may be either broken in, trained, and mechanically taught, or he may be really enlightened. Horses and dogs are broken in, and man, too, may be broken in; it is eminently important that they learn to think.

---

8 *Ibid.*

9 *Ibid.*

10 *Ibid.*

11 *Ibid.*

That leads to the principle from which all transactions proceed. Thus we see that a real education involves a great deal. But as a rule, in private education, the fourth and most important point is still too much neglected, for children are substantially educated in such a way that moral training is left to the preacher. And yet how infinitely important it is that children be taught from youth up to detest vice, not merely on the ground that God has forbidden it, but because it is in itself detestable." [12]

Kant believed in experimental schools, which

"must be established before we can establish normal schools. Education and instruction must not be merely mechanical; they must be based on fixed principles. Yet education must be not entirely theoretical, but at the same time, in a certain sense, mechanical.

"People commonly imagine that experiments in education are not necessary, and that we can judge from our reason whether anything is good or not. But this is a great mistake, and experience teaches that the results of our experiments are often entirely different from what we expected. Thus we see that, since we must be guided by experiments, no one generation can set forth a complete scheme of education." [13]

FICHTE

Johann Gottlieb Fichte (1765-1814) was more subjective than his compatriot, Kant; he emphasized the practical intellect rather than our speculative reason.[14] Fichte reached importance not only as a philosopher, but also as a supporter of German nationalism, and as an educational reformer. He emphasized the superiority of the German culture in his *Addresses to the German People.*

From the standpoint of religious education, his most significant books are *The Vocation of Man, The Way Towards the Blessed Life,* and his *Wissenschaftslehre.* To Fichte, idealism was the only meaningful philosophy, for it stresses the dignity of man, while all naturalistic philosophies picture man as being subject to blind forces. The source of reality, according to Fichte, is the Absolute Ego, which postulates its own existence. The Absolute Ego is identified with God, whose desire for self-consciousness creates the empirical ego and the non-ego, a subject and an object. The non-ego has largely a negative meaning; it exists mainly as a field for man's moral endeavor. In Fichte the activistic strains are strong; *doing,* thus, is more important than thinking. The moral life itself constitutes a perennial challenge to the educator.

---

12 *Ibid.*

13 *Ibid.*

14 Regarding Fichte's philosophy see Adamson, *Fichte;* Everett, *Fichte's Science of Knowledge.*

Man is composed of two parts. On the one hand, he strives for pleasure and is essentially selfish. On the other hand, he contains within himself the seeds of morality. The highest moral law is the law of duty. Eternal and universal, the law of duty should be followed not because of selfish considerations, but because in this way man realized his destiny. The religious life is not one of intellectual contemplation. In fact, the intellect can never understand completely the reality of the divine world. Knowledge is symbolic; it cannot give us the core of our inner nature. The intellectual life frequently leads to doubts which we must overcome if we are to be saved.

We experience real life only when we live with the eternal:

"That Eternal Will is thus assuredly the Creator of the World, in the only way in which He can be so, and in the only way in which it needs creation:—in the infinite reason. Those who regard Him as building up a world, from an everlasting inert matter, which must still remain inert and lifeless, —like a vessel made by human hands, not an eternal procession of His self-development, or who ascribe to Him the production of a material universe out of nothing, know neither the world nor Him. If matter only can be reality, then were the world indeed nothing, and throughout all eternity would remain nothing. Reason alone exists: —the Infinite in Himself— the finite in Him and through Him." [15]

It is impossible to define supreme reality. To understand God, we must be like children with a completely open perspective:

"Sublime and Living Will! named by no name, compassed by no thought! I may well raise my soul to Thee, for Thou and I are not divided. Thy voice sounds within me, mine resounds in Thee; and all my thoughts, if they be but good and true, live in Thee also. In Thee, the Incomprehensible, I myself, and the world in which I live, become clearly comprehensible to me; all the secrets of my existence are laid open, and perfect harmony arises in my soul.

"Thou art best known to the child-like, devoted, simple mind. To it Thou art the searcher of hearts, who seest its inmost depths; the ever-present true witness of its thoughts, who knowest its truth, who knowest it though all the world know it not. Thou art the Father who ever desirest its good, who rulest all things for the best." [16]

In education Fichte is especially important in his teachings on *The Vocation of the Scholar* and the *Nature of the Scholar*. Fichte made a clear distinction between the teacher and the pragmatic scholar. The teacher is concerned with the promotion of ideas, while the pragmatic scholar uses ideas for the welfare of mankind. The scholar in his life, Fichte maintained, embodies a Divine Idea. He is the agent of progress and the symbol of genuine morality.

---

[15] *Vocation of Man,* Book III, Part IV.
[16] *Ibid.*

Education, according to Fichte, is to be administered by the state. The training of our body is not to be neglected nor should we overlook our manual capacities. Education should be based upon love of knowledge and love of our fellow man. Such a system has a transcendental basis. for it is incomplete without a religious and an ethical foundation. Fichte's advocacy of co-education was advanced for his time, although he felt that girls should have a different training from boys.

Between 1807 and 1808 he delivered his *Addresses to the German Nation,* which were fundamental in the creation of a new German system of education based upon discipline, exact scholarship, and state control of the schools. To Fichte, education has three major goals. 1. It develops esthetic interests and creates awareness, 2. it stirs our moral nature and develops a knowledge of our sense of duty, and 3. it points to our relationship with God, for man is a spiritual creature.

The teacher, according to Fichte, has an awesome task. He must exemplify the highest spiritual ideals and he must mediate between the student and the discipline of the subject matter. Theory alone in education is inadequate; what is needed above all is *concrete application.*

HEGEL

The most encyclopedic of the idealists was Georg W. F. Hegel (1770-1831). Among his works we find *Phenomenology of the Spirit, The Encyclopedia of Philosophic Sciences, Philosophy of Right, Esthetics, Philosophy of History, Philosophy of Religion, Science of Right,* and *History of Philosophy.* The most difficult of his works is probably his *Science of Logic.*

Hegel basically believes that reality is rational and that the universe is not the product of chaos, that rather it is governed by logical laws.[17] Reason itself is not limited to apprehension of phenomena, and it can understand the structure of reality. It was the aim of Hegel to give a *unitary* description of philosophy. He thought that mere analysis was not enough, he wanted to synthesize man's mind and nature—the subjective and objective aspects of our existence, and art, religion, and philosophy.

The principle of reality in Hegel is called the Absolute, which is not to be conceived as a subjective force, rather it is to be identified with the world structure. It is the dynamic principle, which is in a constant state of flux and which is forever searching for perfection.

A prominent feature of Hegel's philosophy is his consciousness of history. To him history was not merely a collection of unrelated events,

---

17 Cf. Stirling, *The Secret of Hegel;* Caird, *Hegel;* Croce, *What is Living and What is Dead in the Philosophy of Hegel.*

but it contained intellectual and moral significance. Thus, Hegel was primarily concerned with ideas and their relationship to culture and education. History, according to Hegel, presents us with a drama of opposition; we have two opposing forces—thesis and antithesis. To make the matter clear, imagine that Oriental religion represents the thesis, while Greek religion represents the antithesis. According to Hegel, both would be synthesized by Christianity. In short, Christianity, in its emphasis on God's intervention, would bring about a mediation between the Oriental concept that God is far distant, and the Greek concept that the gods are revealed in nature.

The nationalistic spirit was strong in Hegel, who did not accept any type of world government.

> "The nations of Europe," [he wrote,] "form a family according to the universal principle of their legislation, their ethical code, and their civilization. But the relation among States fluctuates, and no judge exists to adjust their differences. The higher judge is the universal and absolute Spirit alone—the World Spirit.
>
> "The relation of one particular State to another presents, on the largest possible scale, the most shifting play of individual passions, interests, aims, talents, virtues, power, injustice, vice, and mere external chance. It is a play in which even the ethical whole, the independence of the State, is exposed to accident. The principles which control the many national spirits are limited . . . Out of this dialectic rises the universal Spirit, the unlimited World-Spirit, pronouncing its judgment—and its judgment is the highest— upon the finite nations of the world's history; for the history of the world is the world's court of justice." [18]

Hegel believed that man's freedom is only realized in the service of the state. In fact, the state exemplifies the ideals of God.

> "The State is the realization of the ethical idea. It is the ethical spirit as revealed, self-conscious, substantial will. It is the will which thinks and knows itself, and carries out what it knows, and in so far as it knows. The unreflected existence of the State rests on custom, and its reflected existence on the self-consciousness of the individual, on his knowledge and activity. The individual, in return, has his substantial freedom in the State, as the essence, purpose, and product of his activity." [19]

In all these views Hegel almost appears as a forerunner of modern National Socialism.

To Hegel, education is a process whereby freedom is achieved. It should be remembered that to Hegel freedom is not self-direction, but

---

[18] *The Philosophy of Law.*

[19] *Ibid.*

identification with a Universal Idea. In the first phase of education, the parents are in control. This represents an external process. The child develops habits and the fundamentals of civilized behavior. In the second phase, the school takes over, and this coincides with a new stage in the child's development. Now he becomes conscious of his own powers and his own individuality. He feels estranged from nature. This is a phase of excessive subjectivity.

The teacher creates a synthesis. He helps the student to develop his own powers and, at the same time, to apprehend universal concepts. A truly liberal education, especially through Greek and Latin, creates objectivity and an understanding of cultural permanence. The life of scholarship then combines objectivity and subjectivity, and both the teacher and the student find themselves in subordination to a universal cause.

Education to Hegel is a rigorous process; the student must reconcile nature and spirit, and he must rise from the sensate to permanent ideals and to a knowledge of absolute principles. Hegel favored thought control. The individual student should be taught to obey the authorities of the state. We fulfill ourselves only as we serve a superior institution.

The teacher, according to Hegel, is to use the methods of discipline. The student tends to be wayward and must be reminded that reason demands self-control. The ultimate aim of the teacher is to interpret the ways of the Absolute to the world.

Hegel's philosophy of education has had a strong impact upon the American philosopher Josiah Royce, who regarded loyalty as the greatest virtue of the teacher. Likewise, Gentile, the minister of education under Mussolini, was a confirmed Hegelian and indicated that the state should control all educational activities. Gentile, a profound thinker, wholly supported the fascist program.

Idealism, as the experiments of Gentile indicate, may be a doubtful blessing. Frequently, idealistic thinkers have supported the authority of the state and have created what Hoeffer calls "The True Believer." On the other hand, some idealistic thinkers, like Kant, have encouraged democratic tendencies by pointing to man's limitless possibilities for creative growth in his personal and intellectual life.

QUESTIONS FOR DISCUSSION AND INVESTIGATION

1. Define the basic assumptions in the philosophy of idealism.

2. What usually were the idealists' stand in religion and social views?

3. Discuss Leibniz' theory of knowledge and metaphysics.

4. What stand in education did Leibniz take?

5. Discuss Kant's main works in philosophy.

6. Sketch briefly Kant's system of knowledge as a prelude to his moral theories.

7. What are Kant's arguments on the existence of God, and what type of reasoning does he employ in support of his beliefs?

8. Describe Kant's educational views.

9. Contrast Fichte's philosophical idealism with Kant's main principles.

10. Describe the basic tenets in Hegel's philosophy and relate them to his ideas on education.

Chapter 21

Pestalozzi

The educational ideals of Johann Pestalozzi (1746-1827) are a reflection of his own life. Since his father, a physician, passed away when the boy was five, he was brought up by his mother, who encouraged his sensitivity. He hated the Latin school which he attended in Zürich, but he enjoyed his college years at the Collegium Humanitatis and the Collegium Carolinum. He tried several professions, including the ministry, law and politics, but he was unsuccessful. He took up agriculture and developed a farm at Neuhof, but he was threatened by poverty, a fact which did not diminish his idealism.

His labors at Neuhof, which became an orphanage, at Stanz, where he was in charge of poor children and orphans, at Burgdorf, and at last at Yverdun, where he conducted a boarding school, convinced him that a new approach was needed in education. His last period was spent at Neuhof, after Yverdun had experienced financial difficulties. There he died in 1827.

His most significant works are *Leonard and Gertrude, How Gertrude Teaches Her Children, Swan-Song,* and *Evening Hours of a Hermit.*

The educational ideals of Pestalozzi rest upon his social philosophy. Unlike Rousseau, Pestalozzi did not glorify the state of nature for it was not an ideal Utopia, rather it tended to be brutish. Primitive man, according to Pestalozzi, often acted like an animal in a jungle. He even killed members of his own family if his survival were threatened. Pestalozzi in his views of primitive man was far more scientific than Rousseau, who was carried away by vague romantic dreams.

The next stage of man, Pestalozzi maintained, is that of society, which is not a convenience but a dire necessity. Because man has animal drives and is a passionate creature he has to be tamed. Thus, laws are invented and enforced; religion creates tabus and restrictions; we develop a sense of right and wrong. However, often society enforces the wrong laws and protects the guilty. Pestalozzi felt that the claims of society are not absolute, for only too often they conflict with our ethical ideals.

Like Comenius and Kant, Pestalozzi had utopian tendencies. He wanted to establish a truly ethical society in which God was worshipped, morality was recognized, and human creativity was stimulated.

Within all of us there are three drives: we have primitive impulses, we are social beings, and also we have ethical yearnings. Education was the process whereby ethics triumphed over our animal impulses. This did not imply artificial training; on the contrary, it meant inward development, for, according to Pestalozzi, we all have sparks of creativity and a capacity for love and understanding.

The model for the school is the home, according to Pestalozzi. Let the teacher act like a loving father, let him develop initiative on the part of the student, let him stress the importance of ethical behavior, let him be an example in all activities. Just as co-operation and understanding govern a good home so these ideals are to be applied to the schoolroom.

The ideal of love governs the educational philosophy of Pestalozzi. Such love is to be unrestrained; it is to include the successful as well as the poor student; it is to be unfailing even when students misbehave. Pestalozzi was especially fond of the children of poor parents and he did everything in his power to improve their lot.

The individual, Pestalozzi taught, develops through the head, the hand, and the heart. The head stands for intellectual development. Like Locke, Pestalozzi refuted the concept of innate ideas; we learn through sense expressions, but it must be remembered that the mind is active in its adjustment to the external world. Form, number, and language are the bases of the educative process. This means that qualitative elements and the power of communication should be stressed. Like Rousseau, Pestalozzi approached education from the standpoint of the interests of children rather than the logic of adults.

He taught a new concept of geography. Often he would take children on walks and in this way they would become conscious of their environment. He used clay models to portray mountains and rivers and he tried to make this study as dramatic as possible. In mathematics he started with concrete objects; thus he would point to two students to develop a concept of the number two. He showed that abstraction can come only when concrete ideas have been mastered.

This is the basis of our contemporary instruction in arithmetic. We do not force the child to remember by rote; rather we try to show how arithmetic is involved in daily living. Thus, the child goes to the store and has to have the correct change. In the schoolroom, a model of a bank will be constructed, and children will act out the roles of bank president, tellers, and customers. In this manner they will learn the concrete meaning of concepts in arithmetic. This type of instruction dates back to Pestalozzi.

Pestalozzi also emphasized the importance of art in the curriculum. This was not only an outlet for the creative talents of children, but it also gave them a consciousness of their powers and it developed intellectual discipline. Children had to participate in art and not be mere bystanders. Instead of learning about melodies they should be encouraged to sing and play instruments. By necessity, their progress would be slow, and their ideas would differ from the ideas of adults, but the teacher should never exhibit an attitude of disapproval or condescension. Again, this meant a revolution in the curriculum. It implied an emphasis on the integrity of the student and a stress upon his creative abilities.

Pestalozzi stressed the importance of concrete situations. He felt that what we see and visualize we remember more vividly than what we hear. Thus, in language training he started with objects like apples and trees. He was certain that knowledge moved from the concrete to the abstract. He made several innovations: he used slates and pencils and taught letters of the alphabet by using cards. Instead of instructing one student at a time he organized specific classes.

He emphasized the need for manual training not just for the children of the laboring classes, but for all, for he believed that our hands are just as important as our intellect, and that we develop excellent work habits when we are busy with manual activities.

However, without the development of the heart, according to Pestalozzi, education is incomplete. We must cultivate our capacity to love. This we first learn at home; hence, the ideals and attitudes of our parents, especially of our mother, are so important. The child must feel a sense of belonging; otherwise emotional difficulties will develop. Religion is to be part and parcel of education. It does not stand for any particular dogma, rather for a feeling of dependence upon God; in this view Pestalozzi echoed the ideas of Schleiermacher. Religion, he felt, is measured by its capacity to stimulate ethical action. Profession of faith meant nothing if it was not followed by constructive action.

In short, the test of education, according to Pestalozzi, is ethical actuality. Are we becoming more tolerant? Are we developing a spirit of compassion? Are we able to live in peace and charity with our neighbor? Are we becoming more spiritual in our philosophy of life?

The approach to education, Pestalozzi taught, must be that of integration: The head, hand, and heart should develop harmoniously. More important than specific instruction is *general education,* for we all meet life in its complexity. As we mature, we become masters of our environment. Knowledge thus means power, not merely an abstract contemplation of the universe.

Critics might feel that Pestalozzi overlooked the importance of discipline and effort. Pestalozzi thought that the teacher was like a gardener, and the pupil like a plant which had to be carefully nurtured. It was so easy to destroy the creative capacities of the individual. Instruction should proceed step by step according to the ability of the child, and nothing should be forced.

Pestalozzi was one of the originators of the modern idea of "readiness." Psychological research indicates that not all pupils are able to read at the same time, that they mature according to varying rates. To force them into one mold or one pattern would be a mistake. Pestalozzi was conscious of the importance of individual differences.

However, we must re-examine our concept of readiness in the twentieth century. Today, children mature more rapidly; they are exposed to far more stimuli than they were in the time of Pestalozzi. They are conditioned by television and the motion picture and thus their readiness for intellectual labor has been intensified. By under-educating our students we only add to the cultural lag of our time.

THE IDEALS OF PESTALOZZI

Pestalozzi's educational philosophy is based on the ideal of liberty.

"Be in no hurry to get on, but make the first step sound before moving; in this way you will avoid confusion and waste. Order, exactness, completion—alas, not thus was my character formed. And in the case of my own child in particular, I am in great danger of being blinded by his quickness, and rapid progress, and, dazzled by the unusual extent of his knowledge, of forgetting how much ignorance lurks behind this apparent development, and how much has yet to be done before we can go farther. Completeness, orderliness, absence of confusion—what important points!

"Lead your child out into Nature, teach him on the hilltops and in the valleys. There he will listen better, and the sense of freedom will give him more strength to overcome difficulties. But in these hours of freedom let him be taught by Nature rather than by you. Let him fully realize that she is the real teacher and that you, with your art, do nothing more than walk quietly at her side. Should a bird sing or an insect hum on a leaf, at once stop your walk; bird and insect are teaching him; you may be silent.

"I would say to the teacher, be thoroughly convinced of the immense value of liberty; do not let vanity make you anxious to see your efforts producing premature fruit; let your child be as free as possible, and seek diligently for every means of ensuring his liberty, peace of mind, and good humor." [1]

1 *Diary.*

Nature, Pestalozzi taught, is to be our guide:

"Man! in thyself, in the inward consciousness of thine own strength, is the instrument intended by Nature for thy development.

The path of Nature, which develops the forces of humanity, must be easy and open to all; education, which brings true wisdom and peace of mind must be simple and within everybody's reach.

Nature develops all the forces of humanity by exercising them; they increase with use.

The exercise of a man's faculties and talents, to be profitable, just follow the course laid down by Nature for the education of humanity.

This is why the man who, in simplicity and innocence, exercises his forces and faculties with order, calmness, and steady application, is naturally led to true human wisdom; whereas he who subverts the order of Nature, and thus the due connection between the different branches of his knowledge, destroys in himself not only the true basis of knowledge, but the very need of such a basis, and becomes incapable of appreciating the advantages of truth.

Thou who wouldst be a father to thy child, do not expect too much of him till his mind has been strengthened by practice in the things he can understand; and beware of harshness and constraint." [2]

God is the measure of all education, and Jesus should be our main example:

"A man's greatest need is the knowledge of God.

The purest pleasures of his home do not always satisfy him.

His weak, impressionable nature is powerless without God to endure constraint, suffering, and death.

God is the Father of humanity, and his children are immortal.

Sin is both the cause and effect of want of faith, and is an act opposed to what a man's inmost sense of good and evil tells him to be right.

It is because humanity believes in God that I am contented in my humble dwelling.

I base all liberty on justice, but I see no certainty of justice in the world so long as men are wanting in uprightness, piety, and love.

The source of justice and of every other blessing in the world, the source of all brotherly love amongst men, lies in the great conception of religion that we are the children of God.

That man of God who, by his sufferings and death, restored to men the sense that God is their Father, is indeed the Saviour of the world. His teaching is justice itself, a simple philosophy of practical value for all, the revelation of God the Father to his erring children." [3]

---

[2] *The Evening Hours of a Hermit.*
[3] *Ibid.*

Knowledge depends upon its motivational foundations; words are only secondary instruments:

> "I have generally found that great, noble, and high thoughts are indispensable for developing wisdom and firmness of character. Such instruction must be complete in the sense that it must take account of all our aptitudes and all our circumstances; it must be conducted, too, in a truly psychological spirit, that is to say, simply, lovingly, energetically, and calmly. Then, by its very nature, it produces an enlightened and delicate feeling for everything true and good, and brings to light a number of accessory and dependent truths, which are forthwith accepted and assimilated by the human soul, even in the case of those who could not express those truths in words.
>
> "I believe that the first development of thought in the child is very much disturbed by a wordy system of teaching, which is not adapted either to his faculties or the circumstances of his life. According to my experience, success depends upon whether what is taught to children commends itself to them as true, through being closely connected with their own personal observation and experience. Without this foundation truth must seem to them to be little better than a plaything, which is beyond their comprehension, and therefore a burden." [4]

The deep compassion which Pestalozzi felt was expressed by an autobiographical incident when he was head of the orphanage at Stanz:

> "We wept and smiled together. They forgot the world and Stanz; they only knew that they were with me and I with them. We shared our food and drink. I had neither family, friends, nor servants; nothing but them. I was with them in sickness and health, and when they slept. I was the last to go to bed, and the first to get up. In the bedroom I prayed with them, and at their own request, taught them till they fell asleep." [5]

SIGNIFICANCE

Pestalozzi's ideas had an international impact. He was made a citizen of the French Republic, and he was knighted by the Tsar of Russia. Maine de Biran, M. A. Julien, and Chavennes spread his ideas in France; in England, Dr. Charles Mayo and Elizabeth Mayo experienced the impact of his concepts; the Prussian government sent teachers to be instructed by Pestalozzi, and in Switzerland, Baron von Fellenberg established an agricultural school at Hofwyl which reflected the ideals of Pestalozzi.

In the United States, William Woodbridge, Joseph Neef, William McClure, Horace Mann, John Griscom, and especially Edward A. Sheldon felt the power of Pestalozzi's educational concepts. Oswego, New

---

[4] *Ibid.*
[5] *Letter on His Work at Stanz,* 1799.

York, where Sheldon was superintendent, became a center for the promotion of a progressive system of education.

Pestalozzi's impact ultimately cannot be defined. In his own time he was misunderstood. His contemporaries thought that he was a radical and a visionary. He was too emotional for them and took education too seriously. Scholars thought that his ideas were muddled and obscure. He was intoxicated by his fame and he lacked detachment.

Still, he had one of the most inspiring conceptions of education and life in the history of humanity. He believed in the greatness of the individual who had unlimited possibilities if he developed harmoniously. Like Comenius, Pestalozzi called not only for a reconstruction of education, but also for a transformation of society. Creativity is to prevail not merely in the schoolroom, but in all activities of life.

Education, thus, cannot be separated from ethical instruction. As Pestalozzi states in eloquent terms:

"Do not hesitate to touch on the difficult questions of good and evil, and the words connected with them. And you must do this especially in connection with the ordinary events of every day, upon which your whole teaching in these matters must be founded, so that the children may be reminded of their own feelings, and supplied, as it were, with solid facts upon which to base their conception of the beauty and justice of the moral life.

"The pedagogical principle which says that we must win the hearts and minds of our children by words alone, without having recourse to corporal punishment, is certainly good, and applicable under favorable conditions and circumstances; but with children of such widely different ages as mine, children for the most part beggars, and all full of deeply-rooted faults, a certain amount of corporal punishment was inevitable, especially as I was anxious to arrive surely, speedily, and by the simplest means, at gaining an influence over them all, for the sake of putting them all in the right road. I was compelled to punish them, but it would be a mistake to suppose that I thereby, in any way, lost the confidence of my pupils.

"Elementary moral education, considered as a whole, includes three distinct parts: the children's moral sense must first be aroused by their feelings being made active and pure; then they must be exercised in self-control, and taught to take interest in whatever is just and good; finally, they must be brought to form for themselves, by reflection and comparison, a just notion of the moral rights and duties." [6]

Pestalozzi was a dreamer with a vivid sense of actuality. He noted how most individuals live unhappy and frustrated lives and how they are guided by irrational passions. For example, in his novel *Leonard and Gertrude,* Leonard is a serf to drunkenness and cannot control his appetites. We rise above our passions, according to Pestolozzi, when we identify ourselves with mankind and when we see education as man's eternal quest for meaning, significance, and enlightenment.

[6] *Ibid.*

QUESTIONS FOR DISCUSSION AND INVESTIGATION

1. What aspects of Johann Pestalozzi's background influenced his ideals on education?

2. Define Pestalozzi's social philosophy.

3. What are the three drives in all of us, according to Pestalozzi?

4. How does love play a vital role in education according to Pestalozzi?

5. What was Pestalozzi's concept of geography?

6. What subjects did he emphasize in the educational curriculum?

7. Define his concept of "readiness" and show how it applies to twentieth-century educational institutions.

8. Elaborate on Pestalozzi's ideal of liberty as constituting the basis of educational philosophy.

9. Describe the international impact of Pestalozzi's ideas.

10. How does he prove that education cannot be separated from ethical instruction?

Chapter 22

Herbart

Johann Herbart (1776-1841) became the champion of realism in education. Unlike Fichte and the romantists, he was not given to an expression of emotional feelings. A university professor and successor to Kant, he expressed the ideals of the academic life. In every way he was systematic, and his writings inspire more by their depth than by their emotional content.

Among the works of significance to educational thought we find *The Application of Psychology to the Science of Education, Outlines of Educational Doctrine, The Science of Education,* and *Textbook in Psychology.*

He founded an important teacher training institution in which he stressed his fundamental ideal of education: the development of character. Morality, to Herbart, was the foundation and end of education. It implied a sense of balance between reason and emotion, between today and the future, between the demands of God and those of man. Extremes were to be avoided; in this viewpoint Herbart followed the ideals of Aristotle. But character development could not be accomplished without self-control, for man's passions and desires constantly stood in the way of philosophic enlightenment.

Freedom and authority should be combined, according to Herbart.

". . . Man from his youth onward must voluntarily accept restrictions, particularly as he has to live a communal life. Hence, first: Children must learn to obey. Their natural exuberance must meet enough resistance to avert offense.

"Immediately we meet a new difficulty. The easy means for a child not to offend his parents or teachers is concealment and lying!

"To cut the knot some teachers assume at once that children always lie if they can. Hence, they have to be so closely supervised and watched, and kept so busy from morning to evening, that they have no time for trickery. There is some truth in this, but if it is carried out with too much harshness and exactness one may fail in the first fundamental postulate we have set up, that children's vigor must be preserved! For this they need freedom! Those teachers who restrict freedom to such a degree that all the children's actions are calculated to please the observer, educate babies. Such creatures will have to learn how to use their powers when they are grown up,—and in spite of all their endeavors they will remain timid, helpless, and inferior to free personalities, until eventually they will try to compensate in whatever way they can.

"Consequently, as such a restricting form of education is dangerous, something better must be combined with supervision and occupation.

"One says rightly that well-bred children have not the heart to deceive their father and mother. Why not? They are used to rely on truth and confidence. This, then becomes the keynote of their lives." [1]

Education means development of man's character.

". . . In spite of a certain severity in your guidance, lead the children into a situation which they like and which invites them to be free and confident.

"This is the supreme demand in education; all the rest, whatever one may call it, is only of secondary and tertiary importance; all instruction from the elements of learning to the highest levels of scholarship should tend to this. Hence those schools, whose main function is merely teaching and learning, cannot be considered as serving education in the deepest sense of the word. They are only of assisting value, and this only for such families as have already fulfilled the educational postulates mentioned above . . .

"It follows that education, in order to have a permanent effect, must try to use instruction not only for mere information but also for the formation of *character*." [2]

While Pestalozzi and Rousseau had emphasized the importance of the individual against society, Herbart tried to achieve a balance between the two. The individual should develop his own capacities; at the same time, he owes much to society and finds himself best in service to his fellow man.

Ethics does not imply the establishment of rigid rules, for life is an educational process which is forever incomplete. The moralist may be the enemy of virtue, for he sets up his own standards as ultimates. Rather, Herbart recommends that we constantly redefine our functions and that

---

[1] *Brief Encyclopedia of Practical Philosophy* (tr. by R. Ulich) from *Three Thousand Years of Educational Wisdom* (Cambridge: Harvard University Press, 1954). Reprinted by permission.
[2] *Ibid.*

we retain an exploratory spirit. Nothing is more futile than to specialize in one field or to look at life from one standpoint. The more we cultivate wide interests and wide sympathy the more we shall grow in genuine morality.

To Herbart, ethics is the test of education. This means that pure reason is the prelude to practical reason, and that knowledge is the overture to action. Ideals are not abstractions to be admired platonically; they are patterns for meaningful activity. The educated man, according to Herbart, knows virtue and understands human aspirations; at the same time, he seeks ways and means whereby ideals can be actualized. This demands both intelligence and emotional balance.

EDUCATIONAL PSYCHOLOGY

As a psychologist, Herbart left his most lasting mark upon the history of education. He revolutionized this field in his attempt to make it into an autonomous science and divorce it from metaphysics. Before his time, psychologists had stressed the separate faculties of the mind and had labored under the impact of Aristotle and Aquinas. Herbart's approach was experimental, whereas he showed that education depends on psychological functions.

Without a psychological background we cannot comprehend the learner:

"Those who have no true psychological insight, rarely understand anything of education. They may cherish the obsolete opinion that there reside in a human soul certain powers or faculties which have to be trained in one way or another. These people seemingly have in mind gymnastic exercises which strengthen the muscles, for man has only one kind of muscles. Indeed in each single apperceptive mass (mass or group of ideas) are contained so-called fantasy, memory, and intelligence, but they are not equally distributed. Rather in one and the same person a certain mass of apperceptions may be of more intellectual, imaginative, or of reproductive character; one mass may be penetrated with profound feeling, another with an atmosphere of coolness, etc. Therefore, what educators call formal discipline (Formelle Bildung) would be an absurdity if it meant the training of isolated mental faculties which exist only in some people's imaginations." [3]

Teachers, according to Herbart, should be conscious of the plasticity of human behavior:

". . . It requires a great deal to raise knowledge to the level of erudition; it is a still more difficult task to combine the imparting of knowledge with the formation of character. To achieve this purpose, knowledge must be

---
[3] *Ibid.*

deeply felt and experienced; in other words, the mere quantity of knowledge and the logical and practical training in notions, maxims and principles must affect the whole emotional attitudes of a person. One may show how instruction has to proceed to produce such an effect. (I have shown this in my *Science of Education*.) The degree of success, however, depends largely on the pupil's individuality.

"Only teachers of much experience can imagine how rapidly even carefully and cultivated knowledge vanishes under new conditions. They only can believe how easily new opinions and ambitions emerge and how irresistibly a person is attracted by temptations which appeal to his nature—in spite of all previous precautions. Even superficial experience teaches us that the results of an examination are valid only for the day when it is held . . . Such facts, however, are easily explained through reference to the continual flow of ideas (apperceptive masses) in our mind. Those, who consider the human soul as a fixed and concrete object, will never understand the mutability of the human character; they will easily resort to false remedies which only aggravate the evil." [4]

In this respect, there are important similarities between Herbart and William James. Both viewed education and philosophy from a psychological standpoint, both were opposed to traditionalism, both had had an experimental bent, both were important textbook writers, and both systematized the knowledge of their time. However, James was a voluntarist, fully aware of the impact of the will, while Herbart had a more rationalistic and mathematical conception of psychology.

To Herbart, man's mind is a battleground of ideas or presentations. They fight for dominance, and when they lose they become part of our subconscious. Consciousness is not a simple process; it is like a stage play in which new actors constantly enter and occasionally the old performers reappear. In his concept of the subconscious, Herbart anticipates Freud, only to Herbart it lacked a sexual connotation and the process of repression was on a mechanical plane.

The mind, according to Herbart, has three functions: it knows, feels and wills. However, the will is not a separate faculty; it is the desire which underlies our mental processes and our emotional reactions. The mind moves from sensation to memory, to imagination, and, at last, to conceptual thinking, its highest sphere. When a new concept enters the mind it can be rejected, and thus find its way into the subconscious; or it can be accepted and assimilated with other presentations.

To Herbart, there is no real intellectual creativity. An idea enters the mind and it has to be assimilated; what happens in creative thinking is a synthesis on a higher level. This can be verified by historical examples. There are no radically new inventions; they are usually built upon the past, and represent a redefinition on a more qualitative level. Toynbee uses the term etheralization to describe progress as a form of qualitative simplification in which past ways are modified by present experiences.

IMPLICATIONS FOR THE TEACHER

All this may sound extremely abstract and unrelated to the practical problems of teaching. However, the teacher can greatly benefit from Herbartian concepts. The teacher should be conscious of the fact, Herbart maintained, that learning involves an internal change. New ideas thus must strike a responsive chord in the mind of the student; they must be developed in his imagination which can be accomplished only if the student is truly interested.

Instruction has four phases. It must 1. be concrete, 2. be continuous, 3. be elevating, and 4. have application to life. Herbart maintains that learning should start with illustrations, for our senses have to be stirred; then, continuous exercise is needed, for without effort we do not progress. Yet, as Whitehead later pointed out, we also must be imbued by the adventure of ideas; thus, our imagination should invest facts with a romantic mantle. Lastly, knowledge is to be lived and experienced. This is the lesson of Goethe's *Faust;* action is superior to theoretical contemplation.

Herbart hints at the fact that the individual in his educational development repeats the development of the race. The young child, thus, is like the primitive and lives on a sensate level. The adolescent is like early society and his sense of romance and adventure is important. He needs, above all, disciplined thinking. The third stage corresponds to modern civilization when man achieves a balance between individuality and society, and when he is able to make evaluative judgments.

The difference between the scholar and the average person lies in concentration. Take the example of a scholar writing a book: his ideas are disciplined; his energies are focused upon the project. He is scarcely conscious of the stimulus of his environment, of the room he is working in, and of what time of the day it is. Take, on the other hand, a mediocre student of today studying for a test. He will daydream about his weekend; he may even listen to television; thus, his thoughts are broken up, and only scattered intellectual associations result.

The method of Herbart is formalized in five steps:

1. *Preparation.* The environment is created—both external and internal—for the development of ideas. Old ideas are recalled from the subconscious and attention is cultivated.

2. *Presentation.* The lessons are presented to children with the use of illustrations to make them as concrete as possible.

3. *Association.* Both similarities and differences between old and new ideas are stressed. This develops order and consistency in thinking.

4. *Generalization.* This is a method of qualitative simplification, so that more and more facts can be understood in their wider meaning.

5. *Application.* Knowledge must be used and become part of our daily existence.

What strikes the observer is the balanced viewpoint of Herbart. He was concerned with theory and practice, with ideal and actuality. The curriculum, he maintained, should cultivate both the sciences and the humanities. Through the sciences the students would gain "empirical knowledge," while the humanities would give him sympathy.

Our mind develops in two ways. It grows and expands through a systematic concentration upon facts which have to be mastered and explored. Thus, Herbart especially favored mathematics, which would create rigorous thinking. Yet, at the same time, we have to develop patterns of appreciation, for we are not merely intellectual beings or products of pure reason. Hence, we should study literature, philosophy, the arts, religion and history. Now we become part of the life stream of humanity; our emotions are touched and we learn to identify ourselves with others.

In the American system of education in the twentieth century we overrate empirical knowledge, and we are seduced by facts. The Quiz Kid thus becomes the ideal of many teachers. However, far more important than facts are wisdom and the ability to judge. Life basically is an evaluative process. Without wisdom, we become prisoners of practicality and victims of a false utilitarianism.

The ideal of balanced wisdom stamps the educational philosophy of Herbart:

> "If the teacher succeeds in developing in the pupil manifold interest, then the education becomes a noble task in that it helps mankind to realize the great practical ethical ideas. These ideas will become the more self-evident to the pupil the less it is necessary to teach him merely to swim on the waves of society as was the case with the unsusceptible type. On the other hand, it is necessary to combine exact methods of thinking and self-criticism with the enthusiasm which can be imparted to the susceptible pupil by such means as religion and history. Of particular use for such an examining attitude is the capacity of clear ethical discrimination. For by its own nature the human mind is not so well disposed as to apprehend clearly the ideas of justice, equity, perfection, and sympathy and to act accordingly. In addition, a person with the capacity for inner freedom not rarely abandons traditional ideals and inclines towards eccentric claims and opinions for which, so he thinks, he has to fight and to bring sacrifices in order to carry off the crown of martyrdom. The striving for the unusual and the exceptional is in the spirit of the time, but it does not fit our country. Hence, what education has to do is to preserve in talented youth their natural courage and openmindedness but not to inspire them with burning ambition." [5]

---

[5] *Ibid.*

EVALUATION

American educators who studied in Germany were impressed by the ideas of Herbart, and they tried to introduce his concepts into the American curriculum. Among these men were Charles McMurray as well as Charles de Gammo, who regarded Herbart as the new Aristotle. In 1892, the National Herbartian Society was founded, ten years later it changed its name to the National Society for the Scientific Study of Education. In later years Herbart's influence waned, as Dewey's concepts and the ideals of pragmatism were more widely accepted.

Still, the lasting contributions of Herbart should not be underestimated. He made the study of educational psychology paramount; he developed a more creative technique of classroom teaching; he showed the significance of methodology in instruction; he developed the social perspective in the study of history and the humanities; he pointed to the intimate connection between education and ethics; he had a balanced viewpoint regarding the responsibilities of the teacher and the student. As yet, our knowledge of the human mind is limited and, while we have progressed beyond Herbart, the psychology of learning is still in its infancy. The more we learn about education, the more we appreciate the wisdom of Herbart, who insisted that education should be based upon sound psychological theory and that the human mind acts not according to faculties, but as a unitary whole.

It has often been pointed out, especially by Dewey, that Herbart concentrates too much on the intellectual side of man and that he overlooks the importance of feeling, and that, furthermore, he makes too much of man's rationalistic processes and neglects the role of impulse. But the other extreme in education, which glorifies impulse and neglects rational control, is far more devastating in its social effects than Herbartianism.

To Dewey, as is well known, education has no external goal; it implies the constant reconstruction of experience. To Herbart, on the other hand, education has a moral purpose, which was to be determined by historical experience in the light of man's deepest spiritual longings. To state that education has no purpose is true from a semantic standpoint, but, viewed idealistically, the aims of educators define their effectiveness.

The greatness of Herbart lies in his faith that education ultimately could become a science. This may be impossible, for actually the teacher is a creative artist who attempts to cultivate sensitivity in his students and in society. But we shall never advance in education unless we subject its results to the test of scientific evidence, and unless we concentrate more upon the psychology of learning—a field in which Herbart was a master.

QUESTIONS FOR DISCUSSION AND INVESTIGATION

1. What parts of Herbart's doctrines manifest a more realistic approach to education?

2. Explain the importance of ethics in education according to Herbart.

3. How did Herbart revolutionize the field of the psychology of education?

4. Compare and contrast Herbart and William James.

5. How can the teacher benefit from Herbart's ideas?

6. List and define the four phases of instruction according to Herbart.

7. According to Herbart, what is the difference between the scholar and the average person?

8. List and define the five steps of his method.

9. Explain the two ways in which our mind develops, according to Herbart, and show the weaknesses of American education in reference to this conception.

10. Name the lasting contributions of Herbart and contrast his educational ideas with those of John Dewey.

Chapter 23

Froebel

BACKGROUND

The life of Friedrich Froebel (1782-1852) covers a stormy period in German history. He lived under the impact of the Napoleonic wars, and he witnessed the growing nationalism of the German states.

All his life Froebel suffered from the impact of his mother's death; she had passed away when he was only nine months old. His father, a pastor, had remarried, but coldness prevailed between the boy and his stepmother. He studied at the University of Jena, and later at Göttingen and Berlin.

His educational capacities were stirred when he became a teacher of drawing at Frankfurt, when he worked with three boys at Keilhau, and, later, when he founded several schools in Switzerland. His most important achievement from the standpoint of education, took place in 1837, when he established a kindergarten at Blankenburg.

Among his works, special mention should be made of his *Autobiography, Education by Development, The Education of Man, Mother Play,* and *Pedagogies of the Kindergarten.* He wrote in a mystic style, and his thoughts were not always systematic.

Among the influences which conditioned his thinking, mention should be made of the *Zend-Avesta,* which pictured both unity and diversity, the philosophy of Schelling who gave a speculative account of nature, the ideas of F. C. J. Krause, a neo-Kantian who pictured the unity of man and God, and especially the impact of Comenius, Rousseau, H. G. Heusinger, Pestalozzi, and Friedrich von Schiller.

Most important was the impact of his own experiences. He felt that children frequently lack security and love in the home, and that education should start as soon as possible in order to develop warmth and understanding between parents and children. He was opposed to war and regarded it as an enemy of human culture and education. How could man progress when he was constantly threatened by destruction? How could creativity develop when society emphasized violence? How could family life be strengthened when war killed the best members of society?

His educational ideals rested upon a deep faith in religion. Spiritual ideals could not be defined; they could only be experienced. God, as the Absolute Power, included all parts of nature; man was part of God and God was part of man; this was a clear expression of pantheism.

God was not a static force; He revealed himself in the universe which thus achieved higher and higher levels. Man likewise moved from primitivism to maturity and finally attained self-consciousness.

A law governs all of life:

"In all things there lives and reigns an eternal law. This all-controlling law is necessarily based on an all-pervading, energetic, living, self-conscious, and hence eternal unity. This unity is God. All things have come from the divine Unity, from God, and have their origin in the divine Unity, in God alone. God is the sole source of all things. In all things there lives and reigns the divine Unity, God. All things live and have their being in and through the divine Unity, in and through God. All things are only through the divine effluence that lives in them. The divine effluence that lives in each thing is the essence of each thing.

"It is the destiny and lifework of all things to unfold their essence, hence their divine being, and therefore the divine Unity itself—to reveal God in their external and transient being. It is the special destiny and life-work of man, as an intelligent and rational being, to become fully, vividly, and clearly conscious of his essence, of the divine effluence in him, and there-fore, of God; to become fully, vividly, and clearly conscious of his destiny and lifework; and to accomplish this, to render it (his essence) active, to re-veal it in his own life with self-determination and freedom. *Education con-sists in leading man, as a thinking, intelligent being, growing into self-con-sciousness, to a pure and unsullied, conscious and free representation of the inner law of divine Unity, and in teaching him ways and means thereto.*" [1]

Education depends on the cosmic purpose:

"By education, then, the divine essence of man should be unfolded, brought out, lifted into consciousness, and man himself raised into free, con-scious obedience to the divine principle that lives in him, and to a free representation of this principle in his life. Education as a whole, by means of instruction and training, should bring to man's consciousness, and render

1 *The Education of Man.*

efficient in his life, the fact that man and nature proceed from God and are conditioned by him—that both have their being in God. *Education should lead and guide man to clearness concerning himself and in himself, to peace with nature, and to unity with God;* hence, it should lead him to a knowledge of himself and of mankind, to a knowledge of God and of nature, and to the pure and holy life to which such knowledge leads." [2]

The two most important aspects of man are creativity and freedom. Freedom implies the ability to make wise choices and to avoid evil. Goodness alone is real, according to Froebel, for evil is merely partiality and a distortion of goodness. Man is naturally creative; this is an expression of his basic nature.

These concepts have important educational implications. The child is not evil, on the contrary, waywardness is usually a lack of vision and the result of false values. The child must be taught in such a way that the eternal spark in his soul becomes a living reality.

Education is most effective when it is based on the needs of children. Did not Jesus say that the Kingdom of Heaven is within man? This meant that, as nature unfolds, potentialities appear. It is a modern version of the dictum of Socrates that self-knowledge is the road to wisdom.

To Froebel, education depended on the unity of the family. The most important virtue for the mother was gentleness, while the father had to guide wisely. A home united by love would be the best institution for human progress. When the home failed in its responsibilities, the educator had the duty to instruct the parents in the paths of virtue.

This does not imply puritanism. To Froebel, moral laws were reflections of the Absolute and our human understanding was limited. Humility was a primary virtue. Still, God was our inspiration and we could find him through the study of man, of nature, and of the universe. Like Emerson, Froebel believed in a fundamental unity. To study oneself and to study nature would lead to the same result: a recognition of the moral nature of the universe. The wise man was the good man, for virtue and knowledge were identical.

Our moral education, according to Froebel, is strengthened through association. Hence, children should be brought up in a wholesome environment. They should be imbued with the ideals of co-operation. To Froebel, play activities had primary significance; when a child played, he revealed his inner nature and at the same time developed patterns of socialization.

We learn best by doing; theorizing is a minor aspect of education, according to Froebel. For example, we can talk about the good life to children and yet we will not influence them; what matters is that we *live* the good life and that our school activities are constructive.

---

[2] *Ibid.*

To become truly educated, Froebel asserted, we must cultivate our senses, especially hearing and vision. Too many children become indifferent because they are never aware of the beauties around them and because they do not play creatively.

Education, according to Froebel, means the cultivation of awareness, love, and independence.

> "A child that plays thoroughly, with self-active determination, perseveringly until physical fatigue forbids, will surely be a thorough determined man, capable of self-sacrifice for the promotion of the welfare of himself and others. Is not the most beautiful expression of childlife at this time a playing child?—a child wholly absorbed in his play?—a child that has fallen asleep while so absorbed?
>
> "The aim and object of parental care, in the domestic and family circle, is to awaken and develop, to quicken all the powers and natural gifts of the child, to enable all the members and organs of man to fulfill the requirements of the child's powers and gifts. The natural mother does all this instinctively, without instruction and direction; but this is not enough: it is needful that she should do it consciously.
>
> "The child—your child, ye fathers—follows you wherever you are, wherever you go, in whatever you do. Do not harshly repel him; show no impatience about his ever-recurring questions. Every harshly repelling word crushes a bud or shoot of his tree of life. Do not, however, tell him in words much more than he could find himself without your words . . . To have found one fourth of the answer by his own effort is of more value and importance to the child than it is to half hear and half understand it in the words of another." [3]

The curriculum, Froebel made clear, should develop the foundations of perception. Facts are secondary and memorization is to be avoided. We are stirred only when we directly experience the greatness of life and of the universe.

Froebel was especially concerned with the problem of creativity. Is it an outward or an inward process? Does it demand discipline or spontaneity? Froebel maintained that creativity is one of man's most important needs. We all seek self-expression; we all want self-realization. On the elementary level, it may be represented by a child building a castle in the sand, on a higher level, it may be a scientist developing a new theory of physics or an engineer building a new factory. Creativity thus is a process which starts in infancy and ends in the grave and it can be furthered best if we understand the spontaneous nature of children. Froebel stated that if we encouraged the child when he is young, the chances are that he will develop creative patterns in his mature years. Our interests, according to Froebel, are continuous; one builds upon another, and the wise teacher realizes that the first years of the child are the most important.

[3] *Ibid.*

Life, Froebel taught, is lived on two levels. First, there is the level of actuality which represents the realm of sensation, of what we hear, and smell, and see. Second, is the realm of symbolism, which is a representation of inward urges and wishes. Objects used by children, such as toys, have an inner meaning. Nothing in the universe, according to Froebel, is without significance.

This is an expression of romantic mysticism which goes back to the ideals of St. Francis who preached to the birds, and who had a special love for children. It is part of the ideals of Jesus who desired adults to have the openness of children. To Froebel, as to St. Francis and to Jesus, the universe was an allegory which taught a moral lesson to man.

Education implies the cultivation of the spirit. As he states:

"The debasing illusion that man works, produces, creates only in order to preserve his body, in order to secure food, clothing, and shelter, may have to be endured, but should not be diffused and propagated. Primarily and in truth man works only that his spiritual, divine essence may assume outward form, and that thus he may be enabled to recognize his own spiritual, divine nature and the innermost being of God. Whatever food, clothing, and shelter he obtains thereby comes to him as an insignificant surplus. Therefor Jesus says, 'Seek ye first the kingdom of heaven,' that is the realization of the divine spirit in your life and through your life, and whatever else your finite life may require, will be added unto you.

"Yet human power should be developed, cultivated, and manifested not only in inner repose, as religion and religious spirit; not only in outward efficiency, as work and industry; but also—withdrawing upon itself and its own resources—in abstinence, temperance, and frugality. Is it needful to do more than indicate this to a human being not wholly at variance with himself? Where religion, industry and temperance, the truly undivided trinity, rule in harmony, in true pristine unity, there, indeed, is heaven upon earth —peace, joy, salvation, grace, blessedness." 4

Instruction depends on example, communication, and the cultivation of a pure heart.

"Will is the mental activity, ever consciously proceeding from a definite point in a definite direction toward a definite object, in harmony with the man's nature as a whole. This statement contains everything, and indicates all that parent and educator, teacher and school, should be or should give to the boy in example and precept during these years. The starting-point of all mental activity in the boy should be energetic and sound; the source whence it flows, pure, clear, and ever-flowing; the direction, simple, definite; the object, fixed, clear, living and life-giving, elevating, worthy of the effort, worthy of the destiny and mission of man, worthy of his essential nature, and tending to develop it and give it full expression.

"Instruction in example and in words, which later on become precept and example, furnishes the means for this. Neither example alone nor words

4 *Ibid.*

alone will do: not example alone, for it is particular and special, and the word is needed to give to particular individual examples universal applicability; not words alone, for example is needed to interpret and explain the word which is generally spiritual, and of many meanings. But instruction and example alone and in themselves are not sufficient; they must meet a good, pure heart, and this is an outcome of proper educational influences in childhood.[5]

SIGNIFICANCE

The most lasting contribution of Froebel lay in his development of the kindergarten. This idea found a ready response in the United States. In 1873, W. T. Harris opened one of the first kindergartens as part of the educational system of St. Louis, Missouri. Today we realize the importance of the kindergarten as a socializing force, and we have made it a primary foundation of our educational system.

Critics often object that Froebel is too vague and indefinite in his ideas. There is a vast difference between him and Herbart. Froebel wrote like a poet and his philosophy was an expression of his heart, while Herbart was an analytical scientist. But Froebel was right in his belief that education has a transcendental function; it points not only to man's social nature, but also to his metaphysical ideals. Education thus becomes an expression of man's ultimate hopes.

Such thoughts are important, but they cannot be presented systematically. They are like the intuitions of poetry or like the melodies of music. They have primarily a symbolic, rather than a scientific, meaning.

Perhaps Froebel went too far in his child-centered system of education; perhaps he overrated play activities. In his period, such an emphasis was progressive. In our own time, it would not necessarily contribute to educational advancement.

In the twentieth century, we have gone to the other extreme. We often neglect intellectual discipline and try to make learning too easy. We underrate the importance of subject matter. Thus, part of our education may be an encounter with triviality.

For all this we must not blame Froebel, who had a basic faith in man's capacity for knowledge and culture. The sciences and the arts, religion and philosophy all would contribute to create a harmonious world view.

In a period of disenchantment, the optimism of Froebel is refreshing. As he states:

"Man is by no means naturally bad, nor has he originally bad or evil qualities and tendencies, unless, indeed, we consider as naturally evil, bad, and faulty the *finite*, the *material*, the *transitory*, the *physical* as such, and

---

[5] *Ibid.*

the logical consequences of the existing of these phenomena, namely, that man must have the possibility of failure in order to be good and virtuous, that he must be able to make himself a slave in order to be truly free. Yet these things are the necessary concomitants of the manifestation of the eternal in the temporal, of unity in diversity, and follow necessarily from man's destiny to become a conscious, reasonable, and free being.

"A suppressed or perverted good quality—a good tendency, only repressed, misunderstood, or misguided—lies originally at the bottom of every shortcoming in man. Hence the only and infallible remedy for counteracting any shortcoming and even wickedness is to find the originally good source, the originally good side of the human being that has been repressed, disturbed, or misled into the shortcoming, and then to foster, build up, and properly guide this good side. Thus the shortcoming will at last disappear, although it may involve a hard struggle *against habit, but not against original depravity in man;* and this is accomplished so much the more rapidly and surely because man himself tends to abandon his shortcomings, for man prefers right to wrong. . . ." [6]

There are two types of idealism in the history of education. One type stresses the importance of authority and it plays a strong part in American educational history. From earliest Colonial times, the idealistic tradition was strong. It found an able representative in Jonathan Edwards, a New England theologian; later in, the nineteenth century, it was championed by Emerson and William T. Harris. In the twentieth century, Herman H. Horne, professor of philosophy at New York University popularized some of the educational views of idealism. The idealists emphasized the importance of discipline and they generally reacted unfavorably to the progressive measures of contemporary education. The idealists believe in tradition; there can be no sharp breaks with the past, and the classics are just as valid today as they were centuries ago.

Robert Hutchins, in his criticism of modern education, belongs to the idealistic tradition. Hutchins indicts education for its specialization, its scientific contents, and its neglect of history. To Hutchins, the ideal university would be Paris around 1200 A.D., instead of Harvard or Yale in the twentieth century. His ideas were formative in the establishment of St. John's College, whose educational philosophy is based upon the mastery of the hundred Great Books of Western Civilization; here, professors and students learn together in seminars, and no electives are tolerated.

The idealists today in elementary and secondary education want to return to the "Three R's," which, they charge, are sadly neglected in contemporary education. They believe in a teacher-centered form of education because they think that the student needs guidance and firmness, especially in the period of adolescence. Horne calls for an "ideal-centered" school.

[6] *Ibid.*

The other type of idealism, influenced by Froebel, is best represented by Felix Adler's Ethical Culture movement, which advocates a moral interpretation of education, the constructive way of life. The dignity of the student is to be safeguarded; no religious and racial prejudices are to be allowed. Universalism is the essence of this philosophy, for it stresses that both education and religion transcend intellectual analysis. The rule of love is to be central, and the teacher is to be an example of wisdom and warmth, understanding and tolerance.

Like Froebel, Felix Adler emphasized the creative development of the student. The student should not merely learn facts, but he is to become aware of his duties to his fellow-man. Education without ethical reverence would be a pilgrimage in vanity.

TOWARDS NATIONAL SYSTEMS OF EDUCATION

GERMANY. In nineteenth century Germany, education generally became a concern of the state. The Volksschule became the fundamental institution; only the most capable students could go on to secondary and to higher education.

The eminence of Germany during the nineteenth and part of the twentieth century depended on its system of public instruction. Elementary schools were compulsory; its teachers were carefully trained. Theorists, like Basedow, combined patriotism and religious instruction and believed in complete state control of education. Basedow's school, The Philantropinum at Dessau, which was established in 1774, exercised a wide influence on German education. The school combined scholarly excellence with physical training and emphasized instruction in small groups.

In German secondary education, classical ideals were challenged, and thus the classical gymnasium occupied a secondary place compared with the Realgymnasium. German universities, especially at Bonn and at Heidelberg, provided for first-rate scientific instruction. A close collaboration existed between German institutions of higher learning and German industry.

Until the coming of Hitler, freedom of expression usually prevailed in German secondary schools and universities. When Hitler subordinated the German schools to his political party and jailed thousands of scholars, the educational program suffered and ultimately contributed to German defeat in World War II.

FRANCE. In 1806, Napoleon established the University of France and a national system of secondary education. The Law of 1802 made primary education a responsibility of local communities, while secondary and higher education were to be administered by the central government.

Most important from the standpoint of educational history was a report issued by Victor Cousin in 1830 on *The State of Public Education in Prussia,* which lauded many of the features of German education. Eventually, it led to the central control of primary schools and to better institutions for teacher training in France.

ENGLAND. In nineteenth century England, religious groups agitated for a better system of instruction. Idealistic humanitarians like Robert Owen established free schools. In 1824, the Infant School Society was established. Valuable work was done by the Society for promotion of Christian knowledge; pioneers, like Joseph Lancaster, used the monitorial system of education, whereby one teacher, with the use of student assistants, could instruct a large number of pupils.

Between 1870 and 1902 the government established higher standards for primary and secondary education. Thomas Arnold, headmaster of Rugby, tried to modernize the system of instruction at ancient schools like Eton and Winchester. Scientific education was strengthened when the University of London was founded in 1828. Various commissions were appointed, such as the Clarendon Commission (1861-1864) and the Taunton Commission (1864-1867). These commissions found weaknesses in the English educational structure and recommended higher standards and better methods of supervision.

Agitation for more adequate education continued in the twentieth century. Oxford and Cambridge now emphasized the need for more scientific instruction, and more scholarships were given to deserving students, so that they could obtain the benefits of higher education.

SUMMARY. Idealism was a fundamental motive in the establishment of national educational systems, but, as the nations became more powerful, idealism was subordinated to nationalistic concepts. Thus, history was taught differently by French and German schools, and extreme chauvinism was evident in the textbooks which were used by these nations. Classical ideals were subordinated to the needs of the state. Typical is Emperor William II's demand that German educators bring up "young Germans and not young Greeks or Romans."

QUESTIONS FOR DISCUSSION AND INVESTIGATION

1. Name the influences which conditioned Froebel's thinking.

2. What important implications, according to Froebel, do man's creativity and freedom have upon education?

3. Why, according to Froebel, does education depend upon the unity of the family?

4. According to Froebel, how do we learn best?

5. Discuss Froebel's belief that education implies the cultivation of the spirit.

6. Why do some educators criticize Froebel's child-centered system of education?

7. Define and discuss the pros and cons of the two types of idealism in the history of education.

8. Give examples of how education advanced in nineteenth-century Germany.

9. Describe the educational system in nineteenth-century France.

10. What advancements did England accomplish in nineteenth-century education?

Chapter 24

Agnosticism and Education

FOUNDATIONS OF AGNOSTICISM

The modern temper in religion and education has been influenced by the development of agnosticism. We are guided by doubt rather than by certainty and we have said good-bye to the absolutes of our forefathers.

Matthew Arnold, in an eloquent poem, pictures the dilemma which the agnostic attitude creates:

> "The Sea of Faith
> Was once, too, at the full, and round earth's shore
> Lay like the folds of a bright girdle furl'd.
> But now I only hear
> Its melancholy, long, withdrawing roar,
> Retreating to the breath
> Of the night-wind, down the vast edges drear
> And naked shingles of the world. . . .
>
> Ah, love, let us be true
> To one another! for the world, which seems
> To lie before us like a land of dreams,
> So various, so beautiful, so new,
> Hath really neither joy, nor love, nor light,
> Nor certitude, nor peace, nor help for pain;
> And we are here as on a darkling plain
> Swept with confused alarms of struggle and flight,
> Where ignorant armies clash by night.[1]

---

[1] *Dover Beach*

The intellectual background of agnosticism is connected with the social currents which developed in early modern times. Agnosticism, in a way, is a logical result of the disintegration of the medieval unity, for ever since the end of the Middle Ages, man's concern has been with the facts of this life rather than with supernatural ideals.

The various revolutions aided in producing the agnostic reaction. The Glorious Revolution of 1688 preached a spirit of religious toleration. As yet it was not absolute; for example, Catholics and Jews still suffered discrimination. Locke, the spokesman of the revolution, believed that tolerance should not be extended to those who denied the existence of God, to those who contradicted the principles of social order, and to those who were subject to an alien religion.

The French Revolution increased the spirit of religious skepticism in France; the aristocracy and the Church had been in close association. Thus, the Revolution was directed not only against social privilege but also against religious ideals. In education the influence of the Church was curbed and the schools adopted a secular foundation for instruction.

Those who influenced the revolution, like Rousseau, Diderot, Voltaire, and Holbach, were frequently regarded with great suspicion by the orthodox; Rousseau was looked upon as a menace to established religion. Voltaire fought a perpetual warfare against the established faith and against all types of superstition, in order to uphold independent thinking in education.

Intellectually, the materialists in France, like Helvetius,[2] Holbach,[3] and de la Mettrie,[4] were even more radical, for they thought that any type of supernaturalism would enslave the human being. To them, materialism appeared as a truly moral gospel; it concentrated man's attention upon this life, emancipated him from priestly control, and led to the enjoyment of our physical senses.

It should be pointed out that the American Revolution likewise owed much to the skeptical spirit. The leaders of the American Revolution, like Jefferson, Paine, and John Adams were opposed to traditional religion. In fact, Paine, in *The Age of Reason*, made a bitter attack on both conventional Prostestantism and Catholicism. A deist, Paine rejected miracles, divine intervention, and he felt that religion could be simplified and based on the laws of love. The liberals of the American Revolution put their ideals into practice; through their efforts, the separation of Church and State became an accomplished fact, and it stamped the development of American education.

Besides social conditions, the scientific and educational changes produced a new outlook in modern times. The authority of mathematics was

---

2 Cf. Helvetius, *De L'esprit*
3 Cf. Holbach, *Système de la nature*
4 La Mettrie, *Passions de l'ame*

waning; more and more attention was focused on the natural sciences. Empirical observation replaced mathematical intuition. As in ancient Greece, many scientists felt that the progress of their subject could best be assured through a method of doubt and through tentative opinions, rather than through the spirit of authoritarianism.

In the eighteenth and nineteenth centuries, the social sciences made solid progress. Comte, thus, asserted that the study of sociology would revolutionize our knowledge. Investigation into the social sciences frequently produced a skeptical spirit. Education was studied as a social process which reflected the environment and the biases of its leaders.

The study of comparative ideas was stressed by the Enlightenment. Voltaire felt that Western Europe had much to learn from Confucianism, which he regarded as a model educational philosophy. Did it not stress agnosticism? Did it not develop a strong family life? The German anatomist Wolff likewise lectured upon the Chinese moral system, and he reminded his hearers that they could learn much from the ethical inwardness and the advanced education of the Chinese.

In the nineteenth century, the Oriental influence became even more pronounced. The transcendentalists in America, especially Thoreau and Emerson, had an immense liking for the *Upanishads*. In Germany, Schopenhauer declared that Buddhism with its stark pessimistic spirit was far superior to Western concepts of education.

EVOLUTION. The fundamental event, of course, which encouraged the agnostic reaction, was the theory of evolution. It taught such doctrines as the prodigality of nature, the struggle for existence, survival of the fittest, heredity, and sexual selection.[5] It must be remembered that Charles Darwin, in his theory of evolution, was very much influenced by the Reverend Malthus, who held that the food supply did not keep up with the population growth, and hence that God through his providence would have to check mankind through pestilence, famine, and other means.[6] Darwin himself remained faithful to the Christian faith. However, some of his followers, like T. H. Huxley, took an agnostic position.

IMPLICATIONS FOR PHILOSOPHY. Evolution indicated that historical factors could not be excluded in religious thought. Religion, thus, was a process of slow development, rather than a process of divine inspiration.

Evolution challenged completely man's concept of creation. According to the theory of evolution, there was no validity to the idea that God had created man, the garden of Eden, or that all of history had started

---

[5] Darwin's theories were modified later by Weisman, Mendel, and de Vries.
[6] Regarding the foundation of Darwinism, see Barnes, *History of Western Civilization*, II, pp. 655-657.

six thousand years ago. Instead, it expanded man's time perspective and frequently replaced theology with anthropological considerations.[7]

Evolution challenged the sentimental concept of man. Instead of a stress upon the divine soul and man's unique place in the universe, it placed emphasis upon man's animal ancestry. The thought that man was part of the animal world was indeed a deadly blow to man's pretensions.

The theory of evolution replaced supernatural explanation with a naturalistic view of life. God, instead of being the beginning and end of man's destiny, now was replaced by scientific ideals. It was thought that science could best explain how man had evolved and that there was no need to appeal to supernatural intervention.

Evolution changed man's concept of morality. Historical studies clearly indicated that the laws of nature and the laws of morality could scarcely be combined, for in nature the strong survived while the weak perished.

The evolutionary theory gave a naturalistic foundation to education. Thus, Dewey believed that biology was the basis of the educative process and that man should be studied in his naturalistic adjustment to the environment.

HUME

The prophet of the agnostic movement before the theory of evolution was David Hume (1711-1776). Intellectually, he was a radical; in politics, however, he was conservative; for instance, he opposed the American Revolution.[8]

Among his significant works are his *Treatise of Human Nature, Inquiry Concerning Human Understanding, Inquiry into Morals,* and *Political Discourses.* From the standpoint of religion and education his *Natural History of Religion* and his *Dialogues* are especially significant. They were so radical that he could not publish them during his lifetime —both came out posthumously.

It was the purpose of David Hume to free philosophy and education from vagueness and obscurity. He wanted not merely to destroy the old foundations, but to develop a new method which would be more in harmony with the conclusions of science. Philosophy and education were to be divorced from all supernatural foundations; they were to be *concrete* and *actualistic* in their emphasis.

---

[7] On the influence of the new evolutionary ideals on religion consult Strauss, *Der alte und neue Glaube.*

[8] Cf. Huxley, *Hume;* Knight, *Hume;* Taylor, *Hume and the Miraculous;* Compayré, *La Philosophie de D. Hume.*

Hume carried on a constant warfare against various religious schools. He attacked both Protestantism and Catholicism. Likewise, he tried to show that the deists, with their concept of a rational religion, could not substantiate their conclusions.

Hume's philosophy was based on the concept of impressions, which are fundamental. Ideas, on the other hand, are copies of impressions. Ideas are not unified by the mind, rather they naturally associate themselves together in a mechanical way. How is this association carried out? In three ways: first, through resemblance—we associate ideas which have a similar impact; secondly, through contiguity in space and time; and thirdly, through the law of causality.

It must be remembered that ideas are not independent, but must be traced to the impressions. For example, if we believe in infinite ideas, the sceptic at once will say, "Upon what impressions do they rest?" Even the laws of mathematics, according to Hume, have only an "ideal reality."

Especially important is Hume's attack against the concept of substance. We have no impression of a material substance; likewise there is no soul substance. When I think of myself, I am always dependent upon a specific sensation. We certainly cannot arrive at metaphysical conclusions regarding the self, which consists of a variety of perceptions. Why do we speak of a simple self? This is merely a habit; it is due to the laziness of the imagination. Man's memory, according to Hume, ascribes more unity both to the physical and the mental world than actually can be found.

Just as significant is his challenge of the law of causality. Hume made it clear that there is no necessity in causality. Thus, when I strike someone and the person feels pain, there is no necessary relationship between these two acts. *Causality is subjective, and is based on habit.* The relationship between cause and effect is psychological; it cannot be discovered by the laws of logic.

Hume believed that most people appeal to theology and metaphysics, when in reality, custom is the foundation of human life. Away, then with the abstruse reasoning of the theologians, for their conclusions are mostly based upon their own wishes and desires rather than upon actual events! There can be no absolute certainty either in natural science, education or theology.

This does not mean that Hume was an atheist, or that he wanted to destroy all religion. He did not have radical opinions regarding social institutions, rather it was his purpose to point out the insufficiency of the intellectual arguments for the existence of God. Man should follow his feelings rather than his intellect.

There are intensely pessimistic strains in Hume. He believed that existence for most human beings is a tragic process; poverty, disease, and starvation abound. Even when man enjoys a pleasant experience, he is frequently tortured by a sense of sin, and those who live a happy life are overcome by death. The theist might say that our ordeals add to the glory of providence, but Hume felt that a perfect God would not create such an imperfect world.

Above all, David Hume believed in freedom of inquiry in education. When he was a librarian at Edinburgh, he was censured because he selected so many books by French authors, like the *Contes* by La Fontaine, which were considered obscene by his contemporaries. Censorship to Hume was an unmitigated evil. He maintained in a letter that, if books inferior to La Fontaine had to be removed, the library would be almost completely empty. Education, Hume thought, could progress only when individuals were allowed to think and read for themselves.

Bigotry and superstition were to be eliminated from our scholastic centers. Hume attacked the schools of his time for being "citadels of regression" and for presenting distorted views of life. An educated man would be critical regarding most doctrines of philosophy, religion and education.

Hume believed that the educational curriculum of his time was obsolete. It stressed memorization and repetition. It overemphasized the classics. It dealt too much with the past and neglected the possibilities of the present. He felt that history especially was taught in a most inadequate way. The teacher of history was usually preoccupied with battles and external events. What mattered to Hume, who wrote a celebrated *History of England,* was the cultural foundation of history, the way individuals in various periods thought, lived, and expressed themselves. Basically, history and literature were interdependent, for literature was a key to the ideals and yearnings of human beings and gave a symbolic account of life.

Should the teacher be a supporter of religion? Hume answered in the negative. God did not create man, rather man formed the concept of God in his own image. Theologians give plausible reasons why men's desires should be realized, but on most occasions, according to Hume, their knowledge is based on ignorance. Those who feel that Christianity is more adequate than other forms of religion are mistaken, for frequently Oriental religions, like Buddhism, have been tolerant of other faiths, while Christianity has carried on terrible persecutions. Thus, Hume believed that Greek philosophy with its tolerance and naturalism could teach a basic lesson to modern man, who frequently leans in the direction of fanaticism.

Extremely skeptical was Hume's conception of miracles. He made it clear that we must be guided by definite evidence, and that doubt is the best rule. Without skepticism, there could be no progress in history.

Hume, with all his intellectual powers, attacked the ecclesiastical control over education, which prevailed in many European countries. Such domination only created an anti-scientific attitude and limited the freedom of teachers. How fortunate the Greeks were, because there was no state religion! There could be no infallible viewpoint either in religion or in education, for our ideas were only hypotheses. Furthermore, the rule of authority only created docile minds and submissive teachers. Like Abelard, Hume taught that we find meaning in life by doubting.

Hume believed in a utilitarian concept of education. We learn when we are interested and when we find new ideas useful in our daily existence. Education is not an abstraction, but a practical process. We must learn not only to think well but to live creatively.

Hume lived up to his own educational ideals. He describes himself with accuracy as:

"A man of mild dispositions, of command of temper, of an open, social and cheerful humor, capable of attachment, but little susceptible of enmity, and of great moderation in all my passions. Even my love of literary fame, my ruling passion, never soured my temperament, notwithstanding my frequent disappointments."

What are the educational conclusions of David Hume? Should there be a system of genuine mass education? Can all become rational? He replied in the negative, for the average man lived by his feelings and was guided by custom. Education, to Hume, was basically an aristocratic process. He rejected the concept of utopia. Educational progress at best occurred gradually. The philosopher may question doctrines, and he may challenge fundamental concepts, but generally he will pay due regard to traditions and conventions, and politically he will be a conservative rather than a radical.

COMTE

The spirit of secularism was furthered not only by David Hume, but also by Auguste Comte (1798-1857). Already in his youth, Comte had radical opinions regarding religion and education. He felt that science was the best tool for the enlightenment and emancipation of man. In his later years, he turned to a new faith, which he called the religion of humanity, and he substituted the saints of humanity for the traditional saints of theism.[9]

---

[9] Cf. Pünjer, *Der Positivismus;* Watson, *Comte, Mill and Spencer;* Caird, *The Social Philosophy and Religion of Comte.*

According to Comte, society passes through three stages. The first stage, *theology*, starts in primitive life when we regard nature as being alive, and when we are governed by taboo concepts. After a while, we deify the forces of nature, and thus reach the polytheistic stage. The best manifestation of this spirit can be found in Greece. Later, the gods are united; this is not done in a theological manner; rather this union reflects a fundamental social and political consolidation. Is the theological stage confined to any one period in history? Do we find it only in ancient times? Comte answers in the negative, for man constantly appeals to supernatural forces, and appears to have a basic mistrust for science.

In the second stage, which is dominated by *metaphysics,* we appeal to the forces of nature. Metaphysics assumes a belief in an underlying substance. Philosophers dominate the metaphysical stage, and they give *a priori* answers to the problems of reality. The metaphysical stage discourages the progress of science, for it negates the consideration of phenomenon, disregards specific analysis, and jumps at preconceived conclusions.

The third stage is dominated by *positivism*. This is genuine education. The scientist takes over, and his main concern is to explain relationships and to reduce the laws of nature to a quantitative foundation. The watchword is control and prediction. Comte, like Bacon, believed that man should not be concerned with the causes of nature, rather with the control of nature.

All sciences pass through the three stages:

"There is no science which, having attained the positive stage, does not bear marks of having passed through the others. Some time since it was (whatever it might be) composed, as we can now perceive, of metaphysical abstractions; and, further back in the course of time, it took its form from theological conceptions. We shall have only too much occasion to see, as we proceed, that our most advanced sciences still bear very evident marks of the two earlier periods through which they have passed.

"The progress of the individual mind is not only an illustration, but an indirect evidence of that of the general mind. The point of departure of the individual and of the race being the same, the phases of the mind of a man correspond to the epochs of the mind of the race. Now, each of us is aware, if he looks back upon his own history, that he was a theologian in his childhood, a metaphysician in his youth, and a natural philosopher in his manhood. All men who are up to their age can verify this for themselves." [10]

In the outline of his educational scheme, Comte maintained that it should follow the evolution of the sciences. First come the sciences of

---

[10] *The Positive Philosophy,* Chapter 1.

number (arithmetic, algebra, geometry, and mechanics), then, astronomy, followed by physics and chemistry. Then, biology and physiology appear on the scene. At last, social physics or sociology appears, and this, to Comte, was the most important science. It was not only a summary of all the other sciences, but it gave meaning and coherence to their study.

Comte anticipated John Dewey in his emphasis upon methodology. Since we cannot know the essence of the universe we should be concerned mainly with practical control and scientific ideals. Education thus has a scientific rather than a metaphysical meaning. However, Comte differed from Dewey in that he made mathematics, rather than concrete experiences, the point of departure for the student. Furthermore, Comte was more concerned with humanity as a whole, while Dewey stressed the importance of the individual.

The democratic ideals of Comte are revealed in his advocacy that education should be a universal process in which no class differences were to be recognized. The schools were to be open to the rich and the poor, the young and the old; merit rather than social position was to determine the educational advancement of the student.

The conclusion of Comte is clear. If man is to progress he must avoid all references to superstition; he must abandon mysticism, which indicates vague reasoning; and he must give up the desire for *a priori* answers. Rather, he must use scientific control, especially the resources of sociology.

Positivism, in Comte's viewpoint, will bring about an educational renaissance. It will concentrate on the development of man, it will produce a new spirit in social legislation; in fact, it will be the prelude to a real utopia.

To some extent, Comte was overly optimistic. He thought that the age of religion was past, he felt that man could live by scientific education alone; however, the twentieth century has not verified his prediction. Indeed, as Spengler has shown, man in this century has experienced a second religiousness.

MILL

John Stuart Mill (1806-1873) was very much influenced both by Bentham and Comte. Among his works we should notice his *Essays on Liberty, Principles of Political Economy, Thoughts on Parliamentary Reform, System of Logic, Utilitarianism, Examination of Sir William Hamilton's Philosophy,* and *Three Essays on Religion.* The temper of Mill was secular.[11] Thus, he rejected the existence of a thing-in-itself, for

---

11 Cf. Bain, *John Stuart Mill, a Criticism;* Douglas, *J. S. Mill: a Study of his Philosophy.*

he felt that knowledge refers only to phenomena. He elaborated the principles of inductive logic, and he tried to get away from all *a priori* reasoning. In ethics, likewise, his naturalistic spirit is very evident. He accepted the pleasure-pain principle, although he had a more qualitative view than Bentham. Matter itself he defined as the permanent possibility of sensation; we have no knowledge of a soul substance or of a material substance, and we can neither prove nor disprove the existence of God.

In education, Mill's fame rests upon his *Address* which he delivered when he was inaugurated rector of St. Andrew's University. He made a strong plea for the cultivation of the sciences as well as the study of ancient languages. The sciences would create logical minds and systematic thinking, while the study of ancient languages would be an excellent discipline as well as a stimulus to the imagination of the student. Mill, on the other hand, had far less sympathy for the study of modern languages, which he thought lacked the dignity and splendor of the ancient tongues. As for literature, he regarded its pursuit as being only of secondary importance.

The ideal of Mill was to combine the study of the classical languages with scientific discipline. "Know the past and know nature" were the foundations of his educational philosophy. However, the curriculum which he advocated was so rigorous that the student would not have enough time for scientific pursuits.

Mill believed in liberty in intellectual discussions. In fact, he made a basic contribution to the concept of academic freedom by stressing that no one should interfere with private opinion, and that there was no infallible authority.

In education this meant that all forms of thought control were to be avoided. Teachers should be able to express their own ideas and they were not to be servants of the state. Unlike Hegel, Mill did not believe that obedience was the most important virtue for the student. On the contrary, the student had to develop his own ideas, and he had to cultivate the habit of independent thinking. Only in this way could education progress and become a tool of genuine enlightenment.

SPENCER

Herbert Spencer (1820-1903), the main interpreter of evolution, was as secular as John Stuart Mill, and thus had no liking for orthodoxy. He was a sharp critic of the weaknesses of religion which, according to him, had hindered the progress of education. With vehemence he pointed out that frequently religious believers had not been faithful to their ideals.[12]

---

12 On Spencer, see Bowne, *The Philosophy of H. Spencer;* Watson, *Comte, Mill and Spencer.*

Spencer made a fundamental division between religion and the sciences. Religion deals with the Unknowable, while science deals with quantitative knowledge. Neither field must intrude upon the other; thus, when the scientist invades the field of religion, the theologian can reject this intrusion. Yet, when religion tries to interfere with the sciences, the scientist likewise should protest against this act.

Can we define the Unknowable? Can we explain his attributes? Spencer answers in the negative, for our knowledge is only symbolic, and applies to the relative and to the conditioned. When we call the Unknowable the cause of the universe, we are using symbolic terms.

What is the foundation of religion? Spencer asserted that it arises out of ancestor worship, for primitive man is afraid of death, and he fears the power of those who have passed away. In his dreams he is tortured by the thought that the ancestors whom he has not honored will come back and punish him. Prayer expresses his fear; when this fear is institutionalized, organized religion develops.

Spencer's treatise, *Education,* was a best seller, both in the United States and in England. It became a favorite text for teacher training institutions. He felt that the most important problem is the concept of values and that education was a practical rather than a theoretical pursuit. Quantitative knowledge was to him far more valuable than the study of ancient languages which at best could have only a secondary value. He favored especially concentration upon physics, chemistry and biology. Mathematics, he maintained, would create clarity and order in our intellectual processes.

Spencer called for a change in the training for citizenship. He believed that conventional history was a waste of time and that emphasis upon battles and kings gave us a distorted view of the past. He wanted sociology to be the center of the curriculum, for it would tell us how nations developed and how social factors influence history.

In all of his theories, Spencer was attacking the conventional English curriculum with its classical emphasis and its stress upon the past. Such studies would hinder the progress of science and create a snobbish spirit. The laboratory, not book knowledge, was to be the center of the educational curriculum.

Spencer attacked the ornamental view of education which is symbolized by a preoccupation with the classics.

"Among mental as well as among bodily acquisitions, the ornamental comes before the useful. Not only in times past, but almost as much in our own era, that knowledge which conduces to personal well-being has been postponed to that which brings applause. In the Greek schools, music, poetry, rhetoric, and a philosophy which, until Socrates taught, had but little bearing upon action, were the dominant subjects; while knowledge aiding the arts of life had a very subordinate place. And in our own universities and schools at the present moment the like antithesis holds. We are guilty of something like a platitude when we say that throughout his after-career a boy, in nine cases out of ten, applies his Latin and Greek to no practical purposes . . ." 13

[Far more important than the classics to Spencer is] "the problem how to decide among the conflicting claims of various subjects on our attention. Before there can be a rational *curriculum,* we must settle which things it would most concern us to know; or, to use a word of Bacon's now unfortunately obsolete, we must determine the relative values of knowledge." 14

The conduct of life, Spencer maintained, is central in education.

"Not how to live in the mere material sense only, but in the widest sense. The general problem which comprehends every special problem is, the right ruling of conduct in all directions under all circumstances. In what way to treat the body; in what way to treat the mind; in what way to manage our affairs; in what way to bring up a family; in what way to behave as a citizen; in what way to utilize all those sources of happiness which nature supplies—how to use our faculties to the greatest advantage of ourselves and others—how to live completely? And this being the great thing needful for us to learn, is by consequence, the great thing which education has to teach. To prepare us for complete living is the function which education has to discharge." 15

Self-maintenance, to Spencer, is the basis of education.

"That next after self-preservation comes the indirect self-preservation, which consists in acquiring the means of living, none will question. That a man's industrial functions must be considered before his parental ones is manifest from the fact that speaking generally, the discharge of the parental functions is made possible only by the previous discharge of the industrial ones. The power of self-maintenance necessarily preceding the power of maintaining offspring, it follows that knowledge needful for self-maintenance has stronger claims than knowledge for family welfare—is second to none save knowledge needful for immediate self-preservation." 16

The family comes before the state, according to Spencer.

"The bringing up of children is possible before the state exists or when it has ceased to be, whereas the state is rendered possible only by the bringing up of children—it follows that the duties of the parent demand closer attention than those of the citizen. Or to use a further argument, since the goodness of a society ultimately depends on the nature of its citizens, and

---

13 *What Knowledge Is of Most Worth?*
14 *Ibid.*
15 *Ibid.*
16 *Ibid.*

since the nature of its citizens is more modifiable by early training than by anything else, we must conclude that the welfare of the family underlies the welfare of society. And hence knowledge directly conducing to the first must take precedence of knowledge directly conducing to the last." [17]

Intellectual training, Spencer taught, should stress the humanities.

"And now we come to that remaining division of human life which includes the relaxations, pleasures, and amusements filling leisure hours . . . Without painting, sculpture, music, poetry, and the emotion produced by natural beauty of every kind, life would lose half its charm. So far from thinking that the training and gratification of the tastes are unimportant, we believe that the time will come they will occupy a much larger share of human life than now. When the forces of nature have been fully conquered to man's use—when the means of production have been brought to perfection —when labor has been economized to the highest degree—education has been so systematized that a preparation for the more essential activities may be made with comparative rapidity—and when, consequently, there is a great increase of spare time, then will the poetry, both of art and nature, rightly fill a large space in the minds of all." [18]

Yet the most important part of knowledge, Spencer asserted, is *science*.

"For that indirect self-preservation which we call gaining a livelihood, the knowledge of greatest value is—science. For the due discharge of parental functions, the proper guidance is to be found only in—science. For that interpretation of national life, past and present, without which the citizen can not rightly regulate his conduct, the indispensable key is—science. Alike for the most perfect production and highest enjoyment of art in all its forms, the needful preparation is still—science. And for purposes of discipline— intellectual, moral, religious—the most efficient study is once more— science." [19]

Can a final truth be found? Spencer answers in the negative. Knowledge, at best, represents only an allegorical interpretation. If man wants to progress he must use his scientific resources, adapt himself to his environment, and through intelligent educational action, eliminate the ills of war and poverty.

HUXLEY

Of all the interpreters of evolution, Thomas H. Huxley (1825-1895) fought the most strenuous warfare with the forces of orthodoxy. His own viewpoint was that of agnosticism, which neither denies nor affirms the

---

[17] *Ibid.*
[18] *Ibid.*
[19] *Ibid.*

existence of God. Psychologically, agnosticism results in a suspension of judgment. Our knowledge, according to Huxley, can never include the supernatural, for there is no experimental evidence as to the nature of God and immortality.

In education, Huxley popularized the knowledge of his day. He believed that education was a continuous process and, as chairman of the London School Board, he tried to expand the bases of popular knowledge. He lectured not only to academic circles, but also to laborers, and he was an enthusiastic proponent of adult education.

He called for an improvement on the primary, secondary, and university level. Like Spencer, he urged that science should be the center of the curriculum. A prolific textbook writer, he advocated that educational and scientific ideas be presented in a systematic fashion to the student. By education, Huxley meant that "we learn the rules of the game," and that we increase our mastery of life. He wanted students to develop a cold logical mind and to be interested in the laws of nature. He despised asceticism which only created a perverted perspective. He wanted to develop a liberally educated man who is "full of fire, whose passions are trained to come to heel by a vigorous will, the servant of a tender conscience; who has learned to love all beauty, whether of Nature or of art, to hate all vileness, and to respect others as himself." [20]

Huxley was opposed to the classical curriculum for it was too traditional and conservative. Why study the past when the present was so exciting? Why concentrate upon the Roman empire when England was expanding all over the world? Let the student learn about his own time and become an expert in the social sciences, especially in geography. Let him study economics rather than Greek, let him be prepared for business and the professions. Humanistic knowledge thus was to be replaced by scientific education.

What is Huxley's conclusion? The educated man will not be dogmatic when he faces life. He will be concerned with facts which he can verify. His arena will be the realm of science, not that of the classics. Away then with all dogmatism and all fanaticism! Man can only progress when education becomes a practical way of life.

Scholars, like Huxley, believed in science as a method of controlling nature which would ultimately create a new social system. But science as an inquiry is a neutral tool. It can be used constructively and destructively. In education, the scientific emphasis alone is not adequate. It has to be supplemented by the warmth of literature and by the insights of philosophy. Real creativity in education always goes beyond specialization and depends upon the cultivation of relatedness.

------

[20] *Liberal Education: Where To Find It.*

QUESTIONS FOR DISCUSSION AND INVESTIGATION

1. Explain the social currents which lent the intellectual background to agnosticism.

2. How did the theory of evolution change man's approach to religion and philosophy?

3. What beliefs of Hume helped to free philosophy and education from vagueness and obscurity?

4. What were Hume's ideas on education?

5. Describe the three stages through which society passes, according to Comte, and explain their significance.

6. In what way did Comte anticipate Dewey?

7. What ideals of John Stuart Mill caused his fame in the field of education?

8. Define Spencer's fundamental division between religion and the sciences.

9. Explain Thomas H. Huxley's viewpoint on agnosticism and his impact on education.

10. In Huxley's conclusion what qualities should the educated man possess?

Chapter 25

Tolstoy and Russian Education

SIGNIFICANCE

One of the leading spokesmen for the pre-Soviet Russian civilization and education is Leo Tolstoy. In his realism, based upon minute and penetrating observation, and in his propensity for self-examination, he represents typical Russian traits. His concept of love is much more sweeping than that of the western mind, for love to him means more than affection, more than compassion; it stands for complete self-abnegation. To find a parallel the reader would have to turn to the concept of Bhakti, as found in the *Bhagavad-Gita.* Tolstoy is not alone among pre-Soviet writers in stressing the importance of sacrificial love; Dostoevsky is possessed by the same burning passion, even in the cold despair of Siberia.

Combined with love in Tolstoy is an unsparing frankness. He analyzes society in anatomical terms, penetrates through the veil of social convention and human rationalizations, and investigates the darkest caverns of the institutional system. This candid observation is extended to human emotions. Seldom have they been portrayed more vividly and more picturesquely. Occasionally, the description becomes physiological, as in the *Kreutzer Sonata,* where he describes the sensations of sex with Augustinian clarity. He never spares himself in this process of analysis, and there is an element of autobiography in all of his major works. Usually the conclusions he reaches regarding his own motives are somber and melancholy. He constantly seems to be asking himself, "Why am I doing this? Why do I not live up to my ideals?" And as a result, his life is full of torment and anguish.

Someone has remarked that genius is characterized by perpetual melancholy. In some geniuses this is merely an esthetic gesture, like the tragic declamations of a great actor, in others it has an emotional basis. Tolstoy belongs to the second class. And again here he is more Oriental than European. Like Buddha, he felt the full weight of existence, the futility of life, and the ever present reality of evil. Undoubtedly there is a strain of cosmic pessimism in the works of the major Russian writers, from Chekhov to Gorky, mainly because these men felt and pondered so deeply over the fundamental problems of existence.

What makes Tolstoy especially human is his sympathy for the oppressed, his identification with the underprivileged members of society, and his willingness to sacrifice for them. Gogol wrote, "Pity for a fallen creature is a very natural trait," and the truth of this claim is illustrated by the life of Tolstoy. He belonged to the aristocracy, and yet he found the greatest meaning in life in the present existence; he betrayed the ideals, the expressions, and the interests of his class. Later in life he regretted that he had not been born as a simple peasant. He wanted to overcome all the barriers that separated him from the lowliest man on his estate, and since this was never quite possible, Tolstoy lived in two worlds and experienced the full twilight of human existence.

Finally, in his proclivity for extremes, Tolstoy exhibits another Russian trait. It takes a certain mellowness in civilization to produce moderation, a spirit shown by the Athenians in the Periclean age. The feudalism and the autocracy of the Russian state did not lead to moderation. The harshness of the climate also made life more somber. Very often we find in Russian writers and educators an alternation between extreme sensuality and extreme asceticism, with periods of conversion following soul-shaking crises. Tolstoy experienced the full measure of emotional storms. He did not hesitate to follow his ideas, regardless of the consequences.

But Tolstoy is more than a representative of the Russian mind; he represents the spirit of world brotherhood. What is more important, he realizes that peace demands more than a new adjustment in international relations, more than institutional reorganization, it requires a new philosophy of life and a new system of education.

MAJOR IDEAS

Tolstoy was born in 1828. In his youth he enjoyed all the advantages of the aristocracy. He received an excellent education, mostly by private tutors, and was surrounded by all the luxuries of life. As a boy, he was strong and passionate, and already had a keen power of observation. The memories of his childhood were distinct and clear. When his mother died in 1830, he writes,

"During the service I wept decently, crossed myself, and bowed down to the floor, but I did not pray with my soul, and I was rather indifferent; I was troubled because the little new dress coat that they had made me wear was very tight under the arms. I was careful not to soil overmuch the knees of my trousers and I stealthily made observations on all who were present." [1]

He attended the University of Kazan, where he majored in natural science, law, and philosophy. He was bored by the curriculum of the University, which was too formal and stereotyped, and his real education came through discussions with his fellow students. Already he had taken a liking to Rousseau, who was to become a powerful influence in his life. The ambition of young Tolstoy can be seen by a plan of study he outlined for himself when he left the University of Kazan. Within two years he desired to master the fundamentals of law, of practical and theoretical medicine, French, German, English, Latin and Italian, the principles of agriculture, history, geography, statistics, the principles of mathematics, and to advance his knowledge in music, painting, and natural science. In addition to these efforts, he planned to write a dissertation and treatises on all the subjects he studied—certainly an ambitious program for a young man. He failed to accomplish these goals in the next two years, since he devoted his life to gay social activities. He wrote to his brother a year later, after he went to St. Petersburg, "I did nothing useful there, merely squandered heaps of money and got into debt." But the ambition for learning persisted and his knowledge later on became truly encyclopedic.

In 1851 he entered the army as an officer, rapidly advanced in rank, and fought through the Crimean campaign, during which he took part in the storming of Sevastopol. His three sketches about the campaign, *Sevastopol in December, 1854, and in May and August, 1855,* portray the full horror of war. These sketches are very different from the patriotic exhortations of Tennyson. He pictures fear in all its dimensions, the fear of the army officers leaving for the front, the cowering dread of the common soldiers crawling on all fours, the mute despair of the hospitals.

The awareness of death is one of the distinguishing traits of Tolstoy. Perhaps he is one of the most skillful biographers of death in the history of world literature. As Tolstoy became older, he spoke more fearfully about death, and the desire for immortality became more insistent. It is well to remember that not for a moment of his life did the awareness of the transitory aspects of human existence desert him. Like Buddha, Tolstoy wanted to conquer not only life, but death itself.

He gave up his army career, joined a brilliant literary circle in St. Petersburg, and resolved to become a great author. He traveled abroad,

[1] Tolstoy, *Childhood,* Chap. 27.

visited France, Switzerland, Germany, and Italy. Like Schopenhauer, he saw the darker aspects of existence in those countries; for instance, the picture of a man being executed in Paris remained in his mind. In Switzerland he observed the life of the idle rich, parasites without a constructive purpose in life.

When he returned to Russia he devoted himself to improving the lot of the serfs who had just been emancipated by the order of the Czar. He conducted an experimental school which tried to put into practice individualistic theories of education. "I should give two rules for education," he said, "not only to live well oneself, but to work over oneself, constantly perfecting oneself and to conceal nothing about one's own life from one's children." He also edited an educational journal *Yasnaya Polyana,* which reflected his indebtedness to Rousseau.

He married when he was thirty-four. His wife was more practical than he, and, while they were devoted to each other, there was no close intellectual comradeship. With his passionate mind, he made a very difficult partner in marriage. It was at this time that he wrote *War and Peace.* The fundamental purpose of this book was educational: to show the fallacy of war. Unlike Carlyle, Tolstoy did not believe in hero worship. Napoleon appears as a vain puffed up individual. Kutuzov is pictured as a stodgy, impotent general; both are puppets in the hands of Fate. Tolstoy shows no respect for the military strategy of Napoleon, and with alacrity exposes his mistakes. The battles are viewed by Tolstoy as parts of a gigantic chaos, in which organization and the best-made plans count for nothing. The real heroes of *War and Peace* are the common soldiers. Their endurance, their sacrifices, their comradeship, are described with profound sympathy. The leading character of the story is not Prince Andrey or his friend, Count Pierre Bezukhov, but an illiterate simple peasant, Platon Karatayev. Instinctively, this man fulfilled the requirements of Christianity. "He loved all and lived lovingly with all with which life brought him into contact, and in particular with man— not with any special man, but with men who were before his eyes." To Tolstoy, Platon is the unattainable and eternal embodiment of the spirit of simplicity and real education, and represents a fulfilment in life for which he was constantly striving.

In *Anna Karenina* Tolstoy reaches the full height of his genius. Here we have a philosophy of life crystallized into emotional terms, and a tale of the inevitable decline of a social order. The world of Anna is destined to fall; nothing can prevent that collapse. All those who are identified with this world are doomed. Almost prophetic in his warning, Tolstoy understood the full significance of his time. But there is also the promise of a new society, symbolized by the efforts of Levin and by his pure love for Kitty.

Anna, as the story opens, is married securely to a high government official. She is a pillar of respectability. Marriage has not brought great emotional upheaval, but steady security. Then she meets Vronsky, a handsome army officer, and her love for him becomes the overwhelming feature of her life. She gives herself completely, becomes an outcast from society, and finally finds out that Vronsky is unworthy of her love. The result is suicide.

Quite different from Anna is Levin, who shuns society, lives a peasant existence, and, like Platon, is imbued with the spirit of Christianity. Some critics have called him a Sunday School type, and found him uninteresting and boring. Nevertheless, there are qualities that give him depth and reality; his sense of unworthiness, his tormenting doubts, and his humility. The spirit of Levin is expressed by Tolstoy in the last paragraph of *Anna Karenina*.

"Just as before, I shall get angry with Ivan the coachman, I shall dispute, I shall express my thoughts at the wrong time; there will be the same wall between the holy of holies of my soul and other people, even my wife; just in the same way as before I shall blame her for my own terror and repent doing so; just as before I shall fail to understand with my reason why I pray, and yet I shall continue to pray—but my life now, my whole life, independently of anything that can happen to me, every moment of it, is not only not bereft of meaning, as it was before, but has the undoubted meaning of good, which I have power to implant in it!"

In spite of the success of *War and Peace* and *Anna Karenina*, Tolstoy felt dissatisfied. Not only was he critical regarding his works (he wrote *Anna Karenina* seven times, and would wake up at night and start changing sentences which did not seem perfect) but he was tortured by doubts, and by a feeling of hopelessness. He started to take stock. He was rich; he owned 16,000 acres in the province of Samara, he had a devoted wife, and he was famous as an author; but something was lacking. Buddha felt the same way when he surveyed the treasures of his kingdom. Tolstoy, with almost Faustian ferocity, wanted to know the answers that had tortured philosophers and educators for thousands of years. In 1879, he summarized the questions which are central in education:

1. "Why live at all?" 2. "What is the cause of my existence, and of everyone else's?" 3. "What is the purpose of my existence and of everyone else's?" 4. "What is the meaning of the cleavage into good and evil which I feel within myself, and why does this cleavage exist?" 5. "What should be the plan of my life?" 6. "What is death—how can I transcend it?"

To find the answer to these problems Tolstoy turned to science. More avidly than ever he studied books on biology, chemistry, physics, and psychology. The scientists reduced qualitative relationships to their

quantitative constituents. They measured nature and created order out
of chaos, but they did not solve the basic problems of life. Technical
philosophy had even less to offer; it restated the problem in a more
complicated form, and in obscure terminology concealed its essential
ignorance. Tolstoy's despair grew as he turned to Socrates, Buddha, the
book of Ecclesiastes, and Schopenhauer. In unison they seemed to stress
the vanity of life. Was not Buddha's four-fold truth a commentary upon
the inescapable sorrow of man's existence? Did not Schopenhauer's philosophy end in nihilism? Did not Ecclesiastes stress the utter vanity of
man's strivings? Tolstoy tried to turn to God, but he did not have a living awareness of Him; he also thought that Kant had demolished all the
purely intellectual proofs of the existence of God.

So volcanic was this rebellion that Tolstoy could not find solace in
the mysticism and the superstition of the Church. He was disgusted with
the corruption of the Greek Orthodox priests, their support of the state,
and their tacit approval of war. How different this organization was
from the primitive Christian church! How it neglected the practices of
Christ! Thus, Tolstoy started a revolution against formalism and ritual.
He desired to find the faith of the common man, the essential spirit of
religion which could be universalized and applied to all times. The Sermon on the Mount gave him the substance of his new beliefs.

Faith brought about a transvaluation of values. Riches, fame, physical love—all these things were obstacles in the quest for salvation. Like
Saint Augustine, Tolstoy examined his actions and came to the conclusion that they were sinful. Naturally, he exaggerated. In his *Confessions*,
he tells about the people he killed in war, the money he lost at cards, the
acts of lying, stealing, drunkenness, violence, murder, and above all of
lust, which he had committed. He tells of an aunt who advised him to
have a liaison with a married woman, and who later urged him to marry
a rich girl so that he could have many servants. That, according to his
Confessions, was his environment. "There was not a crime I did not commit, and for all that I was praised, and my contemporaries have regarded
me as a comparatively moral man." The self-accusation does not stop
here. Asked why he started to compose books, he replied that it was not
for the benefit of the community, but that he was driven by vanity,
avarice, and pride. With pitiless clarity he observed his fellow authors;
not only were most of them immoral and of weak character, but they
were complacent; they thought that they had found the avenue to education when in reality they were only portraying insignificant aspects of
life.

NEW VALUES THROUGH SPIRITUAL EDUCATION

Thus the author of *Anna Karenina* became a writer of moral and
theological tracts. In *Resurrection* we have perhaps the greatest expres-

sion of the new Tolstoy. It is the tale of Prince Nekhludoff, who falls in love with a servant girl. First, their relationship is innocent and very poetic, guided by the idealism of youth. Later, the army spoils his code of ethics. She has a child and he deserts her, according to the code of his class. When her condition is discovered, she has to leave the estate, sinks lower and lower, and enters the darkest stratum of society. The climax of the story occurs when she is accused of a crime of which she is innocent. It happens that Prince Nekhludoff takes part in the trial. He recognizes her again, and now he realizes his own guilt. An innocent woman is being condemned. He tries to help her, because his conscience hurts him, and he wants to save his own soul. She laughs at him. He realizes that he must make a more complete sacrifice and consequently abandons his class and his property, and joins her in Siberia. There she becomes a real woman again because of his kindness and sacrifice.

One might interpret this story theologically as an allegory of the transforming power of love. But the meaning is much deeper. Man must atone, says Tolstoy, not just for the deeds he has committed, but for his indifference and neglect. He wrote from his own personal experiences, seeing as he did for the first time the naked horror of the existence of the lower classes. Moscow in his early period had been a gay city, and he used to drive by the miserable huts of the proletariat without pondering on the meaning of poverty. Siberia was an indifferent word; that people were exiled to this wasteland was a natural act of justice. Now his imagination expanded, and he spoke for the mute sufferings of millions of Russians, for the serfs, laboring under the yoke of the landlords, for the prisoners slaving under the guard of sadistic wardens, for the opponents of the Czar who languished in Siberia; in short, for all the outcasts of society.

It was small wonder that, in 1901, Tolstoy was excommunicated. The official notice stated that Tolstoy, with the zeal of a fanatic, had advocated the overthrow of all the dogmas of the Orthodox Church, and of the very essence of the Christian faith—a strange attack against one of the most religious men of Russia. The ministers of the Czar advised action against the radical theories of Tolstoy, but Alexander III was more judicious, and said that he had no intention of making a martyr out of the famous author.

How could this new order be established? By the help of the intellectuals and educators? Tolstoy claimed that most of them were supporters of the *status quo*. He turned to the artists and found that they lived in ivory towers. One might suppose that he would appeal to political parties. However, when he analyzed the program of the socialists, he realized that they were trying to do the impossible and cure a condition that could not be solved by evolutionary political means. The revolutionary forces appealed to him for aid. Was he not preaching against the wickedness of property, against the oppressions of the state? Did he not favor nationalization of the land and labor for all? Did he not speak of a new Utopia for the common man? Yes, there were many similarities between him and the revolutionaries. But he hated violence and he knew that the overthrow of the system would mean an application of force and bloodshed. He wanted to reform humanity through education; his method, to borrow Koestler's terms, was that *of the Yogi, not of the Commissar.* But, intellectually, he contributed to the growth of the revolution, for he undermined the foundations of the Czarist government. His attacks corresponded with those of Rousseau against absolutism in France. Both had weakened the internal strength of the existing institutional system.

Tolstoy extends his searching analysis to international relations. What is the cause of war? Not acts of aggression or injustice on the part of one nation, not the pressure of population, but the existence of statehood itself. He denounced in bitter terms the Russian war with Turkey, England's campaigns against the Boers, America's conflict with Spain, and Russia's war with Japan in 1904. He spoke against patriotism in all its forms, and saw the full danger of the suspicious attitude of the European nations. How could wars be abolished? In his time, treaties of arbitration were being made. The Hague Conferences were giving new hopes to mankind. But Tolstoy was far more realistic: he urged a more thoroughgoing reform, abolition of violence itself. He writes: "Bethink yourselves and understand that not the Boers, English, French, Germans, Bohemians, Finns, Russians are your enemies, but that the only enemies are you yourselves, who with your patriotism support the governments, which oppress you and cause your misfortune."

CONFLICTING IDEALS

In his later life, Tolstoy's missionary zeal became extremely strong. In an essay on art, he condemned the idea that art was designed for pleasure. Here he reminds us of Plato. He speaks of "Shakespeare's meaningless twaddle," of Beethoven as a "seducer to sensuality." Again he goes to an extreme, but his essay is justified in striking at the root of the impoverishment of modern art, in attacking the sensationalistic and superficial content of much of the art of his time, and in his insistence upon the wider mission of the artist, who should be an apostle for humanity. "The best works of art of our time," he writes, "transmit religious feelings urging toward the union and the brotherhood of man." Hence, he praises the books of Dickens, Hugo, and Dostoevsky, for they are preachers of a universal brotherhood.

There was an abiding conflict in Tolstoy's existence. Although he worked like a peasant, laboring in the fields, he had not abandoned his property, and was living in a luxurious home. Around him was ignorance and abject misery; people were being sent to Siberia, and what did he do? He received interviewers, wrote pamphlets, and enjoyed the comforts of his class. Until the last days of his life, he carried on this process of self-examination. More and more he wrote of leaving his home, renouncing his property, abandoning his art, and walking as a pilgrim on the roads of Russia. Conflict with his family deepened, and in 1910 he left his home in a final dramatic gesture of trying to live up to his ideals. He died from exposure at the wayside railroad station of Astapovo.

TOLSTOY AS EDUCATOR

To criticize Tolstoy is like criticizing the New Testament. We may object to the asceticism of his later life, to his opposition to urban existence, to his Puritanical interpretation of art, to the impractical aspects of his social program, to the fanaticism of his beliefs, to his exaggerated faith in non-violence, but all these things are insignificant when viewed in the total perspective of his life. For there are several Tolstoys: the Tolstoy of *Sevastopol*, the Tolstoy of *Anna Karenina,* and *War and Peace,* the Tolstoy of the *Confessions,* the Tolstoy of the *Resurrection,* and the Tolstoy as seen by his wife—the last, a passionate, idealistic, opinionated, and unpredictable man.

Maxim. Gorky said that Tolstoy's influence, like all that is alive, is growing, forever and ever. Upon Gandhi and Romain Rolland the imprint of his ideas is only too evident. The love that he advocated does not respect the barriers of race, religion, or nationality. His religion is designed not for the West only, but also for the East. His constant search, his accomplishments, and his frailties make him a brother to human struggles everywhere. Above all, Tolstoy is important today because the new world society requires a transformation of existing values, a genuine educational reformation.

The age of Tolstoy was one of educational ferment. Especially important was K. D. Ushinsky (1824-1870), the father of the Russian primary school and a proponent of scientific training for teachers. A liberal, he was influenced by Bacon, Locke, and Spencer, and he stressed the personality of the teacher who was to have an intense faith in his vocation. Other leaders who shared his ideas and those of Tolstoy were V. I. Vodovozov (1825-1886), V. Ya. Stoyunin (1826-1888), V. P. Ostrogorsky (1840-1902), D. I. Pisarev (1841-1868), and P. I. Makushin (1844-1926).

Tolstoy believed that education should cultivate a love of country, but it was not to encourage nationalism. There was no superior nation; patriotism had often been perverted by the teacher. Children were to be taught to love mankind and to look beyond the frontiers of race, nation and civilization.

While some Russian educators emphasized the superiority of the West and glorified the advances of Western technology, Tolstoy, like Ushinsky, stressed the values of Russian civilization. The intellectual had to find deep roots in his own nation and become part of its spirit and its ideals.

Tolstoy believed that education had a spiritual meaning. The ideal was not merely to know, but to apply knowledge in a critical way. He maintained that "only a freely developed personality armed with information and scientific knowledge can change life." The dignity of the individual was to be safeguarded. He was *not* to be indoctrinated; he was never to become the tool of the state. Censorship and suppression of new ideas were to be regarded as absolute evils; for freedom to Tolstoy was the highest good.

Tolstoy demanded that scholars accept a sense of social responsibility. They were not just models of information, but they were to be models of enlightenment. The achievement of truth and wisdom was to be an intensely personal process. How much could the scholars learn from the simplicity of the common man! How much could they benefit from the virtue of ordinary people!

Tolstoy stressed the personality of the teacher. It was far more significant that the teacher should be imbued with the importance of his vocation than that he should be an expert. The teacher should be interested in all aspects of life. He was to be concerned with the problems of man rather than with those of technical science.

The type of school which Tolstoy favored would abolish marks and would have no use for class distinctions. It would be child-centered rather than teacher-centered. Students would learn from experience and the classroom would be like a laboratory. Students would be guided in all their activities by the spirit of kindness and compassion.

In his educational theories, Tolstoy showed the importance of the personality of the teacher. If he was cold and hostile towards the students, he would become a negative influence, and he would be only a taskmaster. On the other hand, if he really loved his vocation and had regard for the personality of the student, and if he saw education as a continuous process—he would become a pillar of enlightenment and civilization.

Knowledge was not to be restricted to the few. Tolstoy felt that all human beings yearned for truth and wanted a better way of life. Thus, he felt that adult education should be stressed and that culture was to be universalized.

Tolstoy taught through precepts. "Be frank with yourselves and be frank with children" was the basis of his educational philosophy. He made it clear that man could progress only through self-examination.

To Tolstoy, religion, education, philosophy, and science—all aimed at the same result. They were designed to make loving individuals who were ever conscious of their responsibilities to humanity. He called for a transvaluation of values so that education would stress warmth and spontaneity rather than formal discipline.

In some ways, Tolstoy was a teacher like Jesus. He had infinite faith in the individual, and he taught through the use of parables. To love man and to love God was the beginning and end of wisdom, according to Tolstoy.

Education, to Tolstoy, was a process of identification. The student realized that he owed a debt to others and that, whenever people suffered and were in need, his assistance was required. Thus, education in Tolstoy had a truly universal function.

BERDIAEV

We must not omit the educational work of Nikolai Berdiaev (1874-1948), who was greatly influenced by Tolstoy and also by Western thinkers, including Nietzsche and Boehme. Personalistic strains are evident in Berdiaev, who emphasized man's creativity.

The career of Berdiaev was extremely stormy. He was a member of the Russian Orthodox Church, and he possessed a brilliant and independent mind. In 1917 he was appointed professor of philosophy at the University of Moscow, but soon he was expelled by the Soviets and from that time on he was a perpetual exile. We find him first in Berlin, where he attracted wide attention, and later in Paris.

Among the works of Berdiaev are: *The Philosophy of Liberty, The New Middle Ages, The Meaning of History, The Destiny of Man, Spirit and Reality,* and *Freedom and the Spirit.*

In his philosophical opinions, Berdiaev showed unusual independence. Among the movements which he attacked were humanism, capitalism, communism, neo-scholasticism, and democracy. Like Nietzsche, he was certain that progress was an illusion and he thought that the concepts of rationalism were utterly unbearable. He made it clear that a culture based purely on reason was shallow and superficial and that the awareness of life must be intensely emotional. He criticized modern man for his worship of the machine and for neglecting religious ideas. While many of his contemporaries looked upon the twentieth century as an age of enlightenment and thought that education would usher in a new age, Berdiaev predicted doom and disaster for modern man.

Berdiaev did not neglect the social side of life. While faith is primary, social ideals cannot be overlooked, and they must be practiced in our relationship with our neighbors.

The teacher's task, according to Berdiaev, is to stir his students so that they will live an examined life and be conscious of their possibilities. Through real education man would learn how to cultivate his essential self and how to become independent of the mechanization which characterizes the twentieth century.

CONTEMPORARY RUSSIAN BELIEFS

The basis of contemporary communist education is quite different from Tolstoy's and Berdiaev's ideals. While Tolstoy proclaimed love, Soviet education believes in the class struggle; while Tolstoy proved an ethical way of life, science is the supreme method for Soviet educators. The aim of Soviet education, according to Kairov, is the creation of leaders who will fight for the proletariat.

Karl Marx is revered in Russia as the prophet of the century; his ideas are fundamental in education. It must be remembered that orthodox Marxists believe that he was not only the most penetrating critic of the capitalistic system, but that his system is a description of all future events. To them, World War II was not merely a struggle for power by ambitious nations, but it represented the last oppressions of a dying cultural system. Like the early Christians, they are not afraid of persecutions, which seem to add power to their movement.

The common people of Russia have special veneration for Lenin, who has become a minor deity in the Marxist faith. His body has been treated with the same respect as that of an Egyptian Pharaoh, and his grave has been the object of countless pilgrimages. Many legends have been spread about his wisdom and kindness during the days of the revolution; for example, how he would distribute food that was sent to him, although he himself was nearly starving. His anti-religious spirit is the model for contemporary Russian education.

In such a society it is important that Marx and Lenin are interpreted in the correct manner and that heresies are avoided. It appears that the liberals consciously misinterpret the meaning of Karl Marx and thus are guilty not only of intellectual dishonesty but of reactionary tendencies. As for the Trotskyites, they are even more dangerous, for it is thought in Russia that they are the real enemies of the proletariat and are willing to make a pact with anyone to overthrow the existing government.

To the average Russian, Lenin has become the symbol of infallibility. Their faith in him is as great as the belief of the fundamentalists in the Bible. Lenin is regarded as authoritative not only in matters of politics and economics, but also in foreign relations, diplomacy, military affairs, and even in education.

The question emerges why the Russians have such a strong faith in leadership. The answer is rather complex. For one thing, their leadership has been successful and has guided them through the dark days of the revolution as well as through the torturous period of the German aggression. Moreover, this leadership is based upon scientific techniques and utilizes constant and detailed planning. Hence, statistics and hero worship combine. Today many Russians look upon Khrushchev as a substitute for the czar; long historical experiences have conditioned them to accept the voice of authority. The greatness of the new leadership is stressed from the time a boy starts school until he dies. Education in Russia is subordinated to political goals and is basically authoritarian.

For Russia World War II was a religious conflict. The hatred of the Germans was fierce and consuming. Reading Ehrenburg, one feels that the Germans attacking Russia were not merely brutal soldiers but psychopathic perverts and rapists of innocent women. Many times Hitler had stressed the theme that the Russians were subhuman and had to be exterminated.

World War II and the Korean crisis have intensified the spirit of Russian nationalism. They have given the Russian citizen an intense appreciation of his own heritage. Even the great czars like Peter the Great and Ivan the Terrible are being regarded as statesmen rather than as oppressors of the proletariat. This trend can be compared with the appropriation of the alien gods by the early Christians. The Russians, like the early Christians, are building their theology upon previous historical patterns.

The Marxist system is based upon a subordination of the individual to the party program. Hence discipline, especially in education, is absolutely necessary. This means that the freedom of the individual is curbed; questioning the decisions of the party becomes a major heresy. Here again the religious tone is evident. For the organization of the communist party is just as much based upon obedience as the early monastic orders.

The orthodox Marxists conceive of the world as consisting of two camps; those who are fighting on their side and those who are against them. The latter, they feel, are bound to be destroyed. This categorical philosophy is like the dualism of medieval Christianity, which conceived of life as a constant warfare between the forces of goodness and evil. Part of this philosophy is derived from Marx's statement in the *Communist Manifesto,* claiming that all of history is a conflict between the bourgeoisie and the proletariat. Ultimately, the orthodox Marxists feel, a new utopia will arise in which there will be no class differences and in which the state will wither away. The class struggle, therefore, has a cosmic setting since the Marxists believe that, even if the present is full of turmoil, the future will compensate and see a final victory. Under such concepts, the socialist governments of Europe are regarded with a veritable scorn. They are Pharisees who follow only the outward symbols of socialism while denying its real spirit. The orthodox Marxist looks upon them as a last refuge of the capitalistic society.

In Soviet education, theory has always played a large part. Important theorists of the 1920's were N. K. Krupskaia, who was the widow of Lenin, S. T. Shatsky, who was in charge of a secondary school at St. Petersburg, Paul Blonsky, who wrote *The Unified Labor School,* and Pinkevich, known best for his *Outlines of Pedagogy.* All of them were influenced by Western ideas; Shatsky, especially, reflected the impact of John Dewey, while Blonsky had immense admiration for Rousseau.

Experimentation dominated the Russian curriculum during the 1920's. The emphasis was upon actual experience and a student-centered curriculum. The influence of the teacher was to be restricted, marks were secondary, and homework was regarded as an obsolete method. The laboratory method found favor in Soviet Russia. Some theorists even believed that the school as an organized institution would eventually wither away.

Paul Blonsky perhaps best represents this spirit. He was a fervent opponent of the pre-Soviet school which stressed memorization and the exact mastery of subjects. He favored an educational system based upon actual experiences, such as Robinson Crusoe's way of life on the desert island. He maintained that the child should be left alone to develop his natural impulses and to become truly creative. Previous systems had been guilty of underestimating the student. Book knowledge certainly was not the goal of education. Specialization was a disease and classes were to be planned co-operatively by the teacher and the student.

KAIROV. Comparing Blonsky's viewpoint with the ideas championed in 1948 by a leading theorist, I. A. Kairov, editor of *Pedagogika,* we find a profound intellectual chasm. Kairov emphasized the love of fatherland. The teacher was an absolute authority whose ideas had to be accepted by the student. The aim of Soviet education, according to Kairov, was to build a scientific society based upon dialectical materialism. Religion was to be abolished, for it rested upon superstition. Faith in immortality was a pre-scientific idea. The world was to be understood according to the laws of matter and the interpretation was to be made by the Communist party.

Kairov evaluated the sciences according to their contribution to a materialistic world view. He especially valued mathematics which would develop "dialectical thinking." Physics would be an aid in giving the student a disciplined viewpoint, namely that the material world does not depend on the mind, but follows its own laws. Geology would disabuse the student of the idea that the world was created by a divine power. Biology would show how we are conditioned by evolutionary factors rather than by spiritual ideals.

To Kairov, as to other leading Soviet educators of our time, science was the model for all studies. It was the tool for progress. Through science, the Russians could surpass the Western nations. Through science, supernatural ideas could be eliminated. Through science, unlimited advances could be made in technology, and the fruits of knowledge could be disseminated to the people. Science meant verified knowledge instead of vague mysticism.

In the social sciences, Kairov stressed especially the importance of history. Naturally, it was to be taught in the Communist manner. History was to demonstrate the superiority of the Russian state and the inevitable decline of capitalistic nations. The student was to be imbued with fervent admiration for the leaders of the proletariat.

The nationalistic spirit was strong in Kairov. While the educators of the 1920's, like Blonsky and Pinkevich, had regarded exaggerated nationalism as a relic of the past, Kairov made Soviet accomplishments the center of his educational theories. Education, to Kairov, meant indoctrination in patriotic ways. Russian ideals, Russian science, Russian political concepts, as interpreted by the Communist party, were to govern school life. Kairov felt that it was the duty of teachers and students to subordinate themselves to the state and to be willing to die for the state if the necessity arose.

This concept of education reminds us of Hegel's view. Like Hegel, Kairov opposed freedom of opinion. Like Hegel, Kairov glorified the forces of nationalism. However, Kairov believed that education was guided by material rather than spiritual forces, and that the Absolute was represented by the Communist party.

In Kairov's educational philosophy special emphasis was placed upon exact mastery of knowledge. Vagueness in all forms was to be avoided and facts were the bases of educational progress. Without discipline no real advancement could be made. This meant a stress upon recitation and memorization. The student was to be attentive in class, obedient to his teachers, and he was to prepare his lessons with diligence and care. The good student was to be rewarded for his efforts, and he was to be encouraged by the state. Marks should be emphasized by the teacher and they should penalize the lazy student who would be failed without mercy.

Kairov's philosophy implies an encouragement of thoroughness and the mastery of solid subject matter. All schools in Russia were to have the same basic teaching program and they were to stress fundamentals, especially mathematics and the physical sciences. No local independence was to be allowed, and experimentation in independent methods was to be discouraged.

RUSSIA TODAY. Quite removed from the progressive ideas of the 1920's, Soviet education today stresses teacher-authority and discourages self-expression on the part of the student.

On the positive side, the Soviets have almost succeeded in wiping out illiteracy, and they have extended the compulsory school age through high school. Their universities are among the best in the world, and their studies in physics, astronomy, and chemistry are of especially high calibre. Adult education has been vigorously promoted and interest is strong in the classics and in scientific literature. Books are relatively cheap and find a wide audience; scientific books are frequently best sellers.

Much expansion has taken place in childhood education in Soviet Russia. With many mothers working, nursery schools and kindergartens have become a necessity. Teachers in these schools appear to be well-trained and enthusiastic about their work. At the same time, graduate work has been intensified and it is not uncommon to find managers of industries who return to the university for advanced degrees.

Russia has always had a tradition of language training. This training starts not in the university, but on the primary level. Local dialects are cultivated as well as the knowledge of Asiatic and European languages. English is a favorite subject for Russian students.

The teamwork approach is emphasized in research problems. When the state determines that advances must be made in certain fields, as in ballistics or rocket research, no effort is spared, and money is spent prodigiously. Scientists and professors of various disciplines work together and this partially explains the Russian success in launching space satellites.

Scientists and teachers have a high status in Russian society. Their work is recognized by the state and their pay is higher than that of most professions. Of course, they cannot defy the party line and develop independent thinking. As long as they produce in their own field, they are left free to pursue their researches.

On the negative side, a dogmatic spirit prevails in Marxism. Political issues are paramount and strict adherence to the party is stressed. The humanities lag behind the sciences and this contributes to the Russian culture lag. Furthermore, knowledge of Western ideas is distorted and conforms to propaganda purposes. Students do not have the freedom and the individuality which prevails in Western educational institutions.

It is possible that a more rebellious spirit may emerge in Russian education. A few years ago, a novel, *Not By Bread Alone* by Vladimir

Dudintsev, expressed the spirit of many Russian students who were rebeling against the state and who demanded more freedom. Like the hero of the book, they wanted more individuality and self-expression, and less thought control.

In *The God That Failed*, outstanding intellectuals, like Ignazio Silone, explained why they were drawn at first to Communism and then rejected it. At first, democratic ideals appeared to be corrupt, but authoritarianism was a far more disenchanting alternative. Thus, Silone explained to a Communist that he yearned for liberty "as the possibility of searching and experimenting, the possibility of saying 'no' to any authority." It is this spirit which is spreading in Russia, as Pasternak's *Dr. Zhivago* indicates.

Russian education is limited in its creativity because of political orthodoxy. But as the standard of living improves, as technology spreads, and as a new managerial class is being produced, freedom of inquiry will become much more important in Russia. In striving for universal education, the Russian rulers may be laying the seeds for the decline of Communism, a decline which may ultimately lead to a creative Renaissance of Russian culture.

QUESTIONS FOR DISCUSSION AND INVESTIGATION

1. Why does Tolstoy lay such great importance on love and idealism?

2. Trace briefly the life of Tolstoy and the birth of his major ideas.

3. What intellectual trials did Tolstoy experience before he felt the inspiration to seek out the faith of the *New Testament?*

4. What profound theme in reference to the plight of man is found in *Resurrection?*

5. What was Tolstoy's theory on international relations and the causes of war?

6. What were Tolstoy's conflicting ideals?

7. Why did Tolstoy stress the values of Russian civilization as an inherent part of the growth of Russian education?

8. What main factors did Tolstoy emphasize for a superior educational system?

9. Explain Berdiaev's philosophy of life and ideas on education.

10. Compare and contrast Tolstoy's and Berdiaev's views on education With those ideas that developed from their time on up to present-day Russia.

Chapter 26

Oriental Education and Spirituality

ORIENTAL IDEAS IN PERSPECTIVE

Eastern thought has frequently encouraged *regressive* social trends. Thus, Hinduism has been the supporter of the caste system, Mohammedanism has encouraged feudalism, and Shintoism has emphasized emperor worship. Confucianism in China was a stumbling block in the achievement of adequate educational reforms and in the introduction of new ways of life and new methods of government.

Social progress in the near East and in the Orient has often been delayed because the common people have been too docile and too lethargic. This attitude is largely caused by educational and religious teachings which encourage the spirit of fatalism and resignation. Obedience to God and to secular authorities is emphasized as the cornerstone of life. Furthermore, the time perspective of the Orient is so vast that the present does not matter, for life on earth is regarded as a minor incident. Especially disturbing is the condition of the outcasts in India, who often live in a more deplorable condition than animals, although, in the twentieth century, determined attempts have been made to better their social and educational status.

Social regression has been intensified by the traditionalism of Oriental education. Very often the past is the criterion of evaluation. This tendency is especially strong in Confucianism which felt that in ancient days a real utopia prevailed and that we can learn from the piety and virtue of the ancient Chinese rulers. In Confucianism, family relationships were regarded as fundamental, and rebellion on the part of children was not encouraged. While this attitude caused an elaborate code of manners, it did not promote change and educational progress. The spirit of traditionalism was even stronger in Shintoism than in Confucianism, for Shintoism taught that the gods were born in Japan, and that they bestowed upon the Japanese people unique insight and a unique code of morality.

It has often been charged that Eastern thought has a basic anti-scientific attitude. Thus, in Hinduism we find that the highest stage of knowledge is intuition, and in Taoism there is an intense contempt for reason. Again and again the *Upanishads* points out that the enlightened sage becomes almost as naive and simple as a child, relying upon a spontaneous insight into reality.

What matters most in Eastern thought is *peace of mind,* not scientific progress.[1] In fact, almost all Oriental philosophies have a contempt for technology. Yet it appears that without an adequate technological system no real advancement can be made by the common man. Of course, the disciple of Eastern ideals will point out that technology is not an unmixed blessing; in fact, that it may be the decisive factor in the disintegration of Western culture.

Furthermore, it has often been charged by the West that Eastern thought is *negativistic.* Thus, in Hinduism, Buddhism, and Taoism, spiritual education implies a loss of all individuality. Nirvana itself stands for the extinction of personality. Practically, such a spirit symbolizes a fatalistic resignation to the events of life. The individual is regarded as insignificant; in fact, his life is of minor importance. This means, especially in Hinduism, that the events of this world are to be disregarded. Everyday happenings should not distress the sage who seeks for a total perspective. When he sees suffering, he is not distressed, for he regards it as part of a vast cosmic cycle, and as the result of the law of Karma.

The detachment of Eastern thought widens the gulf between the saint and the common man. The former often tries to escape from society and, as in Hinayana Buddhism, is primarily concerned with his own salvation. The common man, however, is surrounded by a veil of superstition, and he makes little effort to achieve spiritual insight.

However, all these charges against Eastern thought are only partially correct. For, to some extent, Eastern ideals do not support an outworn social system, are not dominated by tradition, are not anti-scientific, and do not reflect the spirit of negativism. The greatness of Eastern education and religion is probably best reflected by the teachings of Buddha. Certainly, he fought with all his might against social discrimination. Buddha, like Dewey, was intensely positivistic. He was uninterested in metaphysical disputes, and he refused to rely upon supernatural aid.

---

1 Cf. Moore, editor, *Philosophy—East and West.*

Nor can we regard his teachings as being basically negativistic. It is true that he looked upon life as a sorrowful process, but he made it clear that a way, the eight-fold path, can be found to overcome man's sorrows.

Eastern thought and Oriental education are characterized by a spirit of peace and tranquillity. In the West we can benefit from such a spiritual perspective and cultivate an attitude of inwardness. It is also significant that the scholar in the Orient has a higher status than the Western scholar. There are many aspects of Oriental education which should be a guide to Western man in his quest for real education.

Real education in the twentieth century can give us a renewed faith in the dignity of the individual, the sacredness of human life, and the creativity of man's spirit. It can teach us a new respect for alien ideals and alien concepts; for we must learn how to get along, not only with our friends, but also with those who differ from us. As in the past, educational ideals appeal to us to disregard the petty, the superficial, and the transitory, and instead to concentrate upon the perennial issues of life and reality. Genuine education, with its universality and social idealism, can be the unifying force for the atomic age and can thus aid in the survival of civilization.

TRENDS IN MOHAMMEDANISM

In Mohammedanism the conflict between conservatives and liberals is especially strong.[2] The conservatives feel that only tradition can safeguard the interests of the Mohammedan people, while the liberals welcome the advent of Western science and Western democracy. The Mohammedans are reacting strongly to foreign domination. The movement for complete independence stirs Mohammedans from the Near East to Asia.

Most Mohammedans look upon the Zionist movement as a great evil. Does not Zionism favor social legislation? Is not Zionism a movement which will uproot the tranquillity of the past? However, a small minority of Mohammedans regard the Zionists as fellow travelers in their search for progress.

Among those who stirred up the nationalistic ideals of the Mohammedans was Jamāl al-Dīn, born in 1839. He had an excellent education and became Prime Minister of Afghanistan when he was only twenty-seven. Somewhat of a traveler, he spent much time in India, Egypt, Persia, and Germany. He did much in encouraging the independence of Egypt and throughout his life supported the Arab independence movements.

---

[2] Cf. Adams, *Islam and Modernism;* Gibb, *Modern Trends in Islam;* Widmer, *Übertragungen aus der neuarabischen Literatur,* vol. II.

How was this independence to be accomplished? Not by peaceful means, but through revolution. Jamal was extremely fanatical in his beliefs, and he thought that his own culture was far superior to Western ideals.

His thoughts are expressed in a work entitled the *Refutation of the Materialists*. This book tries to demonstrate that Islam is the only revealed religion and that God had spoken through Mohammed. All the modern scientific developments are regarded as insignificant when compared with the spiritual dignity of Mohammedanism. As for Western education, Jamal also opposed the rationalistic and agnostic tendencies of Western education.

Mohammed Abduh was a follower of Jamal and, like him, believed in Arab unity. He traveled widely, and he was often disappointed by the low economic status which most Moslems occupied. Abduh was more tolerant of science than Jamal. Science, however, was not to be appreciated for its own sake, for it was inferior to spiritual truth. He regarded scientific education as an aid in emancipating the followers of Mohammed and ultimately in giving them equality with the people of the West.

To Abduh the rule of authority was not sufficient, rather he favored the use of reason. The doctrines of religion were not to be accepted by blind faith, but were to be examined by man's rational capacities.

Ali Abdul Raziq tried to separate church and state. He explained his basic philosophy in a work entitled *Islam and the Principles of Government*. Raziq stated that the *Koran* does not ordain that religion and government should be united. Islam is basically a spiritually ideal, not a political system. The theocratic form of government, according to Raziq, had prevented material and social progress. In the West the separation of church and state had had most fruitful consequences. The same was to be done in Arab nations, that thus would enjoy a new educational enlightenment and a new renaissance.

The rationalistic spirit of Mohammedanism was probably best represented by Sir Muhammad Iqbal, who demanded a radical reformulation of Mohammedan education. The insights of the West were not to be disregarded. He stressed the fact that the Moslems were to produce a synthesis between Oriental and Western ideals. Unlike the orthodox, Iqbal did not believe in the theory of fatalism, which, he thought, was merely an invention of unscrupulous rulers to support their regressive philosophy.

It is interesting to note that this thinker also gave an allegorical explanation of heaven and hell. Heaven represents nearness to God, a victory over the lower self and the forces of disintegration. Hell itself is a state of alienation; it is not everlasting, for its purpose is to bring the sinner back to God.

In contemporary Moslem education a strong rebellion against Western ideals can be noticed. Thus, at the University of Cairo conservatism prevails and liberal ideas are avoided. As yet, in most Moslem countries, like Iran and Iraq, illiteracy is widespread, and there is a wide gulf between the intellectuals and the masses.

CHINESE TENDENCIES

In China, Western thought has made a deep impact.[3] This is represented especially by the pragmatic theories of Hu Shih. The latter, a student of John Dewey, popularized the teachings of Pragmatism in China.

Hu Shih's main works are *Outline of the History of Chinese Philosophy,* and *The Development of the Logical Method in Ancient China.*

It is interesting to note that this thinker rejected the idea that Oriental civilization is basically more religious than that of the West. He felt that spirituality could not prosper when poverty and ignorance abound. Thus, he advocated that the Orient is to adopt Western technology and Western education and be emancipated from superstition and traditionalism.

He vigorously rejected Confucianism, for he thought that it tied China to the past and that it made for the dominance of obsolete social institutions. He did not believe in the existence of God, and he accepted the agnostic philosophy of Huxley. Man cannot rely upon a supernatural force; he must use his intelligence in an experimental and functional manner.

To Hu Shih knowledge was primarily *hypothetical.* Its purpose was to increase man's power over nature; as for religion, it only gave us illusions and false conceptions. Thus he thought that the modern educational concepts should replace theological ideals.

Opposed to this philosophy were the followers of Confucianism, a system which had an immense revival in the 1930's. The ceremony in honor of Confucius became again a state function in 1934, and the Confucian temples were put in order after many of them had been left in disrepair in the 1920's. It was thought, in the 1930's, that the concepts of Sun-Yat-Sen—democracy, livelihood, and nationalism—could be combined with those of Confucius.

A cardinal event was the establishment of the New Life movement in 1934. It had four fundamental principles.

1. Li—the attitude of the people was to be disciplined. They were to be schooled in the right attitude regarding the state, and they were to be obedient to the nation.

---

[3] For a survey of modern Chinese thought see Hu Shih, *The Chinese Renaissance;* Dubs, "Recent Chinese Philosophy," *Journal of Philosophy,* vol. XXXV, pp. 345-355.

2. Yi—this principle stressed correct behavior. All irresponsibility and disorganization should be avoided. There was to be no extravagance, luxury, and idleness. Bad manners were not to be allowed; likewise, callousness and hypocrisy were taboo. Instead of excessive individualism, national solidarity was to be cultivated.

3. Lien—this principle stands for honesty in all aspects of life. Any dishonesty was to be punished. Honesty is to be taught from the time a child first learns to reason until he dies.

4. Ch'ih—this stands for the principle of honor. We are to feel repentant and ashamed when our actions do not accord with high moral principles. We are constantly to cultivate our own integrity. Even when we feel that we are perfect, we are to try to improve others and to help better the state.

More influential than Confucianism, ultimately, was the materialistic movement which championed the principles of Communism. What were the intellectual evils that were attacked by the materialistic movement? First Confucianism, with its stress upon the past, and which had delayed the full industrialization of China. Secondly, all forms of idealism; thus the materialists in China emphasized that the Buddhist and Taoist philosophies could not be an adequate answer to the problems of modern life.

Generally, Western philosophy was not regarded as a model by the materialists; frequently they reflected the nationalist tendencies of their nation.

The pilgrimage of the materialists is best represented by Chen Tu-hsiu. He was responsible for much of the renaissance of the Chinese thinking; however, in his later life he became a confirmed Marxist and joined the Communist party.

Under Marxist domination, Chinese education has a secular basis. Service to the family has been replaced by service to the state. Every year thousands of Chinese students are now studying at Russian universities. While traditional Chinese thought was based on ethics, today science is the center of the Chinese curriculum. To Chinese educators science is more than a method, it is a tool of emancipation and an organ whereby the West may be surpassed.

JAPANESE IDEALS

In turning to Japan we find that Buddhism appealed to the esthetic sense of the common people. It was extremely colorful and spoke of heaven and hell and established saints who could intercede for the common man. The Japanese Buddhist priest was a teacher who instructed by precept and example. He emphasized the importance of nature in man's moral development. This type of Buddhism almost reminds us of Catholicism; like the latter, it believed in pilgrimages, holy shrines, saints, and it made allowances for the frailties of ordinary men.

In the seventeenth and eighteenth century, the influence of Confucianism became extremely strong in Japanese education and religion. Among its disciples there were Kyuoso, who objected to the Buddhist ideal of withdrawal from the world; Ekken, who represented an agnostic strain in philosophy, and who believed that the humanities should be cultivated in education; Nakaye, who leaned in the direction of pantheism; Ito Jinsai, who generally disliked metaphysics, and who, like Confucius, appealed to moral education and concentrated upon earthly matters; and Ito Togai, who believed in scholarly detachment. Probably the most important of the Confucian scholars was Ogyu Sorai; he stressed that man is naturally evil, but can be reformed through spiritual education.

The national religion of Japan is *Shinto,* which can be translated as the "Way of the Gods." Basically, this faith is polytheistic with a multitude of gods (kami). The most important deity of Shinto is *Amaterasu,* sun goddess and ancestor of the Mikado, whose providence governs the universe. The theology of Shintoism is extremely vague; there are no exact accounts of creation and of a future life. Its main pillars are ancestor worship and deification of the forces of nature. Moral ideals are secondary in Shintoism, which does not possess a systematized creed or infallible books.[4]

A noteworthy character trait emphasized in Shinto education is the ideal of courage. The superior man, according to Shintoism, will never act in a cowardly manner. He will be ready to follow the commands of his ruler regardless of personal danger. In addition to valor, there is strong stress upon loyalty in Shintoism. Treason is condemned both on political and spiritual grounds. Furthermore, loyalty is applied to family relations; the son is to obey his father in every way and must live up to the ideal of filial piety.

Educationally, the Shinto ideal is anything but intellectual. The superior man is more interested in action than in contemplation. He is opposed to the detachment of the scholar.

Among thinkers who have contributed to the philosophical and educational foundations of Shintoism we find Kamo-no-Mabuchi (1697-1769), who combined a Taoist philosophy with a belief in the superiority of the Japanese people. He felt that man has an intuitive knowledge of righteousness and that the study of nature aided in improving man's social institutions. Motoori Noringa, even more strongly than Mabuchi,

---

[4] Some scholars consider the ancient compilations of *Kojiki* and *Nihongi* as sacred in Shintoism.

emphasized the *supernatural* foundations of Shintoism and stressed the divinity of the emperor. Hirata Atsutane (1776-1843) taught that the Japanese culture was unique and that it could not be compared with that of any other nation. In fact, he claimed that the gods were born in Japan and that their main concern was the welfare of the Japanese people.

It must be remembered that in modern times two main types of Shintoism emerged: State (Kokka) Shinto and Sectarian (Shuha) Shinto. In State Shinto, chauvinism played a large role.[5] Special attention was paid to the concept of Japanese superiority, the greatness of the emperor, and the uniqueness of Japanese culture. However, in Sectarian Shinto wide differences of philosophy were encouraged and many sects developed which often absorbed Chinese, Indian and European ideals.

Traditionally, the teacher occupies a unique role in Japanese life. He is regarded not only as a man of wisdom but as a representative of the state. After the Japanese defeat in 1945, more democratic ideals were introduced into the Japanese educational system. There is now less emphasis upon memorization and more stress upon discussion. Also, the teacher has lost some of his ancient privileges.

Today, Japanese education represents an intriguing synthesis between East and West. As in the West, scientific education is stressed and the humanities are cultivated. Co-education is making rapid progress. The new generation is rebelling against their elders. At the same time, Japanese educators still stress the importance of the family; they maintain that knowledge without ethics is a pilgrimage in vanity.

INDIAN IDEALS

RAMAKRISHNA. The ideals of Indian thought are best represented by the Hindu thinker, Ramakrishna. To some extent, he was like St. Francis and, thus, had infinite love and affection for all parts of creation. He was well acquainted with Islam and Christianity and felt akin to all the great prophets of the past, especially to Jesus and Buddha.

To Ramakrishna all men were equal; there were to be no distinctions of class, caste, or nation. He willingly served the outcasts of India, for he thought that they deserved the same education, the same privileges, and the same rights that others enjoyed. Education thus was to be open to all and was to create real enlightenment.

Philosophically, he had respect for the faith of all. The masses might use superstition in praying to God, still their faith was not to be disregarded. Likewise, he did not quarrel with the philosophers when they spoke of God's indescribable unity.

---

[5] Cf. Holtom, *The National Faith of Japan;* Genchi Katō, *A Study of Shinto;* Kaibara, *The Way of Contentment.*

He had little patience with doctrinal disputes, for the rule of love was more important than knowledge. Piety was to change our attitude regarding our own achievements, *the universe, and God.* He did not believe in a conversion to a different type of religion. Man sees God according to his own capacity. Thus the Christian can find God in Christ, the Jew can find God in the prophets, and the Buddhist in Buddha.

VIVEKANANDA. Vivekananda was immensely influenced by Ramakrishna. He was acquainted with Western philosophers, especially with Herbert Spencer and John Stuart Mill. To Vivekananda the essence of real education was not asceticism, but *service to humanity.* Prayer itself is not sufficient; rather we must apply our religious ideals to the betterment of man.

Vivekananda dreamed of a world culture, and he expressed his thoughts eloquently and stirringly at the Parliament of Religions in 1893. He traveled widely in the United States and in Europe; wherever he went he preached his simple doctrine—*love to all men.*

How can we achieve real meaning in life? It can be done in two ways, according to Vivekananda. First, by knowledge and education; second, by activity and love. Still, he was not a radical innovator. Thus he did not intend to destroy the faith of the common people, for they had at least an allegorical knowledge of truth.

His visits to America and Europe convinced him that Western education needed the insights and spirituality of India, for the West was engrossed in materialism and worshipped the machine. The West had to rediscover the basic foundations of life and had to redefine its educational standards.

TAGORE

Tagore represents the union of philosophy, education and poetry. In 1913, he received the Nobel Prize for literature. Tagore, with his life-affirming spirit, opposed the traditional pessimism of Indian religion.

In 1901, Tagore founded *Santiniketan,* which was to embody the best of Indian thought. Later, he made his school into an international center for, like Gandhi, he wanted to create a universal synthesis.

Among the famous teachers of this school we find philosophers such as his brother, Dwijendranath Tagore, and C. F. Pearson, poets such as Bose and Haldar, and authors like Satischandra Ray. Like Rousseau, Tagore emphasized the importance of nature; therefore, much of the instruction was under the open sky. Since his own school life had been too strict, he stressed the significance of freedom: the boys should have their own courts and conduct their own social activities. Social service and dramatic performances were prominent features of the educational ideals of Tagore.

There was a church in the open air dedicated to universal spirituality. The school day opened and ended with a prayer. The students were taught that beauty and spirituality are not vague ideals, but values to be applied in daily living.

Tagore did not favor the caste system, and he rejected the doctrine of transmigration. He believed in the equality of all men and all nations. In every way, Tagore was an apostle of universalism, which is to be achieved through genuine education.

As an individualist, Tagore was independent in his opinions. He condemned the abuses of the English Empire administration, and he yearned for India's independence. In 1919, when British soldiers at Amritsar killed participants in a religious procession, Tagore protested vigorously and subsequently returned all his British decorations to the Viceroy. Yet, he was not blind to the imperfections of the nationalistic movement, and he opposed the chauvinism of many of the young Indians.

In Tagore spirituality was based on morality. He asserted that our beliefs do not matter; of primary importance is our relationship with others and our dealings with society. He wavered between the teachings of science and of the *Vendanta;* he thought that science would aid in emancipating man and would improve his social and economic conditions; at the same time, he felt that scientific education alone was not enough and that man needed the inspiration of poetry and religion.

Tagore was skeptical in regard to the reality of an afterlife. Man should devote himself to this world and not live for an illusory existence. Still, there is a certain form of immortality, according to Tagore, for creativity transcends the boundaries of space and time and brings about a universal comradeship. Tagore thus made it clear that asceticism was not sufficient. Nor, on the other hand, is sensuality the answer. Man must cultivate a sense of idealism and a feeling of true spirituality, for Western Civilization has lost its soul, and is engaged in the pursuit of profit and material goods.

What is progress? Tagore replies that progress cannot be defined according to material standards; rather it consists in educational perfection. Material goods are to be subordinated to the love of humanity, which is to include all races and all nations.

GANDHI

In many ways, Mahatma Gandhi represents the climax of Indian thought. His personality has evoked the admiration of both the East and the West. In every way he lived up to his ideals, and he demonstrated the perennial vitality of faith.

Born in 1869, at Porbandar, he studied law in England. Later, he went to South Africa where he fought against racial discrimination. Upon his return to India, he protested against the oppressive acts of England, and in 1920, he officially started a policy of non-violent non-co-operation. He was sentenced to jail in 1922, for six years, but he was released two years later. As a leader of the National Congress, Gandhi had immense power, and he was the leading spirit in achieving Indian independence. He constantly urged peace between the Moslems and Hindus; when riots broke out after the granting of Indian independence, he personally started a campaign of penance. His pacifistic and moderate attitude infuriated his extreme followers, and he was assassinated by one of them on his way to a prayer meeting.

Romain Rolland has compared Gandhi with Jesus, and there are many parallels in the concepts taught by both men. Like Jesus, Gandhi believed in the love of God and of humanity. Like Jesus, Gandhi had uncomplicated faith; he felt that it was primarily a matter of the heart; complicated theological systems were unnecessary if man were to be saved. Like Jesus, Gandhi had respect for all races and all nations. He believed in a universal God whose providence included all parts of the universe and, like Jesus, Gandhi taught by precept and example.

Gandhi made it clear that God's work was manifested in many different religions. He respected the insight and moral heroism of Mohammed; he was moved to tears by the sacrifice of Jesus; he had an abiding love and understanding for the teachings of Buddha. Nevertheless, Gandhi remained a Hindu and accepted its Scriptures, although he protested against the abuses of the caste system.

Gandhi's moral status was fully revealed during his trial in 1922. The prosecutor had demanded the full penalty of the law and had pointed to Gandhi as the real culprit in causing armed resistance against British rule. Without hesitation, Gandhi accepted full responsibility. He stated that he could not dissociate himself from the acts of the Indian people, and that he should have realized that his speeches and publications would inflame their passions. He did not defend the crimes and outrages which had been committed, because violence outraged his soul. He ended his speech not by pleading for mercy, but by saying that he deserved the full penalty of the law.

Even when he was in solitary confinement, his spirit did not break. He used his time in prison to study Western writers, especially Thoreau, Emerson, Ruskin, and Tolstoy. He found new inspiration in the *Bhagavad-Gita,* particularly in the concept of *Bhakti,* which meant unconditional love of God. Gandhi was certain that man's spirit was more important than his body, and that religion and education could aid him in creating a knowledge and an awareness of man's basic spirituality.

All his life, Gandhi believed in the power of prayer. He did not pray for selfish advantages or for supernatural rewards, nor for the destruction of his enemies; rather he prayed that he might be faithful to his ideals and that his life would add to the goodness and harmony in the universe. To Gandhi, education without prayer was a futile process.

Religion, according to Gandhi, was not a compartmentalized activity. It was not a separate and isolated activity. It was not a vocation for the spiritual aristocracy; on the contrary, to him, life and religion were one. A life without faith would be utterly meaningless and sterile; while religion which was not adjusted to man's daily existence and which only appealed to a few, was utterly worthless.

Gandhi did not have much faith in scientific education. He did not feel that science had created permanent happiness. Around him he saw the evil effects of science, especially the instruments of destruction and mass murder which man's ingenious brain had devised. Furthermore, science had made man skeptical. Gandhi felt that faith in God was all-important and, therefore, should be the center of educational instruction.

Like Tolstoy, Gandhi preached against modern materialism. There could be no real progress when man paid so much attention to his physical comforts and neglected the demands of his soul. Gandhi realized that the temptations of materialism and spirituality were often the same. Did not most denominations stress quantitative expansion? Did not the struggle of the various religions represent a basic atheism? Was there not a frequent union between Western religion and Western imperialism?

True spirituality, according to Gandhi, meant a constant search and an unending quest for perfection. There was no time for a feeling of smugness or superiority. Gandhi believed that the saint shared the imperfection of the sinner and that the work of the saint was never finished. As long as war, disease, and poverty prevailed in society, the saint had not accomplished his mission. The saint, as a spiritual teacher, could not rest upon his laurels; his task was to re-educate mankind.

While Gandhi had many wealthy followers, he was at home with the poor of India. He found that poverty was the most meaningful prelude to spirituality. The rich man was too dependent on his possessions; he was a slave to convention; his values were superficial because they were dominated by social approval. The poor man, on the other hand, was close to nature. The poor man suffered, he toiled, and he knew how to appreciate life.

In his moral ideals, Gandhi, above all, stressed the importance of the good motive. In every way he opposed the teachings of Machiavelli, for he contended that the end does not justify the means. For example, if the caste system created misery and oppression, there was still no justification for its violent overthrow and for a bloody revolution against all those who believed in it. For Gandhi thought that a victory, achieved in this manner, would ultimately become a defeat. Once a policy of bloodshed is adopted, it becomes the dominant technique, and thus it undermines the fruits of conquest.

Like Buddha, Gandhi felt that all life is sacred; not only the life of mankind, but also of animals. To destroy life was to sin against creation. He attacked Western man for his insensibility regarding the life of animals. Of course, this was only an overture to the imperialistic policy of the West, which, throughout its history, had shown little respect for the sacredness of life.

Gandhi believed in a universal religion which included all denominations, all prophets, and all the various revelations of mankind. He believed in one God, but he thought that he was manifested in many different ways. Thus, the Hindus would have an impersonal concept of God, while the Christians would pray to a personal deity. The educated scholar would formulate a theological system of God, while the man on the street would express a spontaneous and emotional view of the Supreme Being.

Gandhi was certain that God was not a distant force, unconcerned with mankind, but that he was constantly creative and that his spirit was forever active. God could best be found in the silence of meditation, when man became conscious of his divine origin and divine destiny. The man who dedicated himself to God, who gave up all comfort and all worldly goods, would find an abiding meaning in life and he would thus achieve already in this existence a vision of true immortality.

In regard to education, Gandhi was not a theorist, but a teacher who believed in action. Knowledge and action had to be combined, for Gandhi's ideal was the development of all-around excellence for the individual. Like John Dewey, Gandhi believed that we learn by doing and that book knowledge is less important than practical experience. Literary education should be based on our knowledge of crafts; self-control and discipline—including celibacy for young students—were indispensable tools for the achievement of real wisdom.

He wanted better libraries, more laboratories, and more research institutions for India; they were to be open to all people with the necessary qualifications. But his real love, the education of villagers, was based upon the ideal of self-sufficiency and the promotion of basic crafts. He did not neglect the arts and music, for to him they were essentially spiritual activities.

Gandhi wanted no narrow theological training; rather he favored ethical education. We teach morality best, he affirmed, by being examples in our conduct. An enemy of narrow nationalism, he maintained that "no culture can live, if it attempts to be exclusive." Culture to him represented a living synthesis of the past and the present, of physical, moral, and spiritual qualities. Man could only progress when he combined the love of society with the love of truth. Moral principles were to be applied to the schoolroom as well as to society.

Gandhi was neither traditional nor progressive in his concept of education. We can learn valuable lessons from the past; at the same time we cannot be guided by its necessities. The true teacher, he maintained, needs an international perspective and should see life under the aspect of eternity.

Education, according to Gandhi, could either impede or advance the cause of humanity. If education only cultivated our analytical powers, it could have negative consequences for man. Scholarship alone was not enough; what mattered was the development of a spiritual attitude whereby ideas had a living reality and became part of our daily existence.

Thoreau had a fundamental impact upon Gandhi's educational ideas. Like Thoreau, Gandhi believed in the simple life of nature and that time "was something we could go fishing in." Like Thoreau, Gandhi believed that the intellect was a cleaver, unable to penetrate the core of reality. Like Thoreau, Gandhi wanted to simplify education so that only essentials would be taught. Like Thoreau, Gandhi was opposed to mere technological education and instead urged the virtues of the contemplative attitude.

Silence and meditation are the centers of education, according to Gandhi. We have a divine source of knowledge within ourselves. Thus, the teacher stirs the innate capacities of students and he reminds them of their essential self. "Know thyself and know God" are the bastions of Gandhi's educational thought.

Gandhi thus opposed a purely rationalistic system of education. The teacher could not neglect the wisdom of the heart. Ultimately, religion and education mean the same. Both aim at the true knowledge of God and the universe.

As for evil, Gandhi thought that, metaphysically, evil is unreal. To be sure, we cannot overlook the oppressions of mankind and the ravages of nature and the imperfections of the institutional system; yet, in the final analysis, only goodness counts. Gandhi asserted that goodness could transmute evil and that the time would come when evil would be completely conquered. All this could be accomplished through education which would teach man the importance of compassion.

The universe, according to Gandhi, represents a moral order. The law of cause and effect operates as much in the moral as in the physical realm. Thus, the evil man does not gain a lasting victory, and he eventually creates his own hell. At the same time, goodness is never in vain, for it creates the seeds for a truly meaningful and universal existence. The evil man only lives for himself and inevitably isolates himself from others; the good man, who is truly educated, is never alone, and he is never without comrades. *His dwelling-place is eternity and his soul is in humanity.*

Gandhi accepted the reality of the mystical experience. The ultimate spiritual stage could not be defined intellectually; it could only be felt and experienced. To the mystic, intellectual ideals were secondary; only the union between man and God was of real importance. Such a union produced in Gandhi a feeling of complete peace and serenity. Education and religion thus end in mysticism, which creates a feeling of oneness and turns us away from materialism and teaches us the virtue of detachment.

To achieve this condition, Gandhi disciplined his body; often he would fast; sometimes he would eat only milk and fruit—he was certain that this asceticism strengthened the resources of his soul. Real insight could not be achieved without abstinence from sensuality.

His love was unconditional—it included his friends and enemies; by his love he overwhelmed even his prosecutors. Evil was not to be resisted by violent means—it was to be overcome by compassion and kindness. To Gandhi, *non-violence was the basis of education and spirituality.* As he stated:

> "For me the law of *Satyagraha,* the law of love, is an eternal principle. For the past thirty years I have been preaching and practicing Satyagraha. The principles of Satyagraha, as I know it today, constitute a gradual evolution . . .
>
> "The term Satyagraha was coined by me in a demonstration of its permanence and invincibility. It can be used alike by men, women and children. It is totally untrue to say that it is a force to be used only by the weak so long as they are not capable of meeting violence by violence. It is impossible for those who consider themselves to be weak to apply this force. Only those who realize that there is something in man which is superior to the brute nature in him, and that the latter always yields to it, can effectively be Satyagrahis. This force is to violence, and therefore to all tyranny, all injustice, what light is to darkness." [6]

Since Gandhi had little faith in modern industry, he urged a return to a simple peasant economy. Together with political self-rule, he believed in home production. However, his followers, like Nehru, realized that the industrialization of India could not be delayed and that it contributed to the emancipation of man.

Gandhi's contribution to philosophy and education should not be minimized. His ideals may be the basis of a union between East and West; they remind modern man of the transcendent significance of the life of faith. For all those who treasure idealism, Gandhi's philosophy is a *tribute to man's creative spirit,* a milestone in man's search for emancipation, and a symbol of the universality of genuine education.

---

[6] *Satyagraha*

QUESTIONS FOR DISCUSSION AND INVESTIGATION

1. Give examples of how Eastern thought has frequently encouraged regressive social trends.

2. Give examples of the strong conflict between the conservatives and liberals in Islam, and name the contributions of those men who advanced the Moslem way of life.

3. Trace the ideological movements in modern Chinese thought.

4. Explain the influence of Buddhism and the Shinto religion on the common people of Japan.

5. What are the Indian ideals in philosophy and religion of Ramakrishna and Vivekananda.

6. Explain Tagore's contributions toward the union of philosophy, education, and poetry.

7. What were Tagore's concepts of morality?

8. Why did Mahatma Gandhi represent the climax of Indian thought?

9. Discuss the religious life-view of Gandhi.

10. What were Gandhi's ideals in education?

Part 4

Ideals
of
American Education

Chapter 27

The Foundations of American Educational Theory

JEFFERSON

Among those who contributed to the development of American education, the Colonial leaders deserve a significant place. The revolution of 1776 was fought in the belief that governments are instituted for the welfare of the individual, and that all men have inalienable rights by nature, such as life, liberty and the pursuit of happiness. Colonial leaders, like Washington and Jefferson, were concerned with the problem of education, for they realized that the future of democracy depended upon a rational citizenry.

Thomas Jefferson (1743-1826), especially, was influential in the development of the American public school system. While serving in the Virginia legislature, Jefferson introduced a measure which would have established free public education for that state. This bill, however, was defeated, for most members of the legislature regarded this as a radical measure.

Jefferson played a great role in the establishment of the University of Virginia, which tried to combine the classics and humanities with scientific instruction. Throughout his career he agitated for the separation of state and church, and for freedom of expression on the part of teachers.

Jefferson envisioned a new type of administrative setup of the local schools which were to be guided by a superintendent. The superintendent of schools was to exemplify profound scholarship, high moral ideals, and loyalty to the State. Also, he was to be in charge of teachers, and he was responsible for maintaining adequate standards for the schools.

Jefferson tried to establish the objectives of primary education:

1. To give to every citizen the information he needs to transact his own business.

2. To enable him to calculate for himself and to express and preserve his ideas, contracts and accounts in writing.

3. To improve, by reading, his faculties and morals.

4. To understand his duties to his neighbors and his country, and to discharge with competence the functions confided to him by either.

5. To know his rights; to exercise with order and justice those he retains; to choose with discretion, candor, and judgment the fiduciary of those he delegates.

6. And, in general, to observe with intelligence and faithfulness all the social relations under which he shall be placed.

Education does not apply merely to the mind.

"I should have performed the office of but half of a friend were I to confine myself to the improvement of the mind only. Knowledge indeed is a desirable, a lovely possession, but I do not scruple to say that health is more so. It is of little consequence to store the mind with science if the body be permitted to become debilitated. If the body be feeble, the mind will not be strong—the sovereign invigorator of the body is exercise, and . . . no one knows, till he tries, how easily a habit of walking is acquired . . . Not less than two hours a day should be devoted to exercise, and the weather should be little regarded. A person not sick will not be injured by getting wet . . . Brute animals are most healthy, and they are exposed to all weather, and, of men, those are healthiest who are the most exposed. The recipe of those two descriptions of beings is simple diet, exercise and the open air." [1]

Learning, above all, must promote science. A knowledge of the classics alone is not adequate.

"When sobered by experience, I hope our successors will turn their attention to the advantages of education. I mean of education on the broad scale, and not that of the petty *academies*, as they call themselves, which are starting up in every neighborhood, and where one or two men, possessing Latin and sometimes Greek, a knowledge of the globes, and the first six books of Euclid, imagine and communicate this as the sum of science. They commit their pupils to the theatre of the world, with just taste enough of learning to be alienated from industrious pursuits, and not enough to do service in the ranks of science." [2]

[1] *Letter to Thomas Mann Randolph, Jr.* August 27, 1786.

[2] *Letter to John Adams,* July 5, 1814.

Jefferson felt that education of the masses provides the best safe-guard for liberty. It must be remembered that in his age, mass-education was regarded as a revolutionary idea.

Generally, his concept of culture was functional and utilitarian. Like John Dewey, he disliked the snobbishness of traditional education. To Jefferson, education was the best safeguard of democracy.

HORACE MANN

Horace Mann (1796-1859), like Jefferson, had faith in the teacha-bility of the individual. He was eminently successful both in politics and in educational affairs. His twelve reports, which he issued as secre-tary of the Massachusetts State Board of Education, have become classics. In these reports he outlined his educational philosophy which was based upon five ideas: 1. education was to be universal for rich and poor; 2. education was to be free; 3. education should be handled by the state, not by ecclesiastical organizations; 4. education depended upon care-fully trained teachers; thus, Mann was responsible for the development of the normal school in Massachusetts; 5. education was to train both men and women; he was one of the pioneers of co-education.

Horace Mann was regarded as a dreamer and visionary by many of his colleagues. When, as president of Antioch College, he opened the door of the college to a variety of religious sects and admitted women on an equal basis with men, many educators felt strongly that this would contribute to the collapse of higher education.

Horace Mann was a strong believer in the common school:

"Without undervaluing any other human agency, it may be safely affirmed that the common school, improved and energized as it can easily be, may become the most effective and benignant of all the forces of civiliza-tion. Two reasons sustain this position. In the first place, there is a univer-sality in its operation, which can be affirmed of no other institution what-ever. If administered in the spirit of justice and conciliation, all the rising generation may be brought within the circle of its reformatory and elevating influences. And, in the second place, the materials upon which it operates are so pliant and ductile as to be susceptible of assuming a greater variety of forms than any other earthly work of the Creator. The inflexibility and ruggedness of the oak, when compared with the lithe sapling or the tender germ, are but feeble emblems to typify the docility of childhood when con-trasted with the obduracy and intractableness of man. It is these inherent advantages of the common school, which, in our own state, have produced results so striking, from a system so imperfect, and an administration so feeble. In teaching the blind and the deaf and dumb, in kindling the latent spark of intelligence that lurks in an idiot's mind, and in the more holy work of reforming abandoned and outcast children, education has proved what it can do by glorious experiments. These wonders it has done in its infancy, and with the lights of a limited experience; but when its faculties shall be fully developed, when it shall be trained to wield its mighty energies for the protection of society against the giant vices which now invade and torment it—against intemperance, avarice, war, slavery, bigotry, the woes of want, and the wickedness of waste,—then there will not be a height to which these enemies of the race can escape which it will not scale." [3]

Mann believed in moral education.

"Moral education is a primal necessity of social existence. The unrestrained passions of men are not only homicidal, but suicidal; and a community without a conscience would soon extinguish itself. Even with a natural conscience, how often has evil triumphed over good! From the beginning of time, wrong has followed right, as the shadow, the substance. As the relations of men become more complex, and the business of the world more extended, new opportunities and new temptations for wrongdoing have been created. With the endearing relations of parent and child came also the possibility of infanticide and parricide; and the first domestic altar that brothers ever reared was stained with fratricidal blood. Following close upon the obligations to truth came falsehood and perjury, and closer still upon the duty of obedience to the divine law came disobedience. With the existence of private relations between men came fraud; and with the existence of public relations between nations came aggression, war, and slavery. And so, just in proportion as the relations of life became more numerous, and the interests of society more various and manifold, the range of possible and of actual offenses has been continually enlarging. As for every new substance there may be a new shadow, so for every new law there may be a new transgression . . .

"The race has existed long enough to try many experiments for the solution of this greatest problem ever submitted to its hands; and the race has experimented, without stint of time or circumscription of space to mar or modify legitimate results. Mankind has tried despotisms, monarchies, and republican forms of government. They have tried the extremes of anarchy and of autocracy. They have tried Draconian codes of law, and for the lightest offenses have extinguished the life of the offender. They have established theological standards, claiming for them the sanction of divine authority, and the attributes of a perfect and infallible law; and then they have imprisoned, burnt, massacred, not individuals only, but whole communities at a time, for not bowing down to idols which ecclesiastical authority had set up. These and other great systems of measures have been adopted as barriers against error and guilt; they have been extended over empires, prolonged through centuries, and administered with terrible energy; and yet the great ocean of vice and crime overleaps every embankment, pours down

---

[3] *Twelfth Annual Report.*

upon our heads, saps the foundations under our feet, and sweeps away the securities of social order, of property, liberty and life." [4]

Still we have not really tried education.

"It is an experiment which, even before its inception, offers the highest authority for its ultimate success. Its formula is intelligible to all; and it is as legible as though written in starry letters on an azure sky. It is expressed in these few and simple words: *'Train up a child in the way he should go; and when he is old, he will not depart from it.'* This declaration is positive. If the conditions are complied with, it makes no provision for a failure. Though pertaining to morals, yet, if the terms of the direction are observed, there is no more reason to doubt the result than there would be in an optical or a chemical experiment.

"But this experiment has never yet been tried. Education has never yet been brought to bear with one-hundredth part of its potential force upon the nature of children, and through them upon the character of men and of the race." [5]

EDUCATIONAL UTOPIAS AND REALITY

This was an age of Utopias. One of the most notable, *Brook Farm,* was founded by George Ripley, a Harvard classical scholar. It was situated in the most impressive surroundings of Massachusetts, amidst splendid meadows and a nearby brook; in the summer, its members could go swimming in the Charles River. The main concern of Brook Farm was a preservation of cultural values. There were classes in philosophy, German, Greek, music, botany, and geography. Among the instructors were Charles A. Dana, who later became editor of the *New York Sun,* Mr. Ripley, who later turned to Catholicism, and Margaret Fuller, who found solace and love in Italy.

The two social reforms which were championed by Brook Farm were equality of wages and the absence of any domestic labor. It was Ripley's ideal to do away with all forms of social oppression; complete equality was to prevail and work would be done, not because of compulsion, but because of a real inner urge. Other utopian communities might preserve social stratification as Owen's community did in New Harmony; it was different at Brook Farm, where real freedom prevailed.

Together with community projects, which usually lasted only for a few decades, education was furthered by the reformers. Horace Mann, as we have seen, aided in the development of the public school, as well as

---

4 *Ibid.*
5 *Ibid.*

in more intensive teacher training. Much was done for the education of women. Also, the kindergarten became an accepted American institution and was vigorously endorsed by Horace Mann.

At the same time, Frances Wright, editor of *The Free Enquirer*, who had spent several years in the United States as an agitator for educational reform, urged that the state should erect schools for children, who were to be taken away from their homes at the age of two. Her proposal caused great opposition, for parents and educators felt that this would destroy the family system.

Bronson Alcott shocked many of his contemporaries by touching upon sex in his instruction. A Harvard professor thought this was a most unfit subject for children. Two Boston newspapers carried on such a systematic campaign against Alcott, that conscientious parents withdrew their children from this school. Despite Emerson's defense of Alcott, the school soon failed completely.

EDUCATIONAL LEADERS

Among the educational leaders in other states, mention should be made of Thaddeus Stevens who fought hard for the public schools in Pennsylvania. Caleb Mills expanded the basis of education in Indiana, Breckinridge made educational history in Kentucky, while Samuel Lewis became the first state superintendent in Ohio. In regard to the education of women, Emma Willard, Catherine Beecher, and Mary Lyon played a leading role.

Henry Barnard (1811-1900), deserves a special note among the pioneers of education, for he tried to accomplish in Connecticut what Horace Mann had achieved in Massachusetts. Later, he became president of the University of Wisconsin and Commissioner of Education of the United States. In 1855, he established the *American Journal of Education*.

Barnard was influential in the establishment of a State Board of Education in Connecticut. He convinced the state of Rhode Island to follow the example of Connecticut and to raise its educational standards. A progressive in his educational philosophy, he believed that children should have greater freedom and that education should follow the methods of nature. He felt that the best guarantee for the future of democracy was the public school.

William T. Harris, like Barnard, was a Commissioner of Education of the United States. An idealist in philosophy, Harris stressed the *vocation of the teacher*. For many years he was superintendent of schools at St. Louis, Missouri. There he was influential in the spread of the kindergarten movement and in raising the standards of teacher preparation.

EMERSON

Ralph Waldo Emerson was more mystical in his outlook than Jefferson; he stressed the power of intuition rather than that of reason. To Emerson the universe was one, and the *Oversoul*—the principle of reality—was active everywhere. As a transcendentalist, Emerson believed that nature is a spiritual process and that it reveals moral purposes.

His Phi Beta Kappa speech at Harvard is probably the most eloquent essay on education ever produced in America. He called for an intellectual declaration of independence. He wanted the scholar to be a symbol of unity:

"The old fable covers a doctrine ever new and sublime; that there is One Man,—present to all particular men only partially, or through one faculty; and that you must take the whole society to find the whole man. Man is not a farmer, or a professor, or an engineer, but he is all. Man is priest, and scholar, and statesman, and producer, and soldier. In the *divided* or social state these functions are parcelled out to individuals, each of whom aims to do his stint of the joint work, whilst each other performs his. The fable implies that the individual, to possess himself, must sometimes return from his own labor to embrace all the other laborers. But, unfortunately, this original unit, this fountain of power, has been so distributed to multitudes, has been so minutely subdivided and peddled out, that it is spilled into drops, and cannot be gathered . . . The tradesman scarcely ever gives an ideal worth to his work, but is ridden by the routine of his craft, and the soul is subject to dollars. The priest becomes a form; the attorney a statute-book; the mechanic a machine; the sailor a rope of the ship.

"In this distribution of functions the scholar is the delegated intellect. In the right state he is *Man Thinking*." [6]

Books, Emerson stated, are not to be worshipped:

"Books are the best type of the influence of the past, and perhaps we shall get at the truth,—learn the amount of this influence more conveniently,—by considering their value alone.

"The theory of books is noble. The scholar of the first age received into him the world around; brooded thereon; gave it the new arrangement of his own mind, and uttered it again. It came into him life; it went out from him truth. It came to him short-lived actions; it went out from him immortal thoughts. It came to him business; it went from him poetry. It was dead fact; now, it is quick thought. It can stand, and it can go. It now endures, it now flies, it now inspires. Precisely in proportion to the depth of mind from which it issued, so high does it soar, so long does it sing." [7]

---

[6] *American Scholar.*
[7] *Ibid.*

Life is the test for our knowledge:

> "Life is our dictionary. Years are well spent in country labors; in town; in the insight into trades and manufactures; in frank intercourse with many men and women; in science; in art; to the one end of mastering in all their facts a language by which to illustrate and embody our perceptions. I learn immediately from any speaker how much he has already lived, through the poverty or splendor of his speech. Life lies behind us as the quarry from whence we get tiles and copestones for the masonry of today. This is the way to learn grammar. Colleges and books only copy the language which the field and the workyard made.
>
> "But the final value of action, like that of books, and better than books, is that it is a resource. That great principle of Undulation in nature, that shows itself in the inspiring and expiring of the breath; in desire and satiety; in the ebb and flow of the sea; in day and night; in heat and cold; and, as yet more deeply ingrained in every atom and every fluid, is known to us under the name of Polarity,—these 'fits of easy transmission and reflection,' as Newton called them, are the law of nature because they are the law of spirit." [8]

What Emerson noted in the educational system of his day was that it was so stereotyped. It did not appeal to man's higher sense; it did not create genuine idealism. Real education, Emerson held, would be like a religious conversion; it would challenge man's total loyalty and it would be a lifelong process.

Man was to accept his place in the universe. This meant that envy and hatred should be avoided and that we should cultivate our own garden. There is so much within us that could give us contentment and peace. Education, to Emerson, was ultimately a process of internal development.

The scholar would of necessity be a rebel. Emerson himself shocked the academicians by his radical sentiments, and when he gave the Divinity School speech at Harvard, his views were so liberal that he was never invited back.

There is an existential note in his philosophy. The scholar belongs to no party: he does not accept any official system of religion; he does not accept the mores of his time. The wise man, Emerson felt, is his own court and creates his own party, and he seeks a direct contact with God.

To Emerson, education was a form of inspiration. It reminded us of our limitless resources; it suggested that man is not defined by his biological heritage and that life itself is a constant process of renewal. Education should make us "brave and free"—yet too often it made us anemic and lethargic and it only cultivated the body. What man needed above all was food for his soul and his spirit. The lesson of education

---

[8] *Ibid.*

should be independence, emancipation from convention. To study literature was inadequate; rather we should create literature. To merely peruse the works of philosophy could be futile; rather we should become independent thinkers. To study the history of religion was superficial; rather we should become spiritual in our outlook on life.

As a follower of Pestalozzi, Emerson showed how education should advance from the home to the school, to society, and ultimately to the universe. Its main element was love and compassion. To advance knowledge, genius and drill were necessary. Genius would supply the foundations of knowledge, while drill would give it form. All studies were interrelated, according to Emerson, just as nature was one.

Emerson believed that there are two types of teachers. First, those who, like Locke, speak from the surface and use the method of analysis. But the second type is more important: teachers like Plotinus who speak from their heart and who create a revolution in our mind. They are our guides and they are the symbols of man's irresistible search for creativity and progress.

JAMES AND PRAGMATISM

Pragmatism has an ancient philosophical history. It can be found as early as the Sophists, who stressed man rather than the universe, and who believed that truth is constantly changing and thus forever relative. Charles Peirce, its American founder, thought that, primarily, pragmatism was a method whereby ideas could be clarified. All his life, Peirce believed in the philosophy of fallibilism: no ideas have an absolute status and concepts should fluctuate according to new scientific insights.

William James became one of the protagonists of pragmatism. He divided thinkers into two types: those who were tender-minded and who believed in free will and immortality, and those who were tough-minded, who accepted determinism and did not believe in a future life. The values which he opposed were those of absolute idealism, best represented by his colleague at Harvard, Josiah Royce. Royce, in *The World and the Individual,* called attention to the fragmentary and partial structure of experience and pointed to an absolute principle which included all of actuality, all of possibility, all of man, and all of science. Royce believed that the community is more important than the individual, and hence the keynote in his social philosophy was the principle of loyalty. To Royce, philosophical values were severely technical, to be understood by only a few; he tried to accomplish the same for American thought that Hegel had done for German philosophy.

William James opposed absolute values on two grounds. First, as a student of psychology, he felt that values arise in the context of human experience; they represent temperamental differences, and hence ideas are dependent on the way we feel and the way we act. Since our insights and experiences are fragmentary, we can have no concept of totality. To speak, then, of the Absolute is an arrogant assumption, one which cannot be substantiated by the researches of psychology. In the second place, James was opposed to absolute values because they represent a state of philosophical smugness and complacency. Too often in the history of philosophy and education the Absolute had terminated all disputes and all reflective inquiry. Too often it merely stood for dogmatism and for the closed mind. James was interested in the cash value of ideas, and hence he constantly asked such questions as "What practical importance do ideas have? How do they influence human behavior? How do they contribute to human happiness and adjustment?"

William James affirmed the values of individualism. He was suspicious of the concept of totality and of standards which maintained the supremacy of the group. In education, he pointed to the importance of the student in his encounter with knowledge. In politics, he fought against the domination of big corporations. In religion, he was opposed to all types of orthodoxy. Eccentric and extraordinary individuals had a special fascination for him, as he pointed out in *The Varieties of Religious Experience*.

William James believed with all his mind that life is worth living. He felt that faith created its own values and its own justifications. He disliked the anemic bystanders, those who were neutral in the drama of life. Human existence was a battle which had to be fought vigorously, a battle in which no neutral values were possible.

The religious ideas of pragmatism are best represented by William James' *The Varieties of Religious Experience* and *The Will to Believe*. Pragmatism generally affirms the values of liberal Christianity, although James was more of a mystic than John Dewey.

William James was not interested in fixed theological values. He was generally unconcerned with the problems of salvation, redemption, predestination, and the trinity. He approached religion from an empirical standpoint. Man, to him, was a creature guided by faith and sustained by hope. In crucial decisions, emotion would triumph over intellect, and the will would be more important than rationality.

The problem of God's existence could not be decided on rational grounds, since His existence could not be proven. Rather, God had to be accepted on the basis of faith and this faith had to make a practical difference to man. A universe without God would leave man in a despairing condition; it would give him no hope and no consolation in periods of chaos; it would be a universe in which might would triumph over right and in which the individual would feel profoundly lonely and desolate. A universe with God, on the other hand, would give man support for his endeavors, encouragement for his ideals, and strength for his vision. William James did not believe in an absolute God; his God was limited and in a process of evolution. Occasionally, he spoke of many Gods and thus returned to the system of Greek polytheism.

In education, James stressed the importance of correct habits which would make for emotional stability. Without good habits a student would be subject to sloppy and superficial thinking. Interest, James taught, could never be neglected by the educator, but it had to be based upon a sound foundation.

Education in the past, James held, was a regressive process because so often it had ignored psychological processes. Essentially, education, philosophy, and psychology were interdependent, for they all aimed at a complete exploration of experience.

The teacher, according to the philosophy of James, had to beware of an absolutistic attitude. Since he was fallible, his function was that of a guide and a friend. Dogmatism should never be encouraged in the classroom. A vigorous proponent of adult education, James believed that it was one of the unfulfilled dreams of democracy.

What attitude is most important in education? James replied that the teacher, above all, should *encourage*. A positive attitude would create real progress, while a negative viewpoint would stifle the development of the student. Kindness and understanding were as important in education as in other activities of life.

William James objected to the curriculum of his time because it overemphasized the classics. The knowledge of languages could not be ignored; but even more significant was the scientific method which might ultimately create a revolution in society. Ideas, to James, were not abstractions, but postulates for creative living.

Still, activism was not the goal of education. The wise man, James taught, would cultivate a spirit of inwardness and he would treasure moments of contemplation. He would develop an attitude of cosmic piety, for he would realize that man, nature, and God were interrelated.

James believed that the real teacher had a universal message. His task was not merely to instruct the elite and to dedicate himself to the ivory tower; rather his mission was to reach a wide audience so that democracy would become a dynamic way of life.

FOREIGN INFLUENCES

Four great thinkers have had a special impact upon American education. Pestalozzi's educational concepts greatly influenced the American, Charles Sheldon, a firm believer in humane discipline. At his school at Oswego, New York, Sheldon emphasized the importance of object lessons and contact with nature. He showed how instruction must start with simple concepts and be based upon correct sense perceptions.

Herbart's influence reached the United States through the work of the McMurrays. In 1892, a National Herbartian Society was established. It changed the methodology of education and emphasized history, geography and the social studies. Its formal technique was challenged by Dewey, who believed in a more plastic methodology in education.

Froebel had great influence on Mrs. Carl Schurz, who established a kindergarten, based on his ideas, in Wisconsin. Elizabeth Peabody established the first English-speaking kindergarten in Boston in 1860.

Another educator who exerted a strong influence, especially upon progressive education, was the Italian educator, Maria Montessori. Like Froebel, she stressed the natural goodness of children. To her, freedom was a cardinal goal of education. She believed that children should proceed at their own rate and that coercion should always be avoided. The individuality of the child was to be safeguarded. She summarized her ideas by the statement: "My method is established upon one fundamental base—the liberty of the pupils in their spontaneous manifestations." To Montessori, no intellectual progress could be achieved without training of the senses. All these views parallel the concepts of Dewey and Kilpatrick who became the leaders of the new American education.

DEWEY

The present dilemmas in educational theory are represented by the conflict between the champions of progressive education and traditionalism. John Dewey, until his death in 1952, best represented the progressive tradition, while Robert Hutchins became the champion of perennialism in education.

Among the important books written by Dewey on education we find *Art and Education, Child and Curriculum, Democracy and Education, Experience in Education, How We Think, The School and Society, The Sources of a Science of Education, Moral Principles in Education,* and *My Pedagogic Creed.* In general philosophy, his *Logic, Reconstruction in Philosophy, Human Nature and Conduct, The Quest for Certainty,* and *Art as Experience* deserve special notice.

Dewey was influenced most strongly by the theory of evolution. Thus, he approached education from a biological perspective. To him, the scientific method had meaning not only in the laboratory, but also in the schoolroom, which was to be guided by the spirit of tentativeness.

Among the educational thinkers who influenced him, William James gave him a psychological orientation and showed him that the old type of education was obsolete. G. Stanley Hall imbued him with the importance of early childhood study. Hegel inspired him to see life as a whole, to look to unity and interaction as a fundamental principle of the universe. Like Bacon, Dewey believed that knowledge is power and that it has to be used experimentally for the benefit of mankind. The seeds of his ideas can also be found in Rousseau, Pestalozzi, and Froebel.

A fundamental idea in Dewey's philosophy of education is his concept of the mind. Man's mind is not a static entity, a thing-in-itself; it is part of our evolutionary development, it is a tool of adjustment. He called his own philosophy *instrumentalism* to indicate his concern with methodology.

Problem-solving is fundamental in Dewey's system; we think when our equilibrium is disturbed.

Thinking involves five steps:

1. A felt need.
2. Analysis of the difficulty.
3. Alternative solutions are proposed.
4. Experimentation with various solutions until one passes the mental test.
5. Action is the final test for the proposed solution, which is to be verified in a scientific manner.

Like James, Dewey was conscious of the social environment of philosophy. It was no wonder that Athens had produced a speculative type of thinking, that, in the Middle Ages, theology was regarded as the most fundamental subject of inquiry, and that, in contempory times, philosophy had adopted a scientific outlook. Dewey maintained that knowledge is explosive and that it has to be used concretely and experimentally for the betterment of mankind. Dewey and his disciples, especially Kilpatrick, stressed the supreme significance of the values of co-operation, open-mindedness, and the dignity of the individual. These were not empty terms, but vital slogans which had as much meaning in the classroom as in political life.

Dewey favored, above all, the public school. Private education had often created snobbishness and narrow loyalties. To educate merely the rich was an inadequate process in a democracy.

The school to Dewey is not a prelude to life, rather it represents a miniature society. Democracy is not to be postponed; in the classroom, the child can learn co-operation and participation in group work. We grow only, Dewey maintained, as we participate, as we work out together common difficulties and common problems. Education, Dewey declared, does not stop with graduation, for life is to be our teacher, and we have to develop a better society. When we stand still we stagnate; only when we seek and look forward can we live a constructive life. The individual and society are not opposed to each other, for man is a social animal and finds expression through group life. Individuality is not given to us; we achieve it through social interaction.

Traditional education had been teacher-centered. The teacher was the basis of the educative process. Dewey advocated that the interests of students should be our starting point and he felt that the curriculum should be liberalized in order to avoid departmentalization. He favored play-activities, use of tools, and acquaintance with real life situations.

In the traditional school the student would be submissive and subordinate his individuality to that of the class. Dewey called for self-expression. This might create disciplinary problems, but, if the teacher motivated the child, real growth would take place. The classroom thus becomes a laboratory. In the progressive school, competition is outlawed; grades are tabu. The social studies, rather than the classics, are the center of the curriculum. Book knowledge is subordinated to actual experience. The slogan is: *We learn by doing*.

According to Dewey, philosophy is not a subject which deals with absolute truth. This is a pre-scientific viewpoint and represents the illusion that reality can be understood through intellectual means. Actually, philosophy is a tool of clarification. It illuminates our moral dilemmas; it is a prelude to understanding; it gives meaning to the struggle between the realm of theory and that of action. Basically, philosophy and education have the same meaning: Both aim at the transformation of experience, so that man can use the scientific method rather than appeal to pre-scientific standards.

Nothing is more fallacious, according to Dewey, than to look upon life as a hierarchy starting with practical values and ending with intellectual ideals. This is a reflection of the medieval concept of life, the concept that human existence starts with the sensate and is climaxed by spiritual ideals. Actually, we have always neglected the means and techniques whereby our ideals were to be realized, and this neglect has contributed to the culture lag. Dewey was especially concerned with the methodology whereby morality and wisdom were to be achieved. Did not science accomplish miracles because it had developed a methodology which allowed for no static conclusions? Was not verification as significant in philosophy and in education as in scientific matters?

Those who, like Horne, believed that education and philosophy depended upon metaphysical ideals, were attacked vigorously by Dewey. There could never be an agreement in metaphysics, which was generally a reflection of religious prejudices. Whether the universe was spiritual or material, finite or infinite, caused or uncaused, would have little bearing upon the progress of education. A naturalist in his outlook, Dewey felt that nature is to be the standard of our values. We should concentrate upon the improvement of this world rather than waiting for the perfection of the Beyond.

Morality, then, implies exercise of spontaneity, not following the dictates of the past. Self-activity should be encouraged by the school. The

traditional school had inhibited moral growth by its static and absolutistic tendencies. It had been based upon the cult of obedience. It had
made rules central; thus, the student could not develop real initiative—
without which genuine morality was impossible.

Dewey was opposed to the stress upon inhibition which prevailed
in so many educational circles. To inhibit and circumscribe development was like thwarting man's creativity. It was to prefer "negation over
affirmation," and "death over life." This did not imply encouragement
of unrestrained hedonism. Pleasure was not the goal of life, rather the
full development of the individual in his intellectual, moral, and esthetic
capacities. A positive end was to be achieved which would give meaning
and coherence to the strivings of the individual.

Mere information, Dewey stated, was useless in the educative process. It created a type of scholar who was preoccupied with the past and
who fought the battle of the footnotes. It created the illusion of knowledge, but only provided for the systematization of ignorance. In short, it
developed intellectual arrogance. To Dewey, information was only the
prelude to the development of judgment which could discriminate between various values and various truth claims. What was important was
to use knowledge concretely so that human life could be improved and
society could be made more rational.

Dewey attacked the schools of his time because they discouraged active investigation and intelligent doing. In this way they perpetuated the
errors of the past and contributed to the cult of authoritarianism. They
thus created dependent rather than autonomous human beings.

The three R's, according to Dewey, stood for cultural regression.
Without a plastic curriculum there could be no genuine responsiveness
on the part of the student. The three R's were static disciplines; far more
important were the social and the esthetic parts of the curriculum. If
educators were really interested in the development of responsiveness
and vitality they would not neglect the extra-curricular activities which
so often were more meaningful to the student than the scholastic enterprise.

Dewey had only contempt for the ideal of discipline which prevailed
in the traditional school. This meant that the teacher imposed his will
upon the class and that no genuine community spirit could prevail.
Dewey was undisturbed by the hustle and bustle of the progressive classroom. He compared this spirit with the activities of a busy workshop.
Here individuals were engaged in constructive work; they were sharing
their conclusions and they freely moved around to accomplish their
tasks. They needed no external control, for they were truly interested in
their work. In education likewise discipline would cease to be a problem
when individuals learned how to share their work and how to become gen-
uinely interested in what they were doing. Continuous interest thus became the keynote to educational progress.

Since the curriculum to Dewey was not a course of set studies, it had to be constantly redefined and reevaluated. Its purpose was to enrich the experience of students. The educator had to abandon the notion that the experience of the student was rigid; rather he had to realize how plastic and fluid the interests of students were and how they could be constantly expanded. Since life meant change, learning likewise implied constant reconstruction in which no final ends were allowed and in which stagnation, above all, had to be prevented.

Drudgery in all forms was to be avoided. Work merely for the sake of work, represented a puritanical attitude. The puritans, according to Dewey, had such a low estimate of man, that they were only interested in curbing his evil impulses. The result was the creation of a joyless and anti-esthetic culture. Play, to Dewey, was a central part of education, for it made for the full enjoyment of life and was the prelude to the flowering of the arts. Recreation was necessary not only from the standpoint of health, but also because it had a creative function in the development of man's intellect.

A critic may ask, is there no absolute truth in Dewey's system? Is it a purely relativistic viewpoint? Dewey believed that there can be many truths and that logic was a process of inquiry which had to be verified in a scientific manner. Truth could not be separated from our experiences and depended upon our insights. To be open to new truths was the mark of the educated man, according to Dewey, while the fanatic would try to coerce experience so that it would conform to his own biases and prejudices.

In Dewey's philosophy all studies have educative value:

"We cannot establish a hierarchy of values among studies. It is futile to attempt to arrange them in an order, beginning with one having least worth and going on to that of maximum value. In so far as any study has a unique or irreplaceable function in experience, in so far as it marks a characteristic enrichment of life, its worth is intrinsic or incomparable. Since education is not a means to living, but is identical with the operation of living a life which is fruitful and inherently significant, the only ultimate value which can be set up is just the process of living itself. And this is not an end to which studies and activities are subordinate means; it is the whole of which they are ingredients . . .

"It equally follows that when we compare studies as to their values, that is, treat them as means to something beyond themselves, that which controls their proper valuation is found in the specific situation in which they are to be used. The way to enable a student to apprehend the instrumental value of arithmetic is not to lecture him upon the benefit it will be to him in some remote and uncertain future, but to let him discover that success in something he is interested in doing depends upon ability to use numbers." [9]

9 John Dewey, *Democracy and Education* (New York: The Macmillan Company, 1916), p. 281. Reprinted by permission.

Education to Dewey stands for the reconstruction of experience, determined by our own growth:

"We reach a technical definition of education: it is that reconstruction or reorganization of experience which adds to the meaning of experience, and which increases ability to direct the course of subsequent experience. (i.) The increment of meaning corresponds to the increased perception of the connections and continuities of the activities in which we are engaged. The activity begins in an impulsive form; that is, it is blind. It does not know what it is about; that is to say, what are its interactions with other activities. An activity which brings education or instruction with it makes one aware of some of the connections which had been imperceptible. To recur to our simple example, a child who reaches for a bright light gets burned. Henceforth he *knows* that a certain act of touching in connection with a certain act of vision (and *vice-versa*) means heat or pain; or, a certain light means a source of heat. The acts by which a scientific man in his laboratory learns more about flame differ no whit in principle. By doing certain things, he makes perceptible certain connections of heat with other things, which had been previously ignored. Thus his acts in relation to these things get more meaning; he knows better what he is doing or "is about" when he has to do with them; he can *intend* consequences instead of just letting them happen—all synonymous ways of saying the same thing. At the same stroke, the flame has gained in meaning; all that is known about combustion, oxidation, about light and temperature, may become an intrinsic part of its intellectual content.

"(ii.) The other side of an educative experience is an added power of subsequent direction or control. To say that one knows what he is about, or can intend certain consequences, is to say, of course, that he can better anticipate what is going to happen." [10]

To Dewey intelligent acting is part of the educative process.

"To talk about an educational aim when approximately each act of a pupil is dictated by the teacher, when the only order in the sequence of his acts is that which comes from the assignment of lessons and the giving of directions by another, is to talk nonsense. *It is equally fatal to an aim to permit capricious or discontinuous action in the name of spontaneous self-expression.* An aim implies an orderly and ordered activity, one in which the order consists in the progressive completing of a process. Given an activity having a time span and cumulative growth within the time succession, *an aim means foresight in advance of the end or possible termination.* If bees anticipated the consequences of their activity, if they perceived their end in imaginative foresight, they would have the primary element in an aim. *Hence it is non-sense to talk about the aim of education—or any other undertaking—where conditions do not permit of foresight of results, and do not stimulate a person to look ahead to see what the outcome of a given activity is to be.*

---

[10] *Ibid.*, pp. 89-90.

"In the next place the aim as a foreseen end gives direction to the activity; it is not an idle view of a mere spectator, but *influences the steps taken to reach the end.* The foresight functions in three ways. In the first place, it involves *careful observation of the given conditions to see what are the means available for reaching the end,* and to discover the hindrances in the way. In the second place, it suggests *the proper order or sequence in the use of means.* It facilitates an economical selection and arrangement. In the third place, it makes *choice of alternatives possible.* . . .

.   .   .   .

"The net conclusion is that acting with an aim is all one with acting intelligently . . ." [11]

Education ultimately is an unending process. Are there any final goals? Dewey replies in the negative except that he favored the ideals of democracy. Only as education would become truly democratic, only as it cherished the ideals of co-operation, equal opportunity, and respect for the individual, would it contribute to the betterment of mankind.

To Dewey, democracy is more than a form of government; it has an intricate connection with education:

"Upon the educational side, we note first that the realization of a form of social life in which interests are mutually interpenetrating, and where progress, or readjustment, is an important consideration, makes a democratic community more interested than other communities have cause to be in deliberate and systematic education. The devotion of democracy to education is a familiar fact. The superficial explanation is that a government resting upon popular suffrage cannot be successful unless those who elect and who obey their governors are educated. Since a democratic society repudiates the principle of external authority, it must find a substitute in voluntary disposition and interest; these can be created only by education. But there is a deeper explanation. A democracy is more than a form of government; it is primarily a mode of associated living, of conjoint communicated experience. The extension in space of the number of individuals who participate in an interest so that each has to refer his own action to that of others, and to consider the action of others to give point and direction to his own, is equivalent to the breaking down of those barriers of class, race, and national territory which kept men from perceiving the full import of their activity. These more numerous and more varied points of contact denote a greater diversity of stimuli to which an individual has to respond; they consequently put a premium on variation in his action. They secure a liberation of powers which remain suppressed as long as the incitations to action are partial, as they must be in a group which in its exclusiveness shuts out many interests." [12]

Dewey made it clear that education represents the processes and structure of life itself. The practices of the classroom could either negate

11 *Ibid.,* pp. 118-120.
12 *Ibid.,* pp. 100-102.

or affirm the ideals of democracy. In an authoritarian classroom the teacher would be a stern disciplinarian: he would be only interested in formal standards; he would treat his students as objects; competition would prevail in a ruthless manner. In a democratic classroom, on the other hand, education would be determined by the interest and outlook of the children; it would be based on the ideals of mutuality and instead of competition, *growth* would be the main concern of the educator.

To Dewey the values of traditional liberal education appeared to be obsolete. Traditional liberal education had stressed book knowledge as against practical experience. It reflected the habits, outlook, and ideals of the elite. It frequently produced scholars who had no real knowledge of the world and who were narrow specialists, unable to cope with the advances of science.

Dewey, like James, believed in a pluralistic society. Totalitarianism of both the left and the right led only to the enslavement of the human spirit and represented pre-scientific modes of thinking. The best society was a balanced society in which progressive legislation was enacted, in which the extremes of wealth and poverty would be avoided, and in which education was the supreme activity.

Dewey, in esthetic education, was opposed to the distinction which is conventionally made between the fine arts and the industrial arts. This meant a great stress upon painting, music, and sculpture, and a neglect of industrial design. To Dewey, art simply meant a heightened state of experience. It was never to be confined to the museum or to the art gallery; rather, its value was its capacity to transform the life of the average citizen.

Esthetic values, then, were not absolute. They arose in the context of inquiry. They could be understood not merely by great geniuses, but by the average man. Art ceased to be the possession of the few, and instead, became the privilege of the many.

With disdain, Dewey spoke of the cult of tradition in art. To say that only the Greeks had a concept of beauty was a fallacy. To admire the splendor of the Gothic cathedrals and to underestimate the contributions of contemporary architecture—these were, according to Dewey, reactionary attitudes. The tastes and discoveries of one period could *never* coerce the outlook of another generation. Style, like philosophy, was forever in a state of flux, and hence, could not be guided exclusively by the insights of the past.

The critic in art, according to Dewey, had often impeded the progress of esthetic consciousness. The art critic had too much faith in his own judgment, and he had often discouraged new ideas and new inventions. The critic, if he wanted to perform a vital function in civilization, had to become as open-minded as a progressive teacher, and as tentative as a pragmatic philosopher.

To Dewey, the artist, the scientist, and the religious person all had the same task. The problem was not how could society be transcended and how bliss could be found in another life, but how could happiness be attained in the present.

Religious ideals, according to Dewey, had to be universalized. Religious endeavor simply meant dedication to a living aspiration and a vital world. It could be achieved by the artist in his studio, by the scientist in his laboratory, by the teacher in the classroom, as well as by the minister. The value of religion was not its theology, but its capacity to transform human behavior so that man could become more humane, more compassionate, and more altruistic.

Traditional moralists and theologians as well as teachers, according to Dewey, had been concerned too much with static definitions. They had given noble definitions of the supreme good and they had divided virtues into various categories, but they had overlooked the instrumental values. How could the good life be achieved? What were the means and processes whereby ideal values were to be attained? How could theory and practice meet in man's moral life?

Dewey objected to the viewpoints of both pessimism and optimism. The pessimists had too sober a view of human nature; they had overemphasized the evil and selfishness of man. Conscious only of the deterministic structure of the universe, they had paralyzed constructive improvement by affirming the vanity of human endeavors. The optimists, on the other hand, had celebrated a premature victory. They had underestimated the evil in man's heart, the inadequacy of social institutions, and the lust for power which has dominated so much the history. To say that evil was unreal or that goodness was all powerful—these were only slogans which appealed to the tender-minded.

Dewey stressed the values of meliorism—an attitude which asserts that the universe is neither bad nor good, but that it can be improved through education. Meliorism is an invitation to action, to concrete improvement. According to Dewey, man is neither good nor evil. The great aspect of man is that he can be changed, that his habits can be transformed, that his outlook can be widened, and that his perspective can become more universal.

Intelligence, according to Dewey and his followers, *is a prime factor in the moral life.* Intelligence establishes new patterns of behavior, replaces immediate goals with more distant goals, and narrows the distance between the self and others. Through the use of intelligence, human happiness can best be attained. In a sense, Dewey, returned to the dictum of Socrates who believed that knowledge is virtue. However, Dewey believed that knowledge and virtue are relative rather than absolute terms.

Related to Dewey's pragmatism is the viewpoint of Reconstructionism ably represented by Brameld in such works as *Patterns of Educational Philosophy* and *Ends and Means in Education*. To Brameld complete neutrality in meeting controversial issues was an impossibility. He
favored "defensible partiality" so that education becomes a primary
method of social change. The tone of his philosophy was future-centered,
and he believed that a planned society in the long run would be more
adequate than one which was based on laissez-faire principles.

Although most pragmatists have been less concerned with political
and economic issues than Brameld was, they have created a real revolution in American education. Through such thinkers, as W. H. Kilpatrick
and Boyd H. Bode, the views of Dewey have become commonplace. Undoubtedly, Dewey has often been misinterpreted. He has been cited as
the champion of vocationalism, of extreme permissiveness in the classroom, and as the enemy of the classics. His aim was, in reality, to make
education more dynamic and democratic so that a truly liberal society
would triumph. Pragmatism is a philosophy of experimentalism; the
curriculum is to be plastic; it is to be co-operatively planned; it is to emphasize the interests and ideals of children.

An episode in a seminar meeting related by Irwin Edman illustrates
the spirit of Dewey's philosophy.

"There was among the group a young lady who had come from England
where she had studied philosophy with Bertrand Russell at Cambridge. She
listened patiently for weeks to Dewey's varied insistence that the truth of an
idea is tested by its use. One day she burst out toward the close of the
seminar in the sharp, clipped speech of the educated English-woman: 'But,
professor, I have been taught to believe that true means true; that false
means false, that good means good, and bad means bad; I don't understand all this talk about more or less true, more or less good. Could you explain it more exactly?'

"Professor Dewey looked at her mildly for a moment and said, 'Let me
tell you a parable. Once upon a time in Philadelphia there was a paranoiac.
He thought he was dead. Nobody could convince him he was alive. Finally,
one of the doctors thought of an ingenious idea. He pricked the patient's
finger. 'Now,' he said, 'are you dead?' 'Sure,' said the paranoiac, 'that proves
that *dead men bleed*.' . . . Now I'll say true or false if you want me to, but
I'll mean better or worse.' " [13]

Edman describes Dewey's lecture method.

"He sat at his desk, fumbling with a few crumbled yellow sheets and
looking abstractedly out of the window. He spoke very slowly in a Vermont
drawl. He looked both very kindly and very abstracted. He hardly seemed

---

[13] *Philosophers' Holiday.*

aware of the presence of the class. He took little pains to underline a phrase, or emphasize a point, or, so at first it seemed to me, to make any. . . . The end of the hour finally came and he simply stopped; it seemed to me he might have stopped anywhere. But I soon found out that it was my mind that wandered, not John Dewey's. . . . I had been listening to a man actually *thinking* in the presence of a class." [14]

HUTCHINS

As against Dewey, Robert M. Hutchins (1899-   ) stressed the importance of great books. Hutchins believed that truth is absolute and that the great books of the past could guide the present. To Hutchins, science offered no magic remedies; instead he recommended the study of metaphysics.

The importance of Hutchins cannot be underestimated. His formal philosophy is perhaps less significant than his fundamental faith and his willingness to experiment in education. When the University of Chicago under his leadership granted the B.A. at the end of the sophomore year in college, an outcry could be heard among the genteel in the educational circles of this nation. The University of Chicago was denounced by a score of educational associations, but the University survived and appeared to prosper.

It was the ambition of Hutchins to develop a community of scholars at Chicago. With disdain he looked upon narrow specialization. He felt that the process of knowledge is always *incomplete* and that real education involves the re-education of the professors, who are usually as isolated and fragmentary in their approach to life as the monads of Leibniz. Naturally, many professors at the University of Chicago objected to re-education, for they felt they already had achieved the *summum bonum of knowledge.*

In an age of fragmentary issues and expediency, Hutchins called for a re-examination of education objectives. He shocked many college presidents when he told them that they should worry less about endowments and athletics and instead consider the fundamental problems of education. For Hutchins realized that expansion without vision in education frequently results in *organized triviality.* Like Emerson he was concerned with principles rather than with techniques. Hutchins felt that the technician often becomes a tool of autocracy and that he lacks perspective. Real education, according to Hutchins, was to improve our understanding, and was to give us a frame of reference whereby we can distinguish between right and wrong and between truth and falsehood.

---

[14] *Ibid.*

As a strong defender of freedom Hutchins allowed no loyalty oaths at the University of Chicago. He believed that no idea is infallible and that error cannot be eradicated by being suppressed. He made it clear in such books as *Education for Freedom* and *University of Utopia* that democracy prospers best in an atmosphere of diversity.

By some of his opponents Hutchins has been charged with being anti-democratic. Actually, this charge is unfounded, for Hutchins, like Jefferson, has an enormous faith in the potentialities of the individual. This explains his interest in the Great Books movement and in the bold adult schemes of the Ford Foundation and the Fund for the Republic. Democracy, to Hutchins, does not imply the same education for all, rather a differentiation in training based upon the capacities of the individual.

Hutchins has been outspoken in his denunciation of some practices in higher education. The cult of athletics, the dominance of vocationalism, the cult of scientism, all these trends were attacked by him in vigorous terms.

The weakness of Hutchins lies in his over-emphasis upon intellectualism. The discipline of reason is important in education, but just as significant is the development of esthetic sensitivity. Maturity implies the total development of man, not just the training of his mind.

EVALUATION

In our time, some scholars have attacked Dewey in vigorous terms. Milton Bestor and Mortimer Smith regarded his philosophy as a mark of regression and as an unfortunate incident in American history. Mortimer Adler, in his defense of perennial ideals, felt that Dewey made too much of change and did not see the need for abiding truths. Robert Hutchins maintained that philosophy should be concerned with the essential nature of life rather than with its transitory manifestations. By some religious thinkers Dewey has been accused of being an atheist. Bertrand Russell, who cannot be accused of any leaning towards orthodoxy, felt that Dewey lacked a sense of cosmic piety.

Actually, Dewey accomplished a Copernican revolution in American education. He showed that philosophy above all must have social relevance. He made education an instrument of democracy. He recognized the unlimited possibilities of the scientific method. He clearly saw the weaknesses of the traditional systems of logic and instead favored the tentativeness of the scientific method in man's search for truth. He favored neither optimism nor pessimism as a philosophy of life, but advocated the attitude of meliorism so that improvability became man's ethical goal.

He influenced education not only in the United States but also in Europe, in the Mid-East, in Russia, and his impact extended even to China and Japan. The Imperial University of Japan invited him to give a course of lectures which were later published as *Reconstruction in Philosophy*. He was one of the most creative thinkers of mankind.

Still, disciple worship is a danger in educational history. Just as Dewey did not spend his time commenting on the strengths and weaknesses of Pestalozzi or Froebel, so we must not become mere commentators and blind followers of his ideas. Unfortunately, today many scholars can be classified as being pro-Dewey or anti-Dewey. Such a viewpoint appears to be limited. We are meeting a new challenge today and we cannot respond to it creatively if we do not develop our own ideas. Since education is a reflection of social change it must be constantly re-examined; otherwise a culture lag results. What is progressive and advanced in educational theory at one time may not be totally adequate in a later period. All this means that greatness in history should not be an overture to imitation, but a prelude to originality.

QUESTIONS FOR DISCUSSION AND INVESTIGATION

1. Why do Jefferson and the Colonial leaders deserve a significant place in the development of education?

2. What were Horace Mann's precepts for education?

3. Describe the educational utopias that were undertaken in the early 1800's.

4. Explain Emerson's philosophy on education.

5. Discuss William James' pragmatic approach to philosophy, religion, and education.

6. Name for four great foreign thinkers who influenced American education and define their ideas.

7. Discuss John Dewey's progressive philosophy of education, emphasizing the areas where he departs from the more traditional systems of education.

8. According to Dewey, why is intelligence to be a prime factor in the moral life?

9. Compare and contrast the ideas of Dewey and Robert M. Hutchins.

10. Explain why Dewey accomplished a Copernican revolution in American education.

Chapter 28

The Role of the Teacher

A teacher's influence can be unlimited. His ideas may affect thousands. They may create a profound change in civilization. They may develop leaders of mankind.

Thomas Jefferson, author of the Declaration of Independence, paid his teacher this tribute: "It was my good fortune, and what probably fixed the destinies of my life, that Dr. William Small, of Scotland, was then Professor of Mathematics."

Another intellectual leader, Charles Darwin, in an eloquent passage memorialized his teacher: "I have not yet mentioned a circumstance which influenced my whole career more than any other, this was my friendship with Professor Henslow. . . ."

Bernard Baruch never forgot the efforts of his teacher, Katherine Devereux Blake. He recalled how she formed his character and gave him a prize for "gentlemanly deportment and general excellence." Baruch climaxed his tribute by declaring: "I wish I could adequately express my thanks and appreciation to that beautiful character. . . . When we go to the Great Beyond, I hope it will be my good fortune to go where Miss Blake will meet me and lead me to my seat, as she did so many years ago."

Abraham Lincoln was conscious of the great debt he owed to a frontier teacher, Mentor Graham, who taught him grammar, surveying, and the fundamentals of law. Lincoln asserted in his March 9, 1832 address to the people of Sangamon County: "Upon the subject of education . . . I can only say that I view it as the most important subject which we as a people can be engaged in."

THE PROBLEM OF RECRUITMENT

One of the foremost problems of education deals with the recruitment and preparation of teachers. Often the profession is unable to attract the most dynamic young people.

To remedy this condition, a national organization, the Future Teachers of America, was established in 1938. This organization, under the auspices of the National Education Association, has branches in many senior and junior high schools throughout the nation. The aim of the organization is to spread interest in teaching as a profession, and to attract a superior person to the academic life.

Still, students often comment that teaching is their last choice. Part of this feeling can be explained by the low salary scale in many states and by the tabus which still plague the teaching profession.

Personal counseling can be of immense value in attracting young people to the teaching profession. There is the case of a lawyer who felt that he was living a useless life and thought that expediency reigned in legal affairs. During an alumni meeting he talked to the dean of men, an extremely friendly and personable man, who suggested that the young man should enter the field of education. At first, the lawyer balked at the idea, but later he changed his mind. Today, he is a brilliant superintendent of schools, eternally grateful to the dean, who first had suggested the possibility of an educational career.

A businessman, apparently very successful, wanted to do something constructive with youth. Someone suggested teaching, for he was intelligent, dynamic, and idealistic. He hesitated at first, since he had only a high school education, but after a while he made up his mind to become a teacher, entered college and graduated with high honors. Today he is a renowned college professor.

TRENDS IN TEACHER TRAINING

In early modern times, teachers were not trained formally: they learned as apprentices; if they wanted to gain a reputation as educators, they established a school, like Sturm at Strassburg. It was not until 1704 that the first teacher training school was established at Halle, Germany. This came about mainly through the agitation of ministers who were interested in the improvement of popular education, and who wanted to combine moral with intellectual training.

It was a minister, the Reverend Samuel R. Hall, who in the United States created the first private training school for teachers. This was done at Concord, Vermont. The United States lagged far behind Germany and other European countries in the training of teachers, mainly because teachers were not highly regarded in Colonial America; they certainly were not indispensable, and their salary was low. Often, they had to fulfill menial duties. Teaching contracts reveal that teachers frequently had to act as janitors; occasionally, a teacher even had to bury the dead. No wonder that no adequate provision was made for teacher training.

In the nineteenth century, Massachusetts took the lead in teacher training, and, in 1839, it created three *normal schools*. These schools were in reality glorified high schools and were designed mainly to prepare teachers for elementary school work. To improve standards and to prepare teachers for high school, the Illinois State Normal University was founded in 1857. The requirements of this university were far stricter than the standards of the normal schools in Massachusetts.

In the twentieth century, the influence of the normal school declined; in recent years, the normal school has almost vanished from the educational scene. Its place has been taken by the teachers college, the most famous of which is Teachers College at Columbia University, founded in 1887. Among its great leaders, we should include Russell, Bagley, Butts, Childs, and Kilpatrick—all of them have made fundamental contributions to education. In the South, one of the most famous institutions is the George Peabody College for Teachers, at Nashville, Tennessee.

Teachers colleges, unlike the normal school, require graduation from high school. Some teachers colleges may grant both a Master's degree and the Doctorate, in addition to the Bachelor degree. Often, teachers colleges specialize in the preparation of college professors and administrators. Offerings are diversified and they include various aspects of professional education, as well as elements of the liberal arts curriculum.

In recent decades, some teachers colleges, especially in California, have become state colleges. They compete with state institutions in offering various majors and in emphasizing general education. San Diego State College, Fresno State College, San Francisco State College, and San Jose State are excellent examples of the high standards of scholarship achieved by the state college today.

Education, as a separate subject in college, did not gain status until the last part of the nineteenth century. In 1837, the University of Iowa created a part-time chair of education. Six years later, the University of Michigan established a full-time department. Today, most large universities have a separate school of education. Major subjects of education covered by these schools include:

Administration
Social foundations of education
Guidance and psychology of education
Tests and measurements
History and philosophy of education

Methods of teaching
Audio-Visual material
Pre-elementary and elementary teaching
Secondary teaching
Junior college and college teaching
School finance and management
School law
Adult education
Supervised student teaching
Teaching of various subjects, like reading, writing, arithmetic, industrial arts, physical education, social studies, etc.
Intercultural education
Educational research

It is important that the prospective teacher not only is familiar with the areas of educational specialization, such as child psychology, methodology, and history and philosophy of education, but also possesses an adequate general education. High school teachers will frequently instruct in various subjects; thus, a broad background will be helpful. At the same time, teachers ought to possess complete mastery of their own field of specialization.

An important part of teacher preparation is student teaching, which is an excellent test of the theories of education. Student teaching is usually undertaken under the supervision of a master teacher. Usually, a professor who is in charge of student teaching will evaluate the practical aptitude and success of the prospective teacher.

Before a teacher can instruct, he has to be certified. Today, certification is generally handled by the state departments of education, whereas in earlier times, colleges themselves would often grant the certificate. Requirements for certification vary with the individual states; however, they usually include an oath of allegiance to the United States as well as health examinations.

It should be remembered that the colleges have to meet the requirements of the state departments of education. The certificate is granted upon the recommendation of the college, but it may be revoked by the state, especially in cases of moral turpitude on the part of the teacher.

IN-SERVICE EDUCATION

In order to prevent stagnation and to encourage skillful teaching, supervision is imperative. Supervisors may vary in their strategy; they may visit the classroom frequently or they may see the teacher only rarely; some supervisors make direct suggestions for improvement, others use an indirect approach and leave a considerable area of freedom to the teacher.

A skillful supervisor will be positive in his approach. He will indicate areas of improvement and he will notice lags, but he will not use destructive criticisms. He will allow for considerable experimentation on the part of the teacher and will not set himself up as the ultimate arbiter of good teaching.

In-service growth of teachers is promoted by periodic Institutes, where topics of discussion may range from contemporary Russia to non-objective art.

Summer school study tends to increase teaching efficiency. However, summer school courses should not be limited to professional education, but also should include the liberal arts. Since there is always the danger that the teacher may become too *one-sided,* it is an excellent idea for a shop teacher to take a course in philosophy, or for a physical education instructor to select a course in art.

Teachers should take an active part in community life. They might join service clubs, or they might support the local drama group. Church activities add to the effectiveness of the teacher. In communities, where the Great Books organization exists, membership may be worthwhile and intellectually stimulating.

However, it should be pointed out that community activities for the teacher are not compulsory. Often the teacher engages in *too many* activities; as a result he lives a life of organized desperation. He needs time to think, to ponder, to relax, and to be away from school and community affairs.

The tendency of the modern school and university is to establish a multitude of committees, ranging from library committees to social committees. Frequently, these committees can be consolidated and integrated. Too much time is wasted in unessential committee meetings.

TRAVEL. For professional growth, travel is important. The Sabbatical year, which has become an established institution in college teaching, should also be instituted in high school and elementary school. There should also be more exchange of teachers between the various states and various nations.

Today, an excellent opportunity exists for teachers to instruct abroad. Fulbright fellowships, the Division of Cultural Relations of the State Department, the Education Committee of the English Speaking Union, the American Friends Service Committee—all these agencies, and many more, may aid the teacher who is looking for a position abroad. There is a great need for teachers to train children of army personnel stationed abroad. Ample opportunities exist for teaching in outlying possessions, like Guam, Samoa, Puerto Rico, Virgin Islands, and the Panama Canal Zone.

For the teacher who goes abroad, it is important that he should learn the language spoken in that nation and also that he should know something about its cultural background. He should not be chauvinistic and always tell about the glories at home. Instead, the teacher must be a constant learner, visiting the educational institutions abroad with a view of adopting some of their constructive methods. For instance, Horace Mann almost created an educational revolution in Massachusetts after he had seen some of the more progressive schools in Europe.

ORGANIZATIONS. It is important that the teacher join at least one professional organization. Of special significance is the National Education Association, which is located in Washington and which publishes a monthly magazine, the *N. E. A. Journal.*

The N.E.A. arose out of an organization of teachers founded in 1857, in Philadelphia. It was formally organized in 1871. The governing body of the N.E.A. is a representative assembly which is designed to reflect the interests of the individual members.

The aim of the N.E.A. is to improve the level of education in the United States and "to promote the cause of popular education." Throughout its existence, the N.E.A. has urged better salaries for teachers, an adequate retirement income, better prepared teachers, more exacting standards in school administration, equal educational opportunity for all races, and adequate school equipment. In recent years, the N.E.A. has urged special concentration upon the United Nations Educational, Scientific and Cultural Organization.

Progressive education in this country has been championed most eloquently by the American Education Fellowship which issued *Progressive Education.* The American Federation of Teachers is part of the A.F.L. and is interested primarily in social and economic reform. It regards the teacher as being part of the labor movement and urges that teachers organize like other labor groups. It publishes *The American Teacher,* a journal with liberal views on political and economic events. In addition to these national organizations of teachers, many state and local teachers' associations exist with the purpose of advancing the cause of education.

We should not omit the honorary organizations of education. Most important is probably Phi Delta Kappa, which is growing rapidly. Its membership is reserved for men, and it specializes in educational research. Every month Phi Delta Kappa issues a magazine, the *Phi Delta Kappan.* Kappa Delta Pi is of more recent origin and admits both men and women. Pi Lambda Theta is open only to women, and has also attracted many outstanding leaders of education.

THE SUPERIOR TEACHER

One of the best definitions of the qualities of the good teacher is contained in a report in 1938 by the Commission on Teacher Education of the American Council on Education. The following traits are enumerated:

Respect for personality
Community-mindedness
Rational behavior
Skill in operation
Increasing knowledge
Skill in mediating knowledge
Friendliness with children
Understanding children
Social understanding and behavior
Good citizenship in the school and society
Skill in evaluation
Faith in the worth of teaching.

Bagley, in *School Discipline,* tells about the judgment of administrators and school employees regarding the desirable traits for teaching:

Sympathy
Personal appearance
Address
Sincerity
Optimism
Enthusiasm
Scholarship
Physical vitality
Fairness
Reserve and dignity.

Frank W. Hart, in his *Teachers and Training,* mentions helpfulness regarding assignments and clarity of exposition as important factors in the success of the teacher. On the other hand, over three thousand high school seniors which he had interviewed mentioned a happy and humorous disposition on the part of the teacher; they regarded crabbiness as the worst trait of a teacher.

While the traits required for teachers vary according to the type of position and the type of school, it can be safely said that certain ancient prejudices regarding teaching should be overcome.

Bagley's tenth point was Reserve and Dignity. Unfortunately, many teachers are too pompous and regard dignity as the *summum bonum* of teaching. To be reserved in teaching often means not to take an active interest in the student. We should always remember that we are educating *human beings, not inanimate objects.*

The superior teacher, above all, is *compassionate.* He realizes that standards are less important than individual development. He has a keen sense of imagination, he is never shocked by his students. He remembers that once he, too, was young, and he may even have been wayward.

The superior teacher has faith in his subject and his enthusiasm is so great that it radiates. A superior teacher, like William James, could make psychology the most fascinating study of education. A superior teacher, like Frank Baxter at the University of Southern California, has introduced thousands of students to the glories of Shakespeare.

A superior teacher is able to relate his subject to our contemporary civilization. Thus, when Baxter gives an account of Shakespeare, the latter becomes a contemporary playwright and his characters become our neighbors.

A STATEMENT OF FAITH

A critic recently listed some of the negative features of the teaching profession. He spoke about the fact that for so many teachers, education had been their second or third choice. He maintained that many prospective teachers have less intellectual ability than those who become lawyers, physicians, or engineers. The pay of the teacher is still less than that of the plumber. The social status of the teacher does not compare with the social position of European instructors. In short, he maintained that it was not at all surprising that every year hundreds of thousands leave the teaching profession and that the shortage of qualified personnel is becoming more acute all the time.

To make the picture even more somber for a moment, we should remember a motion picture, *Blackboard Jungle,* which portrayed a school in which a virtual civil war existed and in which teachers were assaulted. In New York, not so long ago, delinquency was so tortuous a problem that a junior high school principal committed suicide. A reporter of one of the main New York newspapers in a series of articles described a school in which students were drunk and in which the juvenile gangs dominated. When asked whether he would ever want to be a teacher he replied: "The job is too tough for me."

Before we lose hope and generalize about the waywardness of American youngsters, we should realize that delinquency is not a general condition and that the vast majority of American youths are law-abiding. Furthermore, the Christian Science Monitor reported that in the worst delinquency area in New York where racial tensions were prevalent, sensational progress has been made in developing constructive programs of adjustment through improved guidance services, community participation, smaller classes, and, above all, through dedicated teaching. For example, every year one junior high school would send some of the worst delinquents to a neighboring senior high school, where they would specialize in assaults and burglaries. After modern methods of education were adopted in the junior high school, and after scientific methods were used to study behavior problems, the delinquency rate dropped at once. The dean of the senior high school remarked that now he welcomed the students from the junior high school, and that many of them were eager to go on to college.

It may be maintained that waywardness of youth is not confined to slum sections and that behavior problems of children from wealthy homes may be just as serious. The confusion of values in a so-called good neighborhood was portrayed in a graphic way by James Dean in the movie, *Rebel Without A Cause;* the protagonist of this story found no support from his parents and was unable to live by the code of society. Frequently, children in better neighborhoods are just as eager for thrills as are the children in slum sections. No wonder we are producing a beat generation. No wonder that many teachers are bewildered by the ways of youngsters who have adult experiences in their early teens and who often exhibit patterns of premature sophistication.

What is worse, often we find teachers who enter the profession with high hopes, yet a few years later they become tired and disenchanted. Some find that they do not have enough time for personal development; their classes may be too large, and perhaps the I.Q. of the students may be low. Others may complain about unimaginative administrators, too many committee meetings, or too much paper work. Men with families usually hold another job to make a living; some may be tempted by the large salaries of industry, or they may leave classroom teaching for higher paying administrative jobs.

Still, the challenge of teaching is enormous. In no other profession is the satisfaction so great and so lasting. In business we may feel a sense of futility even when we become wealthy, for material possessions may only be the preludes to spiritual insecurity. In law we may feel a sense of disgust, for we may be obliged to defend individuals who are unworthy. But in teaching we transcend our own egos and we are able to see the larger self.

GREAT TEACHING

The importance of teaching is eloquently illustrated by the example of Helen Keller. Before she met her teacher, Helen Keller did not want to live. She was sullen. She had no real feelings for her parents. Her world was one of complete isolation. When she met her teacher, everything changed. She learned the meaning of communication. She learned how to identify objects. She discovered a new universe of knowledge and awareness. Above all, she learned the meaning of love and compassion. Now she understood that the worst blindness is not physical but spiritual, and that even amidst physical limitations man's spirit can be triumphant.

Helen Keller was able to go to college and became a brilliant student. When she graduated she devoted herself to work for the blind, and she travelled all over the world. She became a teacher in the real sense of the word, for wherever she went she radiated understanding and optimism. After World War II, she visited Japan where she was triumphantly received. Children lined the streets of Tokyo; it was a public holiday. Her visit was the conversation everywhere. She had an audience with the emperor who was full of admiration for her accomplishments. She remarked to him that all this would have been impossible without her teacher who inspired her and who encouraged her when her spirits were low.

Most of us are blessed with the full use of our senses and do not have to face the obstacles which Helen Keller faced. Our task is to become aware of our opportunities. Our function is to create love where antagonism prevails, to spread the flame of knowledge where ignorance exists, to make men conscious of their neighbors amidst an atmosphere of moral isolation, and to create humility when so many are smug and self-righteous.

Not so long ago, Menninger wrote a book entitled *Man Against Himself*. Freud, as is well known, spoke of man's Death wish. Everywhere we can see destructive tendencies. This attitude is represented not only by constant crises, but also by the wave of lawlessness, delinquency, alcoholism, and the general unhappiness which prevails in our civilization. We have more conveniences and more comforts, we travel more than ever before, we have more numerous entertainments, and yet we are producing millions of neurotics who find little meaning in life.

The task of the teacher thus becomes more urgent. He must not only communicate ideas, but he must be a representative of a creative way of life, a symbol of peace and serenity in a world which is troubled and tortured. Thus, he becomes the guardian of civilization and the protector of progress.

QUESTIONS FOR DISCUSSION AND INVESTIGATION

1. Cite historical examples of the teacher's unlimited influence.

2. Explain the problems of recruitment and the attempted solutions.

3. Trace the development of techniques and methods in teacher training.

4. What are the important requirements of present-day teacher training?

5. Describe in-service education.

6. Explain the importance of national teacher organizations.

7. What are the qualities of the superior teacher?

8. Explain the reasons for the waywardness of youth in slum sections and in wealthy homes.

9. In spite of negative qualities in some teachers and the waywardness of the youth in a few sections of the country, why can the profession of teaching offer such tremendous satisfaction?

10. How did Helen Keller prove the importance of great teaching?

Chapter 29

Early Education

THE IMPORTANCE OF NURSERY EDUCATION

Psychologists inform us that the early years of the child tend to be the most important, yet often we do not take advantage of the educational opportunities of early childhood.

Traditionally, early education has been the prerogative of the home. However, in modern times the home has often disintegrated through divorce and desertion; in times of war, the need for nurseries and kindergartens has been especially evident.

Nursery education probably dates back as far as Plato. Plato felt that the early patterns are established by the parents and warned them not to tell their children unedifying fairy tales; otherwise, the moral behavior of the offspring might be endangered.

Comenius had a more constructive view of the early childhood period and maintained that mothers could best instruct their own children.

Psychoanalysts today are especially interested in nursery education, for they believe that the child adopts many complexes from his environment and that many of his normal drives are repressed by adults. Teachers in nursery schools guided by psychoanalysts will allow greater freedom to children, and they will not be shocked when children act in a wayward manner.

Public nursery schools are of recent origin; the first was established in 1919. In 1933, a federal nursery school program was undertaken; this was mainly an emergency measure under the sponsorship of the W.P.A. During World War II, nursery education was subsidized by the Federal government under the Lanham act.

Universities like Teachers College, Columbia University, Cornell, Iowa State, and Ohio State have long been active in nursery education. Girls schools like Scripps College and Vassar have trained many of their graduates as teachers in experimental nursery schools.

Various types of nursery schools can be observed in operation. For example, some nursery schools specialize in behavior problems, others are social service units, still others are research centers. Some aid in the teacher training program, some are used in the home economics program, some operate only during the summer, and some are part of the kindergarten. The social influence is noticeable in nursery school education; occasionally nurseries are operated on a co-operative basis with parents doing most of the teaching. Other nursery schools reflect, as has been related, the influence of psychoanalysts; in this case, the schools are administered in close co-operation with psychiatrists.

The advantages of nursery school are apparent:

Parents are able to gain a better perspective regarding their offspring. Yet, the nursery school does not replace the home environment, rather it adds to the home atmosphere. The environment of the nursery school is informal and thus resembles the home.

The nursery school aids in socializing children; especially for the only child it is a most valuable experience.

The physical capacities of the child are strengthened. The curriculum of the nursery school varies play with rest. The meals are carefully planned and out-of-door play is stressed.

The emotional growth of the child is stimulated. The child ceases to depend exclusively upon the parents. Contact with other children adds to the range and depth of emotions on the part of the individual child.

Patterns of co-operation are established in the nursery school. The child learns to share toys with others and thus becomes less egoistic.

The intellectual stimulus of the nursery school may be great. This does not imply formal learning, rather an awakening of curiosity and skillful guidance on the part of adults.

Nursery schools appeal not merely to the rich, but also to members of the middle class. They can be found not only in cities, but also in rural areas. Housing projects often contain nursery schools; thus, even workers can afford this type of education for their children.

A distinction should be made between nursery schools and day nurseries. The latter are used primarily for children whose mothers are working or are otherwise occupied and hence cannot take care of their children. Nursery schools, on the other hand, have a distinctive educational mission, which is not always true in the case of day nurseries.

The teachers of the nursery schools often represent the highest standards of education. In previous decades, people believed that anybody could be a nursery school teacher; today, special training is required. The mental health and the emotional attitudes of the teacher are especially important.

The equipment of nursery schools is constantly being improved. Special care is taken to make the school as attractive as possible and also to provide for the health of the children.

Frequently, nursery schools will employ psychologists and psychiatrists, who give special lectures to the parents of the children. Thus, nursery education adds to parental education.

Today, the nursery school has become more specialized. A large nursery school may employ not only teachers and a principal, but also social workers, dietitians, recreation leaders, nurses, as well as a physician and a psychiatrist.

THE KINDERGARTEN

The beginnings of the kindergarten can be traced to the work of Froebel. Before Froebel, Rousseau had already outlined a new curriculum for children, based on self-expression; but it was Froebel who in 1837 established the first kindergarten in Blankenburg, Germany.

Froebel's views regarding early childhood education were expressed in *The Education of Man, Mother Play and Nursery Songs,* and in his *Autobiography.* To Froebel, children were essentially creative and yet easily corrupted by adults. The play of children had definite educational significance, and Froebel was certain that the school should utilize the adventurous spirit of young children.

In the United States, the first kindergarten was established in 1855 by Mrs. Carl Schurz at Watertown, Wisconsin. It did not become a part of the regular educational system until 1873, when W. T. Harris sponsored the kindergarten at St. Louis, Missouri.

In more recent times, Maria Montessori's influence upon the kindergarten has been pronounced; she emphasized the freedom of the child, Also, W. H. Kilpatrick and John Dewey made a significant contribution to the development of the modern kindergarten. Others who aided in the advance of the kindergarten include G. Stanley Hall, Samuel Chester Parker, Alice Temple, Anne Moore, Laura Zirbes, Patty Smith Hill, Edna D. Baker, and Elizabeth Harrison.

The curriculum of the kindergarten, like that of the nursery school. is anything but rigid. The curriculum aims at creative expression on the part of children. It combines play with work experiences. Personal hygiene still plays a large role in the educational program of the kindergarten. Outdoor games and excursions are encouraged. Music and storytelling are central in the kindergarten.

A more recent development is the utilization of science in the kindergarten. Children often ask questions about the sun and the stars, and they are interested in flowers and birds. Thus, a natural opportunity exists for scientific study. At this stage children are uninhibited in their esthetic expressions; hence, art work is also important in the kindergarten.

Often, social consciousness is developed through the kindergarten. For instance, in 1946, one teacher made a lasting impression upon the children when she told them about a little boy in Germany who was almost starving and who had lost his parents in the war. The children all wanted to help the little boy, and they sent food packages to Germany.

It is not too unusual to hear current events discussed in kindergarten. Most of the children come from homes with television sets and have an excellent memory. Since they see more of the world, they are often far more precocious than their parents were at the same age.

It is a difficult, but a rewarding task to teach children of the preschool age. The teacher should be broad-minded and cosmopolitan; she should avoid a puritanical attitude. If she makes a categorical distinction between right and wrong, if she is a strict disciplinarian, her work will suffer. Naturally she should have a sincere liking for children, but her love should not be possessive. She should be easy-going as a person, and yet be firm when the occasion arises for discipline.

She should have an almost inexhaustible fund of stories, for children can listen to them by the hour. She should encourage self-expression on the part of children in art, music, poetry and drama. She should be an expert in both physiology and psychology, and she should know the symptoms of behavior problems.

Often, the pre-school teacher will have to deal with special problem children. The child may have defective vision, or be crippled, or be stuttering. Other children may look down on the handicapped child and may even be cruel to him. The teacher must see to it that a pattern of cooperation and understanding is established in the school, and that special kindness is shown to the underprivileged child.

THE ELEMENTARY SCHOOL

Many pioneers have contributed to the success of the elementary school. Martin Luther and Calvin both were interested in primary education and they urged that it should include children of the rich and the poor. Both thought that the primary grades should stress religion.

Comenius urged a universal system of elementary education. Many thinkers in his time thought this was utopianism in action. He influenced other educators by his insistence that primary education be conducted in the vernacular, not in Latin.

Rousseau initiated the child-centered program of the modern elementary school, while Pestalozzi indicated the need for a flexible curriculum. At Pestalozzi's school the hard subjects came in the morning, while the easier subjects were discussed during the afternoon. Pestalozzi favored frequent excursions and the study of nature as an object lesson for the child.

Herbart tried to formulate the psychological basis of primary education and he exerted a significant influence upon nineteenth century education. His views, in a modified way, appear in the unit plan of Morrison, whose formula was: "Pre-test, teach, test the results, adopt procedure, teach and test again to the point of actual learning." [1]

Horace Mann studied the German educational system, and his Seventh Annual Report extolled the virtues of the Prussian educational system. He aided in improving teacher preparation for the elementary school and in lengthening the elementary school term.

Henry Barnard, like Horace Mann, was influenced by European education, and in 1854 published the *National Education in Europe*. Like Mann, he tried to improve the standards for teacher preparation, and in 1839 he helped to create the first Teachers' Institute.

Francis Parker was chairman of the University of Chicago school of education and he aided the course of progressive education. He believed that traditional education tended to suppress the individuality of children. He influenced many teachers through his books, especially in *Talks to Pedagogues* and *Talks to Teachers*.

The theories of John Dewey, as we have seen, have been popularized and applied to primary education by W. H. Kilpatrick. Among the works of Kilpatrick we should mention *Foundations of Method, Source-Book in the Philosophy of Education,* and *Philosophy of Education*. Kilpatrick gave impetus to the activity curriculum, and he taught thousands of teachers about the significance of projects in education. The keynote to the elementary school is free activity, according to Kilpatrick. Instead of drill, direct experience is used; instead of textbooks, community knowledge becomes important. Instead of the past, the present becomes the center of elementary education.

Progressive education has had a healthy influence upon primary education. It resulted in new experiments, like the Winnetka plan which emphasized individual advancement and which avoided the failings of the grading system. The Dalton plan, initiated by Helen Parkhurst, stressed the principles of freedom, co-operation, and the budgeting of time.[2] Education, according to Parkhurst, is to utilize the laboratory method; a student keeps track of his time, and his progress is recorded

---

[1] Morrison, *The Practice of Teaching in the Secondary School.*

[2] Parkhurst, *Education on the Dalton Plan.*

every day. Freedom of movement permits the student to freely change classes and pursue his labors in various subject-laboratories.

Free elementary schools are of relatively recent origin. The first state to adopt free elementary education was Pennsylvania, in 1834. The first compulsory attendance law was adopted in Massachusetts, in 1852. However, this law provided only for compulsory part-time attendance; it was not until 1890 that Connecticut passed a *compulsory full-time* requirement. In 1918, compulsory education was adopted in all the states of the Union.

The first three grades of the elementary school usually deal with the mastery of reading. The child also learns the elements of arithmetic and spelling. The social relationships of arithmetic are stressed. In spelling the emphasis is upon common words, rather than upon unusual words. Excessive drill is avoided.

The fourth, fifth, and sixth grades also emphasize reading, but now the stress is mainly upon *comprehension*. Many school systems introduce world history and general science at this level. The child learns how to express himself emotionally as well as intellectually.

The unit system has become popular in the elementary school. A unit may deal with such subjects as Boats and Ships, Living in the Desert, or a Day on the Farm. The unit is designed to relate learning to life experiences and attempts to overcome the limitations of the departmentalization of knowledge. Furthermore, handicraft work is encouraged. The pupils actually learn how to build a tent or how to live on the farm.

In many cities, the seventh and eighth grades have been added to the junior high school. This is a desirable step, for it intensifies the intellectual development of the student. Yet often the junior high school has the same standards as a good elementary school.

The organization of the elementary school tends to be elastic. In many cases the *traditional method* persists with the teacher keeping one grade all day; sometimes the *departmental organization* is favored with the students changing from one teacher to another. Thus, one teacher will specialize in reading, another in arithmetic. (This method cannot be effectively used for the first three grades). Another method is the *platoon system*, where the student spends part of the day with a homeroom teacher, and the rest of the day with special subject teachers. The *block system* tends to combine the departmental and the traditional method of organization. It is often found in schools which have adopted a child-centered system of education.

Ability grouping is frequently used in the elementary school. Thus, the grade may be divided into three sections; one section will consist of the fast learners, another will consist of the average students, while a third may contain the poor students. Parents often object to this type of grouping, especially when their children are in the slow group.

THE PHILOSOPHY OF ELEMENTARY EDUCATION

The progressive movement, as we have seen, has had a profound effect upon elementary education. The traditional emphasis upon the subject matter is almost obsolete. It may be asked: What are the main contributions of progressive thinkers like Dewey and Kilpatrick to elementary education?

The physical environment has been stressed. The atmosphere of the classroom is now more conducive to learning. More flexibility has been achieved in the building program; often special workrooms are provided for children.

The child reads not only one book, but is encouraged to consult a variety of books. He learns to take advantage of the library.

The reading program is more flexible with major attention being paid to *reading readiness;* silent reading, rather than oral reading, is being encouraged.

Arithmetic is not taught through drill, but related to the daily activities of the pupils.

There is less stress upon facts and more emphasis upon the significance of ideals and institutions.

Pupils are evaluated individually, with *growth* becoming the main standard of evaluation. Failing of students is discouraged.

Progress reports stress not formal knowledge, but character development. In progressive schools these reports tend to be more informative and detailed than in the traditional school.

The teacher ceases to be authoritarian and become a guide, rather than the arbiter of knowledge.

There is a tendency to unite various subjects instead of teaching them in isolation. For instance, instead of studying spelling for twenty minutes and then arithmetic for twenty minutes, the class will work on larger units, such as transportation.

Democratic ideals are emphasized, with pupils participating in the government of the school.

Instead of imitation in art, the progressive ideal is self-expression.

Wide use of community resources is urged in progressive education. The pupil actually sees the fire department in operation, and he learns from first-hand experience about the city government.

In writing, the ideal of legibility is stressed.

Discipline tends to be a secondary matter in the progressive school, since it is to be achieved through social awareness.

Freedom of movement is one of the keynotes of the progressive school. Play is part of the curriculum.

Careful guidance of the pupil is one of the objectives of the progressive school.

Activity is encouraged by the progressive educator.

Co-operation is replacing competition as the main incentive for learning.

A concerted attempt is made to make learning as pleasant as possible.

Proponents of the traditional ways of education, like Bagley, charge that the progressive school neglects fundamentals and that it creates a weak generation. Often the graduate of such a school does not know how to read or write adequately, and his spelling may be atrocious. Bagley advocated more discipline, rather than self-expression, for the pupil. Competition is to stimulate learning and the school is to prepare the pupil for the "rugged" atmosphere of adult life.

Still we cannot and should not return to traditionalism in elementary education. The school of the nineteenth century is as outmoded as the Model T Ford in transportation. Experimentation is the foundation of creative education.

QUESTIONS FOR DISCUSSION AND INVESTIGATION

1. In referring to the philosophies of a few historically famous educators, prove the importance of nursery education.

2. Name the advantages of the nursery school.

3. Trace the development of the kindergarten.

4. Name the pioneers of the elementary school and their contributions.

5. Describe the educational goals of the elementary grades.

6. What is the unit system?

7. List the various ways in which an elementary school may be organized.

8. As progressive thinkers, what have Dewey and Kilpatrick contributed toward elementary education? Compare these progressive contributions and ideas with the more traditional methods.

9. As a representative of the traditional method of education, what charges does Bagley make against progressive schools?

Chapter 30

The Challenge
of the High School

EARLY BEGINNINGS IN THE UNITED STATES

In the seventeenth century the first high school in the United States was established in Boston—the famous Latin grammar school which celebrated its three hundredth anniversary in 1935. Like the European schools of the seventeenth century, the Latin grammar school specialized in ancient languages and literature. The method of teaching was harsh, with physical punishment as a prominent feature of instruction. The clientele was carefully chosen; usually, only boys of the upper class attended. While the later high school became a public institution, open to all, the Latin grammar school had a rather aristocratic view of its function.

The support of the school depended upon various means. Wealthy people would often donate money to the school, but tuition also paid for part of its expenses. Furthermore, taxation and land grants aided the school, even lotteries were used for its support.

Latin grammar provided the core for the curriculum of this school. The freshness and vitality of ancient literature were often overlooked. Language instruction was as vigorous as possible and dominated by memorization and drill.

Even today, language instruction is often unimaginative and too much guided by ancient tradition. The student learns mainly the grammar of the foreign language, instead of acquiring a speaking knowledge. A functional approach is overlooked; rather, language training becomes an end in itself.

The main purpose of the Latin grammar school was the training of ministers. Harvard had the same goal when it was established in 1636. Consequently, the curriculum of the Latin grammar school was narrow, and a need arose for a new type of school.

As a result there arose a new type of school, called the academy. Benjamin Franklin was connected with the establishment of the first academy in 1751, in Philadelphia. In these schools the curriculum was broadened to include the sciences and the arts as well as the classics. The stress was upon practical application of knowledge. Boys as well as girls were admitted; this, in itself, was a revolutionary event in American education.

It is interesting to note that the academies also provided for vocational efficiency. Their aim was to prepare not only professional people, but also businessmen; hence, bookkeeping had a prominent place in the curriculum.

The academy reflected the educational philosophy of Franklin, who felt that religious instruction ought to be broadened, and that it should not be dogmatic. The supernatural ideal was subordinated in the teaching of *moral philosophy* in most academies. Students were taught that the essence of religion is the love of God and the love of one's neighbor.

Still the academies, which spread rapidly—over 300 alone could be found by 1850 in the State of New York—did not provide free education. While many scholarships were granted to needy students, ·the tuition was high enough to keep out most children of the laboring class.

The first public high school was established in Boston in 1821. It was open only to boys; five years later a high school for girls was organized. The first co-educational high school was instituted thirty years later in Chicago, in 1856.

An important issue in the development of the high school was the Kalamazoo case in 1872. A taxpayer in a suit maintained that he was willing to pay for the support of the elementary school, but that he did not want to pay taxes for the maintenance of the high school. The Supreme Court of Michigan decided that tax funds should be used for the support of the high school; the decision gave impetus to the development of the public high school.

Harvard has had a significant influence upon American secondary education. In our own time, the famous Harvard Report on Education advocated more general education courses for high schools, and many schools have followed the suggestions of the Report.

Among the educational leaders in the development of the high school program, besides Franklin, was Charles W. Eliot (1834-1926). As chairman of the National Committee of Ten in 1890, he gave impetus to the development of the junior high school. He raised the entrance requirements for Harvard and made them more elastic; he influenced many high schools to change their curriculum and to diversify their offerings.

William Rainey Harper (1856-1906), president of the University of Chicago, like Eliot, tried to liberalize the high school curriculum. He was interested in reducing the number of years spent in the elementary school and in adding two years to the secondary curriculum. He is regarded by many as the real founder of the junior college movement.

In the twentieth century, Thomas H. Briggs of Teachers College, Columbia, chairman of the committee on Orientation of Secondary Education of the Department of Secondary School Principals, strove to make secondary education more comprehensive. Thus, it would appeal to more students, and more students would finish high school.

A most important contribution to American secondary education in the atomic era has been the work of Conant, who has made a systematic survey of the American high school, and who favors higher standards of proficiency, both for academically minded students and for those who do not want to go to college.

JUNIOR HIGH SCHOOL

The junior high school provides an easy transition between the elementary school and the high school. Psychologists recognize that the problems of adolescence are especially grave and difficult during the junior high school period. A lesser, but nevertheless valid consideration is the alleviation of the housing problem which faces so many senior high schools. Also, the junior high school offers a wide field for experimentation, especially in the field of general education.

The main characteristics of the junior high school have been summarized by the National Survey of Secondary Education:

Special flexibility for admission and promotion of students
Arrangement of instruction
Program of studies
Extracurricular program
Educational and vocational guidance
Special features for articulation
Specially trained teaching staff
Supervision of instruction
Special housing and equipment

The prospective teacher in a junior high school should have an excellent knowledge of psychology. The behavior problems of junior high school students often indicate extremes. An extreme inferiority complex may be exhibited by some students; others may be extreme extroverts. The sexual drives blossom forth with vigor in junior high school. Girls may have a multitude of "crushes." Many of them start to date for the first time, which certainly presents a problem both to parents and to the teachers. Junior high school dances tend to be far more sophisticated than the social affairs of elementary school. The junior high school student tends to imitate the ways of the adult world, although he may be emotionally still a child.

It goes without saying that skilled guidance is one of the great needs of the junior high school. The teacher should be friendly, informal, and able to reach the students; at the same time, he should have a constructive philosophy of life so that his views offer at least a platform upon which the student can build his own philosophy.

The best preparation for teaching in the junior high school, besides a specific major as English or history, is a *broad, general education.* The junior high school teacher should remember that his students will be active, and that formal discipline and formal learning are to be integrated into an activity type program.

PRINCIPAL. The principal of the junior high school, like the teacher, should have expert knowledge of the psychological foundations of behavior. The flexibility of the junior high school does not allow for an authoritarian attitude. The principal should know how to improvise, and he should encourage a variety of clubs which can absorb the extra energy of the junior high school pupil. The principal should also understand the problems of youngsters, so as not to talk down to them, and yet to be firm when the occasion arises. He should also be democratic and helpful in his relationship with teachers.

CURRICULUM. The curriculum of the junior high school stresses broad areas of concentration. In science, the emphasis is upon general science and general mathematics. Specialization is less prevalent than in the senior high school.

In literature, appreciation of good books is the goal. The student will be introduced to world literature, and he may obtain a taste of poetry, drama, essays, as well as fiction.

In the shop courses, likewise, specialization is avoided. Also, music and the arts are often taught together. In social studies, world history plays a prominent part. The student learns that history is not the story of kings and battles, but the story of how people lived, how they invented new forms of technology, and how they struggled for freedom.

Social living, thus, is a central part of the junior high school curriculum. A course, or a unit, in social living may include elements of anthropology, history, economics, political science, sociology, literature, psychology, and mental hygiene. The goal in social living is to understand man's relationship to society, and to understand how social institutions, like the family and the state, have conditioned man's behavior.

THE SENIOR HIGH SCHOOL

One of the classic statements of the objectives of the secondary school is contained in a report of the Commission on Reorganization of Secondary Education. The objectives, as we have seen before, are:

Health
Command of fundamental processes
Worthy home membership
Vocational preparation
Civic education
Worthy use of leisure
Ethical character.[1]

How are the high schools meeting these objectives? How successful are high schools in fulfilling the needs of their students?

It appears that too many high schools are still guided by traditional subjects. Too much emphasis is placed upon the past, rather than upon the present. While social studies have improved and are more popular today, the student still is not prepared to understand the fundamental issues of the modern world. Frequently, even geography is not strongly enough emphasized, which leads to disorientation regarding foreign nations.

The task of the high school curriculum is to combine specific knowledge with general education. General education without specific facts tends to be an exercise in generalities. This does not imply that memorization and drill should be encouraged; this would indeed be a step backward; rather, it means that disciplined learning as well as relational learning ought to be encouraged in the high school curriculum.

In high school English courses, the stress has been upon grammar, and the writing of compositions has been made as uninteresting as possible. More creative writing classes are needed in high school. Poetry ought to be encouraged, and dramatics ought to supplement the offerings in English. In reading, analysis should be the foremost concern. Semantics could well be introduced on the high school level.

More foreign languages should be introduced into high school curriculum and correlated with the study of world civilization. Language instruction should stress speaking knowledge, rather than grammatical competence. Audio-visual material could make language instruction far more fascinating than it usually is today.

---

[1] *Cardinal Principles of Secondary Education*, U.S. Bureau of Education Bulletin, 1918, pp. 5-10.

Some school administrators may feel that the study of foreign languages is a waste of time. Does not almost everyone abroad understand English? Such an attitude indicates extreme provincialism. Educational conferences usually reveal that American educators are distinguished by *not* knowing another language.

In history, more attention should be paid to twentieth century events. It is better to start with our own time and then to work backward, than to start with prehistoric man and finally arrive at the nineteenth century.

Moral and spiritual values ought to be stressed more in high school. This does not imply championing one philosophy, one religion, or one moral code, rather an attempt to develop perspective and depth on the part of the student, and to give him a basis for an *affirmative* philosophy of life. The story of the great thinkers might well be included in the high school curriculum.

In science instruction, there ought to be more emphasis on the social relationships of science. The student should know not only the results of science, but how scientists arrived at their conclusions. No student should graduate from high school without understanding the meaning and significance of the scientific method. There ought to be greater concentration upon the ways in which science affects our daily life. This certainly requires a knowledge of at least the rudimentary elements of medicine.

Some high schools are introducing psychology into their curriculum. This is an excellent step forward. The high school student is naturally interested in his own emotional life, and psychology can clarify many personal conflicts. However, psychology courses in high school should also be concerned with our thinking processes. Dewey's great book *How We Think* could be adapted for high school use.

The curriculum of the modern high school is constantly expanding. We might enumerate some of the new areas in Social Living.

Family life
Civics and citizenship
Human relations
Community relations
Safety education
Economics
The problems of Democracy
Sociology
Public affairs
International relations
Radio broadcasting and T.V.
Appreciation of motion pictures and television
Contemporary problems of youth

Consumer education
Character education, and many other courses.

In vocational education, great interest has been developed in driver education and aviation. Specialized high schools have multiplied, such as The Brooklyn High School of Automotive Trades, and the Miami, Florida, Technical High School. The general tendency today is to introduce elements of the liberal arts into the specialized high schools, so that the student obtains a broad, rather than a narrowly specialized education.

The trend in high school, as well as in college, is towards *general education*. This implies a rejection of the departmental approach to knowledge. The main goals of general education in high school are a. preparation for vocational efficiency b. preparation for citizenship c. appreciation of culture d. increase of personal efficiency.

High schools today tend to emphasize both classroom study and community experiences. Thinking and doing are to be correlated. The student is encouraged to watch his own community in operation, instead of only reading about it.

Various approaches are used in the preparation of the high school curriculum. While the departmental organization is still popular in many high schools, attempts have been made to experiment with at least four different types of curriculum organization, namely

The correlated curriculum
The fused curriculum
The core curriculum
The experience curriculum.

The *correlated curriculum* attempts to establish definite relationships between the departments. For example, teachers of English literature may correlate their subjects with English history. The study of civics may be correlated with American literature. The history of music may be correlated with the history of the plastic arts.

The *fused curriculum* attempts to establish a broad field of concentration. World history thus may include the study of ancient, medieval and modern history. Social studies may include parts of sociology, history, economics, and political science.

The *core curriculum* emphasizes the *common* experience of the student. Hence one half of the day might be devoted to the core, which would represent an even broader field than the fused curriculum. In core studies history, social studies, language arts, literature, fine arts, the social relationships of science, and elements of speech might be joined together. The core study usually is required for *all* students. The other subjects are elective.

The *experience curriculum* is more plastic and flexible than the core curriculum. Planning in advance is discouraged. The co-operative spirit is emphasized in the experience curriculum, which is often found in progressive schools. The center of the experience curriculum is *the individual student, not the subject.*

SPECIAL PROBLEMS OF HIGH SCHOOL TEACHING

The discipline problem is particularly grave in high school. Cases are reported of students actually assaulting their teachers. Juvenile delinquency is particularly noticeable in some of the larger cities like New York, Los Angeles, and Chicago. Behavior problems range from profanity on the part of the student to moral offenses.

It must be remembered that many students gain status in their group by acting up in class. They feel that a perpetual war exists between teacher and student; no compromise is possible or desirable. High school students may belong to gangs which have definite criminal tendencies.

Many teachers are perplexed about how to preserve order in the classroom. Here are some suggestions which may prove helpful to the teacher.

The first day of the teacher may be decisive. Too many beginning teachers attempt to act too much on the level of the students. Informality is excellent, but the student should realize that the teacher is not an easy mark, and that he has a *definite* personality of his own.

A teacher should prepare the lesson ahead of time and *vary* the activities of the classroom. Teaching often is like a television program. Thus, a comedian will not continuously tell jokes, rather he will use a singer, or he may put on a skit. The student is easily bored by sameness; change of pace is imperative.

The teacher should know his students. It is most important to know their names; but this is only a beginning—he should know something about their interests, background, and ideals.

The teacher should ensure that his students are occupied. It is important, however, that the tasks assigned are not too heavy or excessive. Often one student may be the trouble maker. It is important for the teacher to counsel with him and to find out why he is rebelling. In almost every class there will be those who are eager to learn, and those who are indifferent, even hostile, towards knowledge. The skillful teacher knows how to utilize the eagerness of the good students; thus, the trouble makers may be curbed by a lack of social approval.

Punishment of the wayward student should be reasonable; it should never be vindictive. The teacher should under no circumstances hate a student, for hatred creates an iron curtain between teacher and student.

The teacher should be personable, and he should make the work dramatic. Human beings love excitement, and when their emotions are aroused they cease to be passive. There is a constant need in teaching to vitalize and humanize knowledge.

The teacher should exhibit interest in the extracurricular life of the students. Too many teachers have a negative attitude regarding sports or social activities. The student may be flattered and complimented when he knows that the teacher has seen him perform during baseball and football games. Interest in extracurricular activities creates a spirit of rapport between student and teacher.

The teacher should be a "salesman" for his subject. His teaching must reflect unbounded enthusiasm. He should almost have a religious faith in the vitality and importance of the course in which he is instructing.

The teacher should encourage student participation. Good teaching represents mutuality in action. The student realizes the importance of the subject or the activity, and he takes over part of the teaching duties. Reports and panels, when skillfully handled, can be significant assets of the educational program.

High schools often are held back by inflexible requirements on the part of colleges. To encourage flexibility of entrance requirements, the Progressive Education Association sponsored an eight year study (1932-1940) of thirty secondary schools. These schools were not obliged to stress the usual college entrance requirements, and they could thus experiment in curricular matters. Many of the schools used the core approach instead of the usual departmental organization. Results of the study indicate that graduates of these schools were as successful in college as the graduates of more orthodox high schools.

Too often state universities, by their admission policies, determine the academic subjects to be stressed in high school. A crying need exists for *liberal* admission policies on the part of colleges.

We must *not* divide our high school population into two sections: those taking a college preparatory course, and those taking vocational courses. Often a student may change his mind, and he may not be interested in the liberal arts until he is a senior in high school. He should not be penalized for this by the colleges. One of the main aims of secondary education should be the establishment of *core* experiences and a *common* background for *all* students, instead of fostering a scholastic hierarchy.

THE EXTRACURRICULAR LIFE

One of the distinguishing marks of the modern high school is the extracurricular spirit. Students often learn more in their clubs than in the classroom. The student government plays an important part in the management and administration of the school.

Emphasis upon sports can be helpful to the school. Athletic events create real enthusiasm on the part of students who often take them extremely seriously. In many small communities, the merchants will close their shops when the local high school team is playing. The coach frequently is one of the most honored members of the community.

Still, the educational values of athletics should be stressed. Merely the desire to win a game is not enough. *Team spirit* should be the primary consideration. Roughness and foul tactics should never be allowed. Students should learn how to be sportsmanlike in their conduct and they should be good losers, for every school will lose ball games.

The coach, especially the coach of the football team, has a serious responsibility. His first duty is to promote character, not athletic victory. He should be interested not only in the star athletes, but also in those who may never make the team. The coach is not training future all-Americans, he is *educating* future citizens.

Participation, rather than the spectator spirit, should be developed in high school. Every student should become interested in a sport, which later may become a major leisure time occupation.

The student council, like athletics can perform a valuable function for the school. The student council should not be a rubber stamp for the administration, nor should it have excessive powers. It should be a training ground for democracy, and it should combine rational insight with emotional conviction.

Above all, it is important that the student council be representative; it should include various groups and various classes. It should establish patterns of mutuality, instead of patterns of antagonism.

Homeroom activities, assemblies, and the direction of the traffic in the corridors—all may have great educational value. Homeroom activities often foster a generous spirit on the part of the student. After World War II, many high school students would write letters during the homeroom period to students in Europe; others would study the organization of the United Nations; still others would send Care packages to Europe.

Assemblies should stress the creative arts, instead of merely entertainment. In this way assemblies can test the learning of the students and they can uncover original talent.

Student traffic control can be used to develop consideration for others. Students thus learn both about their rights and responsibilities.

Musical activities are especially helpful in the educational program. The glee club and the band can foster creative talents. A teacher, by his own enthusiasm and technique, may stimulate his students to join the band or the choir; he may even impart a general appreciation of classical music.

Speech activities may vitalize the curriculum. Dramatics should be especially stressed. Debating can sharpen the mind of the student and develop his powers of expression and concentration. The successful debater in high school is often a very successful student in college.

Certainly, secret social fraternities and sororities should not be allowed in high school. They create an undemocratic spirit, and their initiation ceremony and requirements are frequently barbaric.

Cultural clubs, on the other hand, should be encouraged. Clubs may range from the study of photography to the consideration of international relations. It is important that membership in these clubs be limited, otherwise too much chaos may result.

Honor societies are especially worthwhile. In 1921, the American Torch Society was established for the secondary school; its name was later changed to the National Honor Society. In 1929, a special honor organization was created for the junior high school, the Junior Honor Society. Statewide organizations as, for example, the Arista League of New York City, the Pro Merito Society of Massachusetts, and the California Scholarship Society, attempt to promote scholarship on the part of the students.

THE NEW AND THE OLD HIGH SCHOOL

While the high school of early colonial times emphasized theology, the modern high school stresses social studies. The traditional high school was for the few; the modern high school is for all. Education of women was frowned upon in colonial times; today, co-education is an accepted part of American secondary education.

The stress upon the classical languages has been replaced by an emphasis upon modern languages. The study of grammar is subordinated to the study of the living qualities of literature.

The teacher in colonial times was regarded as an absolute authority; his word was law. In modern high schools the teacher is regarded as a friend and guide. Today, physical punishment of the students is abhorred; instead, guidance is used to solve behavior problems.

The modern curriculum, instead of being subject-centered, is life-centered. Subjects are being integrated as the modern high school moves gradually toward the core-approach.

Instead of a stress upon the past, the modern high school emphasizes the present, although the contemporary spirit still lags behind. Curricular and extracurricular activities of the student, today, are often fused together. The ideal of the modern high school is not just the development of the mind, but the creation of positive attitudes toward society and toward life. The entire individual is to be educated, not only his intelligence.

The modern high school, unlike the Latin grammar school, is not an oasis of learning amidst a desert of illiteracy, but rather a *community center* which attempts to universalize learning.

THE DILEMMAS OF HIGH SCHOOL TEACHING

In our time, the high school curriculum is being examined with thoroughness. Conant, former president of Harvard University and former ambassador to Germany, made a study of hundreds of high schools and spoke to thousands of citizens in his attempt to improve our secondary system. Generally, he felt that the comprehensive high school was a significant asset to American civilization and that it made for real democracy. He did not agree with critics who wanted to separate students as is done in European secondary schools.

Still, Conant made specific criticisms of the secondary system. For example, he favored more guidance facilities and smaller classes, especially in English composition. He championed consolidation of small school districts so that better instructional aids could be given. He maintained that too many students take easy courses which have little academic content. For the top three per cent he recommended more college type courses in high school; for the academically gifted he favored four years of mathematics and emphasis on foreign language study.

While Conant's recommendations were thought-provoking, they should be examined with extreme care. He did not emphasize sufficiently the place of the arts and the social studies in the high school curriculum, and he did not pay sufficient attention to the humanities. Furthermore, rigid requirements are not the answer. Psychology demonstrates that we all have different abilities, and that we must explore our individuality rather than become part of a common mold. Conant's study would have been even more significant if he had started with the primary level; instead he concentrated upon secondary education; only later did he make a survey of our primary schools.

Ever since the sputniks, more attention has been paid to the gifted students in our high school. Pioneering work has been done by a group of school districts in which qualified high school students have taken college work while still pursuing their high school studies. Usually, they have done very well; often, they have surpassed college sophomores and juniors. The Berg Foundation in Chicago started seminars for science students, involving great scientists from industry; this helped to make science live. Colleges and universities, through grants of the National Science Foundation, have held special institutes for high school teachers to help them become more proficient in their work. Through television, introductory courses in physics and chemistry were made more vital; and schools which could not afford adequate science instruction received aid from such world famous institutes as Massachusetts Institute of Technology and The California Institute of Technology.

It appears today that high school students are studying harder and are more serious than their parents were. They know that competition is keen for college enrollment. They know that scholarship is important, and that athletic prowess is less significant than intellectual capacity. Today, the student who is the intellectual leader of the class is more respected than he would have been ten years ago. Homework is becoming harder. While not many students will study as much as 15 hours a week—the average which Conant recommended—there is a tendency among high school youngsters to be more thorough in their assignments.

The joy of high school teaching is the joy of watching adolescents develop in depth and understanding. It is a difficult psychological period; full of doubt and uncertainty. The boy is not yet a man; still he wants to act in a very adult way. The girl is not yet a woman; still she wants to appear very sophisticated.

One student recently described his best high school teacher in these terms:

"When Mr. Smith was a young man he had no plans or intentions of becoming a teacher. He graduated from college as an engineer, and later did some graduate work. He worked for a number of years as an engineer, but the confinement and monotony of the work did not hold his interest. His love of the outdoors and skiing caused him to spend more and more time in the mountains. Finally, he moved to a mountain community, where he lived in a small cabin and did everything from surveying to labor in order to get along.

"After several 'lost' years, the position of custodian and bus driver at the elementary school was open, and Mr. Smith took the job. From the very first the children loved him, and Mr. Smith was happier in this environment than he had been for years. In addition to making the school grounds look better than they ever had before, or have since, he helped the children with skiing in winter, arithmetic problems, and he took a personal interest in all of them.

"A friendship developed between Mr. Smith and the principal, who had been a math major in college, and soon the principal persuaded Mr. Smith to go back to college and get a teaching credential. Acquiring the necessary units in education at night and summer school took two years. But when he was ready, a job was waiting for him, and Mr. Smith started teaching high school in his early forties.

"Undoubtedly, it had taken this man a long time to find himself, however no one could be better suited, more enthusiastic and happier in his work. It is not what he teaches but *what he is* that makes him a wonderful teacher. The personality, inspiration, and outlook that he brings to subjects that are not usually among the most popular courses in high school, makes everyone enjoy his classes. He treats all students as equals and talks as though they knew the answer all the time, but that it had just slipped their memory. He is sensitive to minds that he realizes are less mature than his, and tries to bridge the gap that exists in interests, experience, vocabulary, and maturity or understanding. He is able to make his subject matter live, and somehow the pupils feel that if they don't learn it they will miss something important.

"Outside the classroom he is friendly, understanding, and generous with his time for those with problems. So much so that more and more counseling and guidance work is being given to him. Because he is an excellent skier (something rare in teachers) he is coach of the ski team during the winter season and gives unstintingly of his time to this activity. There is hardly any question but that he would qualify for the best-loved teacher in the school."

Another student found her ideal teacher as a freshman in high school:

"When I picture myself as a teacher I always use Mrs. Brown as my pattern. She was my English and history teacher in my first year in high school. I had just come from junior high, where in my senior year I had had a very poor homeroom teacher, so poor that I was disappointed and discouraged about school. Mrs. Brown was just what I needed! She was young, perhaps twenty-eight or twenty-nine, blond, blue eyed, and exceedingly capable.

"I can't remember well enough to analyze Mrs. Brown's teaching methods, but I know that I always had a good feeling in her class. One reason for this was the fact that she never "taught down" to her students. For the first time a teacher was treating me as if I had the mentality and the capabilities of an adult.

"Mrs. Brown was vitally interested in both American history and literature, and her interest was contagious; soon the entire class was stimulated and enthusiastic. She made history come alive for us. I can still remember the excellent movies and discussions we had on World War II. Although she taught history remarkably well I feel that her forte was literature. She introduced us to wonderful works of literature. We began to value poems, short stories, and novels that before had meant nothing to us. I recall looking forward to the days when she would read some of her favorite stories to the class. This experience, bringing her own favorites to share with us, made the whole class feel warmer toward her and much closer to her as a person.

"Mrs. Brown was not only excellent in handling the subjects she taught, but she had an ability for keeping control of the class, even in the most disturbing moments. As the year progressed, I can remember one disturbing incident in particular, mainly because it was a traumatic experience for me. There was an epileptic in the class, and one day during history he had a seizure. This was, of course, something that very few of us had been exposed to before and most of the students, including myself, were very upset. I still admire Mrs. Brown for the excellent way in which she handled the situation. She seemed to know exactly what to do, and did it. Two or three minutes after the boy had been taken from the room, the class was back to normal, and the incident was out of our mind."

Another student describes her English teacher:

"I remember only one great teacher from my high school days. A woman, who was sensitive, had a great understanding of people and who became a personal friend. Our long hours of conversation after school were the most rewarding, encouraging and satisfying hours in high school. She encouraged me not only to read but to think, write and discuss ideas with others. I began to search for new friends—those who had ideas to share and those who would understand my ideas.

"I became interested in literature, especially contemporary poetry and prose. Miss Jones helped me to understand philosophies of writers as well as helping me to crystallize and expand those ideas which I had gained from a book. Through her I learned that art could not exist without a prolific history, history without people, and people without literature. I learned that there may be a world where philosophy is not a belief but a way of life, beauty is not mistaken for decorativeness, nor virtue for conventionality, nor love for fantasy.

"I shall never forget the moment when I felt that there was a bond between us and I felt that she would understand me and could help me.

"It was early in the year and we had been reading some of the works of Latin American poets. After reading a very lovely poem, she closed her book and said, 'Tonight I want you to go home and make a list of all the things you love. Bring them tomorrow and share them with the class.' For the rest of the day I could think of nothing else and I lay awake that night making notes of those things which I loved. In the morning, when I returned to school, I had a piece of paper with me that was the most precious thing that I had ever had to share with anyone. That morning there was a warmth and closeness in the classroom that I had never felt before nor have I had that feeling since that time. First Miss Jones read 'The Great Lover,' by Rupert Brooke, and then we shared.

"Truly this was a great teacher. She was critical but understanding, she motivated and guided individually, she had time and was interested in the student, she had knowledge, experience, and travel which she shared, she helped her students to organize and gave them suggestions for writing but did not tell them what to write, and she suggested many books to read but was pleased when the student found his own books.

"Her aims were motivation of the individual, creating an understanding of people and their culture-past and present, understanding oneself, and making education a way of life. How fortunate for me that I had this one great teacher during my high school education!" . . .

The counseling function of the high school teacher, thus, is extremely important. Significant vocational choices are made by students during their high school years. Many of them "go steady"; some even get married. They tend to be impulsive and act without too much deliberation. A wise teacher will ensure that they achieve a degree of maturity and that they develop lasting interests. A creative teacher will stress the pleasures of the mind without which life becomes a form of futility.

QUESTIONS FOR DISCUSSION AND INVESTIGATION

1. Trace the problems and solutions in the historical growth of the American High School.

2. What importance did the Kalamazoo Case in 1872 have toward the development of the high school?

3. Describe the purpose, main characteristics, and nature of the curriculum on the junior high school level.

4. Define the objectives of the secondary school as contained in a report of the Commission on Reorganization of Secondary Education.

5. Explain the problems and developments of the high school in relation to these objectives.

6. What are the four different types of curriculum organization?

7. List the suggestions which may prove helpful in preserving order in the classroom.

8. List the positive attributes of the extracurricular life.

9. Compare and contrast the emphasis on knowledge as demonstrated between the old and the new high schools.

10. What have been the dilemmas in our present-day high schools?

Chapter 31

The American University

Religious ideals were fundamental in the founding of the American universities. Thus, the Congregationalists founded Harvard, the Episcopalians helped to establish William and Mary and Columbia University, the Presbyterians founded Princeton, while Brown University was established by the Baptists.

The oldest and best known university is Harvard, founded in 1636. Its establishment is described in the following document:

"After God had carried us safe to New England, and wee had builded our houses, provided necessaries for our liveli-hood, rear'd convenient places for God's worship, and settled the civill government; One of the next things we longed for and looked after was to advance learning and perpetuate it to posterity; dreading to leave an illiterate ministery to the churches, when our present ministers shall lie in the dust. And as wee were thinking and consulting how to effect this great work; it pleased God to stir up the heart of one Mr. Harvard (a godly gentleman, and a lover of learning, there living amongst us) to give the one half of his estate (it being in all about $1700) towards the erecting of a Colledge, and all his Library; After him another gave $300, others after them cast in more, and the publique hand of the State added the rest; The Colledge was by common consent, appointed to be at Cambridge, (a place very pleasant and accommodate) and is called (according to name of the first founder) Harvard Colledge.

"The edifice is very faire and comely within and without, having in it a spacious hall; where they daily meet at Commons, Lectures, and Exercises; and a large library with some books to it, the gifts of diverse of our friends, their chambers and studies also fitter for, and possessed by the students and

all other roomes of office necessary and convenient, with all needful offices
thereto belonging. And by the side of the Colledge a faire Grammar Schoole,
for the training up of young schollars, and fitting of them for Academical
learning, that still as they are judged ripe, they may be received into the
Colledge of this schoole." [1]

Most of the books in the Harvard library in the seventeenth century
dealt with religion; the majority of graduates became ministers. Chapel
was compulsory for students, who were warned against the deadly dangers of atheism, skepticism, and materialism.

Dartmouth College was established for the expressed purpose of con-
verting the Indians to Christianity. Princeton University was the strong-
hold of the Presbyterians. There Jonathan Edwards tried to popularize
Calvinism. Edwards was a famous preacher who was certain that the majority of mankind were destined to land in hell-fire, while only the few
would be saved. Man, according to Edwards, was depraved, while God
was all-powerful and perpetually outraged by the sins of mankind. The
early college students must have heard many sermons about the inevitability of hell-fire for the majority of humanity.

While science was slighted by Harvard in the seventeenth and eighteenth century, William and Mary encouraged both the arts and the sciences and cherished a more humanistic concept of learning. This was
due, to some extent, to the influence of the Deists, who were rather
skeptical regarding supernaturalism and who thought that education
would teach us how to live in this world, rather than how to anticipate
the beyond.

The first non-sectarian university was the University of Pennsylvania
(1755). There, various religious opinions were tolerated; dogmatism was
generally shunned. During the eighteenth century, many universities
were rebelling against ecclesiastical control, and today most of the major
universities are non-sectarian.

The organization of the early universities was patterned after the
college system of Scotland and England. Frequently the tutorial system
was used. Later, especially in the nineteenth century, the influence of
German universities became pronounced. Exact methods of scholarship
were emphasized. Great teachers, like Royce and Bowne, studied in Germany. Education was thought to be incomplete without post-graduate
training in Germany.

National legislation which promoted the spread of higher education is best represented by the Northwest Ordinance of 1787. When under its provisions land was sold to the Ohio Company, sections were set
aside for the support of universities. Ohio University, established in

---

[1] *Collections of the Massachusetts Historical Society* for 1792, vol. I, pp. 242-243.

1803, benefited by the Ordinance. Since then, over a million acres have been given by the Federal Government to the States for the support of higher education.

State universities, which were advanced by the results of the Northwest Ordinance, are a significant part of the American system of education. Some of the state universities, like the University of California, rival Harvard and Yale in scholastic standing and scholarly eminence.

The need for state universities was well expressed by President Tappan in his report to the regents of the University of Michigan in 1856:

"Scholars form a centre of light, and irradiate it far and wide for the glory of their country, and for the good of mankind. They create an atmosphere filled with inspirations to thought, research and culture. Young men who have passed through the intermediate grade, and hence, who have learned the art and formed the habits of study, resort to them, to hear their lectures, to breathe their spirit, to copy their example, and to submit themselves to their guidance. Thus they multiply and perpetuate themselves. They instruct their own country and times; they instruct foreign countries and future generations. They bring to bear the highest powers of mind, ripened and furnished to the highest degree upon those great subjects which embody all civilization, lead on all improvement, and multiply the enjoyments, elevate the condition, and determine the destiny of the race.

"Where only the lower grades of education are found, a nation must ever remain imperfect in its civilization, must fail in the higher ends of social and national existence, and must be in a condition of servile dependence upon the cultivated nations for those works of science, art, and literature which are indispensable to even material prosperity. But more than this; where only the lower grades of education are found, even these cannot be brought to perfection. The highest institutions are necessary to supply the proper standard of education; to raise up instructors of the proper qualifications; to define the principles and methods of education; to furnish cultivated men to the professions, to civil life, and to the private walks of society, and thus to diffuse everywhere the educational spirit. The common school can be perfected only through competent teachers. These can be provided only by institutions like the normal school, which belong to the intermediate or second grade of education. But the teachers of the normal school, again, require other and higher institutions to prepare them, such at least, as the academy, gymnasium, or college; and these, the highest forms of the intermediate grade, can only look to the university for a supply of instructors." [2]

The freedom of the colleges was protected in a decision by the Supreme Court in the Dartmouth case. New Hampshire had appointed a

[2] *Reports of the Superintendent of Public Instruction of the State of Michigan for the Years 1855, '56, '57,* pp. 161 ff.

board of overseers which was to supervise the board of trustees of Dartmouth College. The trustees felt that this meant an abrogation of their rights and they took legal action. Chief Justice Marshall, in a famous decision, declared that the State of New Hampshire could not interfere with the conduct of Dartmouth. In short, the freedom of action of the private college had been safeguarded.

Co-education, which aided in the development of the American university, was first introduced at Oberlin College in 1833. In 1838, Mt. Holyoke College opened its door as the first Women's College. Today, schools like Vassar, Smith, Sarah Lawrence, and Mills College vie with co-educational colleges as centers of learning and liberal culture.

In 1868, the first college in higher education for Negroes was organized. This was the Hampton Institute, designed to promote the culture and vocational efficiency of the Negroes. In 1881, organized graduate work was started by Johns Hopkins, using the German university as a model.

The Federal government aided the development of agricultural colleges by passing the Morrill Act. Under this act, every state either created a separate university or combined an agricultural and mechanical arts college with another institution. The A&M Colleges, like Texas A&M and Oklahoma A&M, gradually offered liberal arts training as well as vocational training in agriculture and in the mechanical arts.

Among the great leaders of higher education we find Andrew D. White at Cornell, James McCosh at Princeton, Angell at Michigan, Noah Porter at Yale, Mark Hopkins at Williams, Mary Lyon at Mount Holyoke, Daniel Gilman at Johns Hopkins, Horace Mann at Antioch, W. R. Harper at Chicago, and Charles Eliot at Harvard.

Eliot deserves special notice. He introduced the elective system at Harvard, made the entrance requirement more flexible, developed graduate training in the liberal arts, and expanded professional training, especially in medicine and law. The elective system has been attacked in our own century, particularly by Hutchins, who thought that the curriculum should have more compulsory courses than Eliot advocated. The Harvard Report on Education represents, to some extent, a departure from the elective system and recognizes the need for general education.

In our own century the work of two college presidents deserves special consideration:

JAMES BRYANT CONANT. Conant's main effort was to popularize science and to give the student a knowledge of the meaning of science in the modern world. Such books as Conant's *Understanding Science* have added greatly to the layman's appreciation of scientific ideals.

NICHOLAS MURRAY BUTLER. Butler aided in the expansion of Columbia University, and during his many years as president of that institution made the university famous, both here and abroad.

THE JUNIOR COLLEGE

One of the encouraging trends in higher education is the spread of the junior college movement. The first public junior college was established in Joliet, Illinois, in 1902. Since that time, junior colleges have advanced rapidly, especially in California and Texas. In 1947, over 400,000 students attended junior colleges.

In 1920, the junior colleges organized a national organization: The American Association of Junior Colleges. This organization publishes the *Junior College Journal,* which has won widespread support and interest among educators. Schools of education today give special courses on junior college problems.

The Foundations, like the Rockefeller Foundation and the Carnegie Foundation, have given special grants to the junior colleges to strengthen their program of general education and to determine their function in the field of higher education.

The main objectives of the junior college are to prepare the student for general college work, and to serve as terminal points for the educational work of others. Junior colleges stress vocational courses as well as the liberal arts. The humanities movement has found a ready response among junior college leaders. (Valuable experimentation in the humanities has been carried on at Bakersfield College, mainly through the stimulation of Professor Frantz and Dr. Koch, also at San Bernardino Valley College through the brilliant planning of Professor Gordon Atkins.)

Public tax support of the junior college has been guaranteed by a decision of the North Carolina Court in 1930. A taxpayer had questioned the right of Asheville, North Carolina to levy taxes for the support of the local junior college. His suit was denied by the Court which held that the same principles applied to the support of the junior college as to the support of public high schools.

It is important that junior colleges develop definite educational objectives. Mere imitation of the four-year college is *inadequate*. A splendid opportunity exists in the junior college for bridging departmental lines. Science and the arts, social studies and English, all should be correlated. The emphasis of the junior colleges should not so much be upon scholastic knowledge as upon broad integration, trying to create a real *thirst for knowledge* on the part of their students.

DILEMMAS OF THE UNIVERSITIES

American universities are expanding at an enormous rate. Their endowment is at an all-time high. Their laboratories and buildings are more magnificent than those of any other civilization. Millions of students are attending, and many schools expect to double their staff and enrollment in periods of less than ten years.

But bigness by itself does not mean greatness. Quantitative expansion may be only a façade to cover up an inner emptiness. Buildings and laboratories are not substitutes for creative teachers and inspired researchers.

Enthusiastic and profound teaching ought to be the center of university life. It ought to be the real justification for higher education. Indeed, every student knows that his education is incomplete if he has not taken classes from a certain great professor. Thus, when Phelps taught literature at Yale, it was like an exciting drama. When Russell lectured at the University of California at Los Angeles, it was like Protagoras visiting Athens. When Emery Stoops discussed modern education at the University of Southern California, his class became a "must" for hundreds of students. But usually, inspired teaching is not valued sufficiently in our colleges.

What are the reasons for this condition? Our academic system is based on publications. The instructor knows that advancement comes mainly as a reward for writing books and scholarly monographs; the more he writes, the more his reputation grows. Quantity of production rather than quality is valued. Furthermore, he realizes that if he becomes too popular with the students, he may incur the jealousy of his colleagues, who may be more at home with mediocre talents than with inspired teachers. There is a prevalent idea among scholars that teaching ought to be restrained, Apollonian rather than Dionysian, to use Nietzsche's terms. There emerges a stereotype of a teacher, who is aloof and objective, who lectures from notes, and who specializes in a narrow subject area. He will regard students as necessary evils who distract him from his research. Thus, he prefers the library to the classroom.

Another obstacle to great teaching lies in the atmosphere of most universities. Committee meetings take an enormous amount of time; routine work has to be done. Because the administrative pay is better, many of the more promising instructors become deans, and even college presidents.

In the nineteenth century, college presidents often taught the senior course in moral philosophy. Thus, Mark Hopkins influenced hundreds of students at Williams College. He demanded exact answers and exact formulation of ideas. He would inspire his students to lead a more elevated way of life. Eliot at Harvard had less direct contact with students than Hopkins had, but he was never afraid to pioneer. He saw that the curriculum of his time was outdated, and hence he instituted the elective system. He realized that a university depended on the quality of its faculty, therefore he tried to attract some of the greatest scholars to Harvard. Harper, at the University of Chicago, one of the most popular teachers and college presidents of his time, knew how to make ordinary courses become very exciting. He also attracted internationally famous scholars by offering them more pay than they would have received at any other institution.

What makes a university great? Certainly, neither buildings nor equipment constitute academic excellence. Certainly, neither reputation nor scholarly productions create a lasting impression upon civilization. Obviously athletics is not a substitute for intellectual inquiry. Not even research is the center of university life.

Real greatness depends on the *motivation and the capacity of the faculty,* their scholarship, their ideals, their love of students, their morale, and their conception of their tasks. Real greatness depends on atmosphere; it is intangible; it cannot be measured in quantitative terms.

However, research is never to be underestimated. Without it, teachers remain on the periphery of knowledge; without it, universities do not become active centers of inquiry. Research need not have immediate utilitarian goals. Today, more than ever, we need an emphasis on basic knowledge. Pure research is the foundation of technological progress; its discipline and disinterestedness and objectivity should inspire the student, who must learn that the language of nature has to be mastered if man is to advance.

COLLEGE PRESIDENTS

A new group of college administrators has evolved in the United States. They are like businessmen, only they deal with education. They enjoy enormous prestige and, in most cases, command enviable salaries. Their opinions are quoted in the newspapers, and journalists interview them about any political, social, or moral issues. Thus, the position of college administrator offers both political and economic opportunities. Frequently, an outstanding college head may become an ambassador, a senator, or even, like Wilson, President.

No wonder that the competition is intense for these positions. For instance, recent newspaper announcements of the death of a certain college president resulted in hundreds of telegrams—not of condolence, but of application—flooding the offices of the board of trustees. One eager contender had not even waited for the death of the president; he had made a long-distance call, informing the committee in charge that he could assume the presidential office as soon as he was needed.

To be president of a major university requires more than scholarly abilities and educational training; almost super-human qualities are needed. There is a constant demand for an internationally famous scholar who will add to the prestige of the university. Even his wife is inspected with critical eyes; if she is an introvert or an eccentric, she could not become a successful hostess.

College presidents, as a rule, are *doers rather than thinkers*. Still, there are notable exceptions. We only have to think of the achievements of Pusey and Conant at Harvard, Case at Boston University, Hutchins at Chicago, and Griswold at Yale. There are also many presidents of state colleges, like Ralph Prator at San Fernando State College, who have served their institutions in a tireless, unselfish, and most brilliant manner.

Yet the time has passed when college presidents, like Hopkins, would influence the entire educational policy of this nation. One of Hopkins' students makes the following statement.

"The influence of President Mark Hopkins at Williams College was astounding. It was in the senior year that the students came in touch with Dr. Hopkins; a large share of that year was in his hands; the seniors met him every day, sometimes twice; in philosophy and ethics, in logic and theology, he was their only teacher. . . . There was nothing sensational in Dr. Hopkins' teaching, his method was quiet and familiar; his bearing was modest and dignified; but he was a past master in the art of questioning; he knew how by adroit suggestion to kindle the interest of his pupils in the subject under discussion, and by humor and anecdote he made dry topics vital and deep waters clear. What his best students got from him was not so much conclusions or results of investigation, as a habit of mind, a method of philosophic approach, a breadth and balance of thought, which might serve as further study." [3]

DEANS AND DEGREES

The modern university has produced a variety of deans. There is not just the dean of the faculty, but the dean of the various divisions, the dean of the Graduate School, and the dean of men and dean of women, together with a host of assistants and associates.

The dean of men and the dean of women used to be strict censors of morals, old dignified souls with a narrow outlook upon life. Today the picture has changed; frequently, the dean of women is in her early thirties, well acquainted with Freud, an expert in modern literature, and not at all frightened by sex. The dean of men may be as efficient as a business executive and as understanding as a psychiatrist. This does not mean that the deans have become genuine humanitarians; their main

---

3 Gladden, *Recollections*.

function is still to protect the fair name of the institution which they serve. When offenders become too troublesome, they are expelled very graciously with some sage psychological advice; their protest will not deter the iron will of the deans who attempt to enforce in a rigorous manner the standards of the university.

The dean of the faculty usually has the task of advising in the choice of the teaching personnel. In this, he is guided by the head of the department and the president, but he shoulders the main responsibility. He places special emphasis on the degrees of the candidate. The Ph.D. degree is most desirable, not only because of the prestige, but also because of the unlimited opportunities it has to offer in the teaching profession.

CONFLICTS

Frequently, the failure of our universities lies in inadequate human relations and faulty communication. Thus, science divisions tend to look down on the liberal arts, and, on many campuses, education professors and liberal arts instructors are engaged in perpetual cold wars. Some professors of classics fervently wish "that somebody would abolish Columbia's Teachers College." They blame Teachers College for the emphasis on educational methodology and the neglect of Latin and Greek and other cultural subjects in our educational system. Actually, educators, like Kilpatrick at Teachers College, have made a major contribution to the art of education, and they have made school life far more exciting and challenging than it was fifty years ago.

What are the causes behind the controversy between liberal arts and professional education? Liberal arts professors accuse education departments of overstressing minute methods courses, and of being anti-intellectual. Education departments are charged with being too lenient in their standards and of being blind followers of Dewey. They are accused of giving inferior degrees and of giving courses which have no genuine academic value. Furthermore, they are charged with not adequately preparing teachers, who will thus charge out into the teaching world equipped only with vague phrases and slogans rather than with detailed preparation and solid foundations.

Education professors, on the other hand, charge that the liberal arts teachers have an obsolete philosophy of education. Do they not believe in petty specialization? Do they not overemphasize subject matter? Do they not ignore the formidable contributions of the public schools? Are they not ignorant about the methodology of modern education?

While not all the practices of departments of education can be justified, it should be pointed out that teacher preparation is one of the *central functions* of any university. The new methods of education have improved our schools. It is impossible to return to nineteenth. century standards in education, just as we cannot return to nineteenth century standards in industry and government. The liberal arts professors who yearn for the rigorous standards which prevailed a century ago forget that, at that time, only a small minority was educated, and that teachers had an even lower status than they enjoy today. Furthermore, a course in the history and philosophy of education can be just as valuable for training in the liberal arts as for preparation in public school teaching.

No department in higher education has a monopoly on wisdom. We progress when we learn from each other and when we share our insights. Let there be more co-operation between liberal arts and professional education; let them exchange instructors, let them teach co-operative seminars. Above all, let the academic cold war cease once and for all, for this conflict only creates educational regression and stagnation.

Actually, our failures in higher education are usually failures in co-operation. We tend to be limited in our vision, and we tend to look upon the universe through the windows of our departments: If we are scientists we want more science requirements; if we are social scientists we want more emphasis on economics, sociology, and history. If we teach philosophy we may feel that this subject should be a requirement for all students. If we are musicians we want more stress on music appreciation. If we teach religion we may feel that theology is neglected in our universities. If we teach the classics we may be enthusiastic advocates of Greek and Latin for all students. This is a version of academic anthropomorphism!

Actually, requirements are less important than the development of lasting interests on the part of students. Only a community of scholars who respect each other and learn from each other and who cultivate real humility can create a great university. Only a community of scholars with real warmth and dedication can have a creative influence on their students.

EXPANSION

Are universities and colleges ready for the period of expansion? Will they be able to cope with the vast influx of students? Are they enthusiastic about the opportunities which such expansion will develop? Are they receptive to creative new ideas? The answer to all these questions must be largely in the negative.

Many administrators feel that only the top ten per cent should be educated, and that an A-minus or B-plus average should be demanded of all prospective college students. Small colleges are restricting their enrollment. Thus, one small college in California declared it will accept only 25 more students by 1965; in a recent newspaper article one of its administrators said that the college would fight in every way to remain small.

The underlying concept of this philosophy is an aristocratic philosophy of education, whose basic idea is the training of only the few and the carefully selected. The Puritans had the same viewpoint when they established Harvard, for they believed themselves to be the select; providence had chosen them for a special task. Proponents of this viewpoint show a general distrust of the average, or "C" student; their main concern is the development of the real elite.

Because of this philosophy, hundreds of thousands of students will be denied a college education. Does it matter whether a college has a student body of 1,000 or 1,600? By today's standards, a college of 1,600 is a small college. Does it matter whether our large universities have a student body of 20,000 or 30,000?

The central need is the development of universities which are centers of warmth and encouragement, in which creativity is treasured, and in which the individual is valued. Let them prize great research and teaching. Let them put a primary emphasis on personality rather than on buildings. Let them stress the art of human relations. Let them cultivate with intensity the arts and the sciences. Let them be genuine centers for adult education and pioneer in geriatrics. Let them bring to their classroom the outstanding scientists, artists, philosophers, and psychologists of our time. Let them stress the importance of independent study and research projects on the part of their students who will be required to become active participants in the quest for culture and enlightenment. Let them apply theoretical knowledge to pressing social problems—then, and only then, shall we have a new culture in America.

Above all, we need universities with a conscience regarding their educative tasks. Of all the goods of life, education is man's supreme achievement. Education is never an abstraction but a concrete process. It is not an exercise in theory, but a pilgrimage in application. Man, as Fichte pointed out in his *Wissenschaftslehre*, is made wise by action rather than by mere reflection. Action depends on social sensitivity.

John Newman, in a notable treatise, *The Idea of a University*, maintained that

> "liberal education viewed in itself is simply the cultivation of the intellect, as such, and its object is nothing more or less than intellectual excellence. . . . Knowledge is capable of being its own end. Such is the constitution of the human mind, that any kind of knowledge, if it be really such, is its own reward." [4]

---

[4] *The Idea of a University.*

Certainly, we should be interested in truth for the sake of truth, as Newman pointed out. But more important is the application of truths to concrete situations, leaving the ivory tower for the market place of action.

Universities with a conscience will be centers of intellectual controversy and creative thinking. They will produce not merely scholars, but students who read the book of the world, students who have a passion for social justice and a brave new world of enlightenment. Their struggle will be against ignorance and bias and antagonism. With wise guidance, unending encouragement, and hard work, they will create a real renaissance in the United States, which will be a beacon of hope in man's struggle for survival and greatness.

QUESTIONS FOR DISCUSSION AND INVESTIGATION

1. List the types of purposes for the establishment of the major universities.

2. What are the educational contributions of James Bryant Conant and Nicholas Murray Butler?

3. Trace the growing importance of the junior college.

4. What have been the obstacles to great teaching in many universities?

5. What has been the change of attitude on the part of college administrators?

6. Describe the main duties of college deans.

7. What are the causes behind the controversy between Liberal Arts and Professional Education?

8. What are our failures in higher education, and why do they come about?

9. Why is the philosophy of some administrators tending more toward aristocratic lines than democratic principles?

10. How can we solve the major problems of higher education?

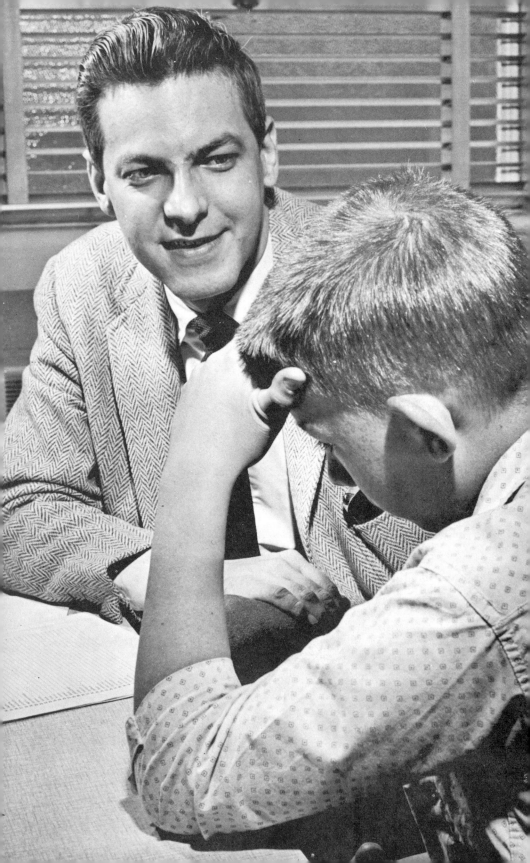

Chapter 32

Guidance
and Educational Problems

THE IMPORTANCE OF PSYCHOLOGY

Psychology, perhaps, more than any other field has influenced the development of modern education. The contributions made to education by eminent psychologists like Wundt, James, Thorndike, Gesell, Pavlov, and Wertheimer, cannot be underestimated.

In 1879, the first experimental psychology laboratory was established by Wundt in Leipzig, Germany. Columbia University students were tested by Cattell and Farrand from 1890 to 1896. In 1896, the University of Pennsylvania opened a psychological clinic. Today, most universities have psychological clinics, and, like Chicago, they may even have a separate department for testing purposes.

Among the pioneers devoted to educational psychology, was J. Mc-Keen Cattell (1860-1944) who during World War I was discharged from the Columbia faculty because of his pacificism. His primary interests lay in the field of measurement of individual differences. At Columbia University, where he headed the psychological laboratory, he trained hundreds of American psychologists.

William James, who has been mentioned already, developed the basis of functionalism in psychology. James regarded the mind, not as an entity, but as a function aiding us in our adjustment to the environment. His approach to psychology, especially in the two-volume *Principles of Psychology*, was eminently concrete and practical.

E. L. Thorndike, at Columbia, made a major contribution to the psychology of learning. In 1913, he published his monumental three-volume *Educational Psychology*. Volume I discusses the foundations of learning; Volume II deals with the laws of learning, and Volume III discusses individual differences as they influence the intellectual development of man. Thorndike's work tended to disprove traditional theories, especially traditional concepts regarding the transfer of learning. His study of more than eight thousand high school students demonstrated that so-called disciplinary subjects, like Latin and mathematics, developed thinking power less than did more practical subjects, like bookkeeping; furthermore, the belief that transfer of learning from one subject to another was easily accomplished was disproven by Thorndike's experiments.

Among the present-day schools of psychology, we should mention structuralism, functionalism, behaviorism, Gestalt psychology, psychoanalysis, and purposivism. *Structuralism* is the oldest school; championed especially by Wundt and Titchener, it emphasizes *introspection*. It is concerned with consciousness—feeling, knowing and willing. Its approach to psychology tends to be static.

Functionalism is more dynamic than structuralism. Championed by such thinkers as James, Dewey, Thorndike, and Judd, functionalism regards the mind in biological terms and emphasizes the mind's adjustment to the environment.

Behaviorism stresses the mechanistic foundation of life. Behaviorism was represented by men like Pavlov, Meyer and Watson. Behaviorism denies the existence of the soul, mind and consciousness. Introspection is regarded as a pre-scientific technique by behaviorists, who are interested primarily in the stimulus and response situation.

Gestalt psychologists like Köhler, Koffka, and Wertheimer have rejected the mechanistic views of behaviorism; instead they stress the whole and the unitary aspects of men's behavior. They regard *insight* as a central factor in learning.

Psychoanalysis was first established by Freud. He stressed the sexual basis of behavior and showed that the conscious mind is often guided by the Id which represents our passions and instincts. The super-ego reflects conventions and the voice of civilization and is constantly repressing the Id. Freud also brought out the symbolic significance of dreams. He pointed out a natural tendency on the part of boys to be in love with their mother (Oedipus Complex), and of girls to fall in love with their father (Electra Complex). Two basic drives compete, according to Freud: The life instinct and the death instinct; apparently the drive towards death is stronger than the drive towards life.

Freud had a *dynamic* view of the mind. He felt that many abnormalities and neuroses are caused by sexual frustrations. His studies of masochism and sadism are especially suggestive. His disciples, like Jung, Adler, Horney, Alexander, and Fromm, differed with him in some respects, but they all recognized his importance.

Purposivism is less important than psychoanalysis. The main champion of this school is McDougall, who stressed the creative drives of man. Man's behavior, McDougall stated, cannot be understood in a naturalistic frame of reference, rather it requires a spiritual explanation. What counts is man's *inner purpose*.

In educational psychology the attempt has been made to establish the mathematical basis of man's behavior. Perhaps the best known example is the Binet Test for Intelligence, as revised by Terman of Stanford University. The Stanford Revision of the Binet Test has two fundamental parts, one the Mental Age (MA) and the other, the Intelligence Quotient (IQ). The Mental Age is an indication of the intellectual growth of the child, while the IQ determines the degree of his intelligence. For example, a child with an IQ of 165 would be in the genius class, while an IQ of 108 would indicate average intelligence.

Psychologists have argued for a long time about the influence of the environment upon IQ tests. Apparently a good educational situation can advance the IQ, but certain limitations exist which are dependent upon the native endowment of the individual.

Group tests were developed during World War I. The Army Alpha Test, to which Thorndike, Terman, and Otis contributed, was given to thousands of G.I.'s at that time.

Specific abilities have also been tested; thus, Seashore of the University of Iowa tried to determine musical ability; Stenquist devised mechanical aptitude tests, and Thurstone attempted to discover talent for clerical work.

Attitudes have been measured by scholars like Bogardus, who was concerned with social distance, Lasker who stressed racial issues, Droba, who dealt with militarism, and Velter, who measured political attitudes. Perhaps the greatest contribution in this area has been made by Professor Thurstone of the University of Chicago.

The degree of introversion and extroversion in personality traits has been measured by Bernreuter. Tendencies in the direction of dominance and submission have been measured by G. W. Allport and F. H. Allport. Strong has contributed a series of vocational interest tests. An especially important clue to our personality is the Rorschach Test, widely used by psychological clinics.

This list is only a small sample of the variety of tests used in psychological research. How do the tests aid educators? How can they improve the standards of our schools?

They give us a basis for evaluation of the educational program.

They develop objectivity on the part of the teacher.

They create more exact analysis of educational problems.

They may verify or negate educational philosophies.

They measure the quantitative growth of the student.

They can give us an indication of the effectiveness of the teacher.

They aid the student in choosing the right profession.

They may uncover, as in the Seashore Test, original talent.

They uncover the areas of personality maladjustment.

They aid us in framing general laws of learning and behavior.

EMOTIONS AND LEARNING

In earlier days, reason was considered to be a static element, and the role of emotions was often disregarded. Pascal already indicated the wisdom of the heart, and Gassendi maintained that existence depends on feeling.

In the nineteenth century, Schopenhauer, in *The World as Will and Idea,* demonstrated the emotional basis of rationality. Schopenhauer felt that man is the product of will, not of reason, and that reason only justifies our passions and feelings. This philosophy is reflected in Freudianism, pragmatism, and existentialism. It has found supporters in such eminent thinkers as Bergson, James, Sartre, and Heidegger.

The nature of emotions has been analyzed by many psychologists. The James-Lange theory held that bodily changes precede mental changes, but most psychologists today accept the Cannon-Dana theory which regard bodily changes as *concomitants* of mental changes, in other words, bodily and mental reactions *occur together.*

Among students we can find the gamut of emotions. Some are isolationists, interested only in ideas; they represent *introverted* tendencies. Others are boisterous, they like to join clubs and hate to be alone. They are the *extroverts.*

A skillful teacher will be able to deal with the various emotional constitutions of the students. Thus, the student in love, who can only think of his girl, the "summum bonum" of life, may be stimulated to sublimate his drive in a more creative manner, such as writing poetry or starting a novel.

To achieve emotional health, good habits are essential. Habits of hard work, concentration, and self-discipline should be emphasized by the teacher.

The attitudes of the student are important. Is he selfish or altruistic? Is he optimistic towards life or pessimistic? Does he accept himself or is he masochistic? Is he interested in others or is he indifferent towards people? Is he domineering or submissive?

The teacher's attitude towards the class may also be decisive. The good teacher is never dictatorial and authoritarian. He likes students even when they oppose his own viewpoint. The good teacher respects the opinion of his students and encourages diversity, for he realizes that unanimity is undesirable in education.

Many teachers use fear as a teaching device. They constantly threaten their classes with tests and remind their students that a certain number of them will flunk. Fear creates dislike of learning and, ultimately, antagonism towards education.

Every teacher should understand the importance of *motivation* on the part of the student. Competition and rivalry were the common incentives in the traditional school. They led to the survival of the fittest, but they did not produce real learning. What matters is the advancement of the individual and his acquisition of permanent interests in knowledge and culture. Instead of competition, the ideals of mutuality and service should be stressed.

We should be imbued by the feeling that our task is important. Futility is the beginning of nihilism. The individual who sees no purpose in life is almost inevitably frustrated. Our great intellectual leaders, like James, Dewey, and Kilpatrick, were all men with a sense of *vocation* and a sense of *purpose*.

Leisure is another aspect of today's education that should not be underestimated. When we relax from our work, we can gain perspective. To be a slave to work is to be a serf to routine; freedom, as Aristotle realized, implies sufficient leisure for meditation and contemplation.

How can the teacher improve the learning of the class? Above all, the teacher should understand the importance of readiness. Thus, at a certain stage a child is ready to read. Experiments demonstrate that arithmetic lessons should be postponed to the second or third grade until the child is more mature. Readiness implies not just intellectual but also social and emotional adjustment. Exercise, as Thorndike has often pointed out, strengthens learning. However, care should be exerted by the teacher not to regard exercise as a goal in itself. Often we become fatigued and reach a plateau. At this point we should rest and take time out, then we may return in a refreshed mood to our task.

Pleasure and pain, as Locke pointed out, influence learning. We repeat what we like, and we tend to give up tasks and lessons which we find distasteful. Again, a word of caution. The teacher can influence the student to be patient and not to be discouraged by early failures.

Much of our learning is accomplished through the trial and error method. We try one solution after another, constantly seeking for truth; occasionally, a flash of insight will occur, the solution is found, and we recognize a pattern in the problem under investigation. It should be made clear, however, that insight is not a magic capacity, rather it demands intellectual discipline.

There is a distinction between primary and concomitant learning, as Kilpatrick insisted in *The Educational Frontier*. Primary learning takes place as we do an assignment; for example, we might write an essay on the French Revolution. The task itself represents primary learning. *Concomitant learning is the growth which results from the assignment.* It may give us an insight into our own time, it may provide us with a philosophy of history, it may aid us in creative thinking and in developing an exact research technique. Thus, the real goal of education is concomitant learning.

SPECIAL PROBLEMS AND GUIDANCE

One of the most encouraging trends in education is the modern treatment of handicapped children. Special schools have been established for the blind and for crippled children; for example, the Boettcher School in Denver represents a scientific approach to the problems of the crippled child. School health examinations tend to be more thorough, and exact charts are kept of the children's health.

The teacher should be able to detect symptoms of disease, especially with the younger children. He should also know the symptoms of mental disorders, such as hallucination, phobias, amnesia, dissociation, schizophrenia, and many other neuroses and psychoses. Understanding mental disorders will make it easier for the teacher to deal with the child, or, if necessary, to suggest psychiatric treatment.

We have become more enlightened in our treatment of stuttering. In earlier times we regarded it either as an aberration of the child or as an organic defect; today, through the research of scholars like Travis and Parker, we can trace speech difficulties to the home. Authoritarianism and puritanism on the part of parents will often be direct causes of speech disorders. Hence, speech clinics will deal with parents as well as children.

Unless a child is badly crippled, teachers try to integrate him into the normal school program. Mental defectives, unless their intelligence is extremely low, are likewise kept in the schoolroom and are not isolated. Generally, modern education tries to prevent discrimination against unfortunate children.

Every teacher may come into contact with handicapped children. John may have a cardiac condition, Mary may have glandular trouble. Jim may suffer from a nervous disorder. Sometimes it may be advisable to keep children at home, or to give them special medical care, or to devise a special physical education program. A delicate child needs periodic check-ups and should be encouraged to rest frequently.

Individual differences of handicapped children should be recognized, but these children should never be regarded as outsiders or pariahs.

All this indicates the significance of guidance and counseling. Today, guidance is one of the major activities of the school, and we need thousands of trained counselors. Not every teacher is a counselor; often the teacher is overworked and hence has little time for counseling.

Vocational counseling started in 1908, in Boston, when Frank Parsons assisted the youth of that city in attempting to solve vocational problems.

Various types of guidance can be found. Besides vocational guidance, concerned with the choice of a future vocation, we have educational guidance, selecting the right type of school, determining the major, type of curriculum, etc. Health guidance is intended to improve our health habits. Character guidance leads to the development of ethical traits. Family guidance improves our efficiency at home. Civic guidance is designed to establish maturity in political affairs. Consumer guidance improves our buying habits. Religious guidance attempts to achieve insight regarding man's relationship to society, to ecclesiastical organizations, and to God. Leisure time guidance attempts to establish worthwhile habits and hobbies for our spare time. Social guidance is designed to improve our manners and our sense of etiquette. More and more guidance counselors are stressing the importance of love and altruism. Thus, Sorokin at Harvard established an Institute of Altruistic Research.

There are two views that conflict in regard to the nature of guidance. J. J. Jones[1] feels that counseling deals mainly with the solution of crisis problems, while Professor John M. Brewer[2] uses the term guidance in the same sense as education. More and more counselors are using the approach of Carl Rogers, and thus they favor non-directive therapy.

What are the qualities of a superior counselor? What type of technique does he use? No exact formula can be given, but here are a few suggestions:

The superior counselor does not despair; he has faith in human nature, psychology, science, and education.

The superior counselor is imaginative and invariably sympathetic.

The superior counselor avoids either-or distinctions; he is anything but dogmatic and he is never shocked.

The superior counselor has mastered the art of listening.

The superior counselor uses tests as aids, but not as absolutes.

---

[1] Cf. Jones, *Principles of Guidance*.

[2] Cf. Brewer, *Education as Guidance*.

The superior counselor is conscious of the vast role of the environment. He is interested in the social, as well as in the psychological factors that condition human behavior.

The superior counselor is able to radiate insight. The person being guided develops his own solutions and is able to recognize the sources of his problem.

The superior counselor appeals to the creative drives of the person who seeks guidance. Thus, counseling establishes creative opportunities in work and leisure time pursuits.

The superior counselor regards his work as a co-operative enterprise; he works with the physician, social worker, minister, and the family members.

The superior counselor is interested in values as well as in facts. He realizes that modern man may be suffering from *valuational frustration* as well as emotional frustration.

THE IMPORTANCE OF COUNSELING

In a democratic society, counseling thus is of utmost importance. We are all counselors, whether we are parents or teachers; as a matter of fact, anyone concerned with the future of society has an interest in that field. In a totalitarian society the state may determine what the individual should do and what occupation he must select. In our civilization, the individual has to make the choice and he can follow his own interests.

Counseling does not mean merely giving advice. The more information we have about the client, the better we are able to guide him and to understand his drives and motives. Modern tests and measurements are extremely important in giving us detailed information. Still, we must also trust our intuitions and develop a feeling of reciprocity with the client.

Take, for example, the counseling efforts of two deans at a large Western high school. The Dean of Men is a former coach; he is firm with the boys, yet he gets to know them as individuals. When they get into trouble, he is always understanding. They respect him for his leadership ability. On the other hand, the Dean of Women, who has an excellent scholastic background and who has taken innumerable advanced courses in guidance and psychology, has a rigid personality. She is prudish and excessively rigid in her standards. The girls do not feel at ease with her. She has very little personal warmth. She preaches to offenders and scolds them for their waywardness. As a result she is one of the most unpopular persons in the school.

The point is not that advanced work is unnecessary. On the contrary, the more we study psychology, physiology, child development, as well as tests and measurements, the more we learn about human behavior. But at the same time we must develop a humane and enlightened outlook and not regard youngsters as if they were naturally wayward. There is no substitute for sympathetic understanding and for open-mindedness. To be a counselor means to be a friend to youth; it means to be imaginative and creative in our approach to human relations; it means unwavering faith in human nature.

QUESTIONS FOR DISCUSSION AND INVESTIGATION

1. Trace the growing importance of psychology in our educational system.

2. Name and define the major present day schools of psychology.

3. Explain the mathematical approach that psychology has lent to man's behavior.

4. Trace the developing concept on handling emotions as related to learning.

5. Give suggestions on how the teacher can improve the learning of the class.

6. What are Kilpatrick's distinctions between primary and concomitant learning?

7. Explain the newly developed methods of handling handicapped children.

8. Name the various types of guidance.

9. List the qualities of a superior counselor.

10. Why is counseling of utmost importance in a democratic society?

Chapter 33

Leadership

FOUNDATIONS OF ADMINISTRATION

Leadership is a basic element of education. A great leader can inspire entire communities; his influence radiates, and he exemplifies in his own life the ideals of education. A mediocre leader radiates indifference, even antagonism towards education. Many bond elections have been lost because of inadequate leadership and because educational leaders have been unable to interpret the needs of their profession.

Among leaders in education who have made a distinguished contribution and who have left their mark upon our system there are three names that stand out: John Whinnery at Montebello, who became president of Phi Delta Kappa, C. C. Trillingham at Los Angeles County, who was elected president of the American Association of School Administrators, and Lawrence Derthick, who guided national education in the Eisenhower era. All three had certain traits in common: They worked day and night; they were scholars; they cultivated the art of public relations; they were democratic with their associates; they were warm as human beings, and they were imbued with an unwavering faith in the possibilities of American education.

American education is decentralized. The tenth amendment has resulted in state control of education. This distinguishes the American system from the system of European nations like Germany, France, and England, in which education is controlled by the central government. FEDERAL LEGISLATION. Still, the federal government has been active in promoting the cause of education. In 1787, the Northwest

Ordinance was passed, which tried to further education. In the case of Ohio, the ordinance provided that the sixteenth section of each township was to be used for the support of public schools. Since the sixteenth section might be of little economic value, Congress later made direct grants to the newly admitted states.

In 1802, West Point was founded for the education of army officers; in 1845, the navy followed suit with the establishment of Annapolis.

The Morrill act of 1862 provided for land-grant colleges, while the Hatch Act of 1887 gave aid to agricultural experiment farms. Agricultural education also was aided by the Smith-Lever Act in 1914. Two years later, the Smith-Hughes Act gave impetus to the development of vocational education, which was further promoted by the George-Deen Act in 1936. While the United States was in the midst of an economic crisis in the thirties, emergency grants were made to the states by the Federal government. Under Franklin D. Roosevelt, the government set up the National Youth Administration and the Civilian Conservation Corps.

In 1941, Congress made special appropriations for education in defense areas. The G. I. Bill of Rights, which was passed after World War II, provided government support for college study on the part of veterans. In 1952 some of the same benefits were granted to veterans of the Korean campaign.

OFFICE OF EDUCATION. We must not overlook the activities of the United States Office of Education. First set up in 1867, it was, at that time, called the "Department of Education." Its name was changed two years later to the "Office of Education," and in 1870 it changed to the "Bureau of Education." In 1929, the name reverted again to the "Office of Education." The Office of Education is now part of the Federal Security Agency under a separate cabinet department.

Many believe that the Commissioner of Education should have cabinet status; they feel that this would give educators a more dominant role in national affairs and that it would assure more financial support of education. Others assert, however, that such a step would involve education in too much politics and that it might result in excessive Federal control over our school system.

United States Commissioners of Education have made significant contributions to the American school system. Among them we find Henry Barnard, who served in the administration of Andrew Johnson, John Eaton, who was appointed by Grant, N. H. R. Dawson, who was part of Cleveland's administration, W. T. Harris, who served under the presidency of Benjamin Harrison, E. B. Brown, who served under Theodore Roosevelt, P. P. Claxton, who was the appointee of Taft, J. J. Tigert, who served in Harding's administration, W. J. Cooper, who administered the office under Hoover, G. F. Zook and J. W. Studebaker, who were appointees under Franklin D. Roosevelt, Earl J. McGrath, who was a capable commissioner in the Truman era, and Samuel Brownell and L. Derthick, who were appointed by Eisenhower, Sterling McMurrin who served under Kennedy, and Francis Keppel who ably aided Johnson.

The Office of Education perennially collects valuable statistics and information regarding the state of United States education. It also issues a journal, *School Life,* and prepares *Annual Reports* and *Biennial Surveys.* The Office has administered various federal acts, like the Smith-Hughes Act, and it has promoted adult education. It sponsors the Future Farmers of America. It contributed funds for the training of war-workers, both during World War II and in the crisis following the outbreak of the Korean War. In the field of educational research, the Office has aided both states and local communities.

STATE CONTROL. Still, in regard to the control of education, the United States Office of Education is far less important than the individual state. The schools are mainly regulated by the state authorities who determine the standards of certification, the way in which taxes can be raised, the manner in which schoolhouses should be built, and the procedure by which textbooks can be ordered. This does not imply direct control, for considerable local autonomy exists in education.

The first State Board of Education was set up by New York in 1784. This board was mainly in charge of secondary and higher education. In 1837, under the leadership of Horace Mann, a state board of education was established by Massachusetts. Two years later, Connecticut followed in the wake of Massachusetts. The powers of the state board vary; in some states it supervises primary and secondary education; in others, the state board controls higher education.

The method of selection of members of the state board also varies with the individual states. In thirty states, the governor *appoints* the members of the board; in five states, they are *elected.* In some states, particularly Florida and Mississippi, certain state officials, like the attorney general, the secretary of state, and the superintendent of public instruction, are *ex-officio* members of the board. Members of the board range from three as in Mississippi, to twenty-one as in the case of Texas.

The State Superintendent of Schools has an important role in education. This may be reflected by his salary, often over twenty thousand dollars a year. The State Superintendent is either appointed by the State Board of Education as in Colorado or Texas, or he may be an elective official as in Utah and Alabama.

The leader, among the states, in expanding the school structure has been Massachusetts. In 1642, a law was passed by the Massachusetts colony providing for schools in the various towns of the colony, schools which would instruct children in the principles of religion and citizenship. In 1643, a law was issued which made it compulsory for a community with over fifty families to employ a teacher, and for communities with more than one hundred families to set up a grammar school. Massachusetts was also the first state to pass a compulsory school attendance law in 1852.

LOCAL CONTROL. The administration of the school depends to a large extent upon local practices. In many Southern states the *county* is the fundamental unit, while in Delaware, for instance, the state assumes the main administrative functions. In other states the dominant control is being exercised by the township or the local school district. A state, like Colorado, may have over seventeen hundred school districts; occasionally there are even more school board members than local teachers. Since the United States has thousands of school districts, an urgent need exists for *consolidation*.

Consolidation of school districts offers many advantages. Consolidation can contribute to a better salary scale for teachers, feature a more diversified program, cut costs, and provide for special services, such as hearing clinics, professional counseling, etc. Consolidation can aid in overcoming the financial irregularity which results from small school districts, attract more capable administrators, provide better audio-visual facilities, and create more stimulation for the teachers. Small school districts are not only uneconomical, but they develop a spirit of isolationism so incompatible with genuine education. It should be remembered that the small district developed in colonial times; it was justified in days when transportation facilities were inadequate. It cannot be justified in the atomic age, when transportation has been mechanized and universalized.

The National Commission of School District Reorganization of the National Education Association set up *ten thousand pupils per district* as the best foundation for a balanced school program; twelve hundred students per district were regarded as a minimum. Yet some districts have less than a hundred students. As a result, the services of the district, especially in health, library facilities, and aid for handicapped children, tend to be *inadequate*.

An important link in the local administration of schools is the Board of Education. Occasionally, members are appointed by the mayor, as in the case of New York, Chicago, and Baltimore. This procedure may involve the Board of Education in city politics. In Chicago, especially, corruption for many years dominated the Board of Education. Thus, it is desirable to provide for popular election of the Board of Education. This is done in such cities as Los Angeles and Cleveland.

Members of the school board should exhibit, above all, a sense of *integrity*. Pressure groups will constantly try to interfere with the administration of education, and they will always urge a return to the good old days. They are forever fearful that textbooks may undermine the political morals of the young, and, as in Pasadena, California, they may agitate for the removal of liberal administrators.

Members of the school board should represent various educational ideals; unanimity is not the ideal in education. However, all members should be dedicated to the *expansion of public education*.

SUPERINTENDENT. The superintendent of schools should be forward-looking in his educational philosophy; he should be well versed in both liberal arts and professional education; he should have teaching as well as administrative experience, and he should be well acquainted with school laws, school finance, school budgeting, and school management.

The various duties of the superintendent include the nomination of assistant superintendents, principals, business managers, supervisors, and teachers. He signs the contract when a teacher is hired, and he determines the dismissal of the teacher. While he cannot vote, he attends all the meetings of the Board, as of its sub-committees. He selects, with the aid of the administrative staff and the teaching personnel, the textbooks, although, occasionally, the state officials carry through this task. With the approval of the Board, he determines boundaries of school attendance districts. He is in charge of the preparation of the budget. He selects principals for the various schools, and gives approval to all purchases and expenditures. He recommends to the Board the building of new schoolhouses; he makes monthly and annual reports to the Board on the state of the schools. He determines whether school facilities may be used by outside organizations; he establishes rules for the administration of the schools; his approval is needed for the courses authorized by the Board of Education; in short, his responsibilities are heavy. Hence, an outstanding educator is needed for the position of superintendent of schools.

PRINCIPAL. The efficiency of the school system depends, to a great extent, upon the principal. The principal is in charge of the teachers, he presides at faculty meetings, he is responsible for the academic standards of the school, he directs the activities of the custodial staff, and he is responsible for the keeping of records. Pupils come to him when they have a complaint against a teacher. Parents will besiege his office in case they are dissatisfied with the conduct of the school. Community organizations will send delegates when they feel the school is not run properly. Hence, one of the main functions of the principal is to mediate between school and community and to serve as an ambassador of good will for the educational system.

What are the traits of a successful administrator? How does he actualize high educational objectives?

The outstanding administrator believes in academic freedom and he resists pressure groups.

The outstanding administrator recognizes that he is fallible and is willing to learn from others.

The outstanding administrator builds a feeling of good will and co-operation in the community.

The outstanding administrator believes in team spirit. He knows how to share responsibilities with others.

The outstanding administrator will guide his subordinates indirectly; he will exhibit a sense of humility.

The outstanding administrator thinks more of objectives and goals than of routine affairs.

The outstanding administrator will encourage new ideas and new concepts of education.

The outstanding administrator is invariably friendly, and his advice is sought freely by his associates and subordinates.

The outstanding administrator is concerned more with the *philosophy of education* than with the techniques of education.

The outstanding administrator is altruistic, and he exemplifies the democratic way of life in action.

SCHOOL PLANS AND FINANCES

In 1925, the National Education Association appointed a Committee on School House Planning. In its report the Committee mentioned nine standards for an adequate schoolhouse:

Adaptation to educational needs
Safety
Healthfulness
Expansiveness
Flexibility
Convenience
Durability
Economy
Aesthetic fitness.

Among the standards mentioned, safety is an especially significant factor. In earthquake areas, as in California, special precautions must be taken, and special standards must be met by the school buildings. Fire is a constant danger to school buildings, and each building should have proper safety provisions.

In the style of architecture, modern schools emphasize informality and functional design. The ideal is to make them as cheerful as possible. The traditional school often looked like a jail and featured rather austere colors.

The features of educational organization will often determine the architectural design of the school. Thus, when rooms in the elementary school are set aside for laboratory work, shops, art, and music, special provisions should be made in the design of the school.

Many schools today are community centers. Thus, the auditorium may be used for visiting lecturers, and the playground may be utilized by adults as well as by children. The question always is: Can the facilities of the school be expanded? What will be the building needs twenty years from now? In states where the school population is constantly expanding the consideration of future needs is especially important.

The site of the school building is an essential consideration. In this connection, several factors have been enumerated by the Pennsylvania State Department of Public Instruction:

Location
Drainage
Nature of soil
Size and shape
Convenience
Location and orientation of buildings
Development of grounds and landscaping.

Schoolhouse construction has become a big business affair. Some of the great architects of our time, like Gropius and Wright, have made constructive suggestions for the development of truly modern school buildings. Even colleges are abandoning the traditional styles of construction, and, in many cases, they have lost the Gothic look. Many state departments of education now have a division in charge of the physical and architectural aspects of schoolhousing and thus are giving valuable assistance to local school districts.

Here the problem of finances emerges. How are the schools supported? How do we pay for the cost of instruction? There are three main sources: 1. local taxes derived from real estate property, 2. funds from the states, and 3. funds from the federal government.

Gross inequalities exist in the financial support of the schools. Some districts may pay a high school teacher four thousand dollars a year; others may pay eight thousand dollars a year. A district may have back of each student only two hundred and fifty dollars assessed valuation, others more than forty thousand dollars assessed valuation. The property tax may vary from more than three thousand five hundred dollars per teacher to twenty dollars per teacher. Some believe that the state makes up the difference; this is not the case, however, in many states. Frequently, the poor district obtains only one half more state aid than does the wealthy district.

Professor Mort of Columbia University suggests that minimum standards be set up by the states to meet the financial needs of the district. The plan would work as follows: The state department of education would make a survey of the minimum costs of an adequate educational structure. The amount might be one hundred and twenty dollars per student in regular daily attendance. District A might have a tax rate of one hundred and twenty dollars, in which case no aid from the state might be required. District B, however, might have only eighty dollars per pupil; thus, the state would contribute forty dollars. District C might have only fifty-five dollars per student, in which case the state would contribute sixty-five dollars to make up the difference.

Equalization of educational opportunities is the goal of constant pressures exerted by the National Education Association for Federal Aid to Education. Such a step, it is argued, would establish more equal opportunities for American school children. Some go to school only six months a year, others ten months. Some pupils cannot go beyond the eighth grade; some go to school in unsafe buildings; some have only elementary school graduates as teachers. Some states lack manufacturing centers; thus their tax rate is bound to be low. Let us compare, for example, the amount of money spent on education by New York and the money spent by Mississippi. Is this fair to the children who may live in a poor state?

Still, strong arguments can be heard against Federal aid to education. Would such a step not increase our tax burden? Would it not add to centralization? Would it not endanger local autonomy?

The issue of Federal aid is a crucial one and will be raised again and again in the future.

TEACHING AIDS

Among the teaching aids used by the schools, the textbook is of primary importance. Some of the early textbooks in the United States were the *New England Primer, McGuffey's Readers,* Noah Webster's *Elementary Spelling Book,* and *New England's Perfect School-Master.* These texts tended to be moralistic, and they stressed memorization.

Modern textbooks, on the other hand, emphasize readability and comprehensive treatment of the subject, with a wider use of illustrations. Objectivity is the keynote to modern texts. Often they are so objective that they become anemic and colorless. *McGuffey's Readers* thus dramatized education more than many modern textbooks do, for many texts today are factually correct, but emotionally uninspiring.

All this should not obscure the advances in textbook writing and manufacturing. Especially on the primary level, textbooks use the full advantages of audio-visual aids.

The library ought to be the center of the school but many students go through high school and college with only a superficial acquaintance of its library resources. Open shelves add to the attractiveness of the library. The librarian should not only have a technical knowledge of books, but she should have an excellent general education and a real *enthusiasm* for books and reading. Too many librarians are unimaginative; their main interest is to collect books and manuscripts rather than to have them used by the students.

Teaching in our time has been made more fascinating through audio-visual means. We use the blackboard more today. Exhibits by students add to the educational program. Maps, globes and charts are a necessary part of the social sciences. Laboratory demonstrations in science make this field more enjoyable to the student. Music appreciation courses have been aided by radio and television programs, like the New York Philharmonic concerts or the Metropolitan Opera performances. The tape recorder has improved the teaching of foreign languages. Thus, the student hears himself speak, and he can improve his accent. The tape recorder also has aided· speech correction work, and it has preserved many lectures for posterity.

Art appreciation would be lost without slides whereby the student obtains a better visual knowledge of the great paintings, cathedrals, and statues of world civilization. Popular magazines, like *Life,* add to art appreciation through their excellent reproductions of the great masters.

The motion picture now is widely used in education. Special companies are engaged in the production of educational films. It takes skill, however, to use motion pictures in the classroom. They should be *selected carefully* and be pre-tested by the teacher. The class should be prepared for the film, and afterwards, the film should be evaluated by the students. The teacher should ask questions regarding the motion picture to test the reaction and comprehension of the audience.

Television promises to revolutionize education. While some of the early programs of television were infantile, featuring mostly cheap materials, the ultimate effect of television will be *positive* in educational terms. Many educators feel that children are too influenced by the gangster stories and by the Westerns which they watch on television. Night after night, they are exposed to brutal acts of violence and sadism. Adults are also exposed to mediocre fare on television and tend to prefer Westerns.

Still, the educational possibilities of television are unlimited. Courses given by Baxter and White have attracted hundreds of thousands of viewers. "Wisdom" and "Omnibus" have enriched American culture. Music appreciation has been intensified through the efforts of Leonard Bernstein. Edward R. Murrow and Chet Huntley have humanized and dramatized political developments. Television, indeed, promises a reconstruction in education.

ADULT EDUCATION

Television raises the problem of adult education, which is as old as the town meetings of the Pilgrims. Adult education did not gain real impetus until 1826 when the first lyceum was held in Massachusetts. The Transcendentalists, especially Emerson, were all interested in adult development.

New York, in 1859, established public forums; fifteen years later, the Chautauqua Institutes, which provided for "educational" camp meetings, were started by Bishop J. H. Vincent. In 1876, several universities started extension courses. These have expanded rapidly in the twentieth century.

In 1924, the National Education Association organized a special adult division; two years later, the American Association of Adult Education was formally established. The N.E.A. publishes the *Adult Education Bulletin;* the American Association of Adult Education publishes the *Adult Education Journal.*

Adult education was strongly promoted by the Roosevelt regime. The Works Progress Administration, for instance, entered various fields of adult education, such as lectures, forums, literary classes, home-making, and a multitude of other activities.

During World War II, the United States Armed Forces Institute provided correspondence study to all the branches of the armed forces. Textbooks and lessons were furnished without cost to the students, and the fee for a course was only two dollars. Usually the Institute assigned a teacher to serve as adviser to the student when he enrolled in the Institute.

In our period, the Ford Foundation has stressed adult education. The following areas in particular are being emphasized: 1. International Relations, 2. Human Relations, 3. Radio and Television programs, 4. Humanities, and 5. The American Ideal of Freedom. The policy of the Foundation is to emphasize liberal adult education. Considerable grants have been made to the American Library Association, the Great Books Foundation, as well as to other organizations, to develop adult interest in the liberal arts.

Adult education in the United States is very much concerned with Americanization programs. The ideal is not just to teach the immigrant the English language and to prepare him for naturalization, but to give him an understanding of the American way of life.

Adult education classes on the part of high schools are popular. They teach everything from typing to recreational dancing. Lately, in some states, protests have been made against the so-called frills of adult education, but this may only represent a temporary reaction.

Adult education programs are particularly strong in New York, Pennsylvania, Michigan, and California. In California, the State Department of Education has a Special Division of Adult Education. The State Legislature has given the same type of aid to adult classes as to regular school programs. Other states with a well-organized adult program include Maine, Connecticut, Delaware, Minnesota, Nebraska, New Jersey, North Carolina, Oregon, Oklahoma, Rhode Island, Virginia, Wyoming, and Utah.

In a period of automation and unparalleled leisure, adult education becomes more urgent than ever. It is possible that in the future we may work only twenty hours a week; a hundred years from now even this time may be shortened. Adults can either be bored by leisure or use it creatively to improve their minds. In the future, millions more will go back to school; college will appeal to mature citizens as well as to youngsters. Adult education is bound to expand and it will challenge the most creative teachers in education.

QUESTIONS FOR DISCUSSION AND INVESTIGATION

1. What active part has the federal government played in promoting the cause of education?

2. Discuss the duties and contributions of the Office of Education.

3. Trace the controls of education from the duties of the state down to the administrators within a school.

4. What are the traits of a successful administrator?

5. Describe the inter-relatedness of educational organization and the style of architecture for school buildings.

6. How would Professor Mort's financial plan be worked out?

7. List the various teaching aids.

8. How may television revolutionize education?

9. Trace the historical growth and importance of adult education.

10. Why has adult education become more urgent than ever?

Part 5

Conclusion

Chapter 34

Philosophy and Education

It has often been remarked that the United States has made only minor contributions in philosophy. Many believe that the American contribution to critical thinking is insignificant compared with American achievements in science, industry, and technology. Thus it has become fashionable to compare the United States with Byzantine civilization. Do we not find the same emphasis on practical matters? Are not both cultures essentially eclectic? Are not both cultures parasites mentally? Are not both cultures mainly interested in application of thought rather than in original speculation?

To some extent, this viewpoint can be justified. Much of American philosophy is somewhat eclectic and represents merely a restatement of European systems. In fact, the great systems of American philosophy usually originated in Europe: for example, Transcendentalism owed much to the inspiration of Hegel and Kant, Puritanism was largely dependent on Calvin, and pragmatism owed at least a partial debt to Comte, Schopenhauer, and Renouvier.

Furthermore, the status of the philosopher in the United States is not a very high one. In colonial times his main task usually was to rationalize religious truth and to fight against heresy. Hence, theology and philosophy were scarcely separated. To be sure, there were already independent thinkers like Woolman, but they were in a minority and their views were regarded with suspicion by the orthodox majority. In reading the works of most colonial thinkers we find that many of them were ministers in disguise. This certainly does not invalidate their systems; on the contrary, we can certainly admire their scholarship and their speculative depth. However, this dependence upon theology, especially in the case of Edwards, set definite limits to their inquiries. Reason was restricted and was forbidden to challenge certain dogmas. It became the task of philosophy to substantiate the insights of the Bible, to defend God's providence, and to justify God's eternal damnation of sinners. Thus philosophy in this period was rather harsh. Such dogmas as those of original sin, the existence

of a literal hell, the eternal doom of the sinners, the working of predes-
tination indicated a somber view of man and of his ultimate destiny.
These views find significant echoes today, especially in the works of
Reinhold Niebuhr.

The emphasis of American thought changed in the revolutionary age.
The old Puritanism became rather unfashionable; instead, Deism and
even a strain of materialism dominated the American mind. It was a
rather optimistic age; hence thinkers like Jefferson stressed the essential
equality of man and insisted upon the fact that it is the task of governments
to promote the welfare of the individual. This period almost witnessed
the emergence of philosopher-kings. In fact, Jefferson and John Adams
were not only outstanding statesmen but also thinkers with an international reputation. The philosophers of this period were opposed to all types
of fanaticism and objected to narrow denominationalism. In the main,
they had a secular concept of politics, religion, and philosophy.

Thinkers like Townsend often object to the philosophy of the enlightenment because of its naturalistic emphasis. Townsend, for example,
thought that social philosophy was overemphasized by Franklin, Jefferson,
and Paine and that metaphysics was neglected in a scandalous manner. All
this may be true; yet we cannot overlook the fact that philosophy in the
revolutionary period was intensely alive and that it had a vivid grasp of
actuality. Philosophy was not merely the concern of college professors;
it appealed to the most brilliant leaders of American civilization.

The culture lag which became so noticeable in later times had not yet
emerged. Ideas and technology were harmonized. The American intellectual received a humanistic education and he was not a narrow specialist,
interested merely in a fragmentary interpretation of the universe. The
leaders of American civilization had a fervent faith in education—both in
the classics and in the sciences, for they knew that democracy without
reason represents the dictatorship of mediocrity and vulgarity.

The emphasis in philosophy changed again in the period of Transcendentalism. The naturalistic gospel had lost its appeal; metaphysics became
more and more significant. It must be remembered that the American
Revolution had ended in a rather conservative manner and that political
life in the first half of the nineteenth century was anything but edifying.
It is not surprising that Emerson had distrust for all political parties and
that he believed that anarchy represents the ideal form of government. No
wonder that Thoreau tried to escape from the genteel atmosphere of Boston and sought refuge in the isolation and calmness of Walden.

This period in some ways represented the victory of the Platonic
spirit in the United States. Like Plato, the Transcendentalists were believers in the existence of eternal Ideas and, like the great Greek philosopher, they had a disdain for the shifting pattern of the actual world. Everything that was in a state of flux was subordinated by the Transcendental-

ists to a changeless realm of absolute truth, absolute beauty, and absolute purity. Like Plato, the Transcendentalists believed in a Utopia and they measured all existing institutions according to an absolute pattern of perfection. Living in this atmosphere of Olympian detachment, the Transcendentalists were rather unconcerned with the problems of the average man.

Yet we must not forget that there was a touch of rebellion in many of the Transcendentalists. Hence, Emerson shocked most theologians by his religious views, and Alcott's educational theories were viewed with profound distaste by the respectable schoolmasters of his time. Nor can we neglect the philosophy of Thoreau, who was a fervent opponent of all types of slavery and who encouraged John Brown's rebellion.

Transcendentalism contributed to the growth of philosophical idealism in the United States. Hegelian thinking became the fountainhead of Royce's system, and for decades Harris tried to apply Hegelian patterns to educational theory. Idealism inspired many thinkers with lofty moral views and thus Harris, as United States Commissioner of Education, tried his best to raise the level of education in the United States and to inspire teachers with an intense sense of vocation. To the idealists, materialism was a dangerous philosophy which, if successful, would become subversive not only in technical thinking but also in political and economic matters.

At the same time a rebellion against the Hegelian spirit took place. Thus Bowne felt that Hegel had neglected the importance of the individual and that the German thinker had made a Leviathan of society. Personalism, as represented by Bowne and by his later followers like Brightman and Flewelling, insisted upon a spiritual interpretation of reality, and it rejected the concept of the Absolute. God thus became more like a constitutional monarch who had constant concern for the welfare of the individual. Furthermore, the personalists thought that the absolute idealists had been too much concerned with a rationalistic approach to reality; instead, personalism emphasized that man above all is an emotional being who feels before he thinks.

Yet while personalism was attracting fervent followers, naturalism was again moving forward. The theory of evolution produced a vigorous controversy, and it indicated to many thinkers that a purely scientific interpretation of man and history was possible. Philosophers like James and Peirce were dissatisfied with the dogmatism of the idealists, and they thought that philosophy could learn much from the insights of the laboratory and the modesty of the scientist, who regards his conclusions in a rather tentative manner.

It must not be forgotten that pragmatism, at least at first, was primarily a methodology to clarify ideas. Undoubtedly, it had a rather healthy effect upon philosophy. It challenged obsolete ways of thinking; it replaced theology with biology; and it fought a strenuous warfare against the closed mind. In education, pragmatism developed a child-centered system of education which emphasized democratic ideals in the learning process.

TWENTIETH CENTURY DILEMMAS

In the twentieth century the role of philosophy tends to be vague. The sciences have become more powerful than ever; thus ethical problems now have often been taken over by the psychologists, anthropologists, and sociologists. The philosopher frequently appears to be isolated and we find few philosopher-kings in American civilization.

The decline in American philosophy is not due to the lack of scholarship; on the contrary, philosophy in the United States is extremely technical and the journals like the *American Philosophical Review* and the *Journal of Philosophy* compare favorably with the scholarly philosophical magazines of Germany, France, and England. However, there is a lack of creativity and originality in American philosophy—almost a sense of decadence.

In this century there is still an intense warfare between the idealists and the realists, and between the new-scholastics and the materialists, but the controversy is less significant than before. Many scientists and writers in semantics feel that the philosophical controversies arise mainly because of verbal fallacies and that many philosophical disputes represent a systematic misuse of words. Especially attractive has been the appeal of the logical positivists, who believe that it is the task of thinkers to clarify linguistic and scientific concepts. It can be readily seen that the logical positivists have a profound distaste for metaphysical reasoning, which, they believe, originated in a pre-scientific age.

Without underestimating the achievements of the logical positivists, especially on the part of Carnap and Reichenbach, it is important that philosophers do not disregard the realm of values and of social philosophy. As Schweitzer has pointed out so eloquently, part of the decay of our civilization is due to the shallowness of contemporary philosophy. Philosophers should be the guardians of civilization; instead, they have been frequently destructive critics of civilization.

FUNCTION OF AMERICAN PHILOSOPHY
IN EDUCATION

It may be asked now what can philosophy accomplish for American civilization? How can philosophy strengthen the positive factors of American life?

In the first place, philosophy can counteract the unexamined life which is so popular in the United States. The lack of strenuous thinking is noticeable not only in politics and economics, but also in education, law, and religion. Yet as Socrates has shown so well, the unexamined life is not worth living, and it ultimately leads to the downfall of civilization. To think critically is a primary necessity. In an age dominated by advertising and television, there is a natural tendency to be conditioned by the social environment and to accept without reservation the slogans of our time. Yet we must not forget that much of the progress of American civilization is due to the achievement of heretics like Thoreau, who felt that the individual should not be seduced by material temptations, but instead should cultivate the resources of the spirit.

This does not mean that we should lose faith in the capacities of reason; on the contrary, we should not be swept away by the irrational idols which are so popular in contemporary life. In this way the American philosopher can learn much from the splendid faith of the enlightenment, which stressed the rational potentialities of man.

In the second place, philosophy can contribute to the life-affirming strains of our civilization. It can instill in us a reverence for the dignity of humanity and a fervent desire for peace and international harmony. It can and should imbue us with a fervent love not only of those who agree with us but also of those who oppose our viewpoints. This certainly implies more charity and humility in philosophical disputes.

Humility is important not only in philosophy but also in other fields of inquiry. There is too much arrogance in our society. As we survey the rise and decline of civilization we note that no institution is eternal. The more we realize our limitations, the more we feel that we can learn from others; and the more we accept the insights not only of Europe but also of Asia, the more we become cosmopolitan in our outlook upon the world. Philosophy should encourage the spirit of universalism which will make possible the survival of man.

Universalism, however, should not be coercive. For it is impossible to establish one pattern of thought or civilization. The story of philosophy is a story of immense diversity. The more we allow for diversity and for a conflict of opinions, the more we establish a genuine form of cosmopolitanism.

AIMS

To realize these goals the American thinker should have a positive attitude regarding man and society. Above all, he should have faith in the potentialities of the individual. He should see the creative powers in every person. Such a gospel may appear too idealistic in an age which emphasizes a Machiavellian concept of human nature and which often stresses the evil aspects of man. Still, it appears that man has not yet completely emerged in the twentieth century and that the future may witness a renaissance of human culture.

Let the thinker beware of narrow allegiances and the gospel of hatred. Undoubtedly many contributions have been made by philosophers like Machiavelli and Nietzsche, who were extremely skeptical of the power of compassion and who urged a defiant and warlike attitude in life. To Nietzsche, love of man meant negation and ultimately a triumph of the weak and the impotent. But the twentieth century has seen only too clearly what these teachings imply when they are applied on a large scale as they were in Nazi Germany. To survive, modern man needs not a gospel of antagonism but a gospel of cooperation and sympathetic understanding.

The American thinker has relied too much upon the past. He has idolized frequently the spirit of Greece and Rome and the Middle Ages. He must learn to live confidently in the present and to approach his subject from a contemporary viewpoint.

As Thoreau remarked:

"To be a philosopher is not merely to have subtle thoughts, nor even to found a school, but so to love wisdom as to live according to its dictates, a life of simplicity, independence, magnanimity, and trust. It is to solve some of the problems of life, not only theoretically, but practically."[1]

Critical thinking should be applied to all aspects of our institutional system. It should create more rationality in politics, more enlightenment in economics, more humanity in our legal system, and more cosmopolitanism in our religious institutions. It should make us more humble as a nation and less self-righteous in dealing with other civilizations. It should give us a feeling of responsibility and concern, for to a great extent the destiny of the world depends upon American wisdom.

Ultimately, education is the test for philosophic thinking. The great controversies of education depend on our philosophic perspective. We have the choice today of being guided by authoritarianism or making democracy the dominant reality.

Education is an attempt to relate ideal and reality. Education appeals to man's creative possibilities. As the bastion of democracy, the study of education, guided by philosophical ideals, is the most *significant* study of the curriculum.

---

1 *Walden.*

QUESTIONS FOR DISCUSSION AND INVESTIGATION

1. To what extent may the viewpoint that the United States has made relatively minor contributions to philosophical thought be justified?

2. How did the emphasis of American thought change in the revolutionary age?

3. Explain how Transcendentalism contributed to the philosophical growth of the United States.

4. Give examples of how twentieth-century American philosophy has declined in vitality.

5. How can philosophy strengthen the positive factors of American life?

6. How is the lack of challenging thinking noticeable in the United States?

7. Why is humility of such great importance in philosophy and in our way of life?

8. Explain how it is impossible to establish coercive universalism in civilization.

9. What are to be the aims of the great American thinker and leader?

10. Why should education ultimately be the test for philosophic thinking?

Chapter 35

Art and Education

Art is the foundation of education. It unites our reason and feelings; it excites our imagination; it transforms our environment. Long after material achievements are forgotten, art remains as a symbol of our inward attitudes. In every way art is a testimony to man's search for immortality.

Emerson looked upon art as the core of morality. "The question of Beauty takes us out of surfaces to thinking of the foundations of things. Goethe said, 'The beautiful is a manifestation of secret laws of Nature which, but for this appearance, had been forever concealed from us.' And the working of this deep instinct makes all the excitement—much of it superficial and absurd enough—about works of art, which leads armies of vain travelers every year to Italy, Greece, and Egypt. Every man values every acquisition he makes in the science of beauty, above his possessions. The most useful man in the most useful world, so long as only commodity were served, would remain unsatisfied. But as fast as he sees beauty, life acquires a very high value.

"I am warned by the ill fate of many philosophers not to attempt a definition of Beauty. I will rather enumerate a few of its qualities. We ascribe beauty to that which is simple; which has no superfluous parts; which exactly answers its end; which stands related to all things; which is the mean of many extremes. It is the most enduring quality, and the most ascending quality. We say love is blind, and the figure of Cupid is drawn with a bandage round his eyes. Blind: yes, because he does not see what he does not like; but the sharpest-sighted hunter in the universe is Love, for finding what he seeks, and only that; and the mythologists tell us that Vulcan was painted lame and Cupid blind, to call attention to the fact that one was all limbs, and the other all eyes. In the true mythology Love is an immortal child, and Beauty leads him as a guide: nor can we express a deeper sense than when we say, Beauty is the pilot of the young soul."[1]

Artistic creativity can be stimulated through the social environment.

---

[1] *Beauty*

Thus certain ages like the age of Pericles in Greece, the Renaissance in Italy, and the Enlightenment in France produced a flowering of geniuses. We observe, on the other hand, that certain ages have been extremely unproductive. This holds true for the Thirty Years War, the early Middle Ages, and the period of the Puritan domination in the United States. Some civilizations like those of Sparta and Assyria have made very few contributions to world civilization. They were mainly interested in the art of warfare, and hence they neglected the realm of the spirit.

The flowering of the periods of creativity was usually brief; thus the age of Pericles lasted roughly from 460 to 429 B.C. This was an age when the traditions of Greece were being re-examined. To Athens came the merchants of the Middle East, and they brought with them not only goods but also *new* ideas. The old aristocracy was supplanted by the new merchant class; intellectual tolerance was practiced; there was no infallible book and no dogma which had to be believed by all. Man became the measure of all things, and man's ideals and needs were studied not only by the thinkers, but by the artists and the scientists. Athens became the school of Greece. The citizens took a personal interest in the adornment of the city-state, hence the dramatists did not create for a select audience, but were judged by all the Athenians.

This golden age was bolstered by a frank interest in this world and by a wave of skepticism which arose amidst the diversity of social, political, and economic opinions. This period, however, had also its disadvantages, for it was based upon slavery and social exploitation. Tolerance even in Athens was limited, as can be seen by the persecution of Anaxagoras who was accused of impiety because he denied that the moon is divine and explained the planets according to scientific facts.

The Renaissance in Italy, like the Age of Pericles, was also a period of rebellion. In the Middle Ages it was thought that man's main task was to glorify God and to escape from the temptations of the devil. All this was reversed during the Renaissance. Power (virtu) replaced virtue and humanism became the keynote of the age. Did not Rabelais preach the gospel of self-expression? Did not Erasmus attack the follies of ecclesiasticism? Did not Leonardo da Vinci represent a universal way of life?

Again the Renaissance lasted only briefly. It was succeeded by the reign of Puritanism and, later on, the Thirty Years War created a wasteland in European culture. The class struggle became stronger than ever, and nationalism was inflamed by the Napoleonic wars and by the growing tide of romanticism, which glorified patriotism.

There are certain common features in all these ages of creativity. They all encouraged nonconformity; Epicureanism became a way of life; intellectual tolerance was practiced; and science made rapid progress and replaced an obsolete theology. The pleasures of this world were emphasized, man was conscious of his failings, and yet he did not despair because of them. These were ages of rebellion; and it appears that rebellion is the first condition of genius.

What can be noticed also is that in all these ages the audiences took a more active part in culture. In the Middle Ages the artists were dependent mostly on the Church or upon a few aristocrats. In the Renaissance, on the other hand, the merchant class and a variety of prices competed in patronizing the thinker. Erasmus was honored not only by scholars but by kings and princes who asked him for advice, not only on political but also on intellectual matters. In the eighteenth century, kings, such as Frederick the Great, were eager to be instructed by Voltaire, and Catherine of Russia wrote complimentary letters to the famous French philosopher.

OBSTACLES TO CREATIVITY

The obstacles to happiness and creativity are not only conditioned by the social environment, but also by individual attitudes. Man appears to object to novelty and instead finds an abiding security in the past. We think of a paradise in which we lived in complete bliss, free of sin and corruption, and in this way we idealize the early condition of mankind. We speak of the knowledge of ancients as if they had possessed an absolute key to wisdom. In our technology we certainly do not use the inventions of two thousand years ago, but in our system of morality and in our basic educational patterns, we feel more secure when we can appeal to the insights of the past.

Another road block in the achievement of creativity lies in the constant occurrence of wars. In modern times these conflicts have become more bloody and more costly than ever before. They involve not only the soldier at the front but also civilians. Thousands of great artists, thinkers, and educators are killed prematurely. Furthermore, dedication to destruction prevents the realization of purely cultural goals. It is true that inventions multiply in wartime, but most of them are used for destructive rather than constructive purposes.

It cannot be forgotten that wars usually result in the enslavement of individuality. The soldier becomes part of a machine, he must submerge himself to the demands of the group, and he must learn to curb his own desires, his own needs, and his own creativity. Life thus becomes a biological struggle for existence. Nothing matters but *survival*.

The effect of war upon the creative spirit is most eloquently portrayed by Erich Maria Remarque in *All Quiet on the Western Front*. It is more than an impressive condemnation of war; it is a description of the pilgrimage of the German mind. Three characters stand out in the tale. The first is Kantorek, the schoolmaster, who is full of patriotic phrases, a believer in Pan-Germanism, and a preacher of hate. He would never change his opinions, regardless of the master he served. Later, under the Weimar republic his followers would speak of the shame of the defeat and the wrongs of the Versailles treaty. His religion consisted in a belief in Germany's greatness, and he thought that it was his duty to spur on young people to be chauvinistic. The tragedy is that while Kantorek was able to grasp facts and had a thorough training in history and humanities, he was essentially a barbarian.

Even more terrifying than Kantorek was Corporal Himmelstoss, the prototype of an SS man, who loved to show off his authority. Essentially, he was sadistic, and he received great pleasure in torturing the new recruits, especially those who would not acknowledge his authority. In civilian life he was a postman, and he must have had a sense of frustration for which he sought to compensate with brutality. As an individual he was harmless, but as a cog in the military system he was like the warden of a concentration camp, a complete automaton.

The main character of Remarque's story was Paul Bäumer. Paul was representative of the high traditions of German civilization. His main interest was in acquiring knowledge, and in school he displayed remarkable literary gifts. He was only eighteen when he volunteered; hence his ideas were plastic, and his mind unformed, and his philosophy of life incomplete. The military training took him away from books and gave him a new sense of values. Latin, philosophy, science, poetry, and mathematics were unimportant now; what mattered was drill and bayonet practice. Slowly, his creative tendencies were erased and he was indoctrinated with the gospel of militarism.

At the front the transformation into a robot was completed. Now his knowledge was limited to death, and in the strange ritual of warfare he attacked and retreated and killed. He fought with frenzy, not because he wanted to kill, but because he clung to life. He met death most intimately in the hospital where his friend Kemmerich was dying. They had enlisted together and Kemmerich's mother had cried when they left for the front. He tried to comfort him, tried to tell him that he would get better, but in vain. Kemmerich knew that his condition was hopeless. In his death the full futility of war was revealed. The hospital was so overcrowded that the doctor could not wait to get his bed for another patient.

Often death came even more violently, and so Paul saw headless bodies, and a Frenchman died beside him in a foxhole they shared together. These sights he could not forget. War to him was not a romantic adventure, but full of graves and disease and starvation.

What was most important was the emotional change in Paul. That a few years ago he should have been concerned with school work and writing poetry seemed ironic amidst the bayonet attacks. That he could have thought of a profession, of a career, of serving humanity, of being creative, he could not understand. The future, like the past, was blurred. He had experienced war for such a long time, and it had made such an impact upon his mind, that he could not visualize the possibility of peace.

Paul tried to escape from war, but he found that escape was impossible. It followed him in his rest camps, even in his love making. Making love became like a purge, like a temporary relief, but it brought no pleasure. It only intensified the pain, because subconsciously he realized that there could be no lasting attachment.

Thus life became a biologic process, with a stress upon eating, drinking, and sleeping. Conventions and laws were abandoned. Existence was reduced to a primitive foundation; his emotions were now based upon brute instinct. War robbed him of his creativeness, he became indifferent, a soldier first and then an individual. He developed a philosophy of utter skepticism. How could he believe in decency, kindness, and cooperation when he saw the slaughter around him? How could he believe in God amidst the injustice of war?

Thus he relied upon himself, upon his own resources, and the external God of Chance, and trusted that the next bullet would not hit him.

When the war ended, Paul was part of a lost generation. An intellectual and emotional wasteland had been created. The seeds of futility had been sown.

LAGS OF CULTURE

Puritanism like war is an enemy of genuine culture and creativity, for the Puritan has a harsh conscience and he feels that art cannot be combined with salvation. Thus Calvin at Geneva was opposed to all forms of art and he even objected to such innocent pleasures as gambling. During Cromwell's Commonwealth in England the theatres were closed, because they were regarded as dens of iniquity by the Puritans.

In early New England, theology was the most important subject of inquiry while secular books were regarded as temptations of the devil. The witchcraft craze revealed an incredibly primitive mentality. Naturally, the Puritans were opposed to the critical scientists because the latter had no patience with superstitions and attempted to apply reason to all aspects of life.

The Puritan is absolutistic in his evaluation of life. Diversity is strictly punished. However, a creative attitude in life leads to an appreciation of opposing traditions and of diverse views of life. The mature teacher sees the moral complexity of most issues and he realizes that human motivation is extremely complicated and not as simple as the Puritans asserted.

Creativity in civilization has also been hindered by over-reliance upon the machine. While mechanical inventions such as printing have made the spread of culture possible, they have also added to uniformity of thinking. It is very doubtful that the contemporary American who reads his newspaper is actually better informed than his ancestor who was exposed to a more rigorous way of communication. We read more, but this does not mean that we think more or that we analyze in a more adequate manner. What is most dangerous is that we have the illusion of knowledge and of certainty, when in reality our conclusions may be prejudiced and may be based upon an insufficient amount of evidence.

More and more our life is dominated by gadgets. For culture we turn to the motion picture and to television. The international situation is explained in fifteen minutes by glib commentators. Einstein is popularized in a lecture of two hours. We learn about the complexities of Spain in an evening lecture by correspondents who visited that nation for two weeks. We can witness the proceedings of Congress through television. We can actually hear the sound of battles, airplanes flying overhead, and in a minute we can be informed about the latest developments in the various capitals. But all this does not add to our own creativity; it only establishes patterns of uniformity and mediocrity.

Mechanical gadgets have made the unexamined way of life more attractive than ever before. Creative conversations in the family circle are limited; after dinner the middle-class family often watches television and is amused by light comedies or by the antics of wrestlers. Who has time to think in this busy world about the essential meaning of life? *Yet we should remember that gadgets are no substitute for genius and that mechanical invention is no compensation for vision.*

TOTALITARIANISM AND ART

In modern times the most determined attack against art was made in Nazi Germany. Hitler had very definite ideas about modern art: in fact, he regarded himself as an expert in that field. He was certain that such movements as cubism, surrealism, and Schönberg's new music were utterly decadent. Liberal artists like Grosz were persecuted because they believed in a democratic approach to life and they satirized the pretensions of the military class and the Nazi party.

Under the Weimar Republic, Germany had made immense strides in art. Contemporary music, contemporary painting, and contemporary sculpture were encouraged. There was feverish literary activity as can be seen from the works of Mann and Remarque. But this renaissance came to an end in 1933 when Hitler's party took over and when art was regulated by political considerations. The artist now had to glorify the state; he had to portray the virtues of total war and the attractions of motherhood. An intellectual and psychoanalytical approach to art was strictly outlawed.

Through Hitler's persecutions some of the most talented German artists were driven into exile. The censorship was so strict that creativity was almost completely stifled in literature, music, and painting. This, indeed, was a dark cultural period for Germany.

The effect of political control upon art can also be noticed in twentieth-century Russia. In the 1920's there was great sympathy in Russia for the new creative movements in painting and music. But in the 1940's and 1950's traditionalism was emphasized and the glories of Russian art were stressed with vigor and intensity. Such artists as Shostakovich and Prokofiev were censored for being influenced too much by "decadent" patterns of music and for not creating music that would appeal to the masses. Both promptly recanted their mistakes and told the authorities that they would change their compositions so that they would promote the needs of the Soviet system.

TOLSTOY AND ART

Critics of modern art, like Tolstoy, believe that the creative spirit is utterly lacking in contemporary painting, literature, and music.

"The organ of art," Tolstoy wrote, "has been perverted, and therefore the upper classes of society have to a great extent been deprived of the effect that it should have produced. The diffusion in our society of enormous quantities, on the one hand of those counterfeits of art which only serve to amuse and corrupt people, and on the other hand of works of insignificant exclusive art, mistaken for the highest art, has perverted most men's capacity to be infected by true works of art, and has thus deprived them of the possibility of experiencing the highest feeling to which mankind has attained, which can only be transmitted from man to man by art."[2]

Tolstoy felt that modern art contributed to vice. "The first consequence, plain for all to see, is the enormous expenditure of the labor or working people on things which are not only useless, but, for the most part, are harmful; and more than that, the waste of priceless human lives on this unnecessary and harmful business."[3]

Furthermore, Tolstoy contended, modern art only serves the idle rich:

"The second consequence is that the productions of amusement—art, which are prepared in such terrific quantities by the armies of professional artists, enable the rich people of our time to live the lives they do, lives not only unnatural, but in contradiction to the humane principles these people themselves

2 *What is Art?*
3 *Ibid.*

profess. To live as do the idle rich people, especially the women, far from nature and from animals, and with enfeebled vital energy, would be impossible
were it not for what is called art—for this occupation and amusement which
hides from them the meaninglessness of their lives, and saves them from the
dullness that oppresses them."[4]

Another consequence of the decadence of art is that values are perverted among the common people. Peasants instinctively, according to
Tolstoy's view, uphold virtue, but the modern artist praises vice and lives
a degenerate life. People thus believe in beauty instead of cultivating
morality. Tolstoy asserted that modern art ultimately leads to superstition.
"Look carefully into the causes of the ignorance of the masses and you
may see that the chief cause does not at all lie in the lack of schools and
libraries, as we are accustomed to suppose, but in those superstitions, both
ecclesiastical and patriotic with which the people are saturated and which
are unceasingly generated by all the methods of art."[5]

What is the solution? How can real creativity be achieved? This is
what Tolstoy recommends:

"A real work of art can only arise in the soul of an artist occasionally, as
the fruit of the life he has lived, just as a child is conceived by its mother.
But counterfeit art is produced by artisans and handicraftsmen continually,
if only consumers can be found.

"Real art, like the wife of an affectionate husband, needs no ornaments.
But counterfeit art, like a prostitute, must always be decked out.

"The cause of the production of real art is the artist's inner need to
express a feeling that has accumulated, just as for a mother the cause of sexual
conception was love. The cause of counterfeit art, as of prostitution, is gain.

"The consequence of true art is the introduction of a new feeling into the
intercourse of life, as the consequence of a wife's love is the birth of a new
man into life. The consequences of counterfeit art are the perversion of man,
pleasure which never satisfies, and the weakening of man's spiritual strength.

"And this is what people of our day and of our circle should understand in
order to avoid the filthy torrent of depraved and prostituted art with which
we are deluged."[6]

ART AND LIFE

Unlike Tolstoy, I believe that we are living in one of the most exciting
ages of human creativity. It is so overwhelming—especially in painting,
architecture, and music—that we have been unable to comprehend its full
significance. Undoubtedly, composers like Hindemith, Shostakovich, Si-

[4] *Ibid.*
[5] *Ibid.*
[6] *Ibid.*

belius, and Bartok, writers like Lewis, Hemingway, and Thomas Mann, painters like Picasso and Rivera, will rank among geniuses of mankind. Still most of us look back to the past while neglecting the greatness of contemporary art.

Art does not have primarily a moral function; rather, it serves as a key to subjective and objective reality. By showing man as he is, by picturing him without presuppositions, modern art has given us a more faithful representation of man and civilization than the art of previous periods. Santayana observed correctly that "the artist is a moralist, though he need not preach." When the artist becomes a categorical moralist as Tolstoy did in his later period, especially when he wrote *Resurrection*, he loses part of his creative genius.

Contemporary artists should not look back to the past as a golden age, rather they should exhaust the possibilities of the present. At first, contemporary art, especially in music and painting, will bewilder the observer who may object to the pluralism of esthetic patterns and to the lack of objective meaning. But the schizoid tendencies of contemporary art are only reflections of the lags in contemporary culture. The chaos of art is a representation of the chaos of our soul.

Educators often follow Tolstoy in urging censorship of contemporary art. Only the beautiful is to be allowed; naturalism is to be discouraged; immoral literature is to be outlawed. They forget that art cannot live in the ideal realm.

The Athenians in some ways were blessed by a lack of historical perspective. They did not invariably compare the work of their creators with that of Babylonian or Egyptian artists. They did not imitate styles of painting and architecture; rather they had confidence in their own culture. Unless we cultivate the same confidence in our own time, we shall always be eclectic and second-rate.

We should remember that art belongs to an autonomous realm. "Art," Goethe asserted, "sticks to the surface of natural phenomena; but it has its own depth, its own power; it crystallizes the highest moments of these superficial phenomena by recognizing in them the character of lawfulness, the perfection of harmonious proportion, the summit of beauty, the dignity of significance, the height of passion."

APPLICATIONS OF ART

To counteract the overly practical strains of our civilization we must have a new faith in the fine arts which should be given a much wider and more extensive place in the curriculum.

Recently a little boy in a painting class painted a green horse. Upon noticing this an unimaginative teacher said to the youngster: "But there are no green horses." To which the boy replied: "This is how the horse looks to me." The approach of the teacher clearly indicated her inability to understand genuine creativity. What matters in the fine arts is not technique, but the stimulation of *insight* and *imagination*.

Emerson observed that art depends on a mystical experience, which can only be partially communicated.

> "Art is the path of the creator to his work. The paths or methods are ideal and eternal, though few men ever see them; not the artist himself for years, or for a lifetime, unless he comes into the conditions. The painter, the sculptor, the composer, the epic rhapsodist, the orator, all partake one desire, namely to express themselves symmetrically and abundantly, not dwarfishly and fragmentarily. They found or put themselves in certain conditions, as, the painter and sculptor before some impressive human figures; the orator into the assembly of the people; and the others in such scenes as each has found exciting to his intellect; and each presently feels the new desire. He hears a voice, he sees a beckoning. Then he is apprised, with wonder, what herds of daemons hem him in. He can no more rest; he says, with the old painter, 'By God it is in me and must go forth of me.' He pursues a beauty, half seen, which flies before him."[7]

Since we are living in a period of technicians, we often mistake form for substance in art. Technical competence can be taught in our schools and colleges, but the inspiration of great art can only be communicated through personal contact with great painters, great composers, and great writers.

In art as in science an understanding of basic relationships is more important than technical proficiency. We kill the genius of our creative students by overwork and routine, by not exciting their imagination, and by stressing conformity, instead of individuality.

---

[7] *The Poet*

QUESTIONS FOR DISCUSSION AND INVESTIGATION

1. Discuss the ways in which art is the foundation of education.

2. Explain how artistic creativity can be stimulated through the social environment.

3. Name and discuss the environmental factors which are obstacles to creativity.

4. Discuss the plot and theme of *All Quiet on the Western Front*.

5. List and discuss the various aspects of religious and philosophical trends which create lags of culture.

6. Describe the effect of political control upon art in Nazi Germany and Communist Russia.

7. Why did Tolstoy consider modern art to be decadent?

8. What does Tolstoy recommend in finding 'real' creativity?

9. How and why does art primarily serve as a key to subjective and objective reality?

10. Explain how in art an understanding of basic relationships is more important than technical proficiency.

Chapter 36

Science and Education

The realm of art deals with values; the realm of science is concerned with verifiable facts. Art progresses through intensification of individuality, whereas science advances by the exclusion of human preferences. Science represents a method of discovery; it is an instrument of knowledge whereby nature can be controlled. Science as such is ethically neutral; its uses are determined by the social environment in which it develops.

In education we find two extreme attitudes regarding science. Some educators feel that questions of value can be eliminated, that all of knowledge can be reduced to a quantitative basis. They believe that measurement is the heart of knowledge. However, it should be realized that education mediates between the subjective and objective poles of existence, and educational research is determined to a great extent by valuational preferences. Our motives and aims govern the postulates of research in education as well as in the other areas of inquiry.

The other extreme in education is represented by the neo-scholastic view that science deals only with the phenomenal world, and that since education deals with wisdom, science is a mere prelude to philosophy. Instead of speaking of the methodology of science, thinkers like Adler stress the pluralistic methodologies of scientific inquiry. Undoubtedly, various methodologies exist; for example, biology is based largely upon induction, while mathematics relies upon deduction; but the scientific spirit is the *same* for all areas of inquiry. The scientific spirit stresses open-mindedness, controlled experimentation, and a rigorous method of verification.

Descartes already stressed the identity of science and wisdom. In an eloquent passage he asserted:

"The sciences taken all together are identical with human wisdom, which always remains one and the same, however applied to different subjects, and

499

suffers no more differentiation proceeding from them than the light of the
sun experiences from the variety of the things which it illumines."[1]

The march of science has been so rapid and breathtaking that it is
almost impossible to comprehend its significance and its implication for
the future of our culture. What stamps our civilization most is its mechanical content and its reliance upon the inventions which science has made
possible. While the advancement of science has been spectacular, it has
not changed the basic attitudes and the fundamental ideas of men. Our
machinery is up-to-date, but our attitudes and morals date back thousands
of years.

This split personality and cultural lag of modern man was best revealed in Nazi Germany. Here, indeed, was superb organization and unusual inventive genius. Science was performing miracles, yet at the same
time the Nazi morals were barbarian. The same efficiency that produced
new chemical substances was used in building gas chambers to exterminate
millions of Jews and other minorities.

The march of science in earlier times was relatively slow; it was based
upon certain fundamental inventions such as the use of fire and the
development of the fist hatchet. Especially important was the use of
metals which took place when civilization became settled; this invention
influenced the conduct of warfare and made large-scale industry possible.

Of the ancient nations the Egyptians perhaps were the most progressive in their use of science. Besides developing the elements of mathematics
they made advances in medicine, and they used in that field, as the *Book
of Surgery* indicates, experimentation and observation.

The Greeks, unlike the Egyptians, were more interested in the *theory*
of science. They developed a definite method of inquiry; they systematized
it and at the same time carried on experiments. But the main occupation
of the Greeks was intellectual speculation; they were rather uninterested
in practical inventions which they regarded as being of minor importance.
Hence Aristotle believed that the main goal of life was contemplation, not
power over nature. Greek science was hindered by too many *a priori* ideas
about man and the universe. This spirit can be found especially in Aristotle, who in the Middle Ages became the foremost authority in science
for the Western World.

In the Middle Ages experimental science experienced almost a total
neglect. The main occupation was theology, and superstition reigned
supreme not only among the common people but also among the scholars.
Astrology was particularly popular; mathematics and the physical sciences
were almost completely disregarded.

A few outstanding minds like Roger Bacon stood out, but they were
regarded with great suspicion by the Church. Small wonder that Bacon

---

[1] *Regulae ad directionem ingenii*

had vast contempt for the prevailing knowledge of his time and he thought that he could learn more from the man in the street than from renowned scholars. He felt that the only road to truth lay in experimentation, not in abstract statements about God, the soul, and angels. While predicting the invention of the airplane, the submarine, and the motor car, he urged also the study of mathematics to give a quantitative basis to science. Still he was suffering from the limitations of his time. His main purpose in science was to substantiate the truth of the Bible and he believed in experimental science to ward off the onslaughts of Anti-Christ.

In the Renaissance a new outlook in science was achieved mainly through advances in mathematics, through new inventions like the telescope, and through the formation of scientific societies which led to an international exchange of ideas and researches. Curiosity now was not held back by prevailing religious customs, but was stimulated by a new interest in nature.

In early modern times the advance of physical science was most spectacular, while in the nineteenth-century biology made rapid headway. In our own century the barriers between the sciences are being eliminated. Thus we find the development of biophysics, biochemistry, and astrophysics. One of the most important advances lies in the insight that mass can be converted into energy—a principle which was formative in the development of the atomic bomb.

Roughly speaking, modern science has passed through four phases. At first it was influenced by its religious origin; for example, even Newton wrote a book on the topography of hell. Later, science was used to develop a theory of metaphysics; being part of natural philosophy it suffered from an abundance of abstractions. Then the sciences became autonomous; the main interest of researchers was not in the explanation of causes and essences, but in the pragmatic function of science.

In the twentieth century the sciences have been subjected to a wave of skepticism. Today we have pluralistic systems of mathematics and the scientist is uncertain about the ultimate constitution of matter, the origin of the universe, and the nature of life. The principle of indeterminacy, as expressed by Heisenberg, maintains that causal determinism cannot be applied to the measurement of electrons. Science in our time has become concerned with semantic meaning as can be seen by such titles as *The Meaning of Meaning* by Ogden and Richards, *Die Philosophie der Symbolischen Formen* by Cassirer, *Philosophy and Logical Syntax* by Carnap, *Language, Truth and Logic* by Ayer, *Symbol and Existenz der Wissenschaft* by Noack, *Philosophy in a New Key* by Langer, and *Tractatus Logico-Philosophicus* by Wittgenstein.

It should be remembered that modern science started with dualistic assumptions which were perhaps best represented in the philosophy of Descartes. Descartes described two realms: The world of matter, which was guided by the laws of mechanics and the realm of mind, which was determined by teleology. This "bifurcation of nature," to use Whitehead's term, had unfortunate consequences for the development of modern culture, for it made a sharp distinction between science and religion, values and facts. Progress so far has been rapid in the realm of matter, but extremely slow in the realm of values.

Scientists in modern times were generally uninterested in the moral implication of their researches. Scientists like Einstein who have taken an active interest in politics and education have usually been in the minority. The divorce of philosophy and science, ideals and actuality, subjectivity and objectivity, has given a schizoid basis to modern culture.

Some thinkers like Reichenbach believe that the same method which governs physical science is to dominate philosophy. Value judgments thus are to be excluded from philosophic inquiry, and empiricism is to govern our thinking. However, sensory knowledge is not the only criterion of truth, for science like art, as Langer points out, is concerned with *symbols*.

The progress of science depends on the advancement of methods of quantification. New mathematical discoveries have greatly contributed to the advancement of physical science. But quantification introduces a fictional principle into science, as Vaihinger observed in *The Philosophy of as If*. We act as if quantification could be extended to all realms of nature, but we realize that certain qualities are irreducible. Measurement consequently is more important in the physical sciences than in psychology and education. The inorganic realm is the realm of quantities, while man is guided by purposes and ideals and is part of the realm of qualities.

Furthermore, it should be pointed out that the laws of social science are different than those of physical science. This insight was expressed by Comte:

"In all social phenomena we perceive the working of the physiological laws of the individual; and moreover something which modifies their effects, and which belongs to the influence of individuals over each other—singularly complicated in the case of the human race by the influence of generations on their successors. Thus it is clear that our social science must issue from that which relates to the life of the individual. On the other hand, there is no occasion to suppose, as some eminent physiologists have done, that social physics is only an appendage to physiology. The phenomena of the two are not identical, though they are homogeneous; and it is of high importance to hold the two sciences separate. As social conditions modify the operation of physiological laws, social physics must have a set of observations of its own."[2]

All this has a profound implication for education. Real educative growth is like the *Tao* of Lao-Tse. The *Tao* is everywhere, yet it cannot

---

[2] *Cours de Philosphie Positive*

be defined. It governs both man and nature; it is infinite and infinitesimal. Real education likewise is intangible; it starts with a sense of vastness and knowledge and ends with a recognition of the mystery of life.

While science is concerned with externality, education dwells upon inwardness. Emerson makes the same point in his essays when he remarks: "The great distinction between teachers sacred or literary, —between poets like Herbert, and poets like Pope, —between philosophers like Spinoza, Kant, and Coleridge, and philosophers like Locke, Paley, Mackintosh and Stewart, —between men of the world who are reckoned accomplished talkers, and here and there a fervent mystic, prophesying half insane under the infinitude of his thought, —is that one class speaks 'from within' or from experience as parties and possessors of the fact; and the other class 'from without,' as spectators merely, or perhaps as acquainted with fact on the evidence of third persons. It is of no use to preach to me from without. I can do that too easily myself. Jesus speaks always from within, and in a degree that transcends all others. In that is the miracle. I believe beforehand that it ought so to be. All men stand continually in the expectation of the appearance of such a teacher."[3]

THE PIONEERS

The development of science has been made possible, above all, by the insight and boldness of a few great men who dared to defy tradition and who almost single-handedly discovered new worlds and new horizons.

Important among these leaders was Copernicus who had an insatiable love for knowledge. He attended several universities including Cracow and Bologna, and he was instructed by teachers who had grave doubts concerning the viewpoint of Aristotle that the earth is the center of the universe. Copernicus studied the ancient astronomer Aristarchus, who believed that the earth moves around the sun.

At first his heliocentric theory did not cause a shock in the Church. Martin Luther, however, was very indignant and regarded it as preposterous. Did not Joshua command the sun to stand still? Did not the Bible point out that the earth is the center of the universe?

Galileo was even more audacious than Copernicus. At an early age he became a professor at Pisa University. He was known as a radical who protested against the academic ritual and who had fun in destroying the accepted ideas of his colleagues. The story is well-known of how he dropped two objects from the Tower of Pisa and they both reached the earth at the same time. The prevailing idea was that the heavier object would fall faster. His colleagues witnessed the experiment, but since it disproved their theories they refused to accept it.

---

[3] *The Oversoul*

Galileo developed a telescope to substantiate the new astronomical insights. The professors refused to look through the telescope; they thought that Aristotle had settled the matter long ago. Later Galileo defended the Copernican theory by a dialogue which was supposed to be impartial, but the character who defended the old theory was a simpleton and sounded suspiciously like one of the main Church leaders.

At this time Galileo was old and in failing health, but he was ordered to Rome to appear before the Inquisition. The authorities sent a Doctor to Galileo who certified that he was in good health and able to travel. Still Galileo hesitated; he finally made up his mind when he heard that he might be taken to Rome in chains. There he was subjected to intense cross-examination and to physical torture. At the end he acknowledged his errors and promised to recant his doctrines and even to inform the authorities if others followed the new theory.

Nevertheless, the new theory of the universe could not be suppressed. It was strengthened by the researches of Brahe, Kepler, and Newton, and it was destined to change the outlook of western man.

What was its ultimate implication? Man's horizon was expanded immeasurably; his world ceased to be the center of the universe. Philosophers like Bruno became intoxicated with the concept of infinity. Bruno suffered for his audacious theories by being burned at the stake in 1600. Before he died he told his accusers in a prophetic vein: "You who pass judgment upon me, feel greater fear than I upon whom it is passed." History sustained the faith of Bruno, not the faith of the Inquisition.

Another great change in science came about through the work of Darwin. He studied at Cambridge, and at first was destined for the ministry. Instead, he became a naturalist studying plant and animal life. For many years he collected various species and kept prolific notes about his biological and botanical studies. His theory of evolution stated that man had descended from an animal ancestry; it also contained the concept of natural selection, the prodigality of nature, and the survival of the fittest. When he pointed out that the Biblical story of creation could not possibly be true, an outcry could be heard. Some bishops charged that he was an atheist, a perverter of morality, and that his theories certainly would be disproven by serious scientists. A famous debate took place between Wilberforce and Huxley. The former was an extremely pious bishop, but somewhat limited in science. Huxley was an outstanding scientist whose religious opinions were lukewarm. He was devastating in the defense of Darwin and had the bishop at a grave disadvantage.

The controversy regarding evolution is still going on in some localities of the United States. In the 1920's a trial took place involving Scopes, a Tennessee teacher of biology who advocated the theory of evolution. His lawyer was Clarence Darrow while his bitter opponent was William Jennings Bryan, who combined with political radicalism a faith in extreme religious conservatism. The case was judged by jurors who were violently opposed to the theory of evolution and who naturally ruled against Scopes.

The theory of evolution had a lasting impact upon educational patterns. Now man was viewed not through the light of the theology but through the sober perspective of his biological ancestry. More attention was paid to primitive culture and to man's animal origin than ever before.

Another blow to accepted traditions came through the researches of Freud who indicated that man is not governed by reason and that much of our thinking is repressed and remains on a subconscious level. He showed how important sex is as a motivating factor and that dreams have a definite relation to our character. Besides exploring infant sexuality he demonstrated how psychoanalysis could be used in religion, art, and other areas of culture. Freud was afraid to publish *Moses and Monotheism* because he knew that it would upset orthodox opinion in religion. He was called an atheist, a man with a dirty mind, and many of his colleagues laughed and ridiculed him when he first propounded his theory.

Einstein met less hostility than Freud, although at first he lived a rather obscure existence as a clerk at the patent office in Bern. His imagination was stimulated by his reading of Poincaré and Mach, and his genius was so great that he outlined a new universe for modern man. Instead of absolute space and time, he spoke about a space-time continuum, and in his theory of relativity he indicated that mass and time vary with velocity and that both depend upon the frame of reference of the observer.

The theories of Freud and Einstein have changed the philosophical views of man. Gone is the world of static entities; skepticism has been reinforced by these theories. How can there be absolute statements either about the universe or about man's nature?

Relativity and Infinity are the keynotes of the 20th-century culture. Relativity indicates the importance of change and the significance of the point of view both in the physical and in the social sciences. The concept of infinity demonstrates that man is not the measure of the universe, that if man wants to survive in a precarious age, he needs a sense of cosmic piety.

This preoccupation with infinity is found in a memorable poem by Leopardi, a poet who anticipated the intellectual mood of the twentieth century:

> "Dear to me always was this lonely hill,
> And this hedge that excludes so large a part
> Of the ultimate horizon from my view,
> But as I sit and gaze, my thought conceives
> Interminable vastnesses of space
> Beyond it, and unearthly silences,

And profoundest calm; whereat my heart
almost
Becomes dismayed. And I hear the wind
Blustering through these branches, I find
myself
Comparing with this sound that infinite
silence;
And then I call to mind eternity,
And the ages that are dead, and this that now
Is living, and the noise of it. And so
In this immensity my thought sinks drowned:
And sweet it seems to shipwreck in this sea."

IMPLICATIONS OF SCIENCE

The scientific method depends upon attention to all aspects of life. The man in the street is often puzzled by the concentration of the scientist upon insignificant details. For example, Pavlov devoted almost all his life to the study of the flow of saliva in dogs. Some might say that nothing could be more useless and unfruitful than to investigate such an unimportant subject. But they do not realize that in this way Pavlov established almost a new foundation for physiological psychology.

No object in life is immune from the curiosity of the scientist. Uninfluenced by his emotions, he examines with tireless patience the universe as well as his own body. Recently, a professor in a major medical school found out he was suffering from cancer. He kept an exact diary of the progress of the disease, noting its symptoms and the effect of the treatment. He kept up his notations until the day before he died. As a last gesture of scientific faith he willed his body to the medical school.

Theories in science are developed slowly; innumerable guesses are made which prove to be wrong. Error is almost as fruitful as correct deductions. The conclusions are made on a tentative basis with new areas and possibilities of research being suggested. Science depends upon the cooperative spirit. For example, not even Einstein could have advanced the theory of relativity without the previous work of Lobachevski, who had developed the elements of non-Euclidean geometry. The achievements of Freud would have been impossible without the researches of Charcot and Bernheim.

Science has profoundly human implications. This is especially true in medicine, for the modern physician has to deal with man's mind as well as his body. Some doctors believe that the best attitude in medicine is one of complete detachment and objectivity with the physician looking upon the patient as a guinea pig. If necessary he is brutally frank with him. Yet such an attitude is reprehensible, for the physician should be a real humanitarian.

A young doctor in Brazil who found that he was suffering from an incurable disease was examined in New York by outstanding specialists and they announced that he had only half a year more to live. He flew back to Brazil and when he arrived he told reporters how now he appreciated even more his home and his family and such values as love and understanding. He continued to carry on his medical practice; he was not overcome by self-pity. To see him in action one would have thought he was living a perfectly normal life; he was cheerful and good-humored, kind and understanding with his patients, yet all the time he was living under the shadows of death.

The physician must struggle forever against commercialism. His educational training should stress the need for idealism so that he regards his profession as a service to humanity. He must be a constant learner, for the new developments in medicine are truly breathtaking.

The dilemmas of the medical profession are best illustrated in *Arrowsmith* by Sinclair Lewis. All types of doctors are described in this novel, from Martin Arrowsmith who yearns for truth and who is idealistic and who wants to apply his researches to humanity, to Pickerbaugh, the health-officer who is a politician in disguise, to the professor of medical salesmanship, to Professor Gottlieb who believes in complete objectivity and who had no use for human feelings and human passions. Martin Arrowsmith constantly finds that medicine is perverted by sensationalism, professional rivalry, and political corruption. He discovers that scientific discovery cannot be combined with the life of a socialite. At the end of the book he leaves his wealthy wife, to carry on his experiments in medicine.

SCIENCE FOR PROGRESS

It may be asked, how can science aid the progress of education? Can scientific principles be applied to our school system? In the first place, no student should graduate from high school and college without an understanding of the scientific method and its place in modern civilization. He should comprehend the social application of science and its relationship to human welfare. This demands a humanization of science courses. Too many instructors in the physical and natural sciences plan their curriculum as if it were only designed for their majors instead of appealing to the general student, who often looks upon science courses as obstacles to be overcome, rather than as challenges to be met in a creative manner.

In the second place, more attention should be paid to the history of science. Books like Wiener's *The Human Use of Human Beings*, Whitehead's *Adventures of Ideas* and *Science and the Modern World*, Russell's *ABC of Relativity*, Reichenbach's *From Copernicus to Einstein*, not only popularize scientific theories, but give an account of the historical genesis of modern science. The scientific enterprise in this way is related to the total cultural pattern.

In the third place, more scientific principles should be used within the educational process. A pressing need exists for more adequate testing. Too many departments still use true and false tests, especially in introductory courses, too many psychologists still have a blind faith in the I.Q. Both objective and subjective testing methods should be used to achieve an adequate measurement of educational progress.

In the fourth place, the isolation of the science departments should be overcome. Science is not merely the concern of specialists but is part of the humanities. Instructors of science should combine with professors in other departments to develop integrative courses both on the undergraduate and graduate level so that the student understands the impact of science upon society. It must be remembered that scientific asceticism is as outmoded as moral rigorism. The ultimate test of the effectiveness of science lies in its capacity to change society from an attitude of conformity and irrationality to one of openmindedness and genuine enlightenment.

QUESTIONS FOR DISCUSSION AND INVESTIGATION

1. Discuss the two extreme attitudes regarding science in education.

2. How did Nazi Germany manifest the split personality of man in his scientific progress on the one hand and his moral backwardness on the other?

3. Trace the historical phases of the scientific approach.

4. How has the divorce of philosophy and science given a schizoid basis to modern culture?

5. Trace historically the great theorists whose scientific principles revolutionized societies.

6. How did the theory of evolution have a lasting impact upon educational patterns?

7. Discuss how the theories of Freud and Einstein have changed the philosophical views of man.

8. How can science have profound human implications?

9. What dilemmas are found within the twentieth century medical profession?

10. What should education do in order to derive the greatest benefits from science?

Chapter 37

Education
as a Creative Endeavor

In a time of crisis we seek scapegoats. Thus, many Athenians blamed Socrates for the corruption of their youths; many Romans regarded the Christian gods as responsible for the decline of their society. Today, some eminent people outside the academic world are blaming professional educators for the ills of our society.

Some look upon Dewey as a "perverter of education"; others regard progressive education as a "subversive movement"; still others regard free public education as an impossibility; a small minority even looks upon American education as being godless and immoral. Some critics want to save society through more rigid requirements, especially through a stress upon science and mathematics. To them the three R's form the substance of educational redemption.

Actually, universal public education is one of the main contributions of American civilization. We are just starting in that direction. Professional educators do not need destructive criticism but rather constructive, philosophical guidance, so that their vision may expand and so that they may become conscious of the unique opportunities of the moment.

Two extreme attitudes should be avoided. One is an attitude of smugness and complacency which represents a type of moral isolationism; this may resemble Leibniz's viewpoint that this is the best of all possible worlds. Such a viewpoint is contrary to the ideals of genuine education, which depends on constant self-examination. The other extreme is the attitude of deep pessimism regarding American education. Those

511

who want to go back to the educational system of the last century are neither realistic nor enlightened. Those who hold up Russian or European
education as a shining example are seldom informed about the negative
aspects of the educational system which they so blindly admire. Those
who advocate magic formulas do not see the complex issues of American
education, which has a social as well as an individual mission.

We must not be seduced by the immediate challenges of our time.
Perhaps a boy in Germany or France may have more factual knowledge
when he graduates from high school than his American counterpart. But
should not the real test of education be: What type of society does it produce? Does it create real human beings? Imitation is an impossibility; we
must learn to stand on our own feet and develop *our own educational
philosophy*.

Throughout American history there has been a conflict between two
types of philosophy. On the one hand, thinkers like Edwards, Royce, and
Niebuhr have stressed the importance of rigid standards and of absolute
truths; on the other hand, thinkers like Jefferson, Emerson, and James
have affirmed the sovereignty of the individual, and an educational system based upon independent thinking with an essentially futuristic emphasis. To Jefferson, Emerson, and James, standards were only preludes
to man's individuality. To them, democracy was more than an abstract
slogan; it was a way of life which was to be realized in the classroom as
well as in society.

Undoubtedly, we need higher standards on all levels of education.
But this is not the central problem. We can be mediocre in an elective
system and in one which has a multitude of requirements. The real need
is to change the atmosphere of our educational institutions so that creativity will be cherished and so that our society will be rational and enlightened. The real struggle is not between those who favor the three R's
and those who believe in progressive education, but between the champions of creativity and those of apathy. Our aim thus must be extremely
ambitious: it is to create a great culture which will make a permanent
contribution to world civilization.

A Buddhist saint one time was asked whether he would want to go
to heaven or hell. His answer was unequivocal. He wanted to go to hell,
because there his help and compassion were needed. This view has important implications in education. As long as a part of society faces the
hell of poverty, delinquency, and general unhappiness, as long as strife
prevails in the world, the task of the educator is to identify himself with
all those who are suffering and to develop the foundations of a rational
society. The only meaningful war in our time is the war against ignorance, and this war has to be fought on all fronts.

THE EXISTENTIAL IDEAL

In *Zadig,* one of the immortal books by Voltaire, two teachers are contesting for the loyalty of a student. Each one explains his philosophy of education and what his basic goals are in philosophy and education.

The first one asserts: "I will teach him the eight parts of speech, logic, astrology, pneumatics, what is meant by substance and accident, abstract and concrete, the doctrine of monads, and the pre-established harmony."

The second maintains: "For my part I will endeavor to give him a sense of justice, and to make him worthy of the friendship of good men." The second teacher is the agent of progress and the voice of enlightenment, for he sees education as a total undertaking, as a moral enterprise, rather than as an isolated activity.

There is a need for a change of values in our system of education. Instead of buildings, we should stress great teachers and great administrators; instead of equipment, we should be concerned with motivation; instead of quantitative tests, we should be concerned with qualitative achievement; instead of a curriculum dedicated to the past, our studies should be based upon the great books and great ideas of the present.

American education has passed through five main phases: The first was a religious phase dominated by Puritanism; theology occupied the center of the curriculum. The second was social and political, in the era of Jefferson. The third was literary, in the time of Emerson and the transcendentalists. The fourth was scientific, and arose through the stimulation of the pragmatists. Since the 1930's, we have been in the fifth period, which is eclectic and which has been characterized by timidity and lack of the experimental spirit.

We can only hope that we may move into a genuine creative phase of education. How can this be accomplished? What methods should be used? What should be our main concerns? We must become conscious of the main elements of creativity. It is not a process reserved for the few, the elite; rather it can be found in art as well as in science, in human relations as well as in statesmanship. Creativity represents an attempt to live life on a qualitative level; to become intense and awakened.

Creativity starts with self-definition. We do not merely want to exist, we want to live on a higher plane. Atmosphere is all important, as the Renaissance experience indicates. An environment of stimulation develops concern and concentration among students.

Discipline is a basic element in unique achievement, for without it we do not accomplish our goal. Contemplation, likewise, is an important attitude, for it is an antidote to an over-emphasis upon subjectivity. In the final stage of creativity we experience almost a mystical element; we

feel a sense of identification and union with the problem we are studying; at the same time, we realize the incompleteness of our researches.

Are our schools and universities truly creative centers of study? Are
they producing enlightened individuals? Are they creating a rational society? Are they developing a great culture? The answer cannot be entirely positive. Part of the failure is due largely to an atmosphere of indifference and specialization, and it is caused by the fact that our schools are
dominated by technicians.

The aim of education is enlightenment. To accomplish this objective a creative and dedicated minority has to be developed; concurrently,
an appreciative audience is needed for culture to progress. The *liberal
arts* must be the center of the curriculum; not all subjects have the same
educative value. Just as an individual should have an essential self, what
the Indians call the *Atman,* education needs a core—the liberal arts—
those studies which truly humanize and enlighten.

We must supplement Dewey's emphasis on the scientific method by
a stress on intuition. Intuition does not refer to a vague feeling, but to insight disciplined by reason. Knowledge rises from sensation to reason, to
antecedent intuition, and then to consequent intuition; all the time we
have to be guided by scientific evidence and by an attitude of fallibilism,
which means that our theories are not final statements of truth.

Our concept of education must be based on an *existential* viewpoint.
Education is an intimate process between student, teacher, and knowledge,
a process of inter-stimulation. It demands liberation of our subconscious
powers. While the objective part of education—scientific measurement—
is significant, the subjective part—motivational growth—is more basic.
Education is truly important when it creates an internal change in the
student which is comparable to a religious experience.

We must agree with Karl Jaspers that philosophy is not an external
activity but an attitude of dissatisfaction with any attempt to categorize
knowledge and ideas. As Jaspers remarked so eloquently: "The only significant content of philosophizing consists in the impulses, the inner constitution, the way of seeing and judging, the readiness to react by making choices, the immersion in historical presentness, which grow in us,
recognize themselves, and feel confirmed on the way past all objective
contents." Objectivity in philosophy thus becomes a prelude to subjective involvement.

We must have greater regard than Dewey for metaphysics, which is
not a science, but a form of cosmic poetry. Man, as a metaphysical animal, wants to go beyond the present and the foreground, and seeks a
perennial perspective. Pragmatic ideals thus are supplemented by a
mystical perspective.

At the same time, man remains a pleasure-loving creature; hence,
enjoyment should be basic in the curriculum. We repeat what pleases us.

Pain and negative incentives have no genuine educative functions. However, pleasure is not a final attainment, but a process which is the accompaniment of meaningful activity. The greatest pleasure lies in an expansion of sensitivity so that the distance between the ego and the non-ego, between man and nature, is overcome.

The fine arts must be the central core in knowledge; here again, our viewpoint must differ from Dewey's. Not all arts are on the same plane, and contact with poetry, literature, painting, and music creates a feeling of sublimity. Art must become a way of life and not be an activity confined to the elite. The basic problem of art and morality is the same: How can we create awareness, and awareness of awareness? How can we actualize the spark which is within us?

Dewey's standpoint that education simply is growth is inadequate. We need tentative affirmations, such as humanitarianism and the need for enlightenment. Intellectual growth without moral maturity may be a doubtful good. Education is a process of *universalization,* both on the emotional and intellectual plane.

All this should not detract from the permanent contributions of Dewey, who demonstrated in a most brilliant way the equivalence of philosophy and education. But we may differ from Dewey as Dewey differed from James. Let our philosophy be a romantic version of pragmatism. Let it be based on the centrality of the teacher and unwavering humanitarianism. Let it be existential rather than methodological, affirming an optimistic philosophy of life.

THE NEW EDUCATION

Psychiatric insight indicates that a reconstruction is needed in our concept of educational processes. This implies a reformulation of our views regarding the nature of intelligence. We realize today that intelligence is not a composition of abstract capacities, but that it is connected with moods, intuitions, and motivation. Bergson, the noted French philosopher, indicates that behind all of life is a vital drive—the *élan vital.* This idea can be applied to intelligence, for it is determined largely by emotional factors. Intelligent living implies capacity to change, to re-examine attitudes.

The most pernicious aspect of this process is preoccupation with the past, which results in a dogmatic attitude, and thus we disregard the possibilities of the present. Materialism likewise is a constant road block, for ultimately education is a spiritual process. It goes beyond technology; it transcends sensate satisfaction; it views life and man under the aspect of totality.

Likewise, authoritarianism is dangerous; it inhibits and limits inquiry. The teacher is not an absolute guide but a fellow pilgrim.

Another insidious enemy is the ritualistic element of education which creates enormous boredom. Education must create genuine excitement and genuine drama, for the teacher is, in effect, the dramatist of ideas. A staid and smug attitude in education only means a return to medieval standards.

We create too many iron curtains in education. Let us realize that the educative process is one process. Just as life consists of actually no levels, no departments, so education, too, is a total undertaking. The more we transcend specific subject matter, the more we develop mutuality, the more enlightened we become.

Education primarily is a vision of intangibles. Behind every fundamental advance is a soul-searching question. The order which we impose upon life and the categories which we use in our concept of knowledge are only postulates, not signposts of reality. Methodology has value as a means of clarification both on the semantic and the empirical plane, but it is not a substitute for basic ideas and basic analysis.

The fundamental problem of education is the problem of life. Education, to use the German terms, depends upon *Lebensanschauung* (life view) more than on *Weltanschauung* (world view). The task of the teacher is not merely to transmit knowledge, but to create an awareness of the possibilities of life. As human beings, all of us have essential encounters. We must answer such questions as: What is my essential self? What is my vocation? What is my relationship to my fellowman? What is my road to happiness? One may object that most individuals are condemned to live in a cave of egocentricity and tribalism, but this is a very despairing view of life and education. The eternal hope of education is to broaden our vision so that we move from the self to society and ultimately to the universe. Education and philosophy have the same goal: They both aim at our liberation from pettiness and superficiality; they are both protests against tribalism and the irrational way of life. They both depend not merely on theory, but on application. Merely to describe the universe, or to analyze Utopia, is inadequate; what matters is how fruitful our ideas are in practice.

Without a basic simplicity, the educational process will be a failure. The wise man knows his limitations; he also knows, like Thoreau, about the things he can do without. Yet our economic processes in the West constantly create new desires which cannot be satisfied. We want more technology, more conveniences, and more comforts; still we do not find fulfillment. The more we attain, the more dissatisfied we are, and, like Faust, we are tormented by doubts and by inner dissatisfactions.

We maintain that we must educate the whole man, which in some cases may mean organized superficiality. What is of equal significance is stress on a few central values and development of *intensity* of concern. For example, if we are interested in intellectual matters, we usually will not be too concerned with athletics, and if we surpass in science we may be less skilled in art. "One world at a time" was the advice which Thoreau gave to his disciples, and this view should be applied to education.

Practically, this means we should teach less and teach it more profoundly. Instead of encouraging dilettantes, we should stress basic capabilities. What the student learns himself has supreme value. Genius itself is a state of exaggeration whereby we deliberately concentrate upon one aspect of the problem. Thus, Kant saw life in an epistemological light; St. Augustine saw education and the universe through a religious perspective; and Dewey stressed the scientific method as man's greatest good.

This does not imply an encouragement of excessive specialization, for the more we become conscious of facts the more we realize their interrelationships. To excel in one field of knowledge is a necessity for a creative person; at the same time, we should keep an open perspective so that we may avoid intellectual isolationism. The more we cultivate a capacity for learning, the more our existence becomes an adventure in wisdom and in human relations. We can teach only what we feel intensely, what matters to us in our quest for enlightenment.

Still, many teachers have reached premature certainty, and they have the illusion of knowledge when it is mere pretension. On the lower level, the teacher tends to be preoccupied with methodology and an activistic life. On the higher level, teachers tend to be concerned with minute research and insignificant footnotes. The tragedy is that both types lack imagination; to them the educative process has become stereotyped. They have lost the spark, the curiosity, and the enthusiasm without which education becomes a form of empty scholasticism.

REFORMS

The educational philosophy that we have thus professed may have utopian tendencies. However, as we anticipate the world of our dreams, we transform reality. Without a bold vision education becomes a drab undertaking. But dreams must be illuminated by a vivid sense of actuality. The great educators, like Pestalozzi and Froebel, have usually been men of hope and action. They stressed the infinite capacities of human beings; they affirmed that all of us have a creative spark; and at the same time they gave a concrete embodiment to their dreams.

It would be a tragic mistake to model our educational plans upon the Russian example. This would indicate an extraordinary lack of creativity on our part. Certainly, the Russian challenge should not be taken lightly, but we must not forget that the essential goal of Russian society is divergent from ours. Russia aims to create a closed society in which the individual is submerged to the mass; our goal is to create a dynamic society in which independent thinking is treasured and in which the sovereignty of the individual is cherished.

GOALS. To accomplish this goal certain tangible steps should be taken. Mankind's foremost need is survival. This implies, one, that educators everywhere have the obligation to stress a better understanding of other cultures. A world university would be a tangible contribution to the promotion of peace. In such a center, artists, scientists, philosophers, theologians, and educators could work together to find unity amidst diversity, and diversity amidst unity. In our time, understanding and compassion are moral imperatives, and ignorance and bias are aspects of immorality.

Two, we should try to overcome the gulf between our educational centers and society. Knowledge must be lived and applied. Culture is not a luxury but a necessity. This demands a far better utilization of artists, scientists, businessmen, and statesmen, who should take an active part in the educative process. Adult education is especially significant in our period, and it should stress the art of human relations as well as personal and social creativity.

Three, we should welcome the expansion of education which we shall witness in our time. The prophets of despair say that only fifteen per cent of our population can benefit from higher education; these prophets are profoundly wrong. Eventually, as many will attend college as are attending high school today; this represents a real opportunity to create a vast audience for culture and abundant living. Let us realize, however, that mere attendance is inadequate; real education demands intensity, enthusiasm, and discipline.

Four, we allow too much lethargy on all levels of education. There should be an intensive emphasis upon the foundations of perception. This means more stress upon esthetic appreciation, scientific awareness, and memory training.

The more the student becomes aware of his own powers the more he will appreciate his educational experience. In this way objective facts become part of his subjective development. As Thoreau remarked so cogently: "No method nor discipline can supersede the necessity for being forever on the alert." Above all, we should remember that we learn more by creative thinking than by uninspired doing.

Five, in an age of profound anxiety we need thousands of skilled counselors with warm personalities to diagnose the students' needs, as a physician diagnoses the ills of a patient. Counseling should create a close contact between school and home so that delinquency can be curbed. All this will be costly, but ultimately we will save millions of dollars in a reduced bill for crime and mental illness. The new concept of the school is that of a therapeutic as well as an educational center.

Six, we should pioneer in the development of real leadership. The advancement of civilization depends on the inspiration of the few as well as the appreciation of the many. Let those who show special talent in the various disciplines attend school before college for ten years, and college for three years, and obtain a Ph.D. within two years after graduation. Let them enter the professions when they are young and vital, and they will be truly creative. They may lack somewhat in social adjustment; however, would it not be better for our society to produce more *dissatisfied Einsteins* rather than *satisfied Babbitts?*

Seven, we need educated followers as well as educated leaders. As in religion, verbal allegiance to ideals is secondary; what matters most is practice. For the student, this means great stress upon reading good books, appreciating good music, and being intense about great art. In this respect television offers unlimited opportunities; it can make education live and show the vitality of ideas. Education without drama becomes an exercise in repetition; as the dramatist of ideas, the function of the teacher is to show that the life of reason can be as exciting as the life of the senses.

Eight, there should be far closer contact between the various levels of education. Snobbery and traditionalism are needless roadblocks. Education has pluralistic manifestations, but its essence is monistic. We can all learn from each other. Thus, an interchange of instructors on all levels would make the educative process more dynamic.

Nine, our worst mistake has been to under-educate our students. Let them do more independent work, especially independent reading; let them write deep dramas, compose important poetry; let them develop profound philosophical themes. Let them pioneer in the art of human relations, especially in trying to solve the delinquency problem. Let our campuses become truly creative centers where inspiring artists and scientists are in residence. Let education be an exciting process which starts at birth and ends with the grave, and then we shall have a new culture.

Ten, there is an urgent need for intensification for our capable students. We must teach in junior high what we teach in high school; in high school partly what we teach in college, and in college part of the material we absorb in graduate school. New super-graduate centers should be established to rival Plato's Academy in intellectual vitality.

The teacher needs not just spiritual rewards. His efforts should be recognized in tangible ways. The more we advance the profession in material ways, the more we shall contribute to our society. As a leader, the teacher's function is to inspire and to point the path to a limitless future. Mankind will experience either greatness or oblivion. We shall have true greatness when education becomes something more than a ritual or tribal conditioning; when it will be an activity which attracts the most dedicated and the most idealistic students, and when it will become a way of life.

The skeptic may question the feasibility of such goals in a utilitarian society, guided by the drive for success and conformity. But there are precedents which prove that these quests are not unreasonable. Athens demonstrated how a city state could be changed through the influence of great teachers, like Socrates, Plato, and Aristotle, and how the life of reason can create a permanent contribution to culture.

We have far more scientific resources than Athens; we have a more highly developed system of technology; all we need is a change of values so that reason rather than emotion, the arts rather than business, become the center of our strivings. History demonstrates the perennial vitality of dreams and visions, for without them we succumb to the expediency of the moment. History demonstrates that a real renaissance is possible if we have the intelligence, the creativity, and the enthusiasm to live up to our ideals and to make education the center of the twentieth century. History demonstrates that dedication to education is man's highest good, for it overcomes the barriers between individuals and nations and points the way to a lasting peace.

QUESTIONS FOR DISCUSSION AND INVESTIGATION

1. What two extreme attitudes should be avoided in American educational philosophy?

2. Discuss the conflict between two types of philosophy that have persisted throughout American history.

3. How may a Buddhist saint's world view be incorporated into Western education?

4. What fundamental changes should be made in the value system of American society?

5. Delineate the five prominent phases through which American education has passed.

6. How may the goal of enlightenment be achieved in American education?

7. Describe the aims and advantages of the 'new education.'

8. What are to be the tangible steps toward the goal of a dynamic society in which independent thinking is treasured and in which the sovereignty of the individual is cherished?

9. Why is the fundamental problem of education also the fundamental problem of life?

10. In what ways may education develop the foundations of a peaceful world?

Chapter 38

In Defense
of American Education

Recently, I asked my students to write an essay about the outstanding contributions of American civilization. One student wrote that he thought our most significant achievement was in the field of technology. Another class member said our greatest contribution was our high standard of living. A third maintained that our most formidable attainment was our system of democracy. And then, one student remarked that our foremost contribution was our system of public education. He was right. In time, when historians will survey our civilization, as we today survey Rome, Greece, and Alexandria, they probably will regard education as America's main distinction. This should not make us arrogant, because the basic spirit of education has to be a spirit of humility. We become wise, not as we imitate the past, but as we live for the future. Receptivity to new ideas which anticipate the future is one of the distinctive traits of American education.

We are living in a period of crisis and opportunity. The competition which we are facing internationally is extremely severe. We must be first-rate because we are somewhat in the same position as George Bernard Shaw, who, when at seventy he was asked how he felt, said, "Sir, at my age you either feel great or not at all."

To understand the importance of American education, let us look at its historical background for a moment. It is based upon the insights of men like Thomas Jefferson. This man was proud, not so much of his political achievements, but of his part in the establishment of the University of Virginia and of his fight for separation of state and church throughout the United States. Jefferson, even in his seventies, would ride ten miles a day on horseback so that he could fulfill his duties as rector of the University of Virginia. His office was always open, to faculty members as well as to freshmen. There was no stuffiness in him. He was a constant student. At the age of fifteen he had read more profound books than many contemporary leaders of American civilization. Already at that age he had mastered Aristotle and Plato, he had read Voltaire and Erasmus, and he was imbued with the spirit of philosophy.

Jefferson believed that man must live with insistent awareness of the present and that he must use the resources of reason. In a letter he said that a democracy that expects to live must cultivate education. And what did education mean to Jefferson? It meant a stress upon the humanities and the sciences, it meant *the forward look*. It meant a cultivation of freedom as an absolute good.

Jefferson maintained that there are two main guides for mankind: Jesus and Epicurus. Jesus, because he taught us how to live profoundly, and Epicurus, because he taught us that the most important pleasure is that of the mind. These and other beliefs brought forth many vigorous attacks on Jefferson by his contemporaries, attacks that awarded him such labels as "atheist" and "perverter of morality." But his beliefs and his faith have survived these attacks and have become part of our heritage.

Another pioneer in education was Horace Mann. He was a lawyer, who gave up law because, as he said, "his client was humanity." When he started his labors, the school system was extremely inadequate. Pay-rates for teachers were worse than in our own period. Professional preparation was on a very low level.

Mann traveled throughout New England and lectured; often he spoke for only five dollars a night; once he even swept out the lecture hall. Wherever he went, he radiated this conviction that education was man's greatest good. He entered Congress in 1848, and he later became president of Antioch College. In the latter capacity, he tolerated no social or racial distinctions. In a speech, which has now become part of our educational history, he said to students and to teachers: "Be ashamed to die until you have won a victory for humanity." Should this not be the slogan for education in our own time?

CRITICISM

Ours is a period of vigorous criticism of education. Suddenly we have a group of new experts; among them we find admirals, beauticians, and even morticians. After having taught for some years, I still do not know very much about education. I think that intimate acquaintance with education on every level is necessary in order that one may develop tentative theories, tentative ideals, and tentative goals. Part of the criticism in our time is simply based on ignorance. There are some who feel that we can have cut-rate education. For example, near our community, we had a bond election, and the opponents—some of them were conscientious objectors to the twentieth century—claimed that they were opposed to frills. One of the frills apparently was the school nurse. Another frill was the guidance officer. They felt that guidance was an unnecessary part of modern education. One elderly citizen said that, when he was a young boy, he walked ten or fifteen miles to school, so why should modern children have school buses? The newspaper editor, also an "expert" on education, had never really visited a public school, since his own children were brought up in a private school. In an editorial he advised the people to go back to fundamentals. The community followed his advice. The bond election was lost. Since then, delinquency has increased considerably in that community. The lesson is clear: Whenever we try to save money in education, we inevitably spend ten times as much for crime, delinquency, and organized and unorganized neurotics.

Now there are some who remark that private schools are much superior; they feel that America can be saved through a return to the three R's. I believe that some private schools are excellent, but I know of others that are only preludes to the country club, that produce nothing but snobs, and that tend to develop rigid class barriers. One of the foremost aspects of public education is its development of interstimulation and interchange of ideas. To make the matter more concrete, recently, Princeton conducted a survey which compared public school graduates and private school graduates. The survey indicated that in almost every case the public school graduates were superior, for they were yearning for knowledge, whereas some of the private school graduates were only intent upon joining clubs and making "the right social connections."

There are some other critics of education today who feel that our standards are lower than they were a hundred years ago. Again, they are wrong. They should read history. This does not mean that our standards are high enough, but certainly we have advanced quantitatively and qualitatively in the last hundred years.

Today almost every newspaper editorial mentions the competition of Russian education. Let us analyze, for a moment, both the advantages and disadvantages of Russian education. Through extreme rigor they have almost wiped out illiteracy. As we know, the Russian teacher occupies a high place. Russian achievements in technology and science are not to be underestimated. Their language training is excellent. Russian diplomats, who tend to be less stuffy than their Western colleagues, usually know the language of the country in which they are stationed.

But ultimately, our system of education is far superior. It is superior because it is based upon individuality. It is superior because it centers less upon standards. It is superior because it expresses the spirit of democracy.

In the future, there will be far more opposition to the Russian system of thought control than we have experienced at the present time. I have been especially interested in two novels: *Not By Bread Alone* and *Dr. Zhivago.* In *Not By Bread Alone,* the main character is constantly fighting a war against bureaucracy. In Pasternak's novel, the importance of the individual is asserted; the individual must constantly re-evaluate his ideas and loyalties. Pasternak claims that there can be no general truth and that there can be no subordination of the individual to an abstract concept of life. What matters is the uniqueness of life based upon an existential faith which no party nor institution can give to us.

ALTERNATIVES

As we look at the future, we have three alternatives. One alternative is to adopt some of the ideas suggested by Rickover, Bestor, and Mortimer Smith. This alternative would be a prelude to rigidity. For example, not so long ago an article by Mortimer Smith, published in one of our major magazines, attacked some of the most dedicated educators of our generation. Smith championed the idea, based upon incorrect facts, that we can have a great educational system by a magic formula: a return to tradition. Certainly, we cannot return to the traditional curriculum just as we cannot return to the Model T Ford.

The second alternative is to continue the status quo, and this, too, is not a sound program. What distresses me most today—and this goes for almost all parts of our civilization—is the feeling of lethargy and indifference found everywhere, the feeling of intent mainly upon respectability. There is far too much stuffiness and tiredness in the world today. Voltaire one time was asked by an actress how she should act. He said to her, "Mademoiselle, you should act just as though the devil were within you." This is also excellent advice for teachers.

In one of the memorable plays of our time, *Our Town,* the central character returns to earth in the third act. She wants to relive part of her life, although she is warned against it. The day goes by, rather uneventful, dominated by routine. She sees her parents and her community again. It strikes her that we waste time, that we misuse the best moments of our life in triviality and routine. Then she goes back to the other world and asks, "Who really lives profoundly?" The answer is: "Saints and poets." I would add "teachers." Is it not their privilege to see young people develop, to stir them, and to intensify their motivations? Thus, the third alternative is creative teaching through which students unfold in the classroom. I can think of one of my students as a freshman. She was a replica of middletown, a product of what Sinclair Lewis described in *Babbitt*. She called Plato—Pluto. Her spelling was atrocious. Her first test was chaos roughly organized. Her taste in music was influenced by Elvis Presley. Three years later she is reading Kafka, Thomas Mann, and Gide. She has just written a superb essay on Albert Camus. We started an experimental class of having freshmen taught by juniors and seniors, and she is an assistant teacher. These freshmen, mainly because of her influence, are more alert, more interesting, and more vital than many of our graduate students. She is a different person today—alive, vibrant, idealistic. Her progress is an excellent example of what education can do.

A PROGRAM OF ACTION

The real pleasures of education are intangible. Once a friend of mine, who had suffered a heart attack, called me to his office and said to me, "I know that my days are numbered. Will you take my class?" And this I did. He passed away two days later. Then I went through his books and some of his letters and a few of his manuscripts. It occurred to me that it was such a waste that he had died too soon.

Accidentally, I came across a note written by one of his former students, who remarked how he had at first found no purpose in life. He had lived what Thoreau called an existence of quiet desperation; after graduating from college he had become a salesman, and then, after talking to my friend, he had become a teacher. The student ended the letter by saying, "I can never repay you. I can never tell you how much I owe to you. I only hope that I can live up to your spirit."

I realized that my friend had lived gloriously, that he had overcome the boundaries of mortality because he had believed in education, and because he had demonstrated the possibilities of knowledge.

IMPROVEMENTS. In a more concrete way, I would like to outline a tentative program which can improve our system of education. Merely to defend our system is not enough. As Whitehead remarked in the *Aims of Education,* knowledge must appeal to the imagination; it must constantly be redefined so that we can achieve true and lasting greatness. First, I would like to suggest a far more imaginative program for our gifted students. Today we are wasting to a great extent the resources of youth. We are wasting them especially in graduate school because young people who emerge from graduate school are often tired; they have written too many unimportant dissertations upon minor subjects, and they have taken too many uninspiring classes.

When Woodrow Wilson became president of Princeton University, he shocked his contemporaries by hiring fifty young instructors; his colleagues felt that they were immature. But Wilson changed Princeton once and for all. It became a vigorous institution, so vigorous in fact that an alumnus wrote to Wilson saying, "Dear Sir, I object; you're trying to make an educational institution out of my dear old alma mater."

Today, especially in science, some of the most important discoveries are being made by very young men and women. There is no substitute for the vigor of youth. Still, we should remember that youth is a state of perception and expectancy. I have found some individuals at sixty who had more young ideas than young people at twenty and twenty-five.

The second point relates to maturity. In our civilization many individuals go through four stages—pre-adolescence, adolescence, post-adolescence, and senility. A sociologist, not too long ago, declared that adolescence should be extended up to the age of forty-five. He must have had many followers. Undoubtedly, we underestimate the capacities of our students who can do far more at an earlier age. At the same time, we are not taking advantage of the resources of maturity. Today, a man or woman at the age of sixty is not old. This means that we must re-examine our policy of retirement. Some schools, like Hastings Law School, have developed an amazing reputation by hiring retired instructors. At an eastern university a famous professor of education was forced to retire at the age of sixty-five; he is still going strong in his eighties. However, the president of his institution would not retire, although he was stuffy even in his forties. There is a need for re-evaluation of our concept of age. Furthermore, we need more respect for maturity. In our classroom we should never tolerate disrespect because the student who has no regard for the teacher will have no respect for parents, and he will have no understanding of the intangible values upon which civilization rests.

The third point is that we need a new group of master teachers. We always claim that we value the classroom teacher, but a teacher on the primary level may earn as little as $3,000 a year. Why should not a great teacher on the primary or secondary level earn as much as $20,000 a year? If this may sound Utopian, let us remember that there is no more important person than a great classroom teacher. He is the foundation of our system. He is our hope; he represents the fulfillment of our dreams.

The next point is that we must overcome the isolation of the various levels of education. I noticed, for example, while attending conferences of philosophers—which often remind me of conferences of morticians—that professors from eastern universities will look down on midwestern universities, and instructors from midwestern universities will look down on western colleges, and professors from western centers of higher learning look down on junior college instructors.

One of my students last summer was a primary teacher and she said, "I like your ideas, I am really enthusiastic, but I only teach the third grade." I remarked to her, "Young lady, you are far more important than I am because you can reach children in the most impressionable stage of their development."

Every level is equally important. The time has to come—and it should come very soon—when we will have an active interchange of instructors on every level. We must make our schools more personable. Often, when I visit a school, an administrator will say, "Here's our gymnasium, here's our administration building, here's a new science building." But this does not impress me. What he should say is, "We have a great science teacher, and a teacher who dramatizes history." Education, we must remember, is an existential process. It demands a vivid and intense relation between teacher and student. Buildings are of secondary importance.

The next point is that we need, in this period of crisis, a gigantic recruitment drive, for we are losing over a hundred thousand teachers a year. The teaching profession must be glamorized and must be made truly dramatic. We need the co-operation of television, the motion picture industry, advertising, and indeed of all the agencies of communication to indicate the importance of American schools. Furthermore, just as American doctors are represented by one organization, and just as American lawyers are represented by the Bar Association, so we must develop one powerful national organization, like the CTA, to represent all teachers. We must work together and stand together. In unity lies our hope for advancement.

Our responsibilities today extend not only to this nation, but to all of civilization. The issue is *how shall we live:* Shall we live by fear in a cynical atmosphere of mediocrity and conformity or shall we live in an environment of openness? Shall we live with a stress upon ideas and ideals? Our aim must be ambitious, for our goal is not only to teach ideas, but to exemplify a way of life. Education is the quality of relatedness. American education is the result of a creative dream that man can live with charity and understanding, that he can be great if he cultivates reason and wisdom and if he lives not only for today, but for the day after tomorrow.

QUESTIONS FOR DISCUSSION AND INVESTIGATION

1. Why may education be America's most important contribution to civilization?

2. According to Jefferson who are the two main guides of mankind?

3. What are the main criticisms of American education?

4. Evaluate contemporary Russian education.

5. What is the significance of *Dr. Zhivago*?

6. What are the three alternatives of American education?

7. How can education overcome the sense of quiet desperation described by Thoreau?

8. What are the intangible pleasures of education?

9. What are the author's suggestions for the improvement of education?

10. Why is authentic education an existential process?

Glossary
Bibliography
Illustration Credits
Index

Glossary

Absolute: A term used to describe anything which is unconditioned and self-caused.

Altruism: A stress upon the benevolent aspects of man.

Anthropomorphic: Refers to the habit of describing God in human terms. This view was criticized most brilliantly by the Greek thinker Xenophanes.

Antinomy: Implies that two contradictory statements can both be valid. This concept was used by Kant in his discussion of the universe. For example, Kant believed that with equal validity we can assert that the universe is caused and uncaused.

A posteriori: That which comes after experience.

A priori: That which comes before experience.

Atman: Man's essential self in the *Upanishads*. While the empirical self is changing, atman remains forever the same.

Augustinianism: Refers to the philosophy of St. Augustine who stressed the all-powerful nature of God and man's original sin. He believed that outside of the Church there was no salvation. He developed the doctrine of predestination.

Authoritarianism: A stress upon an absolute standard of belief. In education, it opposes all progressive tendencies.

Axiology: Refers to the systematic study of values.

Behaviorism: A school of psychology which is based on a physiological interpretation of behavior.

Brahma: A God in Hinduism; also refers to the personal form of the world soul.

Brahman: The impersonal essence of the universe; also describes a priest.

Calvinism: The philosophy of Calvin who believed in the absolute nature of God and the sinfulness of man. Calvin's main work was *The Institutes of the Christian Religion*.

Catharsis: Derived from the Greek word *katharsis* meaning purgation. This term was used by Aristotle to describe the purgative impact of drama upon the viewer.

Cosmology: An aspect of metaphysics which deals with the nature of the universe.

Cyrenaicism: A school of philosophy which stresses physical pleasure.

Deduction: The process of reasoning from assumed premises. Aristotelian logic is deductive, while Sir Francis Bacon used inductive logic (reasoning from particulars).

Deism: A religious philosophy which stresses reason and which is opposed to superstition. Eighteenth century Deists, like Voltaire and Paine, wanted to establish a religion based upon scientific enlightenment.

Determinism: The view that all relationships in the universe are governed by laws—physical or psychic.

Dialectic: Refers to a thorough examination of the foundations of knowledge and finding truth through a combination of opposing statements. Dialectic reasoning was used by Hegel to indicate the triadic nature of truth. According to Hegel, knowledge implies (1) *thesis,* affirmation, (2) *antithesis,* or negation, and (3) *synthesis,* or a combination of previous ideas in a higher unity.

Dogmatism: The habit of basing ideas upon authoritarian standards.

Eclecticism: Derived from the Greek *ek-lego,* select. Refers to a combination of various philosophical standpoints.

Empathy: A feeling of sympathetic understanding and identification.

Empiricism: Emphasis upon sense experience as the foundation of philosophic inquiry. Locke gave a classic formulation of this view.

Epicureanism: The view that pleasure is the highest good. The most important pleasure is that of the mind.

Essentialism: An educational philosophy which stresses authority and formal standards.

Existentialism: A school of philosophy connected with individuals like Kierkegaard, Jaspers, Heidegger, and Sartre which stresses indeterminism, intuition, and the personal approach to philosophy. To most existentialists, man is the center of the universe. In education, existentialism stresses the personal relationship between teacher and student.

Formalism: The belief in an absolute principle of ethics.

Genetic: Refers to the beginning of an idea or movement.

Gestalt psychology: A school of psychology which stresses the pattern and wholeness of experience.

Hedonism: The view that all human actions are guided by pleasure. Two types of hedonism should be distinguished: (a) *ethical* hedonism, which maintains that pleasure is man's supreme value; and (b) *psychological* hedonism, which asserts that our conduct is determined by the pleasure principle.

Humanism: A term which implies a stress upon man and his capacities. In education, humanists oppose all forms of dogmatism and they uphold the separation of state and church.

Idealism: In a popular sense, faith in the moral quality of the universe. Philosophically, it implies the view that the world depends on man's perception and that the universe has a spiritual purpose. In education, idealism usually champions the authority of the teacher and stresses the importance of formal standards (Horne, Croce).

Instrumentalism: Dewey's concept of pragmatism which emphasizes the importance of scientific verification and that ideas should clarify social issues.

Intuition: A supra-rational approach to truth based upon a spontaneous apperception of reality. This view is especially important in Bergson's philosophy.

Logic: The study of the principles of reasoning.

Machiavellianism: The view of Machiavelli that might makes right and that the end justifies the means. In politics, it stands for expediency.

Materialism: The view that matter is the basic reality. Hobbes reduced nature to matter and motion. Modern materialism was represented by Marx, who championed a theory of economic determinism and who wanted to change the conditions and structure of society.

Maya: A term in Indian philosophy which means illusion, anything which obscures reality.

Meliorism: A concept which tries to find a middle ground between optimism and pessimism. It holds that life is neither good nor bad, but can be improved through concerted efforts.

Metaphysics: A study of reality. Its branches are ontology and cosmology.

Modernism: A view in theology which tries to interpret religion according to scientific evidence. The modernist looks upon dogma as an expression of spiritual truth.

Mysticism: The view that reality can only be achieved through reliance upon intuition and that man's individuality is to be transcended.

Naturalism: The concept which regards nature as the criterion of values and as the standard of measurement. Rejects a supernatural or mystical concept of life.

Neo-Platonism: A school of philosophy founded by Plotinus who believed that reality is ineffable and that evil is unreal.

Nominalism: Stresses the reality of individual things.

Noumenon: Stands for the unconditioned, the thing-in-itself.

Pantheism: The belief that God and nature are one. Its classic formulation can be found in Spinoza's *Ethics*.

Personalism: A school of philosophy which believes that the universe is spiritual and that reality can only be found through a personal communion with God.

Phenomenalism: The concept that we can know only appearance and that our knowledge is limited.

Pietism: Religion based upon emotion.

Polytheism: Faith in many gods.

Positivism: Represents an attempt to reduce philosophy to a scientific basis. Comte believed that humanity passed through three stages: (1) a theological phase, (2) a metaphysical stage, (3) a positive or scientific stage.

Pragmatism: Identified with the philosophy of James and Dewey who stressed the consequences of ideas and who opposed all forms of absolutism. Pragmatism attempts to humanize philosophy. In education, it stresses a child-centered approach and values the scientific method, which is to be applied to all aspects of life.

Puritanism: The view that man is sinful and that his physical drives should be curbed.

Realism: Has various meanings. In epistemology, it implies a stress upon universals. It is the doctrine that objects exist independently of the perceiver. In education, realists stress the importance of scientific measurement.

Reconstructionism: An educational philosophy developed by Brameld who believed in social reconstruction and utopianism.

Skepticism: An attitude of doubt regarding any dogmatic belief or any statement about reality.

Stoicism: The philosophy which stresses reason, resignation, and the curbing of emotions.

Summum bonum: Refers to the highest good.

Supernaturalism: This view affirms the reality of God and regards life as a preparation for existence in the beyond. It opposes all forms of naturalism.

Taoism: The philosophy of Laotse who objected to civilization and who urged a return to nature. Taoism stresses the power of intuition.

Teleology: The consideration of purposes.

Teleological argument: Tries to prove the existence of God through finding a design in the universe.

Theism: The concept that the world is ruled by a personal God.

Theology: The study of the nature and qualities of God.

Thomism: Refers to the view of Aquinas who tried to combine the teachings of Aristotle and those of the Church. His views became authoritative for Catholicism.

Transcendental: Refers to that which goes beyond sense experience.

Transvaluation of Values: Nietzsche's view that a new code of ethics is needed based upon man's quest for power.

Utilitarianism: The view that philosophy should lead to the greatest good for the greatest number. Proponents of this view were Mill, Bentham, and Spencer who were concerned mainly with problems of social philosophy.

Value: Refers to any quality which has significance.

Vitalism: The view that life can be understood only in qualitative terms and that it is the expression of an immaterial substance. Various names for this substance have been given, like *élan vital* and *vital principle.*

Voluntarism: An interpretation of philosophy which stresses the importance of the will as a cosmic and a personal force. This view dominated Schopenhauer's *World As Will and Idea.*

Wholistic: A view which stresses the unity of things.

Zen Buddhism: A version of Buddhism which emphasizes the simplicity of life and the spontaneous apprehension of nature.

Bibliography

Adamson, John William. *A Short History of Education*. New York: The Macmillan Company; 1920.

Adler, Mortimer J. *Art and Prudence*. New York: Longmans, Green & Company, Inc.; 1937.

Alexander, W. P. *Education in England*. New York: St. Martin's Press; 1954.

Apelt, Otto. *Platonische Aufsätze*. Leipzig: B. G. Teubner; 1912.

Aristotle. *Nicomachean Ethics*. Translated by James E. C. Welldon. New York: The Macmillan Company; 1927.

———. *Works*. Edited by Sir William Ross and John Alexander. London: Oxford University Press; 1908-31.

Bagley, William C. *Education and Emergent Man*. New York: Thomas Nelson & Sons; 1934.

Barth, Karl. *Against the Stream*. New York: Philosophical Library, Inc.; 1954.

Beard, Charles A. *The Economic Interpretation of the Constitution of the United States*. New York: The Macmillan Company; 1913.

Bellamy, Edward. *Looking Backward*. New York: Modern Library, Inc.; 1942.

Benne, Kenneth D. *A Conception of Authority*. New York: Columbia University Press; 1943.

Berdyaev, Nicolai. *Freedom and the Spirit*. London: G. Bles, The Centenary Press; 1935.

Berkson, I. B. *The Ideal and the Community*. New York: Harper & Brothers; 1958.

Blanshard, Brand, *et al. Philosophy in American Education*. New York: Harper & Brothers; 1945.

Bloch, Ernest. *Freiheit und Ordnung, Abriss der Sozial-Utopien*. New York: Aurora Verlag; 1946.

Bode, Boyd H. *Democracy as a Way of Life*. New York: The Macmillan Company; 1939.

———. *Modern Educational Theories*. New York: The Macmillan Company; 1927.

Bourne, Randolph. *Untimely Papers*. New York: B. W. Huebsch; 1919.

Boyd, W. *History of Western Education*. New York: The Macmillan Company; 1952.

Brameld, Theodore. *Philosophies of Education in Cultural Perspective*. New York: The Dryden Press; 1955.

Brickman, William W. (ed.). *Religion, Government and Education*. New York: Society for the Advancement of Education; 1961.

Bridgman, P. W. *The Logic of Modern Physics*. New York: The Macmillan Company; 1927.

Brubacher, John S. *A History of the Problems of Education*. New York: Mc-Graw-Hill Book Company; 1947.

———. *Modern Philosophies of Education*. (Second edition.) New York: Mc-Graw-Hill Book Company; 1950.

Butts, R. Freeman. *The American Tradition in Religion and Education*. Boston: The Beacon Press; 1950.

———. *A Cultural History of Education*. New York: McGraw-Hill Book Company; 1947.

Carr, Edward H. *The Soviet Impact on the Western World*. New York: The Macmillan Company; 1946.

Cassirer, Ernest. *An Essay on Man*. New Haven: Yale University Press; 1944.

Childs, John L. *Education and Morals*. New York: Appleton-Century-Crofts, Inc.; 1950.

Cohen, Morris R. *Reason and Nature*. New York: Harcourt, Brace and Company; 1931.

Cole, G. D. H. *A Century of British Cooperation*. London: George Allen & Unwin, Ltd.; 1944.

———. *Europe, Russia, and the Future*. New York: The Macmillan Company; 1942.

Cole, L. *Education from Socrates to Montessori*. New York: Rinehart and Company, Inc.; 1950.

Cremin, L. A. *The Transformation of the School*. New York: Alfred A. Knopf, Inc.; 1961.

Curti, Merle. *The Growth of American Thought*. New York: Harper & Brothers; 1943.

Dewey, John. *Art as Experience*. New York: Minton, Balch and Company; 1934.

———. *Characters and Events*. New York: Henry Holt and Company, Inc.; 1929.

———. *A Common Faith*. New Haven: Yale University Press; 1934.

———. *Democracy and Education*. New York: The Macmillan Company; 1916.

———. *Education Today*. New York: G. P. Putnam's Sons; 1940.

———. *Experience and Education*. New York: The Macmillan Company; 1938.

———. *Experience and Nature*. Chicago: Open Court Publishing Company; 1925.

———. *Human Nature and Conduct*. New York: Modern Library, Inc.; 1930.

———. *Interest and Effort in Education*. Boston: Houghton Mifflin Company; 1913.

————. *My Pedagogic Creed*. (Personal Growth Leaflet, No. 19) Washington, D. C.: National Education Association.

————. *The Quest for Certainty*. New York: Minton, Balch and Company; 1929.

————. *Reconstruction in Philosophy*. New York: Henry Holt and Company, Inc.; 1920.

Dobson, J. F. *Ancient Education and Its Meaning to Us*. New York: Longmans, Green and Company, Inc.; 1932.

Durost, Walter N. *Essentials of Measurement for Teachers*. New York: Harcourt, Brace and World, Inc.; 1962.

Eby, F. *Early Protestant Educators*. New York: McGraw-Hill Book Company; 1931.

Eliot, T. S. *The Idea of a Christian Society*. New York: The Macmillan Company; 1935.

Farrington, Benjamin. *Francis Bacon, Philosopher of Industrial Science*. New York: Henry Schuman, Inc.; 1949.

Frank, Jerome. *Fate and Freedom; a Philosophy for Free Americans*. New York: Simon & Schuster, Inc.; 1945.

Freud, Sigmund. *A General Introduction to Psychoanalysis*. New York: Liveright Publishing Corporation; 1920.

Geiger, George. *Philosophy and the Social Order*. Boston: Houghton Mifflin Company; 1947.

Gilson, Etienne. *The Spirit of Medieval Philosophy*. New York: Charles Scribner's Sons; 1937.

————. *The Unity of Philosophical Experience*. New York: Charles Scribner's Sons; 1937.

Hans, Nicholaus A. *New Trends in Education in the 18th Century*. New York: Grove Press, Inc.; 1951.

Hart, Joseph K. *Mind in Transition*. New York: Philosophical Library, Inc.; 1949.

Heidbreder, Edna. *Seven Psychologies*. New York: D. Appleton-Century Company, Inc.; 1933.

Henderson, Stella. *Introduction to Philosophy of Education*. Chicago: University of Chicago Press; 1947.

Herskovits, Melville. *Man and His Works*. New York: Alfred A. Knopf, Inc.; 1948.

Hertzler, Joyce O. *The History of Utopian Thought*. New York: The Macmillan Company; 1926.

Hook, Sidney. *Education for Modern Man*. New York: Alfred Knopf, Inc.; 1963.

Horne, Herman H. *The Democratic Philosophy of Education*. New York: The Macmillan Company; 1932.

————. *The Philosophy of Christian Education*. New York: Fleming H. Revell Company; 1937.

Horney, Karen. *The Neurotic Personality of Our Time*. New York: W. W. Norton and Company, Inc.; 1937.

Hoskheimer, Max. *The Eclipse of Reason*. New York: Oxford University Press; 1947.

Hutchins, Robert M. *Education for Freedom*. Baton Rouge: Louisiana State University Press; 1943.

————. *The Higher Learning in America*. New Haven: Yale University Press; 1936.

Huxley, Aldous. *The Perennial Philosophy*. New York: Harper and Brothers; 1945.

Huxley, Julian. *Man in the Modern World*. London: Chatto and Windus; 1947.

Jaeger, W. *Paideia: The Ideals of Greek Culture*. New York: Oxford University Press; 1939.

James, William. *The Meaning of Truth*. New York: Longmans, Green and Company, Inc.; 1909.

————. *Pragmatism*. Boston: Longmans, Green and Company, Inc.; 1907.

————. *The Principles of Psychology*. 2 vols. New York: Henry Holt and Company, Inc.; 1890.

————. *Talks to Teachers on Psychology*. New York: Henry Holt and Company, Inc.; 1900.

Jones, Howard Mumford. *Education and World Tragedy*. Cambridge: Harvard University Press; 1946.

Kallen, Horace M. *The Education of Free Men*. New York: Farrar, Straus & Co., Inc.; 1949.

Kilpatrick, William H. *Education and the Social Crisis*. New York: Liveright Publishing Corporation; 1932.

————. *Foundations of Method*. New York: The Macmillan Company; 1925.

Kneller, George F. (ed.). *Foundations of Education*. New York: John Wiley and Sons, Inc.; 1963.

Kohn, Hans. *The Idea of Nationalism; A Study in Its Origins and Background*. New York: The Macmillan Company; 1944.

Korzybski, Alfred. *Science and Sanity*. Lancaster: The Non-Aristotelian Library Publishing Company; 1933.

Lamprecht, Karl. *What is History?* New York: The Macmillan Company; 1905.

Langford, Howard D. *Education and the Social Conflict*. New York: The Macmillan Company; 1936.

Laski, Harold. *The American Democracy*. New York: The Viking Press, Inc.; 1948.

Lauterpacht, H. *An International Bill of the Rights of Man*. New York: Columbia University Press; 1947.

Lewin, Kurt. *A Dynamic Theory of Personality*. New York: McGraw-Hill Book Company; 1935.

Lindsay, A. D. *The Essentials of Democracy*. New York: Oxford University Press; 1935.

————. *The Modern Democratic State*. New York: Oxford University Press; 1943.

Livingstone, Richard. *On Education*. New York: The Macmillan Company; 1944.

Lodge, Rupert. *Philosophy of Education*. New York: Harper and Brothers; 1947.

Lovejoy, Arthur O. *The Revolt against Dualism*. Chicago: Open Court Publishing Company; 1930.

Lynd, Robert S. *Knowledge for What?* Princeton: Princeton University Press; 1939.

Madden, Edward H. *Philosophical Problems of Psychology*. New York: The Odyssey Press, Inc.; 1962.

Malinowski, Bronislaw. *Freedom and Civilization*. New York: Roy Publishers; 1944.

Mannheim, Karl. *Diagnosis of Our Time*. London: Kegan Paul, Trench, Trubner and Company, Ltd.; 1946.

——. *Ideology and Utopia*. New York: Harcourt, Brace and Company; 1936.

——. *Man and Society in an Age of Reconstruction*. New York: Harcourt, Brace and Company; 1936.

Maritain, Jacques. *Art and Poetry*. New York: Philosophical Library, Inc.; 1943.

——. *Art and Scholasticism*. New York: Charles Scribner's Sons; 1933.

——. *Christianity and Democracy*. New York: Charles Scribner's Sons; 1945.

——. *Education at the Crossroads*. New Haven: Yale University Press; 1943.

Matthews, Roderic R., and Matta Akrawi. *Education in the Arab Countries*. Washington: American Council on Education; 1949.

Mayer, Frederick. *A History of Ancient and Medieval Philosophy*. New York: American Book Company; 1950.

——. *A History of Modern Philosophy*. New York: American Book Company; 1951.

——. *American Ideas and Education*. Columbus: Charles E. Merrill Books, Inc.; 1964.

——. *Education and the Good Life*. Washington, D. C.: Public Affairs Press; 1957.

——. *Philosophy of Education for Our Time*. New York: The Odyssey Press, Inc.; 1958.

Meyer, Adolph E. *The Development of Education in the Twentieth Century*. New York: Prentice-Hall, Inc.; 1949.

Miles, D. W. *Recent Reforms in French Secondary Education*. New York: Teachers College, Columbia University; 1953.

Monroe, Paul. *Source Book of the History of Education*. New York: The Macmillan Company; 1923.

Moore, Ernest C. *The Story of Instruction: The Beginnings*. New York: The Macmillan Company; 1936.

——. *The Story of Instruction: The Church, the Renaissances and the Reformations*. New York: The Macmillan Company; 1938.

Mukerji, S. N. *Education in India Today and Tomorrow*. Baroda, India: Acharya Book Depot Opposite Jubilee Garden; 1952.

Mulhern, James. *A History of Education*. New York: The Ronald Press Company; 1946.

Mumford, Lewis. *The Condition of Man*. New York: Harcourt, Brace and Company; 1941.

——. *The Culture of Cities*. New York: Harcourt, Brace and Company; 1938.

————. *The Story of Utopias.* New York: Liveright Publishing Corporation; 1933.

————. *Technics and Civilization.* New York: Harcourt, Brace and Company; 1934.

————. *Values for Survival.* New York: Harcourt, Brace and Company; 1946.

Myrdal, Gunnar. *An American Dilemma.* New York: Harper and Brothers; 1947.

Nakosteen, Mehdi. *The History and Philosophy of Education.* New York: The Ronald Press Company; 1965.

Nef, John U. *The United States and Civilization.* Chicago: University of Chicago Press; 1942.

————. *The Universities Look for Unity.* New York: Pantheon Books, Inc.; 1943.

Newman, John H. *The Idea of a University.* New York: Longmans, Green and Company, Inc.; 1947.

Niebuhr, Reinhold. *Moral Man and Immoral Society.* New York: Charles Scribner's Sons; 1932.

Northrop, F. S. C. *The Meeting of East and West.* New York: The Macmillan Company; 1947.

Orwell, George. *Nineteen Eighty-four.* New York: Harcourt, Brace and Company; 1949.

Otto, Max C. *The Human Enterprise.* New York: D. Appleton-Century Company, Inc.; 1940.

Parrington, Vernon L. *Main Currents in American Thought.* New York: Harcourt, Brace and Company; 1930.

Paulsen, Friedrich. *Geschichte des gelehrten Unterrichts auf den Deutschen Schulen und Universitäten vom Ausgang des Mittelalters bis zur Gegenwart.* Leipzig: Lehmann; 1919-21.

Perry, Ralph B. *Present Philosophical Tendencies.* New York: Longmans, Green and Company, Inc.; 1912.

Plato. *The Dialogues of Plato.* Translated by Benjamin Jowett. 2 vols. New York: Charles Scribner's Sons; 1928.

————. *The Republic.* (Modern Student Library edition.) New York: Charles Scribner's Sons; 1928.

Popper, K. R. *The Open Society and Its Enemies.* London: George Routledge and Sons. Ltd.; 1945.

Powell, J. W. *Education for Maturity.* New York: Hermitage House; 1949.

Rader, Melvin. *Ethics and Society.* New York: Henry Holt and Company, Inc.; 1950.

Randall, John H., Jr. *The Making of the Modern Mind.* (Revised edition.) Boston: Houghton Mifflin Company; 1940.

Reiser, Oliver L. *World Philosophy; A Search for Synthesis.* Pittsburgh: University of Pittsburgh Press; 1948.

Rogers, A. K. *A Student's History of Philosophy.* New York: The Macmillan Company; 1907.

Rousseau, Jean Jacques. *The Social Contract.* New York: G. P. Putnam's Sons; 1906.

Royce, Josiah. *The Spirit of Modern Philosophy*. Boston: Ginn and Company; 1892.

Rudolph, Frederick. *The American College and University*. New York: Alfred A. Knopf, Inc.; 1962.

Russell, Bertrand. *Education and the Good Life*. New York: Boni and Liveright; 1926.

———. *A History of Western Philosophy*. New York: Simon & Schuster, Inc.; 1945.

———. *Selected Papers of Bertrand Russell*. New York: Modern Library, Inc.; 1927.

Sabine, George H. *A History of Political Theory*. New York: Henry Holt and Company, Inc.; 1937.

Sanchez Sarto, Luis. *Diccionario de Pedagogia*. Barcelona; 1936.

Sandys, Sir John Edwin. *A History of Classical Scholarship from the 6th Century B. C. to the End of the Middle Ages*. London: Cambridge University Press; 1920.

———. *A History of Classical Scholarship*. 3 vols. New York: G. P. Putnam's Sons; 1906-08.

Scheler, Max. *Die Stellung des Menschen im Kosmos*. Darmstadt: O. Reichl Verlag; 1928.

Schneider, Herbert W. *A History of American Philosophy*. New York: Columbia University Press; 1946.

Shorey, Paul. *The Unity of Plato's Thought*. Chicago: University of Chicago Press; 1903.

Somerville, John. *Soviet Philosophy*. New York: Philosophical Library, Inc.; 1946.

Spender, Stephen. *Forward from Liberalism*. New York: Random House; 1937.

Spengler, Oswald. *The Decline of the West*. New York: Alfred A. Knopf, Inc.; 1932.

Sumner, William Graham. *Folkways*. Boston: Ginn and Company; 1906.

Tawney, R. H. *The Acquisitive Society*. New York: Harcourt, Brace and Company; 1921.

Tead, Ordway. *College Teaching and College Learning*. New Haven: Yale University Press; 1949.

Thayer, V. T. *The Role of the School in American Society*. New York: Dodd, Mead and Company; 1960.

Thomas Aquinas, Saint. *Basic Writings of St. Thomas Aquinas*. Edited by Anton C. Pegis. New York: Random House, Inc.; 1945.

Thut, I. N. *The Story of Education*. New York: McGraw-Hill Book Company; 1957.

Tillich, Paul. *The Courage To Be*. New Haven: Yale University Press; 1952.

Toynbee, Arnold. *A Study of History*. New York: Oxford University Press; 1939.

Ulich, Robert. *Conditions of Civilized Living*. New York: E. P. Dutton and Company, Inc.; 1946.

———. *History of Educational Thought*. New York: American Book Company; 1945.

———. *Human Career*. New York: Harper and Brothers; 1957.

Van Doren, Mark. *Liberal Education*. New York: Henry Holt and Company, Inc.; 1943.

Wahl, Jean. *A Short History of Existentialism*. New York: Philosophical Library, Inc.; 1949.

Wahlquist, John T. *The Philosophy of American Education*. New York: The Ronald Press Company; 1942.

Ward, Barbara. *The West at Bay*. New York: W. W. Norton and Company, Inc.; 1948.

Warner, W. Lloyd; Marchia Meeker; and Kenneth Eells. *Social Class in America*. Chicago: Science Research Associates; 1949.

Washburne, Carleton. *A Living Philosophy of Education*. New York: The John Day Company; 1940.

Whitehead, Alfred North. *The Aims of Education and Other Essays*. New York: The Macmillan Company; 1929.

———. *Science and the Modern World*. New York: The Macmillan Company; 1925.

Whyte, L. L. *The Next Development in Man*. New York: Henry Holt and Company, Inc.; 1948.

Wilds, Elmer H. *The Foundations of Modern Education*. New York: Farrar and Rinehart, Inc.; 1942.

Wilkins, A. S. *National Education in Greece in the Fourth Century Before Christ*. New York: G. E. Stechert and Company; 1911.

———. *Roman Education*. New York: The Macmillan Company; 1905.

Wrenn, G. Gilbert. *The Counselor in a Changing World*. Washington, D.C.: American Personnel and Guidance Association; 1962.

Zimmer, H. *Philosophies of India*. New York: Meridian Books, Inc.; 1956.

Illustration Credits

PART FOUR   *Photo International Publicity, Inc.*

Chapter 27   *Library of Congress Collection*
Chapter 28   *Free Lance Photographers Guild, Inc.*
Chapter 29   *Brown Brothers, Inc.*
Chapter 30   *Board of Education, Worthington, Ohio*
Chapter 31   *Free Lance Photographers Guild, Inc.*
Chapter 32   *Board of Education, Worthington, Ohio*
Chapter 33   *Library of Congress Collection*
Chapter 34   *Union College, by John Ross Studio*
Chapter 35   *Columbus Board of Education,*
                 Columbus, Ohio
Chapter 36   *International Business Machines Corporation*

PART FIVE   *Philip Gendreau, Inc.*

Chapter 37   *Dick Lebowitz for Educational Services Inc.*
Chapter 38   *Alpha Photo Associates, Inc.*

Jacket photo from Charles Phelps Cushing

Index

INDEX

561

Tolstoy, Leo—*Cont.*
  significance of, 331-332
  spiritual doubts of, 335-336
  War and Peace, 334
Totalitarianism, 492-493
Townsend, 480
Transcendentalism, 479
Transcendentalists, 480-481
Travel, as educational agency, 10
Trillingham, C. C., 463
Tu-hsiu, Chen, 356
Twelfth Annual Report (Mann),
  quoted, 373-375

Understanding Science (Conant), 440
Universalism, 483
Universities, rise of, 156
Universities, American, 437-448
  conflicts of, 445
  dilemmas of, 442-443
  expansion of, 446-448
Universities, Arabic, 173
University, The Idea of a (Newman),
  quoted, 447
Upanishads, 35, 39-44, 47
Ushinsky, K. D., 339
Utopia, educational, 375
Utopia, (More), 229, 481

Vaihinger, 502
Vaisesika, 51
Varieties of Religious Experience, The
  (James), 380
Vedas, 37, 39, 44
  Rig-Veda, 37
  Sama-Veda, 37
  Yajur-Veda, 37
  Atharva-Veda, 37
Velter, 453
Vergerius, Petrus Paul, 181
Versailles treaty, 490
Vincent, Bishop J. H., 472
Virtue, 488
Vivekananda, 56, 359
Vives, Juan Louis, 182
  influence on Comenius, 230, 232
Vocation of teacher, 27
Vocations of Man (Fichte), quoted, 277
Vodovozov, V. E., 339

Voltaire, 2, 252, 253, 489
  Zadig, 513
Voragine, Jacopo de, *Golden Legend*,
  158

Walden, 480
Walden (Thoreau), quoted, 23, 484
War, 489
War and Peace (Tolstoy), 334
War, as educational agency, 10
Weimar Republic, 490, 492
West Point, 464
What Knowledge Is of Most Worth?
  (Spencer), quoted, 325-327
Whinnery, John, 463
White, Andrew D., 440
Whitehead, 16, 502, 507
Wiener, 507
Wilberforce, 504
Willard, Emma, 376
William and Mary College, 438
William of Tyre, 152
William II, Emperor, 311
Will to Believe, The (James), 380
Wissenschaftslehre (Fichte), 447
Wittgenstein, 501
Women, education, 153, 179, 376
Woolman, 479
World and the Individual, The
  (Royce), 379
World as Will and Idea, The (Schopen-
  hauer), quoted, 266
Wright, Frances, 376
Wundt, 451

Xenophon, 89

Yang-Chu, 69, 70
Yajnavalkya, 39
Yasna, quoted, 78
Yogi, 53, 54

Zadig (Voltaire), 513
Zen-Buddhism, 49-50
Zend-Avesta, 77
Zionism, 353
Zirbes, Laura, 411
Zoroaster, 77
Zoroastrianism, 78

A HISTORY OF
EDUCATIONAL THOUGHT